AUSTRIAN BANKING AND FINANCIAL POLICY

EDUARD MÄRZ

Austrian Banking
and
Financial Policy

Creditanstalt at a Turning Point, 1913–1923

translated by

CHARLES KESSLER

ST. MARTIN'S PRESS
New York

Originally published in German as
Österreichische Bankpolitik in der Zeit der grossen Wende 1913–1923
© 1981 by Verlag für Geschichte und Politik Wien

This translation © 1984 by Creditanstalt-Bankverein, Vienna

Printed in Great Britain
First published in the United States of America in 1984

Library of Congress Cataloging in Publication Data

März, Eduard.
  Austrian banking and financial policy.

  Translation of: Österreichische Bankpolitik in
der Zeit der grossen Wende 1913–1923.
  Bibliography: p.
  Includes index.
  1. Österreichische Credit-Anstalt für Handel und
Gwerbe—History. 2. Banks and banking—Austria—
History. 3. World War, 1914–1918—Finance—Austria.
4. Austria—Economic conditions. I. Title.
HG3020.V540475313   1984   332.1'09436   84–15148
ISBN 0–312–06124–2

Contents

CONTENTS

List of Tables

Appendix Tables

List of Diagrams

List of Illustrations

Preface

The reader will have little difficulty in recognizing that the present volume is a continuation of my book *Österreichische Industrie- und Bankpolitik in der Zeit Franz Josephs I – am Beispiel der k.k. priv. österreichischen Creditanstalt für Handel und Gewerbe* (Vienna, 1968). Nevertheless the present work differs in two respects from its predecessor. First, it comprises a substantially shorter, even though particularly eventful and momentous period of Austrian history. Secondly, it rests on an almost incalculable multitude of primary and secondary sources capable of being put into shape only through years of painstaking detailed work. Unlike the initial study, whose publication was often impeded by a serious lack of literature on the subject, the completion of this volume was delayed for several years by a positive glut of useful as well as somewhat less useful specialized studies. Sorting the wheat from the chaff frequently entailed time-consuming research although I was able throughout to count on the help of assistants selflessly devoted to the common objective.

My first attempts to master this subject took place in the immediate post-war period under the benevolent auspices of Professor Joseph A. Schumpeter and Abbot P. Usher. Many years later generous grants by the Austrian Federal Ministry of Science and Research rendered possible my resumption of the study.

At the suggestion of Dr Wilhelm Frank, departmental head in the ministry, and assisted by Frau Wilhelmine Goldmann, B.Com., of the Vienna Chamber of Labour, I focused on the contributions made by Austrian economic, financial, and technical experts to the reconstruction of the First Republic. The preliminary investigations, intrinsically valuable as they proved to be for the overall planning of the present work, were, however, only a relatively small portion of the ground which needed to be covered. Its thorough treatment could not be undertaken until the management of the Creditanstalt-Bankverein made available to me its archives, its valuable store of experience, and its ample material support. Without this financial assistance and intellectual encouragement, the present work would probably never have come to fruition.

As only a comparatively short period was to be covered, the organization of its subject-matter and chronology followed an almost automatic course. Part One gives a brief description of developments in banking and industry during the final years of the Austro-Hungarian Empire. Here I was able to rely on my own earlier work, certain recent studies, and to no small degree on newly opened archival sources. Substantial revision of the conclusions reached in my preceding work did not prove necessary. Treatment of the political events leading to the First World War was of course outside my chosen sphere. In my view, none of the available archival sources offer any confirmation whatsoever of the notion that Austrian high finance was somehow entangled in the militant, not to say aggressive, policy pursued by the Imperial Ministry of Foreign Affairs. This finding suggests that Schumpeter's well-known assertion about the pacific character of the moneyed interests, in such striking contrast to the view held by his compatriot and contemporary Rudolf Hilferding, derived from intimate knowledge of the specifically Austrian background of the *belle époque*.

Part Two concerns the phase of transition from the peace-time to the war economy, i.e., a phase lasting barely half a year. The provisions that were made, or that failed to be made, in the economic field during these few months proved decisive for the Empire's physical conduct of the war. This applies in particular to what it is tempting to characterize as the unprincipled recourse to the central bank. It set in train a destruction of the currency's value which did not come to a halt before the 1922 Geneva Recovery Programme. Likewise, the first experimental forms of organization for mobilizing and managing Austria-Hungary's material resources, that evolved during the succeeding years – although with remarkable tardiness – into a system embracing practically all sectors of the economy, date from this early phase of adaptation and transformation. The outbreak of hostilities foreshadowed already the new role of the major banks. Their task, in conjunction with the central bank, was to provide all the liquid resources available for waging war and for financing the 'Agencies', the public authorities in charge of the war economy.

The enormous loss of physical capital, caused by war, resulted in the impoverishment of practically all classes, firms and establishments, and eventually also affected the Empire's powerful banking world. The history of the economic and psychological exhaustion of the multinational state, culminating in its disintegration, is the theme of Part Three. Accounts of the main economic aspects have been given with exemplary thoroughness in several studies sponsored by the

Carnegie Peace Foundation. I have therefore concentrated on the problems arising for industry, finance, and banking under conditions of total war, and here I was able to make use of certain previously untapped archival sources. In the last chapter I dealt with an episode that has hitherto received short shrift at the hands of Austrian historians concerning the negotiations aimed at a customs union between the Empire and Germany. Professor Stefan Verosta, in a recently published essay, has pointed out that Schumpeter – then a young university professor and a serious candidate for a ministerial appointment – regarded these aims as a serious menace to Austria's political sovereignty. After the Empire's disintegration, in his capacity as Minister of Finance, he opposed with consistency and determin-ation (even if not always with kid gloves) every plan tending to the surrender of Austria's existence.

Parts Four and Five are mainly concerned with the conditions and the prospects for the viability of the new Austria. That a considerable portion of its population, faced by cataclysmic changes, the oppressive exigencies of daily life, and the undisguised animosity of the other nations of the Danube basin, should have looked for 'escape' by leaning towards its still relatively powerful German neighbour can hardly come as a surprise. The reasons, the plans and the methods that were adopted for this Austrian attempt at abandonment of its just-won nationhood have been so frequently examined, particularly recently, that I have refrained from furnishing more than a mere sketch of this many-sided problem. Somewhat more space has been allotted instead to the debate over socialization, because its ideological and social repercussions can still be distinctly felt in the Second Republic. It was also necessary to go into closer detail about the Peace Treaty concluded between the Powers and Austria. Literature on the subject is comparatively voluminous, but little of it offers any real survey of the Treaty as a whole. The desperate situation of the First Republic, though, must be ascribed, in no small degree, to a piece of treaty-making so drafted as to relegate at all cost the small, maimed, and new Austria, itself struggling for survival, to the status of a defeated enemy Power.

The *Anschluss* strategy, in stark contradiction to the spirit inspiring the Treaties of Versailles and St Germain, could consequently be little more than a rhetorical gesture, given the constellation of power following the hostilities. Very soon it was countered by a strategy which seemed at first much more realistic. Its most important supporters, including the long-time Creditanstalt director and internationally recognized financial expert Dr Paul Hammerschlag, spoke for the major Viennese banks. To preserve the Danube basin's ancient economic ties, regardless of the radically altered post-war circumstances, was the notion favoured by this small, highly-paid, exclusive group of bank executives. Their philosophy of 'business as usual' rested on the assumption that, if only on grounds of self-preservation, a gradual commercial *rapprochement* would occur between the Successor States. The conditions for the return of the pre-war prosperity were, they believed, capable of being automatically restored within this big economic area that had been more or less free of trade barriers and now was militarily safeguarded by the Allied Powers. And, they further believed, that the *crédit mobilier* banks would continue to hold the key financial position familiar to them in the past.

Fairly early on the major Viennese banks began to put their new strategy into practice with the help of measures described here. The first move was to exert skill and ingenuity in upholding their positions in the new states. Success was admittedly limited. Secondly, they tried to strengthen their severely weakened capital base by 'partnership' with Western financial circles. Thirdly, they acted as mediators between Western moneyed interests and capital-hungry investors in eastern and south-eastern Europe. Their ambitions had the encouragement of such powerful allies as Monsignor Ignaz Seipel, the leading conservative Austrian politician and subsequent Federal Chancellor, and Montagu Norman, the Governor of the Bank of England who in the twenties exercised a crucial influence over the financial and monetary policy pursued by a considerable portion of the Western world. Whether the politicians or the banking moguls gave the main impetus to this new strategy in the Danube basin is indeed difficult to confirm with any certainty.

Generals, as the saying goes, tend to wage the next war with the weapons of the last. No one to any extent acquainted with the way of life and habits of thought characteristic of élite groups should be surprised by the fixation of these senior bankers (and, incidentally, many major industrialists) on the former Empire's territories which, in the two decades preceding the First World War, had been the scene of swift economic advance. A small minority, headed by Alexander Spitzmüller, that meritorious Nestor of the Austrian banking world whose name will frequently recur in these pages, eloquently warned them against such a course. This course, he asserted, was mistaken in its interpretation of the new economic and political factors prevailing in the Danube area. His warnings failed, however, to elicit the slightest response from his colleagues.

The Geneva Recovery Programme, intended by domestic and foreign financial experts to stabilize an Austrian economy shattered by wartime and post-war inflation, also has to be viewed in the perspective of this strategy. The programme was conceived as a macroeconomic framework, so to speak, for the numerous individual banking and industrial operations were to be launched on the assumption of constant, ever-deepening collaboration between Austria and the West in the Danube basin. The distinctly deflationary bias attaching to the Geneva recovery recipe was of course an expression of the non-intervention philosophy dominant in western as well as in central Europe, and it is likely to have played a not inconsiderable part in the economic malaise of the twenties. The present volume ends with an analysis of the economic problems resulting from the stabilization of the Austrian currency in the year 1923.

It is of course impossible to name the very large number of people and institutions who helped me assemble the material essential for the compilation of this work. I shall thank here only those upon whose generous assistance I relied during every phase of the project. First and foremost there are my constant collaborators, Frau Gundl Herrnstadt-Steinmetz, Dr Hans Kernbauer, and Dr Fritz Weber. Not only did they perform a great part of the archival research and the scrutiny of newspapers and periodicals but they were at all times on hand to give me their sound advice on structuring the material. The late Dr Ernst Lachs' thoroughgoing knowledge of Austrian political affairs and history helped me overcome many difficulties. Finally Dr Heinrich Treichl and Dr Johannes Eder, chairman of the Managing Board and director of Creditanstalt-Bankverein respectively, took the trouble to comment on parts of this study as it progressed, yet without ever hinting at a wish to alter any point once I had arrived at a settled view, an attitude for which I take this opportunity sincerely to thank them.

I have availed myself, for the purpose of the present and earlier works, of many archives within and outside of Austria. Requests for help and information were on all occasions handled with courtesy and great efficiency. If I mention specifically *Hofrat* Dr Walther Winkelbauer, of the Austrian Federal Ministry of Finance Archives, and *Regierungsrat* Anton Nemeth of the *Haus-, Hof- und Staatsarchiv*, it is mainly because they and their staffs have for years shown a lively interest, far beyond their official obligations, in the progress of my work. Lastly, I thank my wife, Maria, not only for all the patience and forbearance that she has so generously displayed during the many years of my preoccupation with the present study and consequent isolation from the outside world, but also for her advice on the elucidation of delicate problems of economic policy. The responsibility for all errors and sins of omission which the reader may find in this book rests of course solely with me.

EDUARD MÄRZ
Vienna

Preface to the English edition

The decline and break-up of the Danubian Monarchy and the subsequent emergence of its 'Successor State', the first Republic of Austria, has been the theme of a vast amount of British and American literature. It will suffice to mention a few authors concerned with this particular chapter of recent European history, such as A. J. P. Taylor, Robert A. Kann, C. A. Macartney and Charles A. Gulick, to indicate the high quality of some of this writing. Yet most of the pertinent studies centre heavily on the political, diplomatic, cultural and social aspects of the Austrian tragedy, while the economic issues, so vital to an understanding of the full scope of the story, are dealt with only sparingly. A noteworthy exception is Jan Walré de Bordes' *The Austrian Crown* (London, 1924) which primarily treats the causes and the main phases of the Austrian post-war inflation (1918–1922).

The present study attempts to trace the economic development of the Habsburg Monarchy during the years immediately before the war, the ultimate stage of the so-called *belle époque*, the economic exertion and exhaustion of the huge underdeveloped realm during four years of total war, and the economic birth pangs of the young Austrian Republic. The greater part of the book is devoted to the latter theme. Among the economic issues, financial and banking policies are accorded pride of place.

This predominance may puzzle English readers unused to considering banking as a pivotal economic activity in view of the supposedly 'passive' role of commercial banking. The heavy emphasis on banking in the present study is justified, in my view, by the pre-eminent role of investment banking in the evolution of modern industry in Central Europe and in particular, in the Habsburg Monarchy. One indeed perceives, as I have tried to show in my book *Österreichische Industrie- und Bankpolitik in der Zeit Franz Josephs I* (Vienna, 1968), a symbiotic relationship between banking and industry in Austria. The close ties between the two economic sectors survived the demise of the empire, but were critically weakened by the great banking crash of 1931.

The Austrian Creditanstalt für Handel und Gewerbe (now named Creditanstalt-Bankverein) which has, since its foundation in 1855, been Austria's largest and by far most dynamic investment bank, serves as a model for elucidating the nature of this special relationship both during its heyday in the pre-war decade and during its decline in the post-war period. The author of the present study has profited enormously from his access to the Creditanstalt archives and to the archives of the Austrian Finance Ministry. But perhaps more important than this insight into the original records was the writer's personal contact with some of the architects of Austrian banking policy in the inter-war period, a contact he was privileged to establish while working on the Festschrift *Hundert Jahre Creditanstalt-Bank-verein* (Vienna, 1957) during the early 1950s.

While the book may, it is hoped, break new ground for the evaluation of the causes of the tragic end of the Austro-Hungarian Empire and of the shaky economic foundation of the First Austrian Republic, it has been written in an earnest effort to reach a readership which transcends the closed circle of historians and economic experts. Thus economic theorems underlying some of the arguments have been carefully explained and a specialist economic vocabulary avoided as far as possible.

It is acknowledged that the publication of this study in English could not have been undertaken without the financial support of Credit-anstalt-Bankverein and the sympathetic encouragement of Dr Hannes Androsch, its general manager, and Dr Heinrich Treichl, his predecessor. Lastly, sincere thanks must be extended to Dr Robert Baldock, Academic Director of Weidenfeld and Nicolson, and Professor Philip Cottrell of Leicester University for their generous help in editing the English version of the book.

E.M.

PART ONE

The Austrian Economy on the Eve of the First World War

CHAPTER I
The Boom Years

In autumn 1912 the long-smouldering Balkan crisis, although locally contained, had erupted into war. Upon this the economy of the Habsburg Empire, already marked by signs of strain in the money, goods, and labour markets, slithered into a 'trade crisis', the term then customary for a more pronounced depression or recession. This debility of the Austrian economy was destined to last until the outbreak of the First World War.

Autumn 1912 was also the culmination of a prolonged period of prosperity such as had rarely been experienced so durably and so intensively in the history of the Austrian economy. After the lengthy depression in the 1870s, industry and trade had expanded quite considerably during the succeeding two decades. Yet at the beginning of the new century even the more industrialized Austrian half of the Austro-Hungarian Empire remained distinctly underdeveloped compared with the leading European industrial nations, a fact reflected in no small degree by the high proportion (53%) of the population engaged in agriculture. The Dual Monarchy's final years of peace, however, were marked by a rapid economic expansion whose strongest growth stimuli appear to have come from the association of large-scale business with modern technology.[1] The financial resources for this investment boom during the Second Expansion Era were to a large degree provided by the crédit mobilier banks.[2] The first signs of upward movement could be felt towards the end of 1903. It reached a temporary peak in 1907, sagged in the following year, then continued in 1909 with mounting strength. Only in autumn 1912 did a distinct slackening occur.[3]

An article by Gustav Stolper, in April 1914, describing progress in the past ten years, attracted much attention:

The decade . . . comprises two clearly demarcated cyclical periods, the first from 1904 to 1908, the second from 1909 until 1912. The first, constructive over a broad front . . . , the second headlong, volatile, speculative, and in the

3

van of uneconomic and non-economic forces. The first dwindled into a faint depression which showed Austria-Hungary, in spite of the political danger (annexation), to be more robust than Germany and the entire West. The second has ended in a crisis which in the long run threatens to cripple the economy's vitality.[4]

This brief heyday, must be seen against the background of a rapidly expanding world economy which promoted an upswing in certain local industries (sugar, textiles, cement, glass, machines, and so on). Nonetheless the Austrian export trade during this same time grew comparatively slowly, one not unimportant reason being the dis-inclination of Balkan markets (Serbia, Romania, Bulgaria, and Turkey) to accept Austria's industrial products in view of the Monarchy's blockade on agrarian imports from them.[5] From 1905 to 1911 exports in real terms increased only slightly. Not until 1912 was there a vigorous growth in foreign trade.[6]

While the export of Austrian finished goods developed conspicu-ously slowly, the import of raw materials and foodstuffs accelerated greatly. Favourable economic conditions appreciably increased in-dustry's independence on coal and raw materials from abroad; the influx was occasioned in part also by the comparatively slow rise in agricultural yields. In the last years of the Monarchy they lagged behind the rapid growth of population. Together the two factors account for the adverse trade balance of 1907 which, initially of small significance, worsened remarkably quickly.[7]

Table 1   Trade balance in million crowns

	Surplus	Deficit		Surplus	Deficit
1906	39.0	—	1910	—	434.0
1907	—	44.0	1911	—	788.0
1908	—	143.0	1912	—	823.0
1909	—	428.0	1913	—	637.0

The sudden imbalance after many years of surplus, with its unfavourable implications in the field of monetary affairs, became a topic of lively public debate.[8] Attention focused on two aspects: the adverse marketing situation in the Balkans arising from the Monarchy's protectionist agrarian policy and the slow rise in agri-cultural productivity although this varied notably from region to region.[9]

Oscar Jaszi, in his well-known book, *The Dissolution of the*

Habsburg Monarchy, attributes the unsatisfactory yields to a veritable conspiracy by the Hungarian land magnates. He alleges that they hoped to derive considerable financial advantage from the import tariffs on agrarian products by a policy of curbing their productive potential. As one of his chief witnesses he cites Count Tisza who, after an analysis of prospective trends in his book, *Hungarian Agrarian Policy* (1897), had come to the 'optimistic' conclusion that 'We can therefore assume with a fair amount of certainty that within a few years the Customs Union' (i.e., Austria-Hungary as an economic unit) 'will be among the category of countries showing a wheat deficit and that consequently our farmers will reap the full benefit of agrarian protectionism.'[10]

Jaszi's conspiracy theory need not be subjected to closer scrutiny. Austrian agriculture's comparative inefficiency (during the war it was to prove the most vulnerable point in the Monarchy's armoury) suggests a simpler, more plausible explanation. The system was burdened with structural weaknesses, relics of the Empire's feudal past. The following data give a picture of the distribution of landed property in this period.

At the beginning of the twentieth century the number of agrarian holdings in Austria-Hungary totalled 5,652,234; they covered 53,890,473 hectares of productive soil. The peasants held 5,591,076 of these holdings, the estate owners 61,153. Of the productive soil 21,493,763 hectares were concentrated in the hands of the estate owners while 32,396,690 hectares were peasant holdings.[11]

The significance attaching to big land-ownership becomes clear only when it is realized that 'estate owners with more than 50 hectares, representing 1.08% of the real estate holders, owned 40.72% of the cultivated soil whereas the peasants, constituting 98.92% of the property holders, had only 59.28% of the entire area under cultivation.'[12] Large estates were a common feature over wide stretches of the Empire. In Slovakia they comprised more than 50% of the acreage, in Bukovina almost 45%, in Galicia and Transylvania almost 40%. On many of these gigantic estates, especially those secured as entail, there prevailed an attitude which pre-dated capitalistic times and seriously handicapped rational management.[13]

The far-reaching fragmentation of tillage land also barred the way to any speedy improvement in productivity. Fragmentation took two forms. In the first place the number of farms had risen steadily in recent decades mainly due to the repeated sub-division of inherited land. A reduction in the average size of small holdings followed because such units, in the light of the big estates' inalienability, lacked any opportunities for expansion. Between 1900 and 1910 the number of farms in the Austrian half of the Empire rose by some 20%.[14] Secondly certain regions, particularly the Sudetenland, the Danubian territories, and Galicia, suffered from the defects of open-field agriculture.[15] According to a conservative estimate made in 1912, 70% of the communes listed in this portion of the Empire's land registries should have been merged and their boundaries appropriately adjusted. A statute passed in 1883 had aimed at encouraging the consolidation of landownership, but along the road to its implementation numerous unforeseen obstacles were encountered. Not a few of them were raised by the peasants themselves.[16]

The Dual Monarchy's trade deficit was clearly not accidental, but a matter of structural weaknesses in the economy deriving *primarily* from land-ownership problems and the inadequate competitiveness of Austrian industry. Stolper's article referred to a parallel development in Germany, where a stubborn trade deficit lasted nearly two decades. Only quite recently the greater efficiency of German industry had managed to overcome this state of affairs. Stolper thought that a similar evolution was imminent in Austria-Hungary.[17]

Austrian industry had indeed, quantitatively no less than qualitatively, made considerable progress during the decade before the war. Its expansion, and that of trade, was probably even more rapid than in the years between 1890 and 1900, although these years were also marked by a very vigorous upward trend.[18] Another author pinpoints the period of biggest industrial growth as the brief space from 1903 to 1907.[19]

The forward leap in metal-working and machine-building was especially impressive; output almost doubled. Textile production, cotton goods in particular, increased substantially although at a more moderate pace. Mining and iron production continued the steady advance observed in earlier decades.[20] Only crude oil extraction was subject to serious fluctuations. The sharp price increases in the products of the food industry probably account for its notably sluggish progress. An exception was sugar, but here a conspicuously high proportion of production had to be sold abroad.[21]

The foundations for the economy's remarkable impetus were undoubtedly laid by Ernest von Koerber, Austrian Prime Minister from 1900 to 1904. His initiation of a large-scale state investment programme had a twofold objective: to stimulate economic activities and to commit the Monarchy's feuding political parties to a common task. 'On 1 June 1901, the Second Chamber voted, not only without any obstruction but in an atmosphere of considerable enthusiasm, two investment bills: one related to the construction of railroads and the other to inland waterways.'[22] On 11 June the two bills, with the Emperor's counter-signature, became law.

The ambitious programme, envisaging the expenditure of 1,000 million crowns, over an extended period, was never wholly implemented. Its key feature was a railroad branching south from the main east-west axis and intended as a second rail link between Vienna and Trieste, the Empire's main outlet to the Adriatic and the Mediterranean. It was to be known as the Tauern-Karawanken Line, on account of the mountain ranges crossed. In addition, the Pyhrn Line, named after a pass lying between the Tauern-Karawanken Line and the principal route to the south, and the Wechsel Line flanking it farther east along the last fringe of the Alps were also contemplated. A Carpathian Line would have been an altogether new venture. Furthermore, local networks were to be expanded, stations enlarged and revitalized, official buildings erected in all Crown Lands, and other projects were to be undertaken along the same line.[23] Two more ambitious projects, the Danube-Oder-canal and the Danube-Moldava-canal, never got beyond the stage of technical planning.[24]

The construction activity inspired by Koerber's schemes provided vigorous stimuli for closely related industries such as cement, glass, and brickmaking. During 1904 a steadily growing international upswing, in whose wake sooner or later nearly all industrial sectors prospered, coalesced with these autonomous growth factors.[25] Then, towards the end of 1908, there was a notable worsening of market conditions: textiles were particularly affected. The result was a reduction in operations mainly in the cotton industry.[26]

The years between 1909 and 1912 saw a new pattern of development. Progress in the consumer goods industries was sluggish and the economic upswing was largely attributable to thriving business in the capital goods sector. Its outstanding characteristics were high employment in firms working on armament requirements, the investments undertaken by the state railways, and the rapid expansion in the electrical industry. Inasmuch as a fair proportion of the order-books in the engineering, electrical, and armament industries were also reasonably full in 1913, the new cyclical set-back remained within narrow bounds.[27] The positive state of affairs during these last years of peace is illustrated by the swift increase in the number of insured employees. From 1,722,925 in 1902 it grew to 2,436,250 in 1911, a rise of some 40%.[28] There was also a high investment ratio. In 1913, when a certain weakness became apparent, 13% of the gross domestic product was invested, more than twice as much as necessary to maintain the capital stock.[29]

The close link between large-scale enterprise and industrial technology has been mentioned in another context. A characteristic of the economy's strong expansion between 1904 and 1913 was the rapid increase in the number of joint-stock companies. In 1904 they numbered (excluding railway undertakings) 573 and represented an investment of 2,217 million crowns. At the close of 1913 the Trade Register contained the names of 822 such enterprises with a capital of 4,378 million crowns. This was an increase of almost one hundred per cent within only nine years.[30] The rate of capital growth during the two upswing phases was, however, very different. Barely 30% of the new resources were accumulated between 1904 and 1908, while more than 70% came between 1909 and 1913. This underlines the fact that investments in the early years of the upswing were principally devoted to the comparatively undercapitalized consumer goods field, while the second wave of prosperity was distinguished by a quickened rate of capital formation in the capital goods sector. The pace-maker role which big industry assumed during the last years of peace is attested by its remarkably high and constantly growing profitability. Between 1902 and 1912 few joint-stock companies showed balance-sheet deficits. The great majority reported substantial and continuously rising profits.[31]

Table 2 Capital and profits of Joint-Stock Companies

Year	No. of Companies	Capital in Cr. m.	Net Profit in Cr. m.	Net Profit % of Capital
1902	539	2.075	148	7.1
1903	549	2.122	164	7.8
1904	560	2.163	177	8.2
1905	567	2.263	188	8.3
1906	584	2.516	235	9.3
1907	618	2.661	281	10.6
1908	629	2.751	276	10.0
1909	635	2.814	280	10.0
1910	656	3.195	332	10.4
1911	707	3.843	403	10.5
1912	707	4.050	461	11.4

In spite of the traditional industries (building, iron production and processing, sugar, *etc.*) being the prime movers of the major upswing during the last pre-war years, the share of the new industries should not be underestimated. Notably fast was the increase in the number of power stations and in electric current generation, in spite of the fact that the origins of this technology dated back only to the 1880s. An official statistic reveals that between 1 January 1907 and 1 January 1914 the number of power stations rose from 446 to 933 and their total output from 168,850 to 540,386 kilowatts.[32] Oil production, the newer branches too of the chemical industry and motor vehicle construction were also passing through a period of rapid expansion. The older branches invested in modern technology; this was especially true within the engineering sector. To an ever greater extent this sector applied itself to the manufacture of electrical motors, generators, gas turbines, and the like. Industry's re-equipment is also exemplified by the vast jump in machine imports, particularly from Germany.[33]

The economy's dynamism was all the more remarkable for its having to struggle against 'home-made' limitations: against a guild-minded policy aimed at protecting small businesses; against a taxation policy that fairly obviously made big industry its target; against a protectionist tariff policy that, in consequence of its adverse effect on prices of foodstuffs, had a negative influence on the level of costs in industry and trade. The 1906 tariff was so high as to recall the bad days of super-protectionism at the dawn of Austrian capitalism. It was calculated to reinforce the traditional Austrian economic policy of autarchy.[34]

The reports of the leading armament concerns throw light on how much the boom of recent years had depended on their activities. These, in contrast with the experience of some 'pure' machine constructors, enjoyed a very lively business. Skodawerke, Pilsen, headed the list. Between 1910 and 1914 this firm invested no fewer than 30 million crowns in plant and equipment. In the summer of 1914, i.e., just before the outbreak of war, it purchased the majority share in one of the Monarchy's main engineering enterprises, Prager Maschinenbau AG (formerly Ruston), and amalgamated this with its own machine factory, boiler shops, and bridge-building establishments. The move occurred almost immediately after the acquisition of a fairly large interest in Ungarische Kanonenfabrik, whose operations were due to start in 1915. Foreign customers included Russia and China, the latter thanks in no small measure to the great esteem in which the Austrian ambassador to Peking was held there. An earlier study has dealt with the support accorded by Austrian banks, not the least of which was the Creditanstalt, to the ramified commitments of the Monarchy's biggest armaments undertaking.[35]

The nature of the 1909–1913 boom becomes perhaps even plainer if one looks at the expansion of Stabilimento Tecnico Triestino, the shipyard based in Trieste with a branch at Linz on the Danube. Buffeted for many decades by marketing problems, Stabilimento had been kept afloat, sometimes at considerable cost, by Creditanstalt. Dividend payments averaged between 3% and 5%. In 1901–1903 they were suspended altogether. The vigorous increase of the Monarchy's expenditure on armaments during the second half of the centry's first decade effected a dramatic change of fortune. The construction of three dreadnoughts – *Viribus Unitis, Tegetthoff*, and *Prinz Eugen* – was entrusted to Stabilimento. (A fourth battleship went to the Danubia shipyard at Fiume.) Orders for torpedo-boat destroyers, motorized tugs, smaller-scale steam launches, and other craft were received from the Austrian, Romanian, and Chinese navies. In 1908 the firm's balance sheet had totalled just under 27.5 million crowns. Four years later, with the capital stock almost unchanged, it reached the record figure of 62 million crowns. The strain on Stabilimento's principal banker arising from its commitment is apparent from this tremendous rise in the volume of business. Progress was however likewise reflected in improved earnings. Between 1910 and 1914 the net profit doubled.[36]

The success of two other 'pure' armament firms merits attention. Towards the end of this period the very full order-books of Hirtenberger Patronenfabrik, dealing in munitions and associated with the Creditanstalt, owed much to extensive foreign contracts. In 1910 its number of employees averaged 1,680; in 1913 it was nearly 3,000; and in 1914, when war had already put its stamp on events, it went still higher. From 1912 to 1913 net profit rose substantially, from 1913 to 1914 it doubled.[37] Not quite so spectacular perhaps was the growth of Österreichische Waffenfabriks-Gesellschaft, with arms factories at Steyr and Letten, but here too employment and profit rose considerably. The firm's alertness to technological developments – the manufacture of machine-guns began at Steyr in 1905 – ensured for it a pivotal position during the First World War.[38]

The history of the merger between Skodawerke and Prager Maschinenbau AG was symptomatic of the economic climate between 1909 and 1913. In 1910 Ruston AG, from which Prager Maschinenbau AG had been created, possessed the relatively modest capital of 3.2 million crowns. By 1914, when Skodawerke took over, this had expanded to 14 million crowns. The liabilities, which were insignificant in 1910, stood by 1914 at nearly 14 million crowns.

Within four years the old Ruston machine factory founded in the 1820s had experienced an astounding transformation. First it acquired the Bromowski, Schulz und Sohr works at Königgrätz. Shortly afterwards it absorbed the well-known Ringhoffer machine works and initiated their large-scale expansion. Concurrently its other works underwent sizeable extension.

Two additional transactions should be mentioned in this breathtaking history. Shortly after the Bromowski, Schulz und Sohr amalgamation, Prager Maschinenbau bought a big block of shares in Ungarische Sangerhäusersche Maschinenfabrik, giving it a foothold in the swiftly developing market in the eastern half of the Monarchy. At the same time it sold its shares in Tanner, Laetsch Maschinen AG (purchased together with Ringhoffer from Creditanstalt), because ever since the disintegration of the short lived machine cartel their possession held out no prospect for an automatic increase in the market share.

Ruston's unprecedentedly quick rise had been rendered possible by the financial backing of a syndicate headed by the Anglo-Österreichische Bank. Then the sudden change of conditions in 1912 resulted in an inadequate utilization of the enlarged, modernized plants and eventually entailed such heavy losses as to impose the need for complete reorganization and a merger with Skodawerke. In the summer of 1914 Creditanstalt – in conjunction with four other major banks which had supported the Prague concern's expansion in one way or another –managed to conclude this task in a way acceptable to most parties.[39]

Several of the old Ruston AG's rivals had estimated the limits of expansion more wisely and therefore did better. Even in the critical year 1912 one of Ruston's fiercest competitors Maschinenfabrik AG, formerly Breitfeld, Daneck & Co., which in two successive years had considerably increased sales and capital, was able to survive quite well because, in addition to obtaining large export orders, it received a contract to fit out a cruiser. A report from 1913 on the state of the machine industry stated that the big firms were, on the whole, not faring badly.

But the performance of these great enterprises cannot be regarded as typical for business in the machine construction industry in general. . . . Labour market statistics show that in the case of medium-sized and small undertakings . . . in the second half of 1913 employment was at a low level not experienced in recent memory.[40]

On the eve of the First World War the machine industry, leaving aside notable instances of expansion and concentration which derived from substantial support by the major banks, consisted predominantly of small-scale firms. This was another weak point in the Monarchy's preparedness for an outbreak of hostilities.

Notes

1 Landes has drawn attention to this connection in his well-known work on Western Europe's industrialization and he regards it as the most important cause of Germany's industrial rise between 1870 and 1913. In Austria it becomes clearly perceptible only during the final years preceding the First World War. Cf. David S. Landes, *The Unbound Prometheus. Technological Change and Industrial Development in Western Europe from 1750 to the Present* (Cambridge, 1969), pp. 197 et seq., 206, and 222.
2 The brief, yet in its consequences far-reaching, boom of 1867–1873 is usually called the First Expansion Era (*'Gründerzeit'*).
3 On the basis of 1913 prices Professor Kausel has made the following estimate of the annual growth rate in real domestic product during the four decades prior to the First World War:

1870–1880	1880–1890	1890–1900	1900–1913
1.7%	2.3%	2.1%	2.4%

See Anton Kausel, 'Österreichs Volkseinkommen 1830 bis 1913', *Geschichte und Ergebnisse der zentralen amtlichen Statistik in Österreich 1829–1979* (Vienna, 1979), p. 700.
4 Gustav Stolper, 'Handelsbilanz und Wirtschaftspolitik', *Der Österreichische Volkswirt*, 4 April 1914, p. 469.
5 Between 1905 and 1912 the four Balkan countries' share in Austria's total exports expanded from 10.5% to 13%. The position as regards Austrian exports to Turkey can probably be ascribed to the boycott movement ensuing on the 1908 Annexation. Cf., *Statistische Nachrichten, betreffend den auswärtigen Handel der wichtigsten Staaten in den Jahren 1903–1907* and *Statistische Übersichten . . . in den Jahren 1907–1911*, published by the Austro-Hungarian Ministry of Trade (Vienna, 1910 and 1914 respectively).
6 Cf. 'Rückblick auf das Jahr 1913', *Statistische Monatsschrift*, New Series, Vol. XIX, Brünn (Brno) 1914, p. 149.
7 Cf. Richard Schüller, 'Die Handelsbilanz Österreich-Ungarns', *Zeitschrift für Volkswirtschaft, Sozialpolitik und Verwaltung*, Vol. XXI, Vienna 1912, p. 7.
8 'For three decades, from 1875 until 1906, the Austro-Hungarian trade balance has always shown a surplus.' Ludwig von Mises, 'Die Störungen des Wirtschaftslebens der Österreichisch-Ungarischen Monarchie während der Jahre 1912/13', *Archiv für Sozialwissenschaften und Sozialpolitik*, Vol. XXXIX, Tübingen 1915, p. 176, footnote.
9 'The yield per acre in the various groups of provinces varied with the greater or

lesser intensity of cultivation.' Hans Löwenfeld-Russ, *Die Regelung der Volks-ernährung im Kriege* (Vienna, 1926), p. 10. The author goes on to show, with the help of figures for average hectare yields 1910–13, that these were highest in Bohemia and Moravia, followed by the Alpine provinces, and then the Carpathian and Dinaric Alps regions.

10 Oscar Jaszi, *The Dissolution of the Habsburg Monarchy* (Chicago, 1929), p. 198.

11 Stefan Pascu, Constantin C. Givrescu, Josef Kovacs, and Ludovic Vajda, 'Einige Fragen der landwirtschaftlichen Entwicklung in der Österreichisch-Ungarischen Monarchie', *Die Agrarfrage in der Österreichisch-Ungarischen Monarchie, 1900–1918* (Bucharest, 1965), p. 8. The authors differentiate between small estates of 50–200 hectares, medium size ones of 200–500 hectares, and large ones of more than 500 hectares.

12 Stefan Pascu et al, *Die Agrarfrage in der Österreichisch-Ungarischen Monarchie*, p. 8.

13 'The great estate owners seldom attend personally to the administration of their real property. On the contrary, this is left to a staff which models itself on the leisurely, routine method of conducting business practised by civil servants. The entail on the estates prevents their transfer to better landlords.' Mises, *Archiv für Sozialwissenschaften und Sozialpolitik*, Vol. XXXIX, p. 179.

14 Cf. Frederick Hertz, *The Economic Problems of the Danubian States* (London, 1947), p. 32.

15 'Precisely in the big arable areas of Bohemia, Moravia, and Galicia there often predominated a far-reaching parcelling into plots of the properties belonging to individual farms that of course made their cultivation more difficult.' Alfred Hoffmann, 'Grundlagen der Agrarstruktur der Donaumonarchie.' See *Öster-reich-Ungarn als Agrarstaat* (Munich, 1978), ed. Alfred Hoffmann, p. 22.

16 Cf. Franz Sommeregger, *Die Wege und Ziele der Österreichischen Agrarpolitik seit der Grundentlastung* (Vienna, 1912), p. 29 et seq.

17 'To me it appears an established fact that the productive capacity of Austrian industry has in recent years grown enormously, and if so far this has not also manifested itself through increased competitiveness in the world market . . . then it is due to specific circumstances.' Stolper, *Der Österreichische Volkswirt* 4 April 1914.

18 For the years 1890–1900 and 1900–1913 Kausel estimates an average annual growth rate for industry and trade of 3.2% and 3.3% respectively. Kausel, *Geschichte und Ergebnisse*, p. 700.

19 'Probably the period of most rapid industrial growth in the entire history of Austria was in the years 1903 to 1907.' Richard L. Rudolph, *Banking and Industrialization in Austria-Hungary* (Cambridge, 1976), p. 32f. The author quotes the following annual growth rates for individual branches:

Foodstuffs	Textiles	Metal Processing	Machine Building	Total
3.7	7.9	9.3	9.8	6.3

20 'In so far as anything is known about the cartelized Austrian ironworks' domestic sales, the figure of more than 900 million kilograms for the year 1912 points to a huge uptrend.' The ironworks accounted for some 97% of production and,

according to this same source, sales in 1904 amounted to 497 million kilograms, in 1908 to 741 million kilograms, diminished in the following year to 666 million kilograms, but then rose again and in 1912 reached a provisional peak of 903 million kilograms. See Rückblick auf das Jahr 1913, *Statistische Monatsschrift*, NF XIX/1914, S160.

21 For example, in the high production year 1906, when the 'quantity of unrefined sugar came to almost 1,340 million kilograms, domestic consumption could absorb only 540 million kilograms'. Cf. the report on industry, trade, and communications in Lower Austria for 1906, *Niederösterreichische* Handelskammer (Vienna, 1907), p. XX et seq.

22 Alexander Gerschenkron, *An Economic Spurt That Failed* (Princeton, 1977), p. 71.

23 See Geoffrey Drage, *Austria-Hungary* (London, 1909), p. 98f.

24 For technical details of the rail and planned canal projects, see Gerschenkron, *An Economic Spurt that Failed*, p. 73 et seq.

25 The continual and rapid growth in the production of Portland cement throws light on the important part played by the building industry during the 1904–1912 upswing:

Production in 000 Tons						
1905	1906	1909	1910	1911	1912	1913
511	590	849	1147	1292	1380	1260

Source: *Compass*, 1915, Vol. 2, p. 13.

26 Cf. 'Die Lage der Textilindustrie', *Der Tresor*, 5 December 1908, and 'Die Abschwächung in der Baumwollindustrie', *Neue Freie Presse*, 24 February 1909.

27 A 'Statistical Chronicle' for 1913 speaks of a 'decline in the relative number of vacancies for practically all occupational grades. . . . The figures in the textile industry reveal a particularly blatant state of affairs. While in 1912 a decrease set in, in 1913 a drop occurred as against 1911 in the relative number of vacancies to nearly one third.' *Statistische Monatsschrift*, New Series, Vol. XIX, p. 169.

28 *Materialien zur österreichischen Produktions- und Betriebsstatistik* (Vienna, 1916), compiled by K.K. Handelsmuseum on instructions from the Ministry of Commerce. (K.K. = 'Imperial and Royal', the ubiquitous acronym preceding the name of all central government bodies.)

29 Kausel-Nemeth-Seidel, in 'Österreichs Volkseinkommen 1913 bis 1963', *Monatsberichte des Österreichischen Instituts für Wirtschaftsforschung*, Sup. 14 (Vienna, 1965), p. 17.

30 In the interpretation of these figures allowance has to be made for the fact that a statistically unascertainable fraction of the capital formation must be reckoned as already existent, not fresh, capital which was simply converted into shares. On the other hand it must not be overlooked that during this period company promotion activity availed itself increasingly of the form of the limited liability company which taxwise enjoyed an advantage over the joint-stock company. Between 1906 and 1913 the capital of limited liability companies expanded from some 17.5 million crowns to 494 million crowns. Cf. *Österreichisches Statistisches Handbuch für die im Reichsrat vertretenen Königreiche und Länder* (Vienna, 1914),

p. 176, published by the Central Statistical Commission.

31 *Materialien zur österreichischen Produktions- und Betriebsstatistik*, p. 8. The table is incomplete inasmuch as it leaves out of account the railway companies and those whose balance sheet results were not available at the time of data collection.

32 *Materialien*, p. 12.

33 In the years 1903–1913 'machine imports into the Monarchy rose from 50.3 to 157.2 million crowns.' Friedrich Hertz, *Die Produktionsgrundlagen der österreichischen Industrie vor und nach dem Krieg* (Vienna, 1917), p. 10. In another context the author states: 'The import of machines and equipment into Austria-Hungary during the five years 1909–1913 amounted to 739.3 million crowns, an annual average of 148 million crowns.' Ibid., p. 162.

34 At the beginning of the twentieth century the Dual Monarchy had among the great European nations the lowest per capita foreign trade quota. Only Tsarist Russia held a still more unfavourable position.

35 Cf. 'Skoda-Ruston' in 'Die Bilanzen', supplement to *Der Österreichische Volkswirt*, 10 April 1915, p. 123, *Der Österreichische Volkswirt*, 6 June 1914, p. 648, and Eduard März, *Österreichische Industrie- und Bankpolitik in der Zeit Franz Josephs I* (Vienna, 1968), pp. 303 and 341ff.

36 'Die Bilanzen', *Der Österreichische Volkswirt*, 15 November 1913, p. 25 and 21 August 1915, p. 265.

37 Cf. *Compass*, 1915, Vol. 2, pp. 470–1.

38 *Compass*, 1915, Vol. 2, pp. 470–1.

39 Cf. 'Prager Maschinenbau AG, vormals Ruston, Bromowsky und Ringhoffer', *Der Österreichische Volkswirt*, 31 January 1914, p. 288, 'Der Fall Ruston', *Neue Freie Presse*, 6 June 1914, and März, *Österreichische Industrie- und Bankpolitik*, p. 343f.

40 Cf. 'Die Bilanzen der Maschinenfabriken', *Der Österreichische Volkswirt*, 27 June 1914, p. 213.

CHAPTER 2
Important Structural Features of Austrian Industry

What were the most important structural features of the Austro-Hungarian economy before the outbreak of the First World War? Information on this point is not extensive because the last industrial census for Austria was held in 1902, at a time when the final spectacular pre-war boom had barely begun. Nonetheless, certain writers – notably Kurt W. Rothschild and Stephan Koren – have sketched a fairly precise picture of the Austrian economy as it was in 1913.[1]

Rothschild describes the country as 'an insufficiently developed agrarian state'. This may be applicable to Hungary, where 69% of the working population were still engaged in agriculture and only 13% in industry. Austria, where agriculture accounted for only 53% of the working population as against 23% in industry and trade, could be more aptly characterized as an agrarian state in a condition of rapid industrial development. The structure of the economy of the Alpine Provinces (including Lower Austria), of Bohemia, Moravia, and Silesia, stood at a level much closer to that of neighbouring Germany than to some underdeveloped regions of the Empire such as Galicia and Bukovina.

That the Austrian part of the Dual Monarchy, in spite of being preponderantly an agrarian entity, was no longer self-sufficient in agricultural products has already been mentioned. Large parts of Austria, especially the constantly expanding capital of Vienna, were dependent on grain imports from Hungary. This was to have fateful consequences when, during the war, Hungary increasingly disassociated itself from Austria. On the other hand, Austria had in Hungary an important outlet for its mass production goods.[2]

In the nineteenth century the economic status of an industrial country was determined primarily by its coal and iron deposits. The Austrian half of the Empire was comparatively well endowed with coal, but a great portion of its fuel reserves consisted of lignite. Particularly in the last years before the war increasing amounts of pit coal had to be imported from abroad.

Table 3   Output, exports and imports[3] (in million tons)

	Pit Coal Output	Exports	Imports	Lignite Output	Exports	Imports
1910	137.7	6.2	98.6	251.3	74.9	0.4
1911	143.8	6.1	108.7	252.7	70.6	0.3
1912	156.6	6.6	118.5	264.2	74.4	0.3
1913	163.4	7.1	136.9	274.1	70.2	0.3

A large share of Austria's fuel came from its own mines. Yet the scale of its industry's dependence on imports grew relatively fast. As industrialization progressed, so rose the need for good cokeable coal which Austria did not produce in adequate quantities. During the war the dependence on fuel supplies from abroad was a disadvantage, but not of too serious a nature because the vast majority of pre-war imports had come from Germany. The situation altered abruptly after the collapse of the Monarchy, inasmuch as only a fraction of previous production fell to the new Austria.[4]

The petroleum industry in Galicia constituted another important branch of mineral extraction alongside mining. A few years before the war an output of nearly two million tons per annum placed Austria among the world's leading oil-producing countries. Shortly before the outbreak of hostilities production declined to a little more than one million tons per annum, though it increased once again during the war, in spite of a temporary Russian occupation of the oilfields. During the war petroleum was one of Austria's few noteworthy exports.[5]

Few things are so clearly indicative of the economy's relative backwardness as the state of the iron industry. One of the oldest in Europe and in the eighteenth century still advanced, its modernization proceeded at a snail's pace. A number of circumstances explain why the process was so protracted during the second half of the nineteenth century. The profusion of woodland favoured the survival of small ironworks. The unfavourable location of coal and ore deposits made for relatively high production costs which worked to the advantage of British and German competitors, particularly in periods of liberalized trading relations. Lastly there was the poor absorption capacity of the home markets, above all in the backward regions where the horse-drawn wooden plough symbolized the outlook and the economic efficiency of the Empire's numerically largest occupational group.

From the end of the 1870s onward protective tariffs and cartelization at almost all levels moulded the industry's development. The following table for the year 1911 shows the extent of concentration in pig-iron production:[6]

Table 4   Pig-iron production

	000 tons	%
Total Austrian production	1,596	100
Alpine Montangesellschaft (Styria)	550	34
Witkowitz (Moravia)	447	28
Präger Eisenindustrie Gesellschaft (Bohemia)	329	20
Österreichische Berg- und Hüttenwerks-Gesellschaft (Silesia)	117	7
Krainische Industrie-Gesellschaft (Trieste)	102	5
Total production of five companies	1,545	97

'The duties on iron' (imports) 'were well above the average tariff rate. In many positions they exceeded 50% of the value, in some cases even 100% and more. For rolling mill materials they were three to five times higher than in Germany', writes Koren.[7] Under these conditions it was clearly not difficult for the tightly organized iron cartels to impose on the finishing industries and on consumers an excessive price burden. In the years 1908–1911 'the most important types of rolling mill materials . . .' (were) 'from a quarter to two thirds dearer than in Berlin although the transport distance from Styria or Bohemia to Vienna was shorter than from the Ruhr to Berlin.'[8]

The consequences of these 'defects' in the Austrian iron industry, conditioned by both natural and historical circumstances, can be summarized in two easily remembered sets of figures: the Empire's per capita production of steel and its pig-iron consumption were substantially lower than in all west European countries.[9]

Per capita steel production (in tons) 1903–1907

Belgium	Germany	Gt. Britain	Sweden	France	Aust.-Hung.
0.24	0.16	0.14	0.07	0.06	0.024

Per capita iron consumption (in tons) 1903–1907

| 0.25 | 0.18 | 0.19 | 0.09 | 0.08 | 0.03 |

As is evident, steel production and iron consumption in Austria-Hungary lay far below the comparable figures for all major European states with the exception of Russia, which, however, during the last few years of peace, made considerable advances. The Dual Monarchy's relatively modest performance was to prove a fatal flaw in the first great war of *matériel* experienced in history.

Reference has been made to the swift progress, during the Empire's final years, in the machine industry. Nevertheless, on the eve of war, small and medium sized firms were also dominant in this sphere. The available figures (generally including those for the electrical industry) are, as for most production branches, scanty and usually inconsistent. According to the 1902 industrial census the 24,907 firms with 161,822 employees in the Austrian half of the Empire had at their disposal a 52,645 h.p. engine capacity. Obviously the majority of these undertakings were small-sized firms. Only 321 of these businesses, i.e., a little more than 1%, were joint-stock companies. These employed 52,441 individuals and had a 28,395 h.p. engine capacity. So a tiny fraction of all undertakings accounted for almost a third of all employees; but even their engine capacity was low.

In 1906 a census of working hours in Austrian industrial installations by the Labour Statistics Office reported that the machine industry consisted of 1,108 plants with 112,797 employees. About a quarter of the plants and 70% of the employees belonged to Categories 3 and 4, in which 100 and 300 workers were engaged respectively. A comparison between the 1902 and the 1906 census is unfortunately not possible because of the entirely different statistical criteria applied, but the 1906 investigation conveys at any rate the impression that the machine industry, so important to the economy's international standing, continued to function on a small-scale basis.

This view is supported by many contemporary opinions. Contemporary writers repeatedly referred to the high prices of iron with which the machine and machine tools, equipment, and electrical industries were burdened.[10] The poor absorption capacity of the numerically large market – one with over fifty-two million potential consumers –was moreover responsible for the lack of specialization and therefore of standardization. The declared objective of the Association of Austrian Machine Manufacturers, founded in 1907 as a quasi-cartel, was to achieve specialization and the transition to cheap mass production.[11] In 1911, faced with quickly mounting dissensions among its members, the Association was dissolved.[12]

The following information, which refers to one of the growth sectors of the machine industry, can be taken as typical of the condition of the industry as a whole. Thus in an oft-quoted Jubilee publication it is stated that even in 1908 a few large-scale automobile producers existed alongside a great majority of small producers.[13] Several big firms, especially in the armaments industry which applied mass production methods, had of course no reason to fear comparison with leading Western European undertakings. Large, efficient managements existed likewise in the fields of boiler, locomotive, carriage, turbine, and other manufactures.[14] Indeed Austria could compete successfully in any foreign market where the nature of a particular item made mass production methods inapplicable. And in the electrical industry there were a number of capable enterprises predominantly in foreign ownership.

The results of the 1900 census and the 1910 census convey a fairly reliable picture of the growth and comparative importance of individual industrial sectors.[15] Whereas the total figure for those employed in industry and trade rose during this decade by 25%, the number of wage and salary earners in engineering went up by nearly 67%, in the foodstuffs and allied products industry by 31%, and in textiles by 16%. The share of these industries for 1910 in the total figure of employed was respectively 5.4%, 9.8% and 14.3%. The textile industry was accordingly by far the most important sector of industry as a whole, and that must be taken as an indication of the state of the Austrian economy's development at this time.

Table 5   Employment in industry, 1900 and 1910

	1900 absolute	in %	1910 absolute	in %	1900–1910 increase in %
Total	2,897,261[a]	100	3,627,816	100	25.22
of this					
Machinery and engineering	117,855[b]	4.07	196,666	5.42	66.87
Textile industry	449,011	15.5	519,860	14.33	15.78
Food industry	272,028[c]	9.39	357,441	9.85	31.40

Sources: census 1900, Österr. Statistisches Handbuch 1905, p. 9ff; Census 1910, Österr. Statistisches Handbuch 1915, p. 16ff.
[a] For reasons of comparability the employees in the catering trade were not included in the figures.
[b] Without employees in public utilities (power and water supply). The share of this category in the total was assumed, on basis of the 1910 census, to amount to 7.3%.
[c] Without the catering trade (according to the industrial census of 1902).

It is apparent from Table 5 that the engineering industry was the leading sector in the last decade before the war. The textile industry however remained the largest single industrial branch although its growth was comparatively moderate. At the end of the Dual Monarchy's last great expansion period the textile industry, though rich in tradition and going back to the seventeenth century, had a significantly smaller productive capacity than its major European competitors. In 1914 the German cotton industry possessed almost three times as many spindles as did Austria-Hungary.[16]

The inability, as Koren rightly emphasizes, of the textile industry to take more than very limited advantage of the 'big market represented by the Empire' complements what has been said about the machine-building industry. 'In consequence of the textile industry's fragmentation, of the manifold national and cultural differences, and of the disparities in the level of income between the various parts of the country, the demand structure was very differentiated and this drawback nullified largely the benefit of the "common market".'[17]

However, the diversity of the national markets and the low purchasing power were not the only reasons for the backwardness of Austrian industry. Another factor was the early and rather rigorous cartelization of many of its sectors, among them quite a few branches of the textile industry. The upshot was the preservation of small scale business and obsolete technology.

Typical too for the economy's low level of development was the strikingly high number of individuals (usually women) who eked out a meagre livelihood in the clothing trade. The 1902 census established that there were 171,711 firms in this line of business. Since the engine capacity totalled 4,840 h.p., these firms must have been of a predominantly handicraft character, and as nearly 400,000 persons were employed – more, that is, than in industry's largest sector, textiles – it follows that there were barely more than two individuals on the pay-roll of each firm. Only eight firms were organized as joint-stock companies.

This brief review of Austrian industry's structural peculiarities before the outbreak of the First World War must end with a reference to the important position enjoyed by the foodstuffs and allied products sector. In 1910 (see Table 5) almost 10% of all persons engaged in industry and trade were in its employ. The most up-to-date and efficient branch was the sugar industry, concentrated practically exclusively in Bohemia and Moravia on account of favourable soil conditions and the availability of cheap labour. In the business year 1912/13 the ouput of nearly 1.9 million tons (unrefined sugar value) from 178 factories set a record. Consumption, also a peak figure, was merely 672,000 tons, i.e., hardly more than 35%. By far the largest proportion of production, 1,091,000 tons or 57.5%, was exported.[18] The low domestic consumption, although varying greatly between regions, can again be taken as an indication of the Empire's backwardness.[19]

The milling, brewing, and spirits industries were other important branches. Whereas the sugar industry must be reckoned as having be en among the technically most advanced in Europe, the dominance of small- and medium-sized undertakings inadequately equipped with machinery was characteristic of the other branches in this sector. None was of course altogether lacking in efficient large-scale enterprises. The Hungarian flour-milling industry in particular had been extensively modernized in the last decades before the war; this enabled Hungary to meet a substantial part of the cereals requirements of the Dual Monarchy's Austrian half.[20] Conditions almost everywhere, though, bore the stamp of tenacious survival by small and obsolete operating units able, thanks to their membership of officially sponsored lobbies, to fend off the swift advance of big enterprises.

It will therefore cause little surprise that no more than a relatively minor fraction (31.7%) of those employed in industry and trade were found in establishments with a working force of more than one hundred.[21] True, circumstances were somewhat better in such sectors as textiles and primary products, but this does not change the unfavourable overall picture in comparison with Western industrial states and Germany. The average was an engine capacity of less than 1 h.p. per worker in nearly all sectors. Mining, metallurgy, and paper manufacture alone made a better showing. Almost half of all employed persons were in textiles, clothing, and foodstuffs production. The machine-building, iron, metal-working, and electrical industries clearly had a comparatively small work force. 'The production structure', Koren properly remarks, was 'typical of an agrarian country in the process of industrialization.'[22]

To summarize: on the eve of the First World War the Austro-Hungarian Empire, in spite of great progress achieved during its last decades, must be called a large 'underdeveloped' economic entity. Comparison between incomes in those days is notoriously hazardous, but the following facts will give some idea of how the Austrian half of the Empire stood internationally: in 1913 the average Austrian per capita income is likely to have been 45% of British, 63% of German, and 36% of North American incomes.[23] However the considerable regional income disparities, more marked than in most Western countries, must not be overlooked. Certain parts of Lower Austria,

Vorarlberg, Bohemia, Moravia, and Silesia probably enjoyed a standard of living not strikingly different from that of Germany.[24] The population in the Empire's industrialized areas (approximately eleven and a half million individuals) amounted however to less than a quarter of the total.[25] Such indicators reflect the unfavourable employment structure. According to the 1910 census, 53% of all employed persons were engaged in agriculture, but only 23% in industry and trade. (In Hungary, agriculture absorbed 69% of the labour market, industry only 13%.)

Industry, as has been seen, consisted, in the main, of small units. More than half of its production came from undertakings with fewer than twenty employees. On the other hand a number of big enterprises in the coal, iron and steel, machine-building, electrical, and armament industries had an outstanding part in the Empire's economic life and were destined to bear the brunt of economic warfare between 1914 and 1918. The picture would be incomplete without mention of the strategic role in economic and financial policy played by the major banks. Their ties, personal and financial, with industry were close. Subsequent chapters will deal with these connections in more detail.

Much has been written about the Dual Monarchy's 'natural handicaps', such as a modest endowment with power resources and raw materials, an unfavourable transportation system, vast tracts of mountainous country, a negligible number of navigable waterways, and other traits barring the way to quick industrialization. To them were added a series of grave structural deficiences with deep historical roots; they have been classified as fiscalism, protectionism, and national antagonism.[26] These symptoms of social disease will be examined cursorily in the following chapters, but their thorough analysis must remain outside the scope of the present work.

Notes

1 See *Österreichische Wirtschaftsstruktur Gestern – Heute – Morgen*, edited by W. Weber (Berlin, 1961). Cf. particularly p. 52ff and p. 259ff.

2 'The Austrian half of the Empire . . . , a major agricultural importer, in 1912 drew 85% of its wheat and cattle imports from Hungary. In reverse it sold there the main part of its most important industries' export surpluses. The textile, ready-to-wear clothing, and leather industries sent 60%, the iron, hardware, and machine industries 57% of their exports to Hungary.' Kurt W. Rothschild, *Österreichische Wirtschaftsstruktur*, p. 64.

3 Cf. 'Statistical Chronicle', *Statistische Monatsschrift*, New Series, Vol. XIX, Brünn (Brno) 1914, p. 158.

4 Lower Austrian pit coal, according to Koren's calculations, contributed no more than half a per cent to the total production. Lignite mines, mainly in Styria, furnished just about 14%. If post-1918 territorial cessions are taken into account, 'today's Austria accounted in the lignite production in this half of the Empire for barely 11%.' Stephan Koren, *Österreichische Wirtschaftsstruktur*, p. 275.

5 Before the outbreak of hostilities Austria's oil industry was undergoing a severe recession. The war brought about an abrupt change due in no small part to the needs of Germany which had been almost entirely isolated from its traditional supply sources. Oil transports however were badly impeded by mobilization measures and traffic difficulties. The second part of this work will deal in greater detail with the oil industry. Cf. 'Die Bilanzen', *Der Österreichische Volkswirt*, No. 42, 17 July 1915.

6 *Verhandlungen der vom K.K. Handelsministerium veranstalteten Kartellenquete* (Vienna, 1912), Pt. VIII, p. 507.

7 Koren, *Österreichische Wirstchaftsstruktur*, p. 280.

8 Koren, *Österreichische Wirtschaftsstruktur*, p. 261.

9 Cf. Nachum Th. Gross, 'Die Stellung der Habsburgermonarchie in der Weltwirtschaft', *Die Habsburgermonarchie 1848–1918* (Vienna, 1973), Vol. I, p. 26. It should be noted that Gross's data refer to Austria-Hungary as a whole, but that the contribution of the Empire's Hungarian half was comparatively modest. In 1903–1907 per capita iron consumption in the Austrian half was 0.036 tons, i.e., above the average figure for the Empire as a whole. In 1908–1911 there was a fast rise of per capita consumption to 0.05 tons in the Austrian half, but then the iron production and consumption increases were also considerable in the other industrial countries mentioned here. Cf. *Compass*, 1913, Vol. 2, p. 37.

10 Cf. Friedrich Hertz, *Die Produktionsgrundlagen der österreichischen Industrie vor und nach dem Kriege* (Vienna-Berlin, 1917), p. 149. Also Otto Bauer, 'Die Teverung', *Werkausgabe*, I, 5720ff.

11 Cf. H. Fischer, 'Die Maschinenindustrie in Österreich', *Die Grossindustrie Österreichs* (Vienna, 1908), p. 97ff.

12 *Compass*, 1913, Vol. 2, p. 80.

13 Cf. L. Lohner, 'Der Waggon- und Automobilbau in Österreich'. *Die Grossindustrie österreichs*, p. 107.

14 Koren, *Österreichische Wirtschaftsstruktur*, p. 292.

15 Sources: 'Die Bevölkerung Österreichs im Jahre 1900', *Statistisches Handbuch* (Vienna, 1905), p. 9ff, and 'Volkszählung 1910', *Statistisches Handbuch* (Vienna, 1915), p. 16ff.

16 Koren, *Österreichische Wirtschaftsstruktur*, p. 288.

17 Koren, *Österreichische Wirtschaftsstruktur*, p. 191.

18 See 'Rückblick auf das Jahr 1913', *Statistische Monatsschrift*, NS, Vol. XIX, p. 155.

19 In 1912 the per capita unrefined sugar consumption in Austria-Hungary was 13 kg., in Britain 42.2 kg., and in Germany 21.6 kg. See *Compass*, 1916, Vol. 2, p. 289. The tax on sugar was however both in Britain and in Germany substantially less than in Austria-Hungary.

20 In 1913 the Austrian half of the Empire imported 800,000 tons of wheat and rye as well as 800,000 tons of flour and other mill products preponderantly from Hungary. See Koren, *Österreichische Wirtschaftsstruktur*, p. 286.

21 The data given here derives from the 1902 Industrial Census. Matters had

undoubtedly improved somewhat by 1913.

22 Cf. Koren, *Österreichische Wirtschaftsstruktur*, p. 265.

23 Cf. Angus Maddison, 'Phases of Capitalist Development', *Banca Nazionale de Lavoro*, Quarterly Review, Rome 1977. According to Bairoch, in 1913 the Austrian per capita real gross domestic product was 57% of German and 61% of British real income. Cf. P. Bairoch, 'Europe's Gross National Product 1800–1975', *The Journal of European History*, 5/1976.

24 The Austrian national income amounted on average in the years 1911–1913 to 520 crowns per capita, but in the German-speaking provinces to 790 crowns, a figure almost corresponding to German per capita income. Cf. Kausel-Nemeth-Seidel, 'Österreichs Volkseinkommen 1913 bis 1963', *Monatsberichte des Österreichischen Instituts für Wirtschaftsforschung*, Sup. 14, Vienna 1965, p. 31.

25 An essay by Heiss, 'Der Nationale Besitzstand in Böhmen', stated that practically all leading Bohemian industries were situated in areas predominantly inhabited by Germans. See *Schmollers Jahrbuch* (Leipzig, 1906), Vol. 30, p. 380.

26 See Eduard März, 'Zur Genesis der Schumpeterschen Theorie der wirtschaftlichen Entwicklung', *On Political Economy and Econometrics. Essays in Honour of Oskar Lange* (Warsaw, 1964), p. 371. Also Matis and Bachinger, who regarded the symptoms of social disease as more harmful than economic crises, 'Österreichs industrielle Entwicklung', *Die Habsburgermonarchie*, Vol. I, p. 140.

CHAPTER 3
A State Living Beyond Its Means

In January 1914 Eugen von Böhm-Bawerk, the great Austrian economist, published in the *Neue Freie Presse* three articles dealing in detail with the disquieting phenomenon of the adverse trade balance.[1] Stolper, as has been noted, ascribed the sudden reversal in the trend of the trade balance to the rapid progress of industrialization and so was prepared to look on this manifestation of disequilibrium as a sign of positive growth.[2] Böhm-Bawerk's viewpoint was a novelty inasmuch as he laid most of the blame for the unfavourable development on the government:

People say, and it is probably correct, that a very large number of private individuals among us are living beyond their means. What is definite is that for some time a very large number of our public authorities have been living beyond their means. The state, for one. It is hardly pure chance that the decades when we continually had a favourable balance of trade approximately coincided with the epoch during which rigorous thrift, much abused in its day, prevailed; thrift is never popular. But the change in our balance of trade – it is not a matter here of a specific year – has occurred roughly at the same time as a change in the spirit in which our economic affairs are conducted. We have undoubtedly become lavish and open-handed in our expenditure.[3]

Böhm-Bawerk was, it may be interesting to record from the point of view of the history of economic thought, in this context a supporter of anticyclical budgetary policy: 'In the fat years of an unclouded boom, instead of accumulating direct and indirect reserves for the never failing demands of a less prosperous future, we squandered amidst our good fortune everything, but everything, down to the last penny, that could still be grabbed by tightening the tax-screw and anticipating future sources of income to the upper limit.'

Then he asked how this had come about:

A whole book could be written on that, and it would have to have for its subject the domestic history, more especially the *domestic political* history, of the past decade, for with us the Exchequer has always been politics' whipping-boy. We have seen innumerable variations of the vexing game of trying to generate political contentment through material concessions. If formerly the Parliaments were the guardians of thrift, they are today far more like its sworn enemies. Nowadays the political and nationalist parties . . . are in the habit of cultivating a greed for all kinds of benefits for their co-nationals or constituencies that they regard as a veritable duty, and should the political situation be correspondingly favourable, that is to say correspondingly unfavourable for the Government, then political pressure will produce what is wanted. Often enough, though, because of the carefully calculated rivalry and jealousy between parties, what has been granted to one has also to be conceded to others – from a single costly concession springs a whole bundle of costly concessions . . .[4]

Böhm-Bawerk's remarks aptly describe what is now known as wheeler-dealer politics.

In parliamentary life the period from 1895 to 1900 was marked by an intensification of political conflict, caused partly by the introduction of a 'Fifth Curia' (elected by universal suffrage) into the Austrian *Reichsrat*.[5] During these years national expenditure in the Austrian half of the Empire rose from 1,330 million crowns to 1,605 million, or by 21%. During the next five years the rate of expansion was slightly less, some 14%, so that even after the introduction of the Fifth Curia it is scarcely possible to talk about a process of expenditure escalation. Only in the succeeding five years occurred what can properly be described as a cost explosion. Expenditure mounted from 1,830 million crowns in 1905 to 2,901 million crowns in 1910, some 59%. From 1910 until 1913 the expansion remained within the same limits.[6]

Thus it seems that the parliamentary tradition of 'give, that you may receive' can hardly have been responsible for the increase in national expenditure during the last years before the war. Some writers ascribe to railway construction and other outlays on infrastructure a special place in contemporary expenditure.[7] Since the 1880s' railway construction had however played a subordinate part in fiscal policy, and the enterprising ideas of Koerber as Prime Minister at the beginning of the century could not achieve any decisive change here.[8]

The solution to the puzzle lies in the continual and considerable increase of expenditure on war preparations and armaments after the Bosnian Annexation Crisis of 1908.[9] The modernization of military equipment, naval construction, and the mobilizations in 1908 and 1912 put inordinate demands on the capacity of the Austrian money and capital markets, all the more so because of the heavy claims made on them until autumn 1912 by the private sector. The Annual Report of Creditanstalt for that year describes the situation as follows:

> The shape of business activity . . . was decisively influenced by monetary conditions. Tightness on the money market which had begun in 1911 . . . did not perceptibly ease at the outset of 1912. On the contrary, the disproportion between capital formation and capital requirements on the part of both the public and the private sectors became of ever greater importance in monetary affairs and eventually led, in conjunction with events on the international money market, to a state of constant stringency. The effects had become distinctly noticeable when at the beginning of autumn a serious political crisis, which badly affected the domestic economy, resulted in consequence of the Balkan War.[10]

The growing demands made during the last years of peace by the state on the capital market are apparent from the table below. Undoubtedly 1912 constituted the climax of this development. The following quotation furnishes a basis of comparison. 'Whereas during the 1890s Austria's official issues averaged annually some 109 million crowns, and during the first decade of our century 149 million crowns, national indebtedness to the extent of 541 million crowns was incurred in 1912.'[11]

Table 6   Summary of State debts incurred, 1910–13 (in Crowns)

	1910	1911	1912	1913
4% Crown Bonds	381,136,200	129,193,400	200,000,000	17,182,100
4% Treasury Certificates			130,000,000	
4½% Treasury Certs ($)			123,500,000	
Loans by Insurance Coys.			87,500,000	25,000,000
4½% 1913 Railway Bonds				144,412,800
Total	381,136,200	129,193,400	541,000,000	186,594,900

That the authorities should have been faced with growing difficulties in the raising of loans is hardly surprising. In 1909 the two Ministers of Finance of Austria and Hungary decided to seek cover for the state's most urgent monetary needs by issuing tax-free Treasury Certificates. The press conjectured that the two independent Administrations wanted to refrain from placing too much of a burden on the bond market so as not to put fresh downward pressure on prices.[12] It proved possible to retain the type of 4% Crown Bond introduced at the beginning of the century, but the terms of issue worsened progressively, and increasingly resort had to be made to short-term financing operations. Towards the end of the critical year 1912 the Austrian Government was forced to strengthen the Austro-Hungarian Bank's gold reserves by floating a loan in the United States.[13]

The years 1910 to 1913 are also characterized by a quite exceptional augmentation of capital invested in stocks, a fact that becomes evident from the following table:

Table 7   Joint-Stock Companies[14]

Close of Year	No. of companies	Nom. Cap.	Incr./Decr. Nom. Cap. on Preceding Year	Incr./Decr. as % of Nom. Cap.
		(in million crowns)		
1900	529	2,065.4	125.5	6.47
1901	551	2,164.6	99.2	4.80
1902	557	2,133.1	− 31.5	− 1.45
1903	569	2,169.2	36.1	1.69
1904	573	2,217.2	48.0	2.21
1905	587	2,411.1	193.9	8.75
1906	609	2,587.1	176.0	7.30
1907	648	2,744.5	157.4	6.08
1908	661	2,823.1	78.7	2.87
1909	668	2,940.3	117.1	4.15
1910	709	3,354.4	414.1	14.08
1911	736	3,904.1	549.7	16.39
1912	780	4,177.1	273.0	6.99
1913	822	4,378.3	201.2	4.82

For the years 1900 to 1909 the increase of capital formation in the shape of shares averaged some 100 million crowns. The comparable figure for the years 1910 to 1913 was 360 million crowns, no less than three-and-a-half times the foregoing amount. This should not be read as a precise measure of capital formation, since capital formation was not confined to joint-stock companies. The statistic fails, moreover, to distinguish between companies concerned with financial affairs and those concerned with industrial affairs. A not insubstantial proportion of the newly-formed capital fell to the share of the former (primarily banks and insurance companies).[15] Finally, the figures shown in the table do not take into account the investments of the railway companies, which, during this period, were not very significant.

The facts quoted so far are sufficient to suggest the degree of excess demand that had crystallized especially during the second upswing period, i.e., from 1909 to 1912. The increasing trade deficit that had caused so much public excitement was of course only one, even if the most serious, of the many signs that manpower and industrial resources were being overtaxed. Other symptoms of economic strain included higher prices, mounting interest rates, growing liquidity problems of the principal financial houses and the restrictive central bank policy of trying – with the usual time lag – to keep the boom from getting out of hand.[16] Austria in short was experiencing for perhaps the first time in its history the phenomenon of a demand inflation that had not – or not yet – been caused by the fatal mechanism of inflationary war financing.

The phenomenon of higher prices, one of the most unpleasant manifestations accompanying the Empire's final boom phase, was one of the themes most frequently discussed in economic journals of the day.[17] 'The uninterrupted rise in prices, gaining ever more ground and affecting all the necessities of life, can surely be called the greatest handicap to a thoroughgoing improvement', complained a report by the Lower Austrian Chamber of Commerce on economic conditions in 1910.

That the increase of prices for foodstuffs in Austria is the direct outcome of the excessive protectionism for agrarian products as well as the nonsensical policy gravitating toward autarchy, and that the enormous sacrifices imposed on consumers confer no benefit on the broad mass of the rural population, but in the main only on the large-scale producers, has become the axiom of the [country's] entire urban and business population. . . . The rise in prices forces the lower and the middle strata to curtail to the utmost outlays which go beyond the necessities of life and it acutely restricts the use that they can make of any manufactured and commercial goods other than for basic needs.[18]

In 1909, the year of vigorous economic revival, the bank rate had been 4%. Step by step it rose to 5.5%. In November 1912, when the Dual Monarchy reacted to the Balkan War by mobilizing its Army, it rose to a rare height of 6%, remaining at that level almost until the close of the following year. Likewise the bank note circulation expanded in 1912 to a record high and was not substantially reduced during 1913. Growing indebtedness abroad, gold and foreign exchange losses, and an intermittent increase above par of the exchange rate in Paris and London were further clear signs of the pressure to which the Austrian economy was subject in the last years of peace.[19]

Indubitably therefore it was not only the balance of trade on merchandise account but also the balance of payments that was in the red at this time; that explains the growing concern with which Böhm-Bawerk and other prominent economists observed developments. Perhaps this chapter may properly close with a reference to the balance of payments situation before 1914, although statistical information is scanty. At the beginning of the eighties the import of capital in conjunction with the trade balance surplus resulted in a balance of payments surplus indicated by the central bank's rising gold and foreign exchange reserves, as well as by holdings, in general on a modest scale of foreign securities. The Empire's capital flows consisted largely of bonds, loans, and shares. Since 1880 the trade balance had shown a surplus, only after 1907 it went into deficit once again. The figures available on the balance of capital transactions permit the conclusion that whereas in 1892, when the crown was introduced as the new monetary unit, some capital export took place, in subsequent years until about 1903 the import of capital predominated. Then for a short while, until about 1909, capital exports again took place; thereafter capital was again imported but on a larger scale.[20]

Computations of the interest and dividend payments, as well as the statistics of securities owned, suggest that for quite a considerable time before the turn of the century substantial capital imports had been occurring. After 1900 interest and dividend payments abroad, according to balance of payments estimates, averaged annually some 350 million crowns. In 1901 Austro-Hungarian securities totalled 19,600 million crowns face value; of which 6,800 million crowns, or 35%, and 2,000 million crowns were respectively Austrian and Hungarian securities in foreign possession. (In the case of the roughly 4,000 million crowns railway bonds even 75% were in foreign possession.) Capital movements after 1900 were, however, no longer one-way. In 1912 Austrian banks and finance houses held foreign securities to the value of about 1,000 million crowns. There was also a flow of capital from the Empire's Austrian half to Hungary, although the Austrian half's overall capital import exceeded its export of capital abroad and to Hungary.

Capital movements were in essence confined to fixed interest securities. Direct foreign investments, i.e., foreign interest in Austrian enterprises, were comparatively unimportant. In 1901, of the total 789 million crowns face value of industrial shares and bonds in circulation and belonging to firms in the Austrian half of the Empire, only 12% were held by foreign investors. In Bohemia the proportion was probably still smaller. With banks the foreign ratio was higher and amounted to about 20% of their shares' nominal value.

A summary of estimates for important items in the Austro-Hungarian balance of payments during the last pre-war years attests to the trend towards a chronic deficit.[21]

Table 8   Estimate of the Austro-Hungarian
balance of payments, 1894–1913
(Total payments for quinquennial periods in crowns million)

	1894–1898	1899–1903	1904–1908	1909–1913
Net Receipts				
Balance of Trade in Goods				
incl. Gold and Coins	205	960	405	—
Remittances by Emigrants	150	200	700	1500
Tourism	200	250	350	500
Bank Profits and Services				
Receipts	200	300	400	450
Transit Traffic	100	150	180	250
Total Net Receipts	855	1860	2035	2700
Net Payments				
Balance of Trade in Goods				
incl. Gold and Coins	—	—	—	2400
Interest and Dividend Payments	1550	1750	1750	1750
Less Earnings and For. Investm.	− 120	− 150	− 150	− 200
Total Net Payments	1430	1600	1600	3950
Bal. of Net Receipts/Payments	− 575	260	435	−1250
Credit/Debit Securities Balance				
(Capital Exports −, Imports)	481	157	− 270	267

Sources: Leo Paswolsky, *Economic Nationalism of the Danubian States* (New York, 1928), pp. 11–13. Ignaz Gruber-Menninger and Gustav Thaa, 'Daten zur Zahlungsbilanz', *Tabellen zur Währungsstatistik* (Vienna, 1904), Pt. 2, No. 3, p. 775, published by the Ministry of Finance. Franz Bartsch, 'Statistische Daten über die Zahlungsbilanz Österreich-Ungarns vor Ausbruch des Krieges', *Mitteilungen des k.k. Finanzministeriums* (Vienna, 1917), No. 22, p. 87f.

Notes

1 Eugen von Böhm-Bawerk, 'Unsere passive Handelsbilanz', *Neue Freie Presse*, 6, 8, and 9 January 1914.
2 Cf. Gustav Stolper, 'Handelsbilanz und Wirtschaftspolitik', *Der österreichische Volkswirt*, 4 April 1914.
3 Böhm-Bawerk, *Neue Freie Presse*, 9 January 1914.
4 Böhm-Bawerk, *Neue Freie Presse*. Italics in the original.

5 On 14 June 1896 the Austrian Parliament passed the law on the constitution of the 'Fifth Curia'. The existent four curias allowed 129 seats for the rural communes, 118 for the municipal electors, 21 for the Chambers of Commerce and Trade, and 85 for representatives of the large landed estate owners. The new curia had 72 seats to represent a new general elector class for which every national who had attained his twenty-fourth birthday was given the franchise. Cf. Richard Charmatz, *Österreichs innere Geschichte von 1848 bis 1907* (Leipzig, 1909), Vol. II, p. 105.

6 The figures are taken from the official Statements of Account. Cf. also Aloys von Czedik, *Der Weg von und zu den österreichischen Staatsbahnen* (Teschen-Vienna-Leipzig, 1913), Vol. III, p. 50f.

7 In 'Die österreichische Finanzpolitik', *Die Habsburgermonarchie 1848–1918* (Vienna, 1973), Vol. I, p. 92, Josef Wysocki writes, 'If there is added to this' (railway expenditure) 'the same kind of outlay on postal, telegraphic, and telephone services, which in 1910 amounted to 175 million crowns or 87.5 million Austrian gulden, i.e., 6.1% of the total state expenditure, the upshot is that some 33% of the total state expenditure in Imperial Austria was applied in a manner clearly identifiable as a trend towards socialization. Activities closely linked with economic development and technical progress turn out to be the chief agents of expansion.' The author overlooks that in the Austrian budget railway expenditure and railway receipts are itemized and that only the balance on them can be taken into consideration for the kind of reflection in which he engages. It is hardly possible to speak of increased expenditure on infrastructure in view of the operating profits shown by the railways in the last pre-war years. A notable expansion in public expenditure occurred in the years 1907 and 1909 primarily on account of the nationalization of the last important private railways.

8 Karl Bachinger, 'Das Verkehrswesen', *Die Habsburgermonarchie*, Vol. I., p. 296, confirms that 'Looking at the whole period since 1882, official construction activity, with a total length of 2,237 kilometres at an outlay of close on 657 million crowns (1910 figures), remained relatively modest.'

9 Cf. 'Das Budget', *Der österreichische Volkswirt*, No. 36, pp. 676–7, 6 June 1914, criticized the budget estimates for the financial year 1914–15, which had to be changed after the outbreak of war (28 July 1914), in the following terms: 'Using net figures for the state undertakings and monopolies, the outcome would be a requirement for the military household exceeding 30% of the overall expenditure. The amount needed for joint outlays and the Home Defence Ministry is higher than the joint total of the budgets for the Ministries of the Interior, Justice, Commerce, Agriculture, and Public Works. In addition the requirement for the National Debt, and especially its increase, is of course attributable in the main to armament activities.' The publication refers in this connection to drastic reductions in capital spending on railways, postal services, and telegraph lines 'although the entire working population is badly hit by the inadequacy of the telegraphic and telephone installations.'

10 *Geschäftsbericht des Verwaltungsrates der k.k. Priv. Österreichischen Creditanstalt für Handel und Gewerbe für das Jahr 1912* (Vienna, 1913), available in the Creditanstalt archives.

11 Cf. 'Rückblick auf das Jahr 1913', *Statistische Monatsschrift*, New Series, Vol. XIX, Brünn (Brno) 1914, p. 142.

12 Cf. 'Wiener Börsenwoche', *Neue Freie Presse*, 28 February 1909, where a

knowledgeable commentator remarked, 'The price for bonds is the criterion for the state's creditworthiness. In 1868 the 4½% State bonds stood at 61, after the unification and consolidation' (a reference to the Compromise from which the Austro-Hungarian Empire emerged, cf. Ch. 1, Note 11) 'they rose without interruption to 87, after the 1894 Currency Reform they reached their zenith at 102, a peak at which with one brief interval they remained until 1905 since when they have incessantly dropped to the low of 80 (today 83).' See Wilhelm Ellenbogen, 'Die österreichische Staatsschuld', *Der Kampf*, Vol. 7, p. 300, 1 April 1914.

13 Cf. Eduard März, *Österreichische Industrie- und Bankpolitik in der Zeit Franz Josephs I* (Vienna, 1968), p. 356. The liberal press observed with great anxiety the growing burden on the economy of governmental financial demands and often vented its disapproval frankly. Gustav Stolper in particular assumed in these years the role of an Austrian Cassandra. In 'Wehrreform und Finanznot', *Der Österreichische Volkswirt*, 11 October 1913, after comparing the Habsburg Monarchy's situation in 1913 with that of the tragic year 1859 (defeat at Solferino leading to the loss of Lombardy and the establishment of a united Italy), he reached the conclusion that 'of recent years the economy has been inspired by a productive urge such as Austria-Hungary has not hitherto experienced. . . . But this time too the military have stood in the way of its consummation. To the immense claims on the capital market for investments relating to the economy, they have added their no less vast demands for an enormous increase in their current and so-called non-recurring, yet constantly recurrent, expenditure as well as on top of this' (the outlays incurred) 'for the twofold mobilization within five years. That was more than the capital market could stomach. It has broken down . . .'

14 'Rückblick auf das Jahr 1913', *Statistische Monatsschrift*, p. 143.

15 The proportion of companies concerned with financial affairs in the formation of capital varied considerably from year to year. E.g., 'Changes in the State of Joint-Stock Companies 1913', a statistic for the period 1912/13, shows that during this time the increase of capital on the part of banks and insurance companies amounted merely to 3 million crowns, that is, barely more than 1.5% of total private capital formation. See *Statistische Monatsschrift*, p. 144.

16 On the Creditanstalt's state of liquidity in 1913, cf. März, *Österreichische Industrie- und Bankpolitik*, p. 337. Also Alexander Spitzmüller, *Und hat auch Ursach' es zu lieben* (Vienna, 1955), p. 89.

17 Otto Bauer ascribes the reason for the rise in prices mainly to two circumstances: first the high duties on cereals and the embargoes on cattle imports from the Balkans; secondly the high tariff protection for manufactures and the cartel practices ensuing from this system. Indubitably Austrian tariff policy was largely responsible for the gap between domestic prices and price levels in Western countries. 'With the coming into force of the new 1906 tariff the difference between the Vienna and the London wheat price has risen from 10.70 to 80.80, the difference between the price of wheat in Vienna and Odessa from 25.80 to 99.10 marks.' (Otto Bauer, 'Die Teuerung', Werkausgabe (Vienna, 1975), Vol. I, p. 729. To the present author, though, the vigorous excess demand, with private investments and steeply mounting state expenditure as the principal components, seems primarily responsible for the quickening pace of prices during the final pre-war years.

18 *Bericht über die Industrie, den Handel, und die Verkehrsverhältnisse in Niederösterreich während des Jahres 1910* (Vienna, 1911), p. 1. A meritorious investigation by Professor Good has shown that the cost of living from 1874 to 1894 dropped about 15%, in the following years stayed more or less stable, and from 1903 to 1912 rose by some 30%. See David F. Good, 'The Cost of Living in Austria: 1874–1913', *The Journal of European Economic History*, Vol. V, No. 2 (Autumn 1976), p. 391ff.

19 Cf. 'Österreichisch-Ungarische Bank', *Die Bilanzen*, Supplement to *Der österreichische Volkswirt*, 8 February 1913, and the same publication's issue of 14 March 1914.

20 Ignaz Gruber-Menninger and Gustav Thaa, 'Daten zur Zahlungsbilanz', *Tabellen zur Währungsstatistik* (Vienna, 1904), Pt. 2, No. 3, p. 775, published by the Ministry of Finance. Franz Bartsch, 'Statistische Daten über die Zahlungsbilanz Österreich-Ungarns vor Ausbruch des Krieges', *Mitteilungen des k.k. Finanzministeriums* (Vienna, 1917), No. 22, p. 87f. The figures comprise the import and export of securities by major banks, but not the direct placement of issues on foreign markets. For a summary, see the Balance of Payments Table at the end of this chapter.

21 Cf. Eduard März and Karl Socher, 'Währung und Banken in Cisleithanien', *Die Habsburgermonarchie*, Vol. I, pp. 356–7.

CHAPTER 4

Austrian Crédit Mobilier Banks During the Boom Years

The narrative has so far been confined to the most outstanding factual aspects of the boom period from 1904 till 1912. The speedy development of the economy could clearly be effected only in closest co-operation with an efficient banking system whose most important representatives were the crédit mobilier banks.[1] After the brief though hectic 'period of prosperity' (*Gründerzeit*) (1867–73) these had withdrawn almost entirely from the promotion of industrial enterprises and instead made the handling of government loans and day-to-day banking activities the main object of their business. Not until the 1880 drew to an end, when governmental credit was visibly improving and dealings with the state showed a constantly declining yield, did their concern gradually veer towards the provision of finance for the industrial sphere, especially since industrial recovery was obviously under way. This trend was reinforced by the growing competition from provincial banks in the fields of discounting and deposits business.[2]

The crédit mobilier banks' approach to industrial company promotion was at this time marked by great caution. Creditanstalt's Board Minutes reveal that in the early 1890s the bank participated as a limited partner in a number of medium-sized undertakings, bought a stearin candle and soap factory at Brno, and built at Trieste a linoleum plant, a form of floor-covering new in Austria.[3] In this period the emphasis in major financing deals, undertaken partly in close collaboration with large German banks, lay on loans to the Italian, Russian, Romanian, and Portuguese Governments for railway construction and similar enterprises.

Around the turn of the century industrial promotion activity became more lively. The Creditanstalt took part in several larger financial operations, such as the reorganization of certain leading firms in the machine industry into limited companies (Emil Skoda at

Pilsen, Tanner, Laetsch & Co. at Prague, Nikolaus Heid at Stockerau), the capital increase of Stabilimento Tecnico Triestino at Trieste, the foundation of Österreichische Fez-Fabriken AG, and so on.[4] The boom period 1904–12, following a brief recession at the century's beginning, witnessed a wave of flotations that gradually came to include practically all branches of the economy. The crédit mobilier banks – with Creditanstalt in the lead – entered into a relationship with industry which bore all the marks of symbiosis.[5]

The interdependence between industry and the banking world, the ground for which had been prepared since the early 1890s, soon led to far-reaching structural changes inside the crédit mobilier banks. After the 1873 Stock Exchange crash the well-to-do classes displayed a distinct reserve towards purchases of stocks, which were regarded as speculative investments. The 1895 Stock Exchange crisis served to increase suspicion attaching to them. The major banks had therefore to proceed with great patience and caution in their efforts to build up a workable stock market.

It was extremely rare for the shares of new companies to be offered on the market immediately after the companies had been founded, the issuing houses had to keep the new securities in their own portfolios until the public had gained confidence in the earning power and the viability of the new firms.[6]

The consequence was a continual rise in the banks' holdings of tied resources. Moreover during these years of prolonged upswing when current business transactions likewise constantly rose, the principal banks were very soon forced to increase their share capital, which for a long time had remained unaltered, quite substantially. In 1899 Creditanstalt set the trend by an addition of 20 million crowns to its share capital, to give a total of 100 million crowns.[7]

During the recession starting in 1900, the share capital of banks grew remarkably quickly.[8] From 1904 onward, when the number of new industrial enterprises soared, this development was most strikingly manifested by the spectacular expansion in the capital of joint-stock banks. Their share certificates met with a readier acceptance by the wealthy public than did most industrial equities. During the second phase of the boom (1909–12) attitudes changed as ever broader sections of the population fell under the spell of the stock market.[9] The following table will give some idea of the fast growth in numbers and capital experienced by the Austrian banking world. (See Table 9 overleaf.)

Table 9   Share capital in thousands of crowns

Year	No. of Austr. Joint-Stock Banks	Total Capital	Capital of Vienna's 12 Largest Banks[b]	% Share of Total Capital	% Increase 1904–1913 All	12 VB
1904	64[a]	874,000	469,000	57.15		
					64.72	86.35
1913	105	1,351,700	874,000	64.66		

Sources: *Compass* 1906, Vol 1; 1915, Vol. 1; 1918, Vol. 1
[a] *Compass* 1915, Vol. 1, p. 129 gives 73 joint-stock banks for 1904 with a total of 822.6 million crowns. Until 1908 savings banks' mortgage departments and other mortgage institutions were classified among limited companies. The rectification has been effected in accordance with *Compass*, 1906 issue, data.
[b] Anglo-Österreichische Bank, Wiener Bankverein, Österreichische Boden-Creditanstalt, Centralbank der deutschen Sparkassen, Creditanstalt, Allgemeine Depositenbank, Niederösterreichische Escompte-Gesellschaft, Österreichische Länderbank, Mercurbank, Unionbank, Verkehrsbank, Lombard- und Escomptebank.

The notable increase in the crédit mobilier banks' share capital was not the only sign of the steadily closer relationship between the world of finance and of industry. The growing connection between the two was also demonstrated by the continual growth in the banks' outstanding loans and deposits and, not least, of capital tied up in their securities portfolios. It is a development which has been fully described before so that a single illustration can suffice here.[10]

Table 10   Vienna joint-stock banks' own securities (in million crowns and in % of the base year)[11]

1895	93.5	100
1905	252.5	270
1913	359.0	384

When the crédit mobilier banks first had come into existence it had been thought that they would have a crucial role to play in Austria's industrial progress. The impression is inescapable, however, that not until the years before the war did they prove capable of performing the tasks intended for them satisfactorily.[12]

This review of the system of Austrian crédit mobilier banking before the war would be incomplete without mentioning the major Czech banks. Initial efforts to build up a national Czech banking system dated back to the period 1867–73.[13] As Richard L. Rudolph noted, the rapid growth of Czech-controlled bank houses did not begin until the turn of the century. Then, in the hot-house climate arising with the 1904–12 period of prosperity, the major Czech banks managed to win a position of equality with the Bohemian, Moravian, and Silesian branches of the Viennese crédit mobilier banks. Thus at the outset of the century the leading Czech institution, Živnostenská banka pro Cechy a Moravu at Prague, showed larger profits than the Creditanstalt branches at Prague and Brno. Between 1900 and 1912 it quadrupled its profits, a far better result than either its fellow national or Vienna-centred competitors were able to achieve.[14] Its status among Czech banks is comparable to that of Creditanstalt among Austrian banks in the early days of the Austrian banking system. In 1913 it disposed of over 35% of all Czech banks' total share capital as well as over 43% of all their deposits. After 1910 Živnostenská banka and three other large Czech establishments, Pražka úverni banka, Ceská prumyslová banka and Sporobanka, became members of a syndicate for the placement of government securities. In 1907 Lopuszanski, one of the best informed men in the Austrian banking community at this time, expressed in a short but informative study the view that two important financial centres, Vienna and Prague, were ever more clearly in the making, and that at the latter crédit mobilier banks were trying to concentrate a part of the overall Austrian banking business.[15]

Here is not the place to go into greater detail about the history of Czech banking in the period prior to the First World War. It is sufficient to note three features of its business policy which differentiated it fairly distinctly from the major Viennese banks and their branches. First, it was to a remarkable degree associated with branches of industry based on the rural economy (sugar, beer, spirits). Secondly, it focused its business of industrial promotion on the Monarchy's backward areas (in particular Galicia, Bukovina, Dalmatia) and in the Balkan territories (especially Serbia) where it found virgin soil hitherto neglected by the old-established financial interests. Thirdly, it solicited with great success the opening of checking and savings accounts so as to tap capital resources to which the Vienna crédit mobilier banks began to turn their attention only around the start of the century.

The development of deposits shows growing competition among the commercial banks and, moreover, among the financial world's major sectors, the savings banks, the credit co-operatives, and the private as well as the joint-stock banks. The savings banks' origins went back to the 1840s and before, but their heyday began in 1872 when a new statute explicitly sanctioned changes in the financial sector which had already taken place – the repeal of the limit on deposits and of the ceiling on interest rates for higher deposits extended savings banks' activities to the higher income classes. From the end of 1866 until the end of 1892 the number of savings banks rose from 124 to 444. Communal savings banks accounted for the majority of the new institutions.[16]

Around the turn of the century a change in relations between the various sectors of banking was occurring. The credit co-operatives and in particular the big commercial banks were now in a position to attract a constantly expanding portion of the deposits. Indeed, the savings banks were able between the end of 1900 and the end of 1913 to raise their deposits by 77% from 3,700 million to 6,600 million crowns, but their share of all savings deposits (i.e., those placed with savings banks, banks, credit co-operatives, and the Postal Savings Banks) was 64% at the close of 1913 as against 71% at the close of 1900.[17] The savings banks' declining share of total deposits was principally a manifestation of two factors characteristic of economic development in the decade before the First World War – the new attention paid by major banks to the promotion of industrial companies together with the ensuing rapid growth in the banks' volume of business, and the shift to 'superior', longer-term forms of capital accumulation. An efficient market for fixed interest securities was at last established, much later than in the main Western countries, and in the hot-house atmosphere following the lengthy period of prosperity, the credit co-operatives succeeded in gaining some ground from the more conservative-minded savings banks. The ever-growing competition for deposits eventually resulted in a rise of the interest rate on deposits during the final pre-War years from 3.5% to a rare peak of 4%.

A paper on the development of savings accounts, which was circulated inside the Ministry of Finance during the war, reported that prior to 1880 the right to issue savings books, irrespective of whether a joint-stock bank was being licensed or being given permission to alter its articles of association, had been accorded fairly indiscriminately. The large banks did not attach special importance to this branch of activity and its growth had been accordingly rather slow.[18]

In the 1880s and at the beginning of the 1890s the Ministry had adopted the opposite view that 'the opening of savings accounts' should be reserved to the savings banks whose business should be separated completely from ordinary commercial banking'. Only in 1896, when the Galizische Aktien-Hypothekenbank again applied for permission to deal in this kind of business, did the Ministry reverse its position. The authorities wanted, though, to maintain far-reaching control over this new activity, by determining 'the minimum amount of acceptable deposits, the form of the deposit book, regulating the handling of the book, and establishing a ratio between the amount of the share capital and the permissible deposit maximum'.

The Ministry paper went on to express regret that in the decade preceding the war these principles had been but little heeded. In the ever more bullish atmosphere then prevailing, every financial house did its best to attract as much deposit business as it could. These efforts were clearly reflected not only by the rise in interest rates, but in the speedy expansion of domestic branch office networks. According to figures quoted in the 1913 issue of *Compass*, the number of branch offices, exchange offices, and other bank outlets mounted by the end of 1912 to the handsome total of 500. The figures for the leading institutions were as follows:

Creditanstalt	21	Böhmische Escomptebank	19
Anglo-Österreichische Bank	43	Zivnostenská banka	31
Verkehrsbank	30	Böhmische Unionsbank	23
Wiener Bankverein	49	Böhmische Industrie-Bank	24
Depositenbank	10	Zentralbank deutscher Sparkassen	14
Österreichische Länderbank	31	Galizische Landesbank	74
Mercurbank	34		

The increased competition between banks for deposits business led to an unprecedented scramble for the 'little man's' nest-egg. At the end of 1900 the banks licensed to handle this kind of business totalled 22 and their deposits amounted to 175.9 million crowns. At the end of March 1914 the number of those engaged in the business had risen to 68 and they now disposed of deposits amounting to 1,318 million crowns. Within thirteen years the business had multiplied eightfold. Some of the major banks who forced this line of activity, like Wiener Bankverein and Anglobank, achieved a disproportionate rise. Others, especially Creditanstalt, which enjoyed a dominant status in many other spheres, displayed remarkable restraint.[19]

That in the fight for customers certain institutions used nationalist slogans is a matter for marginal comment. It is not a reproach that can be levelled at the major Viennese banks and their branches. They were careful to avoid aggravating still further the tension-laden atmosphere of many of the mixed-language territories by one-sided propaganda or staff policies.[20] Such reserve was not exercised by the savings banks of German or Czech origin which often mixed advertising and nationalist agitation in the most blatant way.

In 1901 the Centralbank der deutschen Sparkassen was founded.

Four years later a large number of the German institutions merged in the Reichsverband deutscher Sparkassen in Österreich. The Reichsverband and the Centralbank made it their task not only to uphold the interests of the savings banks *vis-à-vis* Parliament, Government, and rival credit institutions, but also 'to support the savings banks in all national affairs and to preserve the rights of Germans'. The Reichsverband, for instance, exhorted all German savings banks to increase their holdings of shares in the Austro-Hungarian Bank so as not to allow the influence of the Czechs over the central bank to become too powerful.[21] At that point the savings banks were the spokesmen for the German majority in the Central Bank's General Meeting. In 1903, as a counterpart to the Centralbank, an umbrella organization, Ustředni banka ceských spořitelen, had been established for the Czech savings banks. Their importance lagged behind that of the German ones, by the end of 1913 the latter administered 75% of the total deposits in all savings banks in the Austrian half of the Empire, the Czechs some 15%, while the rest were divided among those serving customers of Polish, Italian, and other nationalities.[22]

The 'national' policy of the savings banks, on the principle of 'German money for German purposes', undoubtedly impeded access to and use of all the population's savings. What quantitative significance is to be ascribed to these national influences cannot be determined, but the stronger growth of the non-German savings banks during the Monarchy's last years suggests, however, that in communities where the only savings bank was German, these financial institutions could not count on obtaining in full the savings of the non-German inhabitants. The importance of these handicaps decreased with the vigorous expansion of other credit institutions, capable of raising the potential for deposits and loans in rural places and also with the growing strength of supranational securities markets.[23] The excessively fast rise in the number of banking houses during the long period of prosperity from 1904 to 1912 should not, however, be regarded as an unalloyed blessing. Some of them, which owed their existence to the intervention of a political or otherwise highly-placed personage, handled their clients' money without the care incumbent on a respectable business undertaking and foundered during the brief pre-war crisis. In Vienna the number of private banks climbed from 160 to 230. In the Crown lands such exotic plants blossomed scarcely less than in the capital.[24] In Hungary (not the subject of this study) the bank creation urge sprouted far stranger flora. By 1911 'the total of Hungarian banks and savings banks, which are in essence none other than small banks with a strongly speculative streak' had 'within a decade grown from 1,103 to nearly 2,000,' wrote Gustav Stolper.[25]

In the spring of 1914 detailed comment by the Austrian press on certain bank failures clearly demonstrated the speculative character and questionable practices of these new small-scale institutions. In 1906 the Olmützer Kreditbank had been transformed from a co-operative savings association into a joint-stock bank with a share capital of two million crowns and deposits amounting to some one million crowns. Although of purely local importance, it adopted a style appropriate to a major enterprise. More than a third (750,000 crowns) of its modest capital was spent on a magnificent office building. A connection with a 'big' client, turned down by the large banks as too risky a proposition, led to a far-reaching immobilization of the petty provincial bank's funds, since the client threatened to deal with any demand for payment of overdue loans by notification of his insolvency. Good money had therefore to be thrown after bad until such time as the Kreditbank was no longer in a position to meet its current liabilities.[26] A similar fate befell two local banks which did enjoy a certain regional standing, and Ustredni banka and the Carinthian agricultural credit co-operative. It was an open secret that many of the 'national' establishments were barely able to keep their heads above water, and that solely with the assistance of a befriended bigger financial institution.[27]

It has to be stated with regret that the policy of competition without quarter did not stop at the thresholds of the major banks. Here too the highly overheated atmosphere of the boom years 1909 to 1912 resulted in a policy of expansion that occasionally overstepped the limits of orthodox credit policy imposed by long years of experience. 'The reproach to be levelled at the major banks', said Gustav Stolper,

is that they have allowed themselves to be driven along by events without making even the slightest attempt to exercise any control over them. . . . Whether the applicant for a loan sells machines, ostrich feathers, or artificial manure is treated in most Vienna banking offices as pretty irrelevant, and still more the question as to whether under normal business conditions the applicant will be able without difficulty to repay from reserves the loan that he has taken up. The rise in receivables and the constant need for fresh capital by the banks is in the first place to be traced to the fact that the receivables cannot be recouped even though their security may not be inherently suspect. The banks have financed expenditure on the most unproductive luxury, just as they have backed the most sterile construction and stock exchange speculation; on the other hand, the most essential investments have often not been undertaken because it has proved impossible to raise the financial resources.

The policy of the major banks, he added, was to no small degree explicable in terms of their efforts to survive successfully 'the competitive struggle which has been forced on them by new enterprises acting with the greatest unscrupulousness'.[28] There were already indications of a development which, at a later date and under altogether different circumstances, would involve disastrous consequences for the banking world and the economy.

The curbs imposed by the central bank during the boom years were relatively feeble. In 1909 the average discount rate was 4%, remaining at substantially the same level the following year, and in 1911 rose merely to 4.4%. Not until 1912, and then not least for considerations relating to the foreign exchange rate, was the decision made to put up the interest rate to 5%. The increase of the discount rate in the crisis year 1913 to an exceptional high of 6% had been experienced only twice since the currency reform in 1892. The timing of the bank's restrictive measures suggests however that they were taken at a juncture when they could hardly fail to intensify the severe recession that had begun in the preceding autumn. A senior official is supposed to have asked at the start of 1912 members of the banks' managing boards to 'use their influence towards reducing their credit volume'; this method, in modern banking vernacular, of 'moral suasion' seems to have borne little fruit. For in 1912 the Austro-Hungarian Bank's bills portfolio, as well as the notes in circulation, attained a record peak.[29] Only in the following year, under the shadow of economic decline, did these figures reveal the dimension of the economic setback.[30]

The most important structural change in the Austrian banking system – the assumption by the crédit mobilier banks of the main role in the process of industrialization – had been heralded in the 1890s. It was not however until the so-called Second Expansion Era, from 1904 to 1912, that the major banks began to assume responsibility for this task to any really large extent. They promoted the development of the modern large-scale enterprise by financing new companies and mergers, by encouraging the moneyed classes to invest more and more in the capital market, and by ensuring the liquidity of the firms with which they were associated. They acquired a position of power and influence whose outward manifestation was the close collaboration among the firms concerned. In 1910 an investigation revealed the existence of at least 120 cartels. Almost four-fifths of them had been created within the comparatively brief space of five years, from 1904 to 1909.[31] Occasionally one of the major banks would take over the management of a cartel, openly displaying its very great interest in a 'pacification' of conditions in those branches of activity pertaining to its sphere of influence. The experiences thus gained facilitated the swift organization of the various wartime economic institutions after the outbreak of hostilities.

The major banks' 'pacification' operations were not restricted to industry; they led repeatedly to arrangements among themselves. Thus they formed syndicates to facilitate the frequent mergers among large-scale enterprises, particularly in the fields of coal, iron and steel, machinery and electrical equipment. The degree of industrial con- centration grew, and in wide stretches of the economy there existed a close community of banking interests. During the period prior to the war a notable change occurred in the grouping of the big financial houses. The old alliance of Creditanstalt, the House of Rothschild and the Boden-Creditanstalt fell apart. The responsibility lay with the latter's new governor, Rudolf Sieghart, who inaugurated an excess- ively expansive – and likewise also aggressive – phase of business policy diametrically opposed to the conventions hitherto observed by the main banks. Shortly after his appointment Alexander Spitzmüller, the new Chairman of Creditanstalt's Board of Directors, finalized the inevitable breach between the two long-term allies. He described this episode, which, in the light of subsequent developments was not unimportant, as follows:

I had to agree with my colleague Raumann, who warned me against trying to compete with the industrial plans of Boden-Creditanstalt's new manage- ment as this must lead to a hazardous tie-up of funds, a process that indeed went ahead rather quickly at the Boden-Creditanstalt. By the beginning of the First World War it was already the most unwieldy of the major banks. However, to outward appearances, Sieghart seemed to be most successful and knew well how to keep the press, the dailies and especially the financial papers, constantly on their toes and in a state of suspense. That Creditanstalt also ceased to maintain its former considerateness and obliging attitude towards the Boden-Creditanstalt in its transactions is understandable. Over and above this I continued – particularly after the death of Baron Albert Rothschild – my policy of harmonization with the Länderbank. The upshot was the initiation, with the agreement of Baron Louis Rothschild, of the new Creditanstalt-Länderbank-Bankverein *entente* and the exclusion of the Boden-Creditanstalt from the Rothschild grouping.[32]

The Rothschild grouping must not be confused with the 'Österreicher-

Konsortium'. Under the leadership of the Post Office Savings Bank acting as *primus inter pares* with all the major banks, including Rothschild and Živnostenská banka, this consortium was responsible for the placement of all Austrian public loans. In the Hungarian half of the Empire the Rothschild Consortium retained during the last years of peace the responsibility for the issue of Hungarian bonds.[33]

At the close of this examination into the part played by the major crédit mobilier banks during the boom decade preceding the First World War, the question arises as to what extent demand deposits (M2) – see Table 11 – furnished the fuel for this era's dynamism. An investigation of this kind must nevertheless be mainly speculative, because hard and fast statistical material is lacking.

Analysis is here confined to the leading Viennese crédit mobilier banks whose credit accounts can perhaps most nearly be classified as demand deposits, inasmuch as the main source for these funds derived from the credits on current account and was therefore subject to the mechanism of money creation by banks. The problem is: what at this time were the respective shares of banknotes (M1) and of crédit mobilier demand deposits (M2) in the monetary circulation?

Official data render it very easy to trace the development of banknote circulation.[34] At the outset of the 1880s the money supply (M1 plus M2) in the Empire's Austrian half consisted of 50% in banknotes and the same percentage of crédit mobilier demand deposits. The later evolution was as follows:

Table 11   Average annual growth (in %)

	Bank & Treasury Notes (M1)	Crédit Mobilier Demand Deposits (M2)
1880–1890	2.2	4.4
1890–1900	5.3	6.9
1900–1913	4.4	9.2

After 1880 the crédit mobilier banks' demand deposits grew more quickly than the monetary circulation (including Treasury notes). The growth rates, as can be seen from the table, were very high in both categories during the last years of peace, but the crédit mobilier banks contributed the bulk of the liquid resources and so supplied by far the greater part of the financial fuel for the economy's spectacular growth during the 'Second Expansion'.

In this context one is irresistibly reminded of Schumpeter's famous credit theory. Capital, in his view, is a 'purchasing-power fund' and credit the driving force behind industrial development.[35] The fund of purchasing-power that enabled Austrian entrepreneurs to draw means of production away from their previous allocation and thus to guide the economy along new paths was at this period made available for the most part by the major banks, in the form of industrial credit.

Notes

1 The Société Générale du Crédit Mobilier, founded in 1852, was the forerunner of investment banking – 'One of the nineteenth century's most consequential inventions' (Josef Schumpeter, speaking to the present author).

2 Cf. Eduard März, *Österreichische Industrie- und Bankpolitik in der Zeit Franz Josephs I* (Vienna, 1968), p. 276 et seq. for a more detailed description of this development.

3 At the beginning of the 1890s Creditanstalt acquired the Brünner Stearinkerzen- und Seifenfabrik and later transformed this into a limited company. At Trieste it founded Erste Österreichische Linoleumfabrik and it acquired shares in three medium-sized undertakings that displayed good growth prospects for later days – Hirtenberger Patronen-, Zündhütchen- und Metallwarenfabrik Keller & Comp., the electrotechnical firm Bartelmus & Co. at Brno, and the mechanical looms manufactory A. Hohlbaum & Co. at Jägerndorf (Silesia). März, *Österreichische Industrie- und Bankpolitik*, p. 280 et seq.

4 März, *Österreichische Industrie- und Bankpolitik*, p. 303 et seq.

5 März, *Österreichische Industrie- und Bankpolitik*, p. 340 et seq.

6 März, *Österreichische Industrie- und Bankpolitik*, p. 297.

7 März, *Österreichische Industrie- und Bankpolitik*, p. 295. Also *Compass*, 1913, Vol. 1, p. 390.

8 In 1899, after years of stagnation, there occurred a minor increase in the capital of Viennese joint-stock banks from 397 to 422.7 million crowns. From 1899 until 1904 a vigorous increase of about 14% brought the figure to 483.7 million crowns. Cf. A. K. Löwe, 'Österreichs Banken im Jahre 1905', *Statistische Monatsschrift*, NS, 9th Year (Brünn, 1906), p. 464.

9 'The business year 1911 was characterized by dealings in industrial securities. The preceding year had already shown enormous turnovers in this field and during the year under review the lively activity lasted almost incessantly from the beginning until the close of the year.' 'Die Wiener Börse im Jahre 1911', *Der Tresor*, 28 September 1912.

10 Cf. März, *Österreichische Industrie- und Bankpolitik*, p. 325 et seq.

11 During the years following 1905 the major banks' own securities' portfolios expanded more slowly in consequence of the stock market's upswing during the boom's second phase.

12 Contrary to a widespread misapprehension in economic histories of this period, probably attributable to certain writings by Alexander Gerschenkron, the crédit mobilier banks were not committed, even in their own explicit view to any 'missionary' tasks. Creditanstalt's Annual Report as early as 1856 contains the opinion that it had but a secondary part to play in the promotion of industrial

undertakings: 'You will undoubtedly share our view that the objective of Creditanstalt is not so much to be sought in encouraging enterprise in this direction. Even the establishment of factories is hardly commendable in other than exceptional circumstances and will as a general rule be difficult to prove compatible with our responsibility for promoting commerce and industry as a whole.' Cf. Creditanstalt Archives.

13 As early as in the fifties and sixties of last century important banking establishments were opened in Bohemia and Moravia. In 1857 Creditanstalt, two years after its foundation, set up a branch office at Prague. In 1862 Niederösterreichische Escompte-Gesellschaft was behind the start of the Mährische Escomptebank at Prague. All these establishments had however been initiated by the German-speaking portion of the population. Only in 1867 (at the beginning of the First Expansion Phase) was the Landwirtschaftliche Creditbank für Böhmen instituted under German-Czech sponsorship. Shortly afterwards the first Czech universal bank, the famous Živnostenská banka, was set up. Cf. Richard L. Rudolph, *Banking and Industrialization in Austria-Hungary* (Cambridge, 1976), p. 72.

14 Rudolph, *Banking and Industrialization*, p. 73 et seq.

15 Eugen Lopuszanski, 'Die neueste Entwicklungdes Bankwesens Österreichs', an address held at the Gesellschaft Österreichischer Volkswirte, Vienna 1907.

16 Cf. Walther Schmidt, *Das Sparkassenwesen in Österreich* (Vienna, 1930), a thorough study of the subject, and Hedwig Fritz and others, *150 Jahre Sparkassen in Österreich* (five volumes, Vienna 1969–71).

17 Cf. Schmidt, *Das Sparkassenwesen*, p. 99.

18 AVA, Ministry of Finance file 14167/16, Annex B. Insofar as no other source is given for the quotations that follow, they have been extracted from the same Ministry file.

19 These data are taken from various editions of *Compass* as well as the Ministry paper.

20 Not even 'their most critical opponents', said Gustav Stolper, could reproach the major banks 'with national bias towards any side'. See 'Handelsbilanz und Kreditpolitik', *Der Österreichische Volkswirt*, p. 498, 11 April 1914. Similarly a report of the German consul in Prague, addressed to the then Foreign Minister Bethmann-Hollweg: 'The Management of the major banks is multi-national (*utraquist*), Jewish finance plays a leading role.' Zentrales Staatsarchiv der DDR, Z St A Potsdam, RWM 663, Bl. 26.

21 Schmidt, *Das Sparkassenwesen*, p. 141.

22 Schmidt, *Das Sparkassenwesen*, p. 160.

23 Cf. Eduard März and Karl Socher, 'Währung und Banken in Cisleithanien', *Die Habsburgermonarchie*, Vol. I, p. 363.

24 See 'Banquierbuch', Supplement to *Compass* for the years 1905, 1913, and 1915, Vol. I. The figure of 230 private banks was established for the year 1914.

25 See 'Handelsbilanz und Kreditpolitik', *Der Österreichische Volkswirt*, p. 498, 11 April 1914.

26 See 'Kleinbanken', *Der Österreichische Volkswirt*, pp. 454–5, 28 March 1914. The unsigned contribution is likely to have been written by Walther Federn.

27 Cf. 'Bankenpolitik', *Der Österreichische Volkswirt*, 4 October 1913, on the mania for expansion by the small banks: 'It is also possible to extend all-too-ample loans for productive purposes, not only for investments, but even as short-

term commercial loans, especially loans which are out of proportion to the borrower's own assets. In our view this is a reproach from which hardly a single bank can be wholly absolved. The major banks have of course sinned less herein than those banks of more recent date who, lacking a tradition of dealings with commerce, have out of a mania for expansion or out of national chauvinism – and this is not confined to Slav banks – flooded entire provinces with loans which in part are without any economic justification . . .'

28 'Handelsbilanz und Kreditpolitik', *Der Österreichische Volkswirt*, 11 April 1914, p. 499. In 1913 Creditanstalt too experienced a deterioration in liquidity as against earlier years and at the spring 1914 Annual General Meeting a resolution was passed to increase the share capital from 150 million to 170 million crowns. Cf. März, *Österreichische Industrie- und Bankpolitik*, p. 337.

29 Cf. 'Bericht über die wirtschaftliche Lage Österreichs in den Jahren 1912/13', *Mitteilungen der Handelspolitischen Zentralstelle der Vereinigten Handels- und Gewerbekammern und des Zentralverbandes der Industriellen Österreichs*, Vienna 1914, p. 8.

30 According to the 1913 Annual Report of the Austro-Hungarian Bank the bills portfolio and the banknote circulation during the last pre-war years developed as follows:

	Bills portfolio			Banknote circulation		
	in crowns m.					
	1911	1912	1913	1911	1912	1913
Highest level	1,235.1	1,341.1	1,214.6	2,570.4	2,815.8	2,644.9
Lowest level	560.1	711.4	763.7	2,032.2	2,080.5	2,172.6
Average level	790.1	922.4	896.3	2,230.6	2,298.7	2,349.5

Source: 'Die Bilanzen', Supplement to *Der Österreichische Volkswirt*, 14 March 1914, No. 24 and 21 March 1914, No. 25.

31 Cf. Max von Allmayer-Beck, *Materialien zum österreichischen Kartellwesen* (Vienna, 1909), p. 4. Also Matis Bachinger, 'Österreichs industrielle Entwicklung', *Die Habsburgermonarchie*, p. 137 et seq.

32 Alexander Spitzmüller, *Und hat auch Ursach' es zu lieben* (Vienna, 1955), p. 89.

33 März, *Österreichische Industrie- und Bankpolitik*, p. 354.

34 The calculations below derive from the central bank returns. The share of the Empire's Austrian half was computed – in summary fashion, admittedly – on a demographic basis while the various data to be found in *Compass* served for compilation of the crédit mobilier banks' creditors. The table shows the development of the creditors' position among the nine leading Viennese crédit mobilier banks as well as the bank and Treasury notes circulation in the Empire's Austrian half, readjusted for the Austrian half:

Year	Bank and Treasury notes	Crédit mobilier bank creditors
	in crowns m.	
1880	370.6	341.4
1890	455.3	524.2
1900	761.3	1,017.5
1913	1,339.3	3,178.6

35 Cf. Josef Schumpeter, *Theorie der wirschaftlichen Entwicklung. Eine Untersuchung über Unternehmergewinn, Kapital, Kredit, Zins und den Konjunkturzyklus* (Munich and Leipzig, 1926), pp. 148 and 170.

CHAPTER 5

The Business Policy of Creditanstalt During the Last Years of Peace

In 1899 the Creditanstalt's management found it necessary to propose to the Board an increase of the share capital to 100 million crowns.[1] From the reasons given it was clear that this first capital increase – in its early days there had twice been a capital decrease – was mainly conditioned by the turn towards industrial company promotion. Because the public still adopted a temporizing attitude with regard to stronger involvement in industrial securities, the Bank had no choice but to keep many of the new issues in its own portfolio, where for a number of years they remained as tied capital.[2]

Although business in the initial years of the new century was somewhat sluggish, the Bank's holdings of securities rose rapidly. Whereas in 1900 they stood at 35 million crowns, by 1903 they had expanded to 61.6 millions. (In both instances the amounts shown in the 'Own securities' and 'Payments on securities held under syndicate agreements' items have been lumped together.) This brief phase of remarkably speedy growth in the Bank's securities holdings was, however, no more than the prelude to a development that can without fear of exaggeration be termed dramatic. During the long period of prosperity the upward movement in the aforementioned two balance-sheet items presented the following picture:

Table 12   Own securities (in crowns m.)

1905	24.2	1908	29.5	1911	39.8
1906	22.9	1909	44.2	1912	47.7
1907	27.1	1910	40.9	1913	46.6

Table 13   Payments on securities held under syndicate agreements (in crowns m.)

1905	19.9	1908	59.3	1911	58.1
1906	32.2	1909	33.9	1912	72.5
1907	29.4	1910	62.4	1913	84.8

As can be seen from the above tables, within the short space of eight years the Bank's holdings of securities had increased from approximately 44 million to more than 131 million crowns. Within this period it was the years 1908–12 that showed outstanding dynamism, notwithstanding the fact that it was just at this phase that the Bank managed to place a not insubstantial amount of the newly issued securities among wealthy investors. After the outbreak of the Balkan War (autumn 1912) the boom broke and with it the demand for industrial or any other kinds of securities.[3]

The result was that Creditanstalt, like most of the other major banks, had on the declaration of war in July 1914 a quite considerable stock of securities whose composition will be examined later. Concomitant with the high activity in industrial promotion was an extension of the Bank's range of business which soon included organizational responsibilities on behalf of the companies under its wing. It has already been mentioned that the Bank, sometimes in association with other institutions, promoted a pooling of resources between allied firms by way of mergers or looser forms of collaboration. Sometimes this led to the establishment of a cartel bureau whose management was in certain instances assumed by the Bank. Thus the latter played an active part in the organization of the Galician oil industry, much plagued by marketing crises; other examples are the machine, sugar, textile, matches, and spirits industries. In 1911 the Austrian spirits refineries were with the assistance of Creditanstalt amalgamated into a syndicate; at the same time, a working agreement was initiated between the refineries and the agricultural distilleries. In addition the spirits syndicate assigned to the Bank's Prague headquarters the function of a central marketing agency, resulting in a considerable increase in its volume of business.[4]

The favourable economic climate, the vigorous industrial promotion, the concomitant organizational functions and the constant expansion of the branch office network led to an unusually fast growth in current business, perhaps best exemplified by the continual upward movement in the debtor and creditor items (Table 14).

The table shows how in eight years the number of debtors went up some 90% and the number of creditors nearly 80%, with an especially dynamic note struck between 1909 and 1912. The latter year foreshadowed however a somewhat more restrained policy, which was maintained in 1913. The same applied to bills of exchange business, advances against securities, and – to a lesser degree – advances against goods. Acceptances displayed something of a

Table 14   Debtors and creditors at years-end (in crowns m.)

	Debtors	Creditors
1905	445.3	439.6
1906	578.2	548.2
1907	581.0	522.5
1908	592.5	533.3
1909	596.2	566.9
1910	681.9	650.2
1911	811.9	765.2
1912	828.7	801.1
1913	839.0	783.7

retrograde trend. In 1911 the balance sheet total for the first time exceeded one thousand million crowns, a level at which it stayed until the outbreak of hostilities.[5]

It is clear that in the last years before the war earnings also grew very quickly. This was not only due to high turnover, but likewise to the movement of the interest rate, which was advantageous to the banks' interest earnings as well as, to a lesser extent, those of depositors.[6] Nevertheless Creditanstalt's dividend policy was extremely cautious. From 1909 to 1913, a time of particularly high earnings, the dividend was raised by stages from 10% to 10.63%.[7] This restraint in the distribution of profits can be attributed principally to two circumstances: first, the continually greater expenditure on staff, materials and equipment as well as taxes and, secondly, the commitment of larger funds to industrial projects whose realization – contrary to the expectations of the management – on occasion proved highly protracted. This partial immobilization of resources was especially manifest during the slack period in 1912 and 1913 caused by the Balkan hostilities. 'Economist', the commentator of the *Neue Freie Presse*, had the following to say on the Bank's business situation and policy in 1912:

Creditanstalt has been spared the convulsions following in the train of the warlike occurrences and has, in spite of its widespread commitments, not sustained in its current business any noteworthy losses due to insolvencies. It has however throughout the year imposed restraint on its activities and has not substantially extended the volume of its lending, regardless of the greater claims by its customers. All the figures of the present financial statement testify to the effort to exercise restraint in view of the unsettled political and economic situation. The provisions made for the current year, in which the abnormal situation as regards monetary and credit conditions continues to prevail, have at any rate been a contributory factor to the rigorous balance sheet assessment of last year's earnings.[8]

In these circumstances it is small matter for surprise that the Bank's management repeatedly thought it necessary to increase its capital. In 1906 new shares were issued to an amount of 20 million crowns, fetching a premium profit of 17.8 million crowns. In 1911 a fresh capital increase of 30 million crowns brought a further 27 million crowns premium profit. Three years later, in April 1914, the Annual General Meeting passed a resolution to increase the capital yet again by 20 million crowns; after the outbreak of war the Board of Directors did not avail itself of this authority.[9]

In the light of its capitalization, the multiplicity of its industrial interests, and its dominant position in transactions with the government, Creditanstalt must be regarded on the eve of the First World War as the Dual Monarchy's leading crédit mobilier bank.[10] This does not mean that Wiener Bankverein, Anglo-Österreichische Bank, Österreichische Länderbank, and in particular Boden-Creditanstalt did not make considerable efforts in various fields to oust Creditanstalt from its leading role. In the sphere of industrial companies promotion especially Boden-Creditanstalt adopted distinctly unorthodox methods to obtain the best place in the sun. In bills of exchange business, advances against securities, and deposits Wiener Bankverein, Anglo-Österreichische Bank, Länderbank, and to a growing degree Mercurbank were intent on being in the van.[11] This ambition was reflected by the large number of branch offices, which assured Wiener Bankverein and Anglo-Österreichische Bank of an advantage over the other crédit mobilier banks.[12]

During the final pre-war years, moreover, there was a certain move towards specialization in the industrial companies promotion business, with the result that the crédit mobilier banks acquired, in the eyes of the public, a certain sphere of influence or even power.[13] Anglo-Österreichische Bank was above all predominant in the domain of Bohemian lignite, Niederösterreichische Escompte-Gesellschaft in the Bohemian and Moravian mining industry, Wiener Bankverein in the Hungarian iron industry, and Boden-Creditanstalt in the textiles and sugar, mining and machine-building industries.[14] Creditanstalt was linked particularly strongly to those industries, like sugar, petroleum, brewing, and spirits, which specialized in the processing of agricultural and extractive products; it also held an outstanding position in the machine, textiles, paper, and electrical goods industries. Of this more will be said later.

A detailed description of the Bank's major financial dealings during the last years before the war is superfluous inasmuch as this has been the subject of a previous study.[15] Nonetheless a brief look at the 1913 Annual Report may be of interest because within a few months the nature of the Bank's policy began, under the pressure of external events, to undergo fundamental change. For a long time ahead political interests would be the most important guideline for the management's decisions.

The year 1913 was a year of record results for most of the major Viennese banks. Creditanstalt's balance sheet differed from the rest by showing – for the first time, after a lengthy period of continuous expansion – a slight drop in its total, a consequence of the restraint exercised in its business on current account. The outside resources of 914 million crowns employed by the Bank in 1913 are, among other things, evidence of the favourable turn taken by deposit business since the start of the century.

In the same year its activities in securities and securities held under syndicate agreements attained the unparalleled peak figure of 131.4 million crowns. The increase in the amount of securities held by syndicate agreements was mainly due to unsold holdings of the 4.5% Hungarian Treasury bills, issued in the spring to an amount of 150 million crowns, for which the Rothschild Consortium had, for the time being, not invited subscriptions. On the other hand a subsequent Hungarian issue of tax-free Treasury bills to the same amount had been liquidated in the current year. Included in these agreements was a 4.5% Austrian Government debenture issue as well as Bulgarian and Chinese Treasury bonds, shares in a 5% Royal City of Prague bond issue, et cetera.[16] A participation in Vereinigte Brauereien- Schwechat AG, which had been created by the merger of Dreher AG with the St Marx and Simmering breweries, contributed to the temporary increase of this account. The 4.5% City of Vienna certificates of deposit to an amount of 60 million crowns, taken up together with other domestic and foreign banks in 1912, had however been successfully placed.

During the last years of peace Creditanstalt derived a handsome profit from its close links with some of the Empire's leading armament firms, headed by Skodawerke AG at Pilsen (Plzen, Bohemia) which had, next to Krupp, become the most important producer of ordnance in central Europe. Hirtenberger Patronen-, Zündhütchen- und Metallwarenfabrik, formerly Keller & Comp., and the well-known Stabilimento Tecnico Triestino were likewise at this time enjoying significant sales. The same held good for G. Roth Aktiengesellschaft, which on the eve of hostilities was shifting more and more into armaments production. A contrast was provided by such firms as Aktiengesellschaft der Lokomotivfabrik, formerly G. Sigl, at Wiener Neustadt and K. u. K. Priv. Maschinenfabrik L. Zieleniewski AG at Cracow, machine-builders dependent on government orders, whose business was generally poor. By contrast, A.E.G.-Union Elektrizitäts-Lieferungs AG at Vienna and other undertakings in the same line of business were doing excellently in this relatively new branch of activity.

The adverse business conditions of 1913 affected only a few (for instance the recently reorganized Guntramsdorfer Druckfabrik, Austro-Orientalische Handelsgesellschaft, and Carl Stummersche Zuckerfabriken) of the enterprises affiliated with Creditanstalt in the consumer goods industry. Some of these firms which offered poor financial prospects, like Schnellpressenfabrik Mödling und Rosenthal, were liquidated during the course of the year. 'The overall impression', wrote the exceedingly well-informed financial expert of Der Öster-reichische Volkswirt, 'is that the industrial undertakings affiliated with the Bank have suffered little from the economic pinch and have indeed made good progress despite it.'[17] The year 1913 was also the year of a more momentous company reorganization, the transformation of Berndorfer Metallwarenfabrik into a limited liability company. The transaction involved, in addition to the owner of the firm, the well-known industrialist Arthur Krupp, the Bank, together with associated Austrian and German institutions and the Krupp Works at Essen.[18]

Among the numerous foreign financial deals in which Creditanstalt participated, a transaction involving the two Russian industrial giants, the Nevski Works and the Putilov Works, holds a special place. In 1913 Skodawerke, in conjunction with Niederösterreichische Escompte-Gesellschaft, had approached the Bank with the request that the latter take part in a capital increase for the Nevski Works and the extension of a working capital loan to the Putilov Works. Already in the preceding year generous assistance had been obtained from Skoda towards the enlargement of these enterprises.[19] The intention now was to continue this operation on a still larger scale and to ensure financial aid from the Dual Monarchy's leading bank. Spitzmüller, doubtful about the project's political desirability, sought before its submission to the Board, agreement from the two Ministries competent to judge so bold a proposal. His eventual report to the Board stated that he had 'made contact in the matter with both the Minister for Foreign Affairs and the Minister for War, and both Ministers have declared that from the standpoint of public interest there is no objection to the operation'.[20]

At the beginning of 1914 a number of major French banks approached Creditanstalt to persuade it to become a member of a consortium for a big new deal with the Putilov Works. This time the funds were to be made available for the manufacture of gun-barrels. Herr von Skoda himself, anticipating a larger order for Skodawerke, seems to have advocated the Bank's participation very vigorously, whereas Spitzmüller was highly dubious about it. As he wrote in his memoirs, he could not resist 'something of a shudder at the thought that we were to become at least indirectly a party to the production of weapons that, in case of a military conflict, would be turned on our own soldiers'.[21]

Accompanied by Skoda, he expounded the details of the 'complicated transaction' to the Minister for Foreign Affairs, Count Berchtold, and to his astonishment learned that the Minister saw 'from the viewpoint of foreign policy no reason to reject participation in the transaction'. Possibly Count Berchtold's reply, Spitzmüller added, would have been somewhat 'more reserved' if he had spoken to him alone. At any rate Creditanstalt could now hardly evade giving Herr von Skoda a definite affirmative answer as regards acceptance of a share in the deal. All the more so as prior to his appointment as Foreign Minister, Count Berchtold had been Ambassador to the Court of St Petersburg and as such was considered an expert on Russian affairs. Spitzmüller nevertheless managed by delaying tactics to protract the Bank's formal undertaking until the fateful days of July, when the project evaporated of its own accord.[22]

Notes

1 Through the issue of the new shares it was possible to raise the capital to 100 million crowns and also to set up a capital reserve of 20 million crowns. The purpose of the latter was to cover any balance sheet deficits. Cf. Annual Report 1899, Creditanstalt Archives.
2 Cf. Board Minutes, 4 July 1899, Creditanstalt Archives.
3 The prolonged drop in prices on the Stock Exchange did not however occur until late autumn 1913. Panic on the outbreak of Balkan hostilities initially gave way to an optimistic mood. 'In spring and into the summer stock prices were once again sent up almost to pre-Balkan War level as though the Austrian economy had not suffered losses running into many hundreds of millions, as though practically all branches of industry were not suffering a severe marketing crisis, and as though

there were not unhappily every prospect of the depression lasting a long time . . .
On top of all this year's calamities the public is expiating its thoughtless optimism
with heavy losses.' 'Liquidationsprozess an der Börse', *Der Österreichische
Volkswirt*, No. 6, 8 November 1913.

4 Cf. Board Minutes, 7 June 1911, and Annual Report 1911, Creditanstalt
Archives. 'The establishment of the spirits group, whose entire financial dealings
were entrusted to Creditanstalt,' wrote Alexander Spitzmüller, *Und hat auch
Ursach' es zu lieben* (Vienna, 1955), p. 92, was one of the 'major transactions with
industry'.

5 For further details relating to progress of the Bank's business before 1914 see
Eduard März, *Österreichische Industrie- und Bankpolitik in der Zeit Franz
Josephs I* (Vienna, 1968), p. 335 et seq.

6 März, *Österreichische Industrie- und Bankpolitik*, p. 338.

7 At the 57th Annual General Meeting on 4 April 1913 one of the shareholders,
Albert Hofmann, asserted that the Bank 'is once more in a position to pay a
dividend of 38 crowns such as was distributed twenty years ago'. During the
ensuing discussion a number of other shareholders likewise expressed the wish for
a higher dividend. In his reply Management Chairman Spitzmüller referred to the
tight money market situation caused 'chiefly by the heavy demands of the public
authorities, the provinces and the communes, in both States' (Austria and
Hungary), 'but also in view of industry's needs'. For the rest Spitzmüller reminded
his listeners of a passage in the Annual Report. 'We say in the Report that we must
be extremely cautious as regards our engagements. We believe that we must this
year too, unless there is a totally unforeseen change in the state of the money
market and of the economy, adhere to the same policy.' 'Österreichische
Creditanstalt', *Neue Freie Presse*, 5 April 1913. A year later Spitzmüller said on
the same point: 'In the economic field we have noted signs which render it
imperative for a bank's management to regulate its dividend policy in such
manner that in an emergency the bank's progress and operations need suffer no
set-back and no handicap.' 'Österreichische Creditanstalt', *Neue Freie Presse*, 3
April 1914.

8 See *Neue Freie Presse*, 21 February 1913. The remark by 'Economist' about the
management's 'restraint' is confirmed by Spitzmüller in his memoirs, *Und hat
auch Ursach es zu lieben*, p. 92: 'In the field of industrial financing Creditanstalt,
as already intimated, observed a certain restraint *so as not to imperil its liquidity*'.
(Present author's italics)

9 The Annual Report 1914, p. 10, published – as was then the practice, only a year
later – states, 'For the sake of good order we would finally like to point out that in
present circumstances we do not intend until further notice to avail ourselves of
the authority given to raise the share capital.'

10 In 1913 the Bank's own resources amounted to 243.6 million crowns (150 million
crowns share capital and 93.6 million crowns reserves). Next came Boden-
Creditanstalt with own resources of 174 million crowns, Wiener Bankverein with
some 173 million crowns, and Österreichische Länderbank with some 154 million
crowns. Taking into account merely the share capital, the ranking order was
Creditanstalt with 150 million, Wiener Bankverein with 130 million, Anglo-
Österreichische Bank with 100 million, Niederösterreichische Escompte-Gesellschaft with 75 million, Boden-Creditanstalt with 54 million crowns, and so on.
Cf. *Compass* 1916, Vol. 2, and März, *Österreichische Industrie- und Bankpolitik*,
p. 337.

11 In 1913 Creditanstalt's bills of exchange holdings to a value of some 200 million crowns were still the largest among the major banks. See 'Die Bilanzen – Österreichische Creditanstalt', *Der Österreichische Volkswirt*, No. 21, 21 February 1914.

12 In 1913 Wiener Bankverein had 49 branch offices, Anglo-Österreichische Bank 43, Mercurbank 34, Creditanstalt merely 21. See also the preceding chapter in which the development of deposits has been treated in detail.

13 I have already drawn attention to this point in my *Österreichische Industrie und Bankpolitik*, p. 333 et seq. Here I would only like to add that these trends became manifest only during the last pre-War years and that the specialization process had in 1913 not as yet got very far.

14 Cf. 'Wiener Börsenwoche', *Neue Freie Presse*, 16 June 1912. Sieghart, appointed Governor of Boden-Creditanstalt in 1910, has described as the most important transactions of his early business years the inclusion of the Schoeller & Co. and the Redlich & Berger (Göding) sugar factories in Boden-Creditanstalt's sphere of influence, the expansion of Österreichische Berg- und Hüttenwerks-Gesellschaft by the purchase of Steinkohlen-Gewerkschaft Marie-Anne and subsequently that of Fürstlich-Salmschen Gruben at Ostrava (Ostrau), the incorporation of Prague Waggonfabrik F. Ringhoffer among Boden-Creditanstalt's affiliations and participations, etc. Cf. Rudolf Sieghart, *Die letzten Jahre einer Grossmacht* (Berlin, 1932), p. 164.

15 Cf. März, *Österreichische Industrie- und Bankpolitik*, p. 335 et seq., and the jubilee publication *Ein Jahrhundert Creditanstalt-Bankverein* (Vienna, 1957), p. 117 et seq.

16 The acceptance of Chinese bonds by Creditanstalt and Niederösterreichische Escompte-Gesellschaft served to finance ordnance deliveries by Skodawerke to China. In his memoirs Spitzmüller says, 'I raised objection to the deal because in my view Austria-Hungary was not so well off for funds as to be able to assume responsibility for a large-scale capital export to the East, nor was it possible to obtain any security for the soundness of the Chinese bonds. My resistance was however a solitary effort and I had eventually to drop it because Skoda, wooed on all sides, would, if refused by us, simply have turned to other banks. Österreichische Escomptegesellschaft, who sat with us on the Skoda board, had moreover given its agreement at once and unconditionally.' Spitzmüller, *Und hat auch Ursach es zu lieben*, p. 105.

17 Cf. 'Die Bilanzen – Österreichische Creditanstalt', *Der Österreichische Volkswirt*, No. 21, 21 February 1914.

18 Cf. Annual Report 1913, Creditanstalt Archives, and März, *Österreichische Industrie- und Bankpolitik*, p. 345.

19 Cf. 'Kapitalvermehrung der Skodawerke', *Neue Freie Presse*, 31 October 1912.

20 Cf. Board Minutes, 29 July 1913, Creditanstalt Archives, and März, *Österreichische Industrie- und Bankpolitik*, p. 343.

21 Spitzmüller, *Und hat auch Ursach' es zu lieben*, p. 105.

22 Spitzmüller, *Und hat auch Ursach' es zu lieben*, p. 106. Reference to the inconsistent attitude by the exponents of Austro-Hungarian policy towards that of Russia and the related Serbian problem is reserved for later discussion.

CHAPTER 6
Creditanstalt's Industrial Assets in 1913

The major banks' lively promotion of industrial enterprise during the last pre-war years has been repeatedly referred to. A statistical synopsis on the extent of this activity is to be found in a laudable study of the relations between the banks and industry.[1]

The table opposite shows how in 1908, 1909, and 1911 Creditanstalt led the field. In 1912 and 1913 the Bank, as previously mentioned, practised a self-imposed restraint; the main stimulus came from the Boden-Creditanstalt, Länderbank, and Anglo-Österreichische Bank. If a bank's sphere of influence is gauged in terms of its interests, Creditanstalt's expansion from the beginning of the century was as follows:[2]

Table 16   Expansion of Creditanstalt's interests, 1900–14

Year	Industry	Commerce	Banks	Insurance companies	Communications enterprises	Total
1900	15	—	1	3	—	19
1910	32	4	4	3	1	44
1914	43	5	5	2	2	57

The authors of this analysis, it would seem, took into account majority and minority interests alike. (Their study contains no further information as to their method of computation.) A bank's sphere of influence is, however, a very ticklish concept incapable of being deduced solely from its shareholdings. There are instances of a bank withdrawing from the board and management of a firm without relinquishing its powerful creditor position and minority interest.[3]

An attempt to assess the share of the nine major Viennese banks' individual groups in the Empire's joint-stock companies during the first half of 1914 was made by the well-known Czech economic

60

Table 15 Foundation of Joint-Stock Companies
with bank participation, 1907–13

	1907 No.	Cap.	1908 No.	Cap.	1909 No.	Cap.	1910 No.	Cap.	1911 No.	Cap.	1912 No.	Cap.	1913 No.	Cap.
Niederösterreichische Escompte-Gesellschaft	4	16.1	2	8.0	—	—	1	4.5	—	—	3	18.5[e]	1	2.0
Creditanstalt	5	13.5	4	17.0	3	15.0	2	13.3	5	39.8[a]	2	12.5[f]	3	9.0[j]
Boden-Creditanstalt	1	16.0	1	3.0	—	—	2	20.0	3	21.5[b]	4	19.0[g]	1	3.0
Wiener Bankverein	5	9.2	1	2.5	1	1.5	3	6.4	3	15.0[c]	—	—	2	7.4
Länderbank	3	6.25	—	—	1	1.5	1	2.5	6	12.0[d]	2	3.0[h]	4	20.0
Anglo-Österreichische Bank	3	4.5	3	8.0	1	4.0	—	—	3	3.0	9	14.0[i]	5	11.0[k]
Unionbank	1	1.0	—	—	—	—	—	—	2	8.0	1	5.0	—	—
Verkehrsbank	1	2.0	—	—	—	—	2	9.5	1	0.4	1	1.5	1	1.0
Mercurbank	1	1.5	—	—	—	—	2	9.6	—	—	2	3.2	2	3.0
Böhmische Banken	—	0	—	—	4	6.9	7	12.6	5	13.3	6	18.5	5	14.8

[a] Two with 20.5 m. crowns capital and one with 12.0 m. crowns capital together with Boden-Creditanstalt and Wiener Bankverein respectively.
[b] Two in conjunction with Creditanstalt.
[c] One with 12.0 m. crowns capital and one with 1.5 m. crowns capital together with Creditanstalt and Länderbank respectively.
[d] One with Wiener Bankverein.
[e] One with Boden-Creditanstalt and Creditanstalt respectively.
[f] One with Niederösterreichische Escompte-Gesellschaft.
[g] One with Niederösterreichische Escompte-Gesellschaft.
[h] Two with Anglo-Österreichische Bank.
[i] Two with Länderbank.
[j] One with Länderbank, one with Wiener Bankverein and Anglo-Österreichische Bank respectively.
[k] One with Niederösterreichische Escompte-Gesellschaft.

historian Jurij Křižek, but the value of these calculations is limited because of his reliance on his memory as well as on statistical sources.[4] Nevertheless his data does permit two important conclusions: the first being that on the eve of the war the nine major banks controlled a sizeable portion (possibly about half) of the capital in all Austrian joint-stock companies; and the second that their share in the basic, capital goods, and sugar industries exceeded fifty per cent.

The second conclusion holds good particularly for Creditanstalt whose industrial holdings amounted probably to two-thirds of all holdings in those branches of activity. Křižek's investigation furthermore makes it clear that in the first half of 1914 the Bank held the undisputed lead among the crédit mobilier banks, and is likely to have had some twenty per cent of the major Viennese banks' overall industrial holdings in its possession. Worthy of note too is that those crédit mobilier banks (Mercurbank, Verkehrsbank, Unionbank) which had come late into the industrial promotion business were comparatively weakly established in the capital goods branch.

For the purposes of the following detailed examination of Creditanstalt's industrial assets the concept 'sphere of influence' has been interpreted somewhat more broadly than by earlier authors. A sphere of influence would appear to exist when a bank, irrespective of whether its situation is reinforced by a larger shareholding, is represented on the Supervisory Board of 'outside' companies by persons (managers, Board directors, major shareholders) who are 'close' to it. A bank, it must be recalled, generally disposes of the voting rights attaching to the shares deposited with it by smaller shareholders. The result is that its own assets are only a very unreliable indicator for a bigger financial institution's actual sphere of influence.[5] On the other hand no one of these pieces of circumstantial evidence permits any certain inference as to the extent of the sphere of influence; consequently an inquiry of this kind can merely convey an approximate picture of a bank's ramified connections. In this study, *Compass*, the balance sheet comments in *Der Österreichische Volkswirt*, reports in the *Neue Freie Presse*, the Board Minutes, and the Annual Reports of Creditanstalt have been the main sources used.

Description of the Bank's industrial holdings can begin with the foodstuffs sector. Leaving aside participations arising from unforeseen happenings in current business (like those in Simon Klein & Söhne Mühlen AG and in Milchindustrie AG originating from the Anglo-Continental enterprise Kondensmilch AG), interest centred mainly on three branches – sugar, brewing, and spirit distilleries.

During the final years before the First World War Creditanstalt displayed systematic activity above all in the sugar industry.[6] The outcome was the formation of a large group whose most important members were the Nestomitzer and Peceker sugar refineries, Mährische Zuckerindustrie A G, and Verein *mährischer* Zucker-fabriken und Ökonomien A G. In 1911 the Bank joined a syndicate which, under the leadership of Allgemeine Ungarische Kreditbank, took over 75% of the share capital belonging to Carl Stummer Zuckerfabriken A G, a Hungarian firm. Others in the syndicate were the S. M. von Rothschild bank, the Boden-Creditanstalt, and Schoeller & Co. A G, a component of the latter's industrial group and itself a sugar concern.[7]

In two instances, the acquisition in 1912 of shares in Verein mährischer Zuckerfabriken at Olmütz and that of the promotion in 1913 of Zentralmährische Zuckerfabriken und Ökonomien A G, the Bank proceeded in close contact with Länderbank. The story of the second company's formation illustrates how on occasion the influence exercised by the banks in the industrial world was not free of a certain element of coercion. The plight of Kürschner & Co. at Brno meant, as *Der Österreichische Volkswirt* declared, that one of Austria's biggest businesses had run into financial difficulties. (Contemporaries talked in terms of frozen bank credit totalling between 12 million and 15 million crowns.) Länderbank was the principal creditor. Creditanstalt was chiefly interested in a clarification of the situation because of an outstanding loan to Mödritzer Zuckerfabrik A G, in which Kürschner had the majority shareholding.[8] The initial reorganization plan envisaged the foundation of two limited companies under the auspices of the two major banks, but eventually they agreed on the setting-up of a single joint-stock company in which Rohrbacher Zuckerraffinerie, though not Kürschner, should have an interest.[9] Zentralmährische Zuckerfabriken und Ökonomien A G took over, besides the large Kürschner sugar factories, the shares held by the Brno firm in Mödritzer and Tischnowitzer Zuckerfabrik.[10] (See sugar industry diagram overleaf.)

Creditanstalt had had connections with Gösser Brauerei A G, previously Max Kober, in Göss even before the Second Expansion Phase. In 1909 Gösser Brauerei, together with two other major Styrian breweries (Puntigam, Steinfeld) and the Bank's local branch, partici-pated in founding Brauerei A G Union at Laibach (Ljubljana).[11] Three years earlier the Bank had assisted in the merger of several Moravian breweries from which there emerged Nordmährische Brauerei- und

Diagram 1: Sugar Industry Group

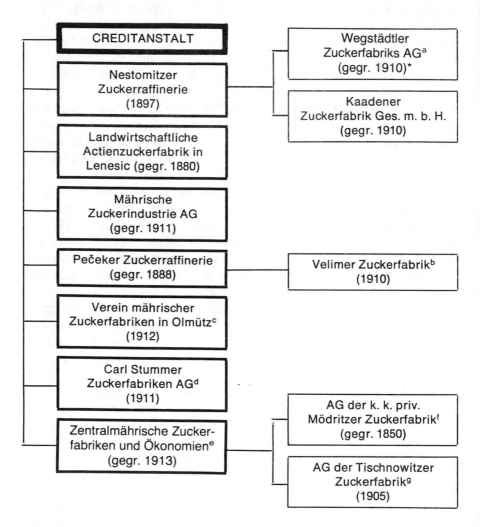

a Shares majority held by Nestomitzer Zuckerraffinerie
b Shares majority held by Pečeker Zuckerraffinerie
c Shares majority together with Österreichische Länderbank
d In 1911 a syndicate led by Ungarische Allgemeine Kreditbank and consisting of Creditanstalt, Ungarische Allgemeine Kreditbank, Boden-Creditanstalt, S.M. v. Rothschild, and Zuckerfabriken Schoeller & Co. AG acquired three-quarters of the share capital
e Joint promotion with Österr. Länderbank and Rohrbacher Zuckerraffinerie AG
f Shares majority held by Zentralmährische Zuckerfabriken
g Ditto
* gegr. = founded

Malzfabrik AG. In 1913 it joined Wiener Bankverein and Niederösterreichische Escompte-Gesellschaft in transforming the family-
owned Anton Drehers Brauereien AG into Vereinigte Brauereien
Schwechat, St Marx, Simmering-Dreher, Mautner und Meichtl AG.
The new undertaking, with a share capital of 36 million crowns, was a
giant among the Danube Monarchy's breweries.[12]

Reference has been made earlier and in another context to the lively
involvement of the Bank in the field of spirits production. (See brewing
and spirits industry diagram overleaf.)

In certain consumer goods branches Creditanstalt was not so
conspicuous. In glass, china and pottery two firms, Stölze's Söhne AG,
glass manufacturers, and Radziwill, Wimmer, Zelensky AG, manufacturers of earthenware and sand products, were within its sphere of
influence. Isolated examples of Bank activity were AG der k.k. priv.
Brünner Stearinkerzen- und Seifenfabrik, previously F. Semmler und
H. Frenzel in soap production, AG der k.k. priv. Brünner Leder-
warenfabrik, previously Max Grünfeld, in leather processing, and
Erste Österreichische Linoleumfabrik in linoleum manufacturing.
The Bank played a larger part in the textile industry. The products of
the AG der Österreichischen Fezfabriken, founded in 1899, were
destined almost exclusively for export to the Balkans. In 1907 this
enterprise expanded its scope by the creation of a working agreement
with the firm of Theodor Pollak in Biala and in 1908 by the purchase
of all the shares of A. Volpini & Söhne. At the turn of the century the
Bank had entered into closer relations with Vöslauer Kammgarnfabrik, which in 1913 became affiliated with the Brünner Kammgarn-
spinnerei AG. On this occasion the share capital was raised from 8.3
million to 9.8 million crowns. The severe crisis prevailing in the textile
industry during the last pre-war years inhibited the lively investment
activity found in other industrial spheres; in 1908 the Bank's
initiatives came virtually to a standstill. Gebrüder Rosenthal AG für
Textilindustrie and Königinhofer Kattundruckfabrik AG, founded in
1905 and 1908 respectively, were such chronically ailing ventures that
in 1913 the Bank decided to dispose of its shares in them.[13] A much
more promising showing was made by Vereinigte Färbereien AG,
founded in 1906. A year later it organized a Hungarian subsidiary; five
years later, it became affiliated to Braunauer Färberei- und Druckerei
Ges.m.b.H. (See textile industry diagram on page 68.)

Creditanstalt had a particularly strong footing in the wood
processing industry. It exercised substantial influence over Erste
Österreichische Aktiengesellschaft zur Erzeugung von Möbeln aus

Diagram 2: Brewing and Spirits Industry

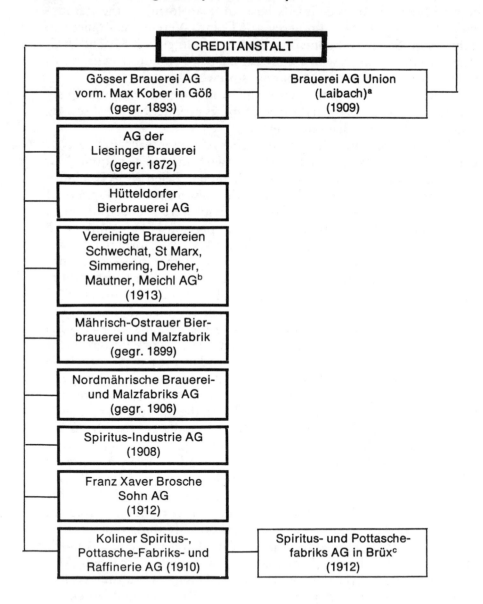

CREDITANSTALT

Gösser Brauerei AG
vorm. Max Kober in Göß
(gegr. 1893)

Brauerei AG Union
(Laibach)[a]
(1909)

AG der
Liesinger Brauerei
(gegr. 1872)

Hütteldorfer
Bierbrauerei AG

Vereinigte Brauereien
Schwechat, St Marx,
Simmering, Dreher,
Mautner, Meichl AG[b]
(1913)

Mährisch-Ostrauer Bier-
brauerei und Malzfabrik
(gegr. 1899)

Nordmährische Brauerei-
und Malzfabriks AG
(gegr. 1906)

Spiritus-Industrie AG
(1908)

Franz Xaver Brosche
Sohn AG
(1912)

Koliner Spiritus-,
Pottasche-Fabriks- und
Raffinerie AG (1910)

Spiritus- und Pottasche-
fabriks AG in Brüx[c]
(1912)

[a] Joint promotion by Creditanstalt, Gösser Brauerei AG, Brauerei Steinfeld, and Puntigamer Brauerei

[b] Other major shareholders were Wiener Bankverein and Niederösterr. Escompte-Gesellschaft

[c] In 1912 all the shares were acquired by Creditanstalt and in the same year re-sold to Koliner Spiritusfabrik

gebogenem Holz, Jacob und Josef Kohn, and its associate in the Polish provinces of Russia. In 1907 it participated in the setting-up of the Austrian and the Hungarian Mundus AG, which incorporated a number of bentwood furniture manufacturers into a single group. In addition to these leading furniture makers the Bank owned the timber production enterprise 'Tisita' Waldexploitations AG in Romania and the business stationery firm König & Ebhardt. The second point of concentration in the wood processing industry lay on the paper manufacturing side. Together with the firm P. Piette, the Bank in 1905 founded the k.k. priv. Papier-Industrie AG Olleschau, whose principal product was cigarette-paper; two years later, the Bank acquired the Seiden- und Zigarettenpapierfabrik L. & O. Holub at Wattens. In 1907 Theresienthaler Papierfabrik Ellissen, Roeder & Co. AG was started; in 1912 it took over the limited partnership shares in the cellulose manufacturing firm Alexander von Peez & Co. at Weissenbach on the Enns. And lastly the Bank, in conjunction with the Wiener Bankerein, participated in the transformation of Diamant & Co. into Mürzthaler Holzstoffund Zellulosefabrik AG. (See timber and paper industry diagram on page 70.)

Both consumer and capital goods firms fell within the purview of the chemical industry. AG der k.k. priv. Brünner Stearinkerzen- und Seifenfabrik, previously F. Semmler & H. Frenzel, which was founded in 1892, belonged to the first category, as did Zündwaren AG 'Helios'. The latter was founded in 1912; besides Creditanstalt the Vienna branch of the Živnostenská banka as well as the Niederösterreichische Escompte-Gesellschaft and its affiliate Industriebank für das Königreich Galizien und Lodomerien were involved in promoting the new enterprise. 'Helios' duly acquired (against contributions in kind) all other Austrian match manufacturers apart from Solo Zündwaren- und Wichsfabriken AG, a member of the Länderbank affiliate group.[14] Eventually the two large-scale enterprises 'Helios' and Solo entered into a cartel agreement and founded a joint sales subsidiary, Österreichische Zündhölzchen-Verkaufs-Ges. m.b.H.

The chemical industry as part of the capital goods sector made a comparatively late appearance. Creditanstalt's first major participation in this area dated from 1902, when it helped to create Holzverkohlungs-Industrie AG at Konstanz. Organized as a combine, the company had a share capital of 18 million marks. A number of chemical and timber firms in Germany and the Dual Monarchy were affiliated. The German undertakings were conducted as limited

Diagram 3: Textile Industry[a]

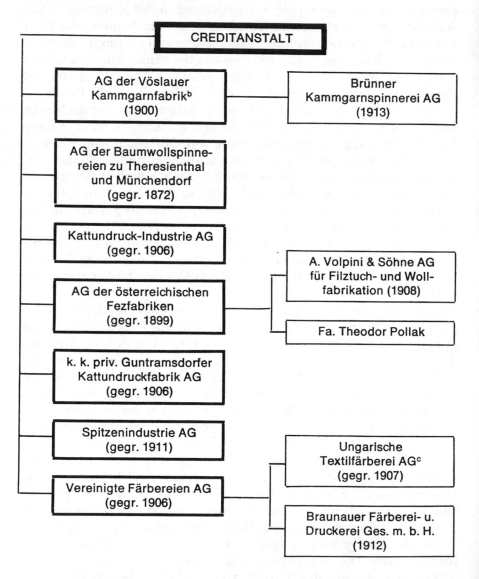

[a] In 1913 the shares of Gebrüder Rosenthal für Textilindustrie and of Königinhofer Kattundruckfabrik AG were unloaded. Both firms had been founded during the first decade of the new century

[b] Dominant influence: S.M. v. Rothschild

[c] Chief shareholder: Ungarische Allgemeine Kreditbank

liability companies; those in Austria and Hungary were conducted as joint-stock companies. Our description is confined to the combine's subsidiaries in Austria-Hungary. The year 1902 witnessed the purchase of all shares in Bantlinsche Chemische Fabriken AG, Union AG für chemische Industrie, and Bosnische Holzverwertungs AG. In 1906 the Konstanz enterprise acquired, together with Österreich-Ungarische Staatseisenbahn-Gesellschaft (a member of the Boden-Creditanstalt's affiliate group) a share in Holzverkohlungs AG Resicza. Two years later the chemical plants of Wagenmann, Seybel & Co. Vienna, were purchased and transformed into a limited company. In 1913 Holzverkohlungs-Industrie AG participated in the reconstruction of Magyar-Bodzaer Buchenholz-Industrie AG, thereby ensuring its own dominant influence in its business management.[15] As early as 1903 a plant operating under the name Perth Amboy Chemical Works, New York, had been established in the United States; 50% of its share capital was held by the Constance undertaking.[16]

Holzverkohlungs-Industrie AG was not Creditanstalt's sole interest in chemical firms located in the capital goods sector. In 1913 Österreichische Chemische Werke AG, founded in 1905, was turned into a limited liability company.[17] In 1911 the Bank joined in the promotion of Adriawerke AG für chemische Industrie and of Kaliwerke AG. Associated with the establishment of the second enterprise were Prince Alexander von Thurn and Taxis and two members of the Bank's affiliate companies, Peceker Zuckerraffinerie and Koliner Spiritus- und Pottaschefabriks- und Raffinerie AG; a third, Franz Xaver Brosche AG, held 10% of the Kaliwerke share capital in 1913.[18] In 1912 the Bank took a leading part in the foundation of Wilsdorfer Gerbextraktwerke AG. Four years earlier it had entered into business relations with 'Kerka' AG for the utilization of Dalmatian hydraulic power, but only in December 1913 did it acquire 27% of the share capital in this company, which operated various chemical plants.[19] (See chemical affiliates diagram, page 72.)

As previously mentioned, the emphasis of Creditanstalt's industrial investment activity shifted during the course of the Second Expansion Phase from consumer goods to the capital goods sector. On the eve of the First World War the Bank's affiliate group comprised some of the biggest, most efficient concerns in the machine construction and armaments industry. The most important was Skodawerke AG at Pilsen. In 1913 it was endowed with a capital (including net profit) of 70 million crowns and more than 53 million crowns outside resources.

Diagram 4: Timber, Timber-Processing, and Paper Industry

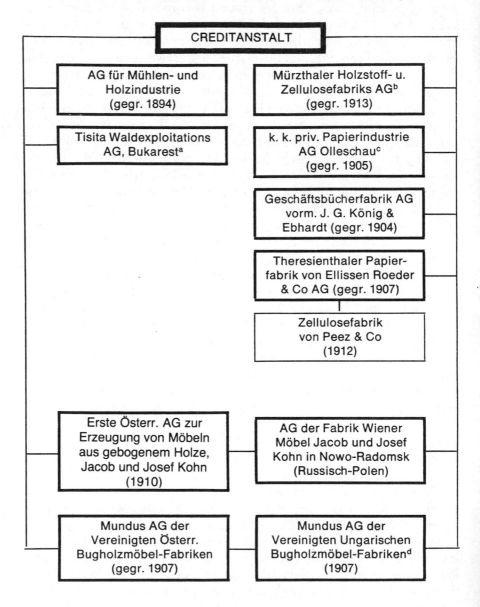

[a] Other major shareholder: S.M. v. Rothschild
[b] Joint promotion with Wiener Bankverein
[c] Joint promotion with the firm of P. Piette
[d] Joint promotion with Ungarische Allgemeine Kreditbank

Between the end of 1910 and 1913 its labour force rose by 60%; before the outbreak of war it totalled over 9,500 individuals.[20]

Affiliated with Skodawerke were a number of well-known machine building firms. In 1906 a group of Galician business men founded, together with Skodawerke and Creditanstalt, the k.k. priv. Maschinenfabrik L. Zieleniewski, which in 1913 bought Prince Lubomirski's machine and iron works at Lemberg (Lvov) and in the same year merged with Erste Galizische Waggon- und Maschinenbau AG at Sanok.[21] Likewise in 1913 Skodawerke purchased the majority shareholding in Österreichische Daimler-Motoren AG from Daimler-Motoren Gesellschaft und J. Mercedes.[22] In 1914 a pooling agreement was reached with Elektrizitäts-Gesellschaft, formerly Kolben & Co., and in June of this same year the majority shareholding in Vereinigte Maschinenfabriken, formerly Skoda, Ruston, Bromovsky und Ringhoffer, at Prague passed into the hands of Skodawerke AG, meaning that the latter now also had possession of the majority in Vaterländische Maschinenbau AG Sangerhausen-Eisele.[23] The foundation of Ungarische Kanonenfabriks AG took place in 1913, but production only began after the outbreak of hostilities. Apart from Skodawerke, Krupp of Essen and the Hungarian Government were also involved in the foundation and establishment of this armament enterprise.[24] Skodawerke's share in Cantiere Navale Triestino, a shipbuilding undertaking, was in 1913 sold at great profit to the Boden-Creditanstalt.[25]

The Bank's second big capital goods affiliate group centred on the shipbuilding yards of Stabilimento Tecnico Triestino, a company with which close relations had subsisted since 1897. Together with Österreichischer Lloyd, Stabilimento in 1910 set up Schiffswerfte San Rocco AG, with the share capital divided 50 : 50 between them. The following year Stabilimento acquired the majority in Societatea Anonima Santeriul Naval G. Fernic, a Romanian concern; in 1912 a majority of the shares in Lokomotiv-Fabrik formerly A. Sigl, which had for many years had close connections with Creditanstalt, passed into the hands of the Stabilimento.[26] Other important members of the Bank's affiliate armament group were Hirtenberger Patronenfabrik, Maschinenbau AG, previously Breitfeld, Danek & Co., and G. Roth AG, founded in 1908.[27]

Alongside the armament firms there were a number of machinery works in the Bank's sphere; of these there may be mentioned Webstuhl- und Webereimaschinenfabrik AG, Fr. Melchiar Sämaschinen-Fabriks AG, and Ringhoffer-Werke AG, in which Boden-

Diagram 5: Chemicals Group

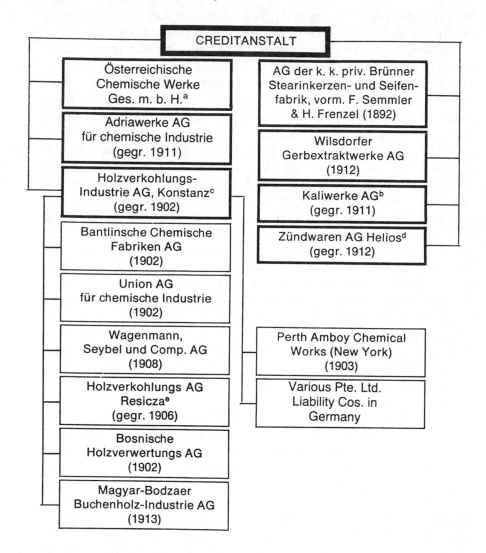

CREDITANSTALT

Österreichische
Chemische Werke
Ges. m. b. H.[a]

Adriawerke AG
für chemische Industrie
(gegr. 1911)

Holzverkohlungs-
Industrie AG, Konstanz[c]
(gegr. 1902)

Bantlinsche Chemische
Fabriken AG
(1902)

Union AG
für chemische Industrie
(1902)

Wagenmann,
Seybel und Comp. AG
(1908)

Holzverkohlungs AG
Resicza[e]
(gegr. 1906)

Bosnische
Holzverwertungs AG
(1902)

Magyar-Bodzaer
Buchenholz-Industrie AG
(1913)

AG der k. k. priv. Brünner
Stearinkerzen- und Seifen-
fabrik, vorm. F. Semmler
& H. Frenzel (1892)

Wilsdorfer
Gerbextraktwerke AG
(1912)

Kaliwerke AG[b]
(gegr. 1911)

Zündwaren AG Helios[d]
(gegr. 1912)

Perth Amboy Chemical
Works (New York)
(1903)

Various Pte. Ltd.
Liability Cos. in
Germany

[a] In 1912 transformed from joint-stock company (*AG*) into private limited liability
    company (*Ges.m.b.H.*)
[b] Joint promotion with Pečeker Zuckerraffinerie (Creditanstalt Group), Pottasche-
    fabriks- und Raffinerie AG (Creditanstalt Group) and Prince Alexander von Thurn
    und Taxis. In 1913 10% of the share capital belonged to Franz-Xaver Brosche AG
    (Creditanstalt Group)
[c] Promotion with participation of German capital
[d] Joint promotion with Živnostenská banka, Niederösterr. Escompte-Gesellschaft,
    and Industriebank für das Königreich Galizien und Lodomerien
[e] Joint promotion with Boden-Creditanstalt and STEG (Staats-Eisenbahn-
    Gesellschaft = State Railways Company, member of the Boden-Creditanstalt
    Group)
[f] See, for individual details, *Compass* 1918, Vol. I, p. 1,240 et seq.

Creditanstalt also had an interest. The earnings situation of two machine-building firms was unsatisfactory, and the Bank rid itself of them. Maschinen-Fabriks AG, previously Tanner, Laetsch & Co., founded by Creditanstalt in 1899, was after a few years sold to Prager Maschinenbau AG and in 1910 transferred to Simmeringer Maschinen- und Waggonfabrik. In 1913 Schnellpressenfabrik Mödling, previously L. Kaiser's Söhne AG, the result of the conversion in 1908 of Creditanstalt's limited partnership Schnellpressenfabrik L. Kaiser's Söhne into a joint-stock company, was sold to a group that included Verkehrsbank, Bankhaus Schoeller & Co., and Würzburger Schnellpressenfabrik König & Bauer.[28] (See machine-building and metal industry on pages 74–75.)

The highest degree of integration among all sectors of industry was to be found in a branch of activity closely related to machine-building, the electrical industry. In the immediate pre-war years the Bank had interests in three enterprises – AEG-Union Elektrizitäts-Gesellschaft (together with Boden-Creditanstalt), and the Austrian and the Hungarian 'Ericsson' Elektrizitäts AG, previously Deckert & Homolka companies, both founded in 1912 jointly with the Swedish firm L. M. Ericsson & Co. The Ungarische Allgemeine Kreditbank took part in the establishment of the Hungarian company. The Bank also had interests in Österreichische Elektrizitätslieferungs AG, founded in 1911 with Boden-Creditanstalt as its second largest shareholder; this firm specialized in the building and purchase of power stations as well as the construction of overhead supply lines. In 1913 'Kerka' AG zur Nutzbarmachung der Wasserkräfte Dalmatiens, founded in 1902, came within the Bank's sphere of influence. This company's resources had proved inadequate for its planned costly investments, and the Bank had extended loans. To redeem them, in 1913 'Kerka' AG issued 15,000 new shares, for which Creditanstalt subscribed.[29] The company did not confine itself to the construction and operation of power stations, but also operated chemical plants where calcium carbide, calcium nitrate, and cyanamide were prepared. It also had interests in the Ungarische Nitrogenindustrie AG, Carbidhandelsgesellschaft m.b.H., and Carbide Trading Co. Ltd., London. (See electrical industry diagram on page 76.)

The firms in the building materials industry in which the Creditanstalt owned an interest were among the most important in the whole Empire. The leading position was held by Wienerberger Ziegelfabriks-und Baugesellschaft, with a large number of brickyards, two ceramic wares factories, and real estate that in 1913 covered

Diagram 6: Machine-Building and Metal Industry

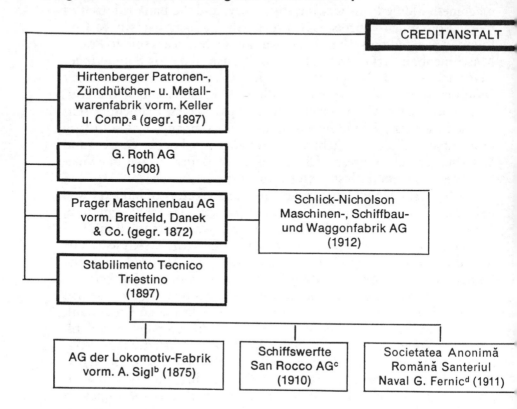

CREDITANSTALT

Hirtenberger Patronen-, Zündhütchen- u. Metall-warenfabrik vorm. Keller u. Comp.[a] (gegr. 1897)

G. Roth AG (1908)

Prager Maschinenbau AG vorm. Breitfeld, Danek & Co. (gegr. 1872)

Schlick-Nicholson Maschinen-, Schiffbau- und Waggonfabrik AG (1912)

Stabilimento Tecnico Triestino (1897)

AG der Lokomotiv-Fabrik vorm. A. Sigl[b] (1875)

Schiffswerfte San Rocco AG[c] (1910)

Societatea Anonimă Română Santeriul Naval G. Fernic[d] (1911)

[a] From 1913 onwards other major shareholder: Anglo-Österreichische Bank
[b] In 1912 the shares majority, hitherto held by Creditanstalt, was acquired by Stabilimento Tecnico Triestino
[c] Joint promotion with Stabilimento Tecnico Triestino and Österreichische Lloyd (Unionbank Group). Each of these held 50% of the share capital
[d] Shares majority held by Stabilimento Tecnico Triestino
[e] With participation of Creditanstalt and Boden-Creditanstalt transformed into joint-stock company
[f] Joint promotion with Živnostenská banka
[g] Other major shareholders: Baron Skoda and Niederösterr. Escompte-Gesellschaft
[h] Promoted with participation by Skodawerke, Creditanstalt and Niederösterr. Escompte-Gesellschaft
[i] In 1913 shares majority acquired by Skodawerke
[j] In 1911 shares majority acquired by Prager Maschinenbau AG and in 1914 devolved on Skodawerke
[k] In 1914 shares majority acquired by Skodawerke
[l] Promoted by Skodawerke, Friedrich Krupp AG, Essen, the Hungarian Government, Creditanstalt, and Ungarische Allgemeine Kreditbank

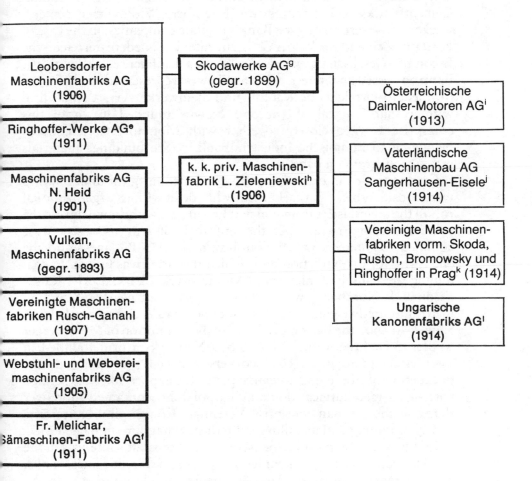

Leobersdorfer
Maschinenfabriks AG
(1906)

Ringhoffer-Werke AG[e]
(1911)

Maschinenfabriks AG
N. Heid
(1901)

Vulkan,
Maschinenfabriks AG
(gegr. 1893)

Vereinigte Maschinen-
fabriken Rusch-Ganahl
(1907)

Webstuhl- und Weberei-
maschinenfabriks AG
(1905)

Fr. Melichar,
Sämaschinen-Fabriks AG[f]
(1911)

Skodawerke AG[g]
(gegr. 1899)

k. k. priv. Maschinen-
fabrik L. Zieleniewski[h]
(1906)

Österreichische
Daimler-Motoren AG[i]
(1913)

Vaterländische
Maschinenbau AG
Sangerhausen-Eisele[j]
(1914)

Vereinigte Maschinen-
fabriken vorm. Skoda,
Ruston, Bromowsky und
Ringhoffer in Prag[k] (1914)

Ungarische
Kanonenfabriks AG[l]
(1914)

approximately 104 hectares.[30] A number of major cement works – Golleschauer Portland-Cementfabrik, Österreichische Portland-Cementfabriks AG at Szczakowa, Stramberg-Witkowitzer Zementwerke AG – were among the Bank's affiliate companies; in the case of Portland-Zementfabriks AG Lengenfeld, Niederösterreichische Escompte-Gesellschaft exercised the crucial influence, although the Bank possessed an interest.[31] It was likewise represented on the Board of Niederösterreichische Kaolin- und Steinwerke AG, a small firm with a share capital of 500,000 crowns founded in 1909; this enterprise worked closely together with Montan-AG, a concern belonging to Böhmische Industrialbank.[32] (See buildings materials industry diagram on page 78.)

Creditanstalt's interests in mining and metallurgical undertakings were considerable.[33] An earlier study has dealt with its organizational role in the oil industry, from which it had in part withdrawn during the years preceding 1914.[34] At the outbreak of war its assets were confined to interests in Mineralölraffinerie AG Budapest and the enterprise for oil extraction with which the latter was linked. In coal mining the Bank had interests in Montanwerke der k.k. priv. Kaiser Ferdinands-Nordbahn, which in 1913 produced nearly 13 million metric hundredweight, and in Ostrauer Bergbau AG, previously Fürst Salm.[35] In 1908 the Bank had a hand in the promotion of Mitterberger Kupfer AG; Eisenwerke AG Rothau-Neudeck, a firm founded in 1909 and employing 2,500 workers engaged principally in the production of iron bars and gauge plates for export, likewise formed part of its metallurgical domain. Its portfolio contained moreover shares in the German enterprise Vereinigte Königs- und Laurahütte AG. (See mining and metallurgical industry diagram on page 80.)

Finally attention must be focused on Creditanstalt's interests in the services sector: trading companies, railways and shipping lines, banks, and insurance companies. Two companies on close terms with the Bank were active in trade with the East. In 1904 the management had decided that a limited partnership share should be taken in Alois Schweiger & Co., which had been in overseas business since the eighties. In 1911 the firm was turned into a limited liability company. The Bank's interest was a capital investment of 2 million crowns and substantial outstanding loans.[36] Austro-Orientalische Handels AG had been founded by the Bank in 1908 and in 1914 this firm and Schweiger were joined in a syndicate, which during the war had but limited scope for its activities.[37]

In 1905 Creditanstalt had assisted in the promotion of Adriatica

Diagram 7: Electrical Industry and Gas Works

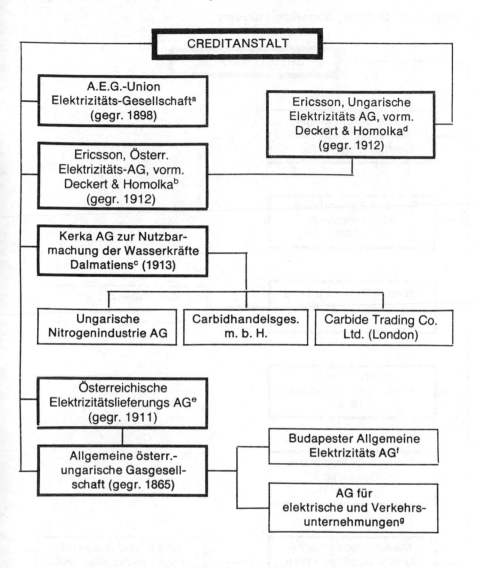

a   Other major shareholders were AEG-Union, Berlin and Boden-Creditanstalt
b   Joint promotion with L.M. Ericsson & Co., Stockholm
c   The company also disposed over various chemical firms
d   Dominant influence: Boden-Creditanstalt. 25% of the share capital was held by Allgemeine österreichisch-ungarische Gasgesellschaft
e   30% of the share capital was held by Allgemeine österreichisch-ungarische Gasgesellschaft
f   An approximately 9% participation by Allgemeine österreichisch-ungarische Gasgesellschaft
g   Other major shareholder: Ungarische Allgemeine Kreditbank

Diagram 8: Building Materials Industry

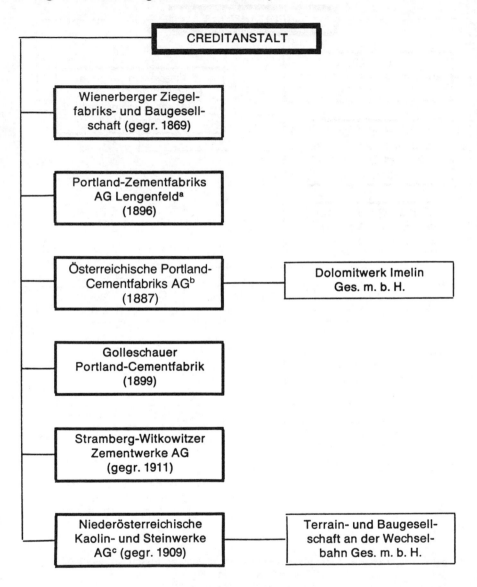

CREDITANSTALT

Wienerberger Ziegel-
fabriks- und Baugesell-
schaft (gegr. 1869)

Portland-Zementfabriks
AG Lengenfeld[a]
(1896)

Österreichische Portland-
Cementfabriks AG[b]
(1887) — Dolomitwerk Imelin
Ges. m. b. H.

Golleschauer
Portland-Cementfabrik
(1899)

Stramberg-Witkowitzer
Zementwerke AG
(gegr. 1911)

Niederösterreichische
Kaolin- und Steinwerke
AG[c] (gegr. 1909) — Terrain- und Baugesellschaft an der Wechsel-
bahn Ges. m. b. H.

[a] Determining influence: Niederösterr. Escompte-Gesellschaft
[b] Other major shareholder: Niederösterr. Escompte-Gesellschaft
[c] Pooling arrangement with Montan AG, Prague, a group member of Böhmische Industriebank

Speditions AG, in which a number of Trieste forwarding agents were amalgamated. Another venture was Wollehandels-Ges.m.b.H., founded in 1912 together with Ungarische Allgemeine Kreditbank. In the preceding year the Bank had joined with Wiener Bankverein in converting the department store A. Gerngross into a joint-stock company with a share capital of 12 million crowns. (See commerce diagram on page 81.)

In shipping, Creditanstalt had an interest in two concerns: Allgemeine österreichische Schiffahrt Gerolimich & Comp. AG, created by the conversion of a family firm at Lussinpiccolo (today's Mali Losinj); and Vereinigte österreichische Schiffahrts AG, previously Austro-Americana & Fratelli Cosulich. Acquiring an influence over the second of these two companies was evidently a matter of national interest. Since 1904 two major German shipping lines, Hamburg-Amerika-Linie and Norddeutsche Lloyd, had possessed a controlling block of shares in Austro-Americana and at the beginning of 1914 had acquired still more of its stock. In the spring of 1914 the Austrian Government arrived at an agreement with the German concerns that they should transfer their shares to a consortium headed by the Wiener Bankverein. The consortium had to pledge itself to retain until 1929 at least a third of the respective share capital in its own hands and moreover to see to it that the majority shareholding in Austro-Americana did not pass into foreign hands.[38] The firm had an interest in the Cantiere Navale Triestino shipyard, whose share majority (as already mentioned) had been acquired in 1913 by the Boden-Creditanstalt, it also held stock in the Greek shipping line Archaia.

On the eve of hostilities only a few local railways belonged to Creditanstalt – Localbahngesellschaft Potscherad-Wurzmes in Bohemia, Überetscher Bahn, Virglbahn and Vigiljochbahn companies in the South Tirol, and Lokalbahn Marci-Arco-Riva on Lake Garda. The year 1910 saw the Bank's participation in the sole major rail construction project, that of the Mittenwaldbahn in the Tirol. (See rail and shipping diagram on page 82.)

In insurance Creditanstalt was in close association with three companies, all of which had been founded in the 1890s: Münchener Rückversicherungsgesellschaft, the Providentia Allgemeine Versicherungsgesellschaft, and Erst österreichische Versicherungsgesellschaft gegen Einbruch. Creditanstalt and Münchener Rückversicherungsgesellschaft were partners in the promotion of the other two enterprises. Boden-Creditanstalt and Versicherungsgesellschaft

Diagram 9: Mining, Metallurgical Plants, Oil Production & Refining

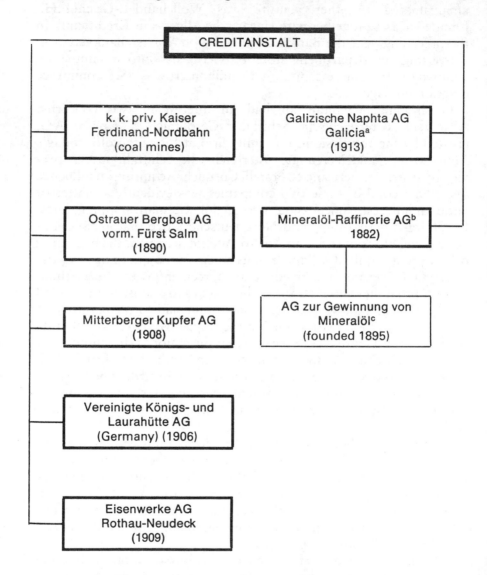

CREDITANSTALT

k. k. priv. Kaiser Ferdinand-Nordbahn (coal mines)

Galizische Naphta AG Galicia[a] (1913)

Ostrauer Bergbau AG vorm. Fürst Salm (1890)

Mineralöl-Raffinerie AG[b] 1882)

Mitterberger Kupfer AG (1908)

AG zur Gewinnung von Mineralöl[c] (founded 1895)

Vereinigte Königs- und Laurahütte AG (Germany) (1906)

Eisenwerke AG Rothau-Neudeck (1909)

[a] Other major shareholder: Bankhaus Ofenheim & Co. (Germany)
[b] Other major shareholder: S.M. v. Rothschild
[c] Promoted by Mineralöl-Raffinerie AG

Diagram 10: Commerce and Transport

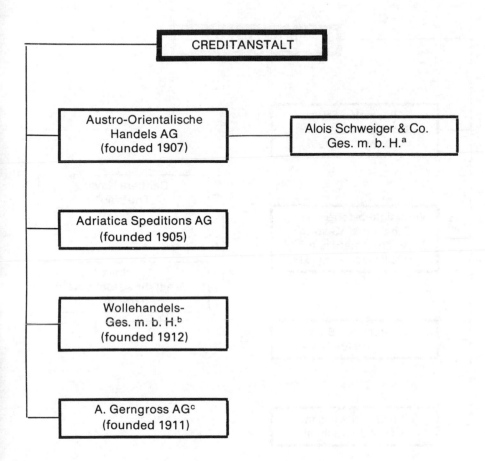

a Ensued on transformation of a limited partnership by Creditanstalt. In 1914 a pooling arrangement with Austro-Orientalische Handels AG and joint business management
b Joint promotion with Ungarische Allgemeine Kreditbank
c Joint promotion with Wiener Bankverein

Diagram 11: Railways and Shipping

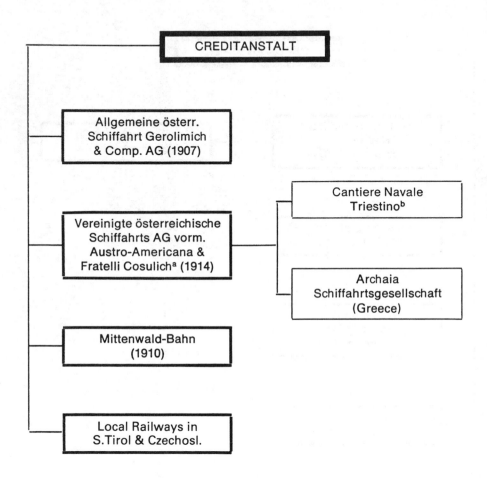

[a] In 1914 a consortium led by Wiener Bankverein acquired the shares majority. Creditanstalt held a 14% participation in the consortium

[b] In 1914 the shares majority devolved on Boden-Creditanstalt

Diagram 12: Banking and Insurance Business

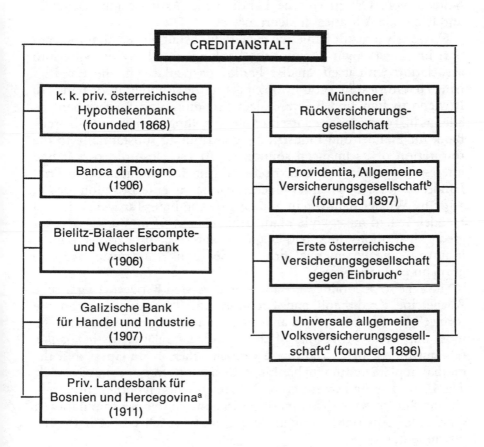

CREDITANSTALT

k. k. priv. österreichische
Hypothekenbank
(founded 1868)

Banca di Rovigno
(1906)

Bielitz-Bialaer Escompte-
und Wechslerbank
(1906)

Galizische Bank
für Handel und Industrie
(1907)

Priv. Landesbank für
Bosnien und Hercegovina[a]
(1911)

Münchner
Rückversicherungs-
gesellschaft

Providentia, Allgemeine
Versicherungsgesellschaft[b]
(founded 1897)

Erste österreichische
Versicherungsgesellschaft
gegen Einbruch[c]

Universale allgemeine
Volksversicherungsgesell-
schaft[d] (founded 1896)

[a] Promoted 1895 by Wiener Bankverein and Ungarische Bank für Handel und Industrie. At the end of 1911 Creditanstalt and Ungarische Allgemeine Kreditbank joined the Board. Creditanstalt had a 20% share
[b] Joint promotion by Creditanstalt, Boden-Creditanstalt, Münchener Rückversicherungsgesellschaft, and Österr. Phönix
[c] Promoted in participation with Creditanstalt and Münchener Rückversicherungsgesellschaft
[d] Promoted by Österr. Länderbank, Assicurazioni Generali, and Riunione Adriatica di Sicurita. The consortium was later joined by Münchener Rückversicherungsgesellschaft. In 1913 Creditanstalt held 1,800 of the company's 10,000 shares

Österreichischer Phönix held interests in Providentia.[39] The Bank and its most important insurance associate, Münchener Rückversicherungsgesellschaft, also had minority holdings in Universale allgemeine Volksversicherungsgesellschaft, whose main shareholders were Österreichische Länderbank, Assicurazioni Generali, and Riunione Adriatica di Sicurita.[40]

Obviously a major bank like the Creditanstalt played an important part in its very own domain, the banking world, by drawing into association with itself smaller banks, particularly in the Empire's fringe territories. In 1906 it took part in the foundation of Banca di Rovigno in Italy and Bielitz-Bialaer-Escompte und Wechselbank in Silesia. In 1907 it assured itself of a controlling interest in Galizische Bank für Handel und Industrie by contributing substantially to the restoration of its financial soundness. At the close of 1911 it had interests, together with Ungarische Allgemeine Kreditbank, in Priv. Landesbank für Bosnien und Herzegowina, an enterprise founded in 1895 by Wiener Bankverein and Ungarische Bank für Industrie und Handel. It had meanwhile made affiliates out of a number of local credit institutions and had acquired interests in various Balkan industrial and commercial firms.[41] (See banks and insurance diagram on previous page.)

Since 1870 a pooling agreement had existed between Ungarische Allgemeine Kreditbank and Creditanstalt. The latter was on the former's Board and received an annual lump commission from it. The most important provisions of the agreement related to the Bank's relinquishment of its right to a branch office in Budapest and the mutual implementation of banking transactions free of commission.[42] The Bank also had interests in Österreichische Hypothekenbank in Vienna and in Banca Commerciale Italiana, in whose foundation a number of Austrian, German, Swiss, and French banks had been instrumental.

Notes

1 See Walter Reik, *Die Beziehungen der österreichischen Grossbanken zur Industrie* (Vienna, 1932), p. 26.
2 Reik, *Die Beziechungen*, p. 21, and Egon Scheffer, *Das Bankwesen in Österreich* (Vienna, 1924), p. 289.
3 Creditanstalt provided financial assistance for Maschinenfabrik Heid, Stockerau. When differences arose with the main shareholder, it withdrew its representative from the Board but retained its powerful creditor status. See *Der Österreichische*

Volkswirt, 'Die Bilanzen', 23 August 1913, p. 279 et seq.

4 See Jurij Křižek, *Die wirtschaftlichen Grundzüge des Österreichisch-Ungarischen Imperialismus in der Vorkriegszeit, 1908–1914* (Prague, 1963), p. 48.

5 Reik, *Die Beziehungen*, p. 47, goes so far as to report that the banks put blocks of shares at each other's disposal for General Meetings.

6 Cf. Eduard März, *Österreichische Industrie- und Bankpolitik in der Zeit Franz Josephs I* (Vienna, 1968), pp. 305 and 349.

7 *Compass*, Vol. 2, 1915, p. 1,255. The rest of the shares were held by Dr Philipp Ritter von Gomperz and the Stummer family.

8 Wrong decisions on the part of the banks extending the loans could not be excluded as a contributory factor because the Kürschner principals were known for their lavish extravagance and indulgence in stock exchange speculation. *Der Österreichische Volkswirt* in this connection criticized the 'reckless lending of the banks in recent years' as a whole. See 'Der Fall Kürschner', *Der Österreichische Volkswirt*, 2 August 1913, p. 984 et seq.

9 *Der Österreichische Volkswirt*, 16 August 1913, p. 1,027. Simultaneously reports were current in the economic press about the sale of the Kürschner sugar factory at Branowitz to Rohrbacher Zuckerraffinerie AG.

10 *Der Österreichische Volkswirt*, 19 July 1913, p. 950; 'Kalendarium' and 'Der Fall Kürschner', *Der Österreichische Volkswirt*, 23 August 1913, p. 1,044.

11 See *Compass*, Vol. 2, 1915, p. 538.

12 *Compass*, Vol. 2, 1915, p. 525. Gösser Brauerei, as a matter of comparison, had in 1913 a share capital of no more than 6 million crowns.

13 'Die Bilanzen', *Der Österreichische Volkswirt*, 21 February 1914, p. 72.

14 See *Compass*, Vol. 2, 1915, p. 569.

15 *Compass*, Vol. 2, 1915, p. 793 (where the company's German interests are also listed) and 'Holzverkohlungs-Industrie AG Konstanz', in 'Die Bilanzen', *Der Österreichische Volkswirt*, 14 December 1918, p. 41.

16 *Der Österreichische Volkswirt*, 14 December 1918, p. 42.

17 See *Compass*, Vol. 2, 1915, p. 570.

18 *Compass*, Vol. 2, 1915, p. 574 et seq. and 'F. X. Brosche AG', in 'Die Bilanzen', *Der Österreichische Volkswirt*, 4 July 1914, p. 225.

19 *Compass*, Vol. 2, 1915, p. 563 and 'Kalendarium', *Der Österreichische Volkswirt*, 7 March 1914.

20 'Skodawerke AG', in 'Die Bilanzen', *Der Österreichische Volkswirt*, 28 March 1914, p. 112 et seq. Niederösterreichische Escompte-Gesellschaft as well as Creditanstalt was represented on the Skodawerke board.

21 *Compass*, Vol. 2, 1915, p. 477.

22 *Der Österreichische Volkswirt*, 10 May 1913, p. 722.

23 Prager Maschinenbau AG, vormals Ruston, Bromowsky und Ringhoffer, although a strongly expansive enterprise, had been in financial difficulties. Prior to Skodawerke's take-over of the shares majority, a dramatic conflict had occurred between the then majority shareholder Sohr and, under the leadership of Anglo-Österreichische Bank, the bank creditors. It ended with Sohr's downfall which in turn rendered the reorganization possible. Cf. 'Prager Maschinenbau AG', *Der Österreichische Volkswirt*, 31 January 1914, p. 288 and the same periodical's issue for 2 May 1914, p. 614 et seq.

24 *Compass*, Vol. 2, 1915, p. 981.

25 See 'Kapitalnot und chinesisches Anleihegeschäft', *Der Österreichische Volks-

wirt, 25 October 1913, p. 75.

26 'Stabilimento Tecnico Triestino', in 'Die Bilanzen', *Der Österreichische Volkswirt*, 15 November 1913, p. 27.

27 In 1913 a conflict arose between Creditanstalt and Anglo-Österreichische Bank which wanted to acquire the majority in the Hirtenberger Patronenfabrik. See 'Hirtenberger Patronenfabrik', in 'Die Bilanzen', *Der Österreichische Volkswirt*, 23 August 1913. Creditanstalt's dominant position was eventually preserved.

28 *Compass*, Vol. 2, 1915, p. 487, and 'Österreichische Creditanstalt', in 'Die Bilanzen', *Der Österreichische Volkswirt*, 21 February 1914, p. 72.

29 *Compass*, Vol. 2, 1915, p. 563, and 'Kalendarium-Nachtrag', *Der Österreichische Volkswirt*, 7 May 1914.

30 *Compass*, Vol. 2, 1915, p. 330.

31 See 'Portland-Zementfabriks AG', *Der Österreichische Volkswirt*, 21 February 1914, p. 328, and *Der Österreichische Volkswirt*, 28 February 1914, p. 356.

32 See *Compass*, Vol. 2, 1915, p. 333 et seq.

33 The affiliate group companies belonging to the other major banks were respectively Priv. österreichisch-ungarische Staatseisenbahngesellschaft (Boden-Creditanstalt), Rimamurányer Eisenwerke (Wiener Bankverein), Prager Eisen-Industrie-Gesellschaft and Alpine Montangesellschaft (Niederösterreichische Escompte-Gesellschaft). In the last case, though, it would be inappropriate to speak of a controlling position by the bank.

34 Cf. März, *Österreichische Industrie- und Bankpolitik*, pp. 307 et seq., 356 et seq.

35 See *Compass*, Vol. 2, 1915, p. 375 et seq.

36 See 'Österreichische Credit-Anstalt', in 'Die Bilanzen', *Der Österreichische Volkswirt*, 3 April 1915, p. 111.

37 See *Compass*, Vol. 2, 1915, p. 765.

38 *Compass*, Vol. 2, 1915, p. 1,754. The consortium was composed as follows: Fratelli Cosulich (38%), Wiener Bankverein (16%), Boden-Creditanstalt (14%), Creditanstalt (14%), Österreichische Länderbank (14%), and Banca Commerciale Triestino (4%).

39 See *Compass*, Vol. 1, 1916, p. 1,542.

40 *Compass*, Vol. 1, 1916, p. 1,560. Apart from this Creditanstalt had some small participations in a series of other big insurance companies.

41 See *Compass*, Vol. 1, 1915, p. 340 et seq.

42 *Compass*, Vol. 1, 1915, p. 541.

CHAPTER 7
Creditanstalt Shareholders and Officials

A complete 1913 register of Creditanstalt shareholders with voting rights, i.e., those who held 25 shares, or more, has been preserved.[1] The list unfortunately contains no hint as to the size of the individual holdings and therefore gives no clue as to the size distribution of shares. All that can be said with certainty is that at this time shares in foreign possession constituted a negligible quantity.[2]

The record of shareholders present at an Extraordinary General Meeting held on 2 March 1911 is more informative.[3] 132 shareholders with voting rights appeared either in person or were represented by proxy. This meant that about two-thirds of all those with voting rights were present for the occasion, representing 72,390 shares. As however an important proportion of those with voting rights is not identified, and as the shareholders (or their proxies) present at the meeting will not all have revealed their holdings completely, this record too allows no more than guesses at the distribution of the shares.[4]

The largest single block of voting rights, amounting to 444 votes or 11,100 shares, was represented by Karl Fritz, the proxy for Bankhaus S. M. von Rothschild. 40 of the 444 votes were the personal possession of Baron Louis Rothschild, who after the death of his father Albert had joined the Bank's board, and who during the First Republic (1918–38) would become its Chairman. The rest were in the possession of the old banking house.

In a wider sense it is probably right to count as part of the Rothschild block, and therefore in addition to the 444 votes, those belonging to interests closely allied to the House of Rothschild. It is not easy after the lapse of almost seven decades to determine the composition of this wider circle of interested parties very precisely. Indubitably, though, its focal point was Max Ritter von Gomperz. His links with Creditanstalt went back more than half a century to

1858 when he had first served as a member of the Board and ultimately became its chairman. In 1913, when he died at the age of 91, he personified the Bank's tradition and was a symbol of Austria's economic progress during the past hundred years.[5]

Max Gomperz had inherited from his father Philipp the banking house of the same name which in 1913 still enjoyed a respected status in Vienna's financial world. Among the numerous members of his family it is his sister Josephine who deserves special mention. Married to Leopold von Wertheimstein, long-standing Rothschild proxy, she became the patroness of a literary circle to which Eduard von Bauernfeld, well-known Austrian poet and playwright, belonged and which on occasion included Franz Liszt. His youngest sister, Sophie, was the wife of the banker Eduard Todesco, and the latter's brother Louis had become a member of the board of the Creditanstalt as long ago as 1858. Theodor Gomperz a younger brother, was professor at the University of Vienna and a recognized authority at home and abroad in the field of classical philosophy. Max Gomperz's son, Dr Philipp Ritter von Gomperz, was his father's partner in Bankhaus Gomperz, managing director of an important fine cloth manufactory at Brünn (Brno) that he had taken over from Max, member of the Board of several large concerns in the textile and sugar industries, and after the death of his father also on the Board of the Bank. In Moravia he was a figure in politics, mainly as a member of the provincial assembly.[6] In the 1911 Annual General Meeting attendance list Max and Philipp Gomperz are shown as having 122 votes and owning 3,050 shares. The Gomperz family was among the few major shareholders of the Creditanstalt. Others disposing of a similarly high number of shares were rare: Wilhelm Ritter von Doderer, industrialist and Austrian university professor; Ernst Kohn, a producer of bentwood furniture; Paul Lücke, German industrialist who was probably on intimate terms with Hannoversche Bank, and the Berlin banking house Mendelsohn & Co. None of these major shareholders had however any influence comparable to that of the Rothschilds and the groups allied with them.

Among the rest of the shareholders two groups particularly attract attention – the Bank's Board members and several leading officials of the closely allied Ungarische Allgemeine Kreditbank. The Bank's articles of association provided that Board members must at the Annual General Meeting prove possession of at least 50 shares, the equivalent of two votes. Many of them had of course a more handsome package. It would be wrong to regard the Board members as a whole as belonging to the shareholders in league with the Rothschilds, but some of them undoubtedly were on a close footing with Baron Albert and, subsequently, Baron Louis Rothschild. This, as has been seen, held good for the two Gomperz, for Julius Blum, manager of the Bank for many years and later its chairman, for the private banker Richard Lieben, and for Baron Paul Schey von Koromla who was known to the public mainly as chairman of Vöslauer Kammgarnfabrik. Two former managers, Ludwig Wollheim and Dr Ignaz Mikosch, are likely to have felt an obligation towards Rothschild interests and so probably did Richard Pollak, a proxy for the Rothschild bank who was Board member on some of the Bank's affiliate enterprises (Stabilimento Tecnico Triestino, AG zur Gewinnung von Mineralöl, Budapest, et cetera).

Certain Board members were in one way or another on close terms with Ungarische Allgemeine Kreditbank. This applies first and foremost to Adolf von Ullmann, a leading official of this important Hungarian bank who was in constant business contact with Julius Blum and then Alexander Spitzmüller. Ullmann sat on the board of various companies within the Bank's sphere of influence (Hirtenberger Patronen-, Zündhütchen- und Metallwarenfabrik, AG zur Gewinnung von Mineralöl, and so on). Merey Alexander von Kaposmere, Board member of long standing, was on the management team of Ungarische Allgemeine Kreditbank. Julius Blum was also one of its vice-chairmen.

A strikingly large number of the Bank's shareholders stood in near relationship to Ungarische Allgemeine Kreditbank. Only a few of the more outstanding personalities can be named here. Klaudius Sebesta, owner of a large packet of Bank shares, was secretary-general of the Kreditbank and may be counted as champion of Austro-Hungarian interests in the Balkans. Vice-chairman of Société Ottomane pour l'Eclairage de la Ville de Constantinople, he was likewise on the board of the city's tramway corporation and of the Turkish railways. Margrave Eduard Pallavicini, vice-chairman of Ungarische Allgemeine Kreditbank, also was one of the prominent Creditanstalt shareholders, and besides holding numerous other business appointments was chairman of the AG zur Gewinnung von Mineralöl, Budapest, closely linked to Creditanstalt. A considerable number of the Bank's shares were moreover in the hands of Joseph von Lukacs and Elemer von Horvath, members of the same Hungarian bank's management; of Ignaz Levai, one of its leading officials; of Geza Kovacs, a well-known Hungarian industrialist, and last, but by no means least, of Baron Paul Kornfeld, who as a member of the Kreditbank's board exercised substantial influence over its policy.

At the Annual General Meeting some of these personalities were often represented by Viennese lawyers with high reputation in Austrian economic life. Dr Rudolf Spiro, himself a shareholder, was proxy for a number of important industrialists, among them Ernst Kohn, Heinrich Janotta, and Pacher von Theinburg, as well as for Schlesischer Bankverein. Dr Spiro was on the board of Gebrüder Rosenthal AG für Textilindustrie, a firm belonging to the Bank's sphere of influence. Dr Hugo Fürth, who possessed a fairly large packet of the Bank's shares and as vice-chairman of AG der österreichischen Fezfabriken undoubtedly had close contact with leading figures in the Bank, acted for Joseph von Lukacs and Julius Klein, another industrialist. Dr Emil Ritter von Fürth was above all prominent on behalf of leading officials in Ungarische Allgemeine Kreditbank and of the German industrialist Paul Lücke. In Vienna Dr Emil Fürth was a member of the Municipal Council and an expert in the field of assistance on housing matters.[7]

Among the many outstanding names on the list of shareholders two in particular attract attention: Ivan Emil Edler von Hofmannsthal and Dr Emil Edler von Hofmannsthal. They were of course close relatives of the poet Hugo von Hofmannsthal. Ivan, a private banker, was his uncle. Emil, son of Ivan, was born in 1884 and so was ten years younger than his cousin Hugo. A recognized expert on Austrian company and bills of exchange law, he wrote several authoritative books on these subjects. In 1915 he founded the Austrian Shareholders Association and was its vice-chairman; since 1912 he had been a member of the International Air Traffic Law Commission; and in 1919 he became a delegate to the League of Nations Conference at Berne. In public life he was best known in his capacity as representative of the International Law Association, a function which he continued to hold also in the United States after his emigration there in 1938.[8]

As these examples show, the shareholders of Creditanstalt constituted a remarkably homogeneous social group linked in part by truly close economic, political, and on occasion family ties. Shareholders' meetings, in accordance with this circumstance, were characterized by a spirit of harmony. Unconditional approval of the Board's and the management's manner of conducting business was the rule. Consequently the Bank's conservative dividend and reserves policy during the last years of peace was questioned by only a few shareholders representing minority interests.

The harmonious relations between shareholders and officials stemmed in no small degree from the fact that in 1913 the Bank's two principal personalities enjoyed an unparalleled public esteem. The careers of Julius Blum, the Board chairman, and Alexander Spitzmüller, the Management chairman, have been fully described in an earlier work.[9] Here it suffices to say that they complemented each other ideally. Blum had begun as a trainee in the Bank's Trieste branch office, was later appointed to its agency at Alexandria, switched to the Egyptian Civil Service, and in 1890 returned to the Bank's headquarters as one of the senior managers. In 1913, after the death of Gomperz, he took over its chairmanship. Spitzmüller, until his entry into the Bank in 1910, had been exclusively a Civil Servant who had wide experience of the Empire's banking and monetary problems as well as of problems relating to the Austro-Hungarian compromise of 1867; he was a leading official in the Ministry of Finance and later head of the Lower Austrian Financial Directorate. His thorough familiarity with such matters is reflected in his numerous publications of which ample use has been made in this study. During the last pre-war years the Bank's management consisted of Dr Alexander Spitzmüller, Dr Paul Hammerschlag, Ludwig Neurath, and Emanuel Raumann. Their deputies were Paul Lechner, Sigmund Löwy, Rudolf Patek, and Alois Wismeyer. At this time Hammerschlag and Neurath were probably, next to Spitzmüller, the Bank's representatives best known to the general public. Hammerschlag, born 1860, had in 1909 become a member of the management team with staff and legal affairs as his main responsibility. From the available documents it is clear that above all he was entrusted with examination of the legal aspects of important business questions. In 1917, when the management was reorganized, the onus for the issue and settlement of domestic bonds fell on Neurath and Hammerschlag.[10]

Ludwig Neurath, born 1868, had held leading positions in various industrial enterprises before his appointment as the Bank's consultant on industrial affairs. In 1909 he was promoted to the management team and was primarily charged with preliminary investigation into industrial projects. Later the department for Foreign Bonds and other Financial Transactions was confided to his (and Hammerschlag's) care. On the outbreak of war he became Director of the Metal and Wool Agencies whose functions will be fully described in another connection. When in 1916 Spitzmüller was given a Ministerial portfolio and resigned from the Bank, the Board appointed Neurath his successor.[11]

Notes

1 The register was added as a supplement to the 1913 Annual Report and will be found in the present study's Appendix, Part I.
2 See *Compass* 1918, Vol. 1, p. 502, where the shares in foreign possession are put at a mere 3.9%.
3 See AVA, K.K. Ministry of the Interior, No. 2544/1910.
4 The record of those present will be found in the Appendix, Part I.
5 Cf. Eduard März, *Österreichische Industrie- und Bankpolitik in der Zeit Franz Josephs I* (Vienna, 1968), p. 359.
6 Profuse data about the family Gomperz's economic and cultural influence is contained in Heinrich Gomperz, *Theodor Gomperz, Briefe und Aufzeichungen* (ed. Robert A. Kann, Vienna, 1974).
7 See *Österreichisches Biographisches Lexikon*. The title 'Ritter' incorporated into the names of three personalities mentioned here denoted knighthood and bore some resemblance to baronetcy in so far as it was hereditary. 'Edler', as a matter of translation analogous to 'The Honourable', may be regarded as an infinitesimal shade higher in status inasmuch as it frequently carried the courtesy appellation 'Baron'.
8 The obituary in the Vienna weekly *Die Furche*, 27 November 1971, said, 'Dr Emilio von Hofmannsthal, our long-standing New York correspondent, died on 12 November of a heart attack. He was 87, a Christian and an Austrian, a promulgator and representative of European culture and Austrian urbanity.'
9 Cf. März, *Österreichisches Industrie- und Bankpolitik*, p. 285 et seq. and p. 359 et seq.
10 Taken from various Board Minutes and the Ehrenfest Case files (No. 26 d. Vr. 6373/31).
11 AVA, various Finance Archives files; Ehrenfest Case files, as above; AVA K.K. Ministry of Trade HL/1390; K.K. Ministry of the Interior 17476/16.

CHAPTER 8

Organizational, Economic, and Financial Preparations for War

During the last decade before the outbreak of the First World War the Austrian economy was, as has been seen, characterized by rapid, almost tempestuous progress. The time was however too short for the lead held by older industrial nations like Great Britain, France and Germany to be decisively reduced. The Dual Monarchy, owing to its economic structure, was poorly prepared for a long-term contest with an alliance of important industrial countries.

This weakness was further underlined by two self-inflicted political handicaps, the nationalities conflict and – accentuating this struggle still further – the Dual institutions. A short account of these two phenomena must suffice here.

In 1867 the 'Dual Monarchy' had emerged on the basis of not quite identical Austrian and Hungarian statutes, with the two halves of the Empire linked to each other by only a few common institutions. They included the person of the ruler (Emperor of Austria and King of Hungary), the Ministry for Foreign Affairs, the Army and military matters, and the financial system in so far as it served to cover the outlay on joint affairs.[1] Because the Hungarian statute (Article 58) definitely proclaimed that economic matters did not constitute 'joint' business, a tariff and trade agreement had to be concluded every ten years between the two countries. Each of the renewal negotiations gave rise to arguments about the parties' respective contribution to the outlay on common affairs. Although the 'quota' problem was not of outstanding importance, it frayed tempers more than anything else and it sometimes seemed as though both sides would rate the negotiations a success or failure by this criterion alone.[2]

The Monarchy's currency system (in the shape of an integrated central bank), fiscal legislation (where indirect taxes were concerned), as well as the salt and tobacco monopoly were also parts of the so-called 'compromise'. Because of the necessity of the periodic renewal of the customs agreement and the constantly growing opposition of powerful groups in Hungary, all of the common institutions came under a cloud of uncertainty. Even the central bank, notwithstanding its excellent management, suffered from this state of affairs. Moreover during the last years of the Monarchy's existence the Austrian Parliament hardly ever proved capable of coming to a binding decision. More and more often an Imperial emergency decree had to take the place of a Parliamentary resolution.[3]

The provisional nature of the economic union and the incitement of opposing viewpoints almost inevitably caused by the periodic negotiations – with the Magyar party usually the stronger because of its greater cohesion – were damaging to the Monarchy's prestige and in part responsible for the derisive epithet 'Monarchy Under Notice'. It was Austrian industry that suffered perhaps most from the uncertainty of the situation. 'It never ceased to deplore', wrote Spitzmüller,

that the short duration of each new customs agreement formed an unstable basis for the maintenance of its most important market, complicating industrial planning and rendering impossible, or barring the way to the realization of projects dependent on the preservation of this market. This complaint was the more justified because the beginning of the current agreement's last three years generally coincided with the start of fresh negotiations, so that public irritation and increased uncertainty as to the future usually arose already after the expiry of seven years.[4]

All the same it would be mistaken to conclude that during the last years of peace these circumstances seriously imperilled the Monarchy's cohesiveness. From his analysis of the trade figures Tremel infers that 'Hungary's exports to Austria before the war remained approximately unchanged – crop yields of course played a part – but Austria's exports to Hungary constantly, though slowly, went up and in the ten years from 1900 until 1910 almost doubled.'[5] In 1913 Hungary took nearly half (45.5%) of Austrian finished goods exports. Till the outbreak of hostilities it continued to be Austria's most important export market. For Hungary, on the other hand, Austria was the outlet for more than 80% of its foodstuffs and raw materials and for more than 70% of its finished goods.[6] Its dependence on imports was however showing signs of falling off somewhat in the last two decades before the war. After the turn of the century imports from Austria accounted for about 70% of the total as against 80 to 85% in earlier years.[7]

With the outbreak of war the picture began to alter drastically. Deliveries of goods in either direction became ever more restricted.

Austria was to a great extent dependent on Hungary for its wheat and flour supplies. The unwillingness of the Hungarian Government to share fairly with its partner its increasingly scarce stocks of foodstuffs contributed crucially to the dangerous supply situation in Austria. The nutrition crisis was nevertheless only one, even though the most serious, symptom of the failure of the common institutions when put to the severe test of total war.

Dualism was indeed workable only to a limited extent. Shortly after its introduction in 1867 it turned out to be a political strait-jacket which no longer left room for a broadminded constitutional solution to the nationalities problem. 'It is safe to say', writes the late Robert Kann, the greatest expert on the Habsburg nationalities problem, 'that after the introduction of the Compromise, a non-revolutionary solution of the monarchy's problem of integration, slight as its chance had been before, now became highly improbable.'[8]

The basic political reason for the Compromise lay in its permanent establishment of two principal nationalities, the German-speaking Austrians and the Magyars. The franchise by separate Curias assured the Polish minority of a privileged position in the Austrian half of the Empire, but likewise the Czechs and other Slav nationalities were able step by step to improve their economic and cultural position through a tenacious struggle increasingly conducted by extra-parliamentary means. To the world at large, though, Austria, on account of these heated battles inside and outside the legislature, presented the picture of a politically disrupted state doomed to destruction. Hungary, on the other hand, adhering to a restrictive franchise and a militant policy of Magyarization towards its Slav majority until the end of the Monarchy, conveyed to the outside world the impression of being a stable and secure state. Jaszi sums up this apparently paradoxical development as follows:

... these national struggles growing in passionate intensity, showed directly opposite tendencies in Austria and in Hungary: in the former, political evolution went on manifestly in the direction of national equalization and federalization, whereas the latter – at least seemingly – evolved towards a unitary, unilingual, Magyar national state in which only one political nation was acknowledged as the force maintaining and directing the state.[9]

Regardless of their growingly vehement character and sometimes spectacular manifestations, the national struggles in Austria were therefore hardly a source of serious danger to the Monarchy's continuance. As long as Tsarist Russia and Imperial Germany endured, Austria offered a better guarantee for the free evolution of

Czechs, Poles, and even Ruthenians than did its powerful neigh-bours.[10] In Hungary matters stood otherwise. Here the national aspirations of the South Slavs, who had been loyal subjects of the Monarchy over a long period, were suppressed in the most flagrant way. The result was that small, backward Serbia began to exercise an ever greater attraction to Serbs, Croats, and Slovenes. The mounting nervousness with which the Austro-Hungarian Ministry for Foreign Affairs reacted to these ever more centrifugal forces is reflected in the economic reprisals – the so-called Pig Wars – imposed against Serbia during the Monarchy's last decade.[11] Gustav Stolper in November 1913 analyzed the Slav question's fateful implications.

The solution of this question affects the basis of our political relations with Hungary because the Hungarian nationalities problem cannot be solved by a little more or a little less tolerance on the part of the ruling aristocratic class. It is the natural consequence of the unnatural fact that in the twentieth century a minority in no way outstanding for its cultural attainment lords it over a majority of the population, which culturally is rapidly in the ascendant. . . . Let however the nationalities in Hungary once attain full equality – and the conflict cannot end before that – then Dualism will have lost its meaning. . . . For the Germans in Austria the only alternative, on which they will have to make up their minds, seeing the way that things are going, is to become Pan-German or Greater Austrian. . . . And if they want to remain faithful to their historic task of being the upholders of the Austrian 'Staats idee' . . . then they must resign themselves to the fact that the Monarchy has a Slav majority with whom a *modus vivendi* has to be found precisely by reason of this idea.[12]

A *modus vivendi* of the two principal nationalities with the Monarchy's Slav majority depended however in the last resort on the readiness of the Magyar upper class to furnish the South Slav peoples with guarantees for their free national development. Subsequently Hugo Hantsch trenchantly summarized what Stolper had so clearly recognized on the eve of the First World War:

For the Hungarian Government there existed only one Magyar national-ities policy, and as little as the Magyar chauvinists grasped that Hungary's entire European status, the esteem for and the power of Magyar culture and civilization, ultimately rested on Dualism and the Monarchy's Great Power position, as blind was it to the justified demands of the nationalities whose demand for recognition it saw as sheer treason. This exaggerated notion of Magyar dominion, this fight against the Imperial concept, was the blade that it directed against the Monarchy, but against its own breast too.[13]

It is hardly surprising that during the last years of peace a mood of uncertainty, doubt and anxious foreboding was felt even by people who had little connection with politics. It will do to quote here just one example, that of the great Austrian poet and patriot Hugo von Hofmannsthal, writing to Leopold von Andrian in 1913 in the following moving terms:

This year has taught me to see Austria as thirty preceding years did not teach me to see it. And I have to put it to you the way that I recently put it to Feri Kinsky – I have completely lost the faith that I had in the top class, the great nobility, the confidence that particularly in Austria it had something to give and to signify, and therewith my respect for this class that I had, God knows from where. I see now the part that it has played in all Austria's catastrophes, in 1805, in 1809, in 1848, as in 1859, and in a different, and I fear clearer, perspective. But nowhere do I perceive the class, no, not even the constituents of the class, that could replace this one in leadership. We have to admit to ourselves, Poldy, that we have a native land, but no fatherland – only a ghost as substitute. The thought that some day perhaps ones children's blood will have to be dedicated to this ghost is bitter. Not that the idea of this old empire falling apart would be desirable or even tolerable to me. But to pledge one's soul to a mere shell, void of any idea, indeed void of any purpose beyond the morrow, indeed beyond today – to the bare substance, without and within – cannot be done, not without doing damage to the soul. As against this, Metternich's era had inspiration because, reactionary or not, it served an idea.[14]

The reproach can hardly be levelled against the Monarchy that during the final years of peace it was among the initiators of the arms race. Not before 1908, the year of the Annexation Crisis when the possibility of a larger-scale military conflict had to be taken into account, were warlike preparations comparable with those of the other European Great Powers made. Henceforward the volume of armaments was raised each year until military expenditure shortly before the outbreak of war claimed almost a third of Austria's entire budgetary outlay.[15] Even at this late hour the Monarchy's state of readiness was relatively modest compared with that of its most important potential opponents. Even those who regarded a passage of arms as inevitable evidently thought that this could be limited both in place and time. Neither the organizational nor the economic and financial preparations give the impression of the authorities having appreciated the full gravity of the impending crisis.

Lacking above all was a joint body which would have been responsible in Austria *and* in Hungary for introducing and controlling war economy measures. The *Kriegsüberwachungsamt* (War Supervisory Office) was meant to form the basic unit for such a body, but its competence remained restricted to Austria and Bosnia-Hercegovina. Richard Riedl, in his knowledgeable study of the Austrian war economy, states:

No one had ventured openly to demand the creation of such a central institution for fear of Hungarian resistance to it. The alternative chosen failed to achieve its object. The Monarchy entered the war without a joint and efficient body to deal with the problems which would decide its outcome – the problems of a war economy.[16]

In 1912, following the example of France, Germany, Italy, and Switzerland, a law was enacted which defined the duties of the population in the emergency of war and the projected modes of compensation.[17] 'These regulations', says Riedl,

subjected in case of war the entire population and the whole of the economy to the military. The Defence Minister . . . could, theoretically at least, without needing to obtain the agreement of other Ministries . . . requisition all stocks, lay claim to all industrial plants, and call upon the services of individuals to whatever extent seemed necessary to him.[18]

The most important feature of the law, from a war economy viewpoint, was the scope it gave for taking over strategic industrial sectors like arms and munition factories, coal mines, and so on, as well as those working there. A war production plant was by definition a defence plant under martial law, meaning that its personnel had unquestioningly to obey orders by the military authorities on pain of disciplinary action.[19]

While peace lasted, the armed forces' supplies of armaments and other commodities were in the hands of certain big firms and consortia consisting of a larger or smaller number of firms engaged in the same branch of activity. The arrangement envisaged that a not inconsiderable share of the supplies should come from smaller businesses. This provision, Riedl comments, would, in the event of hostilities, 'prove an obstacle to the necessary increase in production'. The measure, together with others, also contributed to the preservation of small-scale production structures. Raw materials and semi-finished goods were to be obtained as far as possible from domestic sources. This rule applied even to materials produced under relatively unfavourable conditions.[20] Stockpiling of foreign raw materials was seriously impeded in this way.

The Austrian military authorities clearly thought that their organizational and economic preparations would provide an efficient basis for the conduct of a modern campaign. The early months of the war were to convince them of the inadequacy of these measures.

Most obvious of all perhaps was the unsatisfactory state of the financial preparations or, more correctly, the preparations relating to financial policy on the outbreak of war. Outlay, according to the Compromise, should primarily be defrayed from the joint customs revenue. Whatever could not be met from there would have to be divided between Austrian and Hungary in the proportion established by the 'quota'. The last pre-war agreement provided for a ratio of 63.6% and 36.4% respectively, the larger share naturally falling to Austria.

In his memoirs Spitzmüller recounts discussion of the subject during an audience that he had with the Emperor on 4 June 1908.

> Franz Joseph ... became especially animated when I emphasized the political and military importance of having a single central Bank. 'Yes, militarily too, isn't it?' he said. ... He then began to speak about the Bank having made all preparations in case of mobilization, a fact that as former monetary and banking referee I was able to corroborate, and he palpably thought it out of the question to abandon what had so far been done in this field. He also gave it as his opinion that the Hungarians would ultimately not renounce the advantages accruing to them from the currency union. The audience closed after I had added for good measure that opposition to it was to be ascribed purely to Hungarian chauvinism and that the Bank also constituted a bond of the greatest political importance.[21]

That Spitzmüller should have fortified the Emperor in his conviction that the Austro-Hungarian Bank had made 'all preparations' in case of mobilization is astonishing. Perhaps he had in mind the fact that of recent years the Bank's bullion reserve had constantly grown. A year later it would reach the record figure of 1,442 million crowns, giving 72% cover for the notes in circulation. Later on the ratio deteriorated not inconsiderably.[22]

In October 1908, only a few months after the talk between the Emperor and Spitzmüller, the annexation by the Empire of Bosnia-Herzegovina demonstrated very clearly that the financial preparations sufficed at best to meet the requirements following on a partial mobilization. A former governor of the Austro-Hungarian Bank, Alexander Popovics, has told how at this stage there took place a discussion between representatives from the Empire's two Ministries of Finance, the outcome of which is supposed to have been the basis for later measures in this sphere. In case of a partial mobilization, according to Popovics, 'cash on hand' would first of all be called upon. . . . Issues of treasury bills and increasing the funded national debt would be envisaged. If circumstances at the particular moment should not permit such an issue, the banks should be called upon to take over these bonds; agreement would have to be reached with the central bank to raise the ceiling on collateralized loans, so that the financial institutions lending against the state bonds would be able to maintain their liquidity.[23]

The officials seem however to have realized that in the case of a general mobilization more radical measures would need to be adopted. 'In so far as Government credit could not be utilized in the normal way,' Popovics continues, 'the Austro-Hungarian Bank would have to be called upon. For this purpose the provision . . . that business could be transacted with the' (Austrian and Hungarian) 'Governments only if no extensions of credit were involved would have to be repealed. . . .'[24] Thus it was already apparent in October 1908 – almost six years before the outbreak of war – that in an emergency funds would be required on a scale which must, as on previous critical occasions, lead almost inevitably to the abrogation of the current central bank statutes.

The growing political tensions had an adverse effect too in the field of monetary affairs. While the 1911 Agadir Crisis is said to have led to a recall of French assets from Austria and Hungary, the situation became more serious after the onset of the First Balkan War in 1912. The outflow of foreign capital assumed a proportion where the central bank had to sell large quantitites of gold abroad to uphold the currency. Signs of some domestic anxiety were also to be observed. At the bank's General Council meeting on 25 October

the secretary-general, Pranger, reported that for the first time in decades a loss of confidence in the currency was evident in certain parts of the monarchy. Prime sufferers were the savings banks, where big withdrawals were occurring. . . . Even gloomier was the secretary-general's report two months later. Now, he told the meeting on 19 December, withdrawals from financial institutions had spread like a contagious disease to all parts of the economy. An exodus of capital across the Monarchy's borders was verifiable. . . .[25]

By 31 December the note circulation had reached the record level of 2,816 million crowns. Gold stocks, not taking into account gold foreign exchange, amounted to no more than 1,210 million crowns.[26]

In this atmosphere of crisis representatives from the two Ministries of Finance met once more to examine whether the conclusions reached at the conference in October 1908 held good in the circumstances of the Balkan hostilities. 'The participants', says Popovics, were unanimous that from the viewpoint of preparedness for war the prevailing situation was extremely difficult. Because of the constant monetary strain one could count on the home front to only a very limited extent, and all the less because the withdrawal of deposits from savings banks and financial institutions could in case of a general mobilization assume catastrophic dimensions. Nor was it possible to count to any extent on foreign participation in a loan operation because mobilization by the Monarchy would mean immediate uneasiness in the Western markets and in addition their splitting up according to the political alignments of the Powers.[27]

The funds required for a three months' general mobilization were assessed at some two thousand million crowns. As in 1908, the officials did not think it feasible for such an amount to be raised through normal loan issues. 'The emphasis' would have to be shifted 'towards obtaining help from the central bank', but 'after the restoration of normal conditions the soonest possible re-establishment of the *status quo ante* should be pursued with the greatest vigour.'[28] The central bank's representatives asked what measures should be taken to meet the contingency of hostilities exceeding three months. The question was however left unanswered in light of the preponderant opinion that the state of military technology would lead to 'a war in Europe being brought to a definite conclusion within three months'.[29]

In spring 1913 Popovics, currently governor of the central bank, received confidential information about extensive Russian military preparations. He was sufficiently worried to write identical letters on 9 April to the Austrian and the Hungarian Ministers of Finance. He stressed once again that it would prove necessary 'at the moment of the mobilization order being issued, and before a shot is fired,' to take steps to 'dismantle the legal structure of the monetary system.'[30] On this assertion followed proposals for using the available breathing-space 'to fortify by stages the national cash balances'. Furthermore 'the considerable quantity of government orders abroad should undergo the severest restriction and every participation of domestic capital in foreign loan operations should be prohibited.' Nothing suggests that the governor's warnings met with any appropriate response in either ministry.

For completeness' sake let it be added that on 23 July 1914, the day when the Austro-Hungarian ultimatum was delivered in Belgrade, the management of the central bank invited representatives from the major Vienna and Budapest banks for talks. However, it seems that a detailed discussion about the grave effects on the Monarchy's monetary system and financial situation in consequence of a large-scale military conflict did not occur. The senior bank officials, says Popovics, were requested 'not to pursue a restrictive credit policy, not to confront the central bank with excessive demands, and altogether ... to do everything not to arouse any too great anxiety'.[31] Apparently it was still hoped that the conflict could be localized.

Long-winded treatises have been written about the responsibility – in the narrower and wider sense of the word – for the fateful declaration of war on Serbia. There is no room, not even by way of quotation, for dealing with them here. It is certain that the Monarchy had since the Annexation Crisis proceeded on a probable collision course with Russia and thereby become increasingly dependent on imperial Germany. The latter's foreign policy, manifestly aggressive since the Agadir Crisis of 1911, was observed sceptically and with growing disquiet by wide sections of the Austrian middle class, many of whom had a good insight into the Monarchy's limited economic and military fitness.

Josef Schumpeter, the great Austro-American economist and sociologist, regarded imperialism as a relic from pre-bourgeois days comprehensible solely through the existence and dominance of a bellicose feudal class.

Export monopolism is not as yet imperialism. And in the hands of an unwarlike middle class it would never, even if it had originated without protective tariffs, have evolved into imperialism. That happened simply because the war machine, its social psychology, and the will to war were legacies of the past and because, of all middle-class interests, the warlike ones could ally themselves with a bellicose class which had preserved its ruling position and which had domestic political interests of its own in this direction. The alliance kept alive fighting instincts as well as notions of power, of virility, and glamour of conquest that would otherwise have long been extinct. It led to a state of affairs which may ultimately indeed be explicable in terms of production conditions, but not alone in terms of capitalist production conditions. And it often leaves its imprint on contemporary policy, threatening Europe with constant danger of war.[32]

While this is not the place to enter in greater detail on Schumpeter's theory of imperialism, let it be noted that it very clearly reflects the social and political conditions which determined the Monarchy's foreign policy. The financial world's most prominent representatives were as good as debarred from influence on the nation's foreign affairs. These remained the province of the dynasty and a small exclusive group of the higher nobility, where Hungarian magnates set the tone.

The memoirs of Alexander Spitzmüller and Rudolf Sieghart, the two chief banking personalities on the eve of the war, clearly reflect their lack of influence in the field of foreign affairs. Both of them were indubitably aware that certain personalities in the Emperor's immediate entourage favoured preventive war against Russia. Meeting Conrad von Hötzendorf, Chief of the General Staff, at a dinner-party in the Bavarian Legation, Spitzmüller recalls:

Conrad made no bones about going to war with Russia in good time, seeing that it was inevitable anyway. Now [1912] was however a moment at which it could be hoped to win this conflict because the Russian rail system was not yet sufficiently advanced to enable massive troop concentrations to be brought quickly to the Western frontiers. In a word, Conrad advocated preventive war, a fact rendered the more significant for his speaking quite frankly though we had never before met.

Shortly afterwards the Minister for War, Baron Krobatin, spoke in Spitzmüller's presence to the same effect.[33]

In 1913 Creditanstalt was invited by a foreign consortium to participate in a transaction to extend the capacity of Russia's two biggest munition plants, the Nevski and the Putilov Works. Enlightened but a few months earlier by the War Minister on the need for preventive war against Russia, Spitzmüller was probably no little surprised to hear at the Ministry of War 'that from the standpoint of Government interest there is no objection to the operation.'[34] The Minister of Foreign Affairs expressed the same view.[35]

Spitzmüller seems to have been poorly informed on the course of affairs in and around the Ballhausplatz during the fateful days before the outbreak of war. On the other hand Sieghart, in charge of the Office of the Council of Ministers prior to his appointment as governor of the Boden-Creditanstalt, was probably kept constantly informed about the situation's increasing gravity. He remained convinced, until the actual breach of diplomatic relations with Serbia, that hostilities could, indeed must, be avoided. The Monarchy was to his mind a highly vulnerable structure. 'To the last moment', he writes,

I did not believe that war would happen. I could not imagine that Austria-Hungary, of all the Great Powers that with the weakest periphery, with an exposed situation on several fronts, and with the magnetic attraction exercised by numerous nations beyond its borders on their co-nationals inside them, would plunge into so risky an adventure. I still do not understand the folly of the erstwhile rulers, and least of all their childish faith that Austria-Hungary would be dealing solely with Serbia.[36]

Responsible for the declaration of war on Serbia was, Sieghart thought, a handful of men – the Austrian Prime Minister Count Stürgkh, the head of the Ministry of Foreign Affairs Count Berchtold (and his advisers Forgách, Musulin, and Hoyos), General Conrad and War Minister Krobatin, Minister of Finance Bilinski, and finally too the Hungarian Prime Minister Istvan Tisza, notwithstanding his resistance until the last moment to an armed solution of the conflict.[37] In fairness it should be added that the Austrian and Hungarian statesmen's martial policy could count on the plaudits of leading people and even on broad sections of the German-speaking population. That neither the German ambassador nor his master in Berlin exercised any restraining influence is now a familiar fact. Even the Social Democrat leaders and a considerable portion of their followers subscribed, after brief hesitation, to the patriotic course – supporting the defence of their fatherland.[38] Worthy of mention moreover is the strange mistake, widespread among all classes, that a modern war could last no more than a few months. A book by J. Riesser, the well-known German economist who alleged that scarcity of financial resources made prolonged hostilities impossible, may have nourished this belief. Only the Great Depression has furnished similar examples of misjudgement by economic experts.

Sieghart implies that views of this kind were excusable and intelligible. 'Inexcusable and completely unintelligible' was

that the people around Berchtold and his principal political adviser, Count Johann Forgách, deluded themselves into thinking that it would be a case of facing Serbia alone. I remember very well going horrified to the Ministry of Foreign Affairs, after the expiry of the ultimatum and the departure of Giesel [the Austrian ambassador] from Belgrade, and saying to Count Forgách, 'I am afraid that Russia will intervene and, with Serbia, attack us'. Whereupon Count Forgách replied, with an indescribable mixture of indifference and hauteur, 'Well, let them.'[39]

Sieghart's reaction to the decision by the Ballhausplatz was undoubtedly characteristic of the attitude among the great majority in the financial world. None of the leading bankers seems to have entered the war with the same unconcern as the small clique around Stürgkh and Berchtold. But the Siegharts, Spitzmüllers, Neuraths, Poppers, Prangers, and the rest, were farther removed from the controls of political power than their colleagues in London, Paris, Washington, and Berlin, and they could therefore confide their consternation at the 'folly of the erstwhile rulers' only to their diaries.

Notes

1 Cf. Erich Zöllner, *Geschichte Österreichs* (Vienna, 1974), p. 412.

2 Spitzmüller recounts in his memoirs the reaction of the Hungarian Prime Minister, Alexander Wekerle, to what he regarded as having been too far-reaching a concession in the matter of a quota. 'I shall never forget Dr Wekerle's outburst when he learned that his Minister of Trade had conceded an extensive, in fact hardly justifiable quota increase for some constitutional formulations. "This Kossuth, this fool," he fulminated, "gives good money for beads!"' Alexander Spitzmüller, . . . *Und hat auch Ursach' es zu lieben* (Vienna, 1955), p. 63.

3 In 1897, when the Austrian Parliament brought down the Bánffy-Badeni Compromise, a serious crisis occurred. Széll, Bánffy's successor, declared the Compromise effective until 1907 with the rider that no commercial treaties could be concluded for any period beyond 1907. The possibility of severance was therefore left open for that year. On the Austrian side the Compromise was put into force by Imperial decree. Not until 1907 was the treaty renewed. Spitzmüller thinks that Dualism suffered during the period without contract 'especially in respect of the Germans, who had hitherto looked on it as a bulwark, exceedingly grave damage, and that without the main motive having been to replace it by a better system.' Alexander Spitzmüller, *Der letzte österreichisch-ungarische Ausgleich und der Zusammenbruch der Monarchie* (Berlin, 1929), p. 6.

4 Spitzmüller, *Der letzte . . . Ausgleich*, p. 10.

5 Ferdinand Tremel, 'Der Binnenhandel und seine Organisation', *Die Habsburgmonarchie 1848–1918* (Vienna, 1973), Vol. I, p. 391.

6 Cf. Krisztina Maria Fink, *Die österreichische Monarchie als Wirtschaftsgemeinschaft* (Munich, 1968), p. 63. It should be noted that industrial goods, alongside of foodstuffs, comprised a considerable, constantly growing part of Hungary's exports to Austria.

7 Cf. Ivan T. Berend and György Ránki, 'Ungarns wirtschaftliche Entwicklung 1849–1918', *Die Habsburgermonarchie 1848–1918*, Vol. I, p. 486. Nonetheless these figures reveal one of the roots for the deep dissatisfaction prevailing in Hungarian industrial circles. They viewed the absence of tariff barriers as a serious impediment to their progress.

8 Robert Kann, *The Habsburg Empire – A Study in Integration and Disintegration* (New York, 1957), p. 36.

9 Oscar Jaszi, *The Dissolution of the Habsburg Monarchy* (Chicago, 1961), p. 271.

10 A remark in pre-war days by the well-known nationalist Karel Kramaš is perhaps typical for this feeling as it prevailed among wide sections of the Czech population: 'Nobody can deny the fact, clear and obvious to everyone, that in Austria our nation can live in what are comparatively the best conditions for its cultural, political, and economic development.' Quoted by Hugo Hantsch in *Die Geschichte Österreichs* (Vienna-Graz-Cologne, 1962), Vol. II, p. 502.

11 On the link between the repressive nationalities policy practised in Hungary and the growing strength of the pan-Serb movement, Hantsch writes, 'Magyar chauvinism's anti-national trend created that untenable situation in the Monarchy's south Slav areas which gave the Greater Serbian movement its most powerful impetus and its initial prospect of success.' In *Die Geschicte Österreichs*, Vol. II, p. 482.

12 Gustav Stolper, 'Politisches Resumée', Der Österreichische Volkswirt, No. 7, 15 November 1913, p. 125f.

13 Hantsch, in Die Geschicte Österreichs, Vol. II, p. 485.

14 Hugo von Hofmannsthal–Leopold von Andrian, Briefwechsel (Frankfurt, 1968), 24 August 1913, p. 199 et seq.

15 Cf. Chapter 3, 9f. A State Living Beyond Its Means.

16 Richard Riedl, Die Industrie Österreichs während des Krieges (Vienna, 1932), p. 23.

17 See RGBl (Law Gazette) No. 236, 26 September 1912.

18 Riedl, Industrie Österreichs, p. 9.

19 Riedl, Industrie Österreichs, p. 10 et seq.

20 In spite of this promotion by the military authorities, the production of certain raw materials like flax and sheep's wool was declining in Austria. Cf. Riedl, Industrie Österreichs, p. 6.

21 Spitzmüller, Und hat auch Ursach', p. 69 et seq.

22 In 1909 the bullion reserve, including gold bills, attained the imposing peak of 1,713 million crowns. Gold bills were for calculation of the gold reserves allowed to be taken into account only to a total of 60 million crowns. This lowered the official level correspondingly. In 1912 the cover ratio had dropped to a mere 45%. Cf. K.K. Statistische Zentralkommission, Statistische Rückblicke aus Österreich (Vienna, 1913), p. 64.

23 Alexander Popovics, Das Geldwesen im Kriege (Vienna, 1925), p. 33.

24 Popovics, Das Geldwesen, p. 34. See also Siegfried Pressburger, Österreichische Notenbank, 1816–1966 (Vienna, 1966), p. 277.

25 Pressburger, Österreichische Notenbank, p. 273 et seq.

26 Pressburger, Österreichische Notenbank, p. 275. The central bank's reserves, taking into account its gold bills holdings, still amounted to 1,507 million crowns. They had therefore fallen only 12% below the 1909 peak figure. Cf. Statistische Rückblicke, p. 64.

27 Popovics, Das Geldwesen, p. 35.

28 Popovics, Das Geldwesen, p. 35.

29 Popovics, Das Geldwesen, p. 37.

30 Popovics, Das Geldwesen, p. 40.

31 Popovics, Das Geldwesen, p. 43.

32 Josef A. Schumpeter, 'Zur Soziologie der Imperialismen', in Aufsätze zur Soziologie (Tübingen, 1953), pp. 145–6. This essay was first published in Archiv für Sozialwissenschaft und Sozialpolitik, Vol. 46 (1919), pp. 1–39.

33 Spitzmüller, Und hat auch Ursach', p. 116.

34 Cf. Board Minutes, 29 July 1913, Creditanstalt Archives.

35 Chapter 5 has recounted this incident in greater detail.

36 Rudolf Sieghart, Die letzten Jahrzente einer Grossmacht (Berlin, 1932), p. 168.

37 'Count Stürgkh's own words to me were, "Tisza was the only one against war, but we finally dragged him along too." ' Sieghart, Die letzten Jahrzehnte, p. 173.

38 In his memoirs Sieghart refers (see p. 169 in particular) to the Arbeiterzeitung's patriotic leading articles. Characteristic possibly is a speech by Viktor Adler to the Social Democratic functionaries when he defended the support by the German Social Democratic members of the Reichstag for war loans. 'My view is that I know it has to be so. What I don't know is how to let the words cross my lips. But it has to be. It is a dreadful decision, a dreadful conflict that is imposed not only on us

Germans, but just the same on all proletarians who are involved. There is no other choice, dreadful as it is, because the opposite is worse still . . . I think that probably, at the moment when our people stand out there . . . no one can do other than hope, for we don't want defeat. There is only one thing worse than war, that is defeat. . . . And moreover there is the tremendous fact that Germany is fighting for its existence. . . .' Victor Adler, *Der Parteimann. Reden und Aufsätze*, Vol. IX, Vienna 1929, p. 106.

39 Sieghart, *Die letzten Jahrzehnte*, p. 174.

PART TWO

From a Peacetime to a War Economy

CHAPTER I
Problems of Economic Mobilization

Upon the outbreak of war the bitter national disputes and conflicts seemed as though swept from the political stage by magic. Parliament had been prorogued in February 1914 and the government had since ruled by way of the emergency decree article No. 14. From 16 March 1914 until 30 May 1917, when Parliament was recalled, no less than 181 Imperial ordinances were promulgated without the legislature's sanction.[1] At the beginning of August, at a time when heavy losses were sustained on two fronts, the army took over as the highest political authority. In many parts of the country civil administration fell under the control of the military.[2] Jury proceedings were suspended and public meetings forbidden. The press was subordinated to a severe censorship, which was gradually relaxed in 1917 under different political conditions. Munitions factories, coal mines, and other industrial sectors were put under martial law and officers took charge alongside civilian managers. This, as has been remarked earlier, meant that the personnel in such plants was subject to military discipline.[3] Long-established workers' rights vanished overnight. Notice could not be given nor strikes be called to give emphasis to wage demands. The orders of officers in charge had to be implicitly obeyed.[4] Appeal boards, composed of representatives from employers and employees and empowered to arbitrate claims for pay increases, changes in working conditions, and termination of employment, were not instituted before March 1917.[5]

The Napoleonic Wars were the last time that Austria had fought a life-and-death struggle. The brief campaigns against Italy and Prussia half a century back had revealed disquieting defects in the military machine, but the Empire's power of resistance to total warfare had not then really been put to the test. Growing international tension and the government's policy of expansion in the Balkans had necessitated, particularly after 1908, a considerable rise in military preparedness.

After the start of hostilities it soon became clear though that the resources for a conflict on this scale were not available. The general staff had, significantly enough, never reckoned with the possibility of an all-out challenge. War for two years, under the most adverse circumstances, was the most that had been allowed for. Plans had been laid in such an eventuality to mobilize an army 1.4 million strong. Russia's intervention compelled this same number to be called to the colours by September 1914. More than 4 million men under arms was the 1915 average. The total of those enlisted is assessed at between 7.5 and 8 million.[6]

The unexpected turn of events led to what may be called a mobilization crisis. Not that there were insufficient troops. The army had sizeable reserves which could be mustered comparatively swiftly. The difficulty was to procure the necessary quantities of rations, clothes, and equipment. Late autumn and winter saw an acute scarcity of ammunition, heavy arms, and winter clothing on practically all fronts. The cost in lives for miscalculation of this war's true dimensions was high.[7]

Because senior army opinion held that the show-down would come in a matter of months, mobilization took practically no account of the economy's needs. Individuals with qualifications often indispensable to the smooth running of plants were conscripted willy-nilly. Some activities, like coal mines, iron foundries, engineering works, and so on, whose vital importance for conducting a war of *materiél* and equipment was only later fully appreciated, lost large portions of their labour force from one day to the next.[8] Not until 1915 was an order issued to release miners and iron and steel workers from front line service. By then many of those to whom it applied had become exempt for ever from the disposition of any terrestrial authority.

The War Services Act gave the military administration a suitable implement for dealing with raw materials and other essentials just as nonchalantly as with human beings. The numerous, frequently arbitrary requisitions likewise proved a heavy handicap to building up an efficiently running war economy. 'That such requisitions, especially if they are without a definite plan decreed from case to case by various military authorities and commands, introduce a paralyzing factor of uncertainty into the economy, and retard rather than promote an army's orderly supply, was overlooked.'[9] Any consideration for the needs of the civilian population was moreover in the early phase of the war thought almost superfluous. 'The war economy was incapable of going beyond the notion, inspired by this Act, of coercion and requisition' is Riedl's summing-up.[10]

The difficulties were augmented by a government embargo on the import, export, and transit of raw and other materials required for military purposes. Imposition of the same measures in Germany meant that the key neutral markets in Scandinavia and Holland were closed to Austria-Hungary. There remained its ports at Trieste and Fiume, but these had always played a secondary role in the Empire's economic life. Although the two allies very soon entered into negotiations about repeal of the embargo, many invaluable weeks passed until on 24 September an end was put to this absurd mutual isolation during the course of the Berlin Conference, important in other respects too. By this time the purchase of goods in neutral markets had become distinctly more difficult and costly than at the outbreak of hostilities.[11]

More damaging still was that the Hungarian Government, in the supposed interest of its grain producers, vetoed revocation of the cereals tariffs. Reference has in another connection been made to the structural weaknesses of the Empire's rural economy.[12] The growing grain deficit in Austria during the decade before the war was one such manifestation. The 1914 yields, 10% below the average for 1909–13, were particularly unfavourable and the war years were to see the deficits rising steeply.[13]

A shortage of foodstuffs was distinctly felt in Austria soon after hostilities began. Sudden, large-scale purchases of grain by the military authorities were probably the reason. The public of course demanded immediate suspension of the grain duties so as to enable reserves to be bought from neighbouring countries. For any tariff revision the Dual Constitution required the express agreement of both Governments, but Hungary for the reason mentioned was not prepared to sanction the repeal of the cereals tariff. Wearisome negotiations were formally concluded on 9 October 1914 when the Hungarian officials agreed to unrestricted imports from abroad. Romania had however already imposed an embargo on the export of bread grains and it was difficult to keep open the lines to Italy.[14] An opportunity to supplement the Monarchy's scarce grain stocks had been frivolously wasted.[15]

In a review of the lessons for the war economy derived from the first half-year, Walther Federn, a leading journalist, criticized lack of foresight on the part of the bureaucracy.

In wartime it is not only the flow of goods to the army, but also that on behalf of the civilian population which requires all round measures. This is the more so because the army must not suffer any shortages and any scarcity will therefore fall doubly heavily on the civil population. Had our authorities shown adequate prescience, they would on the outbreak of war immediately have tried to buy abroad every obtainable quantity of goods subject to possible shortages, and they would have encouraged and supported every private initiative inasmuch as they should have told themselves that any sacrifice accepted by the state must prove amply worthwhile. . . . The severest reproach to be levelled at our administrative authorities is their narrow-mindedness in this respect and their deterrence, not encouragement, of private efforts, exemplified by the ordeal of applicants being sent from one door to the next only to meet officials who declare themselves incompetent to deal with matters.[16]

Private industry, in so far as it was not subject to the War Services Act, was badly hit by the mobilization measures, requisitions, and transport restrictions. Many firms had to cut back production sharply; others, though temporarily, to close down completely. Unemployment had thrown its shadow over the scene for the past two years. Now, in spite of mobilization, the spectre became increasingly real. The building trade, the machine and glass industries, as well as branches principally engaged in exports were prominent victims of the mobilization crisis.[17] Only the War Services Act's relief measures and the numerous private welfare activities saved the unemployed from direst need. The lack of an efficient official employment exchange agency was a particularly bitter grievance.[18] Unemployment proved however to be a passing phenomenon. The material requirements of an enormous army and the necessity for supplying the home front with a minimum of foodstuffs and consumer goods led after a brief period of readjustment, to an acute labour shortage.

Before the outbreak of war wheat was being sold in Vienna at the relatively high price of 27 crowns per hundredweight, that is almost 30% higher than at the outset of the year. The main cause was probably the unfavourable harvest. When hostilities began, the price soared still faster in consequence of the sudden mass purchases by the military authorities, speculative stockpiling by major wheat producers and dealers, as well as the lack of foresight on the part of the authorities, which neither took the necessary imports in its own hands nor facilitated such imports by private enterprise. The public's reaction to this alarming development was an even more clamourous demand for maximum prices to be fixed for bread grains. But here too no initiative was possible without the express agreement of the Hungarian Government. Any regulation of maximum prices in the Austrian half of the Empire could clearly be of little avail unless the

Hungarian side adopted similar measures. No Hungarian producer would be prepared to export to the Austrian market as long as there was the slightest prospect of selling his grain at home for a better price. Protracted negotiations between the governments were successfully concluded on 28 November – almost four months after the outbreak of war. By then the price for wheat had reached 42.50 crowns per hundredweight, over a hundred per cent more than at the beginning of the year.[19] A system of ration cards for bread and flour was not introduced until February 1915.[20]

On 1 August 1914 an Imperial decree ordered the ascertainment of stock reserves and invested communes with the right to requisition provisions on hand within their area, a move inspired by food shortages and arbitrary price rises in retail trading. Sanctions against profiteering had likewise been prescribed. The Imperial decree of 10 October furnished an important basis for the introduction of war economy measures. In Riedl's words, it empowered 'the government, in view of the war emergency, to issue ordinances to improve economic activity, especially in agriculture, industry, trade and commerce, and to see to the nation's nutrition.'[21]

On 24 September a decision reached at the Berlin Conference was meant to put the war economy on an entirely new footing. The Central Powers had therefore at a comparatively early stage recognized the fact summarized by Walther Federn a few months later in the trenchant phrase that this war was, above everything, a matter of economics.[22] In August 1914 Walther Rathenau had in the Prussian War Ministry established the Raw Materials Departments responsible for the appropriate distribution of raw materials requisitioned in occupied territories to firms engaged on military orders. Within a few months there evolved from these departments the War Raw Materials Companies. Mixed public and private enterprises, they dealt with the procurement, supply, and distribution of raw materials essential to the war effort for the whole of Germany.[23] The state, conformable to Rathenau's ideas, was from the outset the initiator, organizer, and source of funds for these undertakings whose task was vital to the war's conduct.

The arrangements agreed on 24 September involved as Riedl observes, a number of important administrative tasks for Austria.

The quotas for export conceded by the Germans had to be taken over, financed, and appropriately distributed. They could not be left a prey to the fortuitous grabbing by one firm or another nor to speculative buying. . . . To take proper advantage of the freedom of transit achieved by the agreement, it had to be ensured that the reports reaching departments from neutral countries and those on the miscellaneous offers for goods stored at Dutch, Danish, and Swedish ports . . . would receive expert treatment.

Austria-Hungary's transition to a centrally-controlled economy was the logical consequence. Consistent with this was the incorporation of the following passage in the Berlin Conference agreement:

The Austrian and the Hungarian delegates declare their intention to introduce in Austria and in Hungary raw materials purchasing companies on the German pattern so as to ensure an appropriate distribution of the available raw materials, particularly in those cases where export permits are subject to quota, and to go to work systematically on the procurement of raw materials through supplies from abroad.[24]

While the development of the Raw Materials Agencies – known henceforward simply as the 'agencies' – was therefore following the German example, the Monarchy in several respects followed its own, often distinctly wilful ways. The original idea had been for the agencies to include the whole Empire. Hungary, after some initial wavering, chose to set up independent establishments.[25] Agencies conducted along Dualist lines were a paradox not exactly conducive to strengthening the war potential.

Contrary to the German models, the agencies were constituted as private companies, although the principle of strict official supervision and the limited interest yield on capital subordinated them to the public interest. Baron Engel, the Austrian Minister of Finance who as head of the ministry's Budget Department had earned for himself the nickname of *Der Würgengel* (or the angel of death), viewed with utmost scepticism all unorthodox activities on the part of the state.[26] He turned down flatly any official participation in the raw materials procurement companies, regardless of their indispensability to the war economy. He maintained his opposition until 27 February 1915 when he consented to indirect participation by underwriting the state's liability for any contingent deficit incurred by the new War Grain Transactions Office whose purpose was total control over bread cereals.[27] In August 1915 a Feeding Stuffs Agency was formed on the same pattern.

The agencies faced a new, difficult and thankless task. In neutral foreign countries they had to struggle against the competition of many private firms which drove prices to giddy heights till the infuriated governments threatened vigorous counter-measures. The German Government was also free with threats of transit vetoes and other reprisals. The trouble was only gradually overcome, mainly by granting the agencies a monopoly character similar to that of the German raw materials organizations.[28] The domestic activities of the centres also came under criticism. The charge of bureaucratic rigidity was perhaps the most justifiable. The agencies could not, if only for reasons of governmental supervision, adopt too risky a purchasing and stockpiling policy.[29] Nonetheless their speedy development (towards the end of the war there were about sixty of them), as well as the variety of forms of collaboration between the authorities and private enterprise, must be recognized as an astonishing feat. Heinrich Wittek, one of the greatest experts on this subject, rightly says that the long-standing existence of state monopolies in certain branches of consumer goods as well as the associations, cartels, and trusts characteristic of large-scale industry paved the way for putting into practice the concept of public enterprise. They also helped to make available the organizational infra-structure and the services of a commercially-trained staff versed in business affairs.[30]

The agencies concentrated initially on the procurement of raw materials, especially from abroad. With Italy's entry into the war in May 1915 and the effects of the enemy blockade making themselves more and more felt by spring and summer 1916, it was the distribution problem that increasingly became the hub of war economy management.[31] 'Now the administrative task of handling economically quantities of domestic goods and to bring them under central control, and to ensure their priority use for public needs replaced commercial import activities.'[32] The agencies seemed too orientated towards the private sector of the economy to be entirely suitable for a responsibility conceived on such spartan lines. Alongside them arose compulsory associations, usually called War Associations and comprising all undertakings with a stake in a particular raw material. The boards elected from their midst took, in close agreement with the Ministry of Trade, the decisions pertaining to management of the raw material in question.[33] It should nevertheless be stressed that the agencies – and their allied War Associations – did their best to solve the problems of the war economy in a way compatible with the requirements of specific situations and that for this reason a broad range of organizational hybrids emerged during the war years.

This is not the place to describe the complete structure of Austria's war economy organization in detail.[34] The agencies were the responsibility of the Policy Department in the Ministry of Trade and the description of their operation will be confined to one or two examples. The task of procuring raw materials on behalf of plants placed under military administration since the outbreak of war – munitions, arms, and ordnance factories and the iron, metal-working, and chemical firms co-operating with them – were entrusted, for worse rather than for better, to certain Ministry of War departments.[35] A third variant was the Food Office (later the Ministry of Food). Subordinated to this were a multiplicity of food agencies including the War Grain Transactions Office and the Feeding Stuffs Agency. Their structures displayed enormous heterogeneity, due possibly to the complexity of their tasks.[36]

The Berlin Conference of 24 September 1914 had been the point of departure for the establishment of the raw materials agencies. As early as 3 October 1914 the United Austro-Hungarian Cotton Agency had been constituted by the Association of Austrian Cotton Spinners. It had, according to Riedl, a twofold function. It acted as an association for the fulfilment of commercial objectives and as the representative of all Austrian and Hungarian cotton spinners in all matters concerning the war economy.[37] It is almost superfluous to add that in this sphere too Hungary was soon following its own interpretation of Dualism. Contact with the German raw materials associations remained however the prerogative of the Austrian agencies.

On 29 October 1914 the Wool Agency, Inc. was established.[38] A Ministry of Trade act records that intention was for it to fulfill its 'tasks, like the prototype in Germany where a "War Wool Requirements, Inc." has originated in private initiative . . . in the form of a limited company'. The minutes note that 'prominent industrialists from the Austrian half of the Empire together with the Vienna Creditanstalt' would come forward as the scheme's promoters.[39]

The same act defines the purpose of the new corporation as 'procurement, distribution, and utilization of wool and slub to the extent necessary to meet the army's and the navy's industrial requirements'. The share capital was budgeted at 4 million crowns divided into 10,000 registered shares of 400 crowns each. 'In accordance with the non-profit character of the enterprise,' adds the act, 'distribution of profit to the shareholders does not apply. The net earnings shall be allocated to the Reserve Fund . . . and on the company's liquidation the surplus, after meeting outstanding liabilities and the reimbursement of the paid-up share capital, shall be placed at the disposal of the War Ministry for use towards a public purpose.'[40] The Wool Agency's character of a non-profit enterprise – and that of all the other corporations following in its footsteps – was furthermore guaranteed, as the War Ministry and the Ministry of Trade were given the right to have their representatives on the agency's board invested with a power of veto in the public interest.[41]

On 17 November 1914 followed the foundation of the Metals Agency, Inc.[42] On this occasion the Ministry of Trade, in agreement with the Railway Ministry, licensed a single promoter, the Creditanstalt, to form a corporation 'under the usual arrangements'.[43] The new company's articles differed from those of the Wool Agency only in minor details. The Metals Agency's share capital was also to be 4 million crowns although initially a deposit of only 1 million crowns was foreseen. The Creditanstalt's share in that figure was 150,000 crowns. The rest was contributed by the big arms and munitions manufacturers.[44]

During the following four years the Metals Agency had a very busy and, in the light of its purpose, successful career which contributed substantially to the Empire's astonishing military staying-power. Its articles of association declared it to be charged with the 'procurement, distribution, and utilization of base metals and metal alloys especially in so far as these are required to meet the needs of the army and the navy during the present state of war'.[45] Soon after the agency's foundation it was found as expedient to leave the Ministry of War to decide on the distribution of the metals procured.

The manner in which the Metals Agency performed its task underwent many transformations. At the start the military authorities proceeded with individual requisitions. Later a system of general requisition was introduced and subsequently, the longer the war lasted, extended to ever fresh categories of base metals. The Agency's activities increased in parallel to the requisitions. They included the purchase and the conversion of metals and related materials, their storage, delivery of the War Ministry's allocations to arms suppliers, and the extensive accountancy involved.

The necessity for the establishment of a purchasing agency to cover the whole Empire arose from the fact that most of the materials on hand, in the shape of a huge variety of metal objects, was spread among innumerable owners. The system of compulsory surrender, undertaken by so-called requisition commissions along routine lines, was therefore very soon abandoned and replaced by open market sale 'on the basis of appropriate prices'.[46] That businessmen should at first have been extremely hostile to centralized purchasing is not very astonishing. After a time, though, their resistance could be overcome and scrap metal firms of high repute were enlisted as 'authorized buyers'.[47]

The Agency's complex activities demanded a great capacity for improvization. Its report (the source for most of what is said here) contains much invaluable information on the difficult technical problems connected with the procurement of so-called industrial metals. These were not available in freely accessible amounts. On the contrary, in the shape of electrical wiring, machines, copper equipment and tubings, brass fittings, and so on, they constituted a vital component for many plants. Straightforward dismantling was of course not possible without the provision of substitutes, and here primarily iron, then aluminium, played an important part. In thousands of cases plants had to be re-equipped, and skilled personnel had to be found for this purpose. Wearisome negotiations with managements preceded the technical work. A comprehensive 'Metal Register' was compiled.[48] On the result of all these efforts the Report quotes the following figures: 'The War Metals Purchasing Agencies procured a total of 6,638.7 tons. The overall quantity of metal secured by 30 September 1917 amounts to 101,501.4 tons.' The agency's efforts, with its extremely large set-up, therefore provided only 6.5% of the total procurement of metals. Some conclusion may be drawn from this as to the endeavours spent on attainment of the total yield.[49]

Bearing in mind that more than sixty agencies were faced with very similar organizational and technical problems, although the Metals Agency presented perhaps the most complex example, some idea is obtained of the enormous outlay in ingenuity, concentration, and sheer physical exertion entailed by the establishment of this gigantic war economy infrastructure. This is true for the legion of 'small folk' who in industry and, since the beginning of 1915, in the war economy's speedily sprouting organizations, were faced day after day with conversion problems of the utmost intricacy. Gustav Stolper, in one of his periodic reviews of the Austrian economy, wrote on this aspect: 'There can be no doubt but that the intelligence displayed by the working classes, in part under the pressure of emergency, has been one of the most important prerequisites for the transition of industry from a peacetime to a war economy.'[50] It is true no less for the 'captains of industry' and the principal civil servants whose talent for improvization, readiness to take decisions, and perseverance were put to an altogether exceptional test.

Ludwig Neurath, at the outbreak of war a member of the Creditanstalt management, may be quoted as a typical example of the many leading personalities involved in the Austrian war economy. In autumn 1914 he took over key positions in the Wool and Metals Agencies and simultaneously acted as go-between for the Cotton Agency and OEZEG (Österreichische Zentral-Einkaufs-Gesellschaft, the Austrian Central Purchasing Corporation).[51] His ennoblement and his appointment as management chairman of Creditanstalt on Spitzmüller's retirement reflect the esteem in which he was held during the war years.[52]

The Food Office was naturally the pivot on which the nation's nutritional supplies turned. Here too quasi-public enterprises, called into life mainly by private initiative, assumed numerous important functions. It will be sufficient to mention the two Central Purchasing Agencies (MILES and its successor OEZEG) which held a particularly important place in the war economy. Their creation dated from 2 October 1915. The mobilization crisis seemed overcome, but now serious difficulties in respect of Austrian, especially Viennese, alimentation were perceptible.[53]

MILES' task was to organize the import of foodstuffs from abroad and to distribute as large quantities of vital goods as possible to consumers at a low price while still covering the cost. In this instance too Germany had set the Empire a good example inasmuch as during the early phase of hostilities the German Central Purchasing Agency had assumed responsibility for watching Austria's interests in neutral countries abroad. By autumn 1915 the foodstuffs shortage, particularly in Vienna, was viewed as being so acute as to render it impossible to leave to a German body the buying in the few foreign markets still accessible to the General Powers. In a short time purchasing agencies were founded in Sweden, Denmark, Bulgaria, Holland, and Switzerland. The opening of branch offices followed in Berlin, Budapest, Belgrade, and Constantinople. MILES' purchases, and then those of OEZEG, extended to a wide range of consumer goods like butter, cheese, eggs, poultry, meat and livestock, fish, tinned fish, tinned milk, and groceries.

The agencies' imports were intended to supplement the general state-organized foodstuffs distribution. From the outset there existed the problem of as equitable as possible an apportionment to the lower income brackets of the population. Every conceivable effort was made to coordinate the work of the distribution organizations with that of the public food agencies and the retail foodstuffs trade. Nonetheless the two agencies were subjected to vigorous attacks from major, in part entirely unauthorized, food wholesalers. These had derived large profits from the speculative buying of consumer goods abroad, which lucrative activities were brought to an abrupt end by the agencies' interventions.[54]

Following the Austrian example, a War Products Corporation founded at Budapest was soon in a position to make good its claim to five-twelfths of the central agencies total imports. At the insistence of the Hungarian authorities this distribution ratio had to be observed even in the case of products like butter, cheese, potato flour, tinned milk, fish, and so on. These goods were in especially short supply in Austria and had to be imported largely from Hungary. Small wonder that there occurred 'a lively trade between Austria as buyer and Hungary as seller of victuals imported by Hungary and then passed to Austria at appreciably higher prices'.[55]

The agency concerned with the organization of food supplies from the occupied territories (Poland, Serbia, Romania, and – during the last year of hostilities – the Ukraine) encountered many difficulties due to limited co-operation by the Army High Command. In neutral countries the intensification of the Entente Powers' blockade made purchases increasingly difficult. Large-scale transactions could now be undertaken only on a barter basis, but the agencies' efforts to foster this kind of business met with little success because the amounts of suitable commodities (sugar, mineral oil and timber) on hand in Austria were limited. Barter deals northwards were moreover subject to German transit restrictions.[56]

Creditanstalt – and other major banks too – had, as has been said, personal associations with the quickly proliferating agencies. With a handsome participation in the Wool and Metals Agencies the Bank held a quarter of the MILES share capital, 1 million crowns.[57] In addition it acted as lender to a number of these institutions. In December 1914 the Wool Agency had borrowed 4 million crowns. In 1915 the larger items included a loan of 10 million crowns to finance the War Grain Office.[58] An initial loan to MILES of 20 million crowns was in spring 1916 raised to 30 million crowns, and on the occasion of its transformation into a joint stock company (OEZEG) the Bank placed a credit of 50 million crowns at the new corporation's disposal.[59] In 1917 the sum was increased to 140 million crowns.[60] Although large loans were extended to the Cotton, Metal, and Wool Agencies, they remained far below the level of that to OEZEG. The Creditanstalt Board Minutes record that the Polish Economic Council intended to set up agencies in the Kingdom of Poland and would to this end seek assistance from Austrian and Hungarian banks.[61] The plan does not however seem to have come to anything.

In the first phase of the war, the agencies played a subordinate part. The hope was that a colossal exertion at the front and in the arms and munitions factories would result in a quick, victorious finish to hostilities. No consideration, it was thought, need be given to sectors of the economy not directly concerned with military requirements. The general state of uncertainty also caused a stagnation in many consumer goods branches. The early months therefore witnessed an almost universal decline in production. Output fell below the 1913 level in practically all industries. Coal extraction (including lignite) dropped from 57 million tons to 50.9 million tons and steel production from 2.6 million to 2.2 million tons, reductions of 11% and 15.5% respectively.[62] As the first seven months of 1914 had not been affected by the state of belligerency, the decline in production was confined to autumn and early winter.[63]

On the other hand the major arms and munitions factories, like all enterprises able to adapt themselves swiftly to army requirements, enjoyed flourishing conditions from the very first day of hostilities. Three major ordnance firms stood at the Empire's service – Skodawerke AG, Pilsen, Österreichische Waffenfabriksgesellschaft Steyr, and Ungarische Kanonenfabriks AG, Raab. The third, founded in 1913, took up production after the outbreak of war.[64] The leading munitions manufacturers were Hirtenberger Patronenfabrik, Enzesfelder Munitions- und Metallwerke AG, G. Roth AG, Vienna, and Munitions-, Stahl- und Metallwerke Manfred Weiss, Budapest.

The Austrian war industry's period of rapid expansion began in the year of the great Balkan crisis. Skodawerke especially had with the help of mergers and a highly ambitious investment programme – 30 million crowns were expended from the end of 1910 till the end of 1914 – enlarged its potential considerably.[65] Österreichische Waffenfabriksgesellschaft Steyr was, on the completion of its new plant shortly after the beginning of hostilities, reckoned to be the biggest small arms factory on the Continent.[66]

The Austrian troops' inferior equipment necessitated quick expansion of the arms industry, an expansion not confined to existing arms and munitions producers but entailing the switch of many smaller and larger metal-working firms to ordnance and munitions manufacture. In a surprisingly short time Gebrüder Böhler at Kapfenberg, Arthur Krupp at Berndorf, Brevillier Urban at Neunkirchen, Daimler Motorenwerke at Wiener Neustadt, and numerous less well-known business names had been integrated into one or another branch of war work. Most of them were located in the Vienna and Wiener Neustadt industrial area. By 1916 there were no less than forty-seven large companies specializing partly or entirely in munitions production.[67] The concentration of an important portion of the war industry in a comparatively small area would in post-war years create difficult structural problems.[68]

Notes

1 Cf. Josef Redlich, *The Austrian War Government* (New Haven, 1929), p. 101.

2 'For us the first period of the war was characterized by an actual, even if not formal, far-reaching elimination of the government *vis-à-vis* the military power.' Extract from a report by Prime Minister Seidler to Emperor Charles on 21 November 1917, quoted by Hans Loewenfeld-Russ in *Die Regelung der Volksernährung im Krieg* (Vienna, 1926), p. 300.

3 Cf. Part I, Chap. 8.

4 See Richard Riedl, *Die Industrie Österreichs während des Krieges* (Vienna, 1932), pp. 10–11.

5 Riedl, *Die Industrie Österreichs*, p. 13. On the serious worsening of labour conditions after the outbreak of war, see the instructive article by Walter Schiff, 'Die sozialpolitischen Aufgaben der Gegenwart und der nächsten Zukunft', *Der Österreichische Volkswirt*, Vol. 2, 23 November 1918.

6 Gustav Gratz and Richard Schüller, *Der wirtschaftliche Zusammenbruch Österreich-Ungarns* (Vienna, 1930), pp. 149–151.

7 'During the first months of hostilities a run-down of stocks demanded every ounce of industry's strength' to avert disaster 'and a complete throttling of civilian requirements.' Gratz, *Der wirtschaftliche Zusammenbruch*, p. 124. More details about the shortcomings of the Austrian troops' equipment are contained in Robert J. Wegs, *Austrian Economic Mobilization during World War I, with Particular Emphasis on Heavy Industry* (Ph.D. dissertation, University of Illinois, 1970), p. 156.

8 'A large number of plants with otherwise satisfactorily filled order-books had to close down because senior managers, works managers, foremen, furnacemen, and other indispensable employees were called up. For technical reasons the call-up of a single individual made in many cases the dismissal of all a necessity.' See 'Die Industrie und der Krieg', *Der Österreichische Volkswirt*, 5 August 1914, p. 857.

9 Riedl, *Industrie Österreichs*, p. 14.

10 Riedl, *Industrie Österreichs*, p. 15.

11 Reidl, *Industrie Österreichs*, pp. 24–25.

12 See Part I, Chap. 1, p. 5ff.

13 See Löwenfeld-Russ, *Die Regelung der Volksernährung*, an excellent account of the Empire's nutritional situation during the First World War.

14 Löwenfeld-Russ, *Die Regelung*, p. 48.

15 'At the end of 1915 Tisza spoke about the reproach levelled at the Hungarian Government for its behaviour in this matter. Not a hundred kilograms more cereals would, in his view, have entered the Monarchy if the import duties had been suspended immediately on the outbreak of war because soon afterwards the

development of prices was such that even after the payment of duty imports would have proved of advantage. But nothing could be imported as the war had rendered transactions impossible and all grain-exporting countries had been subject to the most ruthless, brutal control. However that may be, the Hungarian Government's resistance to a repeal of the grain duties is in the final analysis to be ascribed to its mistaken belief about the short duration of the war.' Gratz and Schüller, *Der wirtschaftliche Zusammenbruch*, p. 56.

16 Walther Federn, 'Wirtschaftliche Rückschau', *Der Österreichische Volkswirt*, 2 January 1915, p. 201. Astonishing is that Federn's outspoken criticism did not fall victim to the military censor's pencil.

17 'According to expert estimates the reduction of production at the end of 1914 amounted in the cement industry to 60%, in the cotton spinning industry to 55%, in brewing to 40%, in agricultural machinery manufacture to 80%, in the glass industry to 90%, in the fine paper industry to 50%. Firms working for export and the luxury trade were still worse hit.' Stefan von Müller, *Die finanzielle Mobilmachung Österreichs und ihr Ausbau bis 1918* (Berlin, 1918), p. 8.

18 Federn, *Österreichische Volkswirt*, p. 204.

19 Cf. Alexander Löffler, 'Der Einfluss der Gesetzgebung auf die Kapitalaufzehrung', in *Geldwert und Stabilisierung in ihren Einflüssen auf die soziale Entwickling in Österreich*, Schriften des Vereins für Sozialpolitik (Munich, 1925), Vol. 169, p. 83.

20 Löwenfeld-Russ, *Die Regelung*, pp. 84–106.

21 Riedl, *Industrie Österreichs*, p. 46.

22 'More than ever is this war an economic one. Not only that Britain in particular, is waging it as such and that the hopes of our opponents are pinned almost more on our economic than on our military exhaustion, but in the circumstances of today's intricate credit economy this war is of far more pregnant economic consequences than any earlier one.' Federn, *Der Österreichische Volkswirt*, p. 202.

23 See Julius Hirsch, *Grundriss der Sozialökonomie* (Tübingen, 1918), Sec. V, Pt. 1, pp. 160–161, quoted by Heinrich Wittek, 'Die kriegswirtschaftlichen Organisationen und Zentralen in Österreich', *Zeitschrift für Volkswirtschaft und Sozialpolitik*, 1922, New Series, Vol. 2, p. 27, footnote.

24 Riedl, *Industrie Österreichs*, p. 28.

25 Wittek, *Zeitschrift*, p. 27. As to Hungarian motives, 'The war seemed a welcome occasion to extend Hungary's independence in the political and economic field. This included exploitation of the war economy for the furtherance of Hungarian industries. Thus, starting with spring 1915, there gradually came about a separation of the joint Agencies.' Riedl, *Industrie Österreichs*, p. 33.

26 See 'Der Finanzminister', *Der Österreichische Volkswirt*, 31 October 1914, p. 65.

27 'According to the provisions of the ordinance the office had to manage its affairs in such a way as to cover its expenditure through incoming receipts. At the same time it was laid down that, irrespective of this, a deficit should be met by the state. Here was the basis for raising loan capital from banks.' Riedl, *Industrie Österreichs*, pp. 34–35.

28 'So it happened that in these instances Germany went ahead with monopolistic measures of this kind and faced the Austrian Government with the choice of either taking the same path or accepting the restriction on transit regarded by Germany as necessary to prevent interference with its own activities in certain neutral markets through unregulated demand and unbridled outbidding by private buyers

from Austria and Hungary. In almost all such cases agreement was reached.'
Riedl, *Industrie Österreichs*, pp. 40–41.

29 'It can be required of the state that, in the public interest and for the achievement
of objectives which it has set itself, it shall put up with losses sustained in the
purchase of raw materials just as much as with other war costs. What cannot be
demanded of private capital is that it should sacrifice itself completely for public
objectives if . . . , apart from a modest interest return, every possibility of profit is
docked.' Riedl, *Industrie Österreichs*, p. 40.

30 Wittek, *Zeitschrift*, p. 27.

31 The imports of certain important raw materials declined as follows:

	1913	1916
	in 100 kg.	
Cotton	2,258,000	34,000
Flax, hemp, jute	1,357,000	70,000
Oil seeds	2,300,000	79,000

Quoted by Wittek, *Zeitschrift*, p. 30

32 Wittek, *Zeitschrift*, p. 30.

33 Wittek, *Zeitschrift*, pp. 30–31, and Riedl, *Industrie Österreichs*, p. 69 et seq.

34 Riedl and Wittek give excellent accounts of the agencies' activities and
Löwenfeld-Russ furnishes a supplementary description of the nutrition agencies'
scope of activities. See also Wegs, *Austrian Economic Mobilization during World
War I* (Diss. Ill. 1970).

35 There would have been no objection to the concentration of the war economy in
the hands of the Ministry of War if the latter had 'had the talent for an objective,
methodical way of dealing with matters, possessed the indispensable expertise and
formal training, and all those entrusted with responsibility had had the requisite
respect for the knowledge and capacity of others.' Riedl, *Industrie Österreichs*,
p. 50. Riedl adds that the iron industry, placed under military supervision in spite
of its strict organization as an iron cartel, suffered especially from unco-ordinated
interference by the ministry. 'The confusion in which the iron industry landed in
the later war years is attributable to this unco-ordinated interference in the
production process. It would have been far better in this instance – where a
capable, well-organized body already existed in the shape of the iron cartel – to
follow the example of industrial self-administration elsewhere and to have left it
to the cartel to arrange the production programme according to a schedule of
needs stated by the military authorities by whatever was the most efficient
method. Admittedly this was impossible because the Ministry of War had no such
schedule.' Riedl, *Industrie Österreichs*, p. 51.

36 Cf. Löwenfeld-Russ for the nutrition agencies' methods of operation and scope of
activities. *Die Regelung der Volksernährung*.

37 Riedl, *Industrie Österreichs*, p. 31.

38 See Ministry of Trade file PZ 3815 5/14G, 29 October 1914. As early as 6 October
a Creditanstalt board meeting discussed the impending creation of a Wool Agency
Corporation and a Metals Agency Corporation. See Board Minutes, 6 October,
Creditanstalt Archives.

39 See Ministry of Trade file PZ 37.175 ex 1914 of 21 October 1914. The names of

the promoters are listed in the memorandum of association. They are, apart from Creditanstalt, Theodor Flemmich of Jägerndorf, Theodor Kern of Altenberg, Baron Theodor Liebig of Reichenberg, Rudolf Löw-Beer of Switawka, and Julius Sauerbrunn of Vienna. Ministry of Trade file Zl 38155/14 G, 29 October 1914.

40 The Ministry of Trade file PZ 37.175 ex 1914, carries a marginal note by the department head: 'N.B., unlike the Metals Agency where there is provision for a 5% interest payment.'

41 The right of governmental veto was incorporated in the Articles in the following words: 'The Board consisting of at least ten and no more than fourteen members shall at all events have two representatives from the Austrian Army Board and one representative each from the Hungarian Army Board, the Austrian Militia Board, the Hungarian Militia Board, the Moravian, the North Bohemian, and the Silesian industrial areas ... Moreover one individual designated by the Ministry of War and by the Austrian and Hungarian Ministry of Trade shall be invited to attend all meetings of the Board with a right of veto in so far as representatives from these Ministries are not in any case members of the Board.' Ministry of Trade file PZ 37.175 ex 1914.

42 It is interesting that the Creditanstalt took soundings in this direction as early as 8 September 1914, i.e., more than a fortnight before the Berlin Conference. A letter to the Minister of War contains the following passage: 'With reference to the conversation conducted between Your Excellency and Director Dr Alexander Spitzmüller and Director Ludwig Neurath on the 8th of this month, we take the liberty of appending herewith the draft for the organization of agency for the purchase of copper and zinc and to remark that the principles enunciated in this draft could perhaps be extended also for application to the case of other metals required by the war materials industry.' Ministry of Trade file Z 34714, 1 October 1914. That the possibility of including other base metals in this organization should have been envisaged at this early stage is a noteworthy fact.

43 Ministry of Trade file PZ 39.799 ex 1914, 12 November 1919.

44 Creditanstalt Board Minutes, 6 October 1914, Creditanstalt Archives.

45 Valuable accounts of the Metals Agency's activities are to be found in the previously cited works by Riedl, Wittek, and Wegs. The most detailed description is given in the organization's own Report, *Bericht der Metallzentrale-Aktiengesellschaft über ihre Tätigkeit während der ersten drei Geschäftsjahre* AVA ('Kriegswirtschaftsorganisationen', 1917).

46 See *Bericht der Metallzentrale*, p. 16.

47 *Bericht der Metallzentrale*, p. 17.

48 *Bericht der Metallzentrale*, p. 18 et seq.

49 *Bericht der Metallzentrale*, p. 22.

50 Gustav Stolper, 'Die Industrie im Kriege', *Der Österreichische Volkswirt*, 10 April 1915, p. 449.

51 Ministry of Trade, HL/1390, and Ministry of the Interior, 17476/1914.

52 On Neurath's ennoblement, see AVA, 1629/FM/17. On his appointment as management chairman, see Board Minutes, 28 December 1915, Creditanstalt Archives.

53 This description of MILES' and OeZEG's buying activity rests primarily on the *Bericht über die Entstehung und Tätigkeit der Österreichischen Zentral-Einkaufsgesellschaft* (OeZEG), Vienna, 31 May 1917), AVA 31.617/17.

54 From the OeZEG Report emerges that retail interests managed to mobilize a part

of public opinion against MILES/OeZEG: 'The consumers too had adopted a critical attitude towards the buying agency and it had become a catchword that everything handled by MILES became scarcer and dearer. Unfortunately the catchword corresponded to the facts, but what the public confused was cause and effect. The agency was summoned to act only when the rapid rise in prices and/or the constantly more obvious shortage of the article in question prompted the Governments in Austria and Germany to take steps to bring under control the price movement and to engage in the distribution of foodstuffs. What went unrecognized was that further unpredictable price rises were avoided by the agency's operations and that available stocks did not disproportionately pass into the hands of one section of the trade or public while the rest did without.' OeZEG *Bericht*, p. 6.

55 OeZEG *Bericht*, p. 9.

56 OeZEG *Bericht*, p. 13.

57 Board Meeting Minutes, 12 October 1915, Creditanstalt Archives. The Minutes for 7 December 1915 record an increase in the MILES share capital by 5 million crowns with Creditanstalt participation to 45%.

58 Board Meeting Minutes, 12 May 1915, Creditanstalt Archives.

59 Board Meeting Minutes, 14 June 1916, Creditanstalt Archives.

60 Board Meeting Minutes, 13 February 1917, Creditanstalt Archives.

61 Board Meeting Minutes, 31 July 1917, Creditanstalt Archives. A new Polish state had on 5 November 1916 been proclaimed by Austria-Hungary and Germany.

62 Gratz and Schüller, *Der Wirtschaftliche Zusammenbruch*, pp. 92 and 97.

63 A recent study states that 'At the beginning of the war the capacity of the iron industry was sharply curtailed by the call-ups – they comprised a third of the labour force. The reduction in personnel compelled a cut in production. This drop was especially noticeable in the case of the Prager Industrie Gesellschaft and in that of the Österreichische Alpine Montan Gesellschaft, in the latter to such an extent that it had to reckon with the possibility of an entire standstill in its plants.' See Heinrich Mejzlik, *Die Eisenbewirtschaftung im Ersten Weltkrieg* (Vienna, 1977), p. 42.

64 The Ungarische Kanonenfabriks AG was a state-promoted concern in which Skodawerke AG, Creditanstalt, the Ungarische Allgemeine Kreditbank, and Kruppwerke, Essen, had interests. Members of the Board included Julius Blum, Hugo von Hoffmann, Max Feilchenfeld, and Karl von Skoda. Cf. *Compass*, 1915, Vol. 2, p. 981.

65 Cf. 'Die Bilanzen', *Der Österreichische Volkswirt*, 10 April 1915, p. 123.

66 'Die Bilanzen' *Der Österreichische Volkswirt*, 23 September 1916, p. 281.

67 Cf. Wegs, *Austrian Economic Mobilization*, p. 158.

68 See *Memorandum der Kammer für Arbeiter und Angestellte* (Vienna, July 1925) included as an annex to W. T. Layton and Charles Rist, *The Economic Situation of Austria, Report presented to the Council of the League of Nations* (Geneva, 1925).

CHAPTER 2

Interim Financial and Monetary Policy Measures – the Problems of War Financing

In spring 1915 Dr Emil Lederer, the well-known economist and sociologist, is alleged to have said that those concerned 'with the economic preliminaries to hostilities always had in mind only, as it were, the beginning of the war and therefore attached to measures for keeping afloat the monetary and the credit system an importance which they merited only at the outset . . . in the first excitement.'[1]

The Dual Monarchy, as has been seen, was in the monetary sphere as good as unprepared for a conflict that within a few weeks assumed the dimensions of a continental war. More than a year before its outbreak the governor of the Austro–Hungarian Bank had remarked, in identically worded letters to the Austrian and Hungarian Finance Ministers, on the need to suspend the Bank Act, even prior to mobilization.[2] 'The state of our financial preparedness' he added, 'is undoubtedly known abroad and very apt to damage the Monarchy's international position appreciably.'[3] From this it emerges that Lederer (and he was not alone) was but poorly informed on the true state of affairs in the monetary and credit system.[4]

On 20 July 1914, three days before the ultimatum was presented at Belgrade, the Finance Ministers of the Empire's two halves were in conference at Budapest about the serious consequences for financial policy to be expected from the anticipated grave political move. They resolved to adhere to the principles 'laid down by the two Governments in 1908 on the occasion of the annexation of Bosnia and Hercegovina'.[5] This signified that the hope of being able to satisfy the army's financial requirements via normal loan operations had not yet been abandoned. The directive given on the critical 23 July by the ministers in the course of a discussion with representatives from the major banks can perhaps best be summarized as 'business as usual'.[6]

The banks were not averse to obeying the ministers' watchword, if only because during July a distinctly easier situation had prevailed in the money market.[7] A sounder instinct for the impending change of political weather seems to have existed abroad. In July the withdrawals of foreign assets from Austria–Hungary that had already begun in June accelerated. At the beginning of June the item Other Assets, showing part of the central bank's holdings of foreign exchange, had totalled 215 million crowns. On the fateful 23 July it had drained away to 115 million crowns.[8]

A complete change of atmosphere in the money market ensued on news of the ultimatum to Serbia and, more particularly, after the breach on 25 July of diplomatic relations between the two states. Overnight, so to speak, the demand for domestic funds, foreign exchange, and precious metals rose to gigantic proportions. A part of this sudden need stemmed from perfectly legitimate reasons. The major banks with branches in Western countries had to provide the latter with larger stocks of gold and foreign currencies in order to meet the forseeably increased requirements of their customers. Moreover, Popovics argues, the central bank had to fortify its assets abroad through gold transfers. And at this juncture the central bank still tolerated speculative domestic hoarding of gold and foreign exchange because it feared that a rejection of such requests must create 'panicky effects'.[9]

Most eye-witnesses agree that from the moment that the ultimatum to Belgrade became known an urge to hoard funds of every kind was evident among wide sections of the public. The hoarding of gold, silver, and sometimes even token coins seems to have been especially popular in rural regions.[10] This urge to accumulate cash, born from sheer survival worries by households and sometimes even business undertakings, soon led to an acute shortage of small change and ten crown notes.[11] The sole possible redress was to print one and two crown notes, but this involved time-consuming technical preparations.[12] The Central Bank had to work away at the elimination of the acute cash shortage right into the summer of 1915.[13]

On 26 July the extraordinary meeting by the central bank's general council (Generalrat) decided to raise the bank rate from 4% to 5%. That was all. The bank's foreign exchange and foreign assets had now dropped, as revealed in a report by the Governor, to 101.5 million crowns, an alarming low. Its gold stocks stood however at the still respectable figure of 1,184 million crowns and gave 58% gold backing to the note circulation.[14]

During the following days the Governor, who had been watching the situation with great scepticism, saw his worst fears confirmed. In the last week of July the bank's stocks of bullion and gold foreign exchange were depleted by some 148 million crowns while its bills portfolio rose by 868.2 million crowns and its advances against collateral by 223.6 million crowns. The banknote circulation expanded by 932.6 million crowns. On 31 July, the day of the general mobilization order, the bank took two further steps. One, raising the discount rate by another percentage point, had little effect. The other, amounting to a complete stop on the disposal of foreign exchange as well as of foreign notes and coins, at last ended the financial bloodletting that had become a danger to the Monarchy's existence.[15]

In the early days of August advances drawn against collateral on the central bank assumed such dimensions that the shortage of banknotes, in spite of the hectic activity of the printing-presses, became very serious.[16] On 1 and 2 August such advances were limited initially to 10,000 crowns, then to 1,000 crowns. On 31 July, the first moratorium ordinance was promulgated. It provided for the deferment of debts incurred before the 1 August and falling due before 14 August. A few important exceptions included amounts below 200 crowns in a deposit or current account as well as contractual claims for service, pay and rent. Broad sections of the public were therefore deprived of any opportunity for falling back, apart from small sums, on their assets and savings so as to prevent a run on the banks. As a result the feeling of insecurity among urban populations was sometimes tinged with panic.[17]

The moratorium ordinance bore the marks of hasty drafting. Issued at a date when rent payments became due, it imposed, as Müller points out, 'the obligation on tenants to pay their rent while stripping them of the chance to get at the necessary money by drawing on the banks'.[18] Designed initially to avert a run on banks, the moratorium probably caused a fairly general stalemate in transfers which the major banks, despite their willingness to meet legitimate demands over and above the limits set, could do little to alleviate.[19] In the following months the payments suspension could be lifted only gradually, one important reason being that in autumn and winter parts of Galicia and Hungary were overrun by enemy forces. In 1915 constantly growing liquidity permitted settlement of suspended payments with few difficulties.[20]

On 2 August the central bank felt compelled to raise the bank rate to 8%. Undoubtedly the impetus came from the impression made by news of the Bank of England jacking up its lending rate to the then dizzy peak of 10%. Public reaction was predominantly unfavourable. Through the cessation at this juncture of foreign exchange transactions with abroad the bank had, it was pointed out (rightly, in the present author's view), isolated itself from international transfer payments. However on 20 August the rate was dropped to 6% and in spring 1915 brought back to its normal 5% level.[21] The reason it was possible to lower it so quickly in August was that it had been preceded by a step of the utmost importance. On 4 August the Bank Act was temporarily suspended.

The measure was meant to furnish the guarantee that the central bank's management was able to devote all its energies to the war economy's requirements. The suspension affected in particular Article 84 of the bank's statutes:

The Supervisory Board of the Austro–Hungarian Bank is responsible for seeing that the ratio of the precious metals stocks to the banknotes in circulation shall be such as to ensure complete fulfilment of the obligations defined in Article 83, being conversion of the notes into precious metals. The total of banknotes in circulation must at all events be covered to at least two-fifths by legal metal tender of Austrian or Hungarian origin in accordance with its face value or by domestic commercial gold coinage, foreign gold coinage, or bullion . . . and the rest of the banknotes in circulation, including all short-term liabilities, in accordance with banking practice.

Henceforth the central bank could raise the money in circulation in so far as the total was covered by securities, foreign exchange, and bills. After 4 August loans to the state increasingly constituted the backing for banknotes in circulation, inasmuch as it was only after the suspension of the Bank Act that the central bank was in a position to undertake loans operations with the Empire's two financial administrations directly. Later publications have made it clear that the bank's Supervisory Board agreed with some hesitation to extend what amounted more or less to unlimited credit for the state. Only the conviction that the alternative was an issue of currency notes rendered inevitable the decision advocated by the two governments. The bank insisted on the pledge that calls should not be made on its credit unless no other way was feasible.[22] The management did not, strange to say, find anything dubious about extending comparatively long-term loans which legally required Austrian parliamentary sanction. It may have been influenced by the attitude of the national Debt Control Commission. Not before 26 June 1915 did the latter express serious misgivings about the endorsement of loans 'because they only formally show the character of the pending debt'.[23] Regardless of these doubts, uttered only behind closed doors, the commission brought itself to approve through its own endorsement loans with ever longer maturities. In spring 1917, when the two Houses were recalled, the Commission, as a parliamentary body had to submit to their censure.[24]

It is obvious that the suspension of the Bank Act also invalidated the central bank's legal responsibility 'to ensure with all the means at its disposal, that the value of its notes as expressed in terms of their foreign exchange rate shall remain constantly secure in accordance with the gold parity of the crown'. Since moreover the bank no longer had to issue weekly returns and at the close of 1914 was relieved of its traditional duty to publish its balance sheet as well as other statistical material due at year-end, the state's financial operations during the early years of the war remained wrapped in mystery.[25] The most important data was made available to the public only after the recall of Parliament and the convening of the Austro-Hungarian Bank's general meeting after an interval of almost four years.[26]

At the end of July 1914 the Austrian Government already had to turn to a consortium of Viennese banks to arrange a short-term loan of 200 million crowns to be repaid by the end of August.[27] It was the proverbial drop in the ocean. Many hours were spent at this time in consultation between the two Ministries of Finance and the major banks on how the enormous demands of the military administration could be financed. The flotation of a large loan was at this point practically out of the question because after the moratorium, savings-book holders and other bank creditors had only marginal control over their assets. Nor was a direct approach to the central bank possible as long as the Bank Act remained in force. The outcome was a solution enabling the ministries to tap the central bank's resources indirectly. A group consisting of the Postal Savings Bank and the biggest Austrian and Hungarian banks extended a loan to the Empire's two states against collateral of 950 million crowns, Austria taking 600 million crowns and Hungary the rest. The interest rate was 5% and the maturity date was set at 1 February 1917, but this term had on request to be extended. The two Finance Ministries claimed their respective shares of 85%.[28]

The associated banks could not extend a loan of this size to the state from their own resources. They turned therefore, with official blessing, to the central bank and obtained advances on the Treasury bills. As Pressburger rightly comments, with this transaction the first large-scale financial operation after the outbreak of hostilities set the bank's printing-presses into motion.[29] Nevertheless even this relatively important loan gave the military authorities only a short respite and the government decided, after suspension of the Bank Act, to turn directly to the central bank.

Upon publication of the general mobilization order the military administration's needs rose by leaps and bounds. For the first three months, Popovics reports, 'the requirements for the army, the two militias, and the navy were assessed at 2,500 million crowns.'[30] The two Ministries of Finance now turned straight to the central bank. The latter, on the basis of the 14 August agreement, extended to the two states a loan of 2,000 million crowns against deposits of 5% treasury bills. The Austrian share was 1,272 million crowns, that of Hungary 728 million crowns.[31] This corresponded to the 63.6% : 36.4% ratio in which Austria and Hungary divided the Dual Monarchy's joint expenditure between themselves. Approaches to the bank of this kind were on later occasions also made simultaneously by the two states and in accordance with the same formula.

Towards the end of September this loan too was running dry. Fresh negotiations between the governments and the bank ensued. For all that the two finance ministers Engel and Teleszki gave serious consideration to a public loan flotation, the time did still not seem right for such an operation. In a note to his Hungarian colleague Baron Engel wrote that 'it will not be permissable to obtain the funds needed for the war's conduct exclusively by recourse to the Austro-Hungarian Bank'. He vindicates his view by reference to the inflationary consequences of such a procedure:

Undoubtedly early attention must be paid to countering the unfavourable sequel to a genuine banknote inflation by using appropriate means for rerouting into the state's or the bank's coffers those quantities of notes not required for current transactions, and care must be taken through such measures to replace in some degree the economic mechanism that comes into operation when there is a regular issue of banknotes and which keeps the circulation in balance with current transaction requirements.

He shared the belief of many professional colleagues that 'in the prevailing circumstances this purpose cannot be achieved otherwise than by the flotation of a domestic loan'. Very soon, though, he was to be convinced that the issue of a public loan was not the way even 'to replace in some degree' the mechanism which in normal times maintained the equilibrium between note circulation and current transaction needs.

Engel then gave his reasons for thinking the time not yet ripe for seeking public subscription.

An important success gained in one of the principal theatres of war that will among wide sections of the population cement their faith in a happy outcome to the military undertakings must be awaited before the offer of a major loan is brought forward. At present – in so far as I am familiar with the mood of the public (and the financial houses) – the population's reading of the situation, in the light of the slow progress by German operations in the West and especially following the enemy's occupation of the best parts of Galicia and the Bukovina, is not so positive that I could count with complete confidence on the full success of a subscription offer.

The volume of money, he continued with great perspicacity, had not yet reached a point suggestive of particularly rosy prospects for the placement of a loan.

On the other hand those signs of financial plenty which could be held to indicate symptoms of a favourable disposition by the money market towards the acceptance of loans have not, to my mind, become so clearly manifest as to let the prospects of a loan issue appear outstandingly promising from this angle. Naturally it takes a while before the resources brought into circulation by the military payments accumulate at the focal point of economic activity, and in wartime this process undergoes delay through handicaps on transactions, the exceptionally increased real need for funds, and hoarding tendencies of many kinds. I am therefore inclined to believe that it would be a good thing to await a progressive concentration of the funds put into circulation before attempting the negotiation of big state loan issues.

Engel devoted the final part of his note to a warning against making the question of a war loan the subject of public debate too soon.

Nor do I cherish the hope that the yield of the loans to be offered to the public will suffice to meet in full the monetary requirements of the two governments for the rest of the war. As fresh resort to the Austro-Hungarian Bank for the procurement of further resources will be unavoidable. I think that the sequence of employing the feasible means of obtaining funds should be determined not by theoretical principles but only by purely practical considerations. The latter speak absolutely in favour of postponing subscription. For these reasons I would regard it as advisable to make those internal preparations for the issue of loans that will ensure the timely exploitation of a good moment. I would however urgently warn against notifying the public of this design now at this time, and making the intentions of the governments, which themselves have still to give the most mature consideration to all details, the subject of conferences and discussions with the banks.[32]

It is noticeable that neither in the note from the Austrian Minister of Finance nor in the papers sent by the governor of the central bank to the council of ministers is there a single word about the possibility of meeting the war outlay – even in part – by way of higher taxation. Today no more than a few guesses can be made as to why the Austrian Government exercised such restraint. Perhaps there existed a certain shyness about deciding to increase taxation or even to introduce new taxes on the basis of emergency legislation. The undesirability of putting a damper on the patriotic high spirits prevailing among broad sections of the public by early demands for material sacrifices will doubtless have been a more important influence.[33] At this stage, though, only a few people seem to have recognized that financing the war on the basis of constantly inflating the volume of money was the least rational and most unjust method of spreading the military burden among the various classes of the population.[34]

On 7 October the Ministers of Finance and the central bank reached an agreement whereby the bank extended to both governments a further loan of 2,000 million crowns, this time in the form of a bills discount. On recourse to the loan the ministers had each to deposit twenty promissory notes to amounts of 63.6 million and 36.4 million crowns respectively at the bank's headquarters in Vienna and in Budapest. The interest rate was 1%. The bills' maturity was spread over a longer period so as to give the governments the chance to fulfil their obligations gradually.[35]

Two further clauses in the agreement deserve notice. First, the two governments solemnly promised in Article 13 'at every appropriate juncture to make use of every suitable means for the procurement of funds which will render superfluous the artificial increase of monetary tokens'. This is undoubtedly to be interpreted as an intimation of the early issue of a public loan. Secondly, Clause 10 contains the promise by both governments, should the central bank's prerogative not be renewed.

to pay the amount of 1,520 crowns per share as well as the *pro rata* shares in the reserve fund, which according to the provisions of Clause 1, Para. 14, of Article 107 in the bank's statutes shall be disbursed to the shareholders of the Austro-Hungarian Bank, in actual gold or in an equivalent of the gold value according to the choice of the recipient Governments.[36]

When in 1917 this passage became known, it aroused understandably angry public reaction.[37]

At an early stage in the war a notable deterioration in the Empire's balance of payments set in and continued deteriorating. The trend was clearly recognizable in the first few months. On the one hand the military administration's requirements of war materials and equipment from abroad went up, and a poorish harvest made more foodstuffs imports necessary. On the other hand, the economy's export capacity went down for a number of reasons – industry's far-reaching realignment to the army's needs, the requisition of raw materials by the War Ministry, agriculture's declining export ability, Russian occupation of the Galician oilfields, and so on.

As has been mentioned, the drain on gold and gold foreign exchange persisted until the end of July. Only then does it appear to have dawned on those concerned at Vienna and Budapest that in the case of armed conflict gold reserves acquire an importance over and above the level of monetary policy in the normal sense.[38]

The process of continual diminution in the gold holdings could be decelerated, but of course never completely stopped. An effort to fortify the reserves by purchase of funds abroad was undertaken comparatively soon.[39] The only country where bond operations of any magnitude were still feasible was the neighbouring and allied German Empire. In November 1914 the two governments arranged with a number of large Berlin banks a loan of 300 million marks on the basis of one-year treasury bills.[40] 200 million marks of the total fell to the share of the Austrian, 100 million marks to that of the Hungarian financial administrations.[41] These loan operations were repeated in the succeeding war years.[42]

The note by the Austrian Minister of Finance to his Hungarian colleague had named certain conditions essential for floating a big public loan – an impressive success by the Allied forces, a clear manifestation of inflationary factors, and an advanced concentration of funds in circulation. In autumn 1914 the situation of the Austrian Army on the Eastern front remained unfavourable, but inflation and rising receipts of money at banks and savings banks made it seem advisable to try and channel back into the official coffers a part of the nominal purchasing power that had been created. The flotation by the German Government of a public loan had set a distinct example.

From September onward the two Finance Ministers had in closest conjunction with the whole banking world given thought to and made organizational preparations for the issue of the first war loan. Parliament being prorogued indefinitely, the Austrian Government had to derive its authority to invite public subscription from an Imperial ordinance. This first loan and its two successors were therefore issued in the form of treasury bills which, in the prevalent view, meant that no long-term charge on the national budget was involved. The five years maturity was in subsequent issues stretched to ten and to fifteen years. The pressure of circumstances soon caused the fiction of short-term indebtedness to be abandoned. The press welcomed the subscription conditions as being exceedingly attractive inasmuch as at a time of growing liquidity and falling lending rates the public was being offered a 5½% per annum bond. The yield, allowing for the low price of issue, was close on 6%. As the *Neue Freie Presse* rightly emphasized, it offered 'such a splendid return that its purchase against collateral even to the whole amount of outlay still' gave 'a surplus interest'.[43] It may be added that the central bank's Supervisory Board at its meeting on 19 October – that is, before the loan operation had become officially known – decided 'to lend against war loan securities at the current discount rate to 75% of their face value'.[44]

On 9 November the Austrian Finance Minister invited public subscription to the first war loan. Next day's leading article in the country's most prominent newspaper proclaimed, in brief, that this capital investment should be regarded not simply as an obvious patriotic duty, but as a thoroughly advantageous piece of business for every subscriber. The article's author, probably the paper's well-known editor-in-chief, continued by quoting a number of historical precedents that apparently corroborated his dictum.[45] *Der Economist*, the supplement to *Neue Freie Presse*, in its edition of 11 November was particularly insistent on this aspect: 'The conditions of the loan will ensure this success inasmuch as the subscribers, each to the best of their ability, not only demonstrate the wish to provide the state with the means necessary to wage war, but also obtain through the new securities an unusually profitable capital investment carrying a high rate of interest.'[46]

The same reasoning, though losing much of its credibility with growing inflation, accompanied the seven further war loan issues.[47] The flight into material goods, shares, and foreign exchange, especially during the last two years of war, became the determining factor for the shrinking class of money-makers and capitalists. It is hardly surprising therefore that the placement results during the course of hostilities corresponded less and less with official expectations.[48]

Public subscription began on 16 November and was closed a week later. The amount of issue was unlimited, that is, all subscriptions were accepted and the amounts allocated in full. The entire banking world, the Postal Savings Bank at Vienna and all post offices, Ministry of Finance offices and inland revenue offices, the Austro-Hungarian Bank headquarters at Vienna and its branches, as well as insurance offices and their branches were mobilized so as to afford even the little man the chance to participate in this major loan. Although the smallest denomination was 100 crowns, units to a value of 25, 50 and 75 crowns could be subscribed at post offices.[49]

The large banks made their staffs and material resources available to a great extent. They canvassed their customers for as big a commitment as possible and themselves invested in both the Austrian and the Hungarian loan.[50] The total of subscriptions at the leading financial institutions was as follows:

Austro-Hungarian Bank	about 40 million crowns
Creditanstalt	over 190 million crowns
Anglo-Österreichische Bank	over 146 million crowns
Wiener Bankverein	over 180 million crowns
Niederösterr. Escompte-Gesellschaft	over 159 million crowns
Österreichische Länderbank	over 200 million crowns
Unionbank	over 61 million crowns
Mercurbank	over 61 million crowns
Verkehrsbank	over 65 million crowns
Depositenbank	over 24 million crowns
Böhmische Unionbank	over 86 million crowns
Živnostenská banka	over 26 million crowns
Lombard- und Escomptebank	over 7 million crowns
Zentralbank der deutschen Sparkassen	over 59 million crowns

All the above banks subscribed large amounts to the Hungarian loan. The strikingly high total received at the Länderbank includes 25 million crowns from the City of Vienna and other municipalities as well as the contribution from the Austrian Pensions Institution.[51] The Creditanstalt's impressive figure, which follows right after, is probably attributable to keen participation by many of the firms belonging to its industrial group.[52] A surprise is to find the Bankverein, with the largest number of branch offices among the major banks, running only third. Subscriptions by small depositors and savers are nevertheless likely to have been substantial. This emerges from the figures of the Erste österreichische Sparkasse in Vienna whose total of 37 million crowns represented 67% of its deposit assets.[53] The modest amount attained by Živnostenská banka, the leading Czech financial house, is a striking feature and the suspicion that it reflects the apathy of Czech customers towards an operation viewed far and wide as a touchstone for the will to resist by the Austro-Hungarian community of peoples, is hardly likely to miss the mark.[54] Yet the overall total is notable. For Austria the first war loan had netted 2,153 million crowns, for Hungary 1,185 million crowns.[55]

According to Spitzmüller, the outcome allowing for all relevant circumstances, brought the Monarchy within thoroughly respectable distance of the German Empire whose financial effort was rightly regarded as exemplary. He ascribed the success of the loan primarily to awareness permeating all classes of the threat to their existence.

Therefore it was the overwhelming greatness of the moment that summoned the entire population to the battlements of financial mobilization. . . . Everyone of us had opportunity to experience how in truly sacrificial spirit precisely those in straightened or humble economic station, with patriotism high in their hearts, thronged the subscription counters. . . . Thus it came about that literally almost the entire clientèle of the Postal Savings Bank, the savings banks, and the financial institutions answered the call and that there even arrived at the banks large numbers of small subscribers who hitherto had as such kept away from the gilt-edged and every other kind of securities market.[56]

The accumulation of ready money in the hands of the public, the banks, and industry, it should be added, furnished the basis for the loan's success. By November 1914 reassurance as to the financial situation had moreover spread to wide sections of the public and the cash hoarded at the outbreak of war was gradually reappearing.

As has been seen, the participation by the Czech portion of the population is not likely to have conformed to Spitzmüller's description. Still more strongly does this apply to the other Slav nations of the Monarchy, not least because their notorious poverty can have enabled them to contribute but slightly to the success of the loan. Indubitably the vast majority of subscribers came from Vienna and the Alpine regions, from the German-language parts of Bohemia and Moravia, and from the Empire's Magyar area. Even in these territories some financially well-off classes, like big landowners and farmers with large-scale holdings, remained comparatively aloof.[57] Commitment by the small subscriber, so outstanding a feature of the first loan operation, proved ever more difficult to obtain as the war proceeded. The mainstay of every subscription proved to be those who invested between 10,000 to 50,000 crowns. The upper strata, especially the German-speaking Austrian middle class, were undoubtedly the ones who demonstrated a high degree of self-sacrifice.[58] And the banking world as well as industry did invest an important share of its liquid funds in war loan.[59]

The principal financial policy-makers fully realized, notwithstand-ing the operation's success, that in case of the war's prolongation it would be necessary to fall back on the resources of the central bank. Soon after publication of the result, Spitzmüller wrote in the commentary quoted earlier:

We already know that for a very considerable period we can cover the costs of the present war from our economy's liquid assets. That if the war lasts longer, it will prove necessary for the state to depend on the central bank as its main source of funds need not worry us greatly because this will also be unavoidable in countries like France and Britain, hitherto recognized as upholding the highest financial criteria, and we look forward with complete confidence to the outcome of the war at the side of our ally.[60]

Spitzmüller, a former senior civil servant in the financial sphere, seems likely to have had inside information on the central bank's current state of affairs despite the fact that its obligation to publish periodical returns had been suspended at the outbreak of war. On 23 July 1914, the day that the Austrian ultimatum was delivered at Belgrade, the total of banknotes in circulation and of current account deposits as well as of other immediate liabilities was not quite 2,500 million crowns.[61] By 31 December the comparable figure had risen to more than 6,500 million crowns. In five months the volume of money had increased by more than 4,000 million crowns. The war loan issue, having filled the administration's coffers with over 3,000 million crowns, must also in the light of this fact be regarded as uncommonly successful. Nonetheless it lagged – more especially in view of the higher level of prices that necessitated above average cash holdings – considerably behind the growth in fresh monetary funds. Spitzmüller, aware of this, could confidently forecast in case of prolonged hostilities the need for further recourse to the central bank as the state's main source of funds. Later events corroborated his prediction more drastically than he may have surmised in the late autumn of 1914.

There was one circumstance, virtually unnoticed by contemporary writers, which may have contributed to the loan operation's success. On 24 July, the day after delivery of the ultimatum to Serbia, the Stock Exchange Committee closed down dealings in securities for three days. When war broke out the closure was prolonged indefinitely. The stock exchanges at Prague, Budapest, and Trieste followed the Viennese example almost immediately.[62] Share prices had had an unsatisfactory history since the Balkan crisis in 1912.[63] Closure of the stock exchanges at the outset of war was no doubt meant to prevent a complete collapse of the security market. At the beginning of September a relief operation was set on foot by banks, the Postal Savings Bank, and certain large firms to enter into previously concluded deals that in the critical phase after the declaration of war had not been consummated. Later the securities so acquired could be marketed, and in some instances at a profit.[64]

When the war loan was issued the stock exchanges were still closed and the public, with the uncertain economic outlook in mind, viewed with great scepticism the development of share prices. Indeed actual price movements, for as long as the stock exchanges continued to remain closed, were known only to a small circle of professional speculators. In November 1914 there were no hints as yet of the inflation psychology manifested in the war's later stages by panic purchases of goods, shares, foreign exchange, and so on. Abstinence from dealings in securities doubtless assisted the big loan operation.

Notes

1 From Gustav Stolper's 'Zur Beurteilung der Wirtschaftslage', Der Österreichische Volkswirt, 24 April 1915, No. 30.
2 Alexander Popovics, Das Geldwesen im Kriege (Vienna, 1925), p. 38 et seq.
3 Popovics, Das Geldwesen, p. 40.
4 'The outbreak of war put the Austro-Hungarian Bank in a difficult position attributable in part to the central bank's being taken unawares by the political crisis.' See Stefan von Müller, Die finanzielle Mobilmachung Österreichs und ihr Ausbau bis 1918 (Berlin 1918), p. 25. This is one of the best studies relating to the Empire's financial and monetary policy during the war.
5 Popovics, Das Geldwesen, p. 42.
6 Popovics, Das Geldwesen, p. 43.
7 During July the central bank's discount and collateral loans accounts returns showed a downward trend also to be observed in the figures for the note circulation:

1914	Discounts	Collateral Loans	Note Circulation
		(in crowns mill.)	
7 July	829.7	199.4	2,257.3
15 July	773.0	190.4	2,172.4
23 July	767.8	186.4	2,129.8

See Siegfried Pressburger, Österreichische Notenbank 1816–1966 (Vienna, 1966), p. 280.
8 Cf. Müller, Die finanzielle Mobilmachung, p. 26 et seq.

9 Cf. Popovics, *Das Geldwesen*, p. 44.
10 Salcia Landmann, for instance, in her amusing book *Erzählter Bilderbogen aus Ostgalizien* (Munich, 1975, p. 14), recounts how the peasants there proved to be 'financial geniuses': 'Other peasants again brought their meagre savings into town, went from shop to shop, bought everywhere a little something, and accepted silver as change for their banknotes. If one shop had not enough silver, they contented themselves with a fraction of what was owing.'
11 Müller says that the cash shortage was not only due to hoarding. 'The Army's requirements too had tied down great quantities of silver and small change. The available 10 crown notes, silver 5 crown pieces, 1 crown and 20, 10, 2 and 1 heller pieces could not therefore suffice.' *Die finanzielle Mobilmachung*, p. 29.
12 F. F. G. Kleinwaechter speaks, in his memoirs *Der fröhliche Präsidialist* (Vienna, 1925), of the 'appalling scarcity of notes and coins' after the outbreak of war. 'If at this time you went to a café for a coffee, the waiter asked if you had any coins because he could not give you change on a 10 crown note. Only the printing of 1 and 2 crown notes overcame the emergency.' (p. 113)
13 Cf. Müller, *Die finanzielle Mobilmachung*, p. 30.
14 Cf. Pressburger, *Österreichische Notenbank*, p. 281.
15 Cf. Popovics, *Das Geldwesen*, p. 45 and Pressburger, *Österreichische Notenbank*, p. 282.
16 'The printers managed to deliver within a little over a fortnight more than a thousand million (crowns) to the central bank's chief cashier. . . . It shows how, had information about the intention to address an ultimatum to the Serb Government been passed only a few days sooner, this disturbance to monetary activities could also have been avoided.' Popovics, op. cit., p. 48.
17 'Anxiety assumed such proportions that the Mayor of Vienna had an appeal posted in the streets, "Fellow-citizens, don't let the moratorium frighten you!" ' Müller, *Die finanzielle Mobilmachung*, p. 13 et seq.
18 Müller, *Die finanzielle Mobilmachung*, p. 13.
19 The Hungarian Ministry of Finance delegates especially are alleged to have supported a general moratorium. 'The position of banks dealing in deposits business, the majority of which could be placed in awkward straits by a precipitate demand for repayment, is the primary explanation for their attitude.' Popovics, *Das Geldwesen*, p. 49.
20 As early as spring 1915 Walther Federn could write, 'Encashment of the moratorium bills is going ahead very well. Investigations made by certain big banks suggest that in Austria about 90% of the bills falling due are being punctually paid.' See 'Die Zinsfusszermässigung der österreichisch ungarische Bank', *Der Österreichische Volkswirt*, 17 April 1915, p. 477.
21 At this time a high bank rate was indefensible in view of the state of liquidity. Cf. Federn, *Der Österreichische Volkswirt*, p. 477.
22 During the Balkan Wars an agreement of this kind had been reached between the two governments and the bank's management in case of a general mobilization, 'in which connection the guiding idea, upheld in wartime too, was that a claim on the bank shall be made only if every normal form of official credit procurement cannot be applied.' Cf. Walther Federn, 'Die Österreichisch Ungarische Bank im Kriege', *Der Österreichische Volkswirt*, 22 December 1917, p. 198.
23 Discussing in detail the results of a parliamentary committee of inquiry, Federn said, 'A striking fact is that the commission is supposed to have expressed this

misgiving for the first time on 26 June 1915 after having previously endorsed loans for many thousands of millions, including two publicly subscribed War Loans. It seems to have woken up very late to the intrinsically unconstitutional nature of governmental borrowing in wartime without parliamentary authority, and this in spite of our having emphatically pointed out on the occasion of the treasury bills issued before the war that the amount of the debts, incapable of being repaid from current receipts, constitutes the most important criterion for the inadmissibility of their contraction by means of Paragraph 14.' Walther Federn, 'Die Berichte der Staatsschulden-Kontrollkommission', *Der Österreichische Volkswirt*, 29 September 1917, p. 905.

24 Federn sums up the National Debt Control Commission's conduct in the following terms: if the commission can simply endorse war debts, 'then in future the most important constitutional requirement for the recall of parliament in wartime is abolished. And it is downright incomprehensible that the commission appointed by parliament should itself have dared to have shown the way to do it.' Federn, *Der Österreichische Volkswirt*. Müller says, 'On the resumption of parliamentary life the commission was rebuked in the house for having given its approval to the issue of long term treasury bills, and in particular the bonds redeemable in forty years. For this reason a vote of censure was passed.' Müller, *Die finanzielle Mobilmachung*, p. 128.

25 For the regulations on which repeal of the Bank Act was based, see Pressburger, *Österreichische Notenbank*, p. 288.

26 The exorbitant claims made by the state machine on the bank emerge, in addition to the Parliamentary Report, from a detailed report by the bank itself dated 7 December 1917.

27 On 28 July Spitzmüller reported to the Creditanstalt board 'on the situation as affected by the war' and on the loan negotiations of the consortium for official business with the Government. Board Minutes, 28 July 1914, Creditanstalt Archives.

28 The basis for this collateral loan was a Para. 14 ordinance 'which authorized the Austrian Government to obtain by loan funds necessary to meet the expenditure on extraordinary military preparations. This Imperial ordinance was the basis for all later operations required for war financing.' Pressburger, *Österreichishe Notenbank*, p. 284.

29 Pressburger, *Österreichishe Notenbank*, p. 285.

30 Popovics, *Das Geldwesen*, p. 50. 'Militias' refers to the Austrian *Landwehr* and the Hungarian *Honved* which in wartime were placed under the command of the joint Imperial Army.

31 Popovics, *Das Geldwesen*, p. 51 et seq. In this and other parts of the book the reader will find a wealth of additional data on the state's financial operations during the war.

32 Ministry of Finance Archives, Office of the Minister, Imperial Ministry of Finance, file Z.2091/F.M., 12 September 1914.

33 'Until well into 1915 the principle held good that the public, so heavily hit by the war, could not be saddled with a rise in the already crushing burden of taxation.' Müller, *Die finanzielle Mobilmachung*, p. 157.

34 Dr Karl Renner, the first State Chancellor of post-1918 Austria and first post-1945 Federal President, was one of the few sociologists who in the early stage of the war drew attention to the problem of the distribution of the military burden. In

a review of the book by Franz Meisel and Arthur Spiethoff, *Österreichs Finanzen und der Krieg* (Vienna, 1915), there occurs the following passage: 'In our view the public has every reason to concern itself in good time with the problem of the distribution of the military burdens among the individual branches of production and classes of the nation and to forestall disagreeable surprises. Astonishingly enough this project says nothing about a property tax although the German model so often praised by the authors would plainly have suggested it.' Karl Renner, 'Österreichs Finanzen und der Krieg', *Arbeiter-Zeitung*, 14 February 1915. This seems to be the first time that the problem of property taxation, which was to play a great part in subsequent tax reform discussions, was touched upon.

35 Popovics, *Das Geldwesen*, p. 60 et seq.

36 Ministry of Finance Archives, file 789/F.M., 1915.

37 In this connection Federn called to mind the provision in the statute of 8 August 1911 that the gold stocks should if the banknote prerogative was not prolonged, be divided between the two governments. In this way the far more legitimate claims of the banknote owners would be balanced against the claims of the shareholders. 'The bad example given by the bank through its demand is highly regrettable,' the article continued, 'and that the governments agreed to this demand is downright incomprehensible.' Walther Federn, 'Der Finanzausschuss über Kriegsschulden und die Österreichisch-Ungarische Bank', *Der Österreichische Volkswirt*, 8 December 1917, p. 162. Popovics, who as governor of the central bank shared responsibility for the inclusion of Clause 10 in the agreement, in his memoirs defended this uncommonly advantageous settlement for the bank's shareholders as follows: 'This provision has in certain professional periodicals been the subject of adverse criticism by making it a matter of reproach to the bank's management for establishing on its own behalf a privileged position amidst the general depreciation due to the war. Objective judgement of the grounds on which the bank's management raised the claim accepted by the governments must reject this criticism as invalid. It cannot be left out of account that in case that the bank's prerogative had lapsed and consequently (if its banking activities were not assumed by the public administration) a normal liquidation of its business had taken place, there would, after deduction of liabilities, have remained in hand net assets most likely equivalent to the share capital as well as a very sizeable portion of the reserve fund, and those as far as can be foreseen in actual gold.' Popovics, *Das Geldwesen*, p. 630. Let the reader decide which of the two commentators is more convincing.

38 'On the same day' (i.e., 31 July) 'the Bank performed a turn-about as regards the sale of foreign currency and exchange. Until then the central bank had sold considerable quantities of foreign currency and exchange of every kind to meet transaction requirements. Now it said that for the time being it could not supply any fresh foreign currency and exchange.' Müller, *Die finanzielle Mobilmachung*, p. 28.

39 The sale of Austrian securities abroad and the 'export' of crown notes, as long as this was permissible, worked in the same direction.

40 A report by the Austrian Minister of Finance to Emperor Francis Joseph includes the passage: 'Apart from the financial operations mentioned, this same period saw the conclusion of yet another smaller bond transaction which in addition to the procurement of funds for the war's conduct was also intended to serve special financial policy purposes, namely, the marks loan extended against one-year

treasury bills.' See Ministry of Finance Archives, file 1726–1915/F.M., 28 August 1915.

41 Popovics, *Das Geldwesen*, p. 121.

42 A 1915 contract between the Austrian Postal Savings Bank and the major Berlin banks contains the names of the consortium members – Deutsche Bank, Bankhaus Mendelsohn & Co., Disconto-Gesellschaft, and Bankhaus S. Bleichröder. See Ministry of Finance Archives, file 1212/F.M. 1915, 17 June 1915.

43 Cf. *Neue Freie Presse*, 15 November 1914. To reap an interest margin on borrowing against collateral even to the whole amount of expenditure was possible because the central bank extended loans against other securities at a reduced interest rate in so far as the proceeds from the transaction were used to purchase war loans.

44 Cf. Pressburger, *Österreichische Nationalbank*, p. 292 and *Neue Freie Presse*, 30 October 1914. Some writers have concluded from the fact that it was possible for the bonds to be lodged on favourable terms with the central bank as security that this operation too produced inflationary side-effects. This opinion is not however completely sound, inasmuch as the liquidity existing throughout the war years led to little use being made of the chance to borrow from the central bank. At the end of October 1914 commercial advances against collateral by the central bank stood at 312 million crowns, rose by year-end as a result of the November war loan issue in Austria and in Hungary to 670 million crowns, and at the close of April 1915 fell back to 428 million crowns. Only at a later stage of hostilities was greater advantage taken of the collateral deposit opportunity. In October 1918 'the level of collateral lendings, in consequence of substantial amounts of war loan securities being lodged with the bank for settlement at the end of November, soared to 1,927 million crowns.' Cf. Popovics, *Das Geldwesen*, p. 82.

45 'Die österreichische Kriegsanleihe', *Neue Freie Presse*, 10 November 1914.

46 *Neue Freie Presse*, 11 November 1914.

47 On the flotation of the Second War Loan Gustav Stolper coined the later frequently-quoted words, 'Subscribing to the loan is no sacrifice. It serves not only society but self.' See 'Die zweite Kriegsanleihe', *Der Österreichische Volkswirt*, 8 March 1915, p. 529.

48 Walther Federn watched stock exchange speculations during the war with increasing misgiving. Occasional set-backs there nourished in him the hope that capitalists would in growing degree turn to the acquisition of war bonds. As late as November 1917, when the Seventh War Loan was issued, he thought that 'the experience that share prices can drop fast and steep may have opened capitalists' eyes to the danger of investing their fortune in shares and that therefore the disposition to purchase war loans with an interest of 6¼% may possibly have been strengthened.' See 'Die siebente Kriegsanleihe', *Der Österreichische Volkswirt*, 10 November 1917, p. 95.

49 Cf. 'Die Bedingungen der Anleihezeichnung', *Neue Freie Presse*, 15 November 1914.

50 The Creditanstalt board voted to subscribe for its own account 20 million crowns for the Austrian loan and for a 'proportional participation in the 50 million crowns to be subscribed by the Austrian banks to Hungarian war loan'. Board Minutes, 17 November 1914, Creditanstalt Archives.

51 Cf. 'Die Zeichnungen bei den einzelnen Banken', *Neue Freie Presse*, 25 November 1914.

52 'For the rest, the change was principally to be perceived in that the big industrial corporations, whose function in normal conditions can assuredly not be to tie themselves down to any considerable degree in securities, under the influence of their supporting banks ... subscribed very substantial amounts. To avoid however any supposition that this participation, really beyond the limits of ordinary business practice by industrial joint-stock companies, may have been of decisive importance, I would like to point out that according to my estimate the subscriptions by industrial companies are likely at the most to have represented ten per cent of the total subscription for the Austrian war loan.' Alexander Spitzmüller, 'Die Kriegsanleihe', *Neue Freie Presse*, 26 November 1914.

53 Cf. 'Die Zeichnungen der grössten österreichischen und deutschen Sparkassen', *Neue Freie Presse*, 25 November 1914.

54 This suspicion becomes a certainty when the following figures are compared: 'The Zentralbank der deutschen Sparkassen subscribed 170,000,000 crowns to the first war loan, 204,374,500 crowns to the second, altogether 374,374,500 crowns. The Zentralbank der tschechischen Sparkassen subscribed 9,546,000 and 12,030,000 crowns, altogether 21,576,000 crowns.' See Josef Redlich, *Schicksalsjahre Österreichs 1908–1919* (Vienna, 1954), ed. Fritz Fellner, p. 81.

55 Pressburger, *Österreichische Nationalbank*, p. 292. Pressburger's results are somewhat lower than those of Müller and Popovics.

56 Spitzmüller, *Die Kriegsanleihe*.

57 Expert observers have often referred to this aspect. Cf. Gustav Stolper, 'Die zweite Kriegsanleihe', *Der Österreichische Volkswirt*, 8 May 1915. Müller says, 'It has to be noted that as a whole neither the farming class nor the big landowners remotely participated in producing funds for the war loans to the degree commensurate with their financial capacity. As an excuse one may accept the fact that the peasantry in Austria was heavily indebted at the start of the war so that it used the increased income from the strongly inflated prices to lessen liabilities. But the big landowners were before the war not badly in debt and they could certainly have invested considerably greater resources in war loans than they actually did.' Müller, *Die finanzielle Mobilmachung*, p. 138.

58 A certain element of at least moral compulsion may have played a part. 'Banks, joint-stock companies, and big industrialists were under moral obligation to buy a sizeable slice of each war loan.' Cf. Müller, Die finanzielle Mobilmachung, p. 97.

59 A classification of the totals attained by the war loan operations according to financial houses and the amount of the subscription is contained in the Appendix, Table AI.

60 Cf. *Neue Freie Presse*, 26 November 1914.

61 Cf. Popovics, *Das Geldwesen*, Statistical Appendix, Table 2.

62 Cf. Franz Baltzarek, *Die Geschichte der Wiener Börse* (Vienna, 1973), p. 108.

63 A certain improvement in spring 1914 was however followed in May by a bearish tone. Cf. Müller, Die finanzielle Mobilmachung, p. 20 et seq.

64 Baltzarek, *Geschichte der Wiener Börse*, p. 109.

CHAPTER 3
Banking Policy in the Early Phase of the War

The outbreak of war probably took the leading personalities in the Austrian banking world as much by surprise as it did most other figures in public life.[1] The official moratorium was primarily intended to prevent a run on the banks. The larger banks tried however to meet their most pressing obligations, especially in the case of industrial customers, by recourse to the Austro-Hungarian Bank. During the first week of August, when public anxiety threatened to develop into a panic, the central bank's bills portfolio expanded by no less than 592 million crowns.[2] In the following week withdrawals did not substantially exceed the limits set by the moratorium and claims on the nation's central bank were reduced to former levels. This was due largely to the fact that the war administration was able to pay promptly for equipment and armaments purchases and that the recipients, noting the signs of the quick normalization of the money market, entrusted these monies to their banks in the accustomed way.[3]

The banks were confronted with a very complex, highly obscure situation. A sizeable number of firms with whom they were on a close footing were threatened by either restrictions or complete closure because raw materials were lacking and senior staff as well as skilled workers had been called up.[4] The building industry which even before the outbreak of the war had experienced a set-back, now stagnated completely. Mining, together with certain branches of the export and luxury trades, was going through a very difficult time due to supply difficulties and shifts in demand. On the other hand some undertakings, the leading armaments producers and their subcontractors, experienced a lively upswing. But with the spreading of the conflict ever greater sections of industry were integrated into the war economy. After a few months businessmen who saw only this aspect of the mass slaughter began talking about the war as an economic 'blessing'.[5]

The banks, in particular the major Viennese ones, were directly affected by the war. For they had branches, agents, and/or substantial industrial interests in the Empire's north-eastern regions which soon became the scene of fighting. Creditanstalt was probably the worst hit. In addition to its old, well-known branch office at Lemberg (now Lvov), it had a large share in the Galizische Bank für Handel und Industrie.[6] Among its most important industrial interests soon in the firing-line were Vereinigte Fabriken Zieleniewski at Lemberg and Sanok, AG für Mühlen- und Holzindustrie whose sawmills and other lumber works lay on the northern slope of the Carpathians, and 'Tisita' Rumänische Waldexploitation AG whose operations had to be curtailed to a large extent.[7] During the years before 1914 Creditanstalt had pulled out of some of its engagements in the oil industry, but its assets in this field had remained considerable. They comprised interests in Mineralölraffinerie AG, Budapest, in the oil-drilling company linked to the latter, and a small share in Galizische Naphta AG The destruction in the Galician oilfields and refineries was however, as appeared after the Russian retreat, not as grave as had been feared in autumn 1914.[8]

Besides Creditanstalt, Wiener Bankverein, Boden-Creditanstalt, Anglo-Österreichische Bank, and Österreichische Länderbank were the Viennese institutions most affected by events on the Eastern Front. Bankverein, with the greatest number of representations, had branches at Lemberg, Cracow, and Czernowitz (Cernauti), affiliates in six other places on the periphery of the Empire, offices in Constantinople, Smyrna (Izmir), and interests in several Balkan banks. In autumn 1914 an assessment of the risks involved in these commitments was hardly possible.[9] Similarly situated was Boden-Creditanstalt. It had no branch offices, but its mortgage and communal loan transactions in Galicia appeared especially imperilled.[10] Neither Länderbank nor Anglobank were engaged to any major extent in the Empire's eastern and north-eastern territories. For them the sources of most potential loss were their activities in Britain and France. Länderbank was cut off almost completely from its flourishing branches in Paris and London.[11] For the success of Anglobank the profits of its London office were of outstanding importance, inasmuch as during the final pre-war years they had amounted to some 1 million crowns compared to its total profit of some 12 million crowns.[12]

Balancing accounts was in these circumstances a problem which caused experts a certain amount of brain-racking. Most banks, seeing how very unclear the situation was, forewent their usual practice and published no figures for the first half-year 1914.[13] The results for the whole year had of course sooner or later to come out. The question was what criteria should be applied to the first financial statement since war had begun.

On 18 December 1914 experts from the Chamber of Commerce and from the banking world met at the Ministry of Justice to discuss the subject. A day later an inter-ministerial discussion at the Ministry of Finance concluded that no change in the legal provisions on the preparation of balance sheets should be envisaged. The press communiqué ran:

The government has decided, after examining the facts and basing its decision on the opinions given at a meeting of experts attended by representatives from the Chamber of Commerce, the banks, the savings banks, and the credit co-operatives, that it is unnecessary to alter the existing regulations and that the variety of situations as well as other reasons render it inadvisable to issue generally binding regulations.

The guiding principle for a firm's balance sheet valuation should be the 'care which must in general be operative for a conscientious businessman who balances his books'. The ministry allowed that 'on this occasion a market quotation for 31 December 1914 is not imperative', since the Stock Exchange had been closed on the outbreak of hostilities. Nevertheless application of the principle respecting the care of a conscientious businessman would establish as the 'point of departure' the last market quotation, i.e., that of 25 July 1914. The question of how to value securities could indeed have scarcely been handled more cautiously when it is recalled that in the days before the outbreak of war the stock market had dropped to a low rarely recorded before. The communiqué further stated that 'businessmen and companies whose headquarters are in an area directly affected by hostilities are exempt until 30 June 1915 from the duty of presenting their accounts for the current year. . . .'[14] A statutory order by the ministry, dated 25 December 1914, informed the public accordingly. For all other firms with merely main premises, not registered seats, in one of the affected areas, the obligation to prepare their accounts was in principle to hold good.[15]

An analysis of the major banks' balance sheets for 1914 must take into account the many subjective factors colouring the final result to a far higher degree than had been the case in earlier, quieter years. Leaving aside entirely the difficult problems of evaluating losses in the war areas and of the 'real' value of securities on 31 December 1914, the banks had to proceed with particular caution as regards appraising the extent of dubious credits. The proclamation of the moratorium and the factual impossibility of filing suit to recover overdue debts were factors which could not but worry the most experienced accountancy expert. It is hardly surprising that bank managements should in the preparation of their balance sheets have let themselves be guided by fears, wishful thinking, and all-too-familiar 'intuition'.

Creditanstalt was perhaps the most cautious in its estimate of the economic situation created by the war. Net profit for 1914 (including profit brought forward from the preceding year) was put at 10.8 million crowns as against 23 million crowns in 1913. Corresponding to this decline in profits of more than 53%, the dividend was cut drastically from 10.625% to 6.875%. Nevertheless the management thought it necessary to justify even this modest dividend payment by pointing to the formation of the War Loss Reserve (5 million crowns) and to the fact that the value of various securities and syndicate holdings had developed so favourably, because of the boom in certain parts of the war economy, that they made up for the diminution in hidden reserves caused by the fall in security values.[16]*

The management's decision was presumably influenced to no small degree by the views of the Finance Ministry. The latter regarded it as detrimental to the Bank's standing if, with its well-endowed stock of published and hidden reserves, it were to reduce its dividend to the same extent as establishments which had not been able to accumulate hidden reserves to such an extent and to issue new shares at a high premium.[17]

The Länderbank balance sheet showed a similar assessment of the situation. Profit declined from 14.4 million crowns in 1913 to 9.6 million crowns in 1914 and the dividend dropped from 7.5% to 4%.[18] Diametrically opposed was the position adopted by Niederöster-reichische Escompte-Gesellschaft, the sole bank to announce an increase in profit from 10.9 million crowns to 12.7 million crowns, and to maintain an unchanged dividend payment of 10.5%. It could count, *Volkswirt* suggested, on having fewer losses than other banks because its relatively small number of customers enabled the management to evaluate the financial reliability of debtors much more easily and, if need be, to take counter-measures far more quickly than could financial institutions with a ramified branch network.[19] Between these poles were situated Wiener Bankverein, Boden-Creditanstalt, and Anglobank who reported moderate losses and a not too drastic cut in dividends. In the same category was also un-

* As stated by the *Volkswirt*.

doubtedly to be included Živnostenská banka, the biggest Czech establishment. Despite considerable commitments in Galicia and comparatively low reserves, it reduced its dividend from 7.5% in 1913 to 5% in 1914.[20] Considerations of prestige will probably in this as in other cases have influenced the dividend policy considerably.

Yet whatever weight is attributed to subjective factors, the balances struck by the major banks at the close of the first war year show an important change in the economic situation since the stormy August days. The Creditanstalt balance sheet can be regarded as typical in this respect.

The war had led surprisingly quickly to switches in the order of importance attaching to the various branches of banking activities. At the end of 1914 there existed a state of liquidity unknown in living memory. Creditanstalt showed cash on hand of some 73 million crowns as against 31 million crowns in the preceding year. Before the War Loan issue the liquid resources had amounted to more than 150 million crowns. A subscription on its own account of 31.3 million crowns (20 millions and 11.3 millions for the Austrian and Hungarian loans respectively) had raised the holdings of securities to more than 71 million crowns (1913 = 46 million crowns). War loan operations were a proven means of exercising some check over the rising volume of money. Although the banks were indubitably inspired by patriotic motives, the prolongation of the war simply compelled them to give serious consideration to stepping up this progressively more important branch of business.[21]

Receipts on current business, consisting mainly of interest, commissions, and foreign exchange earnings, netted in 1914 a distinctly lower profit than in the year before, foreshadowing a trend that during the course of the war would become ever more marked.[22] The decline in current business, formerly the backbone of crédit mobilier activities, revealed in particular two developments. First there was the decrease in the demand for credits due to the high liquidity of firms, or, expressed in another way, the shorter commitment of bank resources resulting from the speedier settlement of goods and other transactions. Secondly, rising liquidity was accompanied by a falling discount rate. From 1910 till 1913 the interest rate had pointed upward, but in the first six months of 1914 it had displayed a retrograde tendency.[23] After a brief boost to 6% on the outbreak of war, Creditanstalt's average discount rate for commercial bills towards the close of the year was no more than 4.326%.[24]

Dealings in foreign exchange offered some compensation for losses in current business.[25] This lucrative source of activity died down however when in 1916 there was created the Foreign Exchange Agency, a subject to be considered in a later chapter.

Sharper still than the change in current business was the decline of trading in securities. With the closure of the Stock Exchange this activity came practically to an end. As noted, the sale of war loans and the credits extended on such collateral, financed mostly by the banks from their own ever greater liquid resources, furnished a certain, though plainly inadequate substitute.[26] In the second year of war, with rising fears of inflation traditional dealings in securities increased. However, for as long as the Stock Exchange remained closed, this sphere was principally the preserve of bucket-shops and unlicensed dealers who tried to make capital out of the ignorance of the man in the street.

The preceding chapter has recounted how the sale of War Loan, although it yielded relatively little profit, grew into a mainstay of banking activities.[27] Nonetheless fresh opportunities for gain soon arose, such as financing military supplies and stepping up import and export transactions with neutral countries which often proved very profitable. Even more important became the provision of funds for the numerous agencies sponsored by the major banks. This new line of business can without exaggeration be said to have compensated, more so than the voluminous sale of War Loan with its small earnings, for a part of the decline in current activities. The commodities departments of banks, it should be added, made in the early war years considerable profits, whereas mortgage business nearly ceased completely, a state of affairs attributable to the hopeless situation in the building trade.

What was the situation at the outbreak of war with regard to the most distinguished branch of crédit mobilier activities, industrial promotion? In times long past it had been looked on as the raison d'être of these banks. Operations in this field, with the exception of Creditanstalt's interests in the Metals and Wool Agencies and in the *Kriegskredit-Bank*, which will be dealt with later, came to a complete standstill. This development reflected the disinclination to invest that was a predominant feature in the early phase of the war. The leading armaments firms were an exception, but they were in a position to finance their expansion out of their own resources. In January 1915 Creditanstalt board minutes record a decision to acquire a comparatively small interest of 50,000 crowns in an 'aeroplane company' launched by Baron Skoda.[28] Promotions on a larger scale did not however become any too frequent in the later war years either. May

1915 saw discussion of acquiring an interest in a German sleeping-car and restaurant concern, the rare instance of a traditional promotion activity.[29] Normally operations were confined to financing the armaments, ship-, and machine-building industries and the exploitation of raw materials sources in the Empire's peripheral regions or territories under army occupation.

Developments in the savings banks sector have been very expertly described and must here be treated marginally.[30] This sector of banking faced very serious problems at the outset of the international conflict. In the first, critical days they were confronted as much as the crédit mobilier houses with a run on their resources. To some degree the proclamation of the moratorium on 31 July 1914 put a stop to the frenzied urge to hoard which had overtaken the small saver particularly.[31] While the crédit mobilier banks were able to recover comparatively quickly from the blood-letting – by October a general state of liquidity had come about – the savings banks could only retrieve the initial loss of deposits during the course of 1915.[32] Two influences may well account for such strikingly slow recuperation. In the first place, the hoarding instinct was most pronounced among the small savers, secondly many of them were not prepared to buy War Loan on credit. 'If they were going to subscribe to War Loan', they wanted 'actually to put their hands on the bonds and not to content themselves with a confirmation of the amount subscribed.'[33]

Deprived of a considerable portion of their deposits, it was not easy for the savings banks to release as early as November big amounts of cash for the War Loan subscription. The Ministry of Finance therefore instructed the *Kriegsdarlehenskasse* to extend loans to the savings banks against the pledge of gilt-edged mortgage claims. The *Kriegskreditbank* and the *Kriegsdarlehenskasse* were set up to extend credit on reasonable terms to small businesses which had been badly afflicted by the war. The savings banks too were supposed to come to the aid of these classes, who usually had no contact with the commercial banks. To this end the savings banks established special departments for personal loans. Moreover, the central bank stated its readiness to accept commercial bills to a ceiling of 400 crowns from small traders if they were presented through the savings banks.[34]

On the outbreak of war the authorities had taken the view that the existing banking system showed certain structural defects, one in particular being the inability to meet in full the loan requirements of small business. The upshot was the initiative taken by the Ministry of Finance on 19 September 1914 to set up a *Kriegsdarlehenskasse*. (The inspiration probably followed the foundation of similar institutions in Germany a few weeks after hostilities began.) The aim was to furnish credit against goods and securities as collateral. The management of the new institute was entrusted to the central bank. Business was conducted under the supervision of the Minister of Finance and officials appointed by him. The necessary funds were to be obtained by the issue of interest-free certificates of deposit equivalent to the amount of loans. The certificates were accepted in payment by all government offices and the central bank, but their acceptance was not obligatory in non-official transactions.[35]

The institute had been created on the assumption that war would lead to far-reaching immobilization of stockpiles. Yet soon after the opening of the Vienna head office and the thirty-four branch offices it was seen that the call on its facilities was slight. 'Whereas the ordinance of 19 September had fixed the maximum volume of deposit certificates at 500 million crowns, the level of loans did not rise above 128.5 million crowns until the end of October 1918 when the figure leaped to 321.7 million crowns and at year-end attained 470 million crowns.'[36]

Similarly the *Kriegskreditbanken*, established in certain crown lands essentially with the same purpose never achieved special significance in spite of the great expectations accompanying their introduction. The Niederösterreichische *Kriegskredit-Bank*, founded on 28 October 1914, was the first. Of its 6.5 million crowns share capital 40% was paid up immediately. Besides Creditanstalt, certain other leading banks and a large number of important industrial firms were among the shareholders.[37] It was licensed to undertake two types of activity – the discount of bills and the extension of acceptance credits against appropriate security. It was not allowed, however, to deal in securities or to accept deposits. No time limit was specified for its operations, but the articles contained a provision that six months after the cessation of hostilities the Bank must go into liquidation.[38] The realization of this project was assured by a guarantee of indemnity to 4 million crowns, underwritten by the Municipality of Vienna and the Lower Austrian Chamber of Commerce and a rediscount credit to the amount of 33 million crowns by the central bank.[39] However, as in the case of the *Kriegsdarlehenskasse*, its resources were scarcely called upon. Actually the small businessmen were quite able during a period of increasing liquidity to make themselves independent of the services of the bank.

At the close of 1914 the situation of the major banks still looked uncertain. Subscriptions for the first War Loan had indeed proved a surprising success, but neither on the military nor on the economic front had there been a breakthrough. Some sectors continued in an unsatisfactory condition and a call for measures to improve the employment situation could be repeatedly heard.[40] The news of military reverses and the long lists of dead and wounded did the rest to turn initial elation into dejection.[41]

A change of mood had to await spring 1915. Successful transition of the economy to war needs brought a sort of prosperity, causing many to forget the dubious soil from which it sprang. Events at the front contributed to the improvement of spirits generally and 'normalization' was reflected in the banks' activities. Financing of the agencies, large-scale publicity campaigns for War Loan, and certain branches of current business seemed to offer a broad, lucrative sphere of operations. Only at a later stage of development did the war's negative aspects become more manifest.

Notes

1 'One thing is certain. The war took the banks by surprise even though the one or the other, with special sources of information about affairs abroad, was able in good time to reduce its holdings of securities somewhat and to gain elbow-room accordingly.' Stefan von Müller, *Die finanzielle Mobilmachung Österreichs und ihr Ausbau bis 1918* (Berlin, 1918), p. 48.

2 Cf. Siegfried Pressburger, *Österreichische Notenbank, 1816–1918* (Vienna, 1966), p. 290.

3 Müller, *Die finanzielle Mobilmachung*, p. 50.

4 Cf. Part II, Chapter 1, note 8.

5 Gustav Stolper rightly inveighed against such nihilism. 'Optimists who even talk about the war's economic blessings have economics out of focus. (All) they see . . . are the big profits and the scarcity of workers in a large number of industries. A condition which signifies general or widespread deterioration in the masses' standard of living can just as well be called an economic crisis, and *this* is indeed the picture of crisis that meets our eyes as a result of the precipitous rise in the cost of all vital necessities under conditions of straitened consumption.' 'Zur Beurteilung der Wirtschaftslage', *Der Österreichische Volkswirt*, 24 April 1915, p. 489. (The italics are in the original.)

6 Cf. Part I, Chapter 6, *The Creditanstalt's Industrial Assets in 1913*.

7 Cf. 'Österreichische Creditanstalt', *Der Österreichische Volkswirt*, Supplement 'Die Bilanzen', 3 April 1915, p. 109.

8 A review of the situation in the Galician oil industry after the Russians' departure reports only small damage; two thirds of the crude oil stocks remained intact. 'As the material damage in the refineries (especially the state-owned ones), the pipelines, and the pumping-stations is slight and can soon be repaired, work can

be resumed everywhere.' See 'Die Galizischen Rohölvorräte', *Der Österreichische Volkswirt*, 19 June 1915, p. 638.

9 Cf. 'Wiener Bankverein', *Der Österreichische Volkswirt*, Supplement 'Die Bilanzen', 27 March 1915, p. 101.

10 Cf. 'Allgemeine Österreichische Bodenkredit-Anstalt', *Der Österreichische Volkswirt*, Supplement 'Die Bilanzen', 10 April 1915, p. 117. The share in 1914 of Galicia and Bukovina in the bank's total outstanding loans of 437.3 million crowns is put there at '36.2 millions for mortgage loans, 33 millions for communal loans, and 3 millions for industrial loans, making 72.2 million crowns in all.'

11 Cf. 'Die Österreichische Länderbank', *Der Österreichische Volkswirt*, Supplement 'Die Bilanzen', 1 May 1915, No. 31, p. ixi.

12 Cf. 'Anglo-Österreichische Bank', *Der Österreichische Volkswirt*, Supplement 'Die Bilanzen', 17 April 1915, p. 125.

13 At the beginning of November the Creditanstalt management submitted to the board a confidential report on the half-year balance of accounts and on the situation of the bank's affiliated export firms and sugar factories. The minutes unfortunately throw no detailed light on what was discussed at the meeting. See Board Minutes, 3 November 1914, Creditanstalt Archives.

14 Ministry of Finance file 92.190, p. 7 (with memo from Ministry of Justice), 1914.

15 Cf. Müller, *Die finanzielle Mobilmachung*, p. 52.

16 Cf. 1914 Annual Report, Creditanstalt Archives.

17 Cf. 'Österreichische Creditanstalt', *Der Österreichische Volkswirt*, Supplement 'Die Bilanzen', 3 April 1915, p. 109.

18 Länderbank's War Losses Reserve of 8.5 million crowns exceeded in size even the figure chosen by the Creditanstalt, celebrated for its cautious accountancy. Cf. 'Österreichische Länderbank', *Der Österreichische Volkswirt*, Supplement 'Die Bilanzen', 1 May 1915, p. 141.

19 Cf. 'Niederösterreichische Escompte-Gesellschaft', *Der Österreichische Volkswirt*, Supplement 'Die Bilanzen', 6 March 1915, p. 85.

20 Cf. 'Živnostenska banká', *Der Österreichische Volkswirt*, Supplement 'Die Bilanzen', 24 April, 1915, p. 137.

21 The data given here has been taken from the Creditanstalt Annual Report and the series of balance sheet analyses in *Der Österreichische Volkswirt*. The situation of the other major banks was in essence identical with that of Creditanstalt. Cash on hand at Anglobank had inside one year grown from 14 million crowns to almost 49 million crowns, its stocks of securities from 21 to 29 million crowns. Liquidity at Länderbank rose from 20 million crowns to 33 million crowns, its stocks of securities from 54 to 73 million crowns. Here too the expansion in the bank's holdings of fixed interest securities arose from its subscription to War Loan.

22 In 1913 Creditanstalt's earnings on current business had been 18,766 million crowns. In 1914 they amounted to 14,817 million crowns.

23 The average interest rates for 1910–1914 were 3%, 3%, 3.75%, 4.79%, and 5.714% respectively, but at the date of the Stock Exchange closure the rate had dropped to 3.64%. See Müller, *Die finanzielle Mobilmachung*, p. 56.

24 Cf. 'Österreichische Creditanstalt', *Der Österreichische Volkswirt*, Supplement 'Die Bilanzen', 3 April 1915.

25 Creditanstalt's foreign exchange profits were up 30% on the preceding year, according to *Der Österreichische Volkswirt*.

26 The central bank was prepared to accept War Loan as collateral to 75% of face value and at an interest rate of 5% p.a. for a number of years. Banks could therefore extend advances on similar terms against such securities and at any time suggest to debtors that they should borrow from the central bank money to repay an advance. Cf. Walther Federn, 'Die Kreditpolitik der Wiener Banken', *Schriften* Vol. CLXIX, p. 56.

27 'The placement and distribution of War Loans must be described as a determining factor in banking activities during the main part of the war', writes Max Sokal in *Die Tätigkeit der Banken* (Vienna, 1920), p. 5, reprint from the Report by the Lower Austrian Chamber of Commerce and Trade on economic conditions 1914–1918.

28 Board Minutes, 12 January 1915, Creditanstalt Archives.

29 Board Minutes, 26 May 1915, Creditanstalt Archives.

30 Two studies in particular deserve to be mentioned: Walter Schmidt, *Das Sparkassenwesen in Österreich* (Vienna, 1930) and Hedwig Fritz, *et al.*, *150 Jahre Sparkassen in Österreich* (Vienna, 1969–71), in 5 volumes.

31 '... in the last days of July, after the shock caused by the mobilization and Austria's declaration of war on Serbia, the situation had as a whole quietened down rather. When the provisions of the moratorium proclamation became known, withdrawals once again attained an extremely high level which in part exceeded those following the initial shock. By 4 August however the panic had been allayed and henceforward a general rise in deposits with the Viennese savings banks is to be noted.' Fritz, *150 Jahre Sparkassen*, Vol. I, p. 501.

32 The following reduction in deposits between 30 June and 31 December is to be observed among the biggest savings banks: Postsparkasse (Postal Savings Bank), from 195.6 million crowns to 169 million crowns; Erste Österreichische Sparkasse, from 544.4 million crowns to 517.9 million crowns; Zentralsparkasse der Gemeinde Wien (Vienna Municipal Savings Bank), from 184.2 million crowns to 158.9 million crowns. See Müller, *Die finanzielle Mobilmachung*, p. 71.

33 Müller, *Die finanzielle Mobilmachung*, p. 70.

34 Cf. Müller, *Die finanzielle Mobilmachung*, p. 69.

35 Cf. Pressburger, *Österreichische Notenbank*, p. 298.

36 Pressburger, *Österreichische Notenbank*, p. 299.

37 Creditanstalt's management informed the board at the end of September about the impending promotion of the *Kriegskreditbank*. The Bank was to participate with 300,000 crowns in the share capital. At the meeting on 22 October a 'satisfactory outcome of subscriptions for the share capital of the Niederösterreichische Kriegskredit-Bank' was reported. See Board Minutes, 22 September and 22 October 1914, Creditanstalt Archives.

38 Niederösterreichische Kriegskredit-Bank's articles were approved by Ministry of the Interior decrees Z.38522 of 3 October and Z.41110 of 27 October. See Ministry of Finance file Z.82894 of 16 November 1914.

39 Cf. Müller, *Die finanzielle Mobilmachung*, p. 76.

40 'There is another approach according to which the present may be seen as the most suitable juncture. Absolutism in wartime can be viewed one way or another. We in Austria, who have in effect endured it for years, are apathetic to it, and the compulsion to conform to it is perhaps felt less keenly now than in peace-time. The Government's current omnipotence gives it however the opportunity now to take all "necessary" measures solely under the aspect of general utility without heeding

parliamentary currents, parish pump and wheeler-dealer politics that complicate and render more expensive every investment policy because every useful piece of work occasions the creation of many less useful or useless ones.' See 'Der Finanzminister', *Der Österreichische Volkswirt*, 31 October 1914, p. 65.

41 In October the Creditanstalt Management had already to submit to the Board its first report on staff members who had died on the battlefield. See Board Minutes, 30 October 1914, Creditanstalt Archives.

PART THREE

Economic, Financial and Banking Aspects of Total War

Strain and Exhaustion of the Human and Material Resources of the Austro-Hungarian Monarchy

The First World War was 'warfare of a new kind' says Professor Kurt Rothschild in his frequently quoted study on the origins and motivations of the Austrian economy's development.

It was the first war in which the efficiency of industry and of its organization was crucial to management of the war economy and to the successful conduct of war. Huge empires like the Austro-Hungarian Monarchy and Russia, which in earlier times had seemed predestined for military success because of their wealth in human material, now turned out to be unequal to the strains of major warfare due to the weakness of their industrial infrastructure. Signs of economic exhaustion, soon involving a condition of physical and psychological prostration, began in their case to appear much sooner and much more strongly than in France, Germany, and Britain.[1]

In 1915, when the greatest difficulties of organization had been overcome, the war economy looked as though it might be on the verge of a certain consolidation. The production of materials and equipment for the army and the navy accelerated rapidly. The state of under-supply, seriously detrimental to their fighting capacity in the early months, was gradually surmounted.[2] This contributed substantially to the improvement in the Empire's military situation in the spring of that year.[3] On the other hand the food situation, though not as yet critical, was distinctly disquieting. It was a development which set in comparatively early and led to a serious exhaustion particularly among the Austrian half of the Monarchy's urban population.

The subject of food supplies can be treated only marginally.[4] Reference has been made to the very unsatisfactory 1914 harvest.[5] The war years were marked by a continuously growing cereals deficit. In 1918 the crop yield for both halves of the Empire was 47.3% below that in 1913. Austria was in a far more difficult position than

Hungary. Its population amounted to 56% of the Monarchy, but during three successive years its grain production was less than half that of Hungary.[6]

Table 17   Grain production in Austria and Hungary in million cwt.

Year	Austria	Hungary
1914	46.5	43.7
1915	24.3	55.0
1916	20.3	42.6
1917	18.6	43.6
1918	19.0	34.1

As can be seen from these figures there was a dramatic deterioration in Austria, due to a multiplicity of factors like lack of labour, requisitioning of cattle, scarcity of fertilizers and consequent soil exhaustion and the temporary enemy occupation of Galicia. Increasing peasant resistance to bureaucratic control of the grain market may well have affected the extent of deliveries and have been negatively reflected in the official grain statistics.[7]

Germany had managed to establish a fairly equitable system of bread and flour distribution. Given the background and practice of Dualism, an analogous procedure proved utopian. 'Equality of sacrifice' was an inoperative principle in the Monarchy. Hungary, with 44% of the joint population, saved its inhabitants from serious deprivation by withholding grain deliveries in large amounts from its partner. During the first two years, when the crop yield was relatively high, the quantities supplied to Austria were still sizeable, although well below the pre-war level. From 1916 onward Austrian imports of cereals and flour from Hungary were negligible. In 1917 they amounted to only 2.5% of 1913.[8]

Löwenfeld-Russ comments upon this policy of non-cooperation as follows: 'An explanation for these striking and, in light of common statehood and joint conduct of war, disconcerting facts is to be found only in Hungary's traditional separatist policy.'

Hungary's nutritional policy at home was very different from the severe restriction on consumption that Austria had to enforce. For the whole period of the war the per capita quota of the Hungarian bread and flour supply was significantly higher than in Austria. If the Hungarian Government claimed that its population lived almost solely on bread, that justified the higher per capita quotas for those who lived in rural areas, but not for those in cities.

There was no reason why an individual in Budapest had to have a higher bread ration than one in Vienna, Prague, or Innsbruck.'[9]

The flour and bread shortages of 1915 were very soon followed by shortages of other basic foodstuffs because people tried, understandably enough, to substitute one scarce produce with another more easily obtainable. In May 1915 the price for pulses rose by no less than 330% above pre-war days, i.e., July 1914.[10] It was a development to which the government could not remain indifferent. It was clear that a constantly growing number of consumer goods had to be made subject to maximum price regulations. The call for official control of basic foodstuffs seems to have come from the public. 'Threatened by exploitation, [it] demanded measures and action by the authorities, whereas the government shrank initially from interference in complicated mechanism of the economy and accepted the need only reluctantly.'[11]

Fixing maximum prices led with logical inevitability first to an official survey of available produce, then to measures of sequestration and eventually to control of distribution. A flourishing black market developed, which thwarted the official intention to collect as large a quantity as possible of scarce foodstuffs and to see to their fair distribution among all classes. This was, under these conditions, a speedy as well as obvious outcome. The crop yields in the last two years of war were pitiably small; a real crisis occurred in the rationing system and what was worse, in the food situation as a whole. The Austrian population's capacity for resistance might have already collapsed in summer 1917 if conditions had not been somewhat alleviated by grain deliveries from the occupied Romanian territories.[12]

Knowledge of the more favourable state of affairs in Hungary contributed to the general discontent. The fact that at Agram (Zagreb), the capital of Croatia, food rationing existed only on paper, and that even in acutely critical times people there could count on being adequately fed, created nagging doubts about the value of a 'community of nations' apparently lacking the most rudimentary feeling of solidarity. Gustav Stolper's reaction, when in 1920 Hungary tried to make a proposal for alliance attractive to the starving Austrians by dispatching provisions, illustrates the extent of accumulated bitterness at that time: 'It is vain to look for an answer as to where these surpluses were during the four years of war when Hungary's food policy contributed more to the breakdown of the Central Powers than the British blockade.'[13]

Coal and iron were the most important raw materials for the conduct of the war. Coal was vitally important to the standard of living of the masses. Something therefore needs to be said about the production and consumption of this supply of energy and source of warmth for which there was hardly any substitute. It was one of the few raw materials whose decline in production remained within reasonable limits during the hostilities. Imports from abroad (almost exclusively from Germany) did not drop too drastically below the 1913 level.[14] Nevertheless 1917, with an uncommonly harsh winter adding to other difficulties, witnessed serious supply difficulties in the cities, from which not even war industry was spared.[15] In the following year the situation worsened considerably, a circumstance connected with steadily growing transport problems.[16]

At a Joint Affairs Council of Ministers held in June 1917, Emperor Charles had stressed certain grave defects in the use of coal.

Above all, greater economy must be practised. This applies primarily to the railways where, for example, trains often run with only a small complement of coaches. Since 1913 the Austrian railways' coal consumption has risen by 45%. Factories working for the army's requirements also eat up a lot of coal. A factory whose output is only 10% for military purposes, for instance, gets coal for its entire production.[17]

The assumption that these difficulties were caused not so much by the decline of production and imports as by poor management in the transport and distribution systems is probably right.

The story of iron and steel production demonstrates much more clearly than that of coal the strain on, and the exhaustion of, the Empire's economic power of resistance.[18] Coal mining showed relatively negligible fluctuations. The graph of iron and steel production, on the other hand, depicts a rise from a low in autumn 1914 to an unparalleled high in 1916 and 1917, succeeded by a precipitous plunge in 1918.[19] Among practically all the warring nations the decision-making bodies had, in the early stages, been barely conscious of the importance of iron to the conduct of the conflict.[20] Austria-Hungary was no exception. The iron industry's situation, unfavourable in autumn 1914, improved by spring 1915, a turn for the better due in no small measure to investments by the big armaments firms.[21] A growing shortage of scrap iron towards the close of 1915 led at the beginning of 1916 to government control of an input so significant to steel production. Arguments for the regulation of scrap trading were chiefly based on the 'increased demand of the munitions industry for steel production'.[22] In this case too the authorities could rely on an existing organizational framework. Scrap purchases had for many years been concentrated in the hands of the Vienna Scrap Dealers Association.

Spring 1916 saw the need for radical expansion in the supply of munitions. Only now did the High Command recognize the importance of massive material resources in modern warfare. That year's steel production did not even roughly approximate to military requirements. Moreover it became increasingly necessary to substitute steel for certain non-ferrous metals not produced (or at any rate not in adequate quantities) in Central Europe.[23] In October 1916 the decision was finally taken to put iron and steel under state control.[24]

The War Ministry's Iron Section initially confined itself to ensuring the punctual delivery by the iron industry of orders with high military priority. Only a few weeks after its establishment, however, a distinctly more rigorous form of control had to be introduced. Civilian orders were halted and their implementation made dependent on special permission from the ministry.[25] In February 1917 the establishment of a priority scale foresaw a small allocation for civilian purposes. In December 1917 the manifestly mounting iron shortage necessitated imposition of a temporary ban on civilian *and* military orders. The supply of munitions deteriorated as severely as it had done on the outbreak of war when 'the lack of weapons, ammunition, equipment and stores had caused major losses of life'.[26] Gratz and Schüller think that prolongation of the war to December 1918 would have led to the depletion of the last reserves destined for a final emergency. 'From that point onward only the amount of iron needed for the production of 400,000 rounds a month (13,000 rounds per day) would have been available. This meant utter exhaustion.'[27]

The position of light industry is exemplified by the clothing sector. The following concise summary illuminates the stages experienced by almost all branches of the war economy.

Four phases of development in the clothing industry – in textiles and similarly in leather – can be clearly identified. During the last months of 1914 a crisis occurs because the stocks of the war administration have been unexpectedly quickly drained and the newly ordered goods have not yet arrived. In spring 1915 the situation improves because all industrial firms are working to capacity and the raw materials shortage is not yet alarming. In summer 1916 the constant scarcity of raw materials begins to develop into an actual lack of raw materials. Demand and production are no longer in equilibrium. To meet this situation the manufacture of substitutes is introduced, and the quality of clothing reduced. But in the main the armed forces and the civilian population have to suffer and endure shortages. This situation develops gradually into a crisis which, from the middle of 1918 onward, it seems impossible to bring under control. In October 1918 prostration is practically complete.[28]

The armaments industry was prospering even before the war.[29] It was working under a constant strain on its capacity from the day the first shot was fired until the very end of hostilities. Many metal-working firms were very soon able to switch to military requirements. The armaments industry's expansion gave an impetus to the machine industry and, after an interval, to mining. Eventually most consumer goods branches, especially those meeting military needs, shared in the war boom. Only the building trade and certain of its ancillaries, like cement manufacturers, brickworks and glass factories, had almost no part in this war-induced upswing.

By spring and summer 1915 the economy's conversion to wartime requirements appeared in large measure to have been concluded. In a report to the Council of Ministers, the central bank's governor, Popovics, referred to the positive and the negative aspects.

The picture presented by our general economic situation cannot, therefore, be described as unfavourable straightaway. The huge demands of the war economy have both directly and indirectly, served to give individual branches a stimulus. In agriculture, high incomes were earned as long as stocks were on hand. The same is true for the war industry. Even some branches of small-scale manufacture have benefited from this source of income. The allowances for the families of those who have been called up constitute a constant support for retail trade, even in regions not entirely integrated in the money economy. On the other hand some of the firms meeting commercial needs had to cut down on production – the building trade is entirely down.

The Governor began his remarks with a declaration which throws light on the problematic nature of a total war economy.

The war signifies, of course, an enormous interference with the normal run of economic life. This manifests itself in the first place through an accelerated, vast conversion of capital and labour into consumer goods. The dimensions and the duration of the war aggravate the interference and result not only in existing capital undergoing this conversion, but in a line being taken on the future as well.[30]

To this it could be objected that the 'conversion of capital and labour into consumer goods' describes a routine process, namely, the circular flow of the economy. Popovics, however, had something in mind which came to be known during the course of the war as 'depossession', meaning a faulty circular flow where the replacement of worn-out capital goods occurred either not at all or to an insufficient degree. Especially in the last two years of hostilities, the process of depossession assumed proportions that Popovics could hardly have anticipated in 1915. Further reference to this matter will be made at the close of the present chapter.

The story of strain and drain can perhaps be better portrayed at the microeconomic level, that is, by taking certain key enterprises as examples, and here it seems proper to begin with one or two representative armaments firms.

The Skodawerke, Pilsen, had done extremely well during the last pre-war years.[31] In 1913 this firm had some 9,600 employees. Admittedly this figure includes several hundred belonging to a machine factory that became amalgamated with Prager Maschinenbau AG (vormals Ruston) during the course of a reorganization in summer 1914.[32] After outbreak of war the labour force rose to 14,000, working day and night shifts. In 1915 this figure rose to 22,000; in 1916 to almost 30,000, and in 1917 it reached the peak of about 34,000. In 1918 call-up of the younger age groups reduced the numbers to 27,000.[33]

Investment expenditure increased hand in hand with the labour force. Between 1910 and 1914 Skodawerke had spent the large sum of 30 million crowns on new installations. In 1915 outlay on investment amounted to at least 20 million crowns – possibly even more, since smaller purchases were written off during the current year. However, the declining value of money has to be taken into account. The next year, investment activity was weaker, but it is still likely to have been more than 10 million crowns. 1917, a year of even greater production effort, created a record with investments exceeding 40 million crowns. A big slice of the necessary capital, 27 million crowns, came from the War Ministry as part of the so-called 'Hindenburg Programme'.[34] In 1918, the year of attrition, investment by the Empire's greatest armaments enterprise is still likely to have run at over 30 million crowns. More than two-thirds of the outlay was for the purchase of real estate and the construction of factory plant.[35] The management planned to build a locomotives factory, the output of which was to exceed the capacity of all other Austro-Hungarian undertakings.[36] The concern belonged to that category of rare birds which, in the middle of war, made preparations for a wholly uncertain future.

Starting from the second half of 1917, Skodawerke encountered growing difficulties in procuring raw materials. In the autumn, the War Ministry had to intervene on its behalf with Alpine Montan AG to ensure the delivery of half its iron requirements. Because the gun factory at Györ drew on the Pilsen works for some of its inputs, the Hungarian Iron Commission was persuaded to render assistance by occasional deliveries. Wegs rightly notes that at this stage few armaments firms were in a position to assert their claims as effectively as Skodawerke. Yet in autumn 1918, Pilsen lacked the supplies to maintain operations even on severely reduced lines.

The wartime expansion of Österreichische Waffenfabriks-Gesellschaft Steyr was not as breathtaking as that of Skodawerke. By chance a large new plant, built to replace the many scattered and smaller workshops, was ready to go into operation on the outbreak of hostilities. The new situation caused work to be continued on the old sites as well, and soon it proved possible to increase the manufacture of rifles and machine-guns to many times the previous output. In July 1917, as part of the Hindenburg Programme, the record number of 1,500 rifles was produced. In December, though, the figure fell to a mere 700 and in the final months of war to a fraction of the July total.[37] In summer 1917 Steyrwerke was struggling against ever greater shortages of coal and raw materials. From 20 November till 1 January 1918 the works had to be closed and only over a period of months did they reach full capacity again.[38] At the zenith of the armaments boom, the firm had 15,000 employees.[39] Towards the end of the war, the labour force numbered approximately 12,000 and was in part engaged on the construction of premises subsequently to be used for car manufacture. In 1918, aircraft engines and machine-guns were being produced in some of them. The total investment expenditure since the outbreak of war was estimated as having been at least 23,400 million crowns.[40] Like Skodawerke, Waffenfabriks-Gesellschaft Steyr tried to make provision for the days of peace.

The munitions factories had done excellent business prior to the outbreak of war. Hirtenberger Patronenfabrik, a firm with strong ties to Creditanstalt, employed some 3,000 workers in the last year of peace.[41] In summer 1917, when the armaments industry made its last great effort, the labour force was about 8,000 strong. In 1918 it dropped on average to the still relatively high figure of 6,500.[42] Investment activity during the war seems to have remained within narrow bounds. Nevertheless, the balance sheet figure for 1917, when output attained its best performance, was more than seven times that for 1913. G. Roth AG, Vienna, another munitions enterprise on a close footing with Creditanstalt, showed similar evidence of capacities strained to the utmost during wartime. On the other hand, in contrast to Hirtenberger, its balance sheets reveal quite hectic investment activity. The multiplicity of products manufactured at various works (in the Erdberg and Floridsdorf districts of Vienna, at Lichtenwerd, Felixdorf and Pressburg) probably account for this.[43]

From the small number of efficient engineering works it is useful to select Vereinigte Maschinenfabriken AG (vormals Skoda, Ruston, Bromovski & Ringhoffer), not least because its astonishing series of mergers have been described earlier in another connection.[44] On the eve of war, this firm, after its reorganization by Creditanstalt, seemed to have very uncertain prospects. The war was the signal for a development which none of those initiating the reorganization could have foretold in his wildest dreams. Apart from the advantages deriving from its close link with Skodawerke, the army, navy and many large armaments firms were among the most important customers of Vereinigte Maschinenfabriken. It was entrusted with equipping the new gunpowder plant Skodawerke-Wetzler AG. It had orders from the mining industry for a large number of turbo-compressors, winding-engines, sorting, extrusion and rolling plants, and steel structures. In addition, it made considerable deliveries to the foodstuffs industry, including new equipment for the Aussig and Slatenau sugar factories, which had been destroyed by fire. The slow increase in capacity, lack of skilled labour, and ever-increasing scarcity of raw materials appeared to be the only limits to its expansion. During the last two years of hostilities, new factories were built near Pilsen in order to switch to peace production soon after the war. Der Österreichische Volkswirt thought it safe to predict that, in the years ahead, Vereinigte Maschinenfabriken would enter the ranks of Europe's foremost engineering enterprises.[45]

Before leaving the microeconomic level, a look should be taken at the two most important firms in the coal and steel industry, because the latter may well be called the mainstay of any modern war economy. Prior to hostilities, the Österreichische Alpine Montan-Gesellschaft had been the Empire's most efficient steel producer. It did by far the biggest export business and in good times was able to help other metallurgical concerns with deliveries. In wartime it had to cope with greater difficulties than most other firms in heavy industry. During the early war years the management was faced with the difficult problem of recruiting new workers. Replacements were not as easy to find in the thinly-populated Styrian valleys as at the sites of the

Bohemian and Silesian coalfields and steel works. Prisoners of war were eventually taken on, but for obvious reasons their performance did not match that of indigenous labour. At a later stage, the procurement of coal caused such complications that plants, particularly in 1918, could be kept running only at irregular intervals and at extremely high cost. Constantly increasing transport difficulties were responsible for shorter or longer delays in the supply of other materials and in the delivery of finished goods. Towards the close of the war it was hardly possible to talk about rational management.[46]

Precise production figures for Alpine Montan and other major iron and steel works had to await the end of war and complete abolition of censorship. The course of development had been the same in nearly all cases. As a result of unfavourable business conditions in the preceding year and the restrictions that had to be imposed on production in the early months of war, 1914 witnessed a decline. An improvement occurred in the first few months of 1915 and reached its peak in the following year when the 1912 and 1913 figures were exceeded in all sectors (iron ore, pig-iron and steel). A setback in 1917 remained within narrow bounds. 1918 saw a catastrophic slump. Alpine Montan production fell as against 1917, by 33% in the case of iron ore, 35% in that of pig-iron, 48% in that of ingots, and 54% in that of rolled goods. One would have to 'go back to the early years of the century to find similar production figures'.[47]

This development is mirrored, although not completely faithfully, in the changes of the firm's labour force. In 1913, employment had stood at 16,000. In autumn 1914, when the initial mobilization shock had taken its toll, it stood at 11,000; next spring it mounted to 13,000.[48] The figure of some 20,000 in 1917 and 1918 included about 4,000 prisoners of war. In spring 1919 the workforce was still 12,000, although plant capacity was only utilized to a small degree.[49]

Alpine Montan's investment was remarkably low compared with the other leading armaments firms. The explanation lies in the fact that the iron boom started in spring 1915, at a time when large, unused capacities were still available. Later, when it became clear that the efficacy of war management depended to a great extent on a country's ability to produce iron in quantities as large as possible, increasing difficulties in the supply of raw materials and in transport stood in the way of fast expansion. For 1916, total investment outlay was probably some 3 million crowns, more than in the first two years of war, but considerably less than in good peace-time years.[50] In 1917, expenditure rose to almost 5.5 million crowns.[51] In 1918, it climbed to 12 million crowns. Here the particularly strong currency depreciation of that year must be borne in mind.[52] A look at the concern's investment activity during the war as a whole shows that, in real terms, it remained below the figure for 1908 to 1912.

The case of Prager Eisen-Industrie-Gesellschaft, the Empire's second biggest coal and steel works, can be dealt with briefly. Its wartime development was substantially the same as that experienced by Alpine Montan. Initial decline in production was followed in 1916 and 1917 by a marked upswing until eventually a period of strain proved to be the stage prior to complete collapse. However, changes in the scale of operations were less marked than in the case of Alpine Montan. In 1912–13, the labour force stood at 15,300. In the operating year 1917, at the zenith of development, the strength was 16,900, an increase of 10% as against Alpine Montan's 25%.[53] The 1918 decline in production compared with 1917 was 28% for pig-iron and 26% for rolled goods.[54]

What merits attention is that the two concerns, together producing more than 50% of the iron and steel output in the Austrian half of the Empire, constituted a closely-knit group. Prager Eisen had before the war acquired 5,000 shares in Alpine Montan, ensuring for itself a certain influence over policy decisions. The fact that Wilhelm Kestranek, managing director of Prager Eisen, was chairman of the Alpine Montan supervisory board, on which he sat with several prominent board members from the Bohemian undertaking including the well-known industrialists Karl and Paul Kupelwieser, created a particularly close relationship between the giants of the Austrian steel industry.[55]

In spring 1916, Kestranek, on the occasion of Alpine Montan's General Meeting, announced that before the war the two enterprises had discussed plans for amalgamation. In October 1914, a proposal along these lines had been submitted by Prager Eisen to the Ministry of Finance, but no definite answer had been received to date.[56] The Ministry had, it may be supposed, sound reasons of its own for reacting sceptically to this projected 'marriage of giants'.

Walther Federn published two articles on the subject, carefully weighing the pros and cons.[57] Did the proposed merger hold out hopes for greater division of labour and specialization? Federn's answer was in the negative because the two concerns had already been co-operating closely within the cartel. 'For various products they have gone about the exchange of quotas in such a way that only one of the two companies could make use of them. There is nothing to stop the two companies, managed as they are by almost identical boards, from undertaking further swaps whenever the need for such action should arise.' Federn dismissed the argument that 'the desire for amalgamation mainly derives from the difficulties of finding fully adequate junior staff' by pointing out that Austria continued to be able 'to part with first-class managerial staff to take charge of businesses abroad, where, indeed, they can make their way more easily.'[58]

He attached more weight to the problem of how the two firms were to obtain raw materials in the more distant future. Both were already dependent on delivery from abroad of coke, their most important resource. With pig-iron it was different. Alpine Montan enjoyed the advantage of having a rich supply of ore, while Prager Eisen's small site at Nucitz would probably be exhausted within twenty years. An amalgamation, it was feared, would lead to a gradual transfer of operations to the vicinity of the Styrian Erzberg works, and result, sooner or later, in complete abandonment of the Bohemian plants. Such a development would imply grievous discrimination against workers and tradespeople living in the Prager Eisen area. Whatever the advantages for the two groups of shareholders, they could not offer sufficient compensation. But the fundamental problem, Federn concluded, touched on the future of the cartel.

There can be no doubt but that the complete fusion would strengthen the two companies' dominance in the Austrian iron and steel industry still further. This would help to promote mergers by other large enterprises for which perhaps more natural conditions prevail. Consequently, the eventual existence of two enormous trusts and a few small, barely competitive plants might have to be envisaged.[59]

Unlike Federn, the Ministry of Trade thought the merger 'desirable', especially in view of the expected closer economic cooperation with Germany. The dangers of further monopolistic distortion and of an unfavourable influence on prices was not believed to be serious.

Substantial shifts within the iron and steel industry as against the current state of affairs will not occur. In particular, the misgivings as to whether the merger could result in a stronger monopolistic position of the two companies appear to be unfounded. Similarly, an exercise of influence over the costs of iron and steel to the disadvantage of the consumer need not be feared.[60]

Nonetheless the Minister did not think it advisable to recommend the plan during the period of hostilities. His reasoning was primarily politically motivated.

Even if the project for a merger seems harmless from the angle of objective industrial policy, this linkage inside the iron and steel world will be exposed to very acrimonious criticism from the public and especially in parliamentary circles. The public at large will without any doubt most fiercely resist the merger, being little inclined to appreciate the benefits that organization brings to bear on industry's technical development. Looking on Prager Eisen and Alpine Montan as the real protagonists of the iron and steel cartel, it will interpret this as a further step towards attainment of a monopoly status as well as an unrestricted exploitation of opportunities for profit. And it will also take exception to the enhanced power given to certain personalities whose already dominant influence inside the industry will be increased. This is the kind of sentiment, impervious to objective argument, which must at any rate be reckoned with; all the more because public opinion will dispute, *to my mind not entirely without reason*, the need for the reorganization of the companies while the war is on.[61]

The minister's view seems to have been shared by his colleagues. The amalgamation had to be postponed. The disintegration of the Empire rendered the plan obsolete.

The foregoing case-studies have been made so as to give a better idea of the conditions under which the major industries had to operate during the war. If general economic conclusions are drawn from this unrepresentative sample then it is because they are substantially confirmed by a broad collection of statistical data the main findings of which will be summarized here.[62]

The balance sheets of the armaments concerns and their associated supply firms repeatedly refer to the exceptionally heavy wear and tear on machines and other installations, due to constant shiftwork and clumsy handling of equipment by newly-recruited unskilled labour (including a rising number of women) and by prisoners of war. Most armaments firms continued to maintain a sufficiently high level of investment for their equipment to be maintained in a comparatively good state even during the last year of war. This applied to a far lesser degree in the coal and steel industry and the big machine-building enterprises.[63] For the vast majority of consumer goods plants, although they might be meeting military needs, the purchase of new equipment nearly always proved an insoluble problem. In these circumstances there could, of course, be no talk of systematic preparation for the coming tasks – however difficult to predict – of peace.[64] Perhaps the most important aspect of the so-called depossession process was the utterly inadequate investment activity.

The counterpart to this development, although it became manifest only towards the end of the war, was the worsening in the financial situation of most industrial enterprises. Initially, when employment, production and incomes broke records and the military adminis-tration seemed ready to accept the most costly tenders, broad sections of industry and trade basked in a false euphoria.[65] These records were reflected in the balance sheets of many companies in the shape of high profits (gross as well as net) and high dividend payments.[66] During 1916 the shadows closed in and the voices of those talking about the 'blessings of war' faded away. Three factors, frequently mentioned in the press are likely to have effected the change: first, raw materials shortages, higher wages and social contributions, as well as ever more frequent stoppages which, pushed up production costs; secondly, harsher tax burdens; thirdly, an increasingly effective policy of thrift by the military administration.[67]

The trend of companies' 'real net profits' has been published in a series of tables.[68] They derive from summation of the earnings statements by a selection of representative firms for the years 1913 to 1918.[69] The author's conclusions, quoted in full, are as follows:

Here now is the picture shown by the profits, and it is as varied as the variety of their components would lead one to expect. Three major categories can at any rate be distinguished. There are spheres of business whose net profit in the new economic circumstances (including the government's price controls) dwindled heavily and progressively in terms of real value – coal, other forms of mining, electricity, bricks, cement, paper, banks, transport. Then there are spheres where there occurred, temporarily at least, big real war profits – oil drilling and refining (but with a bad year caused by the Russian invasion of Galicia in 1914–15, grain mills, textiles, leather, arms and munitions, machines and locomotives, cars, chemicals. Finally there is an in-between sphere which did neither as badly as the first nor as well as the second – brewing, sugar, spirits, metal goods, glass (with the exception of the bad year 1914), and the wholesale trade.[70]

The author goes on to say that in 1918, and partly in 1917, a striking reduction in real profits becomes evident. He might have added that, *pari passu*, in many firms, the decline in profits was attended by a steep rise in bank indebtedness.[71]

To achieve something like a realistic picture of how far the process of depossession went, estimates relating to the Empire's national income and gross national product have to be added to analysis at the microeconomic level. Winkler calculates the entire war expenditure as having represented 19,300 million peace-time crowns or 77,600 million crowns at current prices.[72] This approximates to Austria-Hungary's total national income in 1914.[73] Allowing for the fact that in 1915 the national income must already have fallen somewhat, irrespective of production records in certain branches of industry, and that this development continued during the following years – particularly in the last year of war – the conclusion can be drawn that war expenditure must have claimed between a quarter and a third of the national income. Because, as Rothschild rightly says, the majority of the population was living not much above subsistence level in peacetime and there can consequently have been only few reserves to hand, a substantial consumption of real capital must have taken place.[74] Its visible manifestation was the reduction in livestock, impoverishment of the soil, depreciation of productive plant especially in industries not directly committed to the war effort, almost total depletion of raw materials, which had to be imported, shrinkage of the gold and foreign exchange reserves, and so on. The loss of life through fighting and the progressive exhaustion of the working population on the domestic front must be regarded as a loss of substance incapable of statistical calculation. What follows can do no more than to give some intimation as to the extent of human suffering caused by the war.

Shortages of foodstuffs and arbitrary retail price rises have been noted as early as the beginning of war. Only in 1915 did the Government bow to pressure of public opinion and introduce bread and flour rationing.[75] During the next two years an ever-widening circle of consumer goods was drawn into the system of state control and price regulation. Most of these measures followed hesitantly and at public insistence. Symptomatic of the inertia with which the bureaucracy approached its new organizational tasks is that the concentration of all matter relating to nutrition in the National Food Office did not take place until *late autumn* 1916, more than two years after the outbreak of war.[76]

The pressure of inflationary forces was so heavy that, regardless of steps taken by the authorities to stabilize prices and to keep demand down, the level of prices constantly moved up. It doubled, broadly speaking, every year. On the eve of the Armistice the purchasing power of the crown had been reduced to something between one-fourteenth and one-sixteenth of its pre-war value. Against this, the upward trend of wages had been very limited during the first two years of war. Not until 1917, when unrest among workers gave cause for alarm, were important wage increases conceded.[77] By June 1918 the general wage level stood between 80% and 100% above that for 1914. In view of simultaneous price rises the increase must be described as totally inadequate. The following, rather meagre statistical compilation throws some light on the movement of wages.[78]

Table 18   Weekly wages in Vienna and Environment (in crowns)

	June 1914	June 1915	June 1916	June 1917	June 1918
Printers	38	38	38	38	44
Drivers	28	34	40	46	46
Brickmakers	34	34	36	36	60
Bakers	38	39	39	56	56
Metalworkers	40	50	56	66	74

Neither the movement of nominal wages nor the calculation of real wages with the aid of price indexes elucidates the workers' actual situation.[79] Their incomes were conditioned by additional factors like overtime earnings, Sunday work, and, to an increasing degree, during the second half of the war cost of living allowances. Another factor was the establishment of canteens and other facilities in many plants essential to the war effort, so as to ensure some degree of sufficient nutrition for the labour force. Nevertheless, the rising scarcity of foodstuffs as well as of other consumer goods rendered ever more desperate the living conditions of those classes whose limited incomes debarred them from access to the black market.

A careful piece of research on the workers' situation reports the first manifestations of bitterness and resistance among the population in spring 1916.

As early as May 1916, a big street demonstration, in which 15,000 workers participated, took place at the Alpine Montan on account of the unsatisfactory food supply. In March 1916, huge hunger risings at Gablonz-Reichenberg [in northern Bohemia] lasted three days. At Pilsen, the proclamation of a state of siege and of martial law were necessary to put an end to wild demonstrations and the plunder of business premises. At the Poldi works in Kladno [Bohemia], a three hours' strike because of inadequate rations was followed by demonstrations repeated towards the end of the year on a far bigger scale. At Steyr, famine led to severe pillaging. In April 1917, a hunger-strike broke out at Warnsdorf. At the same time, work stoppages occurred at Prague because for a week not a gramme of flour and for several days no bread had been on sale. In Vienna itself markets were very often the scenes of noisy demonstrations by women shoppers.[80]

Many expected that the National Food Office, established at the end of 1916, would take upon itself a more equitable distribution of foodstuffs and a reduction of the swiftly rising food prices. 'These prices,' wrote Walther Federn in his review of the year 1916, could come about only in the always insufficiently supplied markets where the buyer was at the mercy of the seller, where whoever had the necessary purchasing power was prepared to pay any and every price for essentials, often even for inessentials, which would no more than have assuaged the most crying hunger of others who saw themselves excluded because they could not compete with the offers accepted by luckier and more ruthless individuals. Profiteering has been more injurious to the broad masses of the population than the actual shortage of foodstuffs. Rational administration and distribution of stocks could put an end to that.[81]

Unfortunately neither the new National Food Office nor its successor, the Ministry of Food, were in a position to fulfil Federn's two demands, namely, more equitable distribution of the food reserves and containment of the price excesses. Löwenfeld-Russ thinks that the basic trouble lay with the price policy of the government, which lacked the courage to adjust official prices to the state of the market.

The greater the shortage of goods on the one hand and the higher the rate of inflation on the other, the less courage the government mustered to adjust official farm prices to prevailing conditions. The bigger became the gap, therefore, between the official price and the free, i.e., black market, rate. That in turn caused an even wider spread of black market practices, whereby ever larger amounts of stocks were withdrawn from official control, and the latter's social objective, equal distribution, was ever more strongly foiled. These mistakes in price policy and their consequences became more and more conspicuous especially during the second half of 1917 and then in 1918.[82]

In Austria, the black market assumed larger dimensions than in most other belligerent countries.[83] Primarily it was a manifestation of the ever more evident shortages, particularly during the later stages of the war, in practically all essential goods. The ubiquity of the evil made its criminal prosecution a completely hopeless endeavour. Soon after Emperor Charles' succession, an effort was made to set a resounding example by the public denunciation of a well-known personality in the financial world. The Kranz Case, like so many other less spectacular ones of this kind, simply revealed the inability of the authorities to enforce respect for legal rules which ran counter to basic human instincts in a situation of acute scarcity.[84]

The growing unrest among the workers culminated in the great wave of strikes in January 1918. They brought the Empire to the verge of economic breakdown. Even previously it had hardly been possible to speak of normal working conditions in the armaments plants and the other important war industries. Most reports told of the failing strength of the workforce, of frequent work interruptions, and of managements' efforts to ensure food supplies, however inadequate, to their employees. A survey of the situation by a major machine-building factory in 1918 describes the exhaustion of industry and its most important resource – human labour.

The board explains the unsatisfactory business result by way of the well-known complaints, recurrent in all industrial reports, of operational difficulties due to lack of materials and their increasing cost. The lack of fuel, particularly, led to stoppages during which the employees had to be kept on the payroll by government decree, thus causing the enterprise further sacrifices. *Regardless of these concessions already made by the company, there were repeated strikes caused by the inadequate food situation as well as by a continuous series of wage claims leading, under the pressure of the Complaints Commissions instituted for enterprises under military control, to precipitous wage rises.* The need also emerged to incur considerable expenditure for the salaries and higher living allowances made to the company's officials. . . . Apart from these circumstances, affecting the financial yield on a large number of products, *the result of the constantly falling performance by the labour force is that the enormously inflated overhead costs, which include substantial outlays and charges for the alimentation of the company's employees, have to be set against a smaller output.*[85]

Yet even in this doomsday mood, the indestructible Austrian sense of humour bubbled over on occasion. On 18 June 1918 Josef Redlich noted in his diary that the following 'Creed' was doing the rounds in the offices:

I believe in the Lord Minister of Food and in the early turnip, provider of the rationed nation's masses, from which alone all blessings flow. I believe in the cognate beet and swede, received from the Holy Food Administration, endured by the Central Buying Association, stored, pressed, spoiled, dropped to the ground and on the third day resurrected as jam, whence it shall come as ambrosia to the long lines of queuing starvelings. I believe in sacred gain and profit, in the universal racketeering community of hoarders, in an increase of taxes, in higher prices for meat, and in the eternal state of war. Amen.[86]

Notes

1 Kurt W. Rothschild, 'Wurzeln und Triebkräfte der österreichischen Wirt-schaftsstruktur', *Österreichs Wirtschaftsstruktur: Gestern – Heute – Morgen* (Berlin, 1961), p. 59.

2 Cf. Part II, Chap. 1, p. 114.

3 The successes in Galicia were however offset by Italy's declaration of war in May 1915. The emergence of a third (southern) front naturally had negative effects on the combat strength of the Imperial Army elsewhere.

4 The facts quoted here are mainly taken from Löwenfeld-Russ, *Die Regelung der Volksernährung im Kriege* (Vienna, 1926).

5 Cf. Part II, Chap. 1, p. 116.

6 Cf. Gustav Gratz and Richard Schüller, *Der wirtschaftliche Zusammenbruch Österreich-Ungarns* (Vienna, 1930), pp. 42–5.

7 'The longer the war lasted, the more the egotism and the hostility of individuals and of groups against whose particularist interests the basic idea of the (control) system contravened had to be reckoned with. And even a much more systematic and better trained administration, given a homogeneous population, would not have been able to overcome their resistance.' Löwenfeld-Russ, *Die Regelung*, p. 83.

8 Cf. Löwenfeld-Russ, *Die Regelung*, p. 61, for the statistical evidence.

9 Löwenfeld-Russ, *Die Regelung*, p. 61 et seq. (The italics are in the original text.)

10 Cf. *Statistische Nachrichten*, published by the Statistische Zentralkommission, July 1915, and Gustav Stolper, 'Eine amtliche Teuerungsstatistik', *Der Österreichische Volkswirt*, 18 September 1915, p. 845.

11 Cf. Löwenfeld-Russ, *Die Regelung*, p. 73.

12 Emperor Charles' remarks, as reported in his diary by the well-known specialist in public law, political expert, and cabinet minister Josef Redlich (1869–1936), may be regarded as characteristic of the situation in summer 1917: 'The emperor discussed the war situation and the need to attain peace with extreme liveliness. Once more it was clear that the Hindenburg policy of "sticking it out" is odious to him because in his opinion it would be futile. He spoke with the utmost emphasis about our losses which totalled 25% of the Empire's able-bodied male population whose working capacity has over and above this been reduced to half. I observed the influence of Prof. Tandler's ideas.' 'On this occasion the emperor stressed again, as in Baden, that our nation's masses were in every respect unsurpassable, so courageous at the front, so patient back home. Only twice had there been firing during the hunger demonstrations, once at Prossnitz and now at Witkowitz, and that, said the emperor,' had always been the fault of inexperienced soldiers. Josef Redlich, *Schicksalsjahre Österreichs, 1908–1919* (Graz-Cologne, 1954), Vol. II, p. 217.

13 Gustav Stolper, 'Das ungarische Bündnisangebot', *Der Österreichische Volkswirt*, 21 February 1920, p. 393.

14 Even in 1917 the Empire's coal production was only 12% below the 1912 level. The surplus of imports over exports was in 1917 some 4.7 million tons, merely 1 million tons less than in 1913. The situation worsened in 1918, but not dramatically. Cf. Gratz and Schüller, *Der wirtschaftliche Zusammenbruch*, p. 92 et seq.

15 In winter 1917–18 even the Steyr armaments works, in spite of their key position in the war economy, could no longer get a sufficient supply of coal. Gratz and Schüller, *Der Wirtschaftliche Zusammenbruch*, p. 96.

16 Until 1918, when signs of exhaustion became clear, a not unimportant factor in the ability of coal-mining to maintain a comparatively high level of output may well have been the special efforts of management to supply sufficient food for the

workers. As early as 1915 certain big firms instituted 'Works Supply-Points' where the sale and delivery of foodstuffs was entrusted to the works administration. After the introduction of rationing miners, like heavy workers in other industries, 'became officially entitled to amounts extra to normal rations'. On further measures in this respect, see Ferdinand Hanusch and Emanuel Adler, *Die Regelung der Arbeitsverhältnisse im Kriege* (Vienna-New Haven, 1927), p. 212 et seq. .

17 Haus, Hof, und Staatsarchiv, PA XL, Carton 314, Council of Ministers Minutes, 28 June 1917.

18 The following details derive mainly from Gratz and Schüller, *Der wirtschaftliche Zusammenbruch*, p. 97 et seq., Heinrich Mejzlik, *Die Eisenbewirtschaftung im Ersten Weltkrieg* (Vienna, 1977), and James Robert Wegs, *Austrian Economic Mobilization during World War I, with Particular Emphasis on Heavy Industry* (dissertation, University of Illinois, 1970).

19 In 1914 the Empire's steel production totalled some 2 million tons, an amount about 500,000 tons below that for 1913. In 1916 it rose to 3.3 million tons. In 1917, irrespective of growing demand, it declined to 2.9 million tons and in 1918 to 1.7 million tons, i.e., below the 1914 level. Gratz and Schüller, *Der wirtschaftliche Zusammenbruch*, p. 97. The War Ministry's official production data differ negligibly from these figures. Cf., Mejzlik, *Die Eisenbewirtschaftung*, p. 216.

20 For the prevalent view in Germany, see Mejzlik, *Die Eisenbewirtschaftung*, p. 41.

21 Gratz and Schüller say that in autumn 1914 a number of furnaces were extinguished. *Der wirtschaftliche Zusammenbruch*, p. 99.

22 See Mejzlik, *Die Eisenbewirtschaftung*, p. 43.

23 'Zinc and lead, for example, were initially substituted for copper. When however this too ran out, it had to be replaced by iron.' 'The military administration resisted for a long time the substitution of iron and steel for copper in munitions because it feared a loss in munitions production due to the difficult processing of iron and steel. Now, at the close of 1916, this measure had also to be introduced. The copper components of machines standing in factories were likewise requisitioned, and in 1916 recourse was taken to church bells and lightning-conductors.' Gratz and Schüller, *Der wirtschaftliche Zusammenbruch*, pp. 104 and 107.

24 Efforts to constitute an Iron Control Office went back to summer 1916, but only at the beginning of October was a beginning made on the War Ministry department to which in mid-November a number of officers and secretaries were posted. This staff soon proved inadequate and in 1917 was much expanded. Mejzlik, *Die Eisenbewirtschaftung*, pp. 50–51.

25 Cf. Gratz and Schüller, *Der wirtschaftliche Zusammenbruch*, p. 103 and Mejzlik, *Die Eisenbewirtschaftung*, p. 51.

26 Gratz and Schüller, *Der wirtschaftliche Zusammenbruch*, p. 105.

27 Gratz and Schüller, *Der wirtschaftliche Zusammenbruch*, p. 105. The Hungarian Prime Minister, Count Tisza, who seems at the beginning of 1917 to have realized perfectly well that the Empire did not possess the industrial capacity to meet the increased material requirements of modern warfare, had an altercation on the subject with the chief of the general staff, Conrad von Hötzendorf. The latter naively argued that Austria-Hungary's resources were unbounded. See Wegs, *Austrian Economic Mobilization*, p. 167 et seq.

28 Gratz and Schüller, *Der wirtschaftliche Zusammenbruch*, p. 124 et seq.

29 Cf. Part I, Chap. 1, p. 9 et seq.

30 Haus, Hof, und Staatsarchiv, PA XL, K.312, Council of Ministers Minutes, 18 June 1915.

31 Cf. Part I, Chap. 1, p. 9 et seq.

32 Cf. Part I, Chap. 1, p. 10 et seq.

33 These facts and those that follow are taken from balance sheet reports quoted in *Der Österreichische Volkswirt*, 22 April 1916, 16 April 1917, and 27 April 1918.

34 Wegs reports that in the period between 1 November 1916 and April 1917 the War Ministry spent a sum of 454,472,039 crowns to increase the production of arms and munitions. The expenditure took the form of outright gifts and subsidies. A number of the bigger items contained grants-in-aid for the gunpowder factories at Blumau, Pressburg, and Magyar-Ovar; for the purchase of machines for the munitions factory at Wöllersdorf; for the construction of workers' houses on behalf of the arms works at Steyr; for additional premises to the artillery plant at Brünn; and for a multiplicity of investments in the occupied territories. The greatest amount of all was invested by the War Ministry in Skodawerke at Pilsen and Ungarische Kanonenfabrik at Györ – 27,077,000 crowns in the former, 32,049,200 crowns in the latter. Wegs, *Austrian Economic Mobilization*, p. 166.

35 'Die Bilanzen', *Der Österreichische Volkswirt*, 17 April 1918, p. 141.

36 Wegs, *Austrian Economic Mobilization*, p. 170.

37 Wegs, *Austrian Economic Mobilization*, p. 169.

38 'Die Bilanzen', *Der Österreichische Volkswirt*, 26 October 1918, p. 13.

39 *Der Österreichische Volkswirt*, 29 September 1917, p. 281.

40 *Der Österreichische Volkswirt*, 26 October 1918, p. 14.

41 Cf. Part I, Chap. 1, p. 10.

42 'Die Bilanzen', *Der Österreichische Volkswirt*, 17 August 1918, p. 263.

43 *Österreichische Volkswirt*, 11 August 1917, p. 251.

44 Cf. Part I, Chap. 1, p. 11.

45 'Die Bilanzen', *Der Österreichische Volkswirt*, 4 November 1916, p. 17 et seq., and 21 September 1918, p. 281 et seq.

46 *Der Österreichische Volkswirt*, 23 March 1918, p. 100.

47 *Der Österreichische Volkswirt*, 5 April 1919, p. 101.

48 *Der Österreichische Volkswirt*, 20 March 1915, p. 93.

49 *Der Österreichische Volkswirt*, 5 April 1919, p. 102.

50 *Der Österreichische Volkswirt*, 10 March 1917, p. 91.

51 *Der Österreichische Volkswirt*, 23 March 1918, p. 102.

52 *Der Österreichische Volkswirt*, 5 April 1919, p. 103.

53 *Der Österreichische Volkswirt*, 12 October 1918, p. 7.

54 *Der Österreichische Volkswirt*, 8 November 1919, p. 21.

55 These facts are taken from a memorandum initialled by Alexander Spitzmüller and giving his views on the planned amalgamation in his capacity as Minister of Finance. Finanzarchiv, File 79129/16.

56 Cf., 'Die Fusion der Alpinen Montan-Gesellschaft mit der Prager Eisenindustrie-Gesellschaft', *Neue Freie Presse*, 5 April 1916.

57 'Das Fusionsprojekt Prager Eisen-Alpine Montangesellschaft', *Der Österreichische Volkswirt*, 15 April 1916, p. 477 et seq.

58 *Der Österreichische Volkswirt*, p. 478.

59 *Österreichische Volkswirt*, p. 479.

60 Finanzarchiv, File 79129/16, Folio 15.

61 Finanzarchiv, File 79129/16, Folio 17, p. 16. The italics are the author's. Spitzmüller, in another part of the memorandum, says that 'the carrying out of extensive financial transactions in the industrial capital market at the present time or indeed during the war must definitely be treated with reserve.' Folio 17, p. 18. The next chapter of the present study deals with the capital market situation.

62 Wilhelm Winkler, *Die Einkommensverschiebungen in Österreich während des Krieges* (Vienna, 1930), p. 165 et seq.

63 The picture drawn by a balance sheet expert with respect to the well-known firm Maschinenbau AG, vorm. Breitfeld, Danek & Co., Prague was probably typical for the situation of the machine construction industry as a whole. 'There is no mention whatever of any significant investment activity at Breitfeld-Danek during the war,' although it was engaged to full capacity on the fulfilment of military orders. See 'Die Bilanzen', *Der Österreichische Volkswirt*, 28 October 1916, p. 15.

64 Notable exceptions like Skodawerke and Steyrwerke have been cited.

65 During the harsh winter of 1916 no less sensitive a personality than Walther Federn voiced satisfaction at the state of business affairs. 'In spite of indignation at those who profiteer from the war, contentment can still be felt that such a boom is possible in wartime, seeing how it had been thought that the whole economic mechanism would break down and famine would within a few months follow on the outbreak of hostilities.' See 'Österreich-Ungarn zum Jahreswechsel', *Der Österreichische Volkswirt*, 30 December 1916, p. 209.

66 Some managements tried to conceal the high dividend distributions by carrying out fictitious capital increases. Such, for example, was the case with Skodawerke when in autumn 1916 the dividend was raised from 34 crowns to 56 crowns. 'Such an increase was announced and the preliminary arrangements made last autumn through the transfer of the capital reserve fund to the share capital account. The point of this purely formal transaction could only be, as we said at the time, to allocate to shareholders a larger portion of the earnings without having to put up the dividend percentage excessively . . . On the nominal capital of 320 crowns, generated without fresh payment by the shareholders, the distributed dividend of 56 crowns amounts to 17.5% whereas the dividend of 34 crowns distributed in the foregoing year on the nominal capital was 17%.' 'Die Bilanzen', *Der Österreichische Volkswirt*, 14 April 1917, p. 127.

67 Winkler thinks that this return to a policy of thrift is also confirmed by official documents. He quotes the reply to a request along these lines from the Prime Minister given in 1916 by the Minister of War on steps taken during the summer in this direction. Cf. Winkler, *Die Einkommenverschiebungen*, p. 172. Similarly Walther Federn wrote that 'In a number of instances the course of the war has enabled the military administration to reach a conclusion as to the fairness of prices. Many suppliers cannot any longer obtain the same high prices as they did during the early months when in the whirlwind of events the military lacked any trained staff to enforce reasonable prices for their mass purchases and simply had to give priority to delivery at top speed, irrespective of all other considerations. That was when spongers of the worst sort managed to infiltrate. Today they probably have no more than occasional opportunity to pocket uncalled-for middlemen's profits.' Cf. 'Österreich-Ungarn zum Jahreswechsel', *Der Öster-*

reichische Volkswirt, 30 December 1916, p. 207.

68 'Real net profits' means profits in terms of the crown's purchasing power. For the calculation of this index cf. the following chapter.

69 See Winkler, *Die Einkommenverschiebungen*, pp. 166 et seq. A selection of the tables is reproduced in Appendix II.

70 Winkler, *Die Einkommenverschiebungen*, p. 171.

71 A passage in a commentary on the Alpine Montan 1918 balance sheet says, 'Currently the three major Niederösterreichische Escompte-Gesellschaft concerns, Prager Eisenindustrie-Gesellschaft, Alpine and Poldi-Hütte, owe their bank some 160 million crowns. Both for the bank and its debtors that is of course, in view of the small prospect for a complete change of circumstances within a foreseeable time, a thoroughly unsatisfactory situation. For Alpine, which now works at an operating loss, these loans constitute a heavy burden. That is why the company, just like Poldi-Hütte, is setting about the reduction of its bank debt by the issue of new shares.' 'Die Bilanzen', *Der Österreichische Volkswirt*, 5 April 1919, p. 103.

72 Cf. Winkler, *Die Einkommenverschiebungen*, p. 231. Winkler made a detailed calculation for individual expenditure categories for Austria and a global estimate for Hungary. Gratz and Schüller, with the assistance of the Winkler method, computed the Empire's total war costs to have been 81,000 million Crowns.

73 Cf. Rothschild, *Österreichs Wirtschaftsstruktur*, p. 60.

74 Cf. Rothschild, *Österreichs Wirtschaftsstruktur*, p. 61.

75 Cf. Part II, Chap. 1.

76 Cf. Löwenfeld-Russ, *Die Regelung*, p. 51. The author adds that only in autumn 1916 did the move towards expanding the control system acquire breadth and depth. 'It will do to quote here a few of the most important measures of this period when the whole problem of foodstuffs control became ever more menacing. Sale of cattle was systematically regulated with application of sanctions and with price ceilings (May 1917). For fats and meat the way led eventually via all manner of restrictions on consumption (meatless days, and so on) to the setting of price ceilings (July 1916) and of ration ceilings in the various provinces (April 1917) to the procurement and distribution of meat in specially created organizations . . . Difficulties in the supply of fruit and vegetables resulted in control of this category also . . . The constantly growing impediments to obtaining basic supplies in the foodstuffs sector rendered necessary official measures for the compressed yeast, coffee substitutes, malt and brewing industry.' *Die Regelung*, p. 57.

77 The establishment by imperial ordinance on 18 March 1917 of the Wages and Grievance Commission can be regarded as a turning-point in the history of wartime labour conditions. 'In the final stage . . . the ever more hopeless military outlook undermined respect for authority and strengthened trade union influence as manifested in repeated and successful strikes for higher wages.' Winkler, *Die Einkommenverschiebungen*, p. 140.

78 See Benedikt Kautsky, 'Löhne und Gehälter', *Geldwert und Stabilisierung in ihren Einflüssen auf die soziale Entwicklung in Österreich* (Verein für Sozialpolitik publications series, Vol. XCLIX, Munich 1925).

79 For tables on the development of real wages during the war, see Winkler, *Die Einkommenverschiebungen*, p. 142 et seq.

80 See *Die Regelung der Arbeitsverhältnisse im Kriege*, edited by Ferdinand Hanusch and Emanuel Adler (Vienna-New Haven, 1927), p. 261.

81 'Österreich-Ungarn zum Jahreswechsel', *Der Österreichische Volkswirt*, 30 December 1916, p. 207.
82 Löwenfeld-Russ, *Die Regelung*, p. 78.
83 Löwenfeld-Russ, *Die Regelung*, p. 96 et seq.
84 Redlich noted in his diary, 'Koerber has learned that Dr Kranz is being indicted at the Emperor's express wish. Until now, they say, powerful patronage – allegedly Archduchess Maria Theresia and Spitzmüller – contrived to shield this daring financial adventurer. The government has in five strenuous sessions adopted an ordinance on profiteering to be published shortly. I hear from Fritz that yesterday the police seized the Fanto Petroleum Company's books. Evidently the aristocratic junta is trying to cover up its purely absolutist schemes and *coup d'état* ideas by a pretence of paternally protecting ordinary folk, whom it is impudently depriving of all their constitutional rights, against exploitation by the rich.' Redlich, *Schicksalsjahre*, p. 195. Reference to the Kranz Case occurs in the next chapter.
85 See 'Maschinenbau A.G. vormals Breitfeld, Danek & Co. in Prag', 'Die Bilanzen', *Der Österreichische Volkswirt*, 5 October 1918, p. 2. (Italics by the present author)
86 Redlich, *Schicksalsjahre*, p. 282.

CHAPTER 2

Meeting the Cost of Total War

The Empire's outlay on armaments during the last years of peace had risen steeply. At the outset of hostilities, expenditure exploded.[1] Its nominal increase continued in the following years to be high. Yet in real terms, according to Winkler's calculations, it receded annually by some 20%. If total military outlay for 1914–15 in million peace-time crowns is put at 100, then the figure for 1917–18 was no more than 39. This demonstrates the catastrophic shrinkage of the Empire's staying-power.[2]

To war costs proper were added the costs incidental to war – outlay by the civil authorities on governmental controls, the transport system, the growing burdens of servicing the War Loan, the payments to soldiers' families (which in Austria were far higher than in Hungary), the pensions for dependents of the war dead, and so on. The Empire, like the other major belligerents, adopted from the start the expedient of seeking to finance war costs and their incidentals by way of loans and recourse to the central bank, while trying to meet routine expenditure via taxation. As the war proceeded, even this modest objective proved incapable of realization.

The calculations of Teleszky and Winkler on Austria-Hungary's war costs do not entirely tally. Winkler presents the following picture for the period from July 1914 until June 1918:

Table 19   War expenditure (in million crowns)

	Austria	Hungary
Quota Contributions	39,000	23,000
War Wounded	730	35
Refugees	1,900	90
Maintenance Contributions	7,000	3,400
Reconstruction in War-Devastated Areas	700	90
War Debt Services	3,500	1,500
Total	52,830	28,025

These figures put total expenditure at 81,000 million crowns. Teleszky arrives at the far higher figure of 90,000 million crowns. The difference is partly explicable through Teleszky taking into account items not included by Winkler. Both methods of calculation were closely scrutinized by Gratz and Schüller, and they seem to incline more towards Teleszky's conclusions.[3]

The Central Powers' war expenditure is known to have amounted to hardly half that of the Entente.[4] This may be regarded as economy in the conduct of hostilities. But this economy did not derive from self-imposed discipline, but from limitation of the material resources at the disposal of the Central Powers. Austria-Hungary, moreover, held a modest place beside its German ally, inasmuch as its military outlay represented barely a quarter of the resources raised by its northern neighbour. It should not be overlooked that by the end of the first war year, the Entente's blockade was already making itself very distinctly felt, and that in due course it led to a total isolation of the Central Powers. The latter could count upon only scanty additional resources from outside their own dominions, in so far as they were able to occupy foreign territory and to maintain some economic contact with the few neutral countries.[5]

The early months of the hostilities pressaged the method of financing military expenditure, which was practically identical among all the major belligerents. The need to have, overnight as it were, large masses of men properly equipped at the front, and to furnish them with armaments and other supplies requisite to the conduct of modern warfare, faced the military authorities with an enormous need for ready money. That the capacity of the central banks to create money should have been turned to account by all the countries involved in this emergency, and that they did not stand on much ceremony as regards any rules to the contrary, can cause little surprise.[6] The technique employed to this end by Austria-Hungary has been described earlier.[7] It suffices to recall that even prior to the suspension of the Bank Act, the financial authorities had to have recourse *indirectly*, i.e., via the big banks, to the central bank's resources. As early as 14 August, the first major direct loan operation between the Empire's two governments and the Austro-Hungarian Bank took place. In October, the bank extended a second loan. Like the first, it took the form of comparatively short-term credit.[8]

In summer 1915, the pleasant illusion that the conflict would last only a short time finally had to be abandoned. This more sober assessment of the situation was demonstrated by the agreement signed on 15 July between the financial authorities and the central bank. It resulted in a new method of raising money which became standard for the remainder of the war. Loans were now put on the footing of promissory notes bearing interest at 1% per annum. No repayment date, says Popovics, could be fixed in light of the previously extended loans. 'It was agreed to begin and to conclude negotiations within six months of the armistice, which would finally settle the modalities and dates for the repayment of these loans.'[9]

Mention must also be made of a procedure giving the central bank a certain, if modest, part in containing the constantly swelling flood of banknotes. In spring 1918, interest-bearing certificates of deposit with three or six months' maturity were issued, their proceeds going to the credit of the two governments' current accounts.

By 26 October 1918, according to Popovics, the central bank's claims against the two governments stood as follows:[10]

Table 20   *Austro-Hungarian Bank claims against Austria and Hungary*

	Austria	Hungary
Syndicate Loans	510,000,000	297,500,000
Loans against Collateral	1,272,000,000	728,000,000
Promissory Notes	1,780,800,000	1,019,200,000
Certificates of Indebtedness	19,634,000,000	6,798,000,000
Certificates of Deposit	1,862,997,276	1,066,243,724
Total	25,059,797,276	9,908,943,724

The two Ministries of Finance, as has been seen, had made preparations at an early stage for the issue of a War Loan.[11] In this they followed the example of Germany, which by September 1914 had adopted the course of skimming off the high liquidity emanating from central bank financing. Britain, Italy and Russia, on the heels of Germany and Austria-Hungary, floated war loans with varying degrees of success. In France, short term *Obligations de la Défense nationale* served their turn until autumn 1915. At that relatively late date the government turned to the public for subscription to a 'funding loan'.[12] Hardach rightly remarks that a rhythm of creating and reducing liquidity was characteristic for war financing as practised in the First World War.[13] In Austria-Hungary and in Germany, though, the process was far more regular than in either Britain or France. Altogether eight War Loans were floated at fairly regular intervals in the Austrian half of the Monarchy. The face value of the securities totalled 35,129,324,600 crowns. The net proceeds were

32,955,576,900 crowns and corresponded to an average rate of issue of 93.8%.[14]

The table below shows that the nominal receipt from War Loan issues could be increased almost constantly. Exceptions were the fifth and the eighth issues, when subscriptions remained well below expectations. On the basis of purchasing power at 1 July 1914, results were fairly satisfactory only in 1914 and 1915. Thereafter they fell further and further below the record figures for the initial years. Increasingly, especially in 1917 and 1918, recourse had to be made to the printing-press.

Table 21   Subscriptions to Austrian War Loans, 1914–18

	Face Value in crowns	Nom. Sub. Index	Purchasing Power at 1 July 1914[a]	Real Proceeds Index
First Issue	2,220,746,900	100	1,805,485,300	100
Second Issue	2,688,321,800	121	1,609,773,500	89
Third Issue	4,203,061,900	189	1,859,761,900	103
Fourth Issue	4,520,292,000	204	1,302,677,800	72
Fifth Issue	4,467,940,000	201	752,178,500	42
Sixth Issue	5,189,066,000	234	679,197,100	38
Seventh Issue	6,045,896,000	272	731,948,700	41
Eighth Issue	5,814,000,000	262	435,832,100	24
Total	35,129,324,600		9,176,854,900	

[a] Based on the index used by Winkler (*Die Einkommensverschiebungen in Österreich*, p. 40 *et seq.*) for the cost of living without rents. Winkler used the consumer price index calculated at the beginning of the twenties by the 'Parity Commission' on Wages and Prices, which the Federal Statistical Office reckoned back to July 1914.

The real proceeds shown above deviate from Winkler (p. 78) inasmuch as in certain instances the purchasing power for two months was computed.

Even the comparatively modest results of the past issues could be attained only by stronger involvement on the part of the institutional investors, in particular the major banks. At the outset the share of the institutional investors had been 40.6% of total subscriptions. In the eighth issue it amounted to some 58.5%.[15] For the first issue there had been almost 55,000 subscriptions by small savers for totals up to 100 crowns. For the second issue the figure dropped drastically, but rose, thanks to the banks' intensive promotional efforts, to 145,000 subscriptions for the third issue. The peak of 258,000 subscriptions for amounts up to 100 crowns was achieved with the fourth issue. Then there was a steep decline in the number of small savers, as they became ever more badly affected by the growing cost of living.[16]

In Hungary, Gratz and Schüller report seventeen War Loan issues.

Thirteen were open to public subscription; four were placed directly by the banks. The proceeds totalled a face value of 18,851,835,850 (net 17,955,885,538) crowns. The average rate of issue was 95.4%.[17] The subscription results were somewhat poorer than in Austria, although the Hungarian securities could, by agreement with the Austrian administration, be placed to some extent in the Austrian market. This simply conformed to an old practice. In pre-war days Hungary had repeatedly had to tap the greater financial strength of Austria.

In April 1916, when the Fourth War Loan was issued, the authorities managed to overcome the resistance of the National Debt Control Commission to the flotation of long-term bonds. Subscribers were offered the choice between 5½% bonds with forty years' maturity, and 5½% treasury bills redeemable within seven years. The price of the bonds was 93, that for the bills 95.5.[18] The procedure of issuing a part of the War Loan as short-term treasury bills was retained until the end of hostilities because it matched the need of the money institutions and commercial firms for an investment which did not permanently immobilize their resources.

The Sixth War Loan saw the introduction of a new feature, the so-called War Loan Insurance. It guaranteed that on expiry of the bond's term the amount would be paid either to the subscriber or, in the event of his prior decease, to his family.[19]

Until the recall of parliament in spring 1917, the government did not have to submit a clear financial programme. On 14 June 1917, Spitzmüller, then Minister of Finance, made public the outlines of such a programme during the course of a major budget speech. He showed himself fully satisfied with the success of subscriptions to the War Loan:

Our financial soundness especially — and that, I may surely say to the surprise of our enemies abroad particularly — has been demonstrated by the fact that we have been able to meet the cost of hostilities mainly by the War Loans subscribed at home. The calls on the central bank in the shape of borrowings are far lower than the sums raised by the War Loans.[20]

At this time, such a view could be held with some claim to plausibility. The state's liabilities to the central bank totalled around 10,000 million crowns while the six War Loans had brought receipts of about 23,000 million crowns.[21] Not until autumn 1917 did the government's indebtedness snowball into an avalanche. Between August and November, the bank advanced almost 3,000 million crowns. A resolution passed by parliament in November forced the government temporarily to cease to avail itself of this expedient. From March 1918 onward, though, it once more had to have recourse to the central bank each month – and sometimes even twice a month.[22] At the time of making his speech, Spitzmüller could have no idea that during the summer months of 1917 there would occur a change in the character as well as the speed of inflationary development.

The war, as the minister told parliament, had broken normal budget bounds. Nevertheless, the government thought that it must do without tapping new sources of revenue. Its efforts were on the whole confined to temporary surcharges on certain important levies like income tax, profits tax on joint-stock companies, land tax, and so on.[23] This method had to be adopted, Spitzmüller explained, because it was a matter of 'provisional decrees and emergency ordinances', and because there were 'certain limits set to the government's activity in this respect'.[24] An exception, he added, was 'the railway transport tax'.

All the same, he plainly intimated that the public should not expect that the problems caused by the war would be solved by improvisation in the long run. The state, apart from the necessity for paying off the large burden of debts, had to assume the task of extending active assistance to those categories of the population worst hit by the long years of conflict. 'Above all, the Minister of Finance will have to make money available where the regeneration of our national strength – and this in the widest sense of the term – is at stake.' Included among the groups of the population needing aid were not only the war injured, the refugees and the dependants of those in the field, but also those in business who had to be reintegrated into the economic process and to whom the state proposed to offer financial aid in one form or another. 'I may say', Spitzmüller concluded in this part of his speech, 'that through these advances and guarantee operations, which are spread over a very broad front, properly speaking a new budget emerges alongside the normal one . . . They are not, however, outlays that directly appertain to the budget. Our hope is that a large part of these guarantees will not be called upon and that a portion of the advances will gradually flow back.'[25]

What were the methods whereby Spitzmüller thought that he could restore financial soundness? He took the understandable view that it would require a great measure of readiness for sacrifice on the part of the nation. These sacrifices should, however, be distributed equitably as far as possible, among all classes:

Probably a system of taxation on consumption and spending, worked out in detail, will be unavoidable. I am aware that this step cannot be taken before a tax on property has been introduced, because the burden of such a system, inasmuch as the broad mass of people will be affected to greater or lesser degree, would be unacceptable unless property were taxed too, though not excessively.[26]

It has previously been mentioned that as early as February 1915, Karl Renner had raised the question of a tax on property.[27] A considerable number of politicians and financial experts had since spoken on the subject and a clear difference of opinions had evolved.[28] Spitzmüller in his speech took sides with the principle of a non-recurrent, radical and progressive levy, but he qualified the statement by adding:

The tax on property must be such that it does not impede the productivity of our capital and our economy in such a way that reconstruction would suffer any handicap. It must be so constructed as not to interfere with, or at any rate alter intrinsically, the hitherto existing relations between the various categories of capital.[29]

The minister announced that his department had a thorough investigation of the subject in hand and he closed his remarks with a forceful admonition.

That is why I must warn against eulogizing the terms 'non-recurrent property tax', 'major radical, progressively rising property tax' into a panacea for all disasters. Not, gentlemen, that I therewith reject the levy on property. On the contrary, I am convinced that we need an extraordinary measure commensurate with the budget situation as with the altogether special currency predicaments.[30]

Spitzmüller's declaration made plain where he stood in Austrian political life. Henceforth he was viewed as a conservative with pronounced social leanings. This lost him the sympathy of many influential circles and led to a political isolation about which he wrote – occasionally with bitter resignation – in his memoirs.[31]

Disclosure to the lower house of the state's enormous burden of debt did not bring any intrinsic change in the methods of war financing. The printing-press remained the most important source of money. Taxation was of secondary importance. Cover for the ever-increasing deficit in the balance of payments had, as said earlier, to be found along more traditional lines.[32] The Entente Powers' blockade had an extremely drastic effect on the Empire's economy, particularly during the last two years of hostilities. Nonetheless it proved possible to import considerable quantities of foodstuffs and other consumer goods from neutral countries. Germany, an important supplier of coal, raw materials, and industrial goods throughout the conflict, was the Empire's chief commercial partner. The control over trade was so lax, however, that until towards the close of 1916 imports of high-class luxury goods like carpets, lace, jewellry, watches, quality furs, scents and similar articles were comparatively easy to obtain.[33] In spring 1917, after the entry of the United States into the war and the complete stoppage of remittances by emigrants, the balance of payments situation became so grave that 'as a matter of principle every import of goods was made contingent on a special permit by the Ministry of Finance'.[34]

Foreign debts could be paid by drawing on the stocks of gold and foreign currencies held by the central bank. The latter had in August 1914 already made international transfers subject to far-reaching restrictions. At the beginning of 1916, Foreign Exchange Agencies (whose original conception and subsequent development will be dealt with later) were instituted at Vienna and Budapest. The prolongation of hostilities and the dwindling of the central bank's gold and foreign exchange reserves placed the Empire in a growing state of dependence on loan operations in Germany and the neutral countries. Sales of securities (War Loan) abroad and the export of crowns played some part, although a subordinate one.

An earlier chapter has described the November 1914 loan operations in Germany.[35] The following years saw further transactions of this kind which resulted, by the end of the war, in Austrian and Hungarian indebtedness to the tune of 2,163,960,000 and 1,336,040,000 marks respectively. The later loans, like the first, were issued in the form of one-year treasury bills whose maturities were extended by special arrangements upon expiry.[36] Yet German financial assistance, in the light of the rapidly accumulating Austro-Hungarian balance of payments deficit, was entirely inadequate. The central bank was forced to purchase larger amounts of marks through sales of gold, a circumstance, according to Popovics, 'to which is mainly to be ascribed the fact that the central bank's holdings of 1,055 million crowns in actual gold at the end of 1914 had diminished by December 1915 to 684 million crowns.'[37] At 31 October 1918, the bank's reserves had dropped still lower to 268 million crowns, whereas the notes in circulation totalled 31,500 million crowns. The banknotes had *de facto* become irredeemable currency.[38]

Under these conditions it is hardly surprising that the Austro-Hungarian ambassador to Berlin repeatedly intervened with the German Government to try and move it in the direction of a more generous credit policy. In spring 1915, Prince Hohenlohe-Schillingsfürst informed Secretary of the Treasury Helfferich of the wish of the Austrian Government to raise a loan of 1,000 million marks. The transaction would, it was hoped, contribute in some degree towards replenishing the central bank's gold stocks.[39]

Seeing that the secretary was not inclined to comply in full with his government's intentions, Hohenlohe turned directly to the Imperial Chancellor, Bethmann-Hollweg, and appealed to him in forcible terms:

I felt it . . . incumbent on me once more to draw his attention, in his capacity as the senior official of the German Empire, to the fact that in my eyes the German Government is adopting from the start an utterly inappropriate attitude in this matter of a loan, which redounds to our direct, and to Germany's indirect, disadvantage. If Herr Helfferich, as watch-dog of the Imperial German Treasury, puts the financial difficulties and the impossibility of lending German capital abroad in the foreground, then from his viewpoint, influenced as it is mainly by financial considerations, this is comprehensible. In reality, though, political interests are paramount here. I simply cannot believe that Germany is not in a position to extend a larger-scale loan to us, and it is up to the German government to overcome the difficulties involved. It would of course be more convenient to shun self-sacrifices and to watch others making them in the common interest. Aware though I am that this is not the German Government's intention, I would nevertheless not like to forbear from warning in good time against incurring the danger of such an opinion among our people . . . By maintaining this uncooperative attitude, it will be Germany itself which will deal the sharpest blow to its ally's financial staying-power.[40]

The ambassador protested in the course of this same meeting against the imputation that his government would abandon territory to Italy – a move which then, prior to Italy's entry into war on the side of the Entente, was seriously considered – in exchange for pecuniary sacrifice on Germany's part. Hohenlohe was explicit in this matter: 'The sacrifice that we are prepared to make by way of territorial surrenders can in no respect be assessed in terms of money.'[41] None of these arguments, however, was capable of inducing the German Government to pursue a loan policy more conformable to Austrian ideas. The German negotiators countered with the – not implausible –objection that Austria-Hungary had failed to introduce as strict a foreign trade régime as Germany had.[42]

Loan operations with neutral countries were naturally on a far smaller scale. Holland supplied loans of 15.6 million guilders, Denmark of 7,350,000 Danish crowns, and Sweden of 1,517,044 Swedish crowns against goods and treasury bills. On the Austrian side, understandably, there existed a strong interest in extending the scope of these transactions. In 1916 Dr Josef Kranz, the leading figure in the Depositenbank and holder of other important functions in the economy, set out to establish an Austro-Dutch bank with head-quarters in Amsterdam. Its principal task was to finance Austrian imports from Holland. The new bank's capital, so ran Krantz's premise, could be raised by the export of alcohol and hops, with the Foreign Exchange Agency releasing the proceeds for this purpose.[43] When Kranz became the principal defendant in a sensational profit-eering trial in 1917, a Creditanstalt director, Regendanz, together with representatives from Boden-Creditanstalt and Niederöster-reichische Escompte-Gesellschaft, began negotiations with Dutch contacts to found an institution with the participation of German, Austrian, and above all Dutch capital.[44] Very soon it became evident that the inauguration of such an undertaking, the purpose of which was to obtain large-scale Dutch loans for trade with Austria-Hungary, was impracticable until after the cessation of hostilities.[45]

Spitzmüller had in his budget address spoken about the 'altogether special currency predicaments'.[46] Such a 'special predicament' had basically existed since soon after the outbreak of war, when the Bank Act had to be suspended. This act absolved the central bank from its statutory duty to exchange its notes at the official gold parity. The central bank nevertheless did its best, in order to conserve the limited gold and foreign exchange reserves, to restrict the sale of foreign exchange. This new practice was not, however, based on any clear strategy.[47]

The longer the war continued, the stricter became the restrictions. Yet the decline in the price for the Austro-Hungarian currency on

Table 22   Average exchange rate of the crown

100 cr. = 105 Sw.Fr.	
August 1914	97.50
June 1915	80.19
June 1916	66.75
June 1917	44.02
June 1918	43.01
October 1918	43.74

foreign markets proceeded, if comparatively slowly, almost inexorably. At Zurich, probably the most important foreign exchange mart at this time, the crown was quoted as above.[48]

Averages are sometimes misleading and often conceal fluctuations that could on occasion be considerable. Such was the case during the final weeks of 1917 and at the beginning of 1918 when the Russian collapse and the Austrian offensive in Italy allowed the Central Powers' military situation to appear in a favourable light. The international bears, who had for some time done considerable business in unsecured forward sales of crowns and marks, had to beat a hasty retreat. The tightness of the foreign exchange markets led to erratic price movements. 'Whereas Vienna's all-time low was 28% of par at Stockholm, 36.4% at Zurich, and 37.3% in Holland, it has since rallied to 70, 72.5, and 80%.[49] The crown's apparently speedy recuperative power fortified many in the belief that after the war the former exchange ratios would be restored.

From the preceding series of figures, it emerges that the exchange restrictions introduced at the outset of war had entirely severed the connexion between the crown's domestic and external value. The progress of inflation, faster in the Empire than in most other European countries especially after 1917, made comparatively small impact on the Austro-Hungarian currency's external value. This was due in no small measure to the stricter control over foreign exchange exercised in the last two years of war.

The decision to establish a central office for foreign currency control was taken relatively late. Previously efforts had been directed towards trying to make do with a series of import and export restrictions. Duties on luxury goods, the import of which in the early years attained a volume rarely recorded, had to be paid in actual gold. That checked, but could not altogether stop, a not inconsiderable source of foreign exchange losses.[50] More effective may have been a regulation aimed at reducing exports by granting permits only 'if exporters undertook to deposit with the Austro-Hungarian Bank the equivalent of what they would receive for their goods in foreign currency'.[51] As the outflow of gold and foreign exchange assumed ever more menacing proportions in spite of these and other measures, preparations were made in February 1916 for the establishment of a Foreign Exchange Agency. In this field too the government at first experimented with an agency acting on the basis of voluntary agreements with banks and other money institutions. On 22 February the central bank announced that 'for the purposes of maintaining a watch on' the amounts of 'foreign currencies available and in demand, and to bring into line the purchase and sale of the same so as to lower their price if possible,' the bank, 'jointly with the Imperial Postal Savings Office and the Austrian banks and bankers in Vienna is establishing a central agency in Austria for dealings in foreign currency which, like the analogous institution founded in Budapest for Hungary, will begin its operations on Thursday, 24 February'.[52] Members of the agency were obliged to hand in all foreign currency received and to approach the agency – with an indication of purpose and submission of the supporting documents – for any requirements. The agency then had to decide whether, and to what extent, the applications for allocation of foreign exchange should be granted. In a newspaper article, Popovics made known the criteria which would be employed. 'In the first place, the requirements for the import of goods will be met; priority will be given to imports for the war administration and to the food imports. The import of luxury goods will on principle be excluded from the provision of foreign exchange.'[53]

A Foreign Exchange Agency based on voluntary agreement, as unfortunately soon became clear, was not able to guarantee the degree of discipline necessary among members to cope successfully with the task in hand. Moreover, when the new agency was founded, it had been overlooked that the 'outsiders' – the smaller banks and money dealers to whom little importance had been attached and who had consequently stayed outside the organization – would at an early stage develop to a position that was bound to call into question the rationing system devised by the central bank experts.

A memorandum from the Minister of Commerce, Dr Stibral, to his colleague at the Ministry of Finance states concisely the most serious deficiencies endemic to the new system.[54] It includes the important declaration that the 'entire weight of the restrictions' is directed 'against the needs of industry', because 'priority is given to requirements of the war administration, the Austrian Central Purchasing Corporation (OEZEG) and the Foodstuffs Agency'. Paradoxically this does not result in improved protection for the Austrian monetary reserves since 'foreign exchange dealings are not actually concentrated among the participants in the agency, but can now, as before, be handled by firms and people remaining outside' its membership. In addition there is 'no strict supervision of the banks who do take part in the agency' and 'transfers of crown assets abroad and their offer for sale there is possible'. The latter circumstance especially – the free export of crowns – increases, in the view of the minister, 'the cost of foreign exchange and depresses the exchange rate of the crown'. Precisely this state of affairs caused discrimination against industry because it is virtually excluded by the agency from its foreign exchange allocations.

Inasmuch as the Foreign Exchange Agency does not trouble itself about the fluctuation of the exchange rate in foreign markets, but continues to adhere to the old rate (with low valuation of the foreign currencies), the outcome is that the allocation of foreign exchange by the agency affords preferential treatment to those who for whatever reasons are the recipients of foreign exchange. For example, whoever on 3 or 4 November applied for and received 100,000 guilders had to pay 330,250 crowns, in accordance with the Foreign Exchange Agency's official quotation. But anybody whose application was rejected and who obtained this foreign exchange on the free market had to expend at least 373,000 crowns, which is 43,000 crowns more.

Whereas firms with stronger resources are able to help themselves through international currency operations, the situation is heavily prejudiced against the small businessman. In this way the standing of the Austrian currency deteriorates abroad and the central bank eventually has to make supporting purchases on the crown's behalf to avoid a collapse. 'The measures of the Austro-Hungarian Bank can, of course, only consist in the surrender of foreign exchange and gold. In the end, circumstances compel the sanction of what the Foreign Exchange Agency's activities are meant to stop. The organization and the effectiveness of the Foreign Exchange Agency cannot, therefore, be deemed other than a failure.'

At the close of his memorandum the minister again drew attention to the fact that the sale of foreign exchange at rates below those prevailing in international markets privileged the favoured parties, whereas the refusal of an allocation imposed a heavy burden on those concerned. It is hardly surprising that he advocated 'reorganization of the Foreign Exchange Agency's structure and practice.'[55]

This massive intervention by the Minister of Commerce was vigorously seconded by the well-informed *Österreichische Volkswirt* and led to measures of the kind taken much earlier in Germany.[56] For practical purposes the Foreign Exchange Agency was transformed into a compulsory system. In December 1916, the Ministry of Finance issued an ordinance requiring foreign exchange deals and every other foreign currency transaction to be executed solely through the agency of banking houses and money-changers who were members of the Foreign Exchange Agency and prepared to let the agency examine their books. Simultaneously, exporters were ordered to deliver to the agency the currency proceeds of their sales abroad. A veto – long demanded by public opinion – was placed on the export of crowns, which during the second half of 1916 had put the Austrian currency under increasing pressure.[57]

In March 1917, the evidence that these steps too enjoyed only limited success produced a drastic decision. All imports were made dependent on a special permit from the Ministry of Finance.[58] Nevertheless, the second half of 1917, as noted in another context, witnessed extensive bear speculations.[59] The average decline in the crown's rate of exchange in 1917 and 1918 was comparatively small, in consequence of the bundle of measures passed in December 1916 and March 1917. However, it must not to be overlooked that the last two years of war proceeded in the ever-deepening shadow of the Entente Powers' blockade, which forced on the Central Powers a – partly unintentional – policy of 'thrift'.

Notes

1 The Empire's expenditure in absolute figures lagged substantially behind that of leading industrial countries, but in percentage terms the burden on the Austro-Hungarian national income was astonishingly high. 'On the eve of war the outlay on armaments in proportion to national income stood in Germany at 3.5%, in Great Britain at 3.6%, in Austria-Hungary at some 4%. Russia spent comparatively still more on military expenditure, some 6% of its national income.' Gerd Hardach, *Der Erste Weltkrieg* (Munich, 1973), p. 162.

2 See Winkler, *Die Einkommensverschiebungen in Österreich während des Krieges* (Vienna, 1930), p. 231.

3 Cf. Gustav Gratz and Richard Schüller, *Der wirtschaftliche Zusammenbruch Österreich-Ungarns* (Vienna, 1930), pp. 165 et seq. and Note 72 of the preceding chapter. It has again to be emphasized that the differences between Teleszky and Winkler are particularly pronounced when they try to assess the *real* war costs. Gratz and Schüller summarize the views of the two authors as follows: 'Austria's war costs, according to Teleszky's calculations, amounted to 31,000 million gold crowns, Hungary's to 18,000 million. Winkler converted the crown totals resultant on his investigations into real money terms and concludes that by the end of June 1918 Austria's military expenditure came to some 12,000 million pre-1914 crowns and that Hungary's must therefore be put at 6,500 million such crowns . . . The difference ensues on Teleszky converting the paper crowns into gold crowns at the average crown rate while Winkler works on the basis of a computation in real money terms, taking into account price changes, during the individual phases of the war. Both methods have their justification, but of course neither calculation is quite correct.' Gratz and Schüller, p. 171.

4 Cf. H. Mendershausen, *The Economics of War* (New York, 1941), p. 305 and Hardach, *Der Erste Welthrieg*, p. 166.

5 Members of the Entente, on the other hand, could count on the help of certain powerful allies. An interesting 1918 study comments, 'Britain and France at a very early stage extended major advances to Russia, Belgium, and the small Balkan states. Britain, the Entente's clearing-house during the first three years of hostilities, also made large loans to France and Italy to facilitate their payments for goods and munitions purchases in Britain and the United States ... After spring 1917 the United States took over the role of banker to the Entente.' Schweizerischer Bankverein, *Die Kriegsbilanz 1914–1918*, Monthly Report No. 5, p. 48.

6 'It was without exception the central banks which furnished the treasuries with the resources for mobilization and for the initial military operations. They [the central banks] were on the whole well prepared for the enormous task in store for them. Advances by the central banks were used, and frequently misused, even after the issue of the first funded loans. The procedure is intelligible in so far as it apparently constitutes the cheapest way of financing war.' *Kriegsbilanz*, p. 50.

7 See Part II, Chap. 2, p. 132 et seq.

8 The first central bank loan, as recorded earlier, had taken the form of one against collateral while the second transaction had been in the form of a bills discount. The redemption dates had in both cases to be prolonged.

9 Alexander Popovics, *Das Geldwesen im Kriege* (Vienna, 1925), p. 75.

10 Popovics, *Das Geldwesen*, p. 79. Appendix II, Table 2 gives a compilation in chronological order of the loans extended by the Austro-Hungarian Bank to the two administrations.

11 See Part II, Chap. 2, p. 136.

12 Cf. *Die Kriegsbilanz*, No. 5, p. 50.

13 Hardach, *Der Erste Weltkrieg*, p. 167.

14 Cf. Gratz and Schüller, *Der wirtschaftliche Zusammenbruch*, p. 176.

15 The share of the institutional investors, taking *Compass* figures as a basis of calculation, will have been 40.6%, 43.6%, 44.5%, 48.3%, 52.1%, 51.4%, and 54.5% for War Loans I to VII respectively. For the Eighth War Loan it was 58.5%, as calculated by Max Sokal, 'Vom österreichischen Bankwesen', *Schriften des Vereines für Sozialpolitik*, Vol. CLXII, p. 45.

16 Cf. Stefan von Müller, *Die finanzielle Mobilmachung Österreichs und ihr Ausbau bis 1918* (Berlin, 1918), p. 145 et seq.

17 Gratz and Schüller, *Der wirtschaftliche Zusammenbruch*, p. 176 et seq.

18 Cf. Müller, *Die finanzielle Mobilmachung*, p. 148.

19 Müller, *Die finanzielle Mobilmachung*, p. 153.

20 Shorthand Minutes of the Lower House, XXIInd Session, 6th Meeting, 14 June 1917, p. 232.

21 Calculated on the basis of statements by Alexander Popovics, *Das Geldwesen*, p. 79.

22 The debts incurred with the central bank between 20 March and 14 October 1918 amounted to some 10,500 million crowns. The two final War Loans netted the comparatively meagre totals of 6,000 and 5,800 million crowns respectively.

23 Cf. Dr Stefan von Licht, 'Die Kriegszuschläge zu den direkten Steuern', *Neue Freie Presse*, 15 March 1918. A systematic description of the fiscal measures adopted during the war will be found in Müller, *Die finanzielle Mobilmachung*, pp. 157 et seq.

24 Shorthand Minutes, 14 June 1917, p. 233.

25 Shorthand Minutes, 14 June 1917, p. 234.

26 Shorthand Minutes, 14 June 1917, p. 237.

27 Cf. Part II, Chap. 2, p. 144 *et. seq.* f.34.

28 The most prominent proponent of a property tax was Richard Goldscheid. In 1917, says Weissel, quoting H. von Beckerath, he was still largely concerned with the amortization of war debt to be achieved by this tax, whereas in 1919 the aspect of socialization came to the fore. Cf. Erwin Weissel, *Die Ohnmacht des Sieges. Arbeiterschaft und Sozialisierung nach dem Ersten Weltkrieg in Österreich* (Vienna, 1976), p. 220 and p. 245, footnote 26.

29 Shorthand Minutes, 14 June 1917, p. 236.

30 A few months later the new Minister of Finance, Baron Dr Wimmer, speaking to the house on the same subject, was distinctly more cautious than Spitzmüller. 'Currently we have a war debt approaching 42,000 millions, and we are budgeting for fresh debts in 1917–18 of 18,000 millions, together therefore 60,000 millions. Even if we were to net 30,000 millions by way of a big property levy, there would still be left 30,000 millions outstanding. Apart from interest due, there has to be added to this the costs of what is needed for reconstruction . . . Were the war debts thereby suddenly to disappear, that would alter matters. There remain, though, the gigantic extra requirements for the national budget and the extra receipts for these colossal burdens. They would have to be met by an economy completely exhausted by such an immense property levy . . . I repeat: the idea of a property tax is not yet topical, it cannot be implemented immediately. In principle I do not reject it, but the subject must be very carefully pondered.' Shorthand Minutes, XXIInd session, 26 September 1917, p. 1,202.

31 As early as December 1917 Walther Federn, generally well-informed, was writing that Spitzmüller, 'the best man in line of succession to National Bank Governor Popovics', had made too many enemies. 'It looks now as if those enemies are trying to keep him from this important economic appointment for which he is predestined.' See Walther Federn, 'Die Österreichisch-Ungarische Bank im Kriege', *Der Österreichische Volkswirt*, 22 December 1917, p. 201.

32 Cf. Part II, Chap. 2, p. 137.

33 For a detailed description of the Empire's 1914–1918 balance of payments problems, see Popovics, *Das Geldwesen*, pp. 107 et seq. The surprisingly large demand for luxury goods originated with individuals who had overnight become rich. Cf. Müller, *Die finanzielle Mobilmachung*, p. 113.

34 Müller, *Die finanzielle Mobilmachung*, p. 119.

35 Cf. Part II, Chap. 2, p. 137.

36 Cf. Popovics, *Das Geldwesen*, p. 122.

37 Popovics, *Das Geldwesen*, p. 123.

38 As Walré de Bordes says, the banknotes represented nothing but the credit of the state. Leaving aside the legal aspects, they were simply currency notes. See J. van Walré de Bordes, *The Austrian Crown, its Depreciation and Stabilization* (London, 1924), p. 51. For data on the notes in circulation as well as on the central bank's 1914–1918 gold and foreign exchange reserves, see Appendix II, Table 3.

39 'I visited today the secretary to the imperial treasury,' reported the Ambassador Prinz Hohenlohe in a confidential report to the Ministry of Foreign Affairs, 'to discuss with him the loan prospects. Herr Helfferich confidently hopes that an Austro-Hungarian loan will prove feasible here, but he fears that the amount of 1,000 million will hardly be attainable . . . He described the request for 300 millions in gold, about which he will in the first instance have to talk to the

chairman of the Reichsbank, as the most difficult of our wishes to fulfil. He is afraid that it will be quite impossible to allow such a sum in gold to leave the country.' Haus-, Hof- und Staatsarchiv, PAI, Box 511, 28 March 1915.

40 Staatsarchiv, 10 April 1915.

41 Staatsarchiv, 10 April 1915.

42 'Admittedly it cannot be denied that the criticism by competent German officials of the attitude of the Austrian and the Hungarian Government on the regulation of trade with other countries was not unjustified. While in Germany steps had been taken in good time to work towards an optimal improvement in the trade balance by facilitating exports and restricting imports, analogous measures occurred only tardily in the Empire.' Popovics, *Das Geldwesen*, p. 124.

43 Gratz and Schüller, *Der wirtschaftliche Zusammenbruch*, p. 182.

44 For details of the Kranz Trial, see next chapter.

45 Abundant material on the planned Austro-German-Dutch banking house foundation is available in the Ministry of Finance archives. See the Ministry file 20.199 for 9 March 1917. Its appendix has a brief draft of the proposed bank's articles of association as well as the names of the likely German and Dutch parent-banks.

46 See above, p. 193.

47 'In foreign exchange matters the Austro-Hungarian Bank lacked during the early period following the outbreak of war the resolute touch shown on other occasions and fancied that it could by way of petty measures overcome the huge problems descending on it. One day the foreign exchange it released was plentiful, the next it again curbed demand, and then it tried to obtain foreign exchange for itself in Germany and in neutral countries by exporting important quantitites of gold.' Müller, *Die finanzielle Mobilmachung*, p. 109.

48 Gratz and Schüller, *Der wirtschaftliche Zusammenbruch*, p. 182.

49 Walther Federn, 'Der Umschwung auf den Devisenmärkten', *Der Österreichische Volkswirt*, 12 January 1918, p. 254.

50 'The demand for foreign luxury goods has expanded exceptionally along with the increasing wealth of a large number of people who have become very free-and-easy spenders and have the necessary purchasing power. These luxury goods buyers will pay any price, and therefore all price increases in the goods and (all) difficulties put in the way of their import through refusing foreign exchange and imposing payment of the actual duty in gold are ineffective. Only a far-reaching restriction on the import of luxury goods and the threat of severe penalties can help here.' Walther Federn, 'Die Devisen-Zentrale', *Der Österreichische Volkswirt*, 28 October 1916, p. 56.

51 Müller, *Die finanzielle Mobilmachung*, p. 119.

52 The exact text of the regulation on the organization of the Foreign Exchange Agency is in the Ministry of Finance omnibus file 13.438 of 24 February 1916.

53 Alexander Popovics, 'Die Neuregelung des Verkehrs in ausländischen Zahlungsmitteln, *Neue Freie Presse*, 23 February 1916.

54 Ministry of Finance omnibus file 84.508/16 of 21 November 1916.

55 The same file contains a detailed analysis of the Foreign Exchange Agency's situation by Dr Hermann Schwarzwald, departmental head in the Ministry of Commerce, who recommended the agency's abolition and the decontrol of foreign exchange.

56 Walther Federn had in his article of 28 October 1916 (see above, Note 50) advanced many of the minister's observations.

57 See Ordinance by the Minister of Finance, in agreement with the ministers concerned, of 19 December 1916 on Trade and Traffic with Foreign Currencies and Restrictions on Traffic with Foreign Countries. The Ordinance was based on the Imperial Ordinance of 24 September 1914 and that of 10 October 1914 published in the Imperial Law Gazette Nos. 251 and 274 respectively. See Ministry of Finance omnibus file 90.822/16 of 14 December 1916. The Ordinance carries the following minute by the competent Finance Ministry official: 'Ordinance I, intended to put the running of the Foreign Exchange Agency on a legal footing and to subject dealings in foreign exchange and foreign notes and coins outside the Foreign Exchange Agency to drastic restrictions, is in essence modelled on the regulation existing in Germany.' He adds that in Austria 90 and in Hungary 40 firms are members of the Foreign Exchange Agency.

58 Cf. Müller, *Die finanzielle Mobilmachung*, p. 125.

59 The Austro-Hungarian Legation at The Hague repeatedly reported on bear operations at the Amsterdam and Rotterdam Stock Exchanges. 'Tallying with a report by Consul Lederer at Rotterdam, the Imperial and Royal Consulate at Amsterdam says that, according to information received there from stock exchange and banking circles about the reason for this sudden fall in prices, there has during the past few days become apparent, besides the unfavourable factors affecting for some longer time past the rate of the crown, a fairly strong bearish speculation in our currency emanating primarily from Rotterdam and Scheveningen where, as stated in Report No. 52/K of 12 January, a systematic crown speculation ring has established itself.' Ministry of Finance file 65.507/17 of 18 June 1917, letter from the Austro-Hungarian Legation at The Hague to the Ministry of Foreign Affairs.

CHAPTER 3
Origin and Course of Wartime Inflation

In his lectures Joseph Schumpeter used to say, 'The state of a nation's monetary system is a symptom of its state.' There can be no doubt that his experiences of the First World War lay behind this pithy aphorism, whose truth subsequent generations can perhaps better appreciate than did the contemporaries of the famous economist. Austria had, since the days of the Napoleonic Wars, been spared the sight of rapidly progressive inflation violently distorting the economy and society. The decade preceding the First World War, characterized by a much remarked wave of high prices, was not one to prepare the less well-to-do classes of the population for the shocks of a cruelly inflationary period.[1]

So often has the mechanism of wartime inflation been described that a brief factual account can suffice here.[2] The government, as has been seen, had to set the printing-press in motion even for its first major financial operation.[3] In autumn 1914, the funds for two additional loans had similarly to be found by the central bank. With the well-known quantity theory in mind, a rise in price levels commensurate with the increased currency circulation might be supposed to have occurred. Initially, though, the rise in prices was confined to two sectors, the armaments industry and agriculture.

In the armaments industry the cause was what is now called the 'bottle-neck effect'. A limited supply capable of only slow augmentation, was confronted by rocketing demand for armaments of every kind. That prices began to mount rapidly is hardly a surprise.[4] The military authorities were fairly powerless in dealings with their commercial opposite numbers and conceded indecently excessive bids without much resistance.[5] Other industrial sectors were infected comparatively late by the inflation germ, because during the war's first stage, considerable unused capacity was on hand almost everywhere.

The early weeks, thanks to the large stockpiles accumulated in the recession years 1913 and 1914, witnessed no acute shortage of manufactured goods. With agriculture the situation was different. Even before hostilities, the poor 1914 harvests had forced up food prices to an uncommonly high level. On the outbreak of war, massive purchases by the military authorities put further pressure on exorbitant cereal prices.[6] The Hungarian Government obstinately opposed suspension of the wheat duties.[7] Little could therefore be done to eliminate this particular bottle-neck.[8] Towards the end of 1914, when the greater part of industry was approaching the state of full wartime employment, inflation seized practically all sectors of the economy.

The government at the beginning had barely any choice other than to print banknotes to finance the overnight flood of demand from the military. Subsequently, large-scale war loan operations were undertaken to try and dam this paper tide. Nevertheless the currency circulation swelled incessantly in spite of variations in the rate of increase.[9]

Table 23   Currency circulation, 1914–18

	Currency in Circulation	Difference in 000m. Cr.	Index Rise
31 July 1914	3,429,227,000		100
31 December 1914	5,563,770,000	2.1	191
30 June 1915	7,138,808,000	1.6	208
31 December 1915	7,435,164,000	0.3	216
30 June 1916	9,663,909,000	2.2	281
31 December 1916	11,313,603,000	1.6	329
30 June 1917	13,125,037,000	1.8	382
31 December 1917	20,398,044,000	7.3	594
30 June 1918	25,436,791,000	5.0	741
26 October 1918	33,528,693,000	7.1	977

In 1911–13 the average figure for banknotes in circulation stood at some 2,300 million crowns.[10] On 23 July 1914, when the army's mobilization was still in an embryonic state, currency circulation amounted to 2,130 million crowns. The dramatic week between 23 July, the date of the ultimatum to Serbia, and 31 July saw a considerable rise in the volume of money. By the end of the year, it had spiralled alarmingly, but in 1915 and 1916 the growth rate slackened perceptibly. This was the monetary reflex to a temporary stabilization, during which armaments productions went up substantially and the flow of vital supplies to the population was assured within tolerable limits. After 1917 the growth rate of the monetary volume expanded faster and the Empire entered a period of rapid economic decline.

Comparison between the currency in circulation on 26 October 1918 and the average for 1911–13 shows an increase of 1,458%.

It has been indicated that the rise in prices did not go completely hand in hand with that in the amount of money issued. This applies especially to the early stage of hostilities when a sudden inflation in the volume of money contrasted with a relatively modest increase in price levels. The development of the latter cannot be considered, however, without a word about the manner of its measurement. To gauge the purchasing power of the crown there are, as Winkler showed in his valuable statistical study, two main price indexes available. They derive from the 'Parity Commission' created in December 1921 to establish a basis for the assessment of salaries and wages.[11] One includes housing costs, the other does not; but the second brings out the rise in prices more strongly, because on the outbreak of war rents were frozen.[12]

Table 24   Cost of living, 1914–18

	Incl. Housing costs	Excl. Housing costs
July 1914	1.00	1.00
January 1915	1.28	1.34
July 1915	1.58	1.73
January 1916	2.21	2.78
July 1916	3.36	3.96
January 1917	5.44	6.59
July 1917	6.71	8.17
January 1918	6.82	8.31
July 1918	11.62	14.34
October 1918	12.85	15.89
November 1918	13.26	16.40

Which index better reflects the development in the cost of living is difficult to say. One reason is that the extent to which black market prices were taken into account, is unknown.[13] Nevertheless, even if the index inclusive of housing costs is thought to provide sounder evidence, the crown's shrinkage in purchasing power is spectacular. The second year of war (July 1915–July 1916), when the cost of living more than doubled, gives the impression of a breached dam even though the increase in currency circulation remained comparatively modest when compared with the preceding twelve months.[14] Subsequently, too, the discrepancies between the growth of money and the movement of the index are glaring. During the second half of 1917 the volume of money grew by some 55%, but the cost of living stayed almost stable. In the first half of 1918, on the other hand, the fresh influx of currency was relatively slight (plus 25%) while the index, including housing costs, leaped upward by a full 70%.[15] This is not the place to trace the reasons for these complicated relations, but even for the phase of galloping inflation they render the unilinear connection between the volume of money and price development so often postulated by simple quantity theorists unconvincing.[16]

Austria's wartime inflation attained a far higher level than in most of the major belligerent nations. During 1914–18, wholesale prices doubled in Germany, Great Britain, Canada and the United States; in France they trebled; in Italy they quadrupled.[17] Austria lacked a wholesale price index for the war and immediate post-war periods. There can however, be little doubt that the Empire had a worse record even than Italy. One important reason for this unfavourable place in the international inflation ranking was the method of meeting war expenditure, characterized as it was by especially strong claims on the central bank. The ratio of public loans to loans by the bank in Austria was 1 : 1, in Germany it was 2 : 1.[18] Another cause was the slow introduction and lax handling of price controls. Only during the second half of 1917 did these controls have an unmistakeable effect on the level of prices. Yet it was precisely in this phase that there arose tensions which from the beginning of 1918 rendered the system of price regulation practically ineffective. In the enforcement of price controls, too, Germany proceeded with far greater rigour than Austria.

The deeper source of the Monarchy's special susceptibility to inflation must be sought in its relatively modest industrial endowment. War, under modern conditions and of long duration, could only be waged with a huge loss of national assets. The state had from the outset to enter into a kind of 'price competition' with the mass of the consumers (ultimate as well as industrial), even if – as later regularly happened – a part of its purchasing power came from the proceeds of War Loan.[19] As the war went on, the means for financing these loans derived to an increasing degree from the capital which, in peace-time, had been destined for the replacement of worn-out equipment and the expansion of productive capacity. This competition became sharper with the constantly growing shortage of stocks, in part because money incomes continually expanded although wages and salaries dropped ever farther behind in the race. Or, putting it differently, the state and consumers were battling for a steadily shrinking pool of use values. One manifestation of the struggle, conducted with increasing bitterness, was the speedy, almost geometric progression in the rise of prices. To be 'inflation-conscious' is nowadays familiar enough. At the beginning of the First World War the hoarding of banknotes was widely practised throughout the Empire. Only gradually did the realization dawn, after the second year of hostilities and then initially among a very small number of people, that the crown's vanishing purchasing power could prove an irreversible process. The Stock Exchange can in this respect be taken as a barometer of opinion.

It had, it will be recalled, been closed indefinitely after the declaration of war.[20] Dealings in securities did not, however, come entirely to a stop. On a very reduced scale such deals continued in coffee-houses in the vicinity of the Stock Exchange. At the beginning of 1915 dealings rose as the favourable employment situation in the armaments industry opened up prospects of increased earnings. Nonetheless a few months later *Der Österreichische Volkswirt* reported on

a complete business low . . . whose deeper cause is presumably the same everywhere. In so far as the war brings firms special profits, this was fully reflected in security prices during the early months of the year. Investments, at present at any rate, leave no room for imagination. For the rest, the realization is slowly breaking through that the unexpectedly long duration of hostilities, with gigantic losses of capital, worsens the general economic prospects more and more and that this must influence market prices.[21]

A very short time was to elapse before Federn would be forced to accept that the development of share prices tended in the opposite direction.

August 1915 saw him again presenting an analysis of market conditions. He had to admit that turnovers were 'extremely large', particularly in view of the fact that the deals were unofficial and quotations lacking. He had however no difficulty in pinning down the true reason for this conspicuous trend. 'Those who today buy shares do so mainly because, with rising inflation, they prefer to participate in enterprises possessing stocks of goods or producing goods to having ready cash *whose purchasing power has during the course of the war become so very diminished.*'[22] Later he was to condemn this market speculation because he thought it prejudicial to War Loan subscriptions. In doing so, he forgot the deeper motive which he had rightly diagnosed.

The authorities could not of course remain unaware of the constantly expanding jobbing activities in disregard of the Stock Exchange's closure. A communication from the Ministry of Finance to the Police President in August 1915 expressed anxiety about the increase in bucket-shops and unauthorized investment dealers. 'Recently the private dealings in securities have become more lively again. The magnitude of deals and the instability of prices admit the firm conclusion that speculative manoeuvres and practices are at work.' The ministry feared that this could 'not only mislead and involve losses for members of the public inexperienced in financial affairs, but prejudice the success of future official credit operations.' Securities transactions had

recently assumed forms contravening the prohibition on unlicensed broker-age contained in the Act, Article 1, of 1 April 1875, Imperial Law Gazette No. 67. In the streets and in coffee-houses bordering on the Stock Exchange there are constant gatherings of persons concerned with the trading of securities and themselves either concluding or negotiating such deals.

This report of the facts was followed by the request 'to prevent these meetings and, if possible, to set a warning example by arresting a number of such demonstrably guilty individuals and indicting them before the appropriate authorities.'[23] Yet neither now nor later was officialdom capable of deciding on really energetic action against those speculative practices which were to take far more exotic forms.

On 14 March 1916 the Stock Exchange reopened an admission by the government that dealings in securities, even without the Stock Exchange, had long since assumed 'peace-time' proportions.[24] Most stock exchanges abroad had also by this time resumed business.[25] Sheer chance determined that in May 1916 the upward trend in securities was halted. Romania's declaration of war on the Central Powers had summoned the bears onto the scene. In early autumn, though, thanks to the Central Powers' military successes and to the rising liquidity of the economy, a bullish trend set in. The banks moreover, with growing liquid resources at their disposal, were prepared to finance speculative securities purchases with compara-tively little cover.[26] At this time speculation 'was on such a scale that the Clearing House Association could barely cope with the settlements'.[27]

1917 and 1918 witnessed an almost continual upward movement in share prices, influenced in part by tremendously hectic activity on the Budapest Stock Exchange. 'For months the Vienna Stock Exchange was completely under the influence of the Budapest Exchange whose motto ran "make sure of shares in those companies where Hungary has a financial interest".'[28] The process of sealing Hungary off from

Austria, which clearly manifested itself during the war, was considerably accelerated by events in the capital markets.[29]

The increase in share prices from the outbreak of war until September 1917 is illustrated by a comparison between the prices quoted on 23 July 1914 and the market value on 20 September 1917.[30] The following is a representative selection:

Table 25   Development of share prices in wartime in million crowns

	25.7.14	20.9.17	Actual Rise	Aver. % Rise
Banks	2,816.3	4,145.1	1,328.8	47
Insurance Companies	82.3	110.5	28.2	34
Shipping Companies	72.7	312.9	240.2	330
Building & Building Materials Companies	139.2	239.3	100.1	72
Breweries	55.6	81.4	25.8	46
Chemical Industries	105.1	249.0	143.9	137
Steel & Metal Companies	851.4	1,708.9	857.5	100
Coal & Mining Companies	397.3	931.3	534.0	134
Mach. & Veh-Buil. Companies	251.5	494.1	242.6	96
Oil Industry	51.8	238.7	186.9	361
Textiles Industry	42.0	90.1	48.1	115
Sugar Industry	74.7	153.3	78.6	105

The compilation shows that share prices in nearly all branches had experienced a considerable upward development. In the industries directly concerned with war production, such as steel and other metals, coal and other forms of mining, machinery, and so on, the movement was particularly hectic. Oil held a special position in the markets because it was also exported in considerable quantities. In 1917 exceptional factors played a part in the case of shipping companies.[31] The comparative lack of demand for bank shares is striking. Probably the explanation lies in the restrained dividend policy pursued by big financial houses.

In summer 1915 Walther Federn had ascribed the feverish activity in securities to the continually dwindling purchasing power of the crown.[32] Thereafter he waged a campaign, as heroic as it was unavailing, against Stock Exchange speculation. When, in September 1917, the banks agreed among themselves to accept buying orders for securities placed with *speculative intent* only against cash payment, he denounced the measure as illusory in light of this proviso.[33] He accused certain bankers like Castiglioni, the recently-appointed managing director of the Depositenbank, of having stirred up movement in the stock market in order to attract public interest in not yet fully matured industrial projects such as aircraft factories and airport companies and so to keep dealings in the shares of these enterprises on the boil. The great journalist displayed a downright uncanny instinct in trying to draw the public's attention to a man who, at this time and later, bore outstanding responsibility for the excesses in market speculation. In November 1917 began the subscription period for the seventh War Loan and Federn thought that 'experience of prices falling suddenly and strongly may have opened the eyes of many capitalists to the danger of investing in shares and may have strengthened the propensity to buy a War Loan with a 6.25% coupon instead of securities with 3 to 3.5% yield'.[34]

The flood-tide of inflation could however at this point no longer be restrained by appeals to reason. Soon Federn had to state resignedly that the public's capacity for subscribing War Loan arose 'in the highest degree illegitimately from the tremendous rise in prices' and that this was at once the cause and effect of the 'constantly growing demand for credit which the state tries to stop with pitiably inadequate measures such as ceiling prices, profiteering laws, and so on'.[35]

During the last years of hostilities it seemed indeed hopeless to resist the inflation psychosis which had now taken hold of practically all well-to-do classes. The symptoms have often been described. Thomas Mann also described them in a few words:

What did people do? Because the future appeared uncertain, because nobody could tell what was coming, because moreover sons and husbands and brothers were at the front and perhaps would not come back, so that it was not really obvious for whom to save, all the less since the war was anyway 'so costly', they bought whatever they could buy and no matter the price. On the black market the German citizen pocketed a pound of rancid butter for twenty marks. In practically every German household the black market dealers played a dominant role and it was thought an impeccable, respectable thing to break the law, live beyond one's rations, and pay insanely for what had been acquired illicitly.[36]

The long unchallenged belief that after the war all would come right again and prices return to their old level began gradually to be shaken. In summer 1917 a soberly worded article in Der Österreichische Volkswirt said that it would not be in the interest of the belligerent countries to bring prices back to their former level.

It is a demonstrable fact that all those states whose peace-time budget absorbed a comparatively large portion of the national income will be able to meet their war debts only if prices and incomes do not return to the peace-time level, and that likewise all other states are interested in at least partial maintenance of the devaluation which has occurred. This is actually perfectly understandable. The origin of big war debts lay in the fact that the warring nations had to buy many times over the amount of several years' production, at hugely increased prices . . . How could they be able to refund or to pay interest on those debts from the national income if prices return to their former level?[37]

Statements of this kind helped to familiarize people with the fact that there existed no method of financing, not even War Loan, which would shift the burden of war expenditure from the shoulders of the present generation to those of future ones.

The Kranz Affair, focusing on the figure of a high-powered profiteer enjoying excellent connections with the political, official, and financial worlds, spotlights the critical situation of the last two years of the war. Emperor Charles I had ascended the throne in 1916. Very soon he let it be known that he proposed to follow militarily, politically, and economically, a new course. An ordinance published on 24 March 1917 severely tightened the regulations on profiteering and the hoarding of goods.[38] The government, as Josef Redlich noted in his diary, had worked out the new measures 'during five laborious sessions'.[39] Shortly afterwards, that is, from 29 March to 4 April, there took place the trial of Josef Kranz and his co-defendants. Undoubtedly these were the most sensational of all proceedings against profiteering so far. About their background Spitzmüller wrote, 'Legal actions against price rises were very popular at this time and I gained . . . the impression that individuals close to the Emperor wanted to use the trial to put the Emperor in the good graces of the masses by making an example of a "profiteer".'[40]

Before the proceedings began, Dr Kranz resigned from his leading position in the Depositenbank. He had before the war already held a number of important posts in the business world. Creditanstalt entrusted him with the organization of the alcohol consortium and he was appointed its first chairman. During the war he had taken over the management of the Alcohol Agency, subsequently becoming also chairman of the Potato Dehydration Agency and the Starch Agency. At the beginning of 1916, on the proposal of the private banking house Reitzes, he was nominated chairman of the Depositenbank Supervisory board. One of his first acts was to persuade the bank to participate in a number of industrial enterprises and in a Budapest credit institution.[41] Kranz's period of office marked the transition of Depositenbank from a respected, rather conservative financial house to a speculative bank of the first water, a development which attained its peak under Kranz's successor, Camillo Castiglioni.[42]

What were the facts fundamental to the Kranz case? Kranz had concluded a big beer deal with the War Ministry and to this end he had created in the Depositenbank a Merchandise Department which functioned, according to the evidence given in court, as the Ministry's *de facto* 'Beer Buying Office'. As such it placed orders with the breweries which by far exceeded the quantities commissioned by the Ministry. The 'surplus' was passed at exorbitant prices to the retail trade via middlemen, Kranz's co-defendants. At a later stage the Merchandise Department did a lucrative intermediate trade in rum and jam.[43]

The Kranz Affair was notable in several respects. A personality with extensive links with the worlds of industry and finance stood in the limelight. In that capacity Kranz was regarded as representing the special relationship that had developed during the war between industry and the War Ministry's senior administrative officials. Captain Lustig, a former 'beer broker', as Der Österreichische *Volkswirt* termed him, had acted as economic assistant to the Minister of War, Baron Krobatin.[44] For his mediatory services Lustig had earlier been rewarded with board membership by certain industrialists.[45] No less than three ministers had to appear in court as witnesses. The Minister of War had been advised by certain of his staff to transmit to the examining magistrate a written statement pronouncing the accused free of all guilt. The compromising document was passed via the public prosecutor to the Minister of Justice, Baron Schenck, who visited the War Ministry accompanied by Spitzmüller. He suggested a change in the statement in the sense that it had been based on declarations by Dr Kranz and had not been the result of an investigation on the part of the ministry. Krobatin readily agreed to follow the recommendation of his influential colleague. In the course of the trial it became clear that the initiative for the War Minister's unusual step had emanated from Lustig and from a departmental head. The latter succeeded also in getting the censorship to suppress certain comments on the Kranz Case.[46]

The chief defendant was in the first instance sentenced to nine months' close confinement and a fine. The judgement was later quashed and the proceedings eventually halted.[47] More embarrassing were the consequences for two ministers. Baron Schenck resigned on 1 April. Baron Krobatin, who had been in office since 10 December 1912 and who was regarded as a supporter of the idea of a preventive war against Russia, followed his example after a few days.[48]

Spitzmüller's memoirs reveal that Prime Minister Count Clam-Martinic and Foreign Minister Czernin were interested in having the proceedings suspended. He writes as follows:

In this difficult situation I intimated to the Secretary of the Prime Minister that I lacked any possibility of intervening in the matter officially. However, as I myself thought the trial inopportune, particularly the manner in which it was now being conducted, I would raise no objections if the Prime Minister proposed to the Emperor to quash the proceedings by invoking the relevant provision of the criminal code. Count Clam did not avail himself of this possibility, but seemed unaccountably to persist in the notion that it was my task to rid the government of this liability.[49]

Understandably the government made no attempt to stage a second show trial of this kind. On the contrary, the impression gained from newspapers and contemporary writings is that during the last year of hostilities no further serious effort was undertaken to stop the more and more shameless black market and profiteering practices. In spring 1918 the leading Austrian morning newspaper published the following fatalistic comment:

The price of flour on the black market is some fourteen crowns. Even larger figures have been quoted in the privacy of places where such business is done. One kilo of flour costs in the contraband market what a hundred did in former days when the protective tariff did not yet make life in Austria costly and miserable. Butter is a nutrient that even well-to-do people can hardly come by. The grapevine says that it costs more than forty crowns. These are figures which will be the subject of talk for generations ahead. Libraries will accumulate books trying to explain such extraordinary events through quotations from present-day reports. Researchers will be amazed at the phenomenon that at a period when whole armies of officials were mustered to keep count on the stocks on hand, to record them by quantity and by weight, and to make these records available in minutest detail, the true state of potential supply was, as the widespread black market proves, never so impenetrable.[50]

The government thought that it could make up for sins of omission relating to price control and rationing by a policy of letting expenditure constantly furnish the economy with fresh, fictitious purchasing power. The above-quoted article continued:

During the past twelve months expenditure has risen eerily. The strange part is that even members of the Lower House, whose financial conscience pricks them and who urge new taxes, seldom raise their voices against outlays which each of them in confidence admits that they ought never to have agreed to and that the decision about their extent was downright frivolous.

Thousands of millions that the fiscal administration had to borrow in the form of notes. *We have afforded the most various levels and classes of society artificial purchasing power.* That is dangerous medicine with narcotic effects detrimental to good health. The effects evaporate, but the body is weakened. It is a policy which 'makes money messy'.[51]

In January 1918 massive strikes convulsed the moribund Austrian economy. The prospect of the Empire's economic, and therewith military, downfall clearly emerged.

Notes

1 The best study of the chronic rise in prices in Austria during the last decade before the First World War continues to be Otto Bauer, *Die Teuerung*, Werkausgabe, vol. I. The author tells how between 1902 and 1909 wheat prices in Vienna rose by 86% (p. 729). This is likely to have been in some degree connected with structural changes in industry. 'The powerful development of cartels and trusts during the last two decades is one of the most important reasons for the high prices' (p. 663). Recently David F. Good, the American economic historian, has tried to construct a cost of living index for Austria during the years 1873–1913. The period of strongest price increases, according to his calculations, was 1904–13 when the annual rate was almost 2%. Cf. David F. Good, 'Stagnation and Take-Off in Austria, 1873–1913', *The Economic History Review*, Second Series, Vol. XXVII, No. 1 (February 1974), p. 87.

2 Some important works on the subject are Constantino-Bresciani-Turroni, *The Economics of Inflation* (London, 1937); Howard S. Ellis, *German Monetary Theory* (Cambridge, 1937); Jan van Walré de Bordes, *The Austrian Crown, Its Depreciation and Stabilization* (London, 1924); Paul Einzig, *World Finance, 1914–1935* (New York, 1935); Elemer Hantos, *Das Geldproblem in Mitteleuropa* (Jena, 1925); Gerhard Hardach, *Der Erste Weltkrieg* (Munich, 1973); Alan S. Milward, *The Second World War* (Munich 1977).

3 Cf. Part II, Chap. 2, p. 133, in particular the quotation from Siegfried Pressburger, *Österreichische Notenbank, 1816–1966* (Vienna, 1966).

4 'The state's creation of money released an inflationary stimulus affecting in the first instance the armaments industry.' Hardach, *Weltkrieg*, p. 167.

5 In a retrospect on the beginnings of wartime inflation Federn wrote that the state – at least at the outset – drove up prices partly consciously, partly from lack of understanding in order to obtain for itself larger quantities of goods. Cf. Walther Federn, 'Kriegsanleihen und Inflation', *Der Österreichische Volkswirt*, 23 March 1918, p. 424.

6 Alois Rašin, the later Czechoslovak Minister of Finance, attributed the rise in agrarian prices also to the fact that 'Straightaway at the start of the war, in order to popularize it, the prices paid for wheat, cattle, horses, transport, and so on, were doubled in the case of military requisition.' Alois Rašin, *Die Finanz- und Wirtschaftspolitik der Tschechoslowakei* (Munich and Leipzig, 1923), p. 14.

7 Cf. Part II, Chap. 2, p. 113.

8 'At Vienna the price for Slovak wheat was in July, prior to the outbreak of war, 13.80 crowns, rose in August to 15.85 crowns, in September to 19.46 crowns, in November to 21.24 crowns, and finally in December to 21.84 crowns per 50 kilograms . . . In this connection it is known that the official quotations even then did not quite correspond to the prices in the open market.' See Gustav Stolper, 'Eine amtliche Teuerungsstatistik', *Der Österreichische Volkswirt*, 18 September 1915, p. 846. During the course of hostilities the discrepancy between official quotations and prices in the open market constantly grew and detracted of course from the value of the various price indexes. This will be referred to later.

9 Cf. Gustav Gratz and Richard Schüller, *Der wirtschaftliche Zusammenbruch Österreich-Ungarns* (Vienna, 1930), p. 181. The authors' figures are not altogether at one with the data given in Table 1 of the appendix to Alexander Popovics, *Das Geldwesen im Kriege* (Vienna, 1925), frequently quoted here. Likewise Walré de Bordes' figures in *The Austrian Crown* do not entirely tally with either Gratz and Schüller or Popovics. In any case the considerable value represented by the certificates of deposit issued in 1918 is not contained in the total given above for currency in circulation. Nonetheless the table gives a fairly good idea of the not discontinuous rise of the money avalanche in the years 1914–18.

10 Walré de Bordes, *The Austrian Crown*, p. 37.

11 Cf. Wilhelm Winkler, *Die Einkommensverschiebungen in Österreich während des Krieges* (Vienna, 1930), p. 38 et seq. A third price index, based on the average food consumption by 100 workers' families in 1912–14, must be left out of consideration because its range is too narrow for present purposes.

12 Winkler, *Die Einkommensverschiebungen*, pp. 40–42.

13 Winkler says that in the preparation of this price index 'black market prices played a part'. (*Die Einkommensverschiebungen*, p. 43.) He omits however any details on the degree to which he took them into consideration and he fails to draw attention to the very considerable discrepancy during the last two years of war between official and actual market prices. See Note 8 above.

14 The 'dam' may have burst because in the second year of war appeals to patriotism wore progressively thinner and producers as well as dealers began to turn the ever-more obvious emergency to their own advantage. 'Part of the official measures against increasing prices is the struggle against efforts by producers and dealers to take excessive advantage of the favourable conditions [*sic*] presented by the scarcity of supplies. Prohibitions as well as the application of penal sanctions have been tried. Criminal proceedings can however only complement organizational measures and it is a waste of effort to try and replace by prosecutions what has been left organizationally undone . . . Only now are the authorities beginning to establish ceiling prices for the retail trade.' 'Der Kampf gegen den Preiswucher', *Der Österreichische Volkswirt*, 24 July 1915, p. 720.

15 The sudden rise in prices probably reflected the acute state of emergency in this phase of the war. The catastrophic worsening of living conditions during the last year of conflict was exemplified by Elise Fränkel, *Zwei Wiener Arbeiterhaushaltungen während des Krieges* (Vienna, 1921), a thesis quoted by Winkler, *Die Einkommensverschiebungen*, p. 158 et seq., by the case of two Viennese workers' families. The first (man, wife, daughter) had in 1917–18 no more than a third of its 1913–14 income. The other (man, wife, and three children) did have a proportionate real income of 59% of its peace-time income, but that had been very low.

16 The objection to a mathematical model in respect of a highly inflationary period is that mass psychological manifestations like loosening of discipline, money-hoarding, and purchases motivated by fear or speculation, reflected mainly through a change in the velocity of money, are hardly capable of being translated into mathematical formulae. Every highly inflationary period has a specific historical character. For a more differentiated treatment of this problem, see Philipp Cagan, 'The Monetary Dynamics of Hyperinflation', in *Studies in the Quantity Theory of Money*, ed. by M. Friedman (Chicago, 1956), p. 25 et seq.

17 See Hardach, *Weltkrieg*, p. 185. Views as to the degree of wartime inflation vary of course from one authority to another. According to Michael Jefferson, *Inflation* (London, 1977), p. 42, price increases during the war amounted in Great Britain to 140%, in Germany and Spain to 200%, in Norway and Sweden to 300%, and in Belgium, France, and Italy to 400% of the pre-war level.

18 See Günther Schmölders, *Psychologie des Geldes* (Hamburg, 1966), p. 169.

19 'Price competition' is not meant here in the normal sense of the term, but was repeatedly used by Walther Federn to describe the phenomenon of mutual escalation of prices for a shrinking supply of goods. 'Lower consumption was enforced through constant battle, through battle by authorities who imposed restrictive measures, rationing, freezes, sequestrations, and so on, through battle between individual sections of the population against one another and against the state, each trying to buy wares from under the other's nose, with certain groups of the would-be buyers unable any longer to make their incomes do and being eliminated from the market.' See Walther Federn, 'Kriegsanleihen und Inflation', *Der Österreichische Volkswirt*, 30 March 1918, p. 412.

20 Cf. Part II, Chap. 2, p. 141 *et seq.*

21 Walther Federn, 'Die Teilnahme der deutschen Banken am Effektengeschäft', *Der Österreichische Volkswirt*, 12 June 1915, p. 620.

22 Walther Federn, 'Die Kurssteigerung auf dem Effektenmarkt', *Der Österreichische Volkswirt*, 14 August 1915, p. 772. (Italics are the present author's.)

23 Ministry of Finance Archives, File No. 54.907/15, 10 August 1915.

24 Stefan von Müller, *Die finanzielle Mobilmachung Österreichs und ihr Ausbau bis 1918* (Berlin, 1918), p. 92.

25 The trend 'eventually endorsed by a majority of the Stock Exchange Committee was that of a slow transition into its old paths of these hitherto entirely unregulated private deals. Those who supported this opinion pointed out that the public had become resigned to the state of war, that the latter was the source of rich profit for various branches of industry, and that the financial consequences feared at the outbreak of this global conflict had not transpired and were quite certain not to transpire now. Business had moreover been resumed, even if with certain restrictions, on all other stock exchanges.' Müller, *Die finanzielle Mobilmachung*, p. 91.

26 A memorandum to departmental heads circulated inside the Ministry of Finance ran as follows: 'Encouragement by banks is likely to have contributed much to the briskness of business. The fact is, as an investigation into the brokers' books has confirmed, that by far the largest part of the comparatively large turnover in shares is accounted for by bank deals. And it would again seem – although banking circles do not want to admit it – that borrowed funds are being used, even though not to the usual extent. For large-scale amounts of capital to be diverted in this way to speculative purposes is, both from a general point of view as well as in

particular from the aspect of governmental flotations at the present juncture, highly deplorable.' Ministry of Finance Archives, File No. 40.968/1916, 5 June 1916.

27 Müller, *Die finanzielle Mobilmachung*, p. 99.

28 Müller, *Die finanzielle Mobilmachung*, p. 103.

29 The favourable situation of Hungarian farmers during the war was the factor determining the enormous purchases on the Vienna Stock Exchange of shares with a Hungarian interest. As Federn wrote, 'Herein too the difference from Hungary is indicative. There the beneficiaries from the depreciation of money predominate, the farmers as debtors and as vendors of their produce, and the banking world which in Hungarian politics is the second major factor and which greatly gains from the large glut of money.' See 'Österreichische und ungarische Finanzfragen', *Der Österreichische Volkswirt*, 3 November 1917, p. 74.

30 The table, compiled by a banker, is quoted by Müller, *Die finanzielle Mobilmachung*, p. 42.

31 S.S. *Bohemia*, *Silesia*, and *China*, vessels of the Austrian Lloyd Shipping Line, stationed in Shanghai since the outbreak of war, were in 1917 sold to a Chinese syndicate. See *Compass*, Vol. III, 1919, p. 1,533. The ships lying in United States harbours, with the exception of one requisitioned by the American authorities, could also be sold on advantageous terms. Compass, p. 1,515. Cf. also 'Österreichischer Lloyd', *Der Österreichische Volkswirt*, 14 July 1917, p. 221.

32 Cf. Note 22 above.

33 Cf. Supplement 'Die Börse', *Der Österreichische Volkswirt*, 19 September 1917.

34 See 'Die siebente Kriegsanleihe', *Der Österreichische Volkswirt*, 10 November 1917, p. 95.

35 'Kriegsanleihen und Inflation', *Der Österreichische Volkswirt*, 30 March 1918, p. 441. (Italics by the present author.)

36 Thomas Mann, *Collected Works* (Frankfurt, 1974), Vol. XIII, p. 182.

37 Alfred Schwoner, 'Die Kriegskosten und die Geldentwertung', *Der Österreichische Volkswirt*, 25 August 1917, p. 822.

38 Cf. Rudolf Bienenfeld, 'Die neuen Bestimmungen über Preistreiberei', *Der Österreichische Volkswirt*, 28 April 1917.

39 Josef Redlich, *Schicksalsjahre Österreichs, 1908–1919* (Gratz, 1954), p. 194.

40 Alexander Spitzmüller, . . . *Und hat auch Ursach' es zu lieben* (Vienna, 1955), p. 230. The *Arbeiter-Zeitung* wrote on the same lines that there had been 'an order from above' to bring Kranz before the courts. It thought that the proceedings were symptomatic of a 'distinct line'. See 'Die Verfolgung des Dr Kranz aufgegeben', *Arbeiter-Zeitung*, 9 April 1918.

41 Cf. 'Allgemeine Depositenbank', Supplement Die Bilanzen, *Der Österreichische Volkswirt*, 12 May 1917, p. 157 et seq. and 13 April 1918, p. 121.

42 It is interesting to record that at the Allgemeine Depositenbank Annual General Meeting, when discussion of Castiglioni's appointment to the management arose, a member of parliament, Ganser, raised the objection that Castiglioni had been involved in dubious affairs. See Ministry of Finance Archives, File No. 47965/1917, where Dr Munk reports on the meeting of 23 May 1917. An important fact is that behind such equivocal personalities as Kranz and Castiglioni stood the Reitzes banking house. 'The serious blunders of the past year are to be ascribed, above all, to the dominant influence which the affiliated banks have been able, thanks to their large share holdings, to exercise over the bank's management.'

'Allgemeine Depositenbank', *Der Österreichische Volkswirt*, 12 May 1917, p. 157.

43 Certain of these facts were already made public at the beginning of January 1917 in the newspaper *Der Abend*.

44 Walther Federn, 'Der Prozess Kranz', *Der Österreichische Volkswirt*, 7 April 1917, p. 461.

45 *Volkswirt*, 7 April 1917. See also *Neue Freie Presse*, 1 April 1917.

46 Cf. *Neue Freie Presse*, 3 April 1917; *Arbeiter-Zeitung*, 9 March 1917; Spitzmüller, . . . *Und hat auch Ursach'*, p. 232 et seq.

47 On 9 March *Arbeiter-Zeitung* reported that the Public Prosecutor had abandoned the case against Kranz and withdrawn the indictment while the judicial authorities had quashed the proceedings. 'What matters', commented the paper, 'is the atmosphere in which proceedings take place. Cleaning up was originally the order of the day. Now it is that of reconciliation. Originally the idea was to show that not even a Kranz can stand in the way of the public interest.'

48 Cf. *Neue Freie Presse*, 2 and 10 April 1917. 'I hear that the War Ministry's whole famous Economics Department has been wound up, Captain von Lustig sent to the front, and Krobatin "is taking his departure" . . . As can be seen, times are hectic in the circles where Austria's masters now have to move.' Redlich, *Schicksalsjahre*, p. 194 et seq.

49 Spitzmüller, . . . *Und hat auch Ursach*, p. 231 et seq.

50 'Die Zunahme des Notenumlaufes – Wachsende Verschuldung des Staates durch Ausgabe von Papiergeld', *Neue Freie Presse*, 24 April 1918.

51 *Neue Freie Presse*, 24 April 1918. (Present author's italics.)

CHAPTER 4

Enlistment of Austrian Banking in Total War

The salient features of the war economy were the constantly intensifying process of 'depossession' and the liquidity markedly apparent even at an early stage of events. This is a simplification, but it seems a permissible one.[1] The second of these phemonena was of course clearly reflected in banking activities.

Table 26   Creditanstalt Balance Sheet Totals in 000 crowns

1913	1914	1915	1916	1917	1918
1,181,173	1,365,932	1,626,133	2,188,882	2,913,011	3,174,340

The most straightforward indicator is that furnished by the annual balance sheets.[2] Among the major banks only Creditanstalt's balance sheet total had in the last year of peace just exceeded 1,000 million crowns. This high level had been achieved after nearly sixty years devoted chiefly to 'routine business'. Only a few Central European banks, like Deutsche Bank, Dresdner Bank, and Disconto-Gesellschaft, could at this time display a substantially broader volume of business.[3] From 1913 to 1918, that is in barely five years, the balance sheet total of Austria's leading bank almost trebled (Table 26).

The balance sheet total of other major Viennese banks showed similarly high growth rates during the war. That of Anglobank rose from 750 million to more than 2,000 million crowns, that of Boden-Creditanstalt from 920 to 1,954 million, that of Länderbank from 821 to exactly 2,000 million, and that of Bankverein from 918 to over 3,000 million crowns. Some of the smaller houses, like Depositenbank, quadrupled their totals. These enormous growth rates appear in a different light when the atrophy of the crown's purchasing power is taken into account. It would however hardly be proper to apply in this connection the previously quoted consumer price indexes, because food prices rose undoubtedly far more sharply than those for industrial goods. Unfortunately no index is available for wholesale prices. Yet even on the assumption that prices for industrial goods (such as armaments equipment) went up only half as fast as those for foodstuffs and vital consumer goods, the major banks' balance sheet totals were in 1918 well below the figures of 1913 in real terms.[4] The satisfaction with which members of the Creditanstalt Board welcomed such 'successful' reports cannot therefore be termed other than a 'big numbers euphoria'.[5] The majority evidently believed that at the end of hostilities the price level would revert to its peace-time positions.[6]

Unless the enormously inflated balance sheet totals of the major banks, a consequence of war financing, are broken up into their components, it is not possible to understand the profound changes in operations which occurred during these years. It has been noted in another connection that at the close of 1914 the banking world had been in a state of liquidity beyond living memory. A state of hyper-liquidity was to remain characteristic of Austria's monetary economy for the duration of the war. The most striking feature was the increase in accounts payable and in deposits which can be classified as 'outside resources'.

Table 27   Creditanstalt outside resources in crowns

1913	1914	1915	1916	1917	1918
Creditors					
783,724,930	799,806,536	1,190,750,107	1,644,480,249	2,274,739,925	2,439,866,92
Deposits					
80,386,705	109,013,252	147,051,291	213,596,801	290,121,151	333,599,44

In the case of Creditanstalt the accounts payable trebled, like the balance sheet total, and deposits even quadrupled (see Table 27). Some of the other large banks experienced an even swifter expansion. At the Anglobank accounts payable grew from 424.6 million in 1913 to 1,508.2 million crowns in 1918, while deposits soared from 74 million to 413.5 million crowns. Bankverein, with the biggest branch network, presented the most spectacular picture with increases from 514.6 million to 2,281.7 and 133 million to 829.6 million crowns respectively. During the first two war years the growth rates were relatively slow, but then they accelerated rapidly, reflecting the increasingly inflationary financing of the war effort (see Tables 28 and 29).

What is the explanation for the increase in outside resources? It was

Table 28 Creditors of the major Viennese banks 1913–18 (in 000 crowns)

Bank	1913[1]	1914	1915	1916	1917	1918
Creditanstalt	783,725	799,807[2]	1,190,750	1,644,480	2,274,740	2,439,866
Bodencreditanstalt	282,933[2]	454,025[2]	545,841[2]	898,604[3]	1,080,632[4]	1,091,500
Escompte-Gesellschaft	254,473	273,113	348,561	607,783	664,023	872,575
Bankverein	514,638	594,902	702,136	1,239,807	1,752,528	2,281,727
Länderbank	409,496	466,255	569,748	808,411	1,030,485	1,286,117
Anglobank	424,649	518,605	659,541	906,023	1,572,862	1,508,528
Unionbank	194,694	196,724	238,947	358,805	489,446	479,436
Mercurbank	143,926	175,958	171,922	263,518	332,003	438,274
Verkehrsbank	164,805	128,977	172,336	324,215	380,393	479,390
Depositenbank	78,722	71,410	71,186	162,921	251,328	621,229
Totals	3,252,061	3,679,776	4,670,968	7,214,567	9,828,440	11,498,642

Source: Compass, 1915–1920
1 Levels as at 31 December
2 Incl. Syndicate Participations
3 Incl. 146,139,000 crowns War Loan Offset Account
4 Incl. 311,559,000 crowns War Loan Offset Account

Table 29 *Deposits and certificates of deposit (in 000 crowns)*

	1913[1]	1914	1915	1916	1917	1918
Creditanstalt	80,382	109,013	147,051	213,597	290,121	333,599
Escompte-Gesellschaft	23,924	29,238	41,940	58,952	73,208	72,997
Bankverein	133,248	167,946	220,407	396,696	643,316	829,680
Länderbank	126,603	133,129	157,380	241,091	336,702	413,783
Anglobank	74,197	83,094	110,533	187,858	283,288	413,502
Unionbank	28,530	34,448	57,557	91,014	124,780	124,889
Mercurbank	42,938	44,850	55,127	84,987	133,667	172,066
Verkehrsbank	71,829	73,865	95,908	146,738	228,544	313,220
Depositenbank	53,629	43,514	51,227	68,779	88,646	142,181
Total	635,280	719,097	937,130	1,489,712	2,202,272	2,815,917
Zentralbank der dt. Sparkassen	163,628	98,671	159,560	165,814	398,673	324,700

[1] Levels as at 31 December
Source: *Compass*, 1915–1920

the direct consequence of the clearance of stocks on hand, of the repayment of bank debts by industrial enterprises enjoying greater financial elbow-room, and of the marked decline in the volume of credit attested by the shrinkage of the bill portfolio and the increase of cash on hand. Moreover many firms, in order to make sure of some interest on money lying idle, left in their bank accounts provisions for tax payments as well as other reserves.[7] Finally agriculture, which during the war enjoyed an unusually high influx of funds, began to avail itself more than before of modern banking facilities.[8]

The outcome of the speedy increase in liabilities was that the ratio of internal to external funds changed drastically in favour of the latter. This abrupt change can again be exemplified by what happened at Creditanstalt. Its last capital increase had occurred in 1911, when the balance-sheet total stood at 986 million crowns. This, according to the 1915 statements, then rose to 1,626 million crowns. In the interval deposits had mounted from 69 to 147 million crowns and overdraft loans from 650 to 1,190 million crowns. Prior to the capital increase, contango and overdrafts on current account had totalled 740 million crowns, but by the end of 1915 all accounts receivable amounted to 1,260 million crowns. In 1906 the share capital of Creditanstalt had been raised from 100 to 120 million, in 1911 to 150 million crowns. Its own resources in 1915, apart from the War Loans Reserve, amounted to 246 million crowns. The ratio of those resources to outside funds, 185 as against 808 million crowns, had before the last capital increase been 1 : 4.3 With the presentation of the 1915 accounts the ratio changed to 1 : 5.5 inasmuch as there were capital resources of 246 million as against 1,380 million crowns of outside funds.

The 1914 Annual General Meeting authorized the Board of Creditanstalt to increase the capital from 150 to 170 million crowns at whatever date seemed opportune. The constant worsening of the ratio between the Bank's own and its outside resources, which had occurred mainly since the outbreak of hostilities, induced the board in the spring of 1916 to avail itself of this authority, and the subsequent Annual Report stated that a premium of 14,579,646 crowns, had resulted from the operation and had been allocated to the Capital Reserve Fund.[9]

In pre-war days one of the main motives for capital increases by the major banks had been their continually expanding purchases of securities and the resultant immobilization of funds in their securities portfolios.[10] After the outbreak of war they were purchasing, with

Creditanstalt in the lead, extensive quantities of Austrian and Hungarian War Loans, but this cannot be regarded as the main reason for their repeated capital increases. In the spring of 1916, when Creditanstalt began the round of capital increases, the Central Powers' military situation appeared promising and a broad section of public opinion believed an end of hostilities to be imminent. The general assumption was that the transition to peace-time conditions would necessitate provision by the major banks of enormous liquid resources. Re-equipping an economy denuded of fuels and raw materials would then be the primary task. Moreover it would be necessary to make available adequate funds for investment projects and the replacement and modernization of industrial plant. As it appeared certain that the settlement of receivables and the recovery of money frozen in War Loans would extend over a longer period it seemed prudent to increase the ratio of the bank's own resources to its outside resources.[11]

Anglobank, Boden-Creditanstalt, Verkehrsbank, Depositenbank and others very soon followed the example of the Creditanstalt, and the reasoning behind their capital increases was in nearly all cases the same as above. Up to a point considerations of prestige may have played a part. During the half-century of the development of the crédit mobilier system a certain hierarchy based on the size of their capital had evolved among the banks.[12] Depositenbank, which had repeatedly increased its capital stock, was clearly out to acquire for itself as fast as it could the widest possible sphere of influence. Wiener Bankverein and Österreichische Länderbank, on the other hand, displayed a more conservative policy inasmuch as only in the last year of the war did they increase their capital to any substantial degree. Niederösterreichische Escompte-Gesellschaft, with its comparatively narrow though exclusive clientèle, saw no need to take such a step, as it had considerably broadened its capital base in 1914.[13]

At the beginning of 1918 Creditanstalt undertook another capital increase of 30 million crowns to 200 million crowns. Its equity (share capital plus reserves, including the War Reserve Fund) now totalled more than 350 million crowns. Besides the above mentioned reasons for enlarging its capital the Board pointed to its plans for the penetration of the South-East Europe and certain overseas territories: 'in the light of the economic situation created by the war we consider eastward and overseas expansion of the Bank's activities appropriate. This has led us to enter into certain commitments which have the character of permanent interests.'[14] Reference was in this connection made to the Bank's interests in the Austro-Hungarian Orient Group, the Deutsche Orientbank-Aktiengesellschaft, the Zuckerfabrik Sofia, the Banque Balkanique, the Belgrader Zuckerfabrik, and certain South American banks which were not explicitly named.[15]

We now turn to the transactions of Creditanstalt in the Balkans and the Near East, directly or indirectly linked to the conduct of the war. In the autumn of 1913 a syndicate consisting of Creditanstalt, Bankverein, and the Hungarian Allgemeine Bank, had at the behest of the Ministry of Foreign Affairs begun negotiations with the Bulgarian Government for the acceptance of 30 million francs 6% Bulgarian treasury bills with one year's maturity. Creditanstalt's share in the transaction was modest.[16]

In the spring of 1914 the same syndicate joined with a German banking group led by the Berlin Disconto-Gesellschaft in negotiations with the Bulgarian Government about a sizeable loan. The talks dragged on until an agreement was signed in early July. The syndicate participated to 25% in the German group and took over altogether 120 million francs 7.5% treasury bills, from the proceeds of which it repaid its previous year's advance of 30 million francs. At the same time it obtained options of 250 million francs each on two 5% government loans to be issued later and with a longer life.[17] Linked to this transaction was a claim to the exploitation of Bulgarian coalfields and to the construction of a railway line to Porto Lagos and the enlargement of its harbour.[18]

Fresh negotiations at the end of 1914 resulted in the 'Bulgarian Syndicate's' agreement to discount 150 million francs in one-year treasury bills shared equally between the German and the Austro-Hungarian groups. The German and Austro-Hungarian governments acted as guarantors for the bills' punctual payment.[19]

Six months later renewed negotiations proved necessary as the bills contracted in the summer of 1914 fell due. The Bulgarian Government floated a 250 million francs 5% gold loan subscribed by the consortium on the strength of its option. The government, it was agreed, should initially make available the amount necessary to redeem the 120 million francs of treasury bills due on 1 August 1915.[20]

Until the summer of 1915 the Bulgarian Syndicate concerned itself exclusively with financial deals at governmental level. Towards the end of that year it began to engage itself in industrial promotion. The Creditanstalt board meeting of 21 December received a report by Mr Hammerschlag on talks held in Berlin. There it was decided to form a company to work the Pernik and Bobowdol mines. The syndicate had been granted an option on the shares until 1 April 1916 by the Bulgarian Government.[21] The new enterprise was constituted in the spring as the Bulgarian National Mining Company.[22]

The founding of the firm appears to have been the end of the activities of the Austro-German Bulgarian Syndicate. Its name never recurred in the Creditanstalt board minutes nor anywhere else. The Austro-Hungarian group now aspired to an interest in the Bulgarian economy, indeed in the Balkans as a whole, free from participation by the German banks, and it is obvious that it had official backing. Symptomatic of the rivalry between the German Empire and the Dual Monarchy, which was kept alive in spite of their military alliance, was the dispute about the 'Oriental Trading Company'. The German Government intended to create this company in order to increase its imports from Turkey and Bulgaria. The Austro-Hungarian Ministry of War wanted the Monarchy to assume an unspecified share in the operation. Spitzmüller had only been briefly in office when at a cabinet meeting he stated that he would regard the appearance at Constantinople of such a company, in which Austria-Hungary was merely represented, as a dubious service to the Monarchy's prestige. He would consider it more appropriate for an Austro-Hungarian company to be founded alongside the German one and for the Monarchy to put in an independent appearance.'[23]

In the spring of 1916, in line with Spitzmüller's advocacy of an autonomous policy, the big Viennese and Budapest banks increasingly shifted their attention to Bulgaria. In 1905 the Banque Balkanique had been founded by Bankverein with certain French, Belgian, and other associates. Creditanstalt and Ungarische Allgemeine Kreditbank came, in 1916, to an agreement with Bankverein about a joint participation of 2 million leva in the capital increase of the Bulgarian bank from 6 to 10 million leva. At the same time the group ensured for itself an option on future shares to a total of 2 million leva.[24] The first package was held by a consortium in which Creditanstalt had a 24% interest. When in the spring of 1917 a further capital increase took place, the option was exercised. Simultaneously the Austro-Hungarian group parted with a nominal 1 million leva of its old share holdings.[25]

The participation in the consortium was undertaken in preparation for a stronger penetration of the Bulgarian industry. The sugar industry, to be reorganized under Austro-Hungarian patronage, was selected as the first target. In February, 1917, Creditanstalt took up

25% of the 8 million leva share capital to finance the purchase of Belgian-owned Zuckerfabrik which was converted into a Bulgarian enterprise ambitiously rechristened National Sugar Industry Corporation at Sofia.[26] However, these ambitious plans were not taken beyond this beginning. The only other transaction of the consortium was the acquisition in Serbia of the Belgrader Zuckerfabrik, then called 'Deutsche Industrie-Aktien Gesellschaft' (German Industrial Corporation).[27]

Creditanstalt and Bankverein were not, however, alone among major Viennese banks in seeking to develop a position of influence in Bulgaria. In 1917 Boden-Creditanstalt decided on a great commercial involvement in the country, which was allied with the Central Powers. In its Annual Report we find the following reference:

The political and economic reorientation caused by the war has prompted us to extend our sphere of interest in the Balkans. We have therefore come to arrangements . . . with the Pester Ungarische Commercial-Bank . . . about our joining in the Banque Générale de Bulgarie, Sofia, founded by it in 1905 in association with friends abroad, and we have participated in this venture through the purchase of an appropriate portion of its 8 million leva capital.[28]

A share in the promotion of two Bulgarian joint-stock companies, Zigarettentabak Handels A.G. and Mühle Sophia A.G., came within the scope of this new field of activities. Further the 'Dunav' Royal Bulgarian Shipping Company was founded by Boden-Creditanstalt in association with the Danube Shipping Company, the Royal Hungarian River and Marine Shipping Co., and Ungarische Allgemeine Kreditbank.

Creditanstalt's participation in the Banque Balkanique was part of a more comprehensive strategy. On 14 June 1916, when the Bulgarian project had been under discussion, the management also told the board of talks on the formation of an Orient Group by Austrian and Hungarian banks. Its principal concern would be to engage in transactions with the Turkish government and with private industry in Turkey.[29] Creditanstalt and Bankverein would be the Austrian members of the group, Ungarische Allgemeine Kreditbank and Pester Ungarische Commercial-Bank their Hungarian counterparts. An arrangement was made with the House of Rothschild providing for an occasional participation in individual transactions of the groups, but a competitive relationship was expressly excluded.[30]

The formation of the Orient Group (like the Banque Balkanique commitment) was an expression of sharper rivalry, now officially encouraged, with Austria-Hungary's financially more powerful German ally.

The concepts associated with the term 'Central Europe' have inspired the group's foundation in two ways. On the one hand a closer link between Turkey and the Balkans with the Central Powers is anticipated in peacetime too. So as to realize the full benefit of the political alliance with Turkey and Bulgaria, whose continuation after the war is believed to be a certainty, the economic potential of the south-eastern members of the alliance must be developed ... Germany, which already before the war outstripped Austria-Hungary as regards economic activity in the Balkans, has during the course of hostilities exploited its dominant military and political position at Constantinople to fill the gap left by the elimination of the Western Powers in Turkey and to establish fresh economic as well as financial contacts there. The danger exists that Austria-Hungary, by reason of the competition of dynamic and financially powerful German firms, will be at a crippling disadvantage. As was often the case before the war, Austrian banks are likely to be carried along in the Orient business merely as subsidiary participants of German banks, without being able to exert any direct influence on the conduct of affairs. The formation of the Orient Group is meant to forestall this danger. The creation of an organization ... capable of carrying through substantial transactions on its own is intended to put Austria-Hungary in a position to act independently in the Balkan peninsula or to co-operate on equal terms with the German groups. The foundation of the group is the prerequisite to satisfactory collaboration in the South-East between the two states.[31]

The Orient Group, in other words, was not founded for a particular transaction, but was conceived of as a permanent institution with a broad range of activities. The year 1916 also witnessed the establishment of two study groups to investigate the Turkish economy for worthwhile investment opportunities. One concentrated on industry and mining, the other on railroads and public construction.[32]

The group's actual performance proved distinctly modest compared with the ambition of its plans. Financing Austria-Hungary's military supplies was its first (and only big) transaction. An advance of 240 million crowns was agreed in September 1916. Boden-Creditanstalt and Niederösterreichische Escompte-Gesellschaft joined the four banks formally representing the group for this purpose. Creditanstalt contributed more than 50 million crowns.[33] A large part of the amount served to settle outstanding Turkish commitments to concerns associated with the group banks for deliveries of war and other materials.[34] Skodawerke was one of the main beneficiaries. By February 1918 the value of the arms deliveries ordered by Turkey from this firm accounted for about 150 million of the 240 million crowns advance.[35]

Only two other group transactions can be traced in the Creditanstalt Board Minutes. In the autumn of 1917 an interest was acquired in the Turkish tobacco marketing company 'Douhan', launched with a capital of 150,000 Turkish lire, of which Creditanstalt subscribed 3%.[36] In December the Bank's management negotiated in the name of the group with the Crédit National Ottoman about participation by the Austro-Hungarian consortium and a German syndicate in this institution's Turkish operations.[37] Neither Creditanstalt's board minutes nor other sources reveal whether in fact the arrangement went through.

Creditanstalt was one of the driving forces behind the Orient Group, but nonetheless thought it expedient to continue to co-operate in certain transactions being carried out by German banking groups in the Balkans. In the autumn of 1916 Director Neurath informed the board of talks concerning the entry of Creditanstalt and Ungarische Allgemeine Kreditbank in the syndicate controlled by Deutsche Orientbank.[38] Members of the syndicate included Dresdener Bank and Nationalbank für Deutschland. During the course of a major reshuffle in 1916, the Schaffhausen'sche Bankverein withdrew. Its place was taken, in addition to the two Austro-Hungarian institutes, by Deutsche Bank and the banking houses Bleichröder, Oppenheim Jr, Levy und Warburg & Co.[39] In November, 1916, Creditanstalt participated to an amount of 3 million marks in Deutsche Orientbank. The headquarters of this bank were in Berlin; it had many branch offices in Egypt and the Near East.[40] Creditanstalt's representatives on the board were the two directors Wilhelm Regendanz and Paul Hammerschlag, who were likewise responsible for looking after the interest of the Vienna bank in the Orient Group.[41] No mention was, however, made in either Creditanstalt's board minutes or its annual reports of Deutsche Orientbank's activities, though this bank survived beyond the end of hostilities.[42]

Briefly it can be said that Creditanstalt's various commitments – and those of other Viennese banks too – in the Balkans and in Turkey became bogged down from the start. The same applies to the proposed foundation in January 1918 of a bank and an oil firm in Romania, with which Creditanstalt was to be associated.[43] Starting out from governmental loan operations, subordinated to the Central Powers' military and diplomatic policies, the major Austrian banks did try – partly in partnership with German consortia, partly in competition with them – to build up positions of strength in south-eastern Europe and in Turkey. Since this business policy was closely linked to the Central Powers' military success, it was bound to fail as soon as their military vigour flagged. After the collapse of the Dual Monarchy there could no longer be any thought of continuing this 'oriental' business on a grand scale.[44] Symptomatic is the fate of the Austrian interest in the Banque Balkanique. As a result of negotiations in 1919 with the bank's major French shareholders the Austrian and Hungarian banks had to turn over a part of their holdings to a French syndicate headed by Banque de l'Union Parisienne and had to content themselves with a secondary role in the bank's management.[45]

Besides financing projects in the Balkans and the Near East, the Austrian banks engaged in commodity and credit transactions with neutral countries. The first of these agreements between a banking syndicate led by Creditanstalt and a Dutch group, was concluded in December, 1916.[46] The arrangement covered the delivery of foodstuffs to Austria for an initial period of nine months. In 1917 it was prolonged.[47] The more sweeping plans for the founding of a bank in Holland to finance exports to Austria-Hungary did not materialize. Soon after the beginning of negotiations by Creditanstalt it became clear that the prospects for bringing such an institution into being before the cessation of hostilities were nil.[48] Hereupon the Austrian syndicate (Creditanstalt, Boden-Creditanstalt, and Niederösterreichische Escompte-Gesellschaft) attempted to set up an Austro-Hungarian-Dutch Trading Company, for which Dutch banks would act as acceptance houses.[49] The project looked to the future inasmuch as the company (according to a letter by Creditanstalt to the Ministry of Trade) would ensure the import of foodstuffs and raw materials into the Empire in the period of post-war 'economic transition'.[50]

In consideration of Holland's neutrality the discussions, begun in late 1916, had to be pursued in greatest secrecy.[51] The founding of a joint-stock company seemed to the Dutch negotiators too conspicuous a step. The three Austrian banks, it was agreed instead, should become sleeping partners in the firm of Vuyk & Co. with far-reaching rights of control.[52] Preparatory work on the project had gone a very long way when the Austrian Government's refusal to give certain guarantees and to provide the necessary foreign exchange via the Central Bank brought about its failure.[53]

There were also attempts to attain similar economic agreements with other neutral countries. At the turn of the year 1916–17 Creditanstalt contacted through the Hamburg bankers M. M.

Warburg & Co., a member of the German Orient Group, the New York banking house Kuhn, Loeb & Co. for the purpose of financing imports from the USA. The latter's entry into the war in April 1917 put an end to this plan.[54]

The negotiations with Denmark and Sweden concerning trade agreements were more successful. Again the services of Creditanstalt were enlisted. In 1917 an Austro-Hungarian-German syndicate concluded agreements on the Dutch pattern with Denmark. In the spring and summer of 1918 two further agreements followed. The loans totalled 90 million Danish crowns. Towards the close of 1917 an agreement was likewise reached with Sweden. It foresaw the provision of 916 million Swedish crowns for the import by the Empire of important goods.[55]

The motives for the notable capital increases of the major banks have already been explained. During the war's final years many large industrial enterprises also regarded it as advisable to improve their equity. They wanted, following the example of the bankers, to be financially prepared for the period of renewal, modernization, and expansion expected to follow the coming of peace. Moreover, the Stock Exchange boom, especially in 1916 and 1917, called up visions of outstandingly high premium profits on operations of this kind.

It is no coincidence that the Creditanstalt board minutes for 1916 to 1918 carry repeated mention of capital increases by affiliated enterprises. In the spring of 1916 the management reported on the issue of 15,000 new Skodawerke shares and the establishment of an underwriting group for 14,000 of these same shares. The Bank would participate 'in the same proportion as hitherto'. The same meeting heard about capital increases by Zündwaren-Aktiengesellschaft 'Helios' (match manufacturers) and Nestomitzer Zuckerraffinerie, one of the largest businesses in the field of sugar refining.[56] Barely a fortnight later the board learnt of substantial capital increases by Ungarische Baumwollindustrie AG (cotton), AEG-Union Elektrizitätsgesellschaft, and A. Gerngross AG (department store). The Bank participated in all these instances with a substantial quota.[57]

Transactions of this kind recur with great regularity in later board reports. Some of the bigger ones were those connected with Österreichische Fezfabriken, Vereinigte Maschinenfabriken AG, formerly Skoda, Ruston, Bromovsky und Ringhoffer (14 June 1916), Carl Stummer Zuckerfabriken (22 September 1916), Wienerberger Ziegelfabrik AG, Österreichische Daimler Motoren AG, Gösser Brauerei AG (30 January 1917), Ungarische Stickstoffdüngerindustrie AG (17 April 1917), a further capital increase by Vereinigte Maschinenfabriken AG (24 April 1917), Mundus AG der Öster- reichischen Bugholzmöbelfabriken (8 May 1917), L. Lang Maschinenfabrik (4 December 1917), Vereinigte Färbereien AG (19 March 1918), Ganz'sche Elektrizitäts AG Budapest (18 June 1918). The Bank's profits on these transactions were clearly considerable, and they compensated largely for the decline in certain branches of current operations.

Company promotion in the traditional sense, an exception in the war's early stage, happened more frequently in later years. This activity was however, as previously mentioned, mainly confined to the armaments, shipbuilding, and machine construction fields as well as to the exploitation of raw materials deposits in the Empire's peripheral regions and in territories occupied by the Austro-Hungarian Army.[58] In June, 1916 the Bank's participation in the founding of Ungarische Erdgas AG, sponsored by Ungarische Allgemeine Bank, was re- ported.[59] In December, 1916 three company promotions were successfully concluded: the establishment of a gunpowder factory with Skodawerke and Anglobank; the construction of an aluminium plant with a share capital of between 25 and 30 million crowns, in which Creditanstalt held a one-eighth share; and the foundation of 'Mitropa' (sleeping and dining cars) in Germany with a capital of 5 million marks that was to be successively raised to 40 million marks. In this undertaking Creditanstalt's share was 5%.[60]

January 1917 brought the promotion of yet another aluminium enterprise, Aluminium Erzbergbau und Industrie AG, in Hungary. Creditanstalt extended a large credit and acquired an option on part of the share capital.[61] A month later the management told the board of a big international tobacco corporation which was to be founded for the purpose of merging the activities of Oriental Tobacco Co. and Ungarische Tabakgesellschaft. The Bank would assume an interest through Ungarische Allgemeine Kreditbank.[62] The spring of 1917 saw the promotion of two more important undertakings. Credit- anstalt participated with Wiener Bankverein in the establishment of a company for Knorr brakes production and, shortly thereafter, of a nettle fibre company working on an experimental basis.[63]

In the summer of 1917 a report was received on the expansion of the Ungarische Allgemeine Maschinenfabrik AG. A portion of the new shares were bought by Creditanstalt. Simultaneously the shipping groups 'Perseveranza' and 'Immaculata' were converted into a single joint-stock company. A part of the 3 million crowns capital was acquired by the Bank's branch office at Trieste. The Eredi di Matteo Premada shipping firm, of Lussinpiccolo, was likewise transformed, with a small participation by the Bank, into a joint-stock company.[64] August, 1917 witnessed some more stock flotations. The Boden-Creditanstalt made preparations for the founding of a company, with a capital of 4 million crowns, to study the chances of exploiting Austria's hydraulic resources. Creditanstalt intended to have a one-seventh interest. The Frankfurt firm Beer, Sondheimer & Co. founded the Metall und Erzgesellschaft, a limited company, with an initial share capital of 1 million crowns. The Bank acquired a quarter interest while also buying a small interest in Österreichisch-Ungarische Osmose Gesellschaft, which had been launched by Depositenbank. Finally in this same month the formation of a group, including the Bank, for the purchase of the Fürstliche Thurn und Taxis'sche Zuckerfabrik took place.[65] In late autumn and winter 1917 the management reported on certain smaller promotional activities such as the transformation of Vereinigung österreichischer Filmfabriken und Leihanstalten (film production and lending business) into a joint-stock company with a capital of 4 million crowns. The Bank acquired shares to the value of 500,000 crowns. On the other hand it sold its holdings of preference and ordinary shares in Mürzthaler Holzstoff- und Papierfabriks A G.[66] Also worthy of mention is the foundation of the Znaimer Stadtbank (Znaim Municipal Bank) with a capital of 3 million crowns, in which the Bank had a 10% interest.[67]

The board minutes for January and February 1918 give particulars of a number of similar transactions. The Bank was a member of consortia for the acquisition of new Boden-Creditanstalt and Öster-reichische Länderbank shares and, jointly with Mineralölindustrie A G, participated in the founding of the Galizische Petroleum Gesellschaft Lifschütz-Segal with 1.75 million crowns. An ambitious reorganization of the Bosnische Kohlenindustrie A G by the Un-garische Allgemeine Kreditbank was supported by a substantial contribution from the Bank. A further considerable increase of capital was undertaken, together with Ungarische Allgemeine Kreditbank, on behalf of Aluminium-Erzbergbau- und Industrie Gesellschaft. The promotion of an Austrian, and also of a Hungarian, import and export corporation was being considered. The Austrian company was to have had a share capital of 15 million crowns and was to take over Alois Schweiger, Austro-Orientalische Handels A G, and Export A G, formerly Janowitzer. The Bank proposed to participate to one-third of each corporation's share capital. In January the capital increase by

Private Landesbank für Bosnien und Hercegovina from 14 to 20 million crowns also took place. The Bank's subscription of new shares amounted to 20%.[68]

There were several smaller transactions in February. The offer by the Disconto-Gesellschaft, Berlin, for a participation in the Bor copper mines in Serbia was accepted by the Bank's assumption of a 6.5% interest in the share capital. The Bank furthermore purchased a small packet of new shares issued by Wiener Bankverein. The Prague branch office exercised its option on shares to a face value of 100,000 crowns issued by Franz Melichar-Sämaschinen-Fabriks-A G. Another interesting transaction by the Prague office was its 1-million-crowns participation as member of a consortium to finance a limited company for the import of grain from the Ukraine.[69]

After the first two months of 1918 Creditanstalt's promotional activities fell off sharply. Indeed no operations of this kind are reported at all during the spring although a number of larger loans were extended to affiliated companies. They included a sizeable credit to Österreichische Daimler Motoren A G, Wiener Neustadt, and one to Österreichische Flugzeug A G.[70] An exception was the underwriting of a new share issue by Maschinenbau A G to the amount of 1.8 million crowns.[71]

Summer and autumn of 1918 were marked by a few isolated instances of promotional business. At the invitation of Ungarische Allgemeine Kreditbank, 2,500 shares were purchased in Schweinegrosschlächterei A G, Budapest. The board minutes also record participation in a German syndicate for harnessing the hydraulic power of the Upper Inn. On the other hand even in this period substantial credits were extended to several firms: to Viktor Mauthner von Markof, C. T. Petzolf Co., Vienna, to Belgrader Zuckerfabrik, to Internationale Import- und Export A G, and to Pulverfabrik Skodawerke-Wetzler A G.[72] The last 'pure' promotional operation in the Empire's era, inspired by Ungarische Allgemeine Kreditbank, was a modest interest in Rabbethge & Gieseke Samenzucht A G, Budapest.[73] The next board meeting, on 22 October 1918, was overshadowed by the Dual Monarchy's impending dissolution.

As a whole, the number of transactions and the sums involved remained far behind those of pre-war years. The Banks' activites concentrated on canvassing and selling war bonds and on extending loans to the large armaments concerns, the government, and the agencies. The considerable effort made by the big banks to place their staffs and material resources at the service of the first War Loan issue has been described.[74] Some sixty per cent of the 2,200 million crowns subscribed were due to the efforts of the commercial banks and the savings banks.[75] The importance of the institutional subscribers tended to increase in proportion to the decline in subscriptions. This fact was rendered manifest on the occasion of the fifth War Loan issue, which also nominally dropped behind preceding subscription totals. Creditanstalt's subscriptions for Austrian War Loan and its share in the overall totals can be seen from Table 30.

Table 30 Creditanstalt Subscriptions to Austrian War Loan for own account

	Face Value[1]	CA % Share in Banks' Subs. for Own Acct.[2]	CA % Share of Institution. Subscribers[2]	CA % Share of All Subscriptions[2]
Ist War Loan	20,000,000	8.72	2.24	0.91
IInd War Loan	30,000,000	8.69	2.56	1.12
IIIrd War Loan	45,000,000	6.68	2.40	1.07
IVth War Loan	50,000,000	6.87	2.29	1.11
Vth War Loan	50,000,000	7.36	2.15	1.12
VIth War Loan	60,000,000	7.69	2.25	1.16
VIIth War Loan	60,000,000	5.97	1.82	1.01
VIIIth War Loan	60,000,000	6.16	1.77	1.03

[1] The figures are taken from the CA Board Meetings Minutes
[2] Author's calculations

The table does not, however, give a complete picture of the Bank's commitment towards financing the cost of the war. Its subscription to the first Hungarian War Loan was 11.3 million crowns, more than one fifth the amount allocated to purchase of the Austrian War Loan, and it continued to subscribe big sums to the succeeding issues. From time to time, like other banks, it unloaded larger or smaller blocks on the public at home and abroad so as to ensure a reasonable proportion among the various investments in its securities portfolio.[76]

The banks' example of an active War Loan policy, closely co-ordinated with the financial authorities, was not always followed by the major institutional investors. Their sometimes slightly under-developed patriotism had to be prodded by a certain degree of 'moral suasion', as it would now be called, on the part of government. The attitude of Skodawerke, the Empire's most important armaments concern, may serve as an illustration. An act of the Finance Ministry shows that the deliveries of this firm to the army from the outbreak of war until 30 June 1917 amounted to 464 million crowns. In addition, there were the deliveries to Turkey as part of the previously mentioned 240 million crowns loan for which the Ministry of Finance had assumed full liability. When the authorities proposed that Skoda-werke should accept 10 million crowns' worth of Turkish bonds for new arms purchases, its management not only rejected the suggestion, but also threatened to stop further sales to Turkey. Hereupon a senior official of the Ministry agreed that this part of the loan too should be financed in the normal way, provided that Skodawerke, which had subscribed 51 million crowns to the first six War Loans, would contribute 10 million crowns more than on foregoing occasions. Finally it is stated in the act: 'This request can of course not be put into writing and His Excellency will make it known verbally to Director Neurath and Baron Skoda.' Whether these two gentlemen – Neurath was Creditanstalt's representative on the board – took the ministry's request into account can today no longer be established.[77]

As has been mentioned before the banks played a truly strategic role in financing the war. In large measure they provided for the sale of War Loans, not least by permitting their customers to purchase war bonds on margin. They also purchased War Loans for their own account. They advanced large sums of money to the state by overdraft facilities. They were the most important lenders of the Agencies and the armaments concerns. The claims of the major banks on the Austrian state and on the Empire as a whole for current loans constituted a formidable amount by themselves. (See Table 31). Otto Steinwender of the Pangerman Party, known for his critical attitude towards the banks, reproached them for failing in their duties, especially at the outbreak of war. Walther Federn, on the other hand, described their performance in table 31.

They have acted as principal agents for the many millionfold subscriptions to War Loans. They have put thousands of millions at the government's disposal through overdrafts. Their merit in these respects is no greater than their alleged failure at the beginning of the war. They have simply obeyed the laws inherent in a modern war economy, which allow the liquidity released by proceeds and profits from commodity transactions to flow into banks, and even given the chance the banks would have found no other use for this liquidity than to place it at the state's disposal.[78]

The manifold contributions of the banks to the war economy went along with their traditional services. The latter underwent substantial structural changes. Bills, foreign exchange, and goods business lost much of their importance. Advances against securities assumed

Table 31 Claims by the major banks on the Austrian State and on the Austro-Hungarian Empire (as at 31 December 1918) in 000 crowns

	Credit-anstalt	Boden-Credita.	Nied. Esc.G.	Bank-verein	Länder-bank	Anglo-bank	Union-bank	Mercur-bank	Verk.-bank	Dep.-bank	Total
Austria	85,756	101,262	—	776,221	—	70,000	132,189	4,130	22,860	4,617	1,197,000
A-H	—	—	—	—	300,103	—	1,531	1,576	—	—	303,210

Source: 'Financial Position of the Austrian Banks as at 31 December 1918' – File 89,309/1919, Ministry of Finance Archives
Striking is the high indebtedness of the Austrian State to the Wiener Bankverein.

Table 32 Securities holdings by the major Viennese banks (in 000 crowns)

	1913[1]	1914	1915	1916	1917	1918	1918 of wh. Aust. War Loan[2]
Creditanstalt	46,600	71,690	113,038	110,471	224,366	179,502	44,860
Boden-Creditanstalt	33,340	50,915	119,449	115,520	73,769	96,017	43,000
Escomte-Gesellschaft	37,586	44,103	35,443	44,025	44,345	37,586	2,743
Bankverein	28,420	40,625	41,444	86,595	199,701	216,914	136,018
Länderbank	54,665	73,704	118,020	112,236	150,235	108,020	93,150
Anglobank	21,052	29,206	63,927	80,818	131,709	87,905	54,000
Unionbank	22,937	34,485	55,449	51,544	53,962	54,577	18,971
Mercurbank	14,568	17,368	19,121	31,317	37,024	35,407	Figures Not Available
Verkehrsbank	15,744	19,022	41,551	81,424	154,475	140,857	206,584
Depositenbank	8,916	9,858	13,630	24,527	34,298	38,658	5,000
Total	283,918	390,976	620,772	738,477	1,103,884	993,803	

[1] Levels as at 31 December
[2] Cf. 'Stand der Banken Österreichs am 31. Dezember 1918', File 89.309/1919, Ministry of Finance Archives – These figures are the banks' *real* holdings, not those shown in their balance sheets.
Source: *Compass*, 1915–1920.

Table 33   Debtors of the major Viennese banks 1913–18 (in 000 crowns)

Bank	1913[1]	1914	1915	1916	1917	1918
Creditanstalt	734,811	721,451	812,235	871,900	991,826	1,667,307
Boden-Creditanstalt	326,407	417,015	363,430	630,219	736,287	785,285
Escompte-Gesellschaft	288,031	330,553	407,647	654,474	698,415	955,331
Bankverein	519,959	580,109	832,712	1,541,881	2,168,670	1,800,455
Länderbank	446,422	469,473	604,315	955,306	1,280,204	1,285,192
Anglobank	525,902	505,344	642,942	1,040,044	1,806,859	1,277,234
Unionbank	191,669	193,847	179,465	280,101	414,271	538,861
Mercurbank	143,926	175,958	171,922	263,518	332,003	438,274
Verkehrsbank	174,565	179,934	220,276	410,445	535,061	493,680
Depositenbank	105,308	105,453	91,045	131,267	218,660	626,438
Total	3,457,000	3,679,137	4,325,989	6,779,155	9,177,256	9,868,057

[1] Levels as at 31 December
Source: Compass, 1915–1920

Table 34 *Bills portfolio of the major Viennese banks (in 000 crowns)*

	1913[1]	1914	1915	1916	1917	1918
Creditanstalt	202,364	215,064	159,607	143,536	194,320	657,853[2]
Bodenkreditanstalt	108,234	127,975	123,254	102,015	99,270	89,778
Escompte-Gesellschaft	66,624	93,083	71,331	82,661	57,191	66,219
Bankverein	218,576	251,306	132,492	101,885	101,917	35,595
Länderbank	173,323	167,022	98,596	92,862	53,158	55,590
Anglobank	159,930	160,688	144,135	100,913	35,034	36,259
Unionbank	90,652	127,303	122,203	79,401	64,089	176,458[3]
Mercurbank	34,875[4]	37,938[4]	32,247[4]	25,648[4]	22,330[4]	159,745[5]
Verkehrsbank	62,308	69,449	85,613	36,429	41,063	56,597[6]
Depositenbank	61,734	46,986	32,915	20,245	14,241	126,267[7]
Total	1,178,620	1,296,796	1,002,413	785,595	682,613	1,460,300

1 Levels as at 31 December.
2 Including approximately 500 million crowns central bank certificates of deposit.
3 Bills and certificates of deposit.
4 Bills and foreign exchange.
5 Central bank certificates of deposit and foreign exchange.
6 Of which 20 million crowns Hungarian State certificates of deposit.
7 Increase mainly due to central bank certificates of deposit.
Source: *Compass*, 1915–1920.

peace-time proportions as the Stock Exchange climate grew friend-lier.[79] Tables 32, 33, and 34 (Debtors, Bills, Securities) furnish a good insight into the shifts in banking activities caused by the war.

These shifts can perhaps be best observed in the development of the securities accounts. In 1917 the total securities holdings of the major Viennese banks were four times that of the last pre-war years. Bills business attained barely 60% of the 1913 level. Yet with some of the banks, such as Creditanstalt, securities business took second place during the last two war years behind loans operations. Without exception the banks availed themselves of the favourable Stock Exchange climate to dispose of old holdings for which prior to hostilities there would hardly have been a market at a handsome profit. For example, Creditanstalt managed to sell their holdings of Ostrau mining and Mitterberg copper shares to Österreichische Berg-und Hüttenwerke (part of the Boden-Creditanstalt Group) and to Berndorfer Metallwerke respectively. Other shares, one commentator remarked, were sold at profits which were likely to have exceeded those shown in the accounts.[80] The comparatively small volume of War Loans held towards the end of 1918 by the Viennese banks, with the outstanding exception of Verkehrsbank, is striking.[81] Besides the systematic sale of such holdings during the course of the war, large amounts had been lodged with the Central Bank as collateral security shortly before the end of the war.[82]

In addition to routine War Loans and the flagging promotional business there were a number of large-scale credit transactions with the Austrian and Hungarian financial authorities, with Bulgaria, with the City of Vienna, and with other bigger municipalities. Most of these operations netted quite substantial profits. Table 35 shows that Creditanstalt's syndicate loans account showed but few fluctuations during the course of the war.[83] The more outstanding transactions included the following ones: in February 1915 German and Austrian banks took over Bulgarian treasury bills to the value of 150 million francs. The Austrian group, consisting of Creditanstalt, Wiener Bankverein, and Ungarische Allgemeine Kreditbank, furnished half the amount.[84] In July 1915 the board was told that the Bank had underwritten, together with other Austrian banking houses, 300 million crowns 4.5% Austrian treasury bills, with an option on another 200 million crowns of the same securities, as well as 412 million crowns 4.5% Hungarian treasury bills.[85] A few months later the Bank joined an Austrian syndicate underwriting 75 million crowns 5.5 Hungarian state certificates of deposit.[86] In February 1916 the

Bank participated in a new issue of China bonds to the modest amount of 100,000 crowns.[87]

Table 35 Creditanstalt syndicate participations in 000 crowns

1913	1914	1915	1916	1917	1918
84,793	71,050	68,696	68,421	67,346	90,834

In spring 1916 the Bank played a major part in the syndicate which, under the leadership of the Österreichische Länderbank, underwrote 100 million crowns 5.5 City of Vienna bonds.[88] Two months later it subscribed 17 million crowns for the fourth Hungarian War Loan. In October 1916 a 240 million crowns advance on behalf of Turkey was concluded.[89] The Austrian and the Hungarian Governments assumed liability toward the banks without the Turkish Government being – officially – informed.[90] At the end of 1916 a large credit, later increased on various occasions, was extended to the City of Trieste.[91] In January 1917 the board received a report on the underwriting of 4.5 million crowns of 4.5 Danube Regulation Commission bonds.[92]

At the start of 1917 the Bank took a 5% share in the 100 million crowns 5% Province of Moravia bond issue.[93] A month later it subscribed 11% of a new 250 million crowns 4.5 City of Vienna bond issue.[94] In spring negotiations began on the floating of a 10 million crowns 4.5% City of Pilsen issue.[95] In autumn the board decided to subscribe 20 million crowns to another 4.5% City of Vienna issue.[96]

During the last year of war financial operations with municipalities and provinces became rarer. In December, 1917 the Bank subscribed 10% of the 20 million crowns 4.5 communal bond issue by Galizische Bank für Handel und Gewerbe.[97] In January 1918 the City of Trieste floated bonds to another 17 million crowns total, of which the Bank took one third.[98] Almost six months passed before there was a bigger bond operation by the Budapest municipality, but the Bank secured no more than minor sub-participation for itself.[99] A short while later it furnished larg-scale loans to the City of Trieste and to the Province of Tirol Purchasing Office. On 19 November, that is a week after the proclamation of the Republic, the board was told by the management of negotiations of a Viennese syndicate with the City of Vienna concerning a 250 million crowns 4.5% bond issue. The Bank's share would be 10%.[100]

The turnover on Creditanstalt's securities and syndicate accounts in wartime was substantial. In 1917 a balance sheet analyst estimated the

Table 36 Receipts and debits of the major Viennese banks in million crowns

	Interest		Commissions		Securities, Foreign Currency, U/writing		Staff Pay & Other Charges		Taxes	
	1917	Increase[1] as against 1913	1917	Increase[1] as against 1913	1917	Increase[1] as against 1913	1917	Increase[1] as against 1913	1917	Increase[1] as against 1913
Creditanstalt	40.7	+15.3	11.8	+4.3	10.0	+6.8	20.1	+10.0	13.7	+9.1
Anglobank	29.9	+13.5	10.8	+2.0	6.8	+5.8	17.2	+ 8.3	7.4	+4.1
Bankverein	31.9	+14.2	8.3	+1.7	9.3	+5.3	20.8	+ 9.6	5.0	+2.2
Bodencredit-anstalt	25.2	+ 8.2	4.1	—	2.9	+1.7	7.2	+ 4.1	8.5	+5.4
Niederösterr. Eskompteges.	17.8	+ 8.8	3.8	+1.3	55.4	+3.8	4.7	+ 2.8	8.0	+6.0
Länderbank	24.3	+ 7.0	6.7	+0.4	9.3	+8.1	10.7	+ 2.7	8.0	+5.2
Unionbank	12.3	+ 5.3	2.6	+0.9	5.9	+4.2	5.7	+ 3.4	6.7	+5.2
Depositenbank	8.9	+ 5.3	12.1	+4.6	—	—	5.8	+ 4.3	3.4	—
Mercurbank	10.7	+ 4.7	4.5	+2.2	3.7	+1.7	6.5	+ 3.3	2.8	+1.4
Verkehrsbank	10.5	+ 4.8	4.4	+1.7	2.2	—	6.8	+ 1.8	2.8	+1.1

[1] in million crowns

yield on these operations to be 'twice as much as in the years of greatest financial gain since the 1870s'.[101] Yet, by omitting to say a word about the *real* value of the superficially astronomic rise in earnings, even this brilliantly informed expert fell victim to the 'big numbers illusion'.

The 1914 bank balance sheets had demonstrated the severe jolts sustained during the war's early months by the Austrian economy. 'Normalization' in 1915 launched an upswing in business reminiscent of the hectic activities in the last two decades before the outbreak of war. Although the discount rate showed a falling tendency as a natural result of the exceptional liquidity, the major banks enjoyed record transactions and record earnings which were not substantially impaired by constantly mounting staff costs and taxation.[102] Table 36 illustrates the profits and the burdens experienced by the banks at the zenith of the war boom.

The unusual extent of interest earnings is explained by the large volume of overdraft business and the rise in savings. Repeated capital increases also furnished the banks with ample means. The profitable investment of these funds was no problem for either Creditanstalt or any other Vienna house. Although the advances to the government and against War Loans (to name only two very important sources of receipts) brought relatively small returns, the enormous volume of these transactions effected a considerable growth in interest earnings. Likewise the commissions deriving from loans, securities, and foreign exchange activities make apparent the huge expansion of banking operations in wartime, even if the yields on this account lag far behind the amount of interest earned. Impressive too are the favourable

Table 37   Dividend distributions of the major Viennese banks

	1913	1914	1915	1916	1917	1918
Creditanstalt	10⅝	6⅞	10	11¼	12³⁄₁₆	7.764
Anglobank	8⅓	6¼	8¾	10	10⅚	6¼
Bankverein	8	5	7	8	8½	5
Boden-Creditanstalt	20	17	10	21	22	18
Niederöst. Escomptegesellschaft	10½	10½	11	11½	12	10
Länderbank	7½	4	6	7½	8	5
Unionbank	8½	5	7½	8½	9	5
Depositenbank	8½	5	8½	9¼	9¾	5
Mercurbank	9	5	7	9	9½	5
Verkehrsbank	7.85	5	6³⁄₇	7⁶⁄₇	8⁴⁄₇	5

All figures are quoted as percentages

proceeds shown in the securities and syndicate agreements accounts. They reflect the tempestuous Stock Exchange activity, which made feasible the profitable sale of shares and liquidations of issuing consortia. Consequently from 1915 onward banking profits showed a rising trend, the effect of which was of course reflected in the distribution of dividends. (See Table 37).

On the 1917 dividend distributions Austria's leading daily newspaper commented that 'Vienna banks' dividends are in all instances at a far higher level than before the war. Sometimes the figures are the highest ever. In certain instances, such as the Creditanstalt or Bankverein, higher dividends were distributed for a time fifty years ago, but since then the level has always been distinctly lower.'[103]

A year later dividends dropped to the 1914 level. The 1918 balance sheets reflected not only the despair and pessimism which gripped large sections of the population after the Central Powers' defeat and the Empire's dissolution, but also, perhaps above all, the desolate state of the Austrian economy after four years of a gruelling war, foreshadowing an uncertain future.

Certain important personnel changes in Austria's banking world had taken place during the war. Spitzmüller's retirement from Creditanstalt has been briefly mentioned. At a special board meeting, called for the occasion of his formal retirement, he stated that he had complied with an appeal from the Emperor, although conscious of the fact that 'to serve in wartime at the head of the Empire's leading banking house is an inspiring, noble, and highly responsible task and that employment in another capacity can hardly offer a more rewarding field of activity'.[104] He left the Bank at the beginning of October 1915 to take over the Ministry of Trade portfolio in the Stürgkh Cabinet.[105] Spitzmüller belonged to that small group of leading personalities, including Anselm von Rothschild, Brestee Hornbostel and Gustav von Mauthner, who tried to harmonize the interests of the Bank and its shareholders with those of society at large. It is fair to speculate as to how the fortunes of Creditanstalt would have fared in the turbulent post-war years if a personality possessing Spitzmüller's integrity and far-sightedness had determined its policy.

Shortly afterwards Ludwig von Neurath was nominated chairman of the management.[106] His career has been sketched in another connection.[107] The appointments of Dr Wilhelm Regendanz and Friedrich Ehrenfest also took place during the war.[108] The former, prior to joining Creditanstalt, had been legal adviser to the well-known banking firm of M. M. Warburg, Hamburg. The Bank had employed him in view of his long experience of Balkan affairs, a region on which it was intended to focus special attention in the post-war years.[109]

During the final years of the conflict Creditanstalt's management was in the hands of Ludwig von Neurath as chairman, Dr Paul Hammerschlag, Paul Lechner, Sigmund Löwy, Friedrich Ehrenfest, and Dr Wilhelm Regendanz. Neurath's responsibilities comprised representing the Bank in dealings with the authorities, the review of new industrial commitments, and the supervision of the affairs of associated firms. Hammerschlag and Regendanz were primarily responsible for the flotation of domestic bonds, foreign transactions, and railway affairs. Hammerschlag in addition looked after legal and tax problems, staff and pension matters, and Creditanstalt's representation in the Banking Association. Lechner, Löwy, and Ehrenfest were responsible for communal and provincial bond issues. Lechner and Ehrenfest were the Bank's Stock Exchange representatives. Löwy kept outstanding credits under control and supervized the Sugar Section of the Merchandise Department as well as the administration of the Bank's properties.[110]

The staff situation inside the Bank became more and more difficult as the war progressed. At the beginning of 1917 Hammerschlag reported to the board that of the 1,366 male employees 828 had been called to the colours in recent years. Their replacement by temporary personnel had proved an unsatisfactory expedient.[111] Of the 828 enlisted staff members 75 were killed at the front.[112]

A year after Spitzmüller's voluntary retirement Dr Rudolf Sieghart, governor of Boden-Creditanstalt, was forced into resignation by the Clam-Martinic Government – at the wish of Emperor Charles, who had recently ascended the throne. The manner of this dismissal met with disapproval from Josef Redlich because 'it smacks strongly of Tsarism'.[113] Yet he had referred to this same man in his diary as 'corrupter general of Austria' (sic). Sieghart had owed his appointment in 1909 to this influential, extremely well-paid position to the recommendation of the then Prime Minister Richard von Bienerth.[114] It was a well-known fact that this had happened in the face of disapproval by the Heir Apparent Archduke Franz Ferdinand, Albert von Rothschild (head of the S. M. von Rothschild banking house), and other people in public life. Emperor Charles seems to have regarded Sieghart's removal as a moral responsibility imposed on him by Archduke Franz Ferdinand. Boden-Creditanstalt had an especially close link to the Imperial House through its responsibility of administering the Habsburg entail. The board tried at first to oppose the young Emperor's order, but its resistance was soon broken after the Prime Minister had prevailed upon the Emperor to grant Sieghart a 'release in grace'.[115] The pill's bitterness was moreover somewhat sweetened for Sieghart by a generous compensation from the board. The latter had also eventually to accept a further Imperial pronouncement, the appointment of the not-very-highly-esteemed former Minister of Finance von Leth to the vacant governorship.

The Sieghart Affair appears to have been the first move towards the other *cause célèbre*, the Krantz affair. In both instances the Emperor and his advisers wanted to offer the badly afflicted Austrian people an expiatory sacrifice and so to lend fresh popularity to the discredited system of government by emergency decree. Joseph Redlich, an implacable opponent of the absolutist régime, draws the following conclusion from this episode:

The strangest part of this government intervention is first, that Clam has all along behaved as though Boden-Creditanstalt's articles of association invest the Emperor, through his right to nominate the governor, with a personal right of action excluding any responsibility of the government, and second, that although all Vienna knows of the event and the Stock Exchange has reacted by a collapse of all shares belonging to the Boden-Creditanstalt group, not one newspaper is allowed to write about it! These two aspects, taken together, give the whole matter a decidedly 'Russian' character. What abyss are the Clams, the Hohenlohes, the Czernins going to lead this country into? The entire affair shows how much alive the aristocratic tyranny is in Austria that between 1848 and 1916 has been responsible for the most grievous catastrophes.[116]

Redlich's bitter comment is reminiscent of Hugo von Hofmannsthal's prophetic words on the eve of war to Leopold von Andrian.[117]

Notes

1 Creditanstalt's 1918 Annual Report summarized developments in the following terms: 'During the period under review the hallmarks of the economy were again vigorous activity coupled with a constantly increasing shortage of raw materials for the industries receiving support to meet war requirements, a further sharp rise in food prices, and a continuous state of liquidity.' See 'Österreichische Creditanstalt', *Neue Freie Presse*, 8 July 1919.

2 The statistical data quoted in the following pages has been taken from Creditanstalt Annual Reports, *Compass, Der Österreichische Volkswirt*, and Max Sokal, *Die Tätigkeit der Banken* (Vienna, 1922).

3 From 1913 to 1917 Deutsche Bank almost trebled its balance-sheet total from 2,200 to 6,200 million marks. In 1918 its share capital (including reserves) was 500 million marks, that of Creditanstalt 285 million crowns. Deutsche Bank was however able during this time to absorb several smaller banking houses including Schlesische Bankverein and Norddeutsche Creditanstalt. See 'Der Krieg in seinen wirtschaftlichen Folgen', *Neue Freie Presse*, 28 April 1918.

4 Obviously even an index of industrial prices does not furnish a very suitable measure for deflation of the banks' balance sheets. The 'true' value of balance-sheet totals can hardly be established with the aid of overall index figures because the individual items of each balance sheet are subject to a highly variable pace of changes in value.

5 Cf., for example, Board Meeting Minutes of 23 April 1918, Creditanstalt Archives.

6 As late as 1918 the Creditanstalt Annual Report speaks, in connection with the steeply risen staff costs, of '*the reduction in the level of prices to be expected* upon the restoration of normal conditions'. See 'Österreichische Creditanstalt', *Neue Freie Press*, 8 July 1919. (Present author's italics.)

7 Industry is no longer the banking world's debtor, but its creditor' is the lapidary comment in 'Entwicklung der Banken im Kriege', *Neue Freie Presse*, 1 January 1918.

8 'Agriculture everywhere has harvested the greatest gains and it is gradually beginning to make use of the modern organization of banking for the administration of its resources. Deposits of farmers are now engaging the banks' attention to an increased extent and they have been turned to account on behalf of the last War Loan in a somewhat larger, even though still inadequate measure.' See 'Der Krieg in seinen wirtschaftlichen Folgen', *Neue Freie Presse*, 7 April 1918.

9 1916 Creditanstalt Annual Report, p. 9, Creditanstalt Archives. As a result of the premium profit the Capital Reserve Fund amounted to 77,195,690 crowns. The Bank's capital totalled 170 million crowns, its reserves 112.6 million crowns, and in addition there was the War Losses Reserve of 5 million.

10 Cf. Part I, Chap. 4, p. 51 *et seq.*

11 In a report to an Extraordinary General Meeting the management chairman, Neurath, made the following statement: 'We have to reckon in post-war days with what is likely to be a steeply rising demand for loans on the part of our industrial customers. They have on the one hand, to a considerable extent invested in War Loan the funds deriving from the liquidation of stockpiles and of outstanding debts. On the other hand they will need large-scale advances to finance their raw materials purchases and for the conversion in many cases of their wartime to peace-time production. Finally, one must allow for the fact that some of the companies belonging to our Group are planning to make important investments, the purpose of which is to render the Austrian economy independent of necessities hitherto supplied from abroad.' 'Österreichische Creditanstalt', *Neue Freie Presse*, 30 January 1918.

12 'A determining factor too was that, once a bank had chosen to undertake a capital increase, others were bound to follow because of mutual jealousy they would not permit any changes which might affect their "social status".' Stefan von Müller, *Die finanzielle Mobilmachung Österreichs und ihr Ausbau bis 1918* (Berlin, 1918) p. 64.

13 See Appendix II, Table 5.

14 Cf. 'Österreichische Creditanstalt', *Neue Freie Presse*, 30 January 1918.

15 The Board Meeting Minutes of 27 February 1917 reveal that they involved (together with Ungarische Allgemeine Kreditbank) a participation in Bank für Chile und Deutschland that was meant in turn to lead to a commitment on behalf of Brasilianische Bank für Deutschland. Creditanstalt Archives.

16 Board Meeting Minutes, 10 September and 4 November 1913, Creditanstalt Archives.

17 Board Meeting Minutes, 21 April, 19 May, 1 and 14 July 1914, Creditanstalt Archives.

18 Cf. Berliner Disconto-Gesellschaft 1914 Annual Report. 'Hereby we have established closer relations with the Bulgarian Government and have paved the way for an association with Germany.' Central State Arch., Potsdam, 31.01 RWM 15729, p. 38.

19 Board Meeting Minutes, 21 February 1915. The minutes disclose the banks' interests: Creditanstalt, Wiener Bankverein, and Ungarische Allgemeine Kreditbank had each one third.

20 Board Meeting Minutes, 24 August 1915, Creditanstalt Archives.

21 Board Meeting Minutes, 21 December 1915, Creditanstalt Archives.

22 See *Compass*, 1918, Vol. I, p. 506.

23 Cabinet Minutes, 12 December 1915, Haus, Hof, und Staatsarchiv, P A X L, Box 312.

24 See Creditanstalt 1916 Annual Report, Creditanstalt Archives. The bank house S. M. von Rothschild also participated in this transaction.

25 Board Meeting Minutes, 17 April 1917, Creditanstalt Archives.

26 Board Meeting Minutes, 13 February 1917, Creditanstalt Archives.

27 Board Meeting Minutes, 28 August 1917, and 1917 Annual Report, Creditanstalt Archives.

28 Boden-Creditanstalt 1917 Annual Report.

29 Board Meeting Minutes, 14 June 1916, Creditanstalt Archives.

30 Walther Federn, 'Eine österreichisch-ungarische Bankengruppe für den Orient', *Der Österreichische Volkswirt*, 4 November 1916, p. 75.

31 *Der Österreichische Volkswirt*, p. 74 et seq.

32 *Der Österreichische Volkswirt*, p. 75.

33 Board Meeting Minutes, 5 September and 3 October 1916, Creditanstalt Archives. Director Neurath reported to the Creditanstalt Board in the meeting of 5 September 1916 that the Austrian government would give the banks a guarantee for the Turkish credit, but Turkey was not supposed to know this. (See also Compass 1918, Vol. I, p. 504.)

34 *Der Österreichische Volkswirt*, 4 November 1916, p. 76.

35 Letter from the management of Skodawerke A G, Pilsen to the Ministry of Foreign Affairs, 25 February 1918, Ministry of Finance Archives, File 25.621/18.

36 Board Meeting Minutes, 23 October 1917, Creditanstalt Archives.

37 Board Meeting Minutes, 24 January 1918, Creditanstalt Archives.

38 Board Meeting Minutes, 17 October 1916, Creditanstalt Archives.

39 Cf. Cen. St. Arch., Potsdam, 31.01 RWM 15691, p. 50, Dresdener Bank 1916 Annual Report: 'An association between the German interests active in the Near East has thus been arranged by the association of the two . . . Austro-Hungarian banks.'

40 *Compass*, 1918, Vol. I, p. 504, and *Ein Jahrhundert Creditanstalt-Bankverein* (Vienna, 1955, p. 140f).

41 Board Meeting Minutes, 1 June 1917, Creditanstalt Archives.

42 *Compass*, 1925, Vol. 1, p. 373.

43 Board Meeting Minutes, 22 January 1918, Creditanstalt Archives. From the Ministry of Finance Archives file 33.434/18, 27 March 1918, it emerges that three banking groups were in competition for the exercise of dominant influence over the future bank – Creditanstalt with Niederösterreichische Escompte-Gesellschaft, Österreichische Länderbank with Unionbank, and Wiener Bankverein with Anglobank.

44 The same applies to the activities of the so-called 'Rouble Syndicate, founded in 1918 by Austrian and Hungarian banks to finance food imports from the Ukraine and dissolved immediately after the defeat of the Central Powers. See *Ein Jahrhundert*, p. 141.

45 *Compass*, 1921, Vol. I, p. 280.

46 Other members of the Austrian syndicate were the Rothschild banking house, Boden-Creditanstalt, Anglobank, Wiener Bankverein, Niederösterreichische Escompte-Gesellschaft, and Unionbank. Subsequently Hungarian banks joined the consortium. The Dutch syndicate consisted of Nederlandsche Handelsmaatschapij, Amsterdamsche Bank, Rotterdamsche Bankvereenigung, and the banking house Lippmann, Rosenthal & Co.

47 *Ein Jahrhundert*, p. 138.

48 In this instance too there was rivalry between Austria-Hungary and Germany. Official circles urged the Viennese banks to go ahead on their own. At a meeting on 14 February 1917 the Creditanstalt representatives pointed out that 'during the negotiations with Dutch friends the talk had so far been about the promotion of a German-Austro-Hungarian-Dutch bank . . . The bank had moreover . . . agreed with its German friends on concerted action and it must therefore as a matter of loyalty notify them prior to negotiations in Holland.' The official representatives, the memo continues, had thereupon pressed Creditanstalt 'to tell its friends that it would continue with the joint project, but that it would ask them to assent to the exclusion of Germany [from it] if their Dutch friends were to profess a preference for the establishment of a purely Austro-Hungarian bank.' Cf. File 20.199/1917 Ministry of Finance Archives.

49 The copy of a confidential letter from Amsterdamsche Bank to Creditanstalt, dated 7 April 1917, is contained in File 36.848/1917, Ministry of Finance Archives. The letter was signed by Director van Hengel who in 1931 was to play a prominent part in Creditanstalt affairs.

50 A copy of the letter, dated 7 April 1917, contained the following passage: 'We have made provision for Austrian peace-time imports from South America in so far as we have put our relations with Brazilianische Bank für Deutschland and Bank für Chile und Deutschland on a closer footing. However, to make sure to an even greater extent of peace-time imports, we have also entered into negotiations with Holland.' See File 45.929/1917, Ministry of Finance Archives. The two banks were closely associated with Berliner Disconto-Gesellschaft. The latter had been Creditanstalt's partner in the 'Bulgarian Syndicate'.

51 The Dutch feared that a joint-stock company 'even though consisting exclusively of Dutch banks would not escape public notice and that therefore it would be advisable to refrain from such a promotion until the conclusion of peace'. Joint

Report by Creditanstalt, Boden-Creditanstalt, and Niederösterreichische Escompte-Gesellschaft to the Minister of Finance Baron Wimmer, 27 April 1917, File 55.726/1917, Ministry of Finance Archives.

52 File 55.726/1917, Ministry of Finance Archives.

53 See File 98.166/1917, Ministry of Finance Archives.

54 *Ein Jahrhundert*, p. 139.

55 *Ein Jahrhundert*, p. 138 et seq.

56 Board Meeting Minutes, 18 May 1916, Creditanstalt Archives.

57 Board Meeting Minutes, 30 May 1916, Creditanstalt Archives.

58 See Part II, Chap. 3, p. 153 et seq.

59 Board Meeting Minutes, 14 June 1916, Creditanstalt Archives.

60 Board Meeting Minutes, 5 and 19 December 1916, Creditanstalt Archives.

61 Board Meeting Minutes, 30 January 1917, Creditanstalt Archives.

62 Board Meeting Minutes, 27 February 1917, Creditanstalt Archives.

63 Board Meeting Minutes, 13 and 27 March 1917, Creditanstalt Archives.

64 Board Meeting Minutes, 9 June, 17 and 31 July 1917, Creditanstalt Archives.

65 Board Meeting Minutes, 28 August 1917, Creditanstalt Archives.

66 Board Meeting Minutes, 6 and 20 November 1917, Creditanstalt Archives.

67 Board Meeting Minutes, 18 December 1917, Creditanstalt Archives.

68 Board Meeting Minutes, 14, 22, and 31 January 1918, Creditanstalt Archiveds.

69 Board Meeting Minutes, 19 February 1918, Creditanstalt Archives.

70 Board Meeting Minutes, 18 June 1918, Creditanstalt Archives.

71 Board Meeting Minutes, 23 April 1918, Creditanstalt Archives.

72 Board Meeting Minutes, 9 July, 1 August, and 9 October 1918, Creditanstalt Archives.

73 Board Meeting Minutes, 9 October 1918, Creditanstalt Archives.

74 Cf. Part II, Chap. 2, p. 138 et seq.

75 Banks and savings banks subscribed more than 1,300 million crowns to the first Austrian War Loan issue. See 'Die Bedingungen der Anleihezeichnung', *Neue Freie Presse*, 15 November 1914.

76 A commentary on the Wiener Bankverein 1917 balance sheet said, 'The second largest item consists of securities holdings. They have far more than doubled, an increase mainly attributable to War Loan, inasmuch as the Head Office's fixed interest securities have risen from 57.4 to 166.8 millions and those of banch offices from 4.4 to 8.4 million crowns. Bankverein has therefore a higher holding of War Loan even if it has *to a greater degree* sold, with sizeable amounts going abroad, the 375.5 million crowns' worth of Austrian and Hungarian War Loan subscribed for its own account.' See 'Die Bilanzen', *Der Österreichische Volkswirt*, 6 April 1918, p. 114. (Present author's italics.)

77 File 24.941/1918, Ministry of Finance Archives. 'H.E.' was Baron Wimmer, Minister of Finance.

78 'Die Banken im Weltkriege', *Der Österreichische Volkswirt*, 16 February 1918, p. 332. One estimate was that at the beginning of 1918 'a good 15,000 million crowns, 70% of banking assets, are serving war finance'. See 'Entwicklung der Banken im Kriege', *Neue Freie Presse*, 1 January 1918, by the newspaper's economic expert.

79 Creditanstalt's merchandise business suffered of course severely through the increasing shortage of consumer goods and of coal. A commentary on the 1917 balance sheet remarks that 'profits on sugar and coal in the Merchandise

Department have again fallen off'. See 'Österreichische Creditanstalt', *Der Österreichische Volkswirt*, 7 April 1917, p. 117.

80 *Der Österreichische Volkswirt*, 7 April 1917, p. 118. Another passage ran, 'As it is, Creditanstalt has in contrast with former years an interest in an only infinitesimal number of poorly profitable enterprises. As early as 1914 its War Loss Reserve made provision for its sole dubious commitment of any importance, the interests in and claims against Schweiger and Austro-Orientalische Handelsgesellschaft, the two export firms which are completely without information as to the fate of their stocks and receivables.' (*Der Österreichische Volkswirt*, 7 April 1917, p. 117.)

81 What must not be overlooked is that the banks' claims against the state, especially by way of overdrafts, exceeded by far the amounts invested in War Loan.

82 See Alexander Popovics, *Das Geldwesen im Kriege* (Vienna, 1925), p. 82.

83 The figures are taken from the Creditanstalt 1913–1918 Annual Reports, Creditanstalt Archives.

84 Board Meeting Minutes, 9 February and 24 August 1915, Creditanstalt Archives.

85 Board Meeting Minutes, 12 May 1915, Creditanstalt Archives.

86 Board Meeting Minutes, 9 November 1915, Creditanstalt Archives.

87 Board Meeting Minutes, 8 February 1916, Creditanstalt Archives.

88 Board Meeting Minutes, 7 March 1916, Creditanstalt Archives.

89 Board Meeting Minutes, 18 May 1916, Creditanstalt Archives.

90 Board Meeting Minutes, 5 September and 3 October 1916, Creditanstalt Archives.

91 Board Meeting Minutes, 19 December 1916, Creditanstalt Archives.

92 Board Meeting Minutes, 16 January 1917, Creditanstalt Archives.

93 Board Meeting Minutes, 30 January 1917, Creditanstalt Archives.

94 Board Meeting Minutes, 27 February 1917, Creditanstalt Archives.

95 Board Meeting Minutes, 4 April 1917, Creditanstalt Archives.

96 Board Meeting Minutes, 9 October 1917, Creditanstalt Archives.

97 Board Meeting Minutes, 18 December 1917, Creditanstalt Archives.

98 Board Meeting Minutes, 4 January 1918, Creditanstalt Archives.

99 Board Meeting Minutes, 4 June 1918, Creditanstalt Archives.

100 Board Meeting Minutes, 19 November 1918, Creditanstalt Archives.

101 The balance-sheet expert of *Der Österreichische Volkswirt* believed the shares flotations of highly remunerative undertakings, on which exceptionally high premiums could be obtained as against their book value, to be the most important source for high profits besides public loans. (Cf. *Der Österreichische Volkswirt*, 7 April 1917, p. 118.)

102 Cf. Max Sokal, *Die Tätigkeit der Banken* (Vienna, 1920), reprint from the report published by the Lower Austrian Chamber of Commerce and Trade on economic conditions 1914–18, p. 38. The author states that in 1917 the discount rate fluctuated between 3% and 1.12% and in 1918 between 4.12% and 2.36%.

103 'Die Banken im Kriege', *Neue Freie Presse*, 4 June 1918.

104 Board Meeting Minutes, 3 December 1915, Creditanstalt Archives.

105 Alexander Spitzmüller, *Und hat auch Ursach', es zu lieben* (Vienna, 1955), p. 136 et seq.

106 Board Meeting Minutes, 28 December 1915, Creditanstalt Archives.
107 Cf. Part II, Chap. 1, p. 91 et seq..
108 Board Meeting Minutes, 1 June 1917, Creditanstalt Archives.
109 Board Meeting Minutes, 14 June 1917, Creditanstalt Archives.
110 See annex to Board Meeting Minutes, 1 June 1917, Creditanstalt Archives.
111 Board Meeting Minutes, 27 February 1917, Creditanstalt Archives.
112 Calculated on the basis of figures given in the 1914–1918 Annual Reports, Creditanstalt Archives.
113 Josef Redlich, *Schicksalsjahre Österreichs* 1908–1919 (Graz, 1953–4), Vol. II, p. 174.
114 Spitzmüller, *Und hat auch Ursach*, p. 82 et seq.
115 Redlich, *Schicksalsjahre*, Vol. II, p. 173.
116 Redlich, *Schicksalsjahre*, Vol. II, p. 194.
117 Cf. Part I, Chap. 8, footnote 14.

CHAPTER 5
Options for the Future

At the beginning of 1918, with the Russians forced by the Central Powers to agree to the humiliating terms of Brest Litovsk, Walther Federn thought that the war had entered its closing stage. The Empire's existence, he noted in his forecast for 1918, was assured for any predictable time ahead as far as the security of its borders was concerned.[1] Otto Bauer, at this juncture openly advocated self-determination for the nations within the Austrian association of states. Like Federn he was convinced that the outcome of the war so far had made certain of Austria's continued existence for the 'foreseeable future'.[2] All critics of the *status quo*, except those belonging to the radical Pan-German wing, were however at one that this association of nationalities must be placed on a new footing permeated by the principles of democracy.

This is not the place to record in detail the variety of views on the form of reorganization appropriate for the multi-national polity. Opinion ranged from those who wanted to adhere to the Dual Monarchy's constitutional structure, apart from some purely cosmetic changes, to the few unrealistic enthusiasts favouring a 'quadralist' solution. The latter group argued that in future the Empire ought to consist, in addition to Austria and Hungary, of a South Slav and a Polish portion. The Polish part should comprise Western Galicia plus the newly-won Polish provinces. The Ukrainian territories would receive autonomy and remain outside the newly formed Polish entity.[3]

The Empire's internal structure was not the only problem weighing ever more heavily on people's minds. Soon after the outbreak of hostilities the German Government took up the frequently-aired notion of a united Central Europe and started discussions by presenting an *aide-mémoire*.[4] Plans for the economic union of the two states had begun in the early decades of the nineteenth century. About the middle of the century they were argued with great emphasis by the brilliant Austrian statesman Baron Bruck, but met with fierce resistance from Prussian quarters. The Austro-Prussian War of 1866 seemed to be the painful end to a particularly unhappy chapter of Austrian foreign policy.

On the conclusion in 1879 of the Triple Alliance between Austria-Hungary, Germany and Italy, the idea of economic harmonization between the first two partners was resuscitated. This time it was German industrial circles and prominent German economists like Gustav Schmoller who advocated plans for closer economic co-operation. The objectors were mainly on the Austrian side.[5] After the outbreak of the First World War the number of partisans in favour of a permanent, close alliance between Austria-Hungary and Germany greatly increased. The most eloquent plea was made in Friedrich Naumann's well-known book *Mitteleuropa*. The initiative taken by the German Government in autumn 1915 followed logically from this concept of 'union' which had, particularly among German industrialists, attracted more and more interest.

The German *aide-mémoire* envisaged a customs union and a far-reaching military convention. It 'created a most unfavourable impression in Austro-Hungarian Government circles', said Spitzmüller in his memoirs.[6]

The inclination to treat the Empire as Germany's war-instrument, or, as Anton Wildgans with poetic pungency later expressed it in his famous oration on Austria, to degrade it to the role of the German Empire's 'shield-bearer', was quite apparent. Above all the German Government sought with this *aide-mémoire* to interfere in Austro-Hungarian domestic affairs and demanded measures against a further 'Slavization' of Austria.[7]

The Ministry of Foreign Affairs' reply was 'distinctly briefer and more reserved in tone'.[8] It spoke of an 'economic convergence between the two states' rather than of a customs union and an economic community. Gratz and Schüller suggest that there was an undercurrent of anxiety in Austria about co-operation with an undeniably stronger Germany which could impair the sovereignty of Austria-Hungary and its independence. The direct answer of the ministry was however that serious negotiations could not begin before agreement had been reached with the Hungarian Government on the renewal of the Compromise Agreement.[9]

The danger of the Empire's 'Slavization', the spectre invoked by the Germans, was rejected in diplomatically discreet, nonetheless unmistakeable terms by Count Burian, author of the reply.

The predominant position of the Germans in Austria rests on their numerical and specific importance. It may be subject to fluctuations, as happens in the life of a multinational state, but it cannot be imperilled. The law and their own activity see to that. The increased importance of other national elements arises with their rising culture of level. It cannot be held back, but must on the contrary be welcomed. It will moreover, as hitherto, not prejudice the external interest of our alliance.[10]

Advocates of the plans for a Central Europe, as familiarized among broad sections of the Austrian public by Naumann's book, included the German-nationalist historian Heinrich Friedjung and the well-known economists Eugen von Philippovich and Gustav Stolper. On the other hand, as Professor Verosta has remarked, social democrats in both Germany and Austria adopted a negative attitude. Rudolf Hilferding, author of *Finanzkapital* and subsequently Minister of Finance in the Weimar Republic, thought that Naumann's Central Europe would lead to a peace which 'would only be the continuation of war by economic means'.[11]

Still more vehement was the reaction of Joseph Schumpeter, then a young professor of economics. In a letter to Heinrich Lammasch, the international lawyer destined to become the Empire's last Prime Minister, he analyzed German political aims as revealed in the *aide-mémoire*.

The points that attracted my attention so strongly are as follows: first of all it is stated here, clearly and concisely, for the first time by that side, that it is the political purpose, that is, our being shackled to Prussia, and not the question of economic utility, which is at the root of the matter. Next, with almost naive bluntness, any hope of intermediate tariffs, which the most modest Austrian soul was surely entitled to entertain, is proved an illusion – nothing must stand in the way of the domination of Berlin banking capital over Austria. The target is 'real, internal, economic dependence' and that this, allowing for the existing ratio of power, cannot be of a 'mutual' nature is obvious. The joint commercial treaty then amounts to a joint policy in all respects – consummation of the *societas leonina*. It would confirm my suspicion that the conquest of Austria is Germany's most important war aim.[12]

That was an uncompromising statement of what Burian, Spitzmüller, and especially the Hungarian Prime Minister Istvan Tisza, who always had great reservations about German foreign policy, may well have thought when reading the *aide-mémoire*.

Renewal of the Austro-Hungarian Compromise Agreement, running out in 1917, had immediate priority. Spitzmüller's condition for joining the Stürgkh Cabinet had been that an effort should be made to put the next economic and trade agreement with Hungary on a longer-term – at least twenty years – basis. Therein he enjoyed the support of his cabinet colleagues and also of many public figures including Wilhelm Ellenbogen, the respected Social Democrat member of parliament.[13] Even in Hungary many leading politicians were friendly to such a new concept of the compromise. There was general realization that the lasting economic unity of the Empire was the prerequisite for its attractiveness as an ally. To the many responsibilities placed by the war on the shoulders of the senior civil servants in the departments of finance and trade were now added the intricate negotiations on political and commercial affairs between representatives of the Austrian and the Hungarian Governments on the one hand and between German and Austro-Hungarian trade experts on the other.

Spitzmüller was the author of an interesting study on the last of the Austro-Hungarian Compromise Agreements.[14] 'At the beginning of the compromise negotiations with Hungary, in February 1916,' he writes, 'there was as yet no firm plan as to the relationship to be sought with Germany.' He goes on to say that, in his capacity as Minister of Trade, he could exercise no influence over the negotiations with Germany because 'these were immediately put on the level of special consultations in which the Ministers had no part.'[15] The possibility cannot be dismissed, even if it should not be possible to give documentary proof, that the desire to exclude people like Spitzmüller from the negotiations originated with the German side. Germany had an understandable interest in keeping at a distance politicians with a pronounced bias towards Austrian autonomy.

The bumpy path of the compromise negotiations will not be followed here. Spitzmüller seems to have nipped in the bud endeavours to impose the new agreement from above, that is, without parliamentary sanction.[16] Not before the end of January 1917 could a settlement be reached on the quota and on cattle imports. Far-reaching concessions had to be made to the Hungarians. Nevertheless, and this they regarded as an act of complaisance on their part towards the demands raised at the outset by the Austrian delegates, the duration of the treaty was extended to twenty years. On 24 February the new compromise was signed.[17] It was however fated never to be sanctioned by the two parliaments, because considerable resistance to its provisions emerged, especially in Hungary, in particular to the lengthening of the term of this agreement. On 2 December the two parliaments merely voted for a two-year extension of the 1907 compromise.[18]

The negotiations on an economic union between the Empire and Germany proved even more difficult than the last compromise talks. At the root of the frequent differences lay perhaps the fact that initially the partners had no common objective. Only in the course of several rounds was a joint formula arrived, as described by Gratz and Schüller as follows:

This formula presented, in the theory and practice of international trade, a new solution to the problem of economic union between independent states. The two states were to constitute as far as possible a free trade area, they were to act in common *vis-à-vis* third countries without relinquishing either their political independence or allowing important sections of their economic life to go to ruin. To avoid this, imperilled branches of production would need protection for a certain period against competition by the partner state and a higher tariff against outsiders than the same branches of production enjoyed within the union'.[19]

On this basis the negotiators at Salzburg on 11 October 1918 concluded a draft convention complete in nearly all details.[20] Today we can only conjecture as to how this comprehensive piece of treaty-making – not quite unobjectionable from the point of view of Austrian industry – would have been received by public opinion. From the start it had of course been clear that only in the case of complete victory would the Central Powers be able to force the rest of the world to accept such an innovation in foreign trade relations.[21]

Whereas the compromise agreement and economic union with Germany were the subject of intensive negotiations, the problem of constitutional reconstruction of the Monarchy – which one would imagine to have been of outstanding importance – remained chiefly the concern of a few statesmen, of political scientists, and of other thoughtful political observers who were deeply worried about the Empire's future. Particularly among the Social Democrats a vehement dispute flared up, which was reflected in a series of interesting publications during the last year of war when the censorship eased somewhat.[22] Spitzmüller, sceptical about a federal solution, nonetheless believed a reorientation of domestic policies 'inevitable, thanks to Wilson's programme of conciliation'. He added, perhaps not altogether convincingly, that 'At that stage, though, the young Emperor really could find no suitable statesmen with the courage to venture now, just in time, i.e., before spring 1918, on the overdue work of reform, the need for which the monarch had himself clearly recognized and called for.'[23]

Serious studies, but of a preliminary character, on the subject were not launched until the formation of the Clam-Martinic (1916–17) and Seidler (1917–18) Cabinets.[24] Baron Hussarek, taking over the thankless task of guiding the affairs of state in summer 1918, devoted his main attention to constitutional reform. In this phase there was hardly any question but that the Empire could be saved from extinction, if at all, only by radical changes.[25]

A small group of advisers close to the Emperor, whose influence can hardly any longer be properly assessed, participated in these efforts. The outcome was Emperor Charles's controversial manifesto of 16 October. It summoned his peoples 'through free co-operation to pave the way for the nation's reorganization in the spirit of the principles pronounced by the Allied Powers in their peace offer'. The basis for the reorganization should be a federal state 'in which every nation shall constitute in its area of settlement its own political community'. Yet directly on the heels of this followed a fatal concession to Hungary, necessitated by the threat from Hungarian Prime Minister Wekerle to cut off all food supplies otherwise.[26] 'The integrity of the lands of the Holy Hungarian Crown is in no way affected.' Finally there was the appeal to the Emperor's peoples 'to participate in this great work of the national parliaments which – composed of the erstwhile members of the Austrian *Reichstag* – are to give effect to the interests of the peoples in their relation to one another and in their dealings with My Government.'[27]

The Emperor's invitation to his peoples to take into their hands their own national destiny gave the signal for the continued speedy dissolution of the Dual Monarchy and thus brought about the opposite of what he had striven for. Josef Redlich's highly penetrating mind grasped this fully on the very day that the draft document became known. The entry in his diary for 16 October reads:

Seidler [the former Prime Minister] gave me the impression of a wily official lacking appreciation of the problem's magnitude, his basic idea being to gain time by compromises of even the most far-reaching nature. There he is in full accord with Hussarek whose speech last week revealed already the court flunkeys' programme – the peoples are to constitute themselves as separate nations and then establish 'the common link' under the guidance of the government. That the constitution of the nations inherently comprehends the annihilation of the central authority proper, of the army, and of the bureaucracy, so that after this act of constitution the government will have neither psychological nor moral power left, that is what the petty-minded manoeuvres in the Herrengasse completely overlook.[28]

The Empire's dissolution proceeded now with something bordering on elemental force. Already on 15 October a South Slav national Council had met and proclaimed an independent Croatia.[29] On 18 October a Ukrainian National Council was constituted and established its sovereignty in Eastern Galicia. On 20 October the Czech National Council assembled at Prague and announced the independence of the Czech and Slovak nationalities. Finally, on 21 and 25 October respectively, the German-Austrian parliamentarians at Vienna and the Hungarian parliamentarians at Budapest announced the formation of their own national polities.[30] The four-hundred-year-old Empire, which had survived the tempests of the Thirty Years War, the eighteenth century Wars of Succession, and the Napoleonic Wars, fell apart completely in less than two weeks. 'Austria-Hungary has ceased to exist and there is no longer any possibility of negotiating with it', such was the lapidary comment on these cataclysmic events contained at the beginning of December in a report by the Foreign Office to the British Government.[31]

21 October 1918 can be called the birthday of the new Austria, inasmuch as it was on this date that the German-Austrian members of the old parliament proclaimed the resolution to organize the political life of their people in the narrower framework of a purely national state. Not as yet clear, though, was the shape the new state would take. The Social Democrats and German Nationalists inclined towards a republic, the Christian Socialists seemed to prefer a constitutional monarchy.[32]

The resolution included a warning that related to the inviolability of German-Austrian soil and referred in particular to the Austrian character of the Sudetenland as this region was regarded as an integral part of Austria in spite of the fact that the German-language territories of Bohemia and Moravia were not a part of the Alpine lands. It was known of course that the Czechs claimed these territories for historical, economic, and strategic reasons and if necessary were prepared to obtain recognition for their claim with armed force. The militancy of the Austrian representatives' declaration could not conceal the fact that they were in no position to prevent the Czech plans for annexation. Their sole hope relied on strict interpretation and implementation of the principles of self-determination enunciated by President Wilson. From the very outset fruitful collaboration between Austrians and Czechs, which would have been the rational expression of a centuries' old, even if not entirely voluntary association, was blocked by the tragic conflict over the Sudetenland.

The assembled former members of the Austrian *Reichstag* reconstituted themselves into the 'Provisional National Assembly of German-Austria', assumed all the prerogatives of a law-giving body until such time as a free general election could provide a legislature and assigned executive power to the committee subsequently called the 'Council of State'. The latter was explicitly authorized to represent the new state in its relations with other states and with the last Austro-Hungarian Government under its last Prime Minister, Lammasch. The reference to the continued existence of such a government was no accident, but was meant to indicate that German-Austria was an entirely new entity not to be confused in any way with the Empire in dissolution. To deliver the new state from the embarrassing role of legitimate heir to the Dual Monarchy, this was also the line adopted by the Austrian delegation to the Peace Conference. The Allies rejected this approach and insisted on Austria's treatment as a defeated country.

A cursory examination of the speeches made on 21 October already shows at this early stage the distressing and apparently insoluble problem of the new Austria's external orientation. The two most important speakers were the German Nationalist Waldner and the mortally ill leader of the Social Democrats, Viktor Adler. Waldner emphasized the new state's 'Germanism', but he failed to declare what the majority of those present probably expected – the consequent need for union with Germany.

It was Viktor Adler who for the first time made a clear, explicit statement on what may be called the 'Austrian dilemma'. 'The German people in Austria' he said,

shall establish their own democratic state, their own German state which shall decide entirely freely how it shall regulate its relations with neighbouring nations and with Germany. It shall enter into association with its neighbouring nations in a free League of Nations if these nations so wish. Should however the other nations reject such an association or agree to it only on conditions incompatible with the economic and the national needs of the German people, then the German-Austrian state which, left to itself, would not be an economically viable entity, will be forced to join Germany as a special associate state. We demand for the German-Austrian state complete freedom to choose between these two possible associations.[33]

Adler had begun his political career as a member of the German Liberal Party whose original objective was perhaps most aptly expressed by Ferdinand Lassalle's famous dictum: 'Greater Germany *moins les dynasties*'. When in 1889 Adler took over leadership of the badly shaken Social Democrat Party at the Convention of Hainfeld, he is likely to have held Karl Marx's view that Austria would lose its right to existence at the moment when revolution had won the day in Russia.[34] But the ageing Viktor Adler, who on the outbreak of the First World War had supported national defence, is likely to have shared the views of Renner and other right-wing Social Democrats who regarded the dissolution of a supra-national state as a historically retrograde step.[35] It was therefore not by chance that in his 21 October speech he recommended preservation of the old family ties and advocated union with Germany only if these could not be renewed, or not renewed on acceptable conditions.

In contrast with his close party friend Otto Bauer, who based his propagation of the *Anschluss* idea on Wilson's, and later Trotzki's, support of self-determinaiton, Adler shifted the emphasis of the argument towards a seemingly unassailable point, the 'self-evident' lack of viability of the rump state German-Austria. Experienced in party affairs as he was, it must have been obvious to him that the nationalist platform of the so-called New Left, which in spring had taken self-determination as its slogan, must signify a severe break with the party's multinational alignment of recent decades. The nickname 'Imperial and Royal Social Democrat Party', implying no more than that something of the mutlinational state's cosmopolitan character attached to it too, was not altogether fortuitous. Adler's ear was also very delicately tuned to the Viennese masses. He was well aware of the unpopularity of the *Anschluss* concept just before the end of hostilities.[36] His recommendation of union with Germany as the alternative to an otherwise impossible economic situation was a considered move. It was the prelude to a debate that continued at varying levels until the last hours of the First Republic.

With certain reservations the Social Democrats had adopted a positive, expectant attitude towards the new state. Their opponents, the Christian Socialists, were in a condition of internal dissension and disorientation. Already before the war this party, once protagonist of the small man's revolt, had to all intents and purposes turned into a pillar of the Dual Monarchy. Even during the most difficult periods of the war it had continued to back the monarchic and semi-authoritarian form of rule practised by the government. Military defeat and the consequent dissolution of the old Empire had thrown this party of the *status quo* into an agonizing crisis of identity.

In this dangerous situation it needed a personality with outstanding leadership qualifications to guide it towards new forms of political association. If it hesitated too long because of its identification with former institutions and values, it might fail to play its part in the new era. Ignaz Seipel, Roman Catholic priest, teacher of theology, and minister in the Lammasch administration, recognized the peril. By the publication of four articles in the organ of the Christian Socialist Party, *Reichspost*, he managed to bring his party into a new, crucial political alignment.

The first article (19 November 1918) of this remarkable series took the old system and its representatives to task with astonishing candour.

Long did the nation wait for the faults of the system to be corrected by those who so often had held out the prospect of constitutional and administrative reform, holding out the prospect of a rosier future. Now it no longer has any confidence in the realization of these reforms and takes its fate into its own hands. It desires to do this simply because it must. And a nation that reaches for self-determination has no better legal title . . . To us, who lived so long under the old system . . . it does not come easy to enumerate the sins that condemned it to death. The war aggravated those sins so greatly and made them so evident that silence can no longer conceal them. In the first place of course there was militarism . . . It was stupid militarism when on the outbreak of war civil authority had to be given over to the military, when the latter harassed honest citizens simply because they protested against infringements of their rights, when people, who may have been excellent marksmen and horsemen but lacked all other abilities, proceeded now with the same assurance as that with which they commanded a company in peacetime to rule over the lives and property of civilians. Militarism was a senseless waste of the taxpayers' money and of the millions of war loans for which the nation would one day have to pay . . . Militarism was military justice with its monstrous institution of special courts which, without possessing the supreme authority of the state or having the guidance of a responsible Minister of Justice in the exercise of their powers, could confirm death sentences . . . The brother of militarism, admittedly far less guilty, was bureaucracy. This bureaucracy, regardless of great individual capabilities, in many instances lacked understanding of ordinary people and had a narrowly formal legal training. It had such exclusive charge of the most important branches of the administration that people must inevitably become opposed to the state, while the latter should never have been other than a commonwealth constituted by the people. And the administrative machinery, then and now so complicated, and its distribution of agenda so unsuitable, that the glut of officials must prove a financial burden on the people . . . To this must be added a residue of feudalism whereby some of the most important offices – think of the governorships – were open, not on the strength of statutory provisions, but in fact, almost solely to members of the higher nobility. That these same circles held all diplomatic appointments, which have the greatest influence over the vital questions of peace or war, and enjoyed a clear advantage in the selection for senior military posts could not but render the nation, gradually succumbing to the burdens of war, ever more discontented. Granted, popular feelings were even more outraged by the fact that even more privileges seemed to attach to money-bags than to pride of birth. This capitalism, not wealth as such, but the presumptuousness and the dexterity to ensure preferential treatment with the help of wealth in areas where everyone and their deeds ought to count equally before the law, aroused bitterness not only against those who tried it and were foolish enough to boast of their success, but also against the system which out of ill-will or weakness was unable to prevail against them. And, finally, the old constitutional state had retained traces of an absolutism which invested the highest authority apparently with a semblance of responsibility which in reality he did not bear either in the sight of God or of his own conscience. The fiction of the Emperor as supreme war-lord, depriving the persons responsible for government of influence over the decision on peace or war as much as over the military command, was upheld too long, all too long . . . The unfortunate dualistic structure of the old monarchy was an additional complication. It forced the sovereign to act simultaneously through three different governments which frequently had to represent opposing interests . . .

At the close of this article, the best concise analysis of the old régime in the last years of its existence, Seipel put the question that was most deeply agitating Christian Socialist party members and, outside their circle, people at large.

What, I ask, remains for a nation that has had such experiences other than to take the law into its own hands, to do away with the past, and to construct a new state from the bottom up? This nation however neither will nor may permit itself to be fobbed off with a few superficial reforms. Merely changing the name of the firm and even putting in new managers is far from a guarantee that the business will be run differently.

Consistently the article ends with a summons to the Austrian people: 'So what is above all called for now is to build up the free, truly democratic state.'

There is no space to deal with Seipel's other three articles, but just one more passage may be quoted from the one published on 23 November 1918. The author was dealing with external affairs.[37]

German-Austria cannot and must not stay isolated. German-Austrians were members of a major state for too long for them to be able suddenly to adapt their psychology to the narrow range of interests appropriate to a small state. And if they could, their country lacks the prime requisite for remaining on its own – economic self-sufficiency. German-Austria will lean on other states, whether to the east or to the west, to the south or to the north, but only as a duly esteemed member of a federation and without allowing itself to be treated other than as an equal. Many reasons, indeed a majority of reasons, argue in favour of union with Germany to whose inhabitants we are attracted by bonds of kinship and the sound of the same mother-tongue. No final decision has, after all, been reached in this matter. On the one hand because the long-term economic requirements cannot as yet be assessed and on the other hand because – and this is the important point – we do not know as yet in what form we can best serve the interests of the German people.

It would be rash to restrict our ability to move in the one or the other direction if we were to bind ourselves irreversibly on the issue of our future status . . .

One must conclude that there was no very wide gap between the declarations of Viktor Adler and Ignaz Seipel concerning the political future of their country. This did not seem an inauspicious point of departure for the new Austria.

Notes

1 'The Empire, as so often when it seemed to its foes an easy prey, has demonstrated its stamina, more indeed than in most of the wars waged during recent centuries . . . Its unimpaired existence is ensured for decades.' Walther Federn, 'Österreich-Ungarn zum Jahreswechsel', *Der Österreichische Volkswirt*, 5 January 1918, p. 226.

2 'Austria's existence, due to the way that the war has gone, is assured for the foreseeable future. The nations can therefore attain self-determination only to the degree that this is feasible within the existing political framework.' Otto Bauer (under the pseudonym Karl Mann), 'Das Selbstbestimmungsrecht der öster- reichischen Nationen', *Der Kampf*, April 1918, p. 205.

3 'My Ministerial colleague, Prince Hohenlohe, vigorously supported the idea of Quadralism, i.e., a programme which envisaged the Empire's organization into four independent states held together by the rights of the Crown, by the joint Ministries (augmented by the Ministry of Trade), and by its customs and economic unity. These four constituent states of the Austrian Monarchy would have been Austria, Hungary, Poland, and Yugoslavia.' Alexander Spitzmüller, *Und hat auch Ursach' es zu lieben* (Vienna, 1955), p. 159.

4 *Aide-mémoire* from the German to the Austro-Hungarian Ministry of Foreign Affairs, 13 November 1915, and quoted by Gustav Gratz and Richard Schüller, *Die äussere Wirtschaftspolitik Österreich-Ungarns* (Vienna, 1925), p. 9.

5 Gratz and Schüller, *Wirtschaftspolitik*, p. 5 et seq.

6 Spitzmüller, *Und hat auch Ursach*, p. 143.

7 Spitzmüller, *Und hat auch Ursach*, p. 144.

8 Gratz and Schüller, *Wirtschaftspolitik*, p. 12.

9 Gratz and Schüller, *Wirtschaftspolitik*, pp. 13–14.
10 Stephan Verosta, 'Joseph Schumpeter gegen das Zollbündnis der Donaumonarchie mit Deutschland und gegen die Anschlusspolitik', in *Festschrift für Christian Broda* (Vienna, 1976), p. 388.
11 Verosta, *Festschrift*, p. 378.
12 Verosta, *Festschrift*, p. 384.
13 Spitzmüller, *Und hat auch Ursach*, p. 147. The author refers in this connection to an article by Ellenbogen in the *Arbeiter-Zeitung*, 14 December 1915, wherein he advocated the 'establishment of the customs union as a permanent institution through taking advantage of the predicament caused by the war'.
14 Alexander Spitzmüller, *Der letzte Österreichisch-Ungarische Ausgleich und der Zusammenbruch der Monarchie* (Berlin, 1929).
15 Spitzmüller, *Ausgleich*, p. 16.
16 Spitzmüller recalls an audience with Emperor Charles: 'My report on objections to imposing the compromise led the Emperor, who in my experience was always open to conviction by quietly, positively, and factually presented arguments, to say after brief thought that he appreciated the need for dropping this plan . . . Procedurally there next followed completion of the compromise negotiations with Hungary right to the end when it was expressly laid down that only parliamentary sanction of the compromise was acceptable.' Spitzmüller, *Ausgleich*, p. 58.
17 Gratz and Schüller, *Wirtschaftspolitik*, p. 32.
18 Gratz and Schüller, *Wirtschaftspolitik*, p. 41.
19 Gratz and Schüller, *Wirtschaftspolitik*, p. 105.
20 Gratz and Schüller, *Wirtschaftspolitik*, p. 106.
21 The prime issue was that of preferences. Under the preferential treatment clause they did not have to be passed on to others.
22 Cf. in particular the articles by Karl Renner and Otto Bauer (under the pseudonyms of Mann, Schulz, and Weber) in *Der Kampf*, 1918.
23 Spitzmüller, *Und hat auch Ursach*, p. 198.
24 Cf. Helmut Rumpler, *Das Völkermanifest Kaiser Karls vom 16. Oktober 1918* (Vienna, 1966), p. 11. Seipel wrote of the manifesto: 'After what the Emperor said on 31 May 1917, constitutional reform was definitely Austria's main preoccupation. And what happened? Every opportunity on which appropriately generous concessions could have regained the confidence of the nationalities was lost. Next to the weakness and desultoriness of successive governments and a certain (at least to us Germans) apparent disingenuousness by non-German representatives, the principal blame – let us be frank – lies with the German parties. Biased by centralist notions, accustomed to an age-old hegemony, incapable of believing in the decline which was perfectly clear to all, they wasted time with pettifogging haggling about district courts and secondary schools, raised a hullabaloo if anyone spoke of Bohemian or South Slav constitutional rights – and now would be extremely glad if anyone had with a strong hand forced them into surrender . . . The whole collapse of Austria could have been avoided if a truly democratic spirit had pervaded our politics.' Ignaz Seipel, 'Die demokratische Verfassung', *Reichspost*, 21 November 1918.
25 Rumpler's book (see above) gives a detailed description of how the 'Nationalities Manifesto' came about. For a short account of the events leading to its publication, see Josef Redlich, 'Heinrich Lammasch als Minister-Präsident', in *Heinrich Lammasch, seine Aufzeichnungen, sein Wirken, und seine Politik*, ed. by

Marga Lammasch and Hans Sperl (Vienna, 1922), pp. 162–64.

26 See Karl F. Novak, *The Collapse of Central Europe* (London, 1924), p. 263.

27 Rumpler, *Das Völkermanifest*, p. 88ff.

28 Josef Redlich, *Schicksalsjahre Österreichs, 1908–1919* (Graz, 1954), Vol. II, p. 302.

29 Otto Bauer regarded 15 October 1918 as the day of Poland's proclamation of independence. See Otto Bauer, 'Die österreichische Revolution', *Werkausgabe* (Vienna, 1976), Vol. II, p. 588.

30 See *Der Österreichische Volkswirt*, Calendarium, 26 October 1918, p. 60, 2 November 1918, p. 76.

31 See David Lloyd George, *Memoirs of the Peace Conference* (New Haven, 1929), Vol. II, p. 588. The same note expresses the wonder of a British diplomat at so unseemly a retirement from history.

32 See Shorthand Minutes of the Constituent Meeting of the German-Austrian Members of the National Assembly, 21 October 1918.

33 Viktor Adler, 'Reden und Aufsätze', *Viktor Adler der Parteimann* (Vienna, 1929), Issue No. IX, p. 264. The 'Austrian dilemma' was of course no new phenomenon. As has been seen earlier, the Empire had until 1866 been confronted with the problem of Western versus Eastern orientation. In 1918 the old dilemma reappeared under entirely new political conditions.

34 'The sole circumstance justifying Austria's political existence since the middle of the eighteenth century, is its resistance to the progress of Russia in eastern Europe – a helpless, inconsistent, cowardly, but tenacious resistance . . .' Karl Marx, *Herr Vogt*, MEW, vol. 14, p. 501f.

35 Renner held as late as spring 1918 that the dissolution of Austria-Hungary into national states 'would always be, as viewed by economically and socially oriented Social Democrats, an economic and social retrogression'. Karl Renner, 'Marx oder Mazzini', *Der Kampf* (Vienna, 1918), p. 304.

36 Bauer was also aware of the slogan's unpopularity. The middle classes and the intelligentsia, he thought, found 'in the hope of *Anschluss* consolation for the downfall of their old ruling structure. The mass of the workers, on the other hand, were still cool towards the idea of the *Anschluss* in spite of Social Democrats having been its initial promulgators. During the war they had hated German imperialism all too deeply to be able now to enthuse for *Anschluss* with the same Germany. Only on 9 November did the idea of *Anschluss* capture the hearts of the working masses. Only when the Emperor had been overthrown in Germany and a Socialist Government, supported by Workers' and Soldiers' Councils, had seized power, when the German revolution seemed at a single blow to have far surpassed ours, did the idea become intelligible that the great, highly industrialized *Reich* could offer the struggle for socialism far more auspicious conditions than could the small, itself semi-agrarian German-Austria helplessly dependent on agrarian neighbours.' Otto Bauer, 'Die österreichische Revolution', *Werkausgabe* (Vienna, 1976), Vol. II, p. 623.

37 Seipel is alleged once to have confided to his last private secretary, Professor August Maria Knoll, that he wrote this series of articles so as to enable the Christian Socialist Party to jump on the bandwagon and prevent its leftward derailment. This was told the present author by Professor Norbert Leser who had had a long talk with Knoll about the series of articles.

PART FOUR

From the Foundation of the First Republic to the Peace Treaty of Saint-Germain

The Economic Consequences of the Habsburg Monarchy's Disintegration and the Dispute about Austria's Viability

The official birthday of the First Republic was 12 November 1918. On that day the Provisional National Assembly proclaimed the new state of 'German-Austria' to be a democratic republic in which all authority emanated from the people. Article II of the resolution, though, stated that German-Austria was a part of the German Republic.[1] This qualification, inserted at the insistence of the Social Democrats, virtually in the same breath put into question the existence of the new Austria. The proclamation of the Republic thus became the prelude to a strange chapter in Austrian foreign policy whose *leitmotif* was the effort to persuade the victorious Powers to grant defeated Germany an important and strategically significant enlargement of territory. Such an attempt was obviously doomed from the outset.[2]

During the very first debate of the Provisional National Assembly, Viktor Adler, the Social Democrats' venerable leader, had uttered the fateful phrase about the 'non-viability of German-Austria'.[3] At the State Council session of 11 November, where the motion to proclaim the Republic and the union with Germany was passed, Chancellor Dr Karl Renner, Adler's closest collaborator, took up the cue. 'What the Entente plans – and our Ministry for Foreign Affairs is very well informed on the point – is frightful,' he declared emotionally,

and a crime against the German people, an act of revenge, the consequences of which the German people can perhaps gradually evade if it is allowed the utmost freedom, the greatest scope for action. At the same time we now already know what their plans are for us. *German-Austria is to be reduced to a poor, completely helpless country* stretching southwards as far as the Brenner at one end, not even as far as Villach, not even as far as Marburg at the other, northwards not even as far as Lundenburg, a state that is not viable, not capable of having any industry other than tourism. Our most ambitious dream for national development could be for us to play porters in Alpine hotels to English lords or to people who wear the clothes of such. And they are not even prepared to make it possible for us to join the great German community. They want to force us to remain a national particle of barely six million.'[4]

Otto Bauer, a far better economist than his party friend Renner, preferred to stress a different argument in his plea for Anschluss, namely that of the immediate perspectives for socialism.

It has become clear that association with these [Slav] peoples with whom we have hitherto constituted a state is no longer possible. Consequently we must seek affiliation there where, according to our history, language, and civilization we belong. And if the middle classes can only slowly bring themselves to recognize this fact, the working classes have reason to enthusiastically proclaim union with Germany. For now it is red, proletarian, socialist Germany which we want to join and which we shall join . . . Joining Germany is joining socialism.[5]

Bauer's chief *Anschluss* argument was however very soon to lose its power of conviction. Thereafter the slogan of Austria's non-viability dominated the debate.

Walther Federn and Gustav Stolper, the knowledgeable editors of *Der Österreichische Volkswirt*, incessantly propagated the idea of *Anschluss*. In 1920 Stolper published his widely-read book *Deutsch-österreich als Sozial- und Wirtschaftsproblem*, based on a selection of his articles. One longer passage presents the quintessence of the economic case for the non-viability of the new Austria in the radically changed circumstances:

German-Austria never lived on its own production. German-Austria's, particularly Vienna's, resources were never drawn from German-Austrian industry, but from that of Bohemia, Moravia, and Hungary. Vienna performed the 'service' functions for the economy of those territories. It financed them, it bought raw materials for them, it distributed their products. And it lived on being the seat of the court, of the military and the central civil administration in an empire comprising fifty-three million people, of a large diplomatic corps, and so on. Among the nations of the former empire, German-Austria was, as it were, the middle class. It supplied them with organizers, merchants, technicians, *savants*, civil servants, officers. German-Austria, in compensation for the middle-class services that it rendered the non-German nations, drew its income from the entire territory of former Austria-Hungary. That was not a parasitic existence, as Czechs often allege. German-Austria hereby performed an essential and useful task. Austria's non-German nations owe it more of what they have and of what they are than they are willing to admit. But moral aphorisms unfortunately do not alter hard facts. German-Austria has now been dispossessed of its characteristic quality because the Successor States to old Austria-Hungary either have taken the conduct of their economic affairs into their own hands, or are trying by every means to get them into their own hands as fast as possible.[6]

In Stolper's view the question of Austria's viability reduced itself to the problem of Vienna's hypertrophic size, more appropriate, it seemed, to an empire with fifty million inhabitants than to the scale of the small new state. Borrowing Stolper's and other analogous arguments, the satirical and contemptuous epithet 'swollen head' Vienna soon found acceptance. Even a politician of Eduard Beneš' calibre, who was normally quite positive in his attitude towards the new Austria's chances of survival, declared in 1920 that 'the solution of the Austrian problem must be sought in the systematically-organized emigration of a million Viennese'.[7]

Dr Friedrich Hertz, well-known as an economist and writer, was one of the few among his fellow economists who in the early days affirmed Austria's viability.[8] In 1921 he submitted the pros and cons to detailed scrutiny. He started with the following proposition:

Obviously the basis of every endeavour to extricate ourselves from our current beggarly existence is the question whether and under what conditions today's German-Austria can live from its labours. The answer of public opinion in Austria is almost unanimously and decisively in the negative. Hardly a day passes without the press, irrespective of party, assuring us that Austria is not viable.[9]

Two principal reasons were advanced for this pessimistic assessment. First, Vienna was 'much too big for today's mutilated Austria' and consisted 'mainly of unproductive elements, that is, an enormous army of civil servants, useless intellectuals, middlemen, and parasites of every kind'. Secondly, Austria was lacking in 'actual productive resources like a fertile soil, mines, and factories'.[10]

Those who have observed Austria's rise since the end of World War II will scarcely be surprised that Hertz did not find it particularly difficult to refute such arguments. He began by comparing Bohemian and Austrian industrial potential. The two countries had approximately identical populations (Austria 6.2 million, Bohemia 6.7 million) and an almost identical number of workers engaged in industry and trade (Austria 740,000, Bohemia 745,000).[11] Even a comparison between contemporary Austria on the one side and Bohemia together with Moravia and Silesia on the other representing the far more densely inhabited territory of Czechoslovakia, is not unfavourable to the First Republic. In 1913 today's Austria accounted for 37%, Bohemia, Moravia, and Silesia for 51% of persons insured for workmen's compensation.[12]

Austria had inherited from the Dual Monarchy not inconsiderable industrial resources. They suffered however from structural weaknesses. The energy basis was slender, agriculture remained underdeveloped, and the industrial centre of gravity lay on metals processing, machinery, electrical plants, and certain branches of consumer goods whose access to traditional eastern markets was severely hampered by the new tariff barriers. Moreover, a point heavily emphasized by those friendly to *Anschluss*, a comparatively large percentage of employment was concentrated in communications, commerce, banking and the public services because Vienna had been the administrative and business centre of a big empire. Many of these functions had to undergo contraction in the new political scene.

Other authors subsequently put forward, far more precisely, ideas of the same nature as did Hertz in 1921. Ernest Waizner, for instance, relying on Fellner's well-known pre-1914 national income estimates, tried to assess the distribution of national income in the Austrian half of the Empire between its Austrian nucleus and the other territories.[13] The new Austria, as can be seen from table 38, with about 22% of the population, accounted for 30% of the total income of the Austrian half of the Monarchy.

Table 38   Austrian and Successor States' average national income, 1911–13

	Domestically Produced National Income in Cr. mill.	Distribution of Nat. Inc. in %	Distribution of Popul. in %
Aust. Half of the Dual Monarchy	15,024.6	100.0	100.0
Austria	4,466.0	29.7	22.3
Czechoslovakia	6,710.3	44.7	34.3
Poland	2,267.7	15.1	29.3
Italy	780.7	5.2	5.4
Jugoslavia	536.8	3.6	5.9
Romania	263.1	1.7	2.8

The Austrian Institute for Economic Research checked Waizner's calculations and concluded that the data for present-day Austria was even more favourable. Its share of the 1911–1913 national income amounted to 33.8% and the *per capita* income to 790 crowns. The corresponding figures for Bohemia, Moravia, and Silesia were 42.8% and 630 crowns, for Galicia 13.7% and 350 crowns, for South Tirol, Trieste, and Istria 4.8% and 450 crowns, for Slovenia and Dalmatia 3.3% and 300 crowns, for Bukovina 1.7% and 300 crowns respectively.[14]

It may be objected that the foregoing reflects the state of affairs during the last pre-World War I years and emphasises to the full the privileged status of Vienna which ceased with the dissolution of the Empire. This is probably what in part induced Professor Rothschild to base his analysis of the new Austria's economic heritage on a compilation by the Central Statistical Commission showing the distribution of certain important resources among the Successor States.[15]

Table 39   Percentage distribution of important resources, 1911–13, among the Successor States

	Austria	Czechoslovakia	Poland	Italy	Jugoslavia
Industrial Plants	32.4	50.7	6.7	4.0	3.6
Boiler Surface	18.3	63.8	12.5	2.1	2.2
Brewing	32.0	55.5	7.2	2.1	2.7
Sugar Production	4.7	94.7	0.7	—	—
Coal Mining	6.3	77.6	12.1	0.4	3.7
Pig-Iron Production (Value)	34.3	53.5	4.5	7.8	—
Arable Soil	17.1	37.7	36.7	1.6	4.0
Meadowland	31.7	20.8	26.6	8.5	8.5
Vineyards	19.2	5.3	—	29.8	45.7
Woodland	30.9	23.0	21.2	8.2	12.1
Cattle	24.2	35.3	28.1	4.0	6.0
Pigs	29.6	27.2	29.3	2.7	7.8

Rothschild demonstrated that the Czechoslovak territories did rather better out of the inheritance than the Austrian. Bohemia, Moravia, and Silesia took over some of the most efficient plants in the heavy metals industry. This emerges from its strikingly high share there of the boiler surface. The share of Czechoslovakia's breweries and sugar refineries was also remarkably large whereas Austria was far behind in sugar production. Pig-iron production was equally divided between the Alpine lands and their Czech neighbours, but unlike the Czechs the former had no bituminous coal reserves worth mentioning, they had to be content with comparatively modest deposits of lignite. On the other hand Austria possessed a high potential of hydraulic power and good prospects for a mineral oil industry, though the deposits had not yet been located.[16]

The above table does not contain any reference to the distribution of the textile plants of the Monarchy; its most important industrial sector. A statistical compilation by the Lower Austrian Chamber of Commerce and Trade shows that the new Austria was endowed with only about a quarter of the previous overall spinning capacity. The major share devolved on Czechoslovakia, which also inherited practically all the large weaving mills.[17] This state of affairs, an accident of the regional distribution of industries in the Empire, burdened Austria with its most conspicuous structural weaknesses. Only with the help of a long-term reconstruction programme did it seem possible to overcome this defect.

Austria was better off as far as its agrarian resources were concerned. Because of its mountainous terrain, it had an above-average share of the Empire's livestock. On the other hand it had a much smaller share of arable land which was less efficiently farmed than in Bohemia or in Austria's western neighbours. 'If Austrian farmers were as good as the Swiss, the country would be almost independent of food imports.'[18] Here too the new state seemed backward but if given a determined economic policy, thoroughly capable of development.

A closer understanding of the structural problems is also seen from a different angle. The Dual Monarchy had been Europe's second largest state in size, its third in population. The new Austria, with an area of 83,833 square kilometres and 6.5 million inhabitants, was one of the continent's smaller states.[19] The Empire had been predominantly agricultural; Austria relied mainly on industry and trade. Neither the 1920 nor the 1923 census contained reliable data on occupational structure, but the gap was well filled by two studies by the Austrian statistician Felix Klezl.[20] Using official and semi-official sources such as publications of the social insurance institutions and periodical trade union reports, he arrived at a figure of 3,025,000 income recipients.[21] Farmers, entrepreneurs, small artisans, and the professions accounted for 730,000 individuals or 24% of the total. Two million individuals, or 66%, were wage and salary earners, salaried staffs, agricultural workers, and family workers in agriculture. 295,000 individuals, or 10%, were in public services, that is, federal, provincial, communal officials, clergymen, railwaymen, and so on. To these should be added the 86,890 civil service pensioners recorded on 1 October 1922.[22] Thus one arrives at the comparatively high figure of 381,890 individuals, or 13% of income recipients, belonging to the public sector.[23]

The ratio between these categories emerges from the following compilation:

Table 40   Distribution of the gainfully employed by economic sectors

		%
Industry & Mining	1,025,000	34.0
Trade & Other Private Services	375,000	12.5
Agriculture & Forestry	1,120,000	37.0
Public Services	295,000	10.0
Professions	210,000	6.5
	3,025,000	100.0

As can now be seen the number of individuals who had derived advantage from Vienna's pre-eminent status was very significant indeed. Employed persons who became supernumerary through the dissolution of the Empire are especially to be found in the second, fourth, and fifth categories listed above. A comparison between the occupational structure in Imperial Austria and the territory covered by the Republic of Austria shows that in the former, 10.5% of the population was engaged in trade and transport as against 16.1% for the Alpine provinces and Vienna. The discrepancy in the case of public services, 8.3% and 12.8% respectively, was similarly very marked.[24]

It has already been seen that, according to Waizner and the Austrian Institute for Economic Research, the average income in the new Austria was considerably higher than in the other countries of the Austrian half of the Monarchy, and it is obvious that this was in large measure due to the administrative, financial, and commercial functions especially exercised by Vienna on behalf of the Empire as a whole. Moreover many of the big joint-stock and private limited liability companies with plants spread throughout the Dual Monarchy, had their headquarters in Vienna.[25] In 1918 the headquarters of 495 joint-stock companies, with a capital of 3,962 million crowns, were situated at Vienna. However 132 of these companies, with a capital of 1,168 million crowns, carried on operations mainly in the Successor States.[26] This centralized administration was even more pronounced in the case of the major banks. Twenty-one of the 68 joint-stock banks in Imperial Austria had their head office in Vienna. These included such giants as Creditanstalt, Österreichische Länderbank, Wiener Bankverein, and Anglobank. Between them they controlled more than two-thirds of all bank capital.[27]

Soon after the Czechoslovak Republic was born in October 1918, systematic attempts set in to do away as quickly as possible with the economic and financial hegemony of the former imperial capital. The intention of the Czech government to naturalize Czech enterprises at utmost speed is documented in detail in a revealing study by Alois Rašin, the first Czechoslovak Minister of Finance. After a somewhat biased account of the reasons for the process of centralization in Vienna, he writes,

It was therefore necessary to put matters in order in the Republic and to see to it that the joint-stock companies hitherto resident in Vienna should transfer their seat to the territory of the Republic. To this end an agreement was reached with Austria to facilitate the procedure for the transfer of the companies' seat to the territory of the Republic. In particular the provision was eliminated according to which a company for the purpose of removal had to be wound up and a liquidation tax had to be paid. Hereupon Law No. 12, 1920, was published and companies whose activities took place within the territory of the Republic were invited to take up residence there and to become naturalized.[28]

Czech efforts to enforce the naturalization of companies will be discussed later.[29]

Leading Austrian economic and financial circles displayed a strangely confident attitude in the face of these undisguised exertions by the Czechs and other former associates to completely break the old economic ties. Very soon there was a slogan in circulation, which was to be heard for a long time ahead, that political and economic frontiers need not necessarily be identical. Towards the end of 1919, Dr Paul Hammerschlag, one of Creditanstalt's executive directors, sent a secret memorandum to the British member of the Reparation Commission Preparatory Committee. He painted the situation in rather rosy colours and, after referring to certain difficulties created by the Treaty of Saint-Germain, continued as follows:

if the aforementioned obstacles are set right, *the future prospects of the Viennese banks can be judged rather favourably.* True, it must not be overlooked that Vienna's banks, as has been frequently stated, were before the war the hub of the entire Empire's financial world and therefore, with the constitution of the successor states and the disruption of the former Austro-Hungarian monetary union, their sphere of activity will in future be more limited. Possibly too certain reorganizations [mergers] will occur for this reason. But at the outset the great business experience of the Vienna banks, and especially the confidence that they enjoy in the international financial world, will presumably help them to maintain this position for the future.

Moreover, out of the economic relations that absolutely must arise between the Successor States and German-Austria, *there will indubitably emerge new stimuli for the activities of the Viennese institutions*. If German-Austria wants to maintain its existence, it will have to develop industrially, create new industries, reorganize others; so here too the cooperation of finance capital will be required.[30]

Two prerequisites were essential for Hammerschlag's optimistic forecast to become reality — a certain willingness by the Successor States to co-operate and a favourable world economic climate. In the coming years both of these requirements were almost totally wanting. The starting conditions for the new Austria were so unfortunate that even a more realistic and determined economic and financial policy than that practised by subsequent governments would not have been able to overcome the severe handicaps placed in the cradle of the First Republic.

Hammerschlag's assessment reflected the opinions of a tradition-ally-minded section of economic and financial experts who included such influential public personalities as Josef Redlich and Joseph Schumpeter. On the other hand Spitzmüller underwent a distinct change of mind on the subject of *Anschluss*. In an address at the beginning of 1919 he gave it his support with the reservation that 'our specifically German-Austrian culture and opportunities for economic development in the Danube basin and in the direction of Trieste should be preserved'.[31]

The outlook at that moment for economic opportunities in the Danube basin did not seem very hopeful even if one took a more reserved attitude towards *Anschluss* than Spitzmüller. The over-riding problem was the supply of foodstuffs and fuel to Vienna, previously drawn in considerable quantities from the Czech and Hungarian areas. The violent reproaches levelled by the Austrian press at Czechoslovakia and Hungary do not seem altogether justified since these countries were also suffering serious supply difficulties. An Inter-Allied Commission on a visit to Vienna, Prague, and Budapest in January 1919 concluded that 'Czechoslovakia and Hungary far from being in a position to supply Vienna, were themselves already in need of large imports of cereals and fats'.[32] As late as May 1920 fuel supplies from domestic sources were not enough to meet the demands of Czech industry. Gustav Stolper, who can hardly be accused of a weakness for the Czech state, wrote that 'as long as important industries in Czechoslovakia are short of coal so that industrial exports and the country's balance of payments are hampered, it is useless to complain about Czechoslovakia' resisting the export of coal from its territory'.[33]

Cereals exports from Hungary were much reduced compared with pre-war days because of the heavy territorial losses. As H. Emil Bacher explained in a series of articles in the Budapest newspaper, *Pester Lloyd*, the Bacs, Torontel, and Temes districts, which had had to be ceded to Romania and Yugoslavia, had been the main source of food surpluses for distribution among the Empire's deficient areas. Given time to adjust itself to the situation, Hungary could undoubtedly have resumed its place among Europe's cereals exporters. There was no possibility, though, for immediate aid to the Austrians in their current emergency.[34]

The Treaty of Saint-Germain forbade the *Anschluss*, but Article 222 envisaged the introduction of a preferential tariff system between Austria, Hungary, and Czechoslovakia for a period of five years. Its advantages would not have had to be granted to other allied states.[35] The French were the main advocates of close co-operation between the three Danubian countries that had constituted the Empire's inner core and they hoped, according to competent observers, that out of closer economic co-operation there would grow a lasting community.[36]

Article 222 remained a dead letter notwithstanding occasional appeals from the League of Nations' Financial Committee for collaboration between the parties concerned.

> The Financial Committee is convinced that the restoration of the economic life of Austria is dependent in large measure upon Austria's ability to trade freely with other countries, and that such trade would be greatly beneficial to all successor states. It urges, therefore, that immediate and effective steps should be taken by the governments of those states and of Austria to remove the trade barriers between them.[37]

Towards the end of the period provided by the Peace Treaty, negotiations on the introduction of a preferential tariff system did begin between Austria and Czechoslovakia. This belated effort miscarried, not least because of Germany's threat of trade reprisals.[38]

The idea of a preferential customs agreement between the Empire's three core countries clearly had from the outset small chance of realization. This was not so much because of the negative attitude taken by Germany or Italy, but because of the ever growing spirit of 'economic nationalism' that engulfed all of the Danube basin. Leo Pasvolsky, a leading expert on Danubian affairs after the First World War, believed the reason behind this new phenomenon derived from fear of Vienna's still evident economic attraction. 'Desire to break away from the economic domination of Vienna was another powerful stimulant of a policy of nationalism. The fear of Vienna as a dominant economic and financial centre was felt in Hungary as well as in Czechoslovakia, Rumania, and Yugoslavia.'[39] Rapid industrialization seemed to offer the best guarantee for economic independence and high tariff walls the best way to implement this policy. In the early twenties Czechoslovakia and Romania introduced tariffs about fifty percent higher than Austria, while the tariffs of Hungary, Poland and Yugoslavia were double those of Austria.[40] The rates were later raised again, by Hungary (1924), Bulgaria and Romania (1926). The increase in Yugoslavia (1925) was of a more modest order. Finally Austria joined the round in 1927 when it introduced a protectionist policy.[41] A number of League of Nations reports described these activities of Europe's central and eastern states as 'most critical'.[42]

The Empire's per capita exports had been far lower than those of any other European country with the exception of Russia. After the collapse of the Monarchy, Rothschild remarks, 'large parts of the Empire' were transformed into 'states highly dependent on exports'.[43] This applied in particular to the First Republic. The question of Austria's viability was consequently very closely linked to its ability to hold its own in the arena of international trade. It is hardly surprising that the public debate on viability was increasingly centred on the country's balance of trade and balance of payments.[44]

To conclude from the foregoing that Austria's efforts to establish closer economic relations with south-eastern Europe were primarily frustrated by the new tariff barriers would however be a mistake. The economic nationalism of the Successor States, although not a handicap to be underestimated, was only one among a number of adverse factors. The traditional consumer goods sector was the focal point of the rival states' industrial ambitions. Austria therefore met with growing difficulties in marketing a part of its customary range of products (textiles, leather goods, paper and paper products, etc.). With capital goods it came up against the superior competition of Germany and other western European industrial giants in what had formerly been its well protected markets. These obstacles too stood in the way of the hesitant attempts at restructuring Austrian industry. Forcing the pace of domestic agricultural production during the second half of the twenties, without doubt an overdue measure, affected unfavourably incomes in the south-eastern countries and thus their receptivity to Austrian industrial products.

Austria's efforts to restructure its economy would doubtless have had greater success if they had occurred in a global climate of expansion, as was the case after the Second World War. Unhappily the twenties were characterized by only weak upward trends. The most outstanding fact, as has been noted by the British economist Derek Aldcroft, was the marked slow-down in growth of incomes throughout the world between 1913 and 1929. Growth was by no means insignificant, but the expansion of both total and per capita incomes (in real terms) was distinctly slower. The period from 1913 to 1929 compared poorly with the long period of growth before 1914 and also with the entire period 1913 to 1959.[45] There were of course obvious regional differences. The period from 1913 to 1929 saw Japan's rise to the status of an economic Great Power. In contrast the growth record of large parts of western, central and south-eastern Europe was strikingly poor. European production increased at about half the world rate and by only a third of the extra-European rate. And most of this poor performance, Aldcroft goes on, must be ascribed to the slow growth in Germany, the United Kingdom, and, with the exception of the Soviet Union and Czechoslovakia, eastern Europe.[46] Especially striking was the slow rise in Europe's export trade. Its growth rate amounted to barely a quarter of that of 1880 to 1913.[47]

The worsening of the world's economic climate in the 1920s has often been the subject of investigation.[48] The consensus of opinion seems to be that it was a period lacking in pioneering innovations – innovations in the Schumpeterian manner, it is tempting to add. The period is not famous for spectacular inventions, but rather for the widespread application of known techniques or production processes.[49] Yet it is doubtful whether this is an adequate explanation for the unfavourable economic situation of the twenties. Actually pioneering innovations were not lacking. Comparatively recent products like rayon, aircraft, and radio spring to mind. Automobiles, which in the United States were an important element of the prosperity of the 1920s, still had rarity value in many parts of Europe.

The destruction caused by war and the resulting impoverishment for much of its population appears primarily to account for Europe's conspicuously disappointing performance. The decimation of the formerly large class of rentiers and the proletarization of the middle classes in wide parts of Central Europe, a logical consequence of inflation, were the underlying causes of the prolonged weakening of a class formerly accustomed to liberal spending and luxury. Orthodox economic policy, sticking to the principle of balanced budgets, furnished no decisive stimuli. International recovery programmes had small effect on attitudes to growth and employment. Comparison with the Marshall Plan, quite differently conceived with the objective of a planned rise in investment rates by the key industries of the western European countries is almost inevitable in this connection.[50]

A brief spell of fine economic weather in the late 1920s was enjoyed by Austria too. By the end of the decade production had nearly drawn level with the final year of peace.[51] Nevertheless even during this phase of development, borne along on a mild breeze of optimism, only a marginal reduction in the high level of unemployment was achieved since the modernization drive of Austrian industry was primarily borne by labour saving investment.[52] The army of chronically unemployed also contained a hard core of dismissed bank officials, prematurely-pensioned civil servants, ex-officers, and higher executives back in their old home from the former imperial provinces. After the end of the stabilization crisis, the effect of which was felt as late as 1925, unemployment did recede slightly, but thereafter it stayed at 10% of the working population until the outbreak of the world economic crisis.[53] Constant under-employment was especially evident in districts where the production structure was characterized by a large share of the iron and metal industry of motor car construction and of engineering firms. In the area between Vienna and Wiener Neustadt, which had been a centre of the armaments industry, a substantial portion of the plant capacity had to be closed down during the course of the 1920s. It is clear that the phenomenon of unused capacities was not confined to Austria and that it stemmed, up to a point, from the 'economic nationalism' practised by nearly all the Successor States.[54]

The pauperization of the middle class (consisting of the small businessmen, the professions, civil servants, and the higher as well as medium-level salary earners) was alleviated by the brief recuperative phase in the 1920s, but then aggravated by the depression beginning in 1929. To the plight of these classes must be ascribed the melancholy, resigned atmosphere reigning at Vienna, often echoed in the literature of the time. How far the mentality of the middle classes can be held responsible for the sluggish investment activity in those days must remain a matter of speculation. In a letter to Karl Seitz, chairman of the German-Austrian National Assembly, the satirist Karl Kraus epitomized the mood of the immediate post-war period.

It's the Republic that is to blame for everything, including stupidity as such, and it transpired on the very first day of its existence that it is incapable of paying the Empire's debts, awakening the Empire's dead, or making undone the Empire's war, and all round it has proved to be unable to attain to the Empire's merits, leaving aside the Empire's condition of mind which, granted, was indestructible . . . The sole conclusion which the local breed, born not to learn from experience, is nevertheless capable of drawing, is that the experience should be had once again. Always forgetting tomorrow on account of today, it now forgets yesterday for the sake of the day before.[55]

The concept of *Anschluss* had of course numerous militant supporters among the middle class as well. It was however the Social Democrats who hoped for a swift healing of the wounds inflicted by war from union with Germany. Part of the First Republic's tragedy is that at a time when the workers' party was beginning to free itself from the *Anschluss* obsession, a sizeable portion of the middle class veered towards this old doctrine of salvation draped now in Nazi brown.

Notes

1 Ludwig Brügel, *Geschichte der österreichischen Sozialdemokratie* (Vienna, 1925), Vol. V, p. 394.

2 German politicians were much more cautious and reserved in their attitude. 'On 13 November already the Council of State had invited the German Government to endorse the *Anschluss* declaration and to enter into negotiations on the earliest possible implementation of *Anschluss*. Reactions in Berlin remained cool and were disappointing for Austrian supporters of the unification. Germany, now experiencing the breakdown phase, had at that moment other worries and rightly feared creating a negative impression in France if in the jaws of defeat another attempt was made at territorial gain. In the German Ministry of Foreign Affairs there was secret jubilation at the Austrian resolution, but outwardly comment was avoided.' Norbert Schausberger, *Der Griff nach Österreich* (Vienna, 1978), p. 55.

3 Cf. Part III, Ch. 5, *Options for the Future.*

4 Brügel, *Geschichte*, p. 395. Present author's italics.

5 *Arbeiter-Zeitung*, 12 November 1918. Subsequently, when *Anschluss* no longer promised immediate, radical social change, Bauer also fell back on the argument of Austria's lack of viability. 'This land . . . cannot exist, a land with seven million people of whom two million live in the capital – that in itself shows the economic impossibility. This is no naturally matured economic entity, but the remains of violent, sanguinary surgery.' Otto Bauer, 'Imperialismus und soziale Revolution', *Works* (Vienna, 1979), Vol. VI, p. 66.

6 Gustav Stolper, *Deutschösterreich als Sozial- und Wirtschaftsproblem* (Munich, 1920), p. 115 et seq.

7 Friedrich Hertz, 'Zahlungsbilanz und Lebensfähigkeit Österreichs', *Schriften für Sozialpolitik* (Munich, 1925), Vol. 167, p. 4.

8 Friedrich Hertz became particularly well-known for his work *Die Produktionsgrundlagen der österreichischen Industrie vor und nach dem Kriege, insbesondere im Vergleich mit Deutschland* (Vienna – Berlin, 1917). This study was published

on the eve of the First World War and within a few years ran through six editions. In one of his last works, *The Economic Problem of the Danubian States* (London, 1947), Hertz dealt once again with the problems of the Austrian economy.

9 Friedrich Hertz, *Ist Österreich wirtschaftlich lebensfähig?* (Vienna, 1921)

10 Hertz, *Ist Österreich*, p. 3 et seq.

11 Hertz, *Ist Österreich*, p. 6.

12 Hertz, *Ist Österreich*, p. 8.

13 Ernst Waizner, 'Das Volkseinkommen Alt-Österreichs und seine Verteilung auf die Nachfolgestaaten', *Metron, International Statistical Journal* (Rome, 1929), Vol. VII, No. 4, pp. 82–3.

14 Cf. Kausel-Nemeth-Seidel, 'Österreichs Volkseinkommen 1913 bis 1963', *Monatsberichte des Österr. Instituts für Wirtschaftsforschung*, 14th Special Issue (Vienna, 1965), p. 31.

15 See *Der Österreichische Volkswirt*, 27 August 1921, p. 904 et seq. and Kurt W. Rothschild, 'Wurzeln und Triebkräfte der österreichischen Wirtschaftsstruktur' in W. Weber (ed.), *Österreichs Wirtschaftsstruktur, gestern-heute-morgen* (Berlin, 1961), p. 54.

16 'Only in 1925 and 1926, on the instruction of the Vacuum Oil Company, did systematic preliminaries on a geological exploration of the Vienna Basin begin. The results gave rise to some hopes. They remained however unknown because later the Company withdrew from central Europe . . .' Stephan Koren, 'Struktur und Nutzung der Energiequellen Österreichs', in Weber, *Österreichs Wirtschaftsstruktur*, p. 177.

17 See 'Wirtschaftsstatistische Materialien über Deutschösterreich', Niederösterreichische Handels- und Gewerbekammer (Vienna, 1919), pp. 19–20.

18 Hertz, *Ist Österreich*, p. 9. Gustav Stolper made a careful study of the official publications for 1909–1913 and calculated an average yield of 13.6 quintals wheat and 135 quintals rye per hectare. See *Deutschösterreich*, p. 65. This is substantially less than German and Swiss yields. It suggests, especially in view of Swiss figures, that the shortcomings due to Alpine topography were aggravated by certain structural flaws in Austrian agriculture.

19 Cf. *Statistisches Handbuch für die Republik Österreich* (Vienna, 1920), Vol. I.

20 Cf. *Statistische Nachrichten*, 25 March 1925, p. 49 et seq. and *Neues Wiener Tagblatt*, 9 May 1925. The 1930 industrial census confirms Klezl's statistical investigations as regards the two most important employment categories, the building and metal workers who accounted for some 37% of all industrial workers. The discrepancies in respect of other categories are slight, e.g., in the case of textile, paper, and food workers, and were conditioned by industrial development in the 1920s.

21 An indeterminate number of home workers, trainees, and retired civil servants were left out of account. *Österreichisches Jahrbuch 1923*, p. 24.

22 Cf. *Österreichisches Jahrbuch 1923*, p. 24 et seq.

23 It should however be noted that 169,937 individuals, i.e., 45% of the total figure for public services employees given above, were engaged on a 'productive' employment inasmuch as they belonged to monopoly enterprises, like the railways, postal and telephone system, power stations, and tobacco plants, in the hands of the central government and territorial authorities.

24 This data has been taken from a recent publication by the Austrian Statistical Office, Anton Kausel, *Österreichs Volkseinkommen 1830 bis 1913* (Vienna,

1979). Kausel's statistical categories include a 'Mixed Group' (public services and the professions) which had to be taken as a basis in the comparison here.

25 This explains why the proportion of salaried employees to industrial workers was particularly high in the Alpine areas. Whereas there were 35 salaried employees per 1,000 industrial workers in the Czech areas, the correponding ratio in Austria was 90 : 1,000. Cf. *Die Gewerkschaft*, 20 January 1920.

26 *Der Österreichische Volkswirt*, 27 August 1921, p. 904.

27 Cf. *Österreichisches Statistisches Handbuch* (Vienna, 1913), p. 269; Rothschild, in *Österreichs Wirtschaftsstruktur* p. 55.

28 Alois Rašin, *Die Finanz- und Wirtschaftspolitik der Tschechoslowakei* (Munich and Leipzig, 1923), p. 141.

29 At an early stage too efforts were consistently made to alter the property structure in Czech industry in favour of Czech nationals. 'Determined efforts are being made to buy out Austrian shareholders in the Bohemian industries until at least 55 per cent of the capital of all large factories is Czech.' See *Economic Conditions in Central Europe*, 2nd Report by William A. M. Goode (London, 1920), Cmd. 641, Misc. No. 6.

30 See Ministry of Finance Archives, File No. 83623/19, 21 November 1919, 'Gegenwärtiger Stand und Zukunft der Banken Österreichs'. (Present author's italics.)

31 Alexander Spitzmüller, *Und hat auch Ursach' es zu lieben* (Vienna, 1955), p. 313.

32 See Goode, *Economic Conditions*, p. 3.

33 Gustav Stolper, 'Donauföderation', *Der Österreichische Volkswirt*, 29 May 1920, p. 666.

34 Cf. particularly *Pester Lloyd*, 15 February 1920.

35 Cf. Karl R. Stadler, *Hypothek auf die Zukunft* (Vienna, 1968), p. 219.

36 Cf. Richard Riedl, *Bemerkungen zu den deutschösterreichischen Friedensbedingungen* (Vienna, 1919), p. 16 et seq.

37 *Report of the Financial Committee of the Council* (Geneva, 1921), p. 26.

38 Cf. Antonin Basch, *The Danube Basin and the German Economic Sphere* (New York, 1943), p. 32. The French ambassador at Vienna later gave it as his opinion that France made a mistake when it failed to make recognition of the Successor States dependent on preservation of the Danube basin's economic unity. Cf. Hertz, *The Economic Problem*, p. 64.

39 Leo Pasvolsky, *Economic Nationalism of the Danubian States* (New York, 1928), p. 73.

40 Cf. Hertz, *The Economic Problem*, p. 70 et seq.

41 Cf. Basch, *The Danube Basin*, p. 26.

42 Basch, *The Danube Basin*, p. 26 footnote.

43 Rothschild, in *Österreichs Wirtschaftsstruktur*, p. 65.

44 Part IV, Chap. 2, pp. 418 et seq. deal in detail with this subject.

45 See Derek H. Aldcroft, *Die Zwanziger Jahre. Von Versailles Zur Wall Street, 1919–1920* (Munich 1978) p. 326.

46 Aldcroft, *Zwanziger Jahre*, p. 339.

47 Aldcroft, *Zwanziger Jahre*, p. 346.

48 Cf. particularly David S. Landes, *The Unbound Prometheus: Technological Change and Industrial Development in Western Europe from 1750 to the Present* (Cambridge, 1969), p. 359ff. also J. Svennilson, *Growth and Stagnation in the European Economy* (United Nations, Geneva, 1954).

49 Aldcroft, *Zwanziger Jahre*, p. 343.

50 In some western European countries, notably Great Britain and to some degree Germany, the excessive share of 'obsolete' industries (shipbuilding, mining, textiles, and so on) is likely to have been in part responsible for the comparatively slow recovery of industrial production.

51 Taking 1913 as the starting-point, the index of production in 1929 was 2% *below* the pre-war level. The differing development between sectors is remarkable. Mining, timber, paper, and chemical products recorded above average growth; iron foundries, iron and metal processing, and most consumer goods industries showed below average increase. Cf. Kausel-Nemeth-Seidel, in *Monatsberichte*, p. 12.

52 The American economist Brady has made a careful study of this phenomenon. Cf. Robert A. Brady, *The Rationalization Movement in German Industry* (Berkeley 1933).

53 See Rothschild, *Österreichs Wirtschaftsstruktur*, p. 81.

54 Examples of surplus capacities in the post-war period are quoted in Walter Layton and Charles Rist, *The Economic Situation of Austria*, Report presented to the League of Nations (Geneva, 1925), p. 13. E.g., 'Hungarian flour mills turned out 20 millions of metric quintals before the war. In 1924 they produced 6½ millions owing to the steps taken by the other states to mill their corn themselves.'

55 Karl Kraus, *Die Fackel* (Vienna, 1919), No. 514–518, p. 23 et seq.

CHAPTER 2
Transitory Measures and Early Reforms

The Republic's first year bore all the marks of the severe sufferings sustained by the capital's population. To the purely physical impact of privation was added the general feeling of insecurity that left its imprint on every aspect of communal life. Large stretches of the frontier hung in the balance of political decision. Neither the shape nor the tenor of national existence had in the early months become sufficiently clear to make the country mature enough for the dangerous phase of an emotionally conducted public debate on fundamental issues. Should it go its own way or should it try and enter into partnership with one or more of its neighbours? Should it belong to the social order of East or West or seek to become a connecting link between the two extremes?

These were questions to which the events of summer and early autumn 1919 brought a provisional answer. They were not the only, and certainly not the most urgent, problems uppermost in people's minds. The struggle for the daily food and coal ration, making sure of employment, and integrating the men back from the front, especially the younger ones, into the productive process, were the truly basic worries that underlay the real focus of life in the newly arisen Republic of Austria still searching for its identity. A large minority had close family and property ties with the Successor States. The Empire's dismemberment faced them with vital problems such as possible emigration, abandonment of professional positions or businesses and loss of possessions.

The 1918 harvest yielded 19.1 million quintals in the western part of the Empire, 57% less than the average for the final five pre-war years.[1] Had hostilities continued another year, Gratz believes, the Empire's food reserves would not have lasted even until March 1919.[2] In the Alpine regions the situation was still more menacing than elsewhere. The 1918 harvest yielded, according to official estimates, no more than 48% of the wheat, 45% of the rye, and 39% of the potatoes of 1913, which meant an increase in the preceding years' nutrition deficit.[3] If the totally inadequate 1918 rations had stretched into 1919, the harvest would have met only one-quarter of the bread, one-fifth of the potato, and one-third of the meat requirements.

The establishment of the Successor States was accompanied by a sharp reduction in their food and fuel exports. The position of Vienna and its hinterland became critical in the extreme. The end of the war did not, contrary to expectations, lead to an immediate lifting of the Allied blockade,[4] the menacing effects of which were now considerably magnified by the neighbouring nations' export restrictions. Political motives were only partially responsible for the uncooperative attitude of these nations. In January 1919 an Inter-Allied Commission had investigated the central European economic situation and found that serious food shortages existed in Czechoslovakia and Hungary.[5] Where surpluses were on hand, it was not possible to transport them straightaway to where the need was greatest because of the many hindrances created by the confusion in the railway system following the cessation of hostilities. Each Successor State had laid its hands on whatever piece of railway equipment was found inside its territory after the Armistice. Rolling-stock was therefore unevenly spread throughout the Empire's former territories. Some states had a large number of railway-engines and comparatively few coaches, others had sufficient coaches but too few engines. The ensuing transport shortage increased the fuel crisis which in turn aggravated the transport problems.[6]

The uneven distribution of the Empire's rolling-stock was the theme of heated controversy. The Czechs especially laboured under the impression that they had come off badly and they demanded that the Austrians should award them a proportionate share of coaches and engines.[7] Probably the complaint was justified. At the end of 1912 the Austro-Hungarian State Railway had owned 119,238 freight and passenger coaches. No less than 49,476 (some 42%, according to the official census of 11 February 1919) had been seized by the new Austrian state. In fulfilment of the provisions of the Armistice 11,085 had to be surrendered to Italy. That still left 38,391 coaches in the hands of Austria in October 1919.[8]

With such a state of affairs it was only natural that every Successor State should try and retain the rolling-stock it had 'inherited' and not be prepared to send it into neighbouring territory without further ado.[9] This attitude led however to a virtual stoppage of through traffic in central Europe. This worsened the already dire situation in Austria because delivery of the meagre quantities of food and fuel agreed after protracted negotiations with its neighbours were then subjected to the delays of a dislocated transport system. Otto Bauer told how he had to conduct five diplomatic discussions with the Czech Government to ensure the transit through its territory of a single coal-carrying train.[10]

The underlying reason for the difficulties with which the new Austria had to contend was its inability to offer its neighbours anything sounder than its debased paper money in exchange for their goods.[11] Industry had initially almost come to a standstill over lack of fuel, since the Czechs had forbidden any coal exports. The economy was in a vicious circle. Lack of fuel meant inability to produce and because of the lack of home-produced manufactures the country could get no coal. A similar relation existed between Austria and the Successor States as between Vienna and its agrarian hinterland. The provinces were by no means self-sufficient as regards foodstuffs, but they were far better off than the country's impoverished capital. The Empire's breakdown had given rise to serious separatist tendencies which could in part be traced to the complex political structure of the new state. As long as its government commanded little respect and had no effective way of asserting its authority, the centrifugal forces had free play. They manifested themselves early in the Republic's history.

On 30 October 1918 Matthias Eldersch, a socialist member of the Provincial National Assembly, reported during its second session that the provincial municipalities had seized trains carrying foodstuffs destined for Vienna.[12] This was the first in a series of arbitrary, unlawful acts by provincial administrations. Using the flimsy argument of democratic liberties, they set about establishing themselves as states within the state. They undertook direct negotiations with other countries, vetoed the export of foodstuffs, and, like the Tirol, issued (or refused) entry visas for foreign tourists – from Vienna, for example.[13]

The unwillingness of the provinces to supply the capital with food other than on a basis of strict reciprocity was not solely due to the opposition of the middle class and peasant groups to the pseduo-proletarian government at Vienna. Hoarding foodstuffs within narrow administrative districts became the core of a touching harmony between Right and Left. Nor, it must be added, did the peasants display any outstanding sympathy for the inhabitants of their own provincial cities. Their main interest lay in selling their surpluses on the black market at prices well above the official ceiling.[14]

Requisitions carried out at the behest of the Workers and Soldiers Councils in the towns were of course bitterly resented by the peasants, but they were accepted, however grudgingly, provided an assurance was given that not a gramme would go to the loathed capital. 'Vehement as the struggles between Workers Councils and Peasants Councils were, they agreed that whatever was handed over should not cross the provincial border.'[15]

Arid statistics cannot illuminate the distress felt by proverbially merry Vienna in the winter 1918–19. The first winter of peace, which ought to have afforded the city's two million inhabitants a glimmer of hope, increased general penury to a level very nearly beyond the limits of endurance. Vienna was a city under siege separated from outside help by no less than three ramparts – the Allied blockade, the boycott of the Successor States, and, perhaps the most oppressive, the self-sufficiency régime of the provinces. The daily ration of bread grains had during the last year of war been 165 grammes plus a modest special allocation for so-called heavy workers.[16] Inadequate though the ration was, it nevertheless represented the vital part of the government's food plan, inasmuch as milk, meat and other high-grade nutritive alimentation had virtually disappeared from the market.[17] Yet because of the threefold blockade this utterly inadequate ration could not be maintained. For some weeks the city's supplies could be ensured only by recourse to the army reserves while efforts to obtain a few deliveries from Germany proved successful.[18] It became obvious that an unsurpassed catastrophe would ensue unless considerable quantities of relief goods could be procured in the shortest space of time.

In this tragic situation the Austrian Government turned to the Allies with a series of appeals and notes in which the *political* implications of the acute emergency were more or less clearly spelt out. Whether the subsequent Allied relief measures were determined by considerations of a political character is difficult to establish. Certain State Department documents, to be found in Volume VII of the Peace Conference Documents, suggest that the broad hint did not miss its target.[19] That is also the impression of David Strong, who considered fear of Bolshevism and of *Anschluss* to have been the crucial motives for the Allied relief operation:

A double-stranded thread, weaving in and out of the official reports of heads of delegations sent to examine conditions in German-Austria, works its way into the committee rooms at Paris and St Germain, and finds its way back to Vienna in official communiqués. One strand of this thread was the realization that unless something of a constructive nature were done for

German-Austria and Hungary, they would draw closer to Germany – a development which in the atmosphere of Paris, 1919, was to be checked at all costs. The other strand was the admitted fear that unless something were done for German-Austria, that small but vital member of the Central-European family of nations might become a convert to Communism.[20]

The Allied relief operation, whatever its determining motives (although humanitarian considerations must have played an important part), got under way comparatively quickly and within bounds proved effective. An Inter-Allied Commission, visiting Vienna at the beginning of 1919, arranged for the immediate delivery of 24,000 tons of wheat, 2,000 tons of fat, and 750 tons of condensed milk to be distributed throughout Austria.[21] Later a permanent Relief Commission was set up at Trieste with the difficult task of organizing under conditions bordering on anarchy the transport and safe conduct of various aid consignments. The arrival of the first deliveries in Vienna did not materially improve the situation. Further resolute operations were necessary. In February an Austrian delegation left for Paris to discuss with Herbert Hoover, in charge of American relief, the possibilities for financing the American food deliveries.[22] The various proposals made by members of the delegation during its stay included a joint Austro-American project for expansion of the country's hydraulic power station resources. Finally the United States extended a loan of 30 million dollars, later increased by another 18 million, to keep Austria going until the next harvest. As American law forbade any loan to a former enemy country, an adroit subterfuge was found by making Great Britain, France, and Italy the direct recipients of the loan and Austria becoming the final beneficiary. In this manner Austria was able to import 360,000 tons of foodstuffs during the critical period from January till September 1919.[23]

The effects of the aid measures were hardly perceptible before late spring 1919. In January and February the nutritional crisis reached its peak. Vienna's meat consumption in pre-war years had been 4 million kilogrammes per week. In the first months of 1919 the figure was less than a tenth of that.[24] By August the 165 grammes daily bread ration dating from the war's worst emergency period had been gradually raised to 235 grammes, but it had then to be reduced again and in December it fluctuated between 100 and 170 grammes.[25] The Allied Food Controller estimated that during the crucial period of spring and early summer the Viennese obtained from their daily rations no more than 1,271 calories in lieu of the vital minimum 2,300 calories.[26] In the provinces the situation was somewhat better.

The four years of war and the dreadful winter of 1918 had appalling consequences for the population's mental and physical condition. All foreign observers agree that, especially among the Viennese, apathy and resignation were the rule.

For the first time in my life I found a whole nation, or what was left of it, in utter hopeless despair. Inability to obtain a ration, in itself insufficient to support human life, and the misery of hundreds and thousands who, in an early winter's snow, shivered without heat or the hope of getting it, were bad enough, but it was nothing compared with the apathy, the helplessness and the loss of all hope that pervaded every class from the highest to the lowest.[27]

The population's state of health gave cause for deep anxiety. 350,000 to 400,000 individuals were suffering from tuberculosis – the so-called *morbus Viennensis* – according to a *Neue Freie Presse* report of 31 May. It meant that at least 800,000 more people who shared housing with the sick, were being put in highest peril of infection.[28] Of 186,000 Viennese schoolchildren who underwent medical examination, 96,000 were graded as severely, 63,000 as clearly, and 19,000 as slightly undernourished. Only 6,732 were described as fairly well fed.[29] Sir William Goode found the hospitals 'full to overflowing with cases of tuberculosis and rickets due to defective food and prolonged undernourishment'.[30] In autumn and early winter a wave of Spanish influenza wrought havoc and, particularly among the capital's inhabitants, caused many deaths.[31]

This unheard of suffering gave rise to violent attacks on official economic policy by political parties, individuals, and newspapers. The Coalition Government had inherited from wartime an enormous bureaucratic machinery whose task had been to regulate and to supervise practically every aspect of the nation's economic life. No drastic changes were made straightaway. Possibly the large number of Social Democrats in the coalition, especially after the February elections to the Constituent National Assembly, may have contributed to this striking propensity for 'continuity'.[32] More decisive, though, is the circumstance that during the first winter of peace there was only one essential component distinguishing it from the preceding war years, the distinct accentuation of their anomalies. The Successor States' boycott, the illegal embargo by the provinces, and the almost general industrial standstill brought the lack of consumer goods to the highest point. At the same time the flood of paper money, constantly swollen during the past four years, continued to rise.

Had the government followed the advice of the conservative press, many rules and regulations would have been abrogated on the day after the Armistice. Such a policy could not however have been given serious consideration by either of the two big parties. In view of the grave shortages at home and abroad, as well as the reluctance of large sections of the peasant community to co-operate, it would have led to mass famine.[33] Even the Christian Socialist Party, despite having drawn remarkably close to the liberal view in economic matters during the last pre-war years, initially supported the retention of ceiling prices, rationing, food requisitioning, and a quasi-monopoly of external trade. Up to a point its attitude was conditioned by regard for its traditional supporters, the small tradesmen and members of the professions, many of whom had invested their savings in Austro-Hungarian War Loan. The peasantry was on the whole able to look after itself as far as alimentation went. The working class was strong enough to defend its standard of living, badly reduced though it was, through reasonable wage adjustments. The burden of rising prices would in the first instance have had to be borne by the groups least able to protect their traditional share of the national income.

While the Coalition Government possessed enough political stamina to ignore the warnings – perhaps more platonically than realistically meant – by the press, it could not remain indifferent to the demands of the peasants because its social basis rested on an unwritten agreement between the Socialists and the representatives of the peasants in the Christian Socialist Party, symbolized in the persons of Karl Renner and Jodok Fink as Chancellor and Vice-Chancellor respectively. Concessions to the agrarians could be made only at the expense of socialist principles. Given an acute food crisis, the peasant representatives changed into stubborn upholders of free market economics. Their clamour for the dismantling of war controls inevitably clashed with the ideas of their social democratic partners. They had their first great success when they forced the government to restrict the programme of food requisitioning. Fixing the quantity of cereals that had to be delivered to the authorities at the official price, the Ministry of Food put the quota for the whole country at no more than 1,800,000 tons of bread grains, that is, only some 18% of the last pre-war average harvests. The Ministry, basing itself on the meagre results of recent requisitions, had assessed the immediate post-war harvest yields at 50% below 1914. But the establishment of the quota at so low a level must have been interpreted by the agricultural representatives as an unspoken admission by the Government that it was virtually powerless in the face of the flourishing black market. The practical abandonment of requisitioning marked the first fatal breach in the imposing structure of wartime regimentation.[34]

The external trade monopoly remained necessary for the time being. For as long as the procuring of foodstuffs, fuels, and raw materials bore the character of diplomatic operations, the prospects for the resumption of private trading could not be more unfavourable. In so far as Austria's neighbours were at all prepared to part with supplies available for export, it was on a *quid pro quo* basis. Large-scale purchases of Czech coal, Czech sugar, or Yugoslav wheat could be made only in exchange for large-scale sales of Austrian iron ore, timber, or magnesite.[35] The rationing of daily consumer goods had its counterpart in the allocation of fuels and raw materials to the vital power, transport, and manufacturing enterprises. The country's economic life was held at a level barely sufficient for the minimum standards of public health and safety. Railway passenger traffic had to be repeatedly stopped for lack of fuel. On 18 January 1919 even freight traffic on the main lines to Italy and Czechoslovakia had to be halted. On the same day the Vienna Municipality was forced to cease all street car traffic.[36] Three days later Alpine Montangesellschaft, Austria's sole pig-iron producer, extinguished its last furnace.[37] Plant stoppages due to lack of coal, the abrupt cessation of armaments production, and the constant stream of men returning from the fronts created an unprecedented rise in the number of unemployed. In December 1918 an official census put the figure at 46,203. Two months later it had risen to 162,104, of whom two-thirds lived in Vienna. In May 1919 unemployment reached its temporary peak of 186,030 individuals.[38]

The Empire had never enjoyed a reputation for bold innovation in the field of social legislation. It had contented itself with following the example of more highly developed countries, in particular that of Germany.[39] Almost at its hour of birth the Republic was faced with a problem of unemployment unparalleled in Austrian history. Past experience offered no help and there was no administrative machinery adapted to this purpose. Such machinery therefore had to be improvized in this hour of need. Particularly critical was the situation created in the industrial areas after the collapse of the Imperial Army. Workers and soldiers, as in other parts of the continent, joined together to form local Councils stormily demanding a new political order. The spontaneous alliance between the former soldiers and the undernourished, in part unemployed urban population was described by a prominent contemporary in the following terms: 'The repatriate feels himself to be a socialist and the worker at home receives him as a comrade. When economic problems impinge on their minds, they make common cause because, repatriate and worker, they are both victims of the war crisis.'[40] The political dynamite inherent in this alliance explains the energy with which the authorities reacted to the challenge of rapidly rising unemployment.

As early as 6 November 1918 an ordinance introduced unemployment benefit for all industrial workers and employees.[41] On 15 November payment of these allowances was in full swing, paid for out of the federal budget. The scale of benefit was adjusted to the sick-pay awarded under the provisions for sickness insurance. According to Karl Přibram the authorities refrained from scrutinizing the claims with respect to the criteria of eligibility. Members of the armed forces obtained the benefit just like other individuals who could furnish no ascertainable legal claim.[42] This generosity partly explains the exceptional rise in the unemployment statistics for spring 1919.

The struggle against unemployment and the dangers connected with it reached their zenith in May 1919 when the example of Soviet Hungary brought thousands into the ranks of the Austrian communists. On 14 May Ferdinand Hanusch issued an emergency ordinance, indubitably interfering more incisively with private ownership rights than any other measure in the immediate post-war period. This ordinance instructed the employers of more than fifteen persons to increase the figure by 20% and to maintain that level unless compelling grounds for reduction could be proved to local authorities.[43] It is difficult to estimate the measure's actual success. Otto Bauer, an experienced observer, believed that it had a stabilizing effect on the labour market.[44] However that may be the number of unemployed did not perceptibly fall in the following months. A marked improvement had to wait until early autumn, but this was, as Přibram explained mainly attributable to the stricter application of the criteria of eligibility to benefit.

The paralyzing fear of the social revolutionary movement disappeared on the day that Communist rule in Budapest broke down. The forbearance which hitherto had to be practiced in Austria on grounds of public safety over the granting of unemployment benefit now lost its justification. The beneficiaries could be reduced from month to month by a suitable tightening of eligibility criteria, and by a system of keeping a check on the circumstances of every single unemployed person.[45]

Unemployment benefit and the employment ordinance were exceptional measures to deal with the needs of an acute emergency. It was soon recognized that full employment would hardly be the normal state of affairs in the post-war period. The trade unions took the initiative in seeing to a definite legislative settlement of the problem. In the second half of 1919 appropriate legislation passed through the various committees and with its passage through Parliament on 24 March 1920 the federal government became responsible for the administration of unemployment welfare arrangements.[46] The Ministry of Finance had to make advances for all expenditure during the fiscal year and was reimbursed afterward by contributions of employers and employees to two-thirds of the total amount advanced. Insurance principles were partly observed inasmuch as there was a connection between the individual's contribution and his or her income. On the other hand no connection was established between unemployment benefit and the size of his or her contribution.[47]

The Social Democrats had been scarcely better prepared for the complete collapse of the old political order than were their coalition partners, the Christian Socialists. As can be seen from the case of unemployment benefit, they practised a pragmatic policy towards the economic and social emergency and adopted whatever reform measures might be appropriate to the most urgent needs of the hour. Indicative of this was their treatment of that stock item in the socialist arsenal, the eight-hour working day, introduced in the first instance as a weapon against unemployment.

Workers' reduced fitness, due to undernourishment and exhaustion after four years of war, was another factor that spoke in favour of cutting hours inasmuch as it was to the disadvantage of both management and labour (as a socialist speaker said) to overstep the limit where a severe drop in performance must follow. Otto Bauer argued on similar lines. 'Cogent reasons existed for an eight-hour working day – to let the generators run a whole long workday, lighting and heating the shops, is a waste of coal if the worker's weakened body cannot make use of the prolonged working time. A shorter, but intensively used, workday had therefore to be the objective.'[48]

The emergency, especially the desperate lack of coal, facilitated achievement of the eight-hour day. In the circumstances, managements had anyway only a short workday to offer their employees. Thus the fuel crisis contributed to the initiation of an epoch-making piece of social legislation. It is no wonder that the draft of the provisional law introduced into parliament on 12 December 1918 met with hardly a murmur from the Right.[49] The definitive bill, turning the eight-hour day into standard practice, met likewise with little opposition,[50] the more so as it had been noted that the eight-hour-day had by that time been introduced in all industrial countries, partly by law, partly by trade union action.[51]

Planned as an emergency measure, the innovation was in fact one of the few pioneering reforms during the Republic's first year of existence. For the working classes it opened the door to the culture of the twentieth century. It furnished the basis for the numerous political, educational, cultural, and sports organizations which were then launched, particularly in Vienna in the fifteen years of its Social Democrat government. It also contributed to a relatively swift improvement in workers' performance and morale, a point confirmed by competent observers in 1920 and 1921.[52] The statute therefore had its attractive side in the eyes of industry too, all the more because of the trade unions' subsequent agreement to certain important amendments which allowed adaptation to special operational requirements – shift work, for example.[53]

Another group of laws concerned workers' health protection. Prime mention must be made here of the workers' holiday law, guaranteeing every industrial employee one week's holiday after one year's engagement and a fortnight after five years.[54] A bill passed on 14 May 1919 forbade night-work by young persons and women.[55] This can however hardly be regarded as a revolutionary innovation since such a law had already been issued in 1911. Certain other measures, like strict regulations against child labour, a veto on night-work in bakeries, and so on, had the same target in mind.

A third category of laws had as its aim, along with abating unemployment and protecting workers' health, the improvement of labour's status in negotiations with management. In this respect the three most important measures related to the establishment of the Chambers of Labour, settlement of the collective agreements and the election of shop stewards.[56] Attention will again be focused on the latter, possibly the most outstanding achievement of the revolutionary period, in connection with the public debate on socialism in the immediate post-war era.

The preparation of most of these measures by the leaders of the Social Democrat party and by the trade union organizations took place in an atmosphere of almost complete passivity on the part of the influential conservative press. Karl Přibram, probably the greatest authority on social affairs in the First Republic and an objective political observer, commented, not without a hint of consternation,

'Faced with this plethora of social innovations . . . it is remarkable that there was hardly ever a word of serious criticism in the conservative press. Indeed the leading morning papers, apart from the working-class journals, barely published more than a meagre note here and there about social legislation.'[57]

Similar passivity was displayed by the Social Democrats' opponents inside and outside the coalition. As a whole they confined their activities to preventing legislation which might prove damaging to the peasants. They succeeded, for instance, in restricting the institution of work councils to industry. During the early phase of the revolution a mixed commission, drawn from the trade unions and the Association of Austrian Industrialists, conferred about many of the reforms proposed by the Minister of Social Administration. (The step can be regarded as an anticipation of the Parity Commission, the joint employers' and employeees' organization, which has been of such great importance for economic policy in the Second Republic.) Naturally the trade unions constituted the more militant group while the industrialists usually remained on the defensive. Ludwig Urban, a well-known, capable and progressive-minded Viennese manufacturer, acted as their spokesman and normally gave the demands of the workers' side a fair hearing.[58] The First Republic's fate might have proved different if these early attempts at institutionalized collaboration between employers and employees had been continued.

A most important reform originating in wartime conditions was the famous Tenants' Protection Act of December 1922.[59] One of this period's most controversial pieces of social legislation, its passage was accompanied by uncommonly fierce public debate. Imperial Austria, like most of the belligerent nations, had thought it necessary to drastically curtail the rights of urban landlords. For practical purposes the freedom of landlords to fix rents and give notice at will was suspended for the duration of hostilities. Soon after the end of the war the small, but noisy landlords' lobby began to push for the immediate abolition of all rent control. When this group realized that public opinion rejected these demands it started a violent campaign against the confiscatory practices of 'Austromarxism'. The question at issue did not however involve only the working classes. Broad sections of the middle class, who as a result of inflation had had to suffer a substantial loss of income, were also unwilling to pay pre-war rents from their present reduced means. Business men, themselves often landlords were in a dilemma. They understood very well that abolition of controls must be followed by unprecedentedly violent wage disputes.

The landlords' lobby faced an opposition which, however heterogeneously composed, seemed at one in being determined to make up their war losses partially at the expense of a single social stratum. None of the middle-class parties was prepared actively to support the interests of the landlords because, as an expert in these matters noted, rent control was 'an economic necessity. Had the various governments not taken it into account, the country would certainly have slid into serious internal struggles'.[60]

The Tenants' Protection Act must be viewed against this political background. The landlords' right to give notice was as good as abrogated. Rent was divided into three elements: one part for maintenance (repair and administration), a second for operating costs (light, chimney-sweeping, and other current expenditure); finally there was ground-rent. This, the landlord's due, was fixed at 1% of its pre-war value in gold. The almost complete standstill in private building was not, as often asserted, the outcome of the act because the statute's provisions did not apply to newly-constructed dwellings. These were moreover exempt for thirty years from the payment of rates.[61] The main reason for entrepreneurial inactivity in this field was the exorbitant costs that private building involved plus the high interest rate. The city of Vienna later undertook an ambitious housing programme which between 1923 and 1927 resulted in the construction of 25,000 dwellings.[62]

Although the achievements of the Austrian revolution in the field of social legislation were significant, broad masses of the population desired a more sweeping reform of the social structure. The novelty of the great political debate in the crisis winter of 1918–19 lay in the central place given to the question of socialization. The degree to which the Austrian working class had acquired political self-confidence during a decade of war and revolution is perhaps best illustrated by the exceptional expansion of the trade union movement. In the German-language Austrian territories its progress was as follows:[63]

Table 41   Trade Union membership (in 000s)

1910	1912	1916	1917	1918	1919	1920
224	257	108	213	295	772	900

In 1920 almost all wage-earners and more than half of the salaried staffs stood behind the Social Democrat trade union leadership.[64]

This state of affairs laid a great responsibility on the party. Should it yield to the demands of a considerable portion of the working class and launch a frontal attack on the weakened capitalist system? There were signs that the Allied Powers were not prepared to tolerate a revolutionary step of this kind. At this juncture, though, it appears that these powers had only limited means of intervention at their disposal. Revolutionary Russia had until now, contrary to all expectations, been able to successfully hold its own. In spring 1919 the revolutionary tide had swept forward as far as Bavaria and Hungary and was surging with growing force against the Alpine lands' ideological defences. Had Austria at this moment followed the path of the two neighbouring Soviet republics, who could have vouched for the prospects of an intervention by the Allies and their partners? The quandary facing the Social Democrats can be seen as the alternative to following Russia or Hungary's example; establishing a Soviet dictatorship in Austria and accepting the risk of an enormous blood toll as well as utter defeat, or not participating in the crusade against capitalism in the hope of obtaining socialist objectives by stages and through the parliamentary machinery. The decision in favour of the latter method appears to have been reached early on.

Otto Bauer, the unchallenged intellectual leader of the Social Democrats after Viktor Adler's death, published between 5 and 28 January a series of contributions to *Arbeiter-Zeitung* which familiarized readers with his plans for socialization. Shortly afterwards these 'dashed-off newspaper contributions' came out as a brochure, *The Way to Socialism*.[65] Bauer's concept, as he recounted in the preface to the pamphlet's twelfth edition, derived from a mixture of the ideas aired by British Guild socialism and the Bolsheviks' plans for economic organization as agreed in May 1918 at the Congress of Economic Councils.[66] The proposal for direct participation by workers in the management of socialized industries amounted to an, at least partial, acceptance of western European syndicalism.[67]

Bauer envisaged socialization as a gradual process. Starting with coal, steel, and heavy industry, it would spread step by step to other sectors. Two important reasons spoke for the immediate socialization of coal and iron mining, and of the iron and steel industry: firstly, their strategic economic role and secondly their high degree of concentration that made it possible for production to be supervised at the highest level from a central location. The management of the socialized enterprises was not to be entrusted to the state which Bauer regarded as a bureaucratic and therefore inefficient manager, but to boards composed of workers' representatives, the consumers and the state. The latter would have the task of settling conflicts between the other two parties.[68] The compensation to be paid to the former owners of expropriated enterprises would be raised by a capital levy on the whole of the capitalist class.

For branches of industry not yet ripe for socialization, on account of their fragmentation, Bauer envisaged the creation of cartel-like associations based on the pattern of the wartime agencies. Workers, businessmen, consumers and official representatives would share equally in the direction of these public companies. Their task would in particular be to see to the concentration of production in the technically most advanced plants. Socialization would then subsequently take place.[69]

With co-determination by the workers envisaged only at the enterprise level, 'workers' committees were to be constituted, as a supplementary measure, in all units with more than twenty employees. These committees were not supposed to interfere with the commercial or the technical management, but simply to enforce the rights already obtained by the unions' spokesmen.[70] In their original form these 'workers' committees' – the later works councils – were not an integral part of any socialization programme. Probably they were conceived as a compensation for the workers' exclusion from the direction of individual firms.

After advancing proposals for the socialization of urban real estate and for the nationalization of large agrarian estates on a co-operative basis, Bauer turned to the banking system. Expropriation of the big financial houses would be the crowning act of socialization. As industry's dependence on the commercial banks was an obvious fact, this 'heretical' reversal of the logical process in socialization needed explanation.[71] Industry, Bauer elucidated, had in pre-war days been subservient to finance capital. Since the war ended this was no longer true because, as a result of their huge purchases of War Loans the banks' assets consisted chiefly of government bonds.

This view did not entirely concur with the facts. By the end of 1918 the major banks had mostly rid themselves of their own War Loan holdings and on the whole retained their dominance over industry.[72] Bauer does not himself seem to have been completely convinced by his argument as, to justify his reasoning, he added that immediate nationalization of the banks might imperil their access to the international capital markets. 'Today, when we need to borrow from abroad for the reconstruction of our economy, it [nationalization] would hardly be as easy to implement and hardly . . . as effective as it would have been in peace-time.'[73]

In the 1920s the difficulties of finding funds for enterprises in social ownership made Social Democrats realize the priority of nationalizing the banks. Käthe Leichter, the Left-Wing Socialist, advocated nationalization,[74] so did Karl Renner, the party's right wing spokesman.[75] Otto Bauer however adhered, though in a diluted form, to his former views.[76]

Bauer's plan for a partial socialization which would progressively bring about a reorganization of the economy in the long term was adapted wholly to Austrian conditions. The dismemberment of the Dual Monarchy had torn apart a large, organic economic entity. Styrian ore was now sundered from Czech coal. Individual firms belonging to large-scale concerns were situated in different Successor States.[77] What Bauer did not consider was the possibility of a vertical socialization comprising the whole process of production from the acquisition of raw materials to the final manufacturing stage.[78] Herein he was undoubtedly inconsistent. On the one hand his plan for socialization was harnessed to the situation of little Austria. On the other, *Anschluss* was presented as the *sine qua non* of socialization. But union with Germany would have made far-reaching structural changes more feasible inasmuch as a large number of German industries met the criterion of being 'ripe for socialization'.

Bauer's ideas had great political importance because they constituted an attempt to present a Social Democrat model opposed to the Communist strategy of dictatorship of the proletariat on Russian lines. Between Bauer's plans for socialization and the Austro-marxist concept of 'radical reformism' existed an internal connection. The revolution that Bauer and his party friends had in mind was to be a gradual, orderly change, a matter of 'creative legislation' capable, so they thought, of being effected without the exercise of dictatorial measures.[79]

Considerations of principle as well as of political realism led Bauer to reject the notion of forcibly imposed, complete socialization. An opponent of clenched fist logic, he did not believe that mere 'socialization of property', meaning the precipitate expropriation of 'claims to surplus value', was the right way to solve the problem of 'socializing production'.[80] The dwindling of purchasing power for luxury goods, rationalization of the distributive sector, and the inevitable concentration and modernization process in the socialized portion of industry would make necesasary structural changes that could be 'consummated only in the course of generations'.[81] It is therefore 'expedient to proceed with the legal acts of socialization only progressively, that is, only at the pace at which the economic process of socialization can be carried through.' Bauer thought moreover that the social production mechanism in western and in central Europe was far more complicated and liable to malfunction than in backward Russia. Proletarian revolution in the West must take care that 'the social metabolism be not interrupted'. It must not 'destroy any capitalist organization . . . before the socialist organization is ready to take over and to continue its proper function.'[82] For all these reasons the period of transition would probably take decades during which 'capitalist and socialist enterprises would exist alongside each other'.[83] Just as remnants of feudalism jutted out from capitalism, so would vestiges of capitalism continue in socialist society. Socialism would be 'a social order of hybrids'.[84]

Bauer's plan for socialization soon became the official programme of the Social Democrat Party. The only resistance worthy of mention came from speakers for the co-operative societies. They foresaw a danger of managerial paralysis in co-determination by workers and employees and they disapproved of workers' committees in their own establishments because they regarded these as being socialized already.[85] Karl Renner, as the party's right wing spokesman, thought socialization at this stage of events impracticable. He was however too heavily engaged with official duties to be able to intervene in the running discussion.[86]

The feeling of a fresh start and radical change was not confined to the ranks of the Social Democrat Party and the trade unions. A programme published at the end of February 1919 by the Christian Socialists shows that during the early months of the Republic the idea that society needed to take over and to retain control of strategic economic positions also met with approval outside the hard core of the working class. 'Communications and industrial construction enterprises serving the general need, as well as those major undertakings manufacturing universally required articles and in the nature of things capable of acquiring a monopoly position, shall be socialized by being placed in the hands of the national, provincial, or local authorities. Other industrial enterprises which, if left in private hands, threaten to become instruments of exploitation shall . . . become subject . . . through participation by the state, the province, or the commune . . .

to public control.'[87] In spring 1919, when the debate over socialization was generating particularly high excitement, a Viennese priest, August Schaurhofer, declared that Bauer's programme rendered it 'possible for Christian circles to make common cause with Social Democracy for a certain part of the way'.[88] Such a demonstration of sympathy for the idea of socialization is in strong contrast to the admission made by Christian Social Vice-Chancellor Jodok Fink, that in 1919 he had 'only jumped on the revolutionary bandwagon in order to put a brake on it'.[89]

At the time of Bauer's publication of his newspaper articles such a radical interference with economic conditions appeared to be still far ahead. Events in February and March nonetheless imposed on the Social Democrat Party the need for action. On 16 February it had won an impressive victory in the elections to the Constituent National Assembly. With 70 out of 162 seats, it was now the strongest group in Parliament. The victory was a clear expression of growing radicalism in the country, especially among the urban population.

There were other signs of increasing impatience among the broad mass of people. The Workers and Soldiers Councils, initially operating on a local basis and fulfilling various administrative tasks, established during the late winter months a country-wide organization. On 1 March an all-Austrian Workers Council at Linz drafted and passed a constitution closely modelled on the Russian Soviet pattern. In the same month membership of the Austrian Communist Party, born of the turbulent days of November 1918 rose considerably. Particularly after the establishment of the Soviet republics in Hungary (21 March) and Bavaria (7 April), the Austrian proletariat reacted more and more positively to communist agitation. There followed a series of wild socializations, the most important affecting the nation's biggest industrial enterprise. On 7 April the workforce of the Alpine Montan-Gesellschaft expelled the senior executives and elected a new management from its own ranks.[90]

On 21 February the Social Democrat party had, under pressure from its radical supporters, published in *Arbeiter-Zeitung* a programme designed to serve as a platform for coalition talks with the Christian Socialist Party. One of its most important demands was for a Socialization Commission.[91] A bill passed on 14 March, on preparations for socialization, gave parliamentary assent to such a body. Next day Otto Bauer was appointed its chairman.[92]

The strategy of the Social Democrat leadership at the height of the revolutionary crisis in spring 1919 can be described in a few words. It sought to channel the 'elemental force of the working class, urging socialization, away from irregular into practicable, attainable, and beneficial paths'.[93] The middle class, on the other hand, was to be forced into vital concessions under threat from the 'elemental working class strength'. These tactics, as has been seen, were highly successful as far as social legislation went. Over socialization however the anticipated, decisive breakthrough did not happen.[94]

In 1919 parliament passed three bills that in the narrow sense can be termed socialization measures: that of 14 March; the Expropriation Act of 30 May; and the establishment of enterprises in collective ownership, by an act of 29 July. To these are generally added the Works Councils Act of 15 May. Preparatory work on the bill was done within the framework of the Socialization Commission, but its final version was worked out by the Social Welfare Ministry. Bauer accorded this bill a key role in long term socialization strategy. Whereas in *The Road to Socialism* he had seen the 'worker's committees' as merely supplementing socialist structural changes, in mid-April he defined works councils for the first time as a necessary preliminary stage to socialization.[95] Henceforward he argued that the councils should 'fulfil an important educational function as the great school for proletarian self-government in the production process'.[96] They should prevent the later emergence of a 'bureaucratic state socialism' which would simply replace 'the entrepreneur's despotism by the despotism of the bureaucrat'.[97] The working class must 'of itself' bring forth 'a team of well-trained and loyal spokesmen capable of taking over the direction of plants without disturbance to production'. That was why it was the 'prime task of a systematic socialization scheme' to create the conditions for developing such a team of potential plant managers.[98]

The bill on the introduction of works councils in industrial and commercial enterprises was passed with a big majority, perhaps because 'it satisfied an urgent demand by the working class without seriously interfering with the capitalist economic order'.[99] The Christian Socialists had assembled sufficient votes prior to the discussion to make the law inapplicable to agriculture.[100] On 22 May the Government announced *ex cathedra* that it had decided in due time to nationalize mining, iron ore production, power stations, major forestry holdings, and the timber industry.[101] Paradoxically this was intended to pacify the business world which had repeatedly called for a statement on the industries that it was proposed to nationalize. Whether the declaration had the desired effect must be left open to debate.

On 30 May a bill was passed on the procedure for the expropriation of enterprises.[102] The Social Democrats had hoped to obtain a general power of expropriation for the Government. However, in the face of hardening opposition by the Christian Socialist coalition partners, they had to content themselves with a purely procedural statute. As, moreover, the Christian Socialist provincial administration were given a voice in this matter the door was wide open to obstruction and delay of socialization measures.

Shortly after the passage of the Expropriation Act a longer interval in legislative activities ensued as a reaction to announcement on 8 June of the crushing Peace Treaty provisions. When at the end of July Parliament again met, the situation at home and in the neighbouring countries had fundamentally changed. The collapse of the Hungarian Soviet Republic was hourly expected. In Germany the danger of revolution appeared to have been banished. In Austria the tide of working class radicalization had turned. Finally, the sale of a substantial packet of the shares of the Alpine Montan-Gesellschaft, the biggest Austrian industrial enterprise, made socialization practically impossible.

Small wonder that the act establishing enterprises in collective ownership was trimmed to the organizational reshaping of existing state enterprises. It was, as Erwin Weissel states, a law that 'did not socialize the existing capitalist enterprises but capitalized the planned socialist enterprises'.[103] Basic reconstruction of society was no longer the purpose.[104] The socialized enterprises it created were in the main plants formerly operated by the army whose biggest assets consisted in their supplies of stocks but which nonetheless rested on a very narrow financial basis.[105] Some socialists described them as 'germ-cells of the future socialist economy'.[106] Realistically seen, though, it was clear that these experimental 'socialized' enterprises could not represent any serious alternative to the prevailing economic order.[107]

The first major socialization debate has been treated in somewhat greater detail because it had some influence on the development of the Second Republic.[108] Some contemporary observers inclined to a negative view of Social Democrat policy in the sense that it was mainly motivated by the wish to appease the workers aroused by events in Hungary. Nearly half a century later Norbert Leser passed a negative verdict on the left wing socialists by reproaching them with lack of a 'real revolutionary will'. His final judgment is damning. 'Yet the will to seize a marginal chance, and so to take the risk involved in such uncertain situations, could not be at hand because, whether before or after, it was not at hand in the case of far less risky and, in the light of socialist convictions, far more morally compelling situations.'[109]

Otto Bauer himself encouraged such interpretations when he justified his consistent rejection of revolutionary action solely by drawing attention to the possibility of foreign intervention and of Vienna's desertion by the peasant provinces. In a letter to Bela Kun, for instance, he wrote that the Allied Powers would begin by stopping coal and food deliveries. 'The masses, literally threatened by famine, would rise against a dictatorship. There is moreover the danger of the isolation of Vienna and the industrial areas which, if dictatorship by the Soviets were proclaimed' must 'probably lead to the immediate breakaway by the preponderantly peasant, and therefore clerical-agrarian, provinces from Vienna.'[110] The truth is that the Social Democrat leadership as a whole was not prepared to compel the middle-class majority into acceptance of the 22 May socialization programme by the use of extra-parliamentary means. It considered itself unconditionally bound by the rules of the democratic game. Socialism, argued the left wing similarly, could not materialize as long as the broad mass of the nation did not consciously desire it.

If the intellectual workers and the agricultural workers join the industrial proletariat, then the class-conscious proletariat in any industrial state is the majority of the nation. Then it can seize and wield power by democratic means. If we are still in a minority, it proves that all-too wide a section of the intellectual and agricultural workers are still outside our ranks. Then the objective social prerequisite to socialism is still not fulfilled. Force is the midwife to every old society spawning a new, but force cannot deliver the new society until it has ripened in the womb of the old.[111]

Notes

1 Gustav Gratz and Richard Schüller, *Der wirtschaftliche Zusammenbruch Österreich-Ungarns* (Vienna, 1930), p. 89.
2 'There is every justification for saying that in the economic year 1918–19 Austria-Hungary would no longer have been able to prevent the complete breakdown of food supplies and the outbreak of a dreadful famine.' *Der wirtschaftliche Zusammenbruch*, p. 89.
3 *Anbaufläche und Ernteergebnisse in der Republik Österreich im Jahre 1918* (Vienna, 1918), published by the State Office for Agriculture and Forestry.
4 Not until 22 March 1919 did the Allies decide to raise the blockade against the territories of the former Empire. See *Der Österreichische Volkswirt*, 23 March 1919, p. 460.

5 Sir William Goode, *Economic Conditions in Central Europe* (London, 1920), p. 3.

6 This phase of post-war confusion is excellently summarized in Goode's report on central European conditions. 'In all the economic chaos of Europe there is no more perplexing vicious circle than that of coal and railways. In countries where I found wagons I found almost invariably a shortage of locomotives; where there were locomotives there was a shortage of wagons. Where coal lay at the pithead awaiting transport there were no wagons and where wagons waited, men were not available to work the coal. For want of coal in Austria whole trains of wagons stood idle on the tracks. In Yugoslavia and Hungary the lines were congested with empty wagons for want of locomotives. In Poland, where efforts were made to stimulate the production of fuel oil there were not enough tank wagons to carry the increased quantity of oil.' Goode, *Economic Conditions*, p. 8.

7 'The Austrians themselves have stripped us of them [railway cars] very nearly completely, and it is they who clamour loudest for coal, yet refuse to hear us when we ask to be provided first with means of transportation.' Letter from Beneš to Hoover, 7 January 1919, A. R. A. Archives, Hoover War Library. Quoted in David F. Strong, *Austria, October 1918–March 1919, Transition from Empire to Republic* (New York, 1939), p. 176.

8 Heinrich Wittek, 'Die österreichischen Eisenbahnen vor und nach dem Kriege', *Schriften des Vereins für Sozialpolitik* (Munich, 1929), p. 116.

9 'The jealousies of the several governments in respect of the use of their railways and rolling stock were, and still are, a formidable obstacle to the renewal of commercial intercourse.' Goode, *Economic Conditions*, Part II, p. 5.

10 Otto Bauer, 'Die Österreichische Revolution' in Werkausgabe (Vienna, 1976), Vol. II, p. 643.

11 '. . . again, in the case of sugar, the Czechoslovakian government had an exportable surplus of sugar. They were under contract to the Austrian government to deliver an amount which would have met Austria's minimal requirements. On the other hand, the Czechoslovakian government . . . is dependent for its national welfare upon imports of raw material, but has no credit with which to buy them. Practically its only security for loans or credits is its sugar crop, and a large quantity of this has now been pledged in return for external loans. Austria is therefore likely to have to obtain sugar by arrangement with the Allied governments if she gets it at all.' Goode, *Economic Conditions*, Part I, p. 9.

12 Shorthand Minutes, 30 October 1918, p. 55.

13 Contemporary newspapers repeatedly mention such incidents. The Tirolese ordinance against Vienna is to be found in *Der Österreichische Volkswirt*, 15 March 1919, p. 403. An earlier issue, 7 February, p. 337, had reported the prohibition of food exports by Upper Austria.

14 'The official prices, which are still nominally maintained, are so low that the peasant producer will not look at them, and the provincial governments are not strong enough to compel him to sell. He therefore sells what he chooses at six or eight or ten times the official price to the well-to-do classes in the town on the black market. What he cannot sell, or does not choose to sell, he allows to rot or gives to his pigs. The callousness of the peasant as to the fate of the towns, and especially of Vienna, must be seen to be believed.' Goode, *Economic Conditions*, Part II, pp. 6–7.

15 Bauer, in *Werkausgabe*, Vol. II, p. 653.
16 Goode, *Economic Conditions*, Part II, p. 4.
17 Goode, *Economic Conditions*, p. 4.
18 Bauer, *Werkausgabe*, Vol. II, p. 644.
19 A United Press dispatch of 18 May 1946, summarizing the contents of some of the documents, had the following to say about Hoover's attitude towards relief matters: 'At the time Mr Hoover was US Relief Administrator but played an important role in international political affairs. As recorded in the volume, his discussions of food at meetings of the Big Five of 1919 – US, Britain, France, Italy and Japan – never were disassociated from politics.'
20 Strong, *Austria*, p. 243 et seq.
21 Goode, *Economic Conditions*, Part II, p. 3.
22 The negotiations with Hoover are described in some detail by Gratz and Schüller, *Der wirtschaftliche Zusammenbruch*, p. 207 et seq.
23 See the report by the Minister of Food, Löwenfeld-Russ, in *Der Österreichische Volkswirt*, 7 February 1920, p. 351. The loans extended to Austria in 1919 and 1920 amounted, according to the International Committee for Relief Aid, to £26,686,690. See Jan van Walré de Bordes, *The Austrian Crown, Its Depreciation and Stabilization* (London, 1924), p. 8. A number of neutral countries and many philanthropic associations participated in addition to the Big Four (USA, Great Britain, France, and Italy).
24 Goode, *Economic Conditions*, Part II, p. 4. Black market sales, although they must sometimes have been huge, are of course not included in this figure. Walther Federn believed that a quarter of the meat consumption came from illegal sources. See *Der Österreichische Volkswirt*, 1 March 1919, p. 373.
25 Goode, *Economic Conditions*, Part II, p. 6.
26 Goode, *Economic Conditions*, Part II, p. 7.
27 Goode, *Economic Conditions*, Part I, pp. 9–10.
28 Quoted in Karl R. Stadler, *Hypothek auf die Zukunft* (Vienna, 1968), p. 202.
29 Bauer, in *Werkausgabe*, Vol. II, p. 644.
30 Goode, *Economic Conditions*, Part II, p. 7.
31 *Österreichisches Jahrbuch 1920*, pp. 24–5. The victims included the painter Egon Schiele, only twenty-nine years old.
32 The outcome of the elections to the Constituent National Assembly on 16 February 1919 was as follows: 70 Social Democrats, 67 Christian Socialists, 25 German Nationalists. See *Chronique des Événements Politiques et Economiques dans le Bassin Danubien, 1918–1938, Autriche* (Paris, 1938), p. 160.
33 'At this time . . . there was a deficit in the production of bread cereals throughout the world. Private companies in Austria which imported cereals did not possess sufficient financial resources to meet the situation, and as they were not in touch with exporters overseas . . . they were unable to obtain credits from them. Finally, the supply of cereals was closely bound up with diplomatic conventions concluded with the Entente Powers. The state was therefore obliged to organize the food supply of the country . . .' *Financial Reconstruction of Austria*, Report by the League of Nations Financial Committee (Geneva, 1920), p. 29.
34 For highly instructive discussions of the Austrian Government's food policy during the first half of 1919, see Walther Federn, 'Defizit aus staatlicher Ernährungswirtschaft' and Gustav Stolper, 'Die Neuregelung des Getreideverkehrs', *Der Österreichische Volkswirt*, 31 May 1919, p. 633 et seq. and 7

June 1919, p. 659 et seq. respectively.
35 A typical communiqué ran, 'The Czechoslovak Ministry of Labour sanctions the daily delivery of 80 wagons of lignite and 50 wagons of pit coal in exchange for the monthly delivery of 100 wagons of magnesite.' See *Der Österreichische Volkswirt*, 15 February 1919, p. 337.
36 *Chronique*, p. 36.
37 *Chronique*, p. 27.
38 Edmund Palla, 'Ein Jahr Arbeitslosenfürsorge in Österreich', *Nachrichten des Staatsamtes für Soziale Verwaltung* (Vienna, 1920), No. 21–22.
39 Karl Přibram, 'Die Sozialpolitik im neuen Österreich', *Archiv für Sozialwissenschaft und Sozialpolitik* (Tübingen, 1921), Vol. XLVIII, p. 615 et seq. 'In regard to social policy the old Austrian Empire, with its conservative tendencies, had observed an anxious reticence' is Přibram's verdict.
40 See Emil Lederer, 'Friedensdiktat und Sozialismus', *Der Kampf*, 24 May 1919, p. 309.
41 Executive directive, Official Law Gazette No. 20, 6 November 1918.
42 Přibram, *Archiv*, p. 638.
43 Official Law Gazette, 16 May 1919.
44 Bauer, *Werkausgabe*, Vol. II, p. 702.
45 Karl Přibram, 'Die gesetzliche Regelung der Arbeitslosenunterstützung', *Der Österreichische Volkswirt*, 3 April 1920, p. 522.
46 Official Law Gazette No. 153, 3 April 1920.
47 For a detailed discussion of the Unemployment Act, see Přibram, *Archiv*, pp. 631–44.
48 Bauer, *Werkausgabe*, Vol. II, p. 702.
49 Official Law Gazette No. 138, 24 December 1918.
50 Official Law Gazette No. 581, 17 December 1919.
51 Bauer, *Werkausgabe*, Vol. II, p. 704.
52 'Many an honest business man will tell you that peace-time performance has practically been attained.' See Walther Federn, 'Wohlleben und drohende Katastrophe', *Der Österreichische Volkswirt*, 13 August 1921, p. 86.
53 Přibram, *Archiv*, p. 628. It must be realized that the provisional eight-hour working day law was confined to factories, whereas the statute applied to all commercial and industrial enterprises, irrespective of size.
54 Official law Gazette No. 395, 7 August 1919. Gulick says that the importance of this law 'can hardly be exaggerated. It rendered it possible for the whole Austrian economy to replenish its reserves in physical man power'. See Charles A. Gulick, *Austria: From Habsburg to Hitler* (Berkeley and Los Angeles, 1948), Vol, I, p. 201.
55 Official Law Gazette No. 281, 24 May 1919.
56 For a detailed discussion of collective agreements and related spheres, see Gulick, *Austria*, p. 219 et seq.
57 Přibram, *Archiv*, p. 626.
58 Přibram, *Archiv*, p. 625.
59 Official Law Gazette No. 822, 15 December 1922.
60 Ernst Wagner-Herr, 'Die Wohnungsverhältnisse', *Schriften des Vereins für Sozialpolitik* (Munich, 1925), Vol. 169, p. 177. In Austrian industrial circles a radical change of opinion occurred as soon as the early twenties. The principal industrialists' association, for instance, published in 1924 a memorandum

culminating in the demand for abolition of rent control. See *Neue Freie Presse*,
31 August 1924.

61 Two Municipality of Vienna ordinances dealt with tax exemption for newly-constructed houses. See Vienna Law Gazette No. 127 of 30 September 1921 and No. 128 of 10 October 1921.

62 *Die Wohnungspolitik der Gemeinde Wien* (Vienna, 1929), p. 27, published by the Austrian Museum for Economic and Social Affairs.

63 *Die Gewerkschaft* (Vienna, 1921), 25 August 1921, and Gulick, *Austria*, p. 202.

64 In comparison the strength of the Catholic trade unions was negligible. In 1920 its members numbered only 60,000. See *Christlich-soziale Arbeiterzeitung*, 10 November 1921. Also Fritz Klenner, *Die österreichischen Gewerkschaften* (Vienna 1951) vol. I, p. 467.

65 Writing about how his socialization scheme originated, Otto Bauer said, 'I was at the time in charge of the young German-Austrian Republic's Ministry of Foreign Affairs. Day after day we had to smoothe out highly dangerous border incidents with the small neighbouring states and to conduct extremely difficult negotiations with the Entente countries. I had great difficulty in wresting a few hours from excessively long working days to dictate a number of articles for *Arbeiter-Zeitung* on the problem of socialization. They were no more than hastily dashed-off newspaper contributions. But these same contributions had unexpected success . . .' Quoted from Otto Leichter, *Otto Bauer, Tragödie oder Triumph* (Vienna, 1970), p. 170.

66 Rudolf Gerlich, *Sozialisierung in der Ersten Republik* (Vienna, 1975), p. 60. On the ideas of guild socialism and the Bolsheviks, see Otto Bauer, 'Bolschevismus oder Sozialdemokratie', *Werkausgabe* (Vienna, 1976), Vol. II, p. 282 et seq. and p. 325 et seq.

67 Cf. Karl Korsch, 'Das sozialistische und syndikalistische Sozialisierungsprogramm', *Schriften zur Sozialisierung* (Frankfurt am Main, 1969), p. 55 et seq.

68 Bauer did not however hold this tripartite management to be an ideal type of organization having everlasting, rigid application to all sectors of production. 'A socialist economy will probably have no uniform industrial organization, but each branch of production will organize itself on its own lines.' See Otto Bauer, 'Einführung in die Volkswirtschaftslehre', *Werkausgabe* (Vienna, 1976), Vol. IV, p. 854.

69 Otto Bauer, 'Der Weg zum Sozialismus', *Werkausgabe* (Vienna, 1976), Vol. II, p. 100 et seq.

70 Bauer, *Werkausgabe*, Vol. II, p. 104 et seq.

71 A short while later, for instance, Schumpeter wrote, 'Above all it makes sense to start with the socialization of banking. In some respects the aforementioned normal banking operation is anyway a good example of how a line of business becomes ripe for socialization.' Joseph Schumpeter, 'Sozialistische Möglichkeiten von heute', *Archiv für Sozialwissenschaften und Sozialpolitik* (Tübingen, 1921), Vol. 48, Part II, p. 342.

72 'Banks which included in their group many large armament firms had primarily engaged in meeting the latter's requirements and had comparatively fewer direct claims on the state. Others, with a large branch office organization and big deposits, had no use for the inflow of thousands of millions other than by way of loans to the state and advances on War Loan issues. It was they who were the

state's creditors for the greater part of their outside resources.' Walther Federn, 'Die Kreditpolitik der Wiener Banken', *Schriften des Vereins für Sozialpolitik* (Munich-Leipzig, 1925), Vol. 169, p. 57.

73 Bauer, 'Der Weg', *Werkausgabe*, Vol. II, p. 121.

74 'These financing difficulties ... have clearly shown that any large-scale socialization is inconceivable so long as it is not possible to tackle socialization of the banks ... that it must stand at the outset of any large-scale work of socialization which is to have a real grip on the economy.' Käthe Leichter, 'Erfahrungen des österreichischen Sozialisierungsversuches', in *Käthe Leichter, Leben und Werk* (Vienna, 1973), ed. Herbert Steiner, p. 423 et seq.

75 Karl Renner, *Die Wirtschaft als Gesamtprozess und die Sozialisierung* (Berlin, 1924), p. 327 et seq.

76 Bauer, 'Einführung', *Werkausgabe*, Vol. II, p. 851. 'The task can always be only that of socializing certain important branches of production. It will be different in every country. In Germany and in America the start would be made with the big banks. In Austria it would need to be considered whether to start there.'

77 The Austrian textile industry, for instance, worked with Bohemian factories on a division of labour basis. The weaving mills were concentrated in Bohemia, the spinning mills in Lower Austria. See Stephan Koren, 'Die Industrialisierung Österreichs – Vom Protektionismus zur Integration', in *Österreichs Wirtschaftsstruktur – gestern-heute-morgen* (West Berlin, 1961), p. 238. Similarly complicated conditions existed in the vegetable oil and fats industry.

78 'And if many in the days of vertical trust formations had thought a vertical socialization right ... this scheme could not but fail in a country where after the revolution there hardly existed a production sector which did not need to have raw materials processing or finishing performed abroad.' Leichter, *Otto Bauer*, p. 388.

79 Bauer, 'Der Weg', *Werkausgabe*, Vol. II, p. 95, described the task of socialization as 'a creative legislative and administrative' one.

80 Bauer, 'Bolschevismus', *Werkausgabe*, Vol. II, p. 344 et seq.

81 Bauer, *Werkausgabe*, in particular p. 342, and p. 344 et seq.

82 Bauer, *Werkausgabe*, p. 314.

83 Otto Bauer at the Social Democratic Party Convention 1926, as quoted by Leichter, *Otto Bauer*, p. 175. In the course of his lectures to the Vienna Workers University, 1927–8, Bauer said, 'Every social order is the outcome of a protracted evolutionary process ... Initially capitalistic and socialistic elements will exist alongside each other. The next development will be that, step by step, socialistic elements will gain ground. *We shall never at a single bound leap from capitalist into socialist society. In between there will necessarily be a long transition period.*' Bauer, 'Einführung', *Werkausgabe*, Vol. II, p. 852. (Present author's italics.)

84 A phrase from an address, quoted by Gerlich, *Sozialisierung*, p. 32.

85 Gerlich, *Sozialisierung*, p. 68.

86 It was Renner who at this time coined the phrase that debts cannot be socialized. See Gulick, *Austria* Vol. I, p. 134.

87 Klaus Berchtold (ed.), *Österreichische Parteiprogramme 1868–1966* (Vienna, 1976), p. 362.

88 Gerlich, *Sozialisierung*, p. 116.

89 Gustav Otruba, 'Bauer und Arbeiter in der ersten Republik', *Geschichte und*

Gesellschaft, Festschrift für Karl R. Stadler (Vienna, 1974), p. 67.

90 Gulick, *Austria*, p. 137, FN 11.

91 Gerlich, *Sozialisierung*, p. 151 et seq.

92 As the rules of the parliamentary game were strictly observed, members of the middle-class parties, including the prominent Christian Socialists Ignaz Seipel and Leopold Kunschak, also belonged to the Socialization Commission. The impression made on the working class by this composition was the same as would have been created 'among Catholics in the case of a Church Council with preponderantly rabbinical representation', says Erwin Weissel, *Die Ohnmacht des Sieges, Arbeiterschaft und Sozialisierung nach dem Ersten Weltkrieg in Österreich* (Vienna, 1976), p. 264.

93 'Sozialisierung', *Arbeiter-Zeitung*, 6 April 1919.

94 The Social Democrats' idea that they could gain a free hand in the matter of socialization by ignoring the agrarian problem – cf. Julius Deutsch, 'Der Geist der Koalition', *Der Kampf*, 1919, p. 684 et seq. – proved an illusion. It was precisely the peasant-dominated provinces with Christian Socialist administrations which played a crucial role in the prevention of impending socialization measures.

95 On 14 April Otto Bauer wrote in *Arbeiter-Zeitung*, 'The introduction of works councils ... does not as such signify any socialization. It is simply a democratization of enterprises' constitutional structure, but it is a basis for socialization on which this can then be built.'

96 Bauer, 'Die Österreichische Revolution', *Werkausgabe*, Vol. II, p. 711.

97 Bauer, *Werkausgabe*, p. 711.

98 Otto Bauer, 'Die Sozialisierungsaktion im ersten Jahre der Republik', *Werkausgabe* (Vienna, 1976), Vol. II, p. 205.

99 Přibram, *Archiv*, p. 647.

100 Official Law Gazette, No. 283, 15 May 1919.

101 *Der Österreichische Volkswirt*, 31 May 1919, p. 642. This was the first step envisaged by Otto Bauer in 'Der Weg zum Sozialismus'. Cabinet Minutes No. 72, 20 May 1919, read 'The two most important sources of power, coal and electricity, and the two most important raw materials, iron and timber, are therefore to be socialized.' German-Austrian Ministry of Finance, File 35472/19, Ministry of Finance Archives.

102 Official Law Gazette No. 381, 30 May 1919.

103 Weissel, *Ohnmacht*, p. 282.

104 Bauer continued for a time to pin his hopes on Article 37 which empowered the government on the foundation of joint-stock companies or on capital increases by existent undertakings to enforce compulsory state participation. The other coalition partners inhibited the article's application after it had attained a number of early successes.

105 In 1921 eight joint enterprises were in operation.

106 Wilhelm Ellenbogen, *Sozialisierung in Österreich* (Vienna, 1921), p. 15.

107 A single pharmaceutical factory survived the years of stabilization and the economic crisis at the end of the 1920s. Ellenbogen's germ-cells theory was in the first half of the 1920s already criticized from the socialist side. Käthe Leichter (*Leben*, p. 390) held that the task of the joint enterprises could only be properly grasped by abandoning from the start any identification with the term 'socialization'. See also Otto Neurath, 'Vollsozialisierung und gemeinwirt-

schaftliche Anstalten', *Der Kampf*, 1922, pp. 54–60.

108 Cf. Eduard März and Fritz Weber, 'Verstaatlichung und Sozialisierung nach dem Ersten und Zweiten Weltkrieg – eine vergleichende Studie', in *Wirtschaft und Gesellschaft* (Vienna, 1978), No. 2, p. 115 et seq.

109 Norbert Leser, *Zwischen Reformismus und Bolschewismus* (Vienna, 1968), p. 304.

110 Miklos Szinai, *Zur Geschichte der Beziehungen zwischen der ungarischen Räterepublik und Österreich – Otto Bauers Brief an Bela Kun* (Budapest, 1972), p. 314 et seq.

111 Bauer, 'Bolschewismus oder Sozialdemokratie', *Werkausgabe*, Vol. II, p. 321. In another passage Bauer took issue with Trotsky's argument that if ultimately it is to the proletariat's advantage to conduct its class struggle and even its dictatorship within the framework of democratic institutions, then this still by no means signifies that history always allows the proletariat such a combination. Bauer's answer was that 'Trotsky's view is undoubtedly correct, but from it follows 1, not that the proletariat at all times and everywhere should aim at dictatorship, but that it should and must opt for it only when history forces it to do so, and 2, that the proletariat should adhere to dictatorship only for so long as historical conditions compel it to do so and that it must, as soon as history allows such a combination, strive to conduct its class struggle and even its dictatorship within the framework of democratic institutions. That, though, is a consequence not drawn by generally accepted Communist doctrine.' *Werkausgabe*, Vol. II, p. 352.

CHAPTER 3
Plans for Budget and Currency Reform – the Bauer-Schumpeter Controversy

During the First World War, and under the impact of the country's desperate financial straits, Schumpeter made a statement which was subsequently often quoted.

It is above all its financial history that constitutes an essential part of a nation's history as such. An enormous influence over the destiny of nations derives from the blood-letting that the needs of the state impose and from the manner in which the results of the blood-letting are employed. The direct bearing of states' financial needs and the continuing influence of their financial policy on the development of their economy, and thus on all modes of life and culture, are in many periods of history more or less the explanation for the broad course of events.[1]

Soon after setting down these words their author, appointed Minister of Finance in March 1919, had occasion to study at close quarters a period of history during which financial policy became the hub of the nation's existence.

If one takes a more detailed look at production, money volume, price levels and currency in the immediate post-war period, that is, the time from the foundation of the Republic to the signing of the Peace Treaty, it may be appropriate to distinguish between two phases:

1, from November 1918 until the end of March 1919, the phase of limited independence as regards monetary policy, and

2, from April till September 1919, the phase of full independence.

Table 42   National Budget 1 Nov. 1918 to 30 Jun. 1919 in crowns m.

Receipts	Expenditure	Deficit
3,068	3,669	601

During the first phase production was almost at a standstill and the lack of consumer goods, bordering on the acute in the last year of war, was aggravated. The government was the foremost agent in bringing about deliveries of foodstuffs and fuels from abroad through barter deals and with American aid, thus saving Vienna from catastrophe.[2] At this point Austria was still linked to the Successor States by a common currency. Their problems, though not on such a serious scale, were of much the same kind and the means they used to ensure foreign supplies were also much the same. With a rigorous system of trade and currency controls operating in the Danube area, neither an adverse trade balance nor the constant increase in the banknote circulation could exert pressure on the crown.[3]

Nevertheless, even in this first phase the crown had to suffer a continual decline of its exchange rate. In November the mean dollar rate at Vienna was 14,330 crowns. By the end of March 25,847 crowns had to be paid for a dollar, a drop of more than fifty per cent in the value of the Austrian currency. The main reason for this swift decline lay in the desperate efforts made by holders of crown notes to sell them for hard currency of any sort.[4] The government was practically helpless against the activities of international speculators, and that increased the pressure. A stern law, passed on 19 December, against flight of capital appears to have had little effect.[5] The Ministry of Finance could in theory intervene in foreign exchange markets by purchasing crowns. The success of such a measure was however dependent, as long as the crown remained the common currency of the Danubian countries, on a concerted defence plan by all the Successor States. In the prevailing political atmosphere this was impossible to achieve.

The rapidly rising flood of paper money and the acute lack of consumer goods were, as in the war years, the driving forces behind the inflationary development of these months. The government's vigorous price controls were virtually useless against these extremely strong pressures.[6] Rising prices and falling exchange rates suggest a causal connection in the sense of Gustav Cassel's well-known theory of purchasing power parities. The mutual dependence of price level and exchange rate remains valid, though, only on the supposition of a freely-operating market. This is clearly illustrated by what happened in the second phase from April to September. Whereas the high budget deficit and the price-wage spiral caused the volume of paper money to rise more than a hundred per cent, the crown's exchange rate remained stable for a longer period. The month of May even saw a distinct improvement in its price at Zurich. The explanation for the palpable inconsistency between rising domestic prices and this comparatively stable exchange rate lies in the intervention by the Ministry of Finance struggling bravely against the international bear speculation and the deserters in the ranks of domestic capital. The intervention in the foreign exchange markets was part of a strategy aimed at the restoration of a balanced budget.[7] Growing domestic political conflicts, partly originating with the appalling Peace Treaty conditions, marked the close of the second phase.

The assumption behind the government's draft of its provisional budget for the first half-year 1919 was that fifty per cent of expenditure could be met from current receipts.[8] Actual developments turned out, as the following figures show, to be rather more favourable.[9]

During the turbulent war years financial experts had become resigned to the phenomenon of unbalanced budgets. It is hardly open to doubt that the new republican régime was at pains to make financial orthodoxy the basis of its budget policy.[10] Three items principally strained the budget to the utmost: the servicing of the Austro-Hungarian public debt; unemployment benefit; and the food subsidies. The last were constituted by the difference between what was paid abroad for consumer goods (or obtained on credit) and the official sales price. Another factor was the strongly overmanned civil service designed to meet the needs of a large empire, which in wartime was expanded to deal with an excess of tasks.

The financial obligations inherited by the government from its Imperial predecessors were assumed to be much more onerous than the emergency expenditure on foodstuffs and unemployment. In spring 1919 the financial authorities had to make 530 million crowns available on behalf of interest and amortization on the war debt.[11] During the course of hyper-inflation the burden became progressively lighter because every claim to valorization of official war and pre-war debt was rejected with the stubborn argument 'A crown is a crown'. The government pay roll also absorbed a constantly shrinking share of receipts as the civil servants, unlike other professional groups, were in no position to bring their incomes into line with the rapidly rising level of prices.[12]

From 18 November 1918 until the beginning of May 1920 federal expenditure for unemployment benefits amounted to 500 million crowns, as Přibram points out in his informative essay. The same sum was needed to cover the wheat imports for the half-year from July to December 1919.[13] This showed at an early stage that food subsidies were by far the greatest burden on the state. Understandably the question of whether this costly form of subsidizing the living standard of the masses should be continued or abolished became one of the most explosive domestic issues.

At the beginning the hope was nursed that a vigorous programme of taxation and tax collection would enable the government to master the budgetary crisis. A considerable portion of the receipts needed for the extraordinary expenditure (food subsidies and unemployment benefit) could, it was thought, be raised by way of traditional fiscal measures. Corporation and income taxes were raised.[14] A novelty, reflecting the new outlook on financial policy, was a tax on rented shoots.[15] Formally there was no change in the taxation of salaries and wages, but this meant in consequence of progressive inflation a radical lowering of the tax burden on this income category. The lump sum levy on business was raised from 37 to 50 million crowns, and proportionate amounts of this sum were assigned to all those territories which the peacemakers would probably recognize as belonging to the new Austria.[16] A further series of measures affected the public directly, such as increased excise duties on beer, wine, and spirits.[17] And finally serious efforts were made to collect wartime tax arrears, evidenced by the act of 12 December providing heavy penalties for tax offences.[18]

The business world reacted with great indignation to this new wave of impositions and the protests reached their peak on 27 January 1919 when, as a sign of resistance, establishments of all kinds remained closed.[19] The new laws proved however to be far more harmless than could have been foreseen at the time of publication. Because of the currency's depreciation and the lax revenue collection the higher taxes were hardly felt. As for the business tax, the protests soon proved entirely misplaced inasmuch as it was never enforced in the form announced.[20]

While the government tried, albeit with little success, to meet most of its financial obligations from current receipts, it contemplated an altogether new approach to the problem of the public debt. The application of orthodox principles seemed likely to fail because the debt itself was among other things a completely unorthodox phenomenon. War financing had contributed to the rapid rise of public debt to such an extent that by the end of hostilities it had reached 58,000 million crowns for the western half of the Empire.[21]

That the debt had assumed a scale justifying the most trenchant inroads on existing conditions of capital ownership was a view already aired during the war. Among conservatives the two Ministers of Finance, Spitzmüller and Wimmer, had supported the idea of a capital levy. Rudolf Goldscheid, an independent Socialist, had pleaded for conversion of the nation's greatest debit item into its greatest asset by using it as a key to socialization.[22]

Goldscheid and his journalist friend Popper-Lynkeus were Utopian Socialists. They did not, like the Marxists, hold a specific theory of the process of socialist transformation,. Popper thought that certain egalitarian aspects of the war economy could be interpreted as the first signs of society's realignment in a socialist mould. The following passage is characteristic of his outlook:

The war has had a shattering effect on everyone's feelings and it has diverted attention from concentration on one's own fate to that of one's fellow human beings. Multifarious government measures and relief initiatives, which may collectively be termed 'war socialism', have taken us along the road to practical socialism. The wheat monopoly, the simplified expropriation procedure, various regulations on matters which were normally private affairs . . . impinge deeply on the rights and habits of the individual for the sake of society . . . It all serves mainly war purposes, but this and that will presumably be absorbed into peace-time practice through the dawning recognition that every citizen should, like every soldier, always as far as possible be safeguarded against want or deprivation.[23]

Goldscheid can be described as the first sociologist of finance. He believed that he had discovered the means to give society a more egalitarian character relatively painlessly. He favoured a capital levy not in the form of money, but by the taking over of assets. The state would thus be turned into the dominant entrepreneur.

Putting a tax on profits means that the nation in the long run has to pay for the cost of war without the state being rescued from its financial distress. Transforming an equivalent part of *productive* private assets into public property will, without impairing the economy or the public interest, affect in the first place the wealthiest and enable the state to consolidate its position economically and financially to a better degree than ever before . . . If the state just once puts a levy on *productive* assets, the profitability of individual businesses stays the same as previously. *Only the shareholders change.* The state instead of private people has become the biggest shareholder.[24]

With the state's partial acquisition of the shares there

devolves on it the right to co-determination as regards the management of the enterprise's without anything else in its economic situation undergoing alteration. As for the state participating in management, this is all to the community's good, because political control by popular representation is thereby turned into effective *economic control* signifying further progress in the direction of democracy.[25]

Goldscheid's ideas have been given a comparatively prominent space because they show how the widely debated question of redeeming the war debt was linked by practically all eminent financial experts to the scheme for a non-recurring capital levy. But only Goldscheid connected fiscal innovation with the purposes of social reform. For Schumpeter too a capital levy was a central point in his reconstruction programme, as he made clear in his first speech as Finance Minister.

In dealing with the state's financial problems our primary task is to implement quickly, energetically, and without much shilly-shally the once and for all major capital levy, this enormous incursion into the private rights of the propertied classes. We have to do it, the public has been prepared, and, even though it might have been a good thing to settle the matter earlier and to put an end to uncertainty, I am now inclined to think that the Fabian approach actually adopted here also has its positive side – the matter has been talked through; everyone, whether have or have-not, is literally demanding it; and we can handle the business in such a way – in particular by combining it with the promotion of appropriate credit institutes – that economic development is in no wise affected by the capital levy.[26]

Schumpeter complemented his remarks by saying that to cut down war debt was a priority task and 'the capital levy must not be used for anything else than for this reduction'.[27]

He familiarized the public with the five most important points of his reform programme within a few weeks of taking office. First the capital levy, to be primarily used for doing away with the war debt. Secondly, the achievement of currency stability in terms of working towards 'a secure currency value, free as far as possible from fluctuations', not the re-establishment of its former parity.[28] Thirdly, the foundation of a central bank with the duty of conducting monetary policy independent of the state.[29] Fourthly, greater use of indirect taxation in order that the broad masses too should make an adequate contribution to putting the budget on its feet. And, finally, the restoration of a climate in which Austrian industry would again have a sound credit rating at home and abroad. 'The supply of credit for industry', he proclaimed in a speech at Vienna University, 'is a problem to which the state must now turn its attention without any reservations.'[30]

The last point however, necessitated preliminary clarification on the extent of the socialization measures that it was proposed to take, and here it seemed as though Schumpeter's views might be subject to a surprisingly swift volte-face. On 20 March he made a statement to Viennese press representatives which hardly differed from the Social Democrat view. 'We shall have to encroach deeply on the private sector of the economy. The course is set for socialization. Imagining this to be a passing idea is utterly hopeless. We have to try and put it into effect, and in doing so we have to go so far that there is no room for those on the Left of us. But, in so far as socialization does not take place, we have to accord the business world full freedom.'[31] On 26 April, that is, about five weeks after expressing such a positive attitude towards socialization, Schumpeter in his university speech argued that, for the sake of foreign capital imports, perhaps a somewhat more cautious course would need to be pursued.

We face the task of reconstruction. The entire economy could, although at the price of immense friction and resistance, be socialized. For my part I confess that professionally I sympathize a good deal with such a move. The alternative is for a radical, vigorous, but *restricted* socialization measure to place certain branches of industry or business at the disposal of the community and to let the rest of privately-owned enterprise go on working as it used to. In our situation certain reasons, which, it has to be acknowledged, are compelling, speak for the latter course, in particular because of the need for those foreign capital imports which would not be obtainable, or not to a sufficient degree obtainable, on behalf of a socialized economy.[32]

Whereas the principle of a capital levy for the reduction of the national debt very soon won general approval, questions as to its extent and especially as to its consequences for the social system were hotly disputed. Another obstacle to this important piece of legislation was the complete uncertainty concerning the economic burdens to be imposed by the impending Peace Treaty. The greatest resistance to the levy came from the representatives of the peasantry who were resolved to protect their voters from any action against their property. The progressive depreciation of the currency, though, diminished the weight of war debt so that Schumpeter's repeated assurances that the state would meet its wartime obligations to the full soon lost credibility among the country's creditors.

The major part of current expenditure had meanwhile to be covered by the issue of three-months treasury bills to the Viennese banks.[33] The banks procured the necessary cash by discounting the official

IOUs at the central bank. In view of the completely obscure political situation there could be no thought of consolidating the rapidly growing floating debt on the pattern of War Loan. Opposition was mounting to the inflationary course of the Austro-Hungarian Bank which had survived the Dual Monarchy's collapse and which has been referred to throughout as 'central bank'. Under the presure of the new national states it had been forced to accept as members of its governing board commissioners from the various parts of the Empire, and these demanded conformity to a strictly anti-inflationary line. In their opinion the central bank must not be allowed to grant a loan to any one of the new governments without the consent of the rest and the bank should abstain from the wartime practice of making advances on War Loan.[34]

This second demand especially led to fierce altercations between the central bank's leading authorities. The Ministry of Finance had, it will be recalled, helped the sale of War Loan by instructing the central bank to extend advances on government bonds to 75% of their face value. Despite the disappearance of the Empire, the bank felt bound by its promise and continued to extend the usual advances, a practice that was particularly questionable when bonds had dropped to 60% and less of their nominal par.[35]

It comes of course as no surprise that banks, private individuals, and others were only too glad to avail themselves of the central bank's readiness to grant loans on the old conditions.

On a single day, 7 November 1918, the Austro-Hungarian Bank made advances of a total of 609 million crowns. In the four month period from 26 October 1918 to 2 February 1919, the advances on War Loan extended by the bank rose from 4,094 million crowns to 9,319 million crowns, meaning that the notes in circulation were expanded by 5,225 million [crowns].[36]

The central bank's insistence on fulfilling their commitments to War Loan holders seems somewhat odd. This was not a time when governments attached much importance to the promises of their predecessors. The bank's policy becomes more intelligible if the new Austria's special interests are borne in mind. Among the Empire's peoples it had mainly been the German-Austrians who had subscribed to War Loan. By insisting on making advances against war bonds, whose value was highly dubious, the governor of the bank protected the interests of his fellow-nationals. The neighbouring states, on the other hand, had hoarded large quantities of Austro-Hungarian currency and held few state bonds. They were especially hard hit by the consequences of uncurbed inflation. The attempt of the governments of the Successor States to restrain the bank's management from a too generous acceptance of War Loan as collateral was in turn a natural move to protect the interests of their nationals.[37]

The bank's inflationary practice caused the Successor States to move towards the separation of their currencies from the crown. It can however be safely assumed that sooner or later they would have done so even if the central bank had adopted a policy more in harmony with their interests. Not one of the new states would have regarded itself as free from Vienna's financial domination as long as the capital of the former Empire had remained responsible for the monetary policy of the Danubian countries.

Yugoslavia was the first to turn its back on the central bank. Between 8 and 20 January 1919, Austro-Hungarian banknotes in circulation in Yugoslav territory were counted and stamped with the national emblem. About 5,000 million crowns showed up and were so carelessly marked that within a year the operation had to be repeated.[38] On that occasion only 4,000 million crowns were submitted for stamping. The missing 1000 millions had probably been smuggled to neighbouring territories on account of the unfavourable ratio between crown and dinar fixed by the Yugoslav authorities.[39]

The Czechoslovak stamping operation lasted from 3 until 7 March 1919 and, unlike the Yugoslav, proceeded with the utmost circumspection. A secret session of parliament authorized the Minister of Finance not only to stamp the notes, but to retain fifty per cent of those submitted and declare them as part of a state loan. During the night of 25–26 February all cross-border traffic was halted. From 26 February till 9 March all postal foreign communications were suspended. By this means any transfer of notes and coins was rendered impossible.[40] An official census established that 7,336 million crowns were in circulation inside the country. Adding a further 1,616 million crowns in bank deposits and 468 million crowns of cash certificates, the volume totalled 9,520 million crowns. Of this amount 2,781.5 million crowns, or some 29%, were kept by the Ministry of Finance.[41] The inconsistency between the government's proclaimed intention to withhold 50% of money in circulation and the actual sterilization of less than 30% is obvious. The explanation lies in the exemption from the forced loan allowed for all sums under 300 crowns.[42]

The stamping campaign had two objectives apart from separating the Austrian and the Czech currencies. On the one hand the Minister hoped to stop the ruinous progress of inflation by abruptly reducing

Second cabinet, Renner, March 1919
Seated (left to right):
  State Secretary Dr. Deutsch
  State Secretary Dr. v. Bratusch
  Undersecretary Glöckel
  State Chancellor Dr. Renner
  State Secretary Hanusch
  Undersecretary Dr. Ellenbogen

Standing (left to right):
  Undersecretary Miklas
  Department Secretary Dr. Horicky
  State Secretary Dr. Schumpeter
  Undersecretary Dr. Waiß
  State Secretary Paul
  State Secretary Zerdik
  State Secretary Dr. Bauer
  Ministerial Secretary Dr. Fenz
  State Secretary v. Loewenfeld-Ruß

Baron Louis Rothschild, 1882–1955

The Banking Hall, Creditanstalt, 1922

Otto Bauer, 1881-1938

Ignaz Seipel, 1876–1932

Joseph A. Schumpeter, 1883-1950

Baron Alexander Spitzmüller, 1862–1954

Creditanstalt, Am Hof, 1875
(destroyed in the 1939-45 War)

the volume of money in circulation, on the other he wanted to secure data needed by the government for the collection of a capital levy.[43] In so far as the government believed that the sterilization measure would straightaway stabilize the exchange rate and the wage-price structure, this expectation was disappointed. The exchange rate continued to fall, while the price level took the opposite direction. The anti-inflation therapy was attributable simply to a crude quantitative analysis of what was ailing the Czech economy.[44] A law passed on 10 April gave legal sanction to the separation of the Czech currency from the Austrian. Article 4 invested the Czechoslovak Government with 'the exclusive right to lodge claims against the Austro-Hungarian Bank'.[45]

The provision made the Czech state the sole debtor vis-à-vis owners of the stamped banknotes and the sole creditor vis-à-vis the former central bank. It acquired a claim on the latter's assets to which the Allied Powers subsequently accorded recognition in Article 206 of the Peace Treaty.

A few days after announcement of the currency separation a new ordinance by the Minister of Finance declared the Austro-Hungarian Bank to be nationalized to the extent that it operated inside Czech territory.[46]

This sudden arrogation of monetary sovereignty did not take the Austrian Government by surprise. For all the secrecy with which the Czech Ministry of Finance laid its preparations, sufficient information was leaked for neighbouring countries to become alarmed. On 15 February, ten days prior to the closure of the Czech borders, an article in *Der Österreichische Volkswirt* predicted with astounding accuracy the impending banknote stamping.[47] Next day the Austrian Government made known its first counter-measure, an ordinance forbidding the import of Austro-Hungarian banknotes and the transfer of any crown deposits from abroad. The sale of Austrian securities to nationals of the Successor States was made subject to official permission.[48] Nonetheless the lack of border supervision must have facilitated the introduction of large quantities of banknotes in defiance of the ordinance. There are indications that many Czechoslovak residents tried to evade the imminent capital levy. No more than a guess can be hazarded as to the number of unstamped notes smuggled into Austria this way.[49] Two days after the closure of frontier traffic between Austria and Czechoslovakia a second ordinance issued by the Vienna authorities gave details related to the stamping of the domestic currency.[50] The operation was timed to take place between 12 and 24 March, but its implementation was then prolonged to 29 March.[51]

Leaving the initiative during this operation to the Czechs put the Austrian Government at something of a disadvantage. It had however no alternative because, more than any other new authority in the Danubian area, it felt bound to respect the Austro-Hungarian Bank's issuing privilege. More important still may have been the circumstance that Austria was the party most interested in the maintenance of a currency federation among the Successor States. When the Czechs and the Yugoslavs abandoned the currency union, the death sentence was pronounced on economic co-operation between the Danubian nations in a closer monetary framework.

The Austrian Government had at first probably no intention of linking banknote stamping to the capital levy.[52] Public criticism forced it however to change its attitude abruptly. On 10 March an ordinance put under control all securities held by banks in open deposit or private safes and blocked fifty per cent of all bank deposits.[53] The object was to furnish the Ministry of Finance with as complete a picture as possible of assets and their distribution, as well as to prevent any assets transfer until the time of implementation of the projected capital levy.[54] The government, lacking the unanimity of its Czech counterpart, cannot however have seriously considered the imposition of a forced loan by way of a mere ordinance. Banks and their clients, who were involved in endless discussions on the procedure to be adopted for the capital levy, regarded the preparatory steps as merely bureaucratic harassment.

The Austrian operation was far less rigorous than the Czech in another respect. The frontiers were not closed and banking operations were not suspended for a full week.[55] The volume of currency submitted for stamping was 4,804 million crowns.[56] This was only one eighth of the Austro-Hungarian Bank's total notes in circulation which at the end of March 1919 amounted to 37,965 million crowns.[57] Many Austrians must have clearly preferred retaining their unstamped banknotes to having them stamped with the new Austrian emblem. Some perhaps, as in Czechoslovakia, may have been reluctant to reveal their cash holdings for fear of the impending capital levy. The majority, though, seem to have had a different motive. With unstamped crowns continuing to be legal tender in many parts of the former Empire, they engaged in profitable smuggling activities or sold their holdings at a premium in the Viennese black market.[58] Many unstamped banknotes were hereupon stamped with forged emblems, enabling them to be used as currency in one of the neighbouring countries. Initially because of the Austrian crown's unfavourable exchange rate only a small number of illegally stamped banknotes found their way into the new Austria's monetary circulation, but during 1920, after Czechoslovakia, Yugoslavia and certain other states had issued new banknotes, Austria too became a victim of these unlawful manipulations.[59]

An ordinance on 25 March established the legal consequences of the stamping operation.[60] Stamped crowns were proclaimed the sole means of payment, all contractual obligations had to be fulfilled in the ratio of one unstamped to one stamped crown.[61] Deposits by foreigners in crowns were until further notice frozen. Banknotes belonging to nationals of the Successor States were repayable in unstamped notes. All other deposits would remain frozen until such time as a general debt settlement had been reached by Austria with the former members of the Empire. This provision provoked a heated controversy between Austria and certain of its neighbours. Reprisals from Czechoslovakia followed fast.[62] The Austro-Hungarian Bank, which had at first protested to all three governments against every measure aiming at a separation of the crown currency, soon set about the creation of a special department to serve the new Austria as its central bank.[63] Article 206 of the Treaty of Saint-Germain conferred subsequent ratification on the separation of the crown currency and provided for the liquidation of the Austro-Hungarian Bank.

Ever since joining the Coalition Government Otto Bauer had been trying to bring about some visible sign of Austria's solidarity with Germany. The division of the crown currency seemed in his eyes to present the first opportunity for moving in the direction of *Anschluss*. At the beginning of March, coinciding with the start of the banknote stamping operation, he visited Berlin in his capacity as Foreign Minister and proposed to the German Government an immediate monetary union. To this end the Reichsbank should extend a loan to a new German-Austrian central bank, putting the latter in a position to sell marks at a fixed parity against Austrian crowns. The German Government rejected the proposal on the ground that it was inadvisable to impose on the Reichsbank burdens of indefinite magnitude before the peace treaty conditions had been made known.[64] Probably the German negotiators declined the spectacular project at this juncture mainly for political reasons.[65]

The consultations on monetary union continued as part of the preparations for *Anschluss*. In mid-April a Mixed Finance Commission session took place. The Austrian delegation was led by Bauer and

Schumpeter. It was instructed to desist from pressing for immediate transition to a mark currency. This should be introduced on 1 January 1920, when a German-Austrian central bank, closely affiliated with the Reichsbank, would be established.[66] On 19 April however the Sub-Committee on Monetary Affairs, appointed by the Finance Commission, went a step farther with its resolution that complete monetary union should be established simultaneously with the political union of the two countries. The two delegations eventually agreed that German-Austria would introduce the mark currency on 1 January 1920.[67] This plan, kept secret for the time being, contrasted strangely with the international situation which permitted the two defeated nations virtually no scope for an independent foreign policy.

Schumpeter had in wartime already been a sceptical observer of efforts to create an economic union between the Empire and Germany.[68] He is hardly likely to have lent active support to the Berlin resolutions. Soon after taking office he had, even though indirectly, adopted an *anti-Anschluss* line by pleading for the retention of Vienna as the financial centre of the Successor States and by emphasizing the need for a close relationship between the Danubian countries. 'German-Austria, and especially Vienna,' he said at a press conference,

will probably have to remain a financial centre for a long time ahead. Nationalizing an economy may be a very fine thing. The Czechs worked at it for years, but often enough to their own detriment and only for the sake of a national ideal. To make a national economy self-sufficient is however only feasible within narrow limits. Becoming independent is far easier politically than economically. *In the end we shall have to find a modus vivendi.* The frontiers of future development can be recognized even today with great clarity. *In this new organism Vienna will have to continue as the financial centre and the political separation will affect only marginally the purely economic relations.*[69]

Seipel had from the outset probably regarded the propaganda for *Anschluss* as a tactical weapon to extract concessions from the Allied Powers at the impending peace negotiations. Meanwhile he had reached a close understanding with Schumpeter. In a letter to Lammasch, who seems to have introduced Schumpeter to him, he wrote, 'I am on good terms with Schumpeter, who is very courageous . . . Bauer's policy has been reduced to sheer nonsense. Below the surface everyone in German-Austria is convinced that nothing will come of *Anschluss*.'[70]

Seipel's letter was dated 1 May. The backing given him by this prominent Christian Socialist politician encouraged Schumpeter still more to openly cast doubt on Bauer's strategy. On 8 May he told *Neue-8-Uhr-Blatt* that *Anschluss* could very likely not be vetoed permanently, but at once added the warning that it would entail great sacrifices and that therefore 'far-reaching concessions' must be obtained from Germany. The crucial point of the interview lay in the statement that 'Our salvation lies in peaceful intercourse with all, and particularly with the neighbouring states'.[71]

Bauer's reaction was a lengthy letter of reproach that his cabinet colleague was expressing views likely to undermine the position of the Austrian delegation to the peace negotiations at Saint-Germain. And he added, with a certain amount of justification, that it had not hitherto been customary for departmental Ministers to pronounce on foreign policy matters without prior agreement with the Minister concerned. 'Should you regard my policy as erroneous, the right way would surely be for you to discuss the subject at issue at a meeting of the cabinet.' He closed with an offer 'to try and come to an understanding through a serious discussion within a smaller circle'.[72]

It is unknown whether such a discussion did take place between Bauer and Schumpeter. At any rate the Minister of Finance seems to have been little impressed by Bauer's rebuke. In the middle of May he was making contact with Sir Francis Oppenheimer, the financier, who at the wish of the British Government had just arrived in Vienna. Schumpeter, according to Oppenheimer, outlined a reform plan which primarily envisaged long-term Western loans and conceded the Allied Powers extensive rights of control. In particular the Allies were to assume management of a new Austrian central bank.[73]

Three weeks after his sensational newspaper interview Schumpeter delivered a major address to the General Meeting of the Vienna Industrial and Trade Association. Even more clearly than before he discussed the details of the commercial and monetary policy that the new régime should adopt. As there are reasons for thinking that on this occasion he was expressing not only his own opinion but also that of conservative domestic and foreign politicians and financiers, a longer extract from the speech is given here.

The states of the Danube basin are undoubtedly dependent on close economic cooperation, whether they like it or not. Development has distinctly pointed in that direction and, in one form or another, economic collaboration will have to take place. We must undoubtedly arrive, if not at free trade, at least at a customs agreement with the Successor States and, if not at monetary union, at least at a monetary convention. People so often say that

German-Austria is not viable as a geographic unit. It is obvious that German-Austria constitutes neither administratively nor otherwise a very organic whole but that is no reason to despair. If independence is imposed on us more or less against our will and if it is absolutely impossible for us to go our own way, it is no reason to believe that this means economic annihilation. It simply must not be supposed that a country, to be viable, need have all the necessary raw materials inside its borders. We must have coal. But even if it lay beneath German-Austria's surface, industry would need to buy it, and more than to buy it is not necessary in the case of Ostrau [in Czechoslovakia] either . . . If we and the others are sensible, it does not matter a jot whether our industry's production basis lies within or beyond our political frontiers . . .

We have above all a major asset in the form of Austrian nationals' owning real estate, factories, and shares in, as well as claims against, enterprises situated in the Successor States. To save those assets is our most vital problem . . . What we want is that we should be able to continue to participate in the operation of these enterprises. They are to provide employment not only to our own advantage, but to the advantage of the countries concerned. These other countries too cannot live without us or our financial mediation. *Financing the trade between the countries of the former Empire and the rest of the world will necessarily have to be mediated by Vienna again*, and if we all have a similar or identical currency, the Vienna foreign exchange quotation will still remain the pivotal one. Only Vienna's banks can play the role of reliable broker for the import of foreign capital . . . If we support that principle which for our country is the only possible one, the principle of economic freedom, we shall very soon return to the normal state of affairs. That is not to say that appreciation of this fact means necessarily being opposed to socialization. What has to be clear is what is to be socialized. Whatever is to be socialized must be socialized quickly and thoroughly, and all the rest must be left utterly free.

Then the socialization measures that the government currently has in mind will, from the point of view of the economy as a whole, however much they may differ from a formal act nationalization, after all amount to nothing else than creating a nationalized sector. The capitalist economy would stand that without its recovery being seriously impeded.[74]

Schumpeter's address did not merely ignore Bauer's conciliatory gesture; it was an open challenge. At this point he seems to have been quite certain of being backed by the Christian Socialist cabinet members and of support by the representatives of Western interests. Bauer, for his part, came to the conclusion that Schumpeter must at the first suitable moment be forced to resign. Writing to Renner on 31 May, he compared the behaviour of his cabinet colleagues. 'Fink, as far as I am able to observe, is loyal. Eldersch is doing very well.

Schumpeter, on the other hand, continues with his intrigues. I am temporizing at present, but after the peace [treaty] it will be unavoidable to have done with him.'[75] He could not guess that his conflict with the Minister of Finance had not yet reached its climax.[76]

Bauer's socialization plans have been discussed in another connection. On 22 May the government announced, no doubt at Bauer's insistence, that it had decided to nationalize in due course mining, iron production, power stations, large-scale forestry holdings, and the timber industry.[77] This programme of partial nationalization corresponded to the first step in a long term socialization strategy contemplated by Bauer in *Der Weg zum Sozialismus* and it did not run counter to Schumpeter's more limited socialization plans which had been repeatedly and publicly proclaimed.

Jodok Fink and other prominent members of the government could not openly oppose this Social Democrat nationalization policy with the working class deeply stirred by events in Hungary. They had to confine themselves to delaying tactics, a task made very much easier by the provincial administrations' resistance to all directives and initiatives emanating from Vienna. Ideas of their own had been evolved at the level of the provincial administrations as to how socialization should be arrived at. Large-scale forestry holdings should not be nationalized, but distributed among the peasants. In some instances steps in this direction were indeed taken. The provinces insisted on a federalist solution for power stations, enabling them to deal separately with individual regions. But since development of the hydroelectric generating stations required the import of a great deal of capital, this sector was soon regarded as unsuitable for socialist experimentation.[78]

The final blow against the programme of 22 May fell when Alpine-Montan-Gesellschaft, the biggest industrial enterprise and almost sole owner of Austrian iron ore deposits, fell into the hands of Italian interests. General Roberto Segré, head of the Inter-Allied Armistice Commission which after December 1918 was based at Vienna, brought off this *coup*. The General had initially concerned himself with collecting art treasures, old manuscripts, and various other cultural assets. His own staff told him that during a century of Austrian dominion these objects had been removed from Italy. Then the General became more and more conscious of the economic opportunities afforded the Allied Powers by hapless Austria.

Certain factors at this time facilitated the penetration of the

Austrian economy by foreign capital. Businessmen as a rule were at pains to attract such capital on the correct assumption that the government would shrink back from nationalizing a firm in which foreigners had invested heavily. Perhaps more important was the fact that the economy's requirements of large-scale imports could not, be balanced by exports at a time of dire need. The more or less automatic consequence was the massive sale of industrial and other tangible assets.[79]

Austria was therefore favourable terrain for the reconnoitering General. He was soon in a position to bring off advantageous deals and to obtain valuable information for further economic exploits.[80] His outstanding success was taking over an important part of the capital of Alpine-Montan-Gesellschaft on behalf of Italian banking and industrial interests. The Austrian iron industry played a key role in victorious Italy's plans for expansion, since it seemed destined to provide heavy industry in the Po basin with the source of raw materials it so badly needed. In spring and summer 1919 Alpine shares could be bought at extremely low prices. The crown was cheap, the Vienna Stock Exchange depressed, and Prager Eisenindustrie-Gesellschaft, which in wartime had been so keen to be on a close footing with Alpine, now was ridding itself of all its holdings in the Styrian concern, thus contributing to the further decline in the value of its shares.

The Alpine transaction has been the source of much conjecture. It proceeded under the aegis of the Ministry of Finance and via the good services of the Viennese banking firm Kola & Co.[81] The latter, which acted as the ministry's foreign exchange agent, in spring and summer 1919 purchased 200,000 Alpine shares on behalf of Credito Italiano, the Milan banking group closely connected with the Fiat concern. Kola remitted the lire proceeds to the Minister of Finance, who badly needed foreign exchange to procure foodstuffs and raw materials.[82] The purchase did not of course pass unobserved and quickly drove up the price of Alpine shares, leading in turn to a general boom on the Vienna market.[83] Prices continued to rise even when in October the government, by virtue of Article 37 in the law passed on 29 July 1919 concerning firms in collective ownership, acquired an interest in Alpine on the occasion of its capital increase. A few weeks later the drama ended with the government relinquishing its interest by selling the shares to a Swiss group headed by an Austrian financier, Dr Felix Somary.[84]

In its 20 August issue *Arbeiter-Zeitung* upbraided the Minister of Finance for indirectly supporting the Kola transactions by his passivity. 'The Ministry of Finance, responsible for such matters, ought to have prevented this entire Stock Exchange orgy. Means would not have been lacking if there had been a prudent, energetic financial administration.' At another point the author of the leading article (presumably the paper's editor) implied that the operation had been directed against the socialization project.

We frankly grant that the sale of German-Austrian securities to foreign capitalists may be unavoidable under certain circumstances. As long as the foodstuffs and raw materials which we have to obtain from abroad cannot be paid for by the products of our labour, we shall often have no choice other than to pay for them with industrial assets and natural resources. But even though this much is granted, it may well be questioned *whether it had to be Alpine shares that needed to be sold to foreigners in spite of Alpine being one of the leading enterprises the socialization of which is planned.*[85]

Several years later Bauer endorsed this censure. 'Schumpeter supported this operation [by Kola] although he knew that we had planned the socialization of Alpine-Montan-Gesellschaft. He supported it without informing the members of the government . . . Schumpeter's action caused a vehement conflict inside the government, with Schumpeter seeking and finding the support of the Viennese Christian Socialists.'[86] Many years later Schumpeter in two letters categorically denied that he had either authorized or recommended the disposal of Alpine shares. A subsequent remark makes clear however that *in the circumstances* he felt bound to regard the prevention of a socialization move as an act of loyalty towards the state, the government, and not least the Social Democratic party.[87]

Bauer's belief that Schumpeter had supported Kola's transactions – 'support' must in this context be understood as passive acceptance – is quite definitely confirmed in a letter by the minister to the Chancellor, Renner, written shortly after publication of the *Arbeiter-Zeitung* article.[88]

At the end of June I was surprised to hear from Richard Kola that he could put at my disposal 15 million lire obtained from an Italian source for the acquisition of Alpine-Montan shares. Although I was very pleased to have our foreign exchange reserves so unexpectedly strengthened, I expressed the wish that these transactions should not lead to a foreign majority in this domestic concern. At the beginning of August Herr Kola twice again made 5 million lire available from the same source. I once more requested Herr Kola not to continue with these transactions . . . I do not in this connection wish to leave unsaid that on the whole I deem it an advantage for foreigners to show an interest in our securities and to take part in our stock exchange operations.

If our securities neither arouse any interest nor are traded abroad, our currency is defenceless against any and all attacks. If there are lively dealings back and forth in our securities, things are different. Let there be such trafficking and a momentary need for foreign exchange will not upset the market. Every drop in the exchange rate *immediately* renders the purchase of securities on the Vienna Stock Exchange profitable for arbitrage deals, so that up to a point every jolt to the currency is cushioned by the traffic in our securities.

Schumpeter ended his detailed letter with a reference to his 'conservative' recovery programme and an appeal to the Chancellor's loyalty.

I know that my programme for a conservative solution to current financial difficulties, which would ensure a smooth, undisturbed reconstruction by a finance plan which would not be damaging to the existing order of society, is faced by important and, I readily admit, convinced opposition. I believe it possible to lead the country out of its difficulties without convulsing the foundations of the national economy and of the credit system. If others do not believe that to be possible, then let this be fought out on factual and political terrain. But you, Mr Chancellor, from the loyalty of your character, I expect you to put an end to the witch-hunt that has been incited against me, the object of which is to finish me off politically by dragging my name in the mud.[89]

The impression given by Schumpeter's letter is that his reiterated request to Kola not to permit a majority of Alpine shares to pass into foreign possession must have lacked emphasis. Had it been otherwise, it is scarcely conceivable that his foreign exchange agent would not have been deterred from continuing with his operation. Rather it seems that Schumpeter let Kola fairly clearly understand that the nationalization of Alpine 'could only aggravate the difficulties of a difficult situation', as the minister phrased it in one of his two letters to Professor Gulick, and that to frustrate this project would therefore be a patriotic act. In fairness it must be added that his silent acquiescence in Kola's deals probably corresponded to the unspoken wish of the moderate wing of the Social Democrat leadership. The latter, as Renner once put it, did not regard the socialization of debts as expedient. In this light the Bauer-Schumpeter controversy presents itself as a show put on for the reassurance and amusement of many. The epitaph on the debate was pronounced two years afterwards by Schumpeter: 'Complete socialization as an immediate programme was in Germany and in Austria never more than political phraseology.'[90]

Schumpeter's 'conservative' recovery programme was known in

broad outline from the time of his taking office. He then repeatedly announced at public meetings the early publication of his definitive version, which earned him the stricture that he could talk but not act. Even his opponents had however to admit that 'till the conclusion of peace the scope for action by the Ministry of Finance was rather limited'.[91]

On 10 October an article in *Arbeiter-Zeitung* subjected the minister's activity (or inactivity) to withering criticism; Schumpeter's resignation followed shortly. The article accused Schumpeter of not having prepared a financial plan – for the time following the conclusion of peace, one would have to add. This reproach did not hold water. On 16 October, the day before his resignation, Schumpeter in a speech to the Christian Social Union put forward a comprehensive financial recovery programme.[92] The following extracts are just a few of the most important ideas contained in this political testament.

Right from the beginning it established the principle that Austria would have to meet its budgetary needs without the issue of paper money. The economy's restoration would take, 'given strenuous efforts by everyone, three, perhaps four, years'. Schumpeter excluded the possibility of national bankruptcy, in whatever form, in spite of the huge debt burden imposed on Austria by the Peace Treaty. The procurement of foreign loans was seen as the key to financial rehabilitation:

That is the only way to restore our economy. Without foreign assets, no currency stabilization, no balancing of the budget. The other way about, to proceed at first to the restoration of domestic order and then to procure credit abroad, would be a road to irredeemable, fatal haemorrhage . . . The vicious circle – no foreign credit, no balanced budget, but no domestic order, no foreign credit – must be broken.

Schumpeter believed that he had found the answer. The procurement of foreign loans was to be linked to the capital levy, in such a way that a capitalist who would put foreign credits amounting to at least forty per cent of his assets at the disposal of the state, or who would subscribe to a new government bond issue to at least a quarter of his assets, would be allowed to spread his payments of the capital levy over a period of thirty years. The capital levy – in view of the fact that it absorbed capital – was to be used solely for the repayment of the war debt.

Schumpeter dwelt on many technical details which do not require mention here. It must be noted that he was quite aware of the extremely severe burden that this levy, in the form proposed by him, would put on the economy. To avoid a grave impairment of the economy, he was prepared to allow any firm, as long as it would 'employ at least as many people as it did before the war or, if the number of employees was in wartime higher, as many as at the time of highest employment' a deferment in return for the payment of interest.

He thought that only the 'international reputation acquired in centuries by the country's 'nationals and their financial institutions' could obtain foreign capital for the state.[93] In this connection he again dealt with the question of socialization.

One may be in favour of socialization without failing to realize that today, when the state acutely needs credits, the socialization of enterprises destroys existing credit foundations without concurrently creating new ones. It remains open to socialized capital to attain in later years a credit standing through gradual positive work and through the achievement of genuine successes.

Schumpeter's recovery recipe contained two further important ingredients: the establishment of a central bank, which should be prohibited from extending loans to the state in any shape whatever, and a stronger enlistment of the poorer classes in carrying the national economic burden by way of indirect taxation. This type of tax 'is nothing but the extension of income tax in a downward direction'. Even though the war debt was to be liquidated almost wholly with the help of the capital levy, that would not alter in the slightest the fact that the main burden of war and defeat would be borne by the rentier class. 'It would be self-deception to try to resist the brute force of this tremendous fact.'

He ended with an urgent appeal:

The financial programme rests on the conviction that we can help ourselves. The well-off members of society must place at the service of the state what they possess, not only the largest part of their fortune, but also their credit and their good name, so as to make possible the preservation of the economic order. Those without property must, by paying indirect taxes, take upon themselves the full sacrifice that will make possible the continued survival of the financial foundations of the state without the creation of paper money. The world at large must be shown that we are ready to help ourselves. Only then will it be prepared to help us.

The appeal fell on deaf ears. A report in *Neue Freie Presse* revealed that Schumpeter had lost support among the Christian Social party too, and that this party was no longer prepared to back his plan.[94] Resignation was the logical consequence of this complete political isolation. Today only a guess can be hazarded as to why a section of the Christian Socialists suddenly withdrew their allegiance. Schumpeter's austere plan for a capital levy probably provoked resistance among the party's peasant representatives. A passage in the above-mentioned article permits that conclusion.[95] Moreover Schumpeter's acceptance, though distinctly conditional, of socialization ideas may have cost him the sympathy of influential conservative politicians.

That the *Neue Freie Presse* described Bauer as the 'chief opponent' of Schumpeter's plan will cause little surprise. For Bauer this was assuredly a welcome occasion to be finally rid of his irksome cabinet colleague after so many months of fruitless squabbles. Yet was Bauer really well advised to do without the collaboration of the man who, among his non-socialist colleagues, approached the capital levy problem with expertise, good will, and a great deal of sincerity? *Der Österreichische Volkswirt* had been puzzled as to how it was that *Arbeiter-Zeitung* treated the capital levy with such conspicuous indifference. Bauer too seems to have belittled the issue's importance for a rapid stabilization of the budget.[96] In addition Schumpeter's repeated warnings that socialization would destroy existing credit foundations probably touched on a raw nerve in the case of Bauer and other leftist socialists. The early withdrawal of this great Austrian economist from politics must ultimately be attributed to the fact that for the one side he was too radical and for the other too pragmatic, too self-willed, and also perhaps too hostile to *Anschluss*.

Notes

1 Joseph Schumpeter, 'Die Krise des Steuerstaates', *Beiträge zur politischen Ökonomie der Staatsfinanzen*, ed. Rudolf Hickel (Frankfurt a. Main, 1976), p. 331.
2 'The first loan — to an amount of 48 million dollars — was extended soon after the Armistice. Germany also assisted with a 7% Treasury loan of 200 million marks.' See Walther Federn, 'Die auswärtigen Anleihen Österreichs', *Schriften des Vereins für Sozialpolitik* (Munich-Leipzig, 1928), Vol. 174, Part III, p. 199. Also Gustav Stolper, *Deutsch-Österreich als Sozial- und Wirtschaftsproblem* (Munich, 1921), p. 26.
3 Between November 1918 and March 1919 the average monthly banknote circulation rose from 33,000 million crowns to 37,500 million crowns, i.e., by some 13.5%. In percentage terms this was the same increase as in the comparable

period from November 1917 to March 1918.

4 'Affrighted by the spectre of Bolshevism which was then hovering over Austria, capital commenced to seek safety in flight. This movement received a strong impulsion from the declaration of the Soviet Republic in Budapest on March 21, 1919.' See J. Walré de Bordes, *The Austrian Crown, Its Depreciation and Stabilization* (London, 1924), p. 140.

5 Official Law Gazette No. 122, 19 December 1918.

6 The price increase during the first three months, from November 1918 till the end of January 1919, was 70%. See 'Indexzahlen der Gemischten Kommission ausschliesslich der Wohnungskosten', *Statistische Nachrichten*, December 1923, p. 195.

7 The author had in 1946 an opportunity of discussing with Professor Schumpeter the problem of the crown's tactical defence in the international exchange markets. Schumpeter was able to bring off the temporary stabilization of the crown rate with marginal amounts of foreign currency because occasional intervention purchases were sufficient to prevent the foreign bear speculation from launching excessive operations. The support purchases formed part only of an ambitious recovery programme the implementation of which Schumpeter was however prevented from undertaking.

8 See Official Law Gazette No. 74, 27 November 1918. Cf. also Walther Federn, 'Der Staatsvoranschlag Österreichs', *Der Österreichische Volkswirt*, 8 February 1919, p. 301.

9 See Alois Gratz, 'Die österreichische Finanzpolitik 1848 bis 1948', in *Hundert Jahre österreichische Wirtschaftsentwicklung* (ed. Hans Mayr, Vienna, 1949), p. 278.

10 Siegfried Strakosch, a bitter opponent of the new republican regime, testified to the orthodox approach of the financial authorities to budget problems. 'During the initial period, from 1 January to 30 June 1919, the authorities anticipated a deficit of 2,700 million Austrian crowns. Everything was still *in statu nascendi*, in a state of flux and of re-grouping. Consolation was sought in the thought that order would not return to the national finances until matters had settled down.' Siegfried Strakosch, *Der Selbstmord eines Volkes* (Vienna, 1922), p. 29.

11 Cf. Walther Federn, 'Die finanzielle Liquidation der Monarchie in Deutsch-Österreichs Finanzen', *Der Österreichische Volkswirt*, 31 May 1919, p. 631 et seq.

12 'Here it need only be pointed out,' wrote one of the First Republic's best statisticians, 'that possibly no class has in consequence of the monetary depreciation had to change its standard of living to such a degree as civil servants. No completely homogeneous picture can be given. As yet officials, especially the highly qualified ones, receive after the conclusion of the pay reform only fifty to sixty per cent of their peace-time salaries. It suffices to show that this class stands in the front line of the war's surviving casualties.' Felix Klezl, 'Die Lebenskosten', *Schriften des Vereins für Sozialpolitik* (Munich and Leipzig, 1925), Vol. 169, p. 160.

13 Karl Přibram, 'Die Sozialpolitik im neuen Österreich', *Archiv für Sozialwissenschaft und Sozialpolitik* (Tübingen, 1921), p. 636 et seq.

14 Official Law Gazette No. 150, 26 February 1919.

15 Cf. John V. Van Sickle, *Direct Taxation in Austria* (Cambridge, Mass., 1931), p. 94 et seq.

16 The peculiarities of the Austrian business tax are described by Van Sickle in the following terms: 'The old Austrian business tax . . . was levied on the earnings of small, or at least unincorporated, businesses and professions according to external indices of profitableness. The government protected itself against loss by assessing a lump sum or quota, and then left it to a central and to district and local commissions to apportion this lump sum among those liable to the tax.' Van Sickle, *Direct Taxation*, p. 88.

17 Official Law Gazette No. 112, 6 February 1919.

18 Official Law Gazette No. 12, 12 December 1918.

19 *Der Österreichische Volkswirt*, 1 February 1919, p. 281.

20 'The failure [to enforce the tax] was due to the inability of the Central Quota Commission to carry out with mathematical nicety its task of reducing the 50 million crowns' quota to fit the new Austria. To do this it was first necessary to know the new boundaries. At the end of 1919 these were still indeterminate in a few places. Though the amount of territory in dispute was insignificant, the Commission did nothing at all. The local commissions, meantime, had worked out their relative figures and only awaited the announcement of their total liabilities to send out their tax bills. But the announcement never came. Thus, at the beginning of 1920, the assessments of 1918 and 1919 were still incompleted, and, according to the strict letter of the law, incapable of completion. But in any case it was not worthwhile proceeding with the assessment, because of the intervening depreciation. Since, however, the local assessment commissions' figures of the local tax base quota were already fixed and were known to amount to about 39.5 million crowns more than the approximate quota, the government recommended (January 1920) that these figures be accepted as the final 1918 and 1919 assessments.' Van Sickle, *Direct Taxation*, p. 90.

21 The war debt was, strictly speaking substantially higher. 'If we include in the Austrian war debt, as we must, such items as bank advances on government bonds which could be rediscounted at the central bank and government liabilities arising from war purchases, then the amount in question exceeds the total of 65,000 million crowns.' Cf. Paul Grünwald, 'Das Finanzsystem Deutsch-Österreichs', *Schriften des Vereins für Sozialpolitik* (Munich, 1919), Vol. 158, p. 70.

22 For a complete description of Goldscheid's views, see Rudolf Goldscheid, *Sozialisierung der Wirtschaft oder Staatsbankrott* (Vienna, 1917) and *Staatssozialismus oder Staatskapitalismus* (Vienna, 1919) as well as various articles by the same author in *Der Kampf*, issues for 1918 and 1919.

23 Joseph Popper-Lynkeus, *Nach dem Kriege – Die allgemeine Nährpflicht* (Dresden, 1915), p. 5.

24 Rudolf Goldscheid, 'Staatssozialismus oder Staatskapitalismus', in *Beiträge zur politischen Ökonomie der Staatsfinanzen*, ed. Rudolf Hickel (Frankfurt am Main, 1976), p. 87 et seq. Editor's italics.

25 Goldscheid in *Beiträge*, p. 108.

26 'Das Programm des Staatssekretärs Schumpeter', *Neue Freie Presse*, 20 March 1919.

27 'Staatssekretär Schumpeter über die Vermögensabgabe', *Neue Freie Presse*, 29 March 1919.

28 'Das Programm des neuen Staatssekretärs für Finanzen (aus einem Gespräch)', *Neue Freie Presse*, 16 March 1919.

29 'Orderly monetary conditions presuppose familiarity with the principles of

saving. Resort must not be made to printing new notes.' *Neue Freie Presse*, 29 March 1919.

30 *Neue Freie Presse*, 27 April 1919. The report noted that the numerous guests included Cardinal-Archbishop Piffl, the French envoy Allizé, Vice-Chancellor Fink, the former ministers Baernreither, Engel, and Redlich, the banker Rothschild, the bank directors Neurath, Sieghart, and Reisch, and so on. 'Austria's old ministerial cohort was present and its new, pseudo-socialist one too. Schumpeter spoke fluently, but very casually and superficially at the start. But when he began to whet his sarcastic remarks against Bauer's policy, he became quite amusing.' Josef Redlich, *Schicksalsjahre Österreichs, 1908–1919. Die Tagebücher Josef Redlichs* (Graz, 1954), Vol. II, p. 342.

31 'Staatssekretär Schumpeter über die wirtschaftlichen Aufgaben der Zukunft', *Neue Freie Presse*, 21 March 1919.

32 *Neue Freie Presse*, 27 April 1919. (Present author's italics.)

33 Creditanstalt also participated repeatedly in large-scale transactions of this kind. In spring 1919 it accepted 19,230,000 crowns' worth of 2.5% three-months treasury bills to a total face value of 250 million crowns. See Board Minutes, 13 May 1919, Creditanstalt Archives. On 15 July there occurred another treasury bill acceptance, again on 19 August, and so forth.

34 Alois Rašin, *Die Finanz und Wirtschaftspolitik der Tschechoslowakei* (Munich and Leipzig, 1923), p. 17.

35 Walther Federn remarked that the central bank officially declared its readiness to furnish advances against state securities 'if a justified need for security against collateral exists on the part of the applicant. It reserves to itself scrutiny of the application. It does not seem to have arrived at a decision to observe in all circumstances the assurances given by the central bank, nor at the opposite decision to disregard these assurances, in particular with respect to the lending ceiling of seventy five per cent of the face value.' 'Das finanzielle Chaos', *Der Österreichische Volkswirt*, 25 January 1919, p. 269 et seq.

36 Rašin, *Finanz*, p. 19.

37 Ludwig von Mises was the first to draw attention to this aspect. Cf., 'Der Wiedereintritt Deutsch-Österreichs in das deutsche Reich und die Währungsfrage', *Schriften des Vereins für Sozialpolitik* (Munich, 1919), Vol. 158, p. 151 et seq.

38 See Richard Kerschlagl, *Die Währungstrennung in den Nationalstaaten* (Vienna, 1920), p. 15.

39 Kerschlagl, *Währungstrennung*, p. 16.

40 Rašin, *Finanz*, p. 25 et seq.

41 Rašin, *Finanz*, p. 29.

42 Rašin, *Finanz*, p. 28.

43 Cf. Friedrich Steiner, 'Notenbank und Staatliche Anleihepolitik in den Nachfolgestaaten Österreich-Ungarns', *Schriften des Vereins für Sozialpolitik* (Munich, 1924), Vol. 166, p. 16.

44 Bendixen initially made this criticism in *Bankarchiv*, Vol. XIX, p. 163 et seq.

45 Rašin, *Finanz*, p. 35.

46 'Zwangsweise Verstaatlichung der Österreisch-Ungarischen Bank in Böhmen', *Neue Freie Presse*, 12 March 1919.

47 Walther Federn, 'Die Währungstrennung und der Wert der Krone', *Der Österreichische Volkswirt*, 15 February 1919, p. 321 et seq.

48 Official Law Gazette No. 114, 16 February 1919.

49 Experts are agreed about the fact itself. 'One of the results of the stamping of currencies in Yugoslavia and Czechoslovakia was an influx of unstamped notes into Austria.' Leo Pasvolsky, *Economic Nationalism of the Danubian States* (New York, 1928), p. 39.

50 Official Law Gazette No. 152, 20 February 1919.

51 Kerschlagl, *Währungstrennung*, p. 38.

52 On 8 March, i.e., four days prior to the start of the stamping operation, Walther Federn sharply attacked the government for its failure to prepare the stamping procedure with an eye to the coming capital levy. He noted incidentally, and interestingly enough, that during the past four months he had not found a single article in *Arbeiter-Zeitung* which had raised any demand for a capital levy. Cf. *Der Österreichische Volkswirt*, 8 March 1919, p. 387 et seq.

53 Official Law Gazette No. 167, 10 March 1919.

54 See Van Sickle, *Direct Taxation*, p. 141.

55 An interesting comparison between the two stamping operations is drawn by Walther Federn, 'Die Sicherung der Vermögensabgabe', *Der Österreichische Volkswirt*, 22 March 1919, p. 429 et seq.

56 Kerschlagl, *Währungstrennung*, p. 42.

57 Walré de Bordes, *Austrian Crown*, p. 42.

58 'In the case of the stamping in German-Austria larger quantities (of notes) in private possession are likely to have been kept back from stamping. The public did not expect any appreciation of value from the marking and the unstamped notes, at that time still legal tender in various Successor States, were subsequently in fact worth more.' Kerschlagl, *Währungstrennung*, p. 40.

59 Reviewing the currency situation a year later, Walther Federn exclaimed, 'Our sole hope, grotesque though it sounds, is that the Hungarian and the Polish crown will soon stand substantially higher and that the Hungarian and the Polish stamp be just as easy to counterfeit as the German-Austrian.' 'Ungestempelte und falsch gestempelte Banknoten', *Der Österreichische Volkswirt*, 1 May 1920, p. 606.

60 Official Law Gazette, 26 March 1919.

61 The provision that a stamped Crown was on a par with an unstamped one was echoed in the popular catch-phrase 'A Crown is a Crown'. The saying later acquired the added meaning that owners of War Loan had a claim on the state for no more than the face value of their bonds plus the accrued interest. 'A Crown is a Crown' now meant the tragic recognition by subscribers that they could not turn to the state for indemnification against the loss of as good as all their savings in consequence of inflation.

62 Rašin, *Finanz*, p. 40.

63 Kerschlagl, *Währungstrennung*, p. 42.

64 Otto Bauer, 'Die Österreichische Revolution', *Werkausgabe* (Vienna, 1976), Vol. II, p. 677.

65 Schausberger summarizes the outcome of Bauer's negotiations with the German Government as follows: 'Otto Bauer was undoubtedly himself conscious of his mission's slight success. When on 12 March 1919 he gave the Constituent National Assembly his account of the negotiation results, he was unable to get beyond professions of political agreement and phrases like "most sincere readiness" and "complete understanding". Actual agreements he had none to show. That extremely over-worked formula about Austria's "own, free, wholly

uninfluenced resolution" remained a platonic utterance for as long as corresponding resolutions were not passed in Germany, and that never happened.' Norbert Schausberger, *Der Griff nach Österreich* (Vienna, 1978), p. 68.

66 Ministry of Finance Archives, File 603/Präs. 1919.

67 Ministry of Finance Archive, File 619/Präs. 1919.

68 Cf. Part III, Chap. 5, p. 258.

69 'Staatssekretär Schumpeter über die wirtschaftlichen Aufgaben der Zukunft', *Neue Freie Presse*, 21 March 1919.

70 Stephan Verosta, 'Joseph Schumpeter gegen das Zollbündnis der Donaumonarchie mit Deutschland und gegen die Anschlusspolitik Otto Bauers (1916–1919), *Festschrift für Christian Broda* (Vienna, 1976), p. 401.

71 Verosta, *Festschrift*, p. 401 et seq. The letter is reproduced in full.

72 Verosta, *Festschrift*, p. 402 et seq. Bauer's letter was dated 11 May.

73 Telegram by Oppenheimer to Keynes, 18 May 1919, Public Record Office, FO 608229/10960, quoted by Robert Hoffman, 'Die wirschaftlichen Grundlagen der britischen Österreichpolitik 1919', *Mitteilungen des Österreichischen Staatsarchivs* (Vienna, 1977), Reprint No. 30, p. 268 et seq.

74 'Staatssekretär Dr. Schumpeter über die industrielle Zukunft Österreichs', *Neue Freie Presse*, 31 May 1919. (Present author's italics.) 'Nationalized enterprises within the framework of a market economy' is perhaps the best way to describe Schumpeter's socialist model, and to that degree both Bauer's and his opponent Schumpeter's ideas have influenced the Second Republic's socialization concept.

75 Haus-, Hof-, und Staatsarchiv, Präs. NPA,K.261, Otto Bauer Papers.

76 Renner too was extremely indignant at Schumpeter's public statements. This can be seen in a telegram from Saint-Germain, 8 June 1919. 'These statements make negotiations here impossible. Painting our financial and economic situation in rosy colours, allegations that it does not matter whether our factories lie within or outside the borders, making light of the coal problem, straightforwardly proclaiming Vienna as the Successor States' future financial centre, it is all too grotesque. I must request categorical retraction, and that in the responsible Parisian press, or some other form of speedy clarification because these utterances make us appear frauds here.' Haus-, Hof-, und Staatsarchiv, NPA, K 349.

77 *Der Österreichische Volkswirt*, 31 May 1919, p. 642.

78 Bauer, *Werkausgabe*, Vol. II, p. 723.

79 'Apart from the modest volume of export goods that we still have and can produce there is nothing left for our need for food and ... raw materials ... In such circumstances it is inevitable that we live on our capital and export our securities so as to procure consumer goods from abroad.' Walther Federn, *Der Österreichische Volkswirt*, 26 July 1919, p. 812. Cf. also Karl Ausch, *Als die Banken fielen* (Vienna, 1968), p. 12.

80 Cf. Roberto Segré, *La missione militare italiana per l'armistizio, Decembre 1918–Gennaio 1920* (Bologna, 1929), p. 76 et seq.

81 Richard Kola, *Rückblick ins Gestrige* (Vienna, 1922), p. 236.

82 Kola, *Rückblick*, p. 247.

83 *Neue Freie Presse*, 26 June 1919 and *Arbeiter-Zeitung*, 20 August 1919. The latter wrote, 'In April the shares were priced at 500 crowns. Today they cost 1,471 crowns. Whoever was lucky enough to put his capital into these miraculous securities has seen it trebled in a few weeks, and that at a time when business is completely prostrate.' A report by a British diplomat also contains an interesting

comment. There were, he said, Austrian critics of the transaction who, without going as far as the Social Democrats, nevertheless held that sale of the shares abroad should have been restricted to a ninth of the total Alpine shares available for purchase. See Public Record Office, FO/371/351/HN 00981.

84 Ministry of Finance Archives, Files 2291/AP/1919 and 87794/1919 Annex C. This gives the most important reasons for Dr Richard Reisch, Schumpeter's successor, agreeing to the sale of the shares to Dr Somary and his Swiss associates. 'Even from the standpoint of cash holdings I must attach the utmost importance not only to recovering the 50 million crowns invested in Alpine, but also to realization of the 58 millions' profit that stand to be gained as well as having at my disposal the lire amounts. To my mind it would be irresponsible, in view of the downright hopeless state of our financial affairs and the currently urgent need for foreign exchange, to let pass this exceptionally advantageous opportunity, more particularly as there are no real counter-arguments.'

85 See 'Börsenorgien', Arbeiter-Zeitung, 20 August 1920.

86 Bauer, Werkausgabe, vol. II, p. 721.

87 'I have never authorized, sanctioned, or suggested anyone's purchase of stock in the Alpine Montan or any other corporation . . . I do not say this because I consider that such an authorization would have been wrong. On the contrary, I consider that, had I prevented a measure that could only have increased the difficulties of a difficult situation, this would have been a service to the country, the government, and, above all, to the Social Democratic party.' Charles A. Gulick, Austria: From Habsburg to Hitler (Berkeley and Los Angeles, 1948), Vol. I, p. 141, footnote 19.

88 Undated Schumpeter letter to Renner, AVA, Bundeskanzleramt, Präsidium, Renner Correspondence, Box 65a.

89 The 'hue and cry' against Schumpeter, to which the Chancellor was to put an end, referred to accusations by Arbeiter-Zeitung. The gravest was that of alleged black market foreign exchange deals with Kola (Arbeiter-Zeigung, 20 August 1919). 'As far as I know,' wrote Schumpeter, 'no charge whatever lies against Kola. What however is a matter of course is that no proceedings can be instituted against Kola for black marketing in foreign exchange and currency because, Kola bought foreign exchange and currency on behalf, and at the instruction, of the Ministry of Finance.'

90 Joseph Schumpeter, 'Sozialistische Möglichkeiten von heute', Archiv für Staatswissenschaft und Staatspolitik (Tübingen, 1921), Vol. 48, p. 342.

91 'Everyone waited for what he was going to do, but they waited in vain. For Schumpeter did – absolutely nothing. Against the frightening growth of the budget deficit, against the fearful increase of notes in circulation, against the catastrophic drop in the exchange rate – absolutely nothing. True, till the conclusion of peace the scope for action by the Ministry of Finance was pretty limited . . .' 'Der Fall Schumpeter', Arbeiter-Zeitung, 10 October 1919.

92 'Der Finanzplan des Staatssekretärs a.D. Dr. Schumpeter', Neue Freie Presse, 18 October 1919. The complete text of the recovery programme, Grundlinien der Finanzpolitik für jetzt und die nächsten drei Jahre, is contained in Appendix I.

93 It is questionable whether the statement held good in 1919. A few years later Federn wrote: 'Only a few large and internationally known Austrian firms are the recipients of direct foreign loans. For the majority of them a foreign loan is attainable only through the mediation of, and assumption of liability by, a

Viennese bank.' Walther Federn, 'Die Kreditpolitik der Wiener Banken', *Schriften des Vereins für Sozialpolitik* (Munich 1920), Vol. 169 p. 69.

94 'Der Personenwechsel im Staatsamt für Finanzen', *Neue Freie Presse*, 9 October 1919.

95 'It became known that during the crucial cabinet meeting Minister Stöckler did not support Dr Schumpeter's budget plans in the way that was to be expected from what he had said at the Peasant Convention.' *Neue Freie Presse*, 9 October 1919. Stockler was the Minister for Agriculture.

96 Bauer seems to have thought of a capital levy solely in connection with his socialization programme. As will be recalled, he wanted to indemnify the owners with a capital levy to be paid by the entire capitalist class. Cf. Part IV, Chap. 2, p. 304.

CHAPTER 4

The Major Banks and Industry in the First Year of the Republic

One week after the proclamation of the Republic, members of the Creditanstalt board assembled for a routine meeting, and the mood of these leading figures of the Austrian economy can be judged from the fact that not a word was spoken about the recent political cataclysm. Two years before two extraordinary meetings had been held in commemoration of Emperor Francis Joseph's death and Emperor Charles' succession. The resolution to open a branch office at Trautenau, a small place in northern Bohemia, is indicative of the board's wish even, at this early date, to adhere, whenever possible, to established practice. Events in the next few months were however, to show that not inconsiderable modifications needed to be made to the motto 'Business as usual'.[1]

One of the next meetings, just before the melancholy 1918 Christmas celebration, was symptomatic of the drastically altered political landscape. The board decided to take over a block of 5% Polish treasury vouchers; the Lemberg (Lvov) Branch was authorized to participate to the extent of 750,000 crowns in a loan of ten millions by the major banks to the Polish Provisional Government Committee; and Creditanstalt subscribed 11.5 million crowns to a German-Austrian Government bond issue totalling 150 million crowns. The economic and social aftermath of upheaval was also clearly reflected in other board actions such as a donation of 50,000 crowns for the victims of the Lemberg pogrom and the contribution of 20,000 crowns to a relief operation for discharged officers of the Austro-Hungarian army.[2]

During the early months of the Republic no conspicuous changes occurred in the scope and character of banking operations. A report by Director Neurath showed the extent of Skodawerke indebtedness to have reached 104 million crowns. No less than 55% was owed to the Bank. Large loans were extended to Ringhoffer Werke, Prague, and the San Rocco shipyard loan was prolonged for another three years.[3] The Bohemian and Moravian sugar factories as well as Waggon-fabriken L. Zielenewski at Cracow, Lemberg and Sanok were recipients of bigger loans.[4] In general the Bank did its best, as in the final war years, to stand by those old clients who only with difficulty and excessive slowness could obtain ready funds for their claims on the military administration. Other major Viennese banks had to adopt a similar course.[5]

In February 1919 the first defensive measure of any consequence had to be taken on account of increasing pressure from the Czecho-slovak Government. 'To protect the company's legal status and for the professional operation of business,' ran a board resolution, 'the Prague Branch is appointed Head Office within the territory of the Czechoslovak State.'[6] At this point it was evidently supposed that such a pseudo-grant of independence for the branch network could still save the substance of banking business inside the Czechoslovak Republic.

The events of barely a month showed that purely organizational steps were insufficient to cope with the shifts of power in the Danubian area. Between 8 and 20 January Yugoslavia had detached its currency from that of Austria. The crucial blow fell on 3 March when Czechoslovakia followed suit. At a time of continuous currency depreciation the major Viennese banks were no longer in a position to maintain, in the conditions arising from currency severance, the essential supply of capital to their important branch offices in Bohemia, Moravia, and Silesia. Means corresponding more closely to the new political state of affairs had to be discovered.

Currency severance furnished go-ahead capitalist interests in the Successor States with promising prospects. Two new laws were promulgated in Czechoslovakia to speed up the 'naturalization' of foreign − usually German or Austrian − capital. The so-called Naturalization Act provided that all joint-stock companies operating inside the boundaries of the country must have their headquarters there. The second statute complemented the first by laying down that any joint-stock company with headquarters in Czechoslovakia must have a supervisory board with a Czech majority and a Czech national for its chairman.[7] The outcome of this dilemma was that many Austrian and German shareholders disposed of their assets. Never-theless Czech financial circles were still too weak relatively to be able, especially in certain notorious instances, to derive due advantage from the Naturalization Acts.[8]

Only the example of Skodawerke will be dealt with here. One authority says that Dr Eduard Beneš, the Czechslovak Foreign Minister, had already during the Paris peace negotiations tried to interest Schneider-Creuzot in a take-over of the undertaking. Talks held concurrently between representatives of Živnostenská banka and Dr Karl Skoda, the main shareholder, induced him to sell his holding to the Czech bank. 'A month after the signing of the Versailles Peace Treaty, Dr Beneš informed the Skoda-Works and the Živnostenská Banka that he had reached full agreement with Schneider's represent-ative, Ing. Victor Champigneul . . .'[9] The transaction, adds the author, became a textbook example for other changes of ownership conditions in Czechoslovakia.[10]

Very soon Creditanstalt, in contrast to other major banks, which sought to postpone any binding decisions as long as possible, took account of the drastic change of circumstances in the Successor States. As early as 15 April 1919 the management reported the sale of the Trieste, Gorizia, and Pola branches to a consortium headed by Banca Commerciale Triestina. The arrangement provided for the assignment to the consortium of all the branches' business, with the exception of current foreign exchange assets and liabilities, as well as the transfer of the Trieste office, for the comparatively modest figure of 4.75 million lire. The consortium 'will for the period of fifteen years render Creditanstalt an annual payment to the amount of 16.66% of the profit attributable to a capital of twenty millions . . . If within fifteen years the sum of these payments does not attain the aggregate of three million lire, the period will be extended until such time as that total has been reached.' It was furthermore agreed that Creditanstalt should act as the consortium's corresponding bank for at least the space of time that payments had to be rendered.[11]

Austrian Lloyd and Austro-Americana, the two major marine shipping firms, had been under state control since Italy had taken possession of Trieste. At the beginning of 1919 the chief Austrian Lloyd shareholders, Union-Bank at Vienna and a Fiume group led by the Cosulich family, saw no other prospect than to negotiate with an Italian consortium. The result was a surprisingly swift sale of the oldest Austrian marine shipping enterprise to Italian interests. *Der Österreichische Volkswirt* thought that 'severe steps by the Italian Government against Austrian Lloyd and no less against the branch office of Union-Bank at Trieste were to be feared' and it had argued on behalf of a speedy conclusion to the deal.[12] In the light of the acute scarcity of foreign exchange, the attraction for the Austrian side was likely to have been the payment in lire. At a later date similar grounds persuaded Creditanstalt to sell its share in Austro-Americana and other coastal shipping assets to Italian financial circles.[13] Although the agreement between the Bank and Banca Commerciale Triestina had envisaged closer mutual relations, their collaboration in subsequent years did not go beyond a very small number of operations.

Not many weeks after the painful loss of capital assets in the Adriatic, the management had to undertake another retreat of momentous consequence. On 20 June 1919 it reported to the board the sale of all its branches in Bohemia, Moravia, and Silesia to Böhmische Escompte-Bank for 8 million Czech crowns.[14] This bank acquired all the real estate as well as furniture and fittings. It pledged itself to retain the entire staff including managers. All assets, liabilities and current transactions passed as per 31 December 1919 into the hands of the new ownership. The latter was however entitled within eight weeks to reject certain receivables.

The main shareholder in Böhmische Escompte-Bank had previously been Niederösterreichische Escompte-Gesellschaft, with its head office in Vienna. The shifts in power that had taken place in Czechoslovakia were now reflected in the bank's ownership structure. Creditanstalt took over from Niederösterreichische Escompte-Gesellschaft 6,749 shares of the Böhmische Escompte-Bank to the value of 1,275 Czech crowns each. Its share capital, hitherto 12 million crowns, was raised in conjunction with Niederösterreichische Escompte-Gesellschaft and Živnostenská banka to 48 million crowns. The new shares issue was purchased by Creditanstalt at the price of 200 Czech crowns each and later apportioned between Živnostenská banka (55%) and Niederösterreichische Escompte-Gesellschaft (22.5%) at the price of 240 Czech crowns each. Creditanstalt retained a minority interest of 22.5%.

This reconstruction of the Czech bank's ownership holdings was also reflected in its new name of 'Böhmische Escompte-Bank und Kredit-Anstalt'. The board consisted of fifteen members, including three each from Niederösterreichische Escompte-Gesellschaft and Creditanstalt.[15] Shareholders were to participate in its operations in proportion to their holding. Živnostenská banka promised to do its best to uphold Creditanstalt's representation in its associated companies to the same degree as before. Creditanstalt in turn undertook not to establish any independent finance house in Czechoslovakia and to persuade clients to perform their Czech business via the reconstructed Böhmische Escompte-Bank.[16]

A Creditanstalt letter to the Ministry of Finance gives further important details of the transaction. Before signing the agreements Živnostenská banka had, it appears, made the 'express declaration that customers of German nationality shall, in respect of meeting their loan requirements or in respect of their claim to business accommodation, be in no way discriminated against or be treated differently than customers and interested parties of other nationality'. This declaration was also made on behalf of the remaining parties to the agreement. The letter also contains the following passage on the takeover of Creditanstalt's important sugar interests:

'The sugar business of Živnostenská banka, Creditanstalt's Prague Office, and Böhmische Escompte-Bank will be operated jointly through a new sugar trading company whose shares will be divided in a ratio of 55 : 45 between Živnostenská banka and Böhmische Escompte-Bank. Creditanstalt in Vienna will in addition receive for a number of years a share in the net profit of the company.[17]

The management's report on its disposal of the Czech branch offices was unanimously approved by the board, but discussion of the matter seems to have included criticisms and expressions of anxiety about the future of the Bank's Czech activities. Philipp Gomperz, who as a former member of the Bohemian Provincial Parliament was probably in a better position to judge the new situation than most of his board colleagues, supported the conclusion of the agreement because 'there is no choice other than compliance'. In Czechoslovakia the Bank was faced with difficulties which would indeed, especially after the currency separation, have proved very difficult to circumvent. In contrast to Wiener Bankverein, it had comparatively few branch offices there and these had never greatly put much effort into the deposits business. Under the influence of chauvinist propaganda, which attained high levels after the establishment of the new state, many depositors began increasingly to divert their capital into Czech banks.[18] Although it counted many large-scale firms among its clientele, Creditanstalt was now even less in a position to uphold its traditional role of being the strongest financial institution in the Bohemian and Moravian areas. Instead it had to watch Živnostenská banka and a number of smaller Czech commercial banks like Prager Kreditbank, Bohemian Industrial Bank and Česka banka encroach almost unhindered on its former preserves.

Other major Viennese banks, with the exception of Wiener Bankverein, had quickly to follow Creditanstalt's example. The branch offices of Bank- und Wechselstuben AG, 'Mercur' were merged in Böhmische Kommerzialbank, a new institution mainly under Czech influence. Two years later Anglo-Österreichische Bank and Länderbank branch offices were subordinated to London and Paris respectively.[19] Wiener Bankverein and Société Générale at Brussels founded the Böhmische Bankverein to take over the Viennese bank's Czech branches.

The Czech banks tried to meet their rapidly acquired responsibilities with the assistance of two measures. In swift succession they launched large-scale capital increases, raising their share capital from just on 400 million Czech crowns at the end of 1918 to 900 millions a year later and to 1,400 millions in 1920; and they looked to the West. Banque de Paris and des Pays-Bas, Crédit Mobilier, Rotterdam'sche Bankvereeniging, and the well-known American banking house Kuhn, Loeb & Co. were among the bigger foreign banks first to enter into commitments with the Czech institutions badly needing support.[20]

Creditanstalt, interestingly enough, was able for almost a year to maintain its close contact with leading firms in the Bohemian-Moravian area. The board minutes for 10 October 1919 record the extension of quite considerable loans to Brünner Königsfelder Maschinenfabrik, F. Ringhoffer, Smichow, Landwirtschaftliche Aktienzuckerfabrik Leneschitz, and so on. Nevertheless in the succeeding months these links became manifestly weaker, as the Czech banks gained in financial stength. For completeness' sake it should be mentioned that at the beginning of March 1920 Director Ehrenfest reported to the board the end of negotiations with the Warschauer Disconto-Bank and Galizische Aktien-Hypotheken-Bank. The outcome was the take-over of the Lemberg branch and a close connection between the two Polish banks and Creditanstalt.[21] Although longer, and less dispassionate, discussions had followed the disposal of the Bohemian and Moravian branches, this final deal in the dismemberment of the Bank's international network of offices was accepted by the members of the Board *nem. con.* By the end of 1920, a year during which the Laibach (Ljubljana) branch had also had to be shed, three exchange offices at Vienna and six branch offices in the Alpine provinces including one at Bozen (Bolzano) were all that remained.[22]

The Republic's first year coincided with the major banks having to relinquish a not inconsiderable portion of their industrial empires and other assets in what had become foreign territory. The Adriatic shipping companies and shipyards, the Near Eastern railways, the Czechoslovak heavy industry enterprises, the Galician oil companies, and the rest had to be wholly or partially surrendered to foreign capital interests.[23] Positions not as yet abandoned appeared severely imperilled, inasmuch as the Austrian economy was only able to pay for a substantial part of its imports of foodstuffs and raw materials by the sacrifice of participations and other capital assets. To the process of 'depossession', the hallmark of suffering of the war years, was now added that of the great 'clearance sale', and one not confined to assets abroad. The share majority in Alpine Montan-Gesellschaft had passed into Italian hands. A British group acquired control of Erste Donau-Dampfschiffahrts-Gesellschaft, Süddeutsche Donau-Dampfschiffahrts-Gesellschaft, the Hungarian and the Yugoslav Danube shipping companies.[24] Berndorfer Metallwerke, Veitscher Magnesitwerke, the bolts, screws, and forges manufacturing firm Brevillier & Urban, to name but a few of the major Austrian undertakings, came partly under foreign control.[25] And the Viennese banks were not always successful in retaining either the residue of their former influence or even their voice in the concerns' financial affairs.[26]

The development of counter-tactics to enable banks to preserve some portion of their old influence across the new national borders has been noted. Some became 'junior partners' in one of the established Czech, Polish, or Yugoslavian commercial banks while others (on the pattern of Wiener Bankverein) made sure they had the support of Western capitalist groups in order to safeguard their interests. Creditanstalt very soon found itself forced to put its relations with Western banking houses on a sounder, more lasting basis.

Dr Paul Hammerschlag, one of the leading directors, had, in a secret report to the British delegate of the Reparation Commission's Preparatory Committee, expressed himself in a surprisingly optimistic manner as to the present state, and the future prospects, of Austria's banks.[27] The economic relations which, so Hammerschlag said, 'must of absolute necessity arise betweeen the Successor States and German-Austria' would 'indubitably result in new stimuli for the activities of the Viennese institutions'.[28] Notable moreover, is that a memorandum around the same date addressed to the Reparation Commission's Organization Committee by leading Austrian financiers (including Hammerschlag), should have ended with the emphatic assertion, 'A combination of foreign capital combined with the knowledge possessed by Austrian business men of market conditions in the new states would not only save the Austrian economy, but ensure opportunities of profit for the Principal Powers' capital.'[29] During the following months Neurath and Hammerschlag, the two authorities at Creditanstalt responsible for foreign relations, devoted their efforts to reorganizing the Bank in line with the foregoing doctrine – Austrian know-how plus Western capital.

In summer 1920 (to anticipate matters somewhat) the management, after protracted negotiations with the banker Max Warburg and representatives of Kuhn, Loeb & Co. as well as the Guaranty Trust Co., New York, told the board that these American financial circles were preparing to acquire a substantial minority holding on the occasion of a major forthcoming Creditanstalt capital increase. A Voting Committee, consisting of Warburg, one nominee from each of the American banking houses, and one from Creditanstalt, would be formed so as to reach agreement on 'co-ordination at the respective general meetings' and to protect these foreign interests. Philipp Gomperz, the board minutes record, described the transaction 'as one of the most important in the history of our Bank'.[30]

The American participants had, as emerged from subsequent newspaper reports, bought shares to the value of 40 million crowns. Barely a year later (March 1921) a Dutch participation to the value of 16 million crowns was undertaken by the banking houses Hope & Co., Amsterdam, and Neederlandsche Handel-Maatschappij. Credit-anstalt's share capital at this stage totalled 400 million crowns. Fourteen per cent was therefore now in foreign hands.[31] This was not yet the end of a portentous development.[32]

The commitment of the American and Dutch banks to Credit-anstalt, dominated by Rothschild interests, was of almost inestimably prestigious and symbolic value, far beyond the figures involved. It accorded the Bank, regardless of harshly reduced participations in central and eastern Europe, recognition by the cosmopolitan high finance fraternity as an equal entitled to count on the moral support, the good services, and in particular the credit lines of leading Western banks. Only now could it bring into play its 'knowledge . . . of market conditions in the new states' through the employment of foreign capital. In time a fairly large number of internationally well-known financial authorities were assembled on the board. Oddly enough the board exercised no serious control over the circumspection with which the Bank's 'credentials' were used.[33]

The foundation of international holding companies in order to save a part of the assets across the new national borders was another of the management's counter-tactics. An early example was the formation of Swiss parent corporations to buy the shares of 'Mundus' Bugholzmöbelfabriken (bentwood furniture factories), Vereinigte Färbereien, and Österreichische Fezfabriken. How this worked in practice is illustrated by the case of Mundus A G.

A Ministry of Finance file makes it clear that five companies partially or wholly controlled by Creditanstalt – Österreichische Mundus A G, Ungarische Mundus A G, Kroatische Mundus A G, Borloörmenyeser Holzindustrie A G, and A G zur Erzeugung von Möbeln aus gebogenem Holze Jakob & Josef Kohn – were combined in a Swiss holding company whose shares were allotted to the various sets of shareholders in exchange for the surrender of their previous interests.[34] 'The whole proceeding can be most warmly welcomed because, irrespective of the fact that all of the joint-stock companies have their plants partly outside Austria, this renders it feasible for them to continue to be directed from here and for the Austrian shareholders' interests to remain as far as possible safeguarded,' minuted the ministry official. The nature of the Swiss parent corporation he defined in a marginal note as 'bogus'.[35]

The year 1919 saw an unprecedented production crisis. Industrial output is likely to have been barely a third of what it had been in the last year of peace, agrarian production about half. In 1920 industry did not achieve even half the 1913 figures while agriculture came to only two-thirds and was able to meet rather less than 50% of domestic requirements.[36] 'A large part of the iron-working industry,' ran the report of the Military Liquidation Office, 'especially the armaments and munitions industry, the aviation motors manufacturing industry and the aircraft industry, a later wartime development which only in 1918 had begun larger-scale production and had consequently hardly completed its investments, let alone partially written them off, were facing the danger of breakdown . . . Austria's iron production', the report continued at another point, 'is substantially hampered, indeed practically halted, by the coal emergency inasmuch as in consequence of the coke scarcity only one of the Alpine-Montangesellschaft's three furnaces is in operation, and then not regularly.'[37] A strange fact is that Viennese banks' balance sheets for the Republic's first year of existence give the impression of the economy going through a highly flourishing phase. Discussing the situation of German banks, *Frankfurter Zeitung* similarly spoke of a 'frightening boom'.[38]

This paradox was of course the outcome of constantly mounting inflation, a development reflected by the 1919 balance sheet totals which had on average doubled. Creditanstalt was one of the few noteworthy exceptions. Its total, below the line, rose from a mere 3,100 million to 3,500 million crowns, a performance due above all to the dramatic loss of almost its entire branch office network.

Like the balance sheet figures, so the net profits and dividend distributions rose. The latter attained the level of the hectic wartime boom years. In this respect too the Bank exercised a certain restraint. Its 11⅞% dividend stood well above that of the final war year (6¼%), but it remained substantially behind the 1917 record of 12³/₁₆%. More than most of its fellows Creditanstalt seems, in view of the uncertain future, to have pursued a policy of systematically expanding its hidden as well as its stated reserves.

What were the focal points of the banking community's business in the crisis year 1919? The boom in the securities market had died down towards the end of hostilities, being replaced by a mood of uncertainty and despondency which continued during the early months of the Republic. Only in spring did the turnover on the Vienna Stock Exchange begin to increase. Events connected with the sale of Alpine shares are likely to have had an uncommonly 'stimulating' effect. But inflation and currency erosion were primarily the factors shaping the enlivenment of the incipient securities activity which was to far exceed the wartime dimensions. The 'flight from the crown', behaviour previously confined to a small class of speculators, profiteers, professional market gamblers, and other peripheral social elements, now spread to ever wider middle-class circles and was encouraged by the growing number of middlemen and bucket shops. The subject will be considered in more detail in the next part of this study.

In several respects the major banks benefitted from the unusual activity in the securities market. Old securities and syndicate holdings could be disposed of advantageously. Interest earnings and commissions leaped up almost everywhere.[39] Creditanstalt's credits on margin recorded a rise by 180% on the preceding year. The Bank and other big credit institutions made handsome profits on a series of capital increases that proved easy to place in a share-starved market. Spring 1920 saw the Bank's own first capital increase after its participation in a number of underwriting syndicates.

Something must be said about the large number of capital increases in industry. After the war many leading enterprises were able to realize their receivables only very slowly. With wages as well as raw materials and fuel prices rising rapidly, the demand on banks for loans grew accordingly.[40] The sequel was a sharp change for the worse in the ratio of own to outside resources in so far as an appropriate adjustment was not undertaken by way of capital increases. The banks of course put some pressure on their borrowers to perform this sort of adjustment as often as possible, because thereby they contrived to restrict their risk and to offload it in the form of shares on investors as a whole. The syndicates formed to underwrite the shares issues were automatically able, with continually rising stock prices, to net considerable gains.[41] And in this situation the banks were also able to convince certain well-known private firms of the advantages to be derived from going public.[42]

Foreign exchange business at a time of continuous, accelerating currency erosion was another pivotal point in banking operations. During the immediate post-war chaos the reins had slid almost completely out of the Foreign Exchange Agency's hands. An idea of the proportions assumed by the black market can be gained from Schumpeter's letter to Renner which, among other things, contains the following striking passage:

When I took office, utter disorganization prevailed in the foreign exchange and foreign notes and coins market. Obviously only those transactions that could not avoid official control passed through the Foreign Exchange Agency. All other deals took place in a so-called free market. Things went so far that official bodies and private individuals were given permission, partly from one case to another, partly with general licence, to obtain their foreign exchange in the free market or to use that which they had already obtained there. The agency's stocks were extremely low. That is why with many imports it was only too glad for the body in question to purchase the foreign exchange itself, precisely because the free market's holdings were enormous and not available to it. This coexistence between the official and the free markets was reflected in the agency's exchange rate always being kept six to seven per cent below the unofficial ones. The result was for the free market's large stocks not to be available for purposes the state regarded as desirable, but for all kinds of private objectives like tax evasion and so on.[43]

This last proves that the authorities had virtually lost control over the foreign exchange market and had abandoned the important function of foreign exchange dealings to banks as well as other, less regular channels. The 'flight from the crown' was able to take its course along these newly opened paths. The report by *Der Öster-reichische Volkswirt* on the business year 1919 that 'Gigantic turnovers and huge profits occurred even in foreign exchange operations' hardly comes as a surprise.[44] Many regarded foreign exchange hoarding as a 'dead cert', worth financing even with the aid of expensive loans. Creditanstalt's increased foreign exchange activities in 1919 may be taken as symptomatic. Profits were ten times those in the preceding year. 'The big margins in the sale of crowns were mainly responsible.'[45]

The debtors' side of bank ledgers showed typical changes. War bonds and war bonds collateral had largely disappeared. The state's indirect indebtedness by way of advance payment on war bonds through the Postal Savings Bank likewise no longer played a prominent part. Loans to the state continued to constitue a substantial item with nearly all major banks, but the crucial contrast between wartime and current conditions lay primarily in the loans taking the form of treasury bills, discountable at the central bank. This lent them an eminently liquid character and meant that they helped to keep the inflationary momentum going.

Clients' need for money, in light of the rapidly mounting prices for coal and raw materials, attained unprecedented dimensions. Three main lines of credit should however be distinguished – loans for working capital, more or less immobilized investment loans, and loans for speculative purposes with a securities base. In the case of certain banks this third category showed a vigorously rising trend. Exceptionally great risk attached to any and every variety of loan operation. Even current working capital loans could not but be hazardous. Should there be any improvement in the price of the crown (which in 1919 actually happened, though only temporarily), then debtors must sustain enormous, possibly ruinous losses of stocks on hand.[46]

The established major banks were also menaced, even if not to the same degree, by the aggressive conduct of medium and small banks which, under the management of wartime parvenus, came swiftly to the fore. Reference has been made to the astonishing career of Camillo Castiglioni, in charge of Allgemeine Depositenbank.[47] *Der Österreichische Volkswirt*'s report on its 1919 balance sheet termed it 'at present nothing short of the leading bank', a description primarily ascribable to the link between the bank's chairman and the Banca Commerciale group at Milan.[48] Depositenbank was able, with this Italian connection, to acquire 'some control, some participations in a large number of enterprises hitherto affiliated to the groups of other banks'. An outstanding stroke was the takeover of the alcohol syndicate in Czechoslaovakia, which formerly belonged to Creditanstalt's sphere of interest. Its earnings paid for a series of fresh Czech acquisitions.[49] In Austria, thanks to help from Anglobank and its friends abroad, the bank secured control over the previous branch establishments of the Skoda group and over Daimler Motoren AG, the Austrian Brown, Boveri works, Fischersche Weicheisen- und Stahlgiesserei AG, and Pulverfabrik Skoda-Wetzler. *Der Öster-*

reichische Volkswirt's balance sheet report mentioned also its influence over such important firms as Kabel und Drahtwerke Felten & Guilleaume and Semperit-Gummiwerke. It was moreover able to join Creditanstalt, Anglobank, and Verkehrsbank in converting the Ternitzer Stahlwerke, the possession of Schoeller & Comp., into a joint-stock comapny with 30 million crowns share capital.[50]

Creditanstalt's policy during the first year of the Republic must, in contrast with Allgemeine Depositenbank, be defined as defensive. This applies particularly to its withdrawal from branch office activities and the sale of its numerous participations in the Successor States as well as the painful shrinkage of current business, especially in the Bohemian-Moravian area. Some of the severed threads could be picked up in later years, but this applied less in Czech than in other neighbouring territories.

A very profitable line of business was the Bank's frequent membership of underwriting groups for the issue at home and abroad of capital increase shares. Let it suffice to quote some of the more important operations.

On 18 March the Bank participated in such an operation by Galizische Bank für Handel und Industrie. The capital increase was from 4 millions to 5 million crowns, with an increase to 30 million crowns planned for the future. Simultaneously the Lemberg office was a member of the underwriting consortium for the placement of 30,000 new shares issued by Industriebank für das Königreich Galizien und Lodomerien. On 15 July (that is, a bare fortnight before the sale of the Czech branches) the Prague office joined the group underwriting 200,000 new shares by Živnostenská banka to an amount of 7.5% (a block of 15,000). Then there was an interval until 16 September before a large-scale deal, the conversion of the family-owned firm, Julius Meinl into a joint-stock company, took place. The Bank's portion amounted to 6.25 million crowns. On 18 October the Bank participated in the underwriting of a capital increase for Maschinenfabrik AG N. Heid. On 4 November the management reported on two issue operations: participation in the underwriting group for new shares floated by Berndorfer Metallwarenfabrik Arthur Krupp to increase its capital from 40 to 60 million crowns, and participation in a capital increase from 4 to 6 million crowns by Sascha-Filmindustrie. Two weeks later the Bank again joined in the fresh capital increase from 160 millions to 200 million Czech crowns by Živnostenská banka. On 21 November the board agreed to participate in an underwriting group on behalf of an issue raising the capital of

Polnische priv. Maschinen- und Waggonfabriken L. Zielniewski at Cracow, Lemberg, and Sanok from 6 to 8 million crowns. Finally the board minutes of 10 December record two further large-scale issue participations. One was for a capital increase by Bielitz-Bielaer Escompte- und Wechselbank from 3 to 20 million crowns. The other was implemented by the Lemberg office (at this date still part of the Bank's network) joining to 5% in a consortium to underwrite the shares issued by Industriebank für das Königreich Galizien und Lodomerien to increase its capital from 50 to 100 million crowns.[51]

The Bank's company promotion, in the proper sense of the word, dropped during the first post-war year almost to nil. That of course faithfully reflected the general state of emergency. On 4 February the management reported the incipient formation of an 'Advisory Office on German-Austria's Hydraulic Power' to which, along with certain other Viennese banks, it proposed to make the modest contribution of 100,000 crowns. The Linz Schiffswerfte AG, detached from Stabilimento Tecnico Triestino, was repeatedly extended moderate loans – between 2 and 3 million crowns – to enable it to enlarge its docks.[52] Sascha-Filmindustrie AG was also the recipient of a limited investment loan.[53]

In spite of its not inconsiderable sales of securities and its conservative assessment practice, the Bank's own securities and investment in affiliated companies rose in 1919 by 36.3 million crowns to 306.7 million crowns.[54] Its portfolio had grown by holdings in Böhmische Escompte-Bank & Credit-Anstalt, Deutsche Erdöl-AG, Julius Meinl AG, Sascha-Filmindustrie AG, and Linzer Schiffswerfte AG, as well as through shares deriving from the numerous above-mentioned capital increases. Participations in Austro-Americana AG, Böhmische Landesbank, Helios Zündwarenfabrik AG, and so on, had been jettisoned partly voluntarily and partly by force of circumstances.

The bills portfolio, unlike that of securities, had diminished by nearly half. Its composition also mirrored the strongly altered character of banking operations. Together with certificates of deposit it contained a decreased amount of German-Austrian treasury bills, old stocks of Hungarian treasury certificates and bills, Turkish and Bulgarian treasury bills, bills issued by the War Wheat Marketing Office, and a batch of 4% Czechoslovak treasury bills which, according to *Der Österreichische Volkswirt*, the Bank had been able to buy on advantageous terms. About half the portfolio consisted of commercial bills and bank acceptances.[55]

The Bank was able to keep the burdens arising from increased salaries, expenses and taxation within tolerable limits mainly because staff numbers had been reduced from 2,185 to 1,645, resulting from the disposal of the branch office network. Nevertheless the optimism so conspicuously displayed by the dividend distribution is distinctly puzzling in view of the not unproblematic situation suggested by the balance sheet figures. In June 1919 certain board members, anxious at the unfavourable state of the peace negotiations, had questioned Neurath about future prospects. His reply was deeply pessimistic. 'It was impossible, seeing the utter uncertainty of the situation, to give a precise answer. A complete collapse of our economy seemed inevitable unless the point [in the Peace Treaty] settling our relations with the Successor States was entirely dropped. *A mitigation of these conditions would not be sufficient to avert catastrophic consequences.*'[56]

Neurath was referring not only to the still obscure problem of how pre-war debts were to be met, but especially to the danger that obligations to the Successor States – Czechoslovakia, in the first place – would have to be valorized. The first version of the Peace Treaty, terms of which became known at the end of June, did indeed envisage such an almost unendurable solution.[57] A year later, at the time of the 1919 balance sheet's presentation, the fact that the pre-war debts question was to be settled in a not unreasonable manner was long familiar.

It can however be surmised that the management's more favourable reading of the situation in spring and summer 1920 did not arise only from the definitive version of the Peace Treaty, which was mainly rejected even in its revised form. The subdued confidence emanating from the balance sheet figures is more likely to have resulted from two other events narrated earlier in this chapter – the new-born, close partnership between the Bank and Western financial groups, and the comparatively satisfactory resolution of ownership questions across the new borders, particularly in Czechoslovakia. On this basis it would, even under the new political conditions once more prove possible – as was undoubtedly the opinion of the Bank's leading men and, along with them, of the Austrian financial world's top personalities – to develop a flourishing banking activity.

The management could justifiably assume that the Bank's capital funds had to a very large extent been secured against currency instability through substantial participation in industrial and banking business as well as through massive foreign exchange holdings. It must again be recalled that soon after the end of hostilities the Bank had succeeded in drastically reducing its own holdings of War Loan and its customers' War Loan collateral. The crown loans extended by the Bank were therefore offset by the funds of their creditors who in essence had to carry the risk of currency depreciation.

Neurath is likely in summer 1919 to have painted the picture in all too gloomy colours. The change of mood emerging in spring and summer 1920, only just on a year later, was to a later generation bound to appear hardly intelligible. The Bank, together with certain other major Viennese financial houses, might in fact have succeeded in transforming a general rout into a more or less orderly withdrawal, but its sphere of activity was incomparably more circumscribed and more hazardous than in pre-war days. Above all there could no longer be any hope of influencing to any positive domestic advantage the economic and financial policies of the Successor States, in whose territories Austrian industry's most important markets continued to be. The Bank's operational policy, as could have been recognized at the end of the first post-war year, was founded on extremely dubious premises.

In autumn 1919 the Bank suffered a severe loss through the death of Julius Blum.[58] He had entered its service in 1862 at the age of nineteen at the Trieste branch, became its principal manager following a rather adventurous career in the Egyptian civil service, and eventually held the chairmanship of the board for many years. His departure, like that of Richard Lieben, vice-chairman of many years' standing, symbolized the end of a brilliant era in the Bank's history.[59] The start of an entirely different epoch of development was indicated by the presence of two new members on the board, Max Warburg and Sigmund Metz. They had been invited to join 'by reason of the agreement with our American friends', as the minutes have it.[60] Possibly an even clearer sign of the times was the attendance at the board meetings of the two staff delegates, Hugo Ehrenfreund and August Machart.[61] Nothing, though, proclaimed the beginning of a new phase as clearly as the decision of the board to change the Bank's name, from *k.k. priv. Österreichische Credit-Anstalt für Handel und Gewerbe* (Imperial and Royal Licensed Loans Bank for Industry and Trade) to the more modest *Österreichsche Creditanstalt für Handel und Gewerbe*.

Notes

1 Board Minutes, 19 November 1918, Creditanstalt Archives.

2 Board Minutes, 17 December 1918, Creditanstalt Archives.

3 Board Minutes, 3 December 1918, Creditanstalt Archives.

4 Board Minutes, 8 January 1919, Creditanstalt Archives.

5 The dimension of these claims is revealed in a report by the Military Affairs Liquidation Office. 'In November 1918 the amount of unsettled claims from Austrian industry as a whole totalled not less than 2,000 million crowns. Two-thirds were due to firms located in today's Austria, either through having their plants or their commercial or their financial headquarters here. During the first half of 1918 payment of claims by the military administration was laggard and irregular. When the collapse occurred, Austrian industry was placed in the worst conceivable situation by these outstanding claims. Plants had to be converted to peace-time work, a longer-term handicap for production. Dismissals of wage and salary workers could for political reasons not be undertaken on any bigger scale because precisely at this point of unproductive activity general overheads had to be carried along and thus could not be reduced.' Ministry of Finance Archives 55021/1920, 17 June 1920. The report (4313/1920) was dated 15 June 1920.

6 The board took its authority for the measure from Article 28 of the Bank's articles of association, an Imperial ordinance of 29 November 1865, and 'certain Czech laws'. See Board Minutes, 4 February 1919, Creditanstalt Archives.

7 Alice Teichova, *An Economic Background to Munich, International Business and Czechoslovakia 1918–1938* (Cambridge, 1974), p. 98.

8 Teichova, *Economic Background*, p. 99.

9 Teichova, *Economic Background*, p. 196.

10 Teichova, *Economic Background*, p. 92 et seq. The author describes the background of the spectacular sale of the Österreichische Berg- und Hütten-werkgesellschaft, formerly controlled by Boden-Creditanstalt, to the Schneider-Creuzot interests. In this case Živnostenská banka succeeded in participating in the deal as junior partner to the powerful Schneider group.

11 Board Minutes, 15 April 1919, Creditanstalt Archives.

12 *Der Österreichische Volkswirt*, 1 February 1919, p. 296.

13 The sale of the Stabilimento Technico Triestino shares, Creditanstalt's biggest Italian asset, did not happen until 1920. Cf., 'Die Bilanzen', *Der Österreichische Volkswirt*, 16 July 1921, p. 169.

14 In the Board Minutes for 30 July 1919 the following branches were named: Prague, Brünn, Karlsbad, Gablonz, Olmütz, Mährisch-Ostrau, Reichenberg, Teplitz, Troppau, and Warnsdorf. In addition there was considerable real estate at Trautenau, Aussig, and Warnsdorf. This, according to the Minutes, 'will be ceded at cost price'. Creditanstalt Archives.

15 'The relationship to Živnostenská banka, incidentally, is abundantly unclear. All that is known is that earlier on it took over 55% of the share capital formerly in the exclusive possession of Niederösterreichische Escompte-Gesellschaft and that it has since then participated in all capital increases with this ratio. On the other hand only two of the board's fifteen members are Czechs and in the management, where the real conduct of business resides, Živnostenská banka has no represent-ation at all. Regardless of the changes in ownership, the management seems to have obtained a high degree of independence.' Cf. 'Böhmische Escompte-Bank und Credit-Anstalt', *Der Österreichische Volkswirt*, 30 July 1921, p. 175.

16 Board Minutes, 30 July 1919, Creditanstalt Archives, and Alois Rašin, *Die Finanz- und Wirtschaftspolitik der Tschechoslowakei* (Munich and Leipzig,

1923), p. 143.

17 Ministry of Finance Archives, File 57606/19. The letter is dated 11 August 1919.

18 'Many depositors who had hitherto entrusted their savings only to the highly capitalized Viennese banks with, for those days, voluminous reserves withdrew their funds because they believed them to be safely invested only with Czech banks.' See Friedrich Weil, 'Das Bankwesen in der Tschechoslowakei', *Neue Freie Presse*, 20 April 1921.

19 The subordination of Anglo-Österreichische Bank's and Österreichische Länderbank's branches to London and Paris respectively was connected with the loss of independent status by the Viennese banks. Part V will deal with this aspect.

20 These facts are taken from the informative article by Friedrich Weil quoted above and from Rašin, *Finanz- und Wirtschaftspolitik*, p. 142 et seq.

21 Board Minutes, 10 March 1920, Creditanstalt Archives.

22 See 'Die Bilanzen', *Der Österreichische Volkswirt*, 16 July 1921, p. 167. The Laibach branch was transformed into the Laibach Creditanstalt für Handel und Industrie. For Creditanstalt its most important correspondent bank now was Kroatische Kreditbank, founded by Ungarische Allgemeine Kreditbank.

23 French interests succeeded very swiftly in ousting Austrian capital from its dominant position in the Galician oil industry. 'The total interests of the oil groups in Galicia under French leadership are currently assessed at nearly 1,000 million francs. That undoubtedly puts France at the top in the Galician oil area.' See 'Galizische Naphta A G Galicia', *Der Österreichische Volkswirt*, 25 December 1920, p. 50.

24 On the sale of 3,000 shares from the Austrian Government's holding in the Süddeutsche Donau-Dampfschiffahrts-Gesellschaft to the Danube Navigation Co. Ltd., a British firm, see Ministry of Finance Archives files 53645/19 and 101.096/20. The transaction led, as the files show, to Danube Navigation's participation in Erste Donau-Dampfschiffahrts-Gesellschaft. In 1924 the Süddeutsche DDSG shares were restored to Austrian possession, 60% into the hands of Erste DDSG. See *Compass*, 1925, Vol. I, p. 1,578 and Foreign Office file FO 371/3550/HN 01008.

25 A major share in the capital of Schranken- und Schmiedewarenfabriks A G Brevillier & Co. und A. Urban & Söhne was acquired only in 1920 by the British concern Guest, Keen, & Nettlefold, Birmingham, and the French company Japy Frères, Paris. See *Compass*, 1925, Vol. I, p. 849.

26 Walther Federn, 'Die Wiener Banken', *Der Österreichische Volkswirt*, 17 July 1920, p. 785.

27 Cf. Part IV, Chap. 1, p. 279 et seq.

28 Ministry of Finance Archives, File No. 83623/19.

29 Finanzarchiv, File No. 87111/19. Report to the Subcommittee of the Reparation Commission's Organization Committee. The other signatories included Moritz Benedikt (*Neue Freie Presse*), Wilhelm Berliner (Phönix), Max Feilchenfeld (Niederösterreichische Escompte-Gesellschaft), Josef Redlich, Wilhelm Rosenberg (Anglo-Österreichische Bank), Rudolf Sieghart, Paul Hammerschlag (Creditanstalt).

30 Board Minutes, 14 June 1920, Creditanstalt Archives.

31 'Österreichische Creditanstalt', *Der Österreichische Volkswirt*, 16 July 1921, p. 167.

32 In May 1931, i.e., before Creditanstalt's financial reconstruction by the Austrian

state, approximately a third of the Bank's shares were held by the Austrian Rothschild banking house and another third was in the hands of the Bank of England, Anglo-International Bank, and Prudential Insurance Company. Kuhn, Loeb & Co. and Guaranty Trust Co., New York, continued to hold the share packet bought in 1920. See report from Vienna by the British Minister, Mr (later Sir) Eric Phipps, Public Record Office file FO/371/15150/02382.

33 Whereas in 1931 the Bank's management consisted solely of Austrian nationals, the Board had eleven foreign members in addition to twenty-nine Austrians.

34 The Austrian company's full name was 'Mundus Aktiengesellschaft der Vereinigten Österreichischen Bugholzmöbel-Fabriken, Wien'. In 1920 it had a share capital of 7.8 million crowns and plants in Czechoslovakia and Poland. See Ministry of Finance Archives, File 46707/1920. (The Hungarian Joint-stock company and the rest mentioned here had a somewhat smaller capital.)

35 Ministry of Finance Archives, File 21623/1920.

36 Kausel-Nemeth-Seidel, 'Österreichs Volkseinkommen 1913–1963', *Monatshefte des Instituts für Wirtschaftsforschung* (1965), p. 5.

37 Ministry of Finance Archives, File 55021/1920.

38 Federn, *Der Österreichische Volkswirt*, 17 July 1920, p. 783.

39 Likewise in respect of interest earnings the Bank recorded comparatively modest increases, a circumstance mainly ascribable to the loss of its branch office network.

40 The report by the Military Affairs Liquidation Office had the following to say about the precipitous rise in industrial production costs: 'The continuous rise in wages and salaries since 1918 has proceeded by leaps and bounds so that the level of wages has gone up almost four times and that of salaries five- and sixfold. All raw materials prices have soared, with plants often being forced to stop operations for lack of coal, but seventy-five per cent of the wages and all the salaries have to go on being paid. The cost of coal has risen such that many firms have had to buy on the black market at exorbitant prices in order to keep working. [All] this has completely exhausted the funds of important and well-known industrial undertakings and has resulted in their having to take up large loans with banks.' Ministry of Finance Archives, File 55021/1920.

41 Cf. Federn, *Der Österreichische Volkswirt*, 17 July 1920, p. 784.

42 Cf. Board Minutes, 16 September 1919, Creditanstalt Archives, on the conversion of the firm Julius Meinl into a joint-stock company. 'The Bank is to take a share to the value of 6.25 million crowns and, together with Anglo-Österreichische Bank, to extend to the new company a loan of 30 million crowns.'

43 From the letter by Schumpeter to Renner quoted in the preceding chapter, p. 336.

44 Federn, *Der Österreichische Volkswirt*, p. 784.

45 Alfred Přibram, 'Österreichische Creditanstalt', *Der Österreichische Volkswirt*, 17 July 1920, p. 162.

46 Přibram, *Der Österreichische Volkswirt*, p. 189.

47 Cf. Part III, Chap. 3, p. 211 et seq. and Richard Lewinson ('Morus'), *Die Umschichtung der europäischen Vermögen* (Berlin, 1925), p. 236 et seq.

48 'Allgemeine Depositenbank', *Der Österreichische Volkswirt*, 12 June 1920, p. 143.

49 The Depositenbank's holdings in Czechoslovakia included spirits distilleries at Neutitschein, liqueur factories at Ostrau, zinc-rolling mills at Oderberg, Vereinigte Schafwollfabriken Jägerdorf-Brünn (wool factories), Glasfabrik

Rindskopf at Teplitz, porcelain clay works at Chodau, Bädergesellschaft Marienbad (spa management) and Scuhfabrik Leona.

50 The previous owners, reported *Der Österreichische Volkswirt*, kept half the shares while receiving a more than hundred per cent interest for the rest. See issue of 12 June 1920, p. 144.

51 These details are taken from the respective Board Minutes, Creditanstalt Archives.

52 Cf. Board Minutes, 18 October and 10 December 1919, Creditanstalt Archives.

53 Board Minutes, 4 November 1919. A loan of 8 million crowns was extended to the film company on 23 December 1919. 1919 Annual Report, Creditanstalt Archives.

54 See Creditanstalt 1919 Annual Report, Creditanstalt Archives.

55 Cf. 'Die Bilanzen', *Der Österreichische Volkswirt*, 17 July 1920, p. 162.

56 Board Minutes, 20 July 1919, Creditanstalt Archives. (Present author's italics.)

57 The next chapter deals in more detail with the economic conditions of the Peace Treaty.

58 Further details on the career of Julius Blum will be found in Eduard März, *Österreichs Industrie- und Bankpolitik zur Zeit Franz Joseph I* (Vienna, 1968), p. 285.

59 Board Minutes, report on the memorial meeting for Blum and Lieben, 21 November 1919, Creditanstalt Archives.

60 Board Minutes, 23 July 1920, Creditanstalt Archives.

61 Board Minutes, 18 October 1919, Creditanstalt Archives.

CHAPTER 5
The Peace Treaty of
Saint-Germain-en-Laye

In the months preceding the signing of the Peace Treaty three main objectives seem to have guided the conduct of Austria's foreign policy, the main architects of which were the leaders of the Social Democratic Party. First, to bring about as soon as possible *Anschluss* with Germany. Secondly, to try to have included within the boundaries of the new Austria all parts of the former Empire populated by German-language inhabitants. And thirdly, to obtain a treaty unencumbered by onerous economic provisions. We have encountered some of the arguments employed by Austrian diplomacy in pursuit of these objectives. There was insistence on a literal interpretation of Wilson's national self-determination principle. It was emphasised that the new state was in no way historically or legally heir to the former Empire, thereby invalidating all possible sanctions against Austria. It was repeatedly and forcibly asserted that the new Republic was in no condition to assume crushing financial obligations. It was implied, without the threat ever being openly uttered, that humiliation might compel Austria to seek its salvation in unorthodox social experiments.

A number of recent studies have shown that these arguments did not altogether fail to make the desired impression.[1] Two points in particular, that of legal succession and that of the economic viability of Austria, led to heated arguments among the Allied and the Associated Powers. The eventual compromise, largely British-inspired, was reflected in the final version of the treaty in a manner not unfavourable to Austria.[2]

Reparations, problems affecting Austria's reconstruction, and the new economic order for the Danube basin were the points in which the discussion initially seemed to turn against the new state. The majority of peacemakers inclined towards the simple, though harsh, solution of incorporating without any changes worthy of mention the reparation provisions of the treaty with Germany into that with Austria. As is well-known, John Maynard Keynes stoutly resisted the efforts to impose on Germany and Austria impossibly high reparations payments. He viewed the draft of the Austrian reparation provisions as the acme of a ridiculous, unrealistic Allied economic policy.[3] His outlook and that of other 'doves', for all that he and they withdrew in resignation from the negotiations, did have, as will be seen, a moderating influence on the treaty's final version.

In spring 1919 Keynes had suggested to the British Treasury the dispatch to Austria of an economic and financial expert who could make an assessment of the situation. This he envisaged as a first step towards internationalizing the problem of Central Europe's reconstruction. The plan foundered on objections from the United States who, it was at this time hoped, would take the lion's share in a multinational plan of reconstruction. A comparison with the totally different American attitude after the Second World War comes to mind readily. Statesmen, it seems, are on occasion able to learn from history.

At the end of April Sir Francis Oppenheimer was after all entrusted with the mission proposed by Keynes. More especially he was, in accordance with Foreign Office ideas, to examine the situation in the light of a possible formation of a Danubian Federation.[4] He arrived at Vienna in mid-May and speedily got in touch with the Minister of Finance.[5] Schumpeter introduced him to representatives of influential industrial and financial circles. Their notions on the country's economic rehabilitation were echoed in Oppenheimer's reports to London.[6]

During the next few years several missions invested with greater powers were to follow on Oppenheimer's heels. Their initial recommendations, indubitably inspired by Schumpeter, lay in part at least at the bottom of subsequent concepts and proposals.[7]

Oppenheimer's reports had virtually no influence on the first draft of the Peace Treaty handed to the Austrian delegation on 2 June 1919. Not only the reparations clauses, but also most of the rest followed more or less closely the German model. Particular consternation was caused among the Austrian delegation by a provision that would have enabled the Successor States to expropriate the assets of Austrian companies and individuals without compensation. Such terms could not but substantially diminish the new state's chances of survival.[8]

The final draft, signed on 10 September by the delegation, was a distinctly milder version of the first draconian document. Only a brief description of the most important economic conditions can be given here; it must be preceded by a word on the treaty's political framework.[9]

Article 177 settled the question of war guilt in language conforming chiefly to the strongly felt convictions of France and the Associate Powers: 'The Allied and Associate Governments affirm and Austria accepts the responsibility of Austria and her Allies for causing the loss and damage to which the Allied and Associated Governments and their nationals have been subjected as a consequence of the war imposed upon them by the aggression of Austria-Hungary and her Allies.' This can be interpreted as the moral vindication for upholding the claim for reparations against Austria which had asserted – rightly, to the present author's mind – the status of a Successor State.[10]

Article 88 dealt with Austria's position as a member of the international community and declared Austria's independence to be 'inalienable' unless the Council of the League of Nations agreed to an abandonment of this provision. Keynes was not slow to realize the ambivalence of this apparently 'fair' solution. Instead of saying that German-Austria was forbidden to unite with Germany unless France agreed (which would not have been conformable to the principle of self-determination), he commented, the Peace Treaty skilfully circumvented the matter by a declaration which sounded quite different although it was not. And who could be certain, he added, whether President Wilson had not forgotten that another clause of the treaty insisted that a decision of this kind had to be passed unanimously.[11]

Articles 27 to 35 defined the national frontiers. The five contested Sudeten territories, Tirol south of the Brenner, and the Marburg (Maribor) basin in southern Styria were detached. A plebiscite held on 10 October 1920 decided the fate of the Klagenfurt basin in favour of Austria. In all Austria retained from the former Empire's western half of 300,000 sq. kilometres no more than 79,580, with a population of six and half million and it had to reconcile itself to the loss of more than 30,000 sq. km with a German-language population of about three million. This was offset by a modest gain of 5,055 sq. km through the acquisition of Burgenland at the expense of Hungary. During the preparation of the treaty this former associate of Austria had incurred the Allies' displeasure by its surrender to Bolshevism, but on the basis of a plebiscite it was eventually able to retain the important district of Ödenburg (Sopron). Austria now comprised 83,833 sq. km.

Articles 177 to 196 were devoted to reparations. It was recognized that the new state's resources were inadequate to assure the full compensation of the Allies for the losses and damage sustained by the actions of the Austro-Hungarian Monarchy. A Reparations Commission was created to consider 'the resources and capacity of Austria'.[12] Clearly implied, although nowhere expressly laid down, was the intention that the commission should fix the amount finally to be paid by Austria. The commission's arrival at Vienna in spring 1920 was greeted by the Viennese with optimistic curiosity rather than with the cold shoulder which might have been expected. The reason was that the impossibility of fulfilling the treaty's reparations clauses had meanwhile become evident.[13]

The fact that reparations payments could not possibly be exacted from the Austrian economy did not lessen the damages arising from the financial provisions of the treaty. The commission, in order to guarantee the reparations payments, was invested with a general lien on Austrian and Hungarian assets. Both countries were suffering, though to a very different extent, from a shortage of foodstuffs. Nevertheless there was a provision that annoyed a part of the British delegation, asking Austria and Hungary to deliver before 1 May 1921 a not inconsiderable number of dairy cows and cattle to the other Successor States.[14]

The Allies furthermore agreed among themselves to concede priority to all claims arising on 'supplies of food and raw materials for Austria and such other payments as may be judged by the Principal Allied and Associated Powers to be essential to enable Austria to meet her obligations in respect of reparations.'

This provision in Article 200 was inserted at the request of those countries which during the first half of 1919 assisted Austria with relief consignments. For the time being the Article destroyed any basis for all-too-badly needed reconstruction credits. The next part of this study will show what intricate negotiations were necessary to obtain the Allies' agreement to suspension of these conditions.

The Allies' apportionment of Austro-Hungarian debts among the countries of the former Empire displayed no inclination to consider the 'reserves and capacity' of Austria as they had promised to do in the case of reparations. Public and private financial obligations were to be liquidated according to the principles of 'legitimacy and justice', and little or no thought was to be given to the solvency of the debtor.[15] But here, too, some water of forbearance was later added to the wine of sternness. Post-treaty arrangements with respect to Austria's public and private pre-war debts brought some notable concessions to the Austrian point of view.

The Treaty distinguished between three categories of the Austro-Hungarian public debt: the pre-war debt, both secured and unsecured, contracted prior to 28 July, 1918; and war debt, contracted prior to 29 October, 1918; and the post-war debt, contracted since 27 October, 1918. Article 203 dealt with the first type of liability. It provided that each of the Successor States should assume responsibility for such portion of the secured debt as in the opinion of the Reparation Commission represents the secured debt in respect of the railways, salt mines, and other properties transferred to that state under the terms of this Treaty or conventions supplementary thereto. If, for instance, a railway was owned in equal parts by the new Austrian and Czechoslovak states, then the liability arising from the respective debt was to be distributed in like proportion among the two countries.

The distribution of the unsecured bonded debt among the heirs of the Monarchy proved a somewhat more intricate matter. Article 203 provided that each of the Successor States should assume responsibility for a portion of the unsecured debt, according to a rather complicated mode of calculation. Subsequently, the Reparation Commission assessed the liability of the Successor States in accordance with the respective yields of the principal direct and indirect taxes and the stamp and registration duties. As a result, liability for the Austrian unsecured debt was apportioned as follows:

Table 43   Apportionment of the unsecured Austrian debt in %[16]

Austria	36.827
Czechoslovakia	41.700
Poland	13.733
Italy	4.087
Yugoslavia	2.043
Romania	1.610

The Reparation Commission's assessments as to the financial capacity of former Austria's various territories coincided with certain investigations by the Central Statistical Commission. And yet the use of this data proved highly injurious to Austria because Vienna, no longer the major commercial and administrative centre of an empire, had current financial receipts in no way comparable to those of the last pre-war years. Still more oppressive were those provisions of Article 203 that dealt with the valuation of the liabilities. Had a debt been incurred in a foreign currency, repayment was to be in that same currency. Had it been payable in Austro-Hungarian gold coin, settlement was to be in equivalent amounts of pounds sterling or gold dollars. Had it been contracted in Austro-Hungarian paper crowns, it must be converted into the currency of the Successor State at the rate at which those crowns were exchanged into the currency of the assuming state by that state when it first substituted its own currency for Austro-Hungarian crowns. This final provision contained the important addition that the 'basis of this conversion of the currency unit in which the bonds are expressed shall be subject to the approval of the Reparation Commission, which shall, if it thinks fit, require the State effecting the conversion to modify the terms thereof'. In everyday language this signified that the commission was empowered to protect the Successor States' foreign creditors against losses arising from the depreciation of the currency.

When the provision on the valuation of pre-war debts became known at Vienna spirits fell another few points beneath their persistent low. Although the pre-war debt might seem slight as compared with the huge financial burdens assumed in wartime, its redemption involved precious foreign exchange and anyway would worsen the new Austria's unfavourable balance of payments still more. The settlement on unsecured pre-war debt took place in 1923 and 1925 at conferences held in Innsbruck and Prague. The relief it afforded Austria compared with the original treaty draft was quite substantial.[17]

Article 205 treated the question of Austria's war debt. Since this was almost exclusively in the hands of the Empire's former nationals, the Allies were in a better position to be more accommodating to the Austrian viewpoint. The Successor States held that only the Austrian and the Hungarian Governments were liable to defray the war debt since the Peace Treaties defined them as the Empire's sole heirs. The Austrian Government argued that it was not in a position to shoulder a proportion of wartime obligations which would exceed its own share of the Empire's assets. It wanted, in other words, a settlement based on economic, not juridical, considerations. In the end the Allies decided in favour of the so-called territorial solution. Austria was to be liable only for that portion of war debt which was actually held by its own nationals or those of states outside the Empire's boundaries.[18] The other states were to withdraw War Loan securities and to replace them with new certificates. This did not imply an obligation to redeem their share of the war debt. The decision on that was left to each individual Successor State. However, even though they might decline to honour the Empire's war debt, no claim thereby arose for their nationals against Austria.[19]

The peacemakers' ruling as to the third part of the Austro-Hungarian state debt was simple. On the assumption that the Empire had been dismembered on 27 October 1918, the stocks issued after that date by the new governments of Austria and Hungary were regarded as their exclusive affair.

The foregoing treaty provisions did not relate to the securities of the Austrian and Hungarian Governments deposited with the Central Bank to serve as legal cover against the note issue. Securities of this type were viewed as an element in the overall settlement of the exceptionally complex problem presented by the Austro-Hungarian currency. Theoretically the peacemakers could have pursued one of two approaches. They could uphold the old monetary union, a solution favoured by Schumpeter and Vienna financial circles, or they could take the dissolution of the former community to its logical conclusion and recognize the monetary independence of the individual states. In the early post-war chauvinistic atmosphere the second course alone was of practical importance. Austria, Czechoslovakia, and Yugoslavia had already at the time of the treaty introduced their own monetary systems. The Allies had hardly any choice but to give these measures their subsequent sanction and to urge the other Successor States to endorse with their stamp those Austro-Hungarian banknotes still in circulation within their territories. (See Article 206)

As with the settlement of the war debts, it was similarly left to the Successor States to replace the former banknotes in whatever manner they pleased. Article 206 established moreover that the 'currency notes issued by the bank on or prior to October 27, 1918 . . . shall all rank equally as claims against all assets of the bank', a decision naturally to the disadvantage of the Austro-Hungarian Bank's owners and of holders of current accounts. The securities deposited with the central bank by the Austrian and Hungarian Governments to serve as a cover for the notes issued up to and including 27 October were declared invalid. Banknotes brought into circulation after 27 October were considered as liabilities of the new Austrian and Hungarian Governments.[20] The latter had to assume liability for notes issued before 27 October and on 15 June 1919 still outside the borders of the former Empire.[21]

The liquidation of the Austro-Hungarian Bank was to be conducted by receivers appointed by the Reparation Commission. Its stamped banknotes, which all the Successor States including Austria and Hungary had to surrender to the commission by a certain date, were to be balanced against the Bank's assets minus the bonds issued by the Empire and declared invalid in accordance with Article 206. The Bank's most coveted asset was of course its bullion reserve. At the end of 1918 it amounted to a mere 261 million crowns, that is, little more than a half per cent of the total banknote circulation including sight liabilities.[22] The Austrian representatives argued that legally the Bank's gold reserve belonged to the Austrian Government and they referred to the territorial clauses of Article 208 which seemed to allow for this view.[23]

Article 206 proved unsuitable as a basis for liquidation of the Austro-Hungarian Bank. It was replaced by agreements between the Successor States contained in the main protocol and two supplementary protocols dated 14 March 1922. The Austrian Parliament sanctioned these on 24 April 1922. The Austrian share in the Bank's net assets amounted under this settlement to some 35 million gold crowns.[24]

Articles 248 and 249 dealt with the property of Austrian nationals in the countries of the Allied and Associated Powers as well as with the problem of private debts. The treaty's original draft had, as has been mentioned, envisaged the total liquidation of Austrian property in the Allied and Successor State territories. The Austrian Delegation offered vehement resistance to this truly Carthaginian clause.[25] The final version did not drop the confiscatory terms of Article 249, but by the insertion of Article 267 its application was restricted to territories outside the borders of the former Empire.[26] Thus the frontal assault of the Successor States on the financial hegemony of the former imperial capital was successfully repulsed.

Article 248 distinguished between two kinds of private obligations, liabilities by Austrian debtors to nationals of the Successor States and those against all other foreign creditors. The latter enjoyed the same preferential treatment as foreign holders of Austrian public debt. Debts were repayable in the original currency or, if incurred in Austro-Hungarian crowns, in the currency of the creditor's country and 'at the pre-war rate of exchange'. The provision fell especially hard on the second category of debtors since it could be assumed that only a few individuals or companies had taken adequate precautions against the crown's depreciation. The final arrangement was comparatively favourable for Austrian private interests. In summer 1920 and in subsequent years British and French creditors made notable concessions in regard to the terms of repayment and the Austrian Government also assumed responsibility for a considerable portion of private indebtedness.[27] As for the liabilities to Successor States nationals, the mutual obligations of Austrians on the one hand and of Czechs and Poles on the other were to be settled by private agreements or, failing any other solution, by arbitration through the Reparation Commission. In respect of the other Danubian states the treaty simply provided that mutual obligations should be resolved at the crown's average rate of exchange in September and October 1918. Nor was this solution unfavourable to Austria either. Its nationals did owe firms in the Successor States substantial amounts in crowns for foodstuffs and raw materials deliveries, but they could in turn claim similar amounts in crowns for their capital investments in those countries.[28]

Turning to the treaty's provisions designed to settle the commercial relations of Austria with the victorious Powers, a start may well be made by reference to the third of President Wilson's famous Fourteen Points. It contemplated 'the removal, as far as possible, of all economic barriers and the establishment of an equality of trade conditions among all the nations consenting to the peace'.

Application of the Wilsonian principle would have precluded all discriminatory economic provisions from the peace treaties. But these treaties were obviously more inspired by the spirit of the Paris Economic Conference held in June 1918 than by the American President's principles. The gist of the resolution of the conference, contained in a document signed by the representatives of France, Belgium, Italy, Japan, Portugal and Russia, and subsequently given British approval, was summarized by Sir Harold Temperley as follows:

They looked forward to an economic alliance of the Allies based in large part upon joint measures of discrimination against the trade of the enemy powers. For the period of reconstruction following the war they proposed to grant priorities in respect of supplies to the Allied countries and especially to the invaded regions, to refuse most-favoured-nation treatment to the enemy countries, to prohibit or restrict importations from those countries, and to exclude enemy subjects from industrial and professional activities in Allied territories. As a permanent policy, the Allies were to take steps to free themselves of any economic dependence on enemy countries, and, without undertaking to grant reciprocal reductions in tariffs, they were to adopt measures for facilitating their mutual trade relations.[29]

Austria, Hungary, and Bulgaria had to grant legal and natural persons of the Allied countries the same rights as their own nationals in trade, industrial and taxation matters. The Allied and Associated states had to be accorded for a period of three years a *unilateral* most-favoured-nation treatment.[30] The victorious Powers were moreover conceded complete equality in all matters related to customs, export and import restrictions, and trade embargoes. Even discrimination by indirect means, like differential duties and differing customs regulations, modalities of payment of duties, tariff classifications, and so on, was forbidden. Similarly all exceptions and privileges enjoyed by any country for the export, import, and transit of goods had to be extended automatically to all Allied and Associated states.[31] Article 284 ensured freedom of transit. A unilateral application of the most-favoured-nation principle was also to hold good for the Austrian railways.[32] The Danube was declared an international waterway. No distinction would be permitted between the treatment of the nationals of the riparian states and their property and that of other countries. Membership of the European Commission which controlled the Danube estuary, was confined by the Danube Convention of 1921 to representatives of Great Britain, France, Italy, and Romania. That meant that only one riparian state had a vote in the affairs of this important body. Delegates from the riparian states sat, together with the members of the European Commission, on the International Commission which had jurisdiction from Ulm to Braila.[33]

It is probably no exaggeration to say that the provisions of the Treaty of Saint-Germain relating to trade were faithfully reproduced from the Treaty of Versailles. Common to both was the thinly disguised Allied intention to take advantage of their current political and military preponderance for the promotion of their commercial and industrial interests.[34] The Allied Economic Commission examined, at the instance of the Austrian Delegation, the question of whether a preferential status could be accorded to Austria, Czechoslovakia, and Hungary in respect of tariff policy. Even the possibility of a customs union comprising all the territories of the former Empire was given serious consideration. Italy rightly pointed out that the realization of this project would necessitate the establishment by itself and certain Successor States of internal tariff barriers.[35] Britain and France, understandably concerned for a stable political order in the Danube basin, backed the plan for preferential tariff relations between the three states named by Austria, but they did not commit themselves very deeply. Czechoslovakia and Hungary, on the other hand, suspected in every initiative of this kind an attempt by Vienna to resuscitate its old leading position.

In the end there was a compromise. The well-known Article 222 in the Treaty of Saint-Germain (Article 205 in the Treaty of Trianon with Hungary) provided for the possibility of establishing a preferential tariff system between Austria, Czechoslovakia, and Hungary for a period of five years. The negative attitude of Czechoslovakia and Hungary rendered this provision a dead letter. Many years later Antonin Basch, in a retrospect on events in the Danube basin during the inter-war years, wrote that clearly these provisions should have been declared mandatory and should have been extended to all the Successor States.[36]

A similar fate attended Article 224. Czechoslovakia and Poland were for fifteen years to assure Austria coal supplies on most-favoured-nation terms in quantities approximating pre-war figures. Austria was in return to supply a certain quantity of unspecified raw materials. (Probably iron ore, magnesite, and timber were meant.) In 1921 Gustav Stolper remarked on the article's practical significance, 'In fact our food industry in 1920 received only 4%, the iron industry 35%, the paper industry 23%, the leather industry 25%, the chemical industry 15%, the textile industry 12% of their normal requirement.'[37] During the succeeding years Austria's coal supply improved, but in response to forces which stood in no causal relation to the treaty's provision.

In this connection Karl Stadler's study refers to Article 208 of the Treaty of Trianon which laid down that for a period of five years Hungary would impose neither duties nor other restrictions on the export of food to Austria. Austrian importers of foodstuffs should be able to obtain these on the same conditions as buyers in Hungary or elsewhere. 'The importance of this article,' Stadler correctly emphasizes, 'was not only that it represented an additional relief measure for starving Austria, but that the Allies thereby acknowledged the complementary character of the central European economy.'[38]

The Austrian Government decided to sign the Peace Treaty because it was convinced that in the prevailing political circumstances no more favourable terms were to be obtained and that Austria must be prepared for the sake of peace to pay the high price demanded. Mgr Hauser, the Christian Socialist chairman of the Constituent Assembly, moving the treaty's acceptance, expressed the official viewpoint. 'The National Assembly has no other choice. Nation and people need the peace which morally and economically again gives access to the world . . . There is also no choice because our country depends on the Great Powers for the supply of food, coal, and industrial raw materials as well as for the restoration of its credit and its currency. Even though it regards the Treaty of Saint-Germain as nationally unjust, politically disastrous, and economically unworkable, the National Assembly must take this exigency into account.'[39]

In truth the Peace Treaty, even in its revised, 'milder' form, imposed a heavy, barely tolerable burden on Austria. At the same time it contributed to the creation in central and eastern Europe of a political landscape offering the new state scant chances of survival.[40] Keynes rightly recognized that the League of Nations could by itself not ensure the lasting existence of the new political order born of the Parisian treaties. An additional institution – a large free trade zone – would have been necessary to put the peace order on a sound footing.[41]

The peacemakers' sins of commission and omission have been pithily, aptly summarized by Richard Schüller: 'The dismemberment of the Austro-Hungarian economic area into seven parts was a fact before conclusion of the Peace, occasioned by the Empire's political collapse. The Peace Treaty gave it legal sanction without . . . creating conditions for the maintenance of the economic connexion between these territories or even making provision for a rational economic and financial liquidation of their mutual relations.'[42]

Notes

1 Particularly valuable among these studies are those by Karl R. Stadler, *Hypothek auf die Zukunft* (Vienna, 1968); Marie-Luise Recker, *England und der Donauraum 1919–1929, Probleme einer europäischen Nachkriegsordnung* (Stuttgart, 1976), Vol. III in the series of publications by the German Historical Institute, London; Robert Hoffmann, *Die Mission Sir Thomas Cunninghames in Wien 1919, Britische Österreichpolitik zur Zeit der Pariser Friedenskonferenz* (dissertation, Salzburg, 1971); Hanns Haas, *Österreich-Ungarn als Friedensproblem. Aspekte der Friedensregelung auf dem Gebiet der Habsburgermonarchie in den Jahren 1918–1919* (dissertation, Salzburg, 1968); Fritz Fellner, 'Die Pariser Vororteverträge von 1919/20', in *Versailles-St. Germain-Trianon*, ed. Karl Bosl (Munich and Vienna, 1971).

2 The British delegate Headlam Morley, for instance, proposed the inclusion in the preamble of a sentence that Austria was a 'free, sovereign, independent and friendly State' which for its part renounced all claims ensuing on the succession to the Habsburg Monarchy. He agreed however to the compromise formulated by the Italian Foreign Minister, Vittorio Orlando, that 'the former Austro-Hungarian Monarchy has ceased to exist and that a republican government has taken its place in Austria.' Cf. Robert Hoffmann, 'Die wirtschaftlichen Grundlagen der britischen Österreichpolitik 1919', *Mitteilungen des Österreichischen Staatsarchivs* (Vienna, 1977), p. 277.

3 Hoffmann, *Mitteilungen*, p. 270. Significant of Keynes' views is a passage in a

note to Sir Maurice Hankey (Secretary to the Imperial War Cabinet). He condemned the draft as a document giving the impression of a purely academic exercise which lacked any relationship to the really shocking state of affairs in Austria. To look at the German treaty and to substitute in the text Austria for Germany without allowing for the immense differences in the situation might be a concession to the mentality prevailing at this tired-out conference, but it would result in meaningless, virtually worthless conclusions. Hoffmann, *Mitteilungen.*

4 Cf. Francis Oppenheimer, *Stranger Within. Autobiographical Pages* (London, 1965), p. 366.

5 Cf. Part IV, Chap. 3, p. 331.

6 To the Austrians it was clear, Oppenheimer reported in a telegram to Keynes, that without assistance from outside to put their house in order they had come to the end of both their financial and their economic tether. Outside assistance would have to be synonymous with complete control. The Minister of Finance was insisting that the Allies should establish a strong financial supervisory body at Vienna armed with a receiver's discretionary powers and able to dispose over long-term reconstruction loans on favourable terms. Direction of the central bank, in whatever shape, should also be assumed. Furthermore he had spoken of a financial administration, on modified lines and to the extent that Austrian pride would not be too wounded by the detailed provisions of such a system, as was operated in Egypt. Hoffmann, *Mitteilungen*, p. 268 et seq.

7 Long term Western loans, a new central bank under foreign ascendancy, and far-reaching control rights by creditor states were the cornerstones of most recovery plans formulated subsequently.

8 In a telegram to Keynes on 23 May 1919 Oppenheimer commented that a draft with financial provisions of this kind must appear to anyone even only superficially acquainted with current conditions in Austria as being founded on erroneous premises. Hoffmann, *Mitteilungen*, p. 270. Cunninghame, head of the British Military Mission, reported from Vienna that the right to confiscate Austrian property in the Successor States had had a 'stunning effect' on the Austrian public. Hoffmann, p. 276.

9 A detailed analysis of the Peace Treaty's provisions is contained in H. W. V. Temperley's *A History of the Peace Conference at Paris* (London, 1920–24), Vol. V, pp. 1–108, and in Karl R. Stadler, *Hypothek auf die Zukunft* (Vienna, 1968).

10 A note by the Allied and Associated Powers accompanying the peace terms of 2 September 1919 said, among other things, '... the war was acclaimed from the moment of its declaration at Vienna, the Austrian people have been ardent partisans from beginning to end, it has done nothing to separate itself from the policies of its government and of its allies until their defeat on the field of battle, proof sufficient that according to the sacred rules of justice Austria should be made to assume its entire share of responsibility for the crime which has unchained upon the world such a calamity.' Quoted from Nina Almond and Ralph H. Lutz (ed.), *The Treaty of St Germain, A Documentary History of Its Territorial and Political Clauses* (Stanford, 1935), p. 244. The circumstance diligently disregarded in the note was that the war on the side of the Central Powers was supported to the bitter end not only by the German-speaking Austrians, but also by the great majority of the Slav nations. The January 1918 strike, briefly mentioned earlier, assumed its biggest and for the war's continuation most disquieting dimensions in Vienna and in the industrial towns of the

Vienna basin. What must not be overlooked however is that the Successor States had been obliged to make 'liberation payments', to be rendered to the Allies in compensation for the 'liberation' of the territories assigned to them. Recker, *England*, p. 122.

11 J. M. Keynes, *The Economic Consequences of the Peace* (London, 1919), p. 50.

12 Cf. Article 180 of the Treaty. No analogous reference to the 'resources and capacity' is contained in the Treaty of Versailles.

13 'It is reported that the people of Vienna, hearing that a section of the Reparation Commission is about to visit them, have decided characteristically to pin their hopes on it. A financial body can obviously take nothing from them, for they have nothing; therefore this body must be for the purpose of assisting and relieving them. Thus do the Viennese argue, still light-hearted in adversity.' Keynes, *Economic Consequences*, p. 219.

14 Two years later, though, Richard Schüller, in his capacity as a senior civil servant, was able to state that Austria had still not complied with this demand. 'It has become evident that currently Austria is not only incapable of making any payments or contributions in kind, but that it could in fact not exist at all without the receipt of food from abroad for which it cannot pay.' Schüller, 'Wirtschaftliche Bestimmungen des Friedensvertrages von Saint-Germain', *Zeitschrift für Volkswirtschaft und Sozialpolitik*, New Series, Vol. I., 1921, p. 42.

15 'It was argued by the Austrian Delegation that the general effect of the financial clauses would be to make Austria bankrupt, and this view was supported to some extent by other authorities. The answer was that in the distribution of the liabilities and assets of the Dual Monarchy among its constituent parts, Austria was given the share that was *justly* hers. If, in the end, she was not in a position to meet her liabilities, the bankruptcy that followed would not be caused by the financial clauses, but by Austria's past history. It was the aim of the conference to make such an agreement as should be fair to all the parties concerned, and if bankruptcy was an inevitable consequence, at least to make that bankruptcy as far as possible an internal and not an external bankruptcy.' Temperley, *History*, Vol. V, p. 20. (Present author's italics.)

16 Leo Pasvolsky, *Economic Nationalism of the Danubian States* (New York, 1928), pp. 42–4.

17 For a general account of the principles determining distribution of the Empire's state debts, cf. A. N. Sack, *Le Mode de repartition des dettes autrichiennes et hongroises* (Paris, 1927).

18 War debt in the possession of nationals outside the former Empire's boundaries affected German nationals almost exclusively.

19 Marie-Luise Recker rightly holds that these provisions were of little practical effect. 'In Austria and Hungary the problem of debt redemption was for practical purposes solved at the cost of creditors by inflation . . . The Yugoslav and Romanian treasuries were likewise, by reason of an extremely disadvantageous conversion rate and of the War Loan bonds not being honoured, hardly burdened by these commitments. At Prague, on the other hand, the government decided to honour these obligations at least partially and linked them to a domestic bond issue and a capital levy.' Recker, *England und der Donauraum*, p. 124.

20 The attempt to implement this provision showed it to be impossible to distinguish between banknotes issued before and after 27 October 1918. The question had to be settled by a special covenant. Cf. Rašin, *Die Finanz- und wirtschaftspolitik der*

Tschechoslowakei (Munich, Leipzig, 1923), p. 62.

21 The problem was solved by the Austrian and the Hungarian Governments each placing 2.5 million gold crowns from their share of the liquidation proceeds at the disposal of the notes' owners. See Nationalrat Shorthand Minutes, Annotation 1170 to the Appendixes, 1922, Vol. III, p. 26.

22 Cf. Jan van Walré de Bordes, *The Austrian Crown, Its Depreciation and Stabilization* (London, 1924), p. 53.

23 The relevant passage in Article 208 runs, 'States to which territory of the former Austro-Hungarian Monarchy is transferred and States arising from the dismemberment of that Monarchy shall acquire all property and possessions situated within their territories belonging to the former or existing Austrian Government. For the purposes of this Article, the property and possessions of the former or existing Austrian Government shall be deemed to include the property of the former Austrian Empire and the interests of that Empire in the joint property of the Austro-Hungarian Monarchy, as well as all property of the Crown, and the private property of members of the former Royal Family of Austria-Hungary. These States shall, however, have no claim to any property of the former or existing government of Austria situated outside their own respective territories.' The Austrian Government's standpoint was supported by three experts who admittedly were civil servants. See Ministry of Finance Archives, File 30.976/1921.

24 Nationalrat Shorthand Minutes, Annotation 1170 to the Appendixes, 1922, Vol. III, p. 23. For a more detailed discussion of the liquidation problem, see A. Zeuceanu, *La Liquidation de la Banque d'Autriche-Hongrie* (Vienna, 1924).

25 The Austrian Delegation replied, *inter alia*, 'As it seems to us, these unheard-of stipulations and others of a similar nature can spring only from a very strange notion: the terms which the victorious states would like to impose on a great conquered power have evidently been applied to the relationship between our new State and the other parts of the former Austro-Hungarian Monarchy with which we were united, until the time of her collapse, by the same political and economic interests . . . It is not only that such a procedure would wrest from us all the remaining securities indispensable to the acquisition of the necessities of life for our inhabitants, but that it would also result in the financial collapse of the State, of all the banks, savings banks, and insurance companies, as well as most of the private enterprises.' Cf. Almond & Lutz, *The Treaty*, p. 207.

26 The relevant passage in Article 267 says, 'Notwithstanding the provisions of Article 249 and the Appendix to Section IV the property, rights and interests of Austrian nationals or companies controlled by them situated in the territories which formed part of the former Austro-Hungarian Monarchy shall not be subject to retention or liquidation in accordance with those provisions.'

27 'By the end of 1924 settlements to a total of £4 million had been agreed upon between British creditors and Austrian pre-war debtors – at least three-quarters of this figure by the borrowing of fresh loans. About ten per cent was compensated by the assignment of Austrian claims on British debtors. Rather less than £500,000 was paid in cash. Austria was able to arrange similar settlements with France, Belgium, and Italy.' Friedrich Hertz, 'Zahlungsbilanz und Lebensfähigkeit Österreichs', *Schriften des Vereins für Sozialpolitik* (Munich-Leipzig, 1925), Vol. 167, p. 35. Karl Ausch thinks that the valorization provision concerning pre-war debts owed to foreign creditors had the regrettable consequence that Öster-

reichische Länderbank and Anglo-Österreichische Bank eventually passed into foreign hands. Cf. Ausch, *Als die Banken fielen* (Vienna, 1968), p. 9. See also Part V of this study.

28 Final settlement of the matters treated in Articles 248 and 249 was reached in bilateral agreements. In August 1921 a convention was concluded with France on the treatment of loans payable in crowns. Other conventions, followed later. Cf. *Der Österreichische Volkswirt*, 13 August 1921, p. 864 et seq.

29 Temperley, *History*, Vol. V, p. 64.

30 Germany in this respect was worse off too inasmuch as it had to concede this privilege to the Allies for five years.

31 Cf. Articles 217–220.

32 A part of Article 312 reads as follows: 'Goods coming from the territories of the Allied and Associated Powers and going to Austria, or in transit through Austria, from or to the territories of the Allied and Associated Powers, shall enjoy on the Austrian railways as regards charges to be collected . . . facilities, and all other matters, the most favorable treatment applied to goods of the same kind carried on any Austrian lines, either in internal traffic or for export, import, or in transit.'

33 Articles 291–308 deal with Danube shipping and its administration.

34 'In reply to the Austrian complaint about lack of reciprocity, the Allies answered on 8 July that "the circumstances arising from the war" excluded for the Allies the possibility of "opening their markets immediately to Austrian products on conditions in every respect as favourable as those which they are in a position to grant other nations". They were however prepared to content themselves' with a restrictive period of 'three years'. Stadler, *Hypothek*, p. 218.

35 'The alternative, to include in their entirety all states which were heirs to the Empire, would have created a kind of customs union stretching from Danzig to Sicily. The notion frightened the Czechs, and Mr Balfour thought that such a solution would afford the participant states greater privileges than the Habsburg Monarchy had ever had.' Stadler, *Hypothek*, p. 219.

36 Antonin Basch, *The Danubian Basin and the German Economic Sphere* (New York, 1943), p. 32. A little more than six years later the London *Economist*, in its issue of 16 December 1925, remarking that not much had recently been heard about plans for a Danube confederation, commented that the real argument against the project lay in the fact, to which Dr Beneš had not long ago referred, that nobody wanted it. Cf. Basch, *Danubian Basin*, p. 33, footnote 24.

37 Gustav Stolper, 'Der Friedensvertrag von St. Germain in seinen wirtschaftlichen Wirkungen', *Schriften des Vereins für Sozialpolitik* (Munich-Leipzig, 1921), Vol. 162, p. 10. As a result of the delay over ratification of the Peace Treaty, Austria was in 1920 still dependent on the European Coal Commission's relief measures.

38 Stadler, *Hypothek*, p. 222.

39 Leopold Kunschak, *Österreich 1918–1934* (Vienna, 1934), p. 57.

40 Two years later one of the experts on trade in the Danubian area felt it necessary to say that 'The state of affairs created by the Peace Treaty has been aggravated by the veto policy of the central European nations far and above the degree envisaged by the Powers at the conclusion of peace.' Schüller, *Zeitschrift*, p. 39 et seq.

41 Keynes, *Economic Consequences*, p. 216 et seq.

42 Schüller, *Zeitschrift*, p. 36.

PART FIVE

Inflation and Stabilization

CHAPTER I

Dissolution of the Social Democrat-Christian Socialist Coalition

On 10 September 1919 the Treaty of Saint-Germain-en-Laye was signed. One month later on 17 October Chancellor Dr Karl Renner formed his second cabinet. The government's prestige had suffered badly from acceptance of the Peace Treaty. So had that of the Social Democratic Party, generally regarded as the main protagonist of the Coalition Government. The establishment of a new administration appeared imperative.

Two prominent ministers in the preceding government were no longer members of the new one. In August Otto Bauer had resigned as Foreign Minister, a step that admitted the failure of his *Anschluss* policy. The summer months had moreover plainly shown that his hopes for a European revolution and the breakdown of the Peace Conference were untenable.[1] In October he withdrew from the Socialization Commission, from which he could hardly expect any further progress.[2] The other retiring Minister was Joseph Schumpeter. The so-called Alpine-Montan Affair had damaged his relations with the Social Democratic Party practically beyond repair. As an independent his resignation, without firm backing from the Christian Socialists, was inevitable.

The retirement of these two personalities made no essential difference to the government's political composition, but the second Renner cabinet must nonetheless be rated as a totally new political entity. Neither the Christian Socialists nor the Social Democrats could be blind to the changes in domestic and external affairs since the formation of the first Catholic-Socialist Coalition. After the collapse of the Hungarian Soviet régime the danger of further communist incursions into central Europe seemed banished for the moment. In western Europe, where the post-war crisis had not assumed so critical a character, the return to normal conditions proceeded speedily. Austria could not remain unaffected by these international trends.

They gave fresh strength to the conservative forces which had begun to stir again in spring 1919.

In February 1919 the Social Democrats had owed their election victory in large measure to their ability to attract, in addition to the hard-core working-class vote, the support of strategically important middle-class groups. Most of these new supporters soon deserted them. The farmers continued to resist fiercely every measure that could be connected with the loathed wartime régime and waged a bitter guerilla campaign against the workers' councils wherever the latter sporadically tried, and normally failed, to requisition food supplies. That alone would have been enough to alienate the property-conscious peasantry from their new socialist allies. Their defection was distinctly accelerated when agricultural labour fell under the influence of trades union organizers.[3] Among the factors contributing to the rapid decline of the Social Democratic Party in predominantly rural districts was also the influence of the Roman Catholic clergy.

The growing anger of the peasants against the 'revolutionary' government in Vienna had one important sequel – consolidation in the ranks of the Christian Socialist Party. After the Empire's disintegration a rift had occurred between the urban and the agrarian wing of this party. The second Renner government saw the party acting once more as a disciplined, united force.[4]

The urban middle class was likewise deeply disillusioned. Socialism and *Anschluss* had been the watchword inspiring fresh hope among broad sections of the intelligentsia after their old world had fallen apart. The Social Democrats could deliver neither socialism nor *Anschluss*. Their party was however thought to be the main dynamo of revolution and it was consequently held more and more responsible for the hardship and misery of the transition period whose principal victims were members of the middle class. While workers could balance the social achievements of the early days of the Republic against current deprivations, businessmen, civil servants, employees, and those in the professions could register no gains at all. To them the Republic meant rapid depreciation of the currency and therefore loss of their savings, shrinkage of their real incomes to a fraction of their original purchasing power, forfeiture of the esteem which the middle class had enjoyed in a powerful Empire, and the prospect of difficult, uncertain years inside the Republic's modest confines. It may appear unjust to have made the Social Democrat leadership answerable for the completion of a tragedy in whose beginning it had played so small a part. Nevertheless, as so often in history, the drudgery of daily life lent the past a false halo. The result was the gradual return by a large portion of the urban middle class to the conservative camp whose atmosphere corresponded much more to their intellectual disposition. The Social Democrats had sought the alliance with their political opponents because it was necessary, according to Friedrich Adler, 'that the middle class should carry a substantial part of the responsibility for the consequences of the horrors of war'.[5]

If the socialist leadership had expected that the government's certain loss of popularity would be evenly distributed between the coalition parties, this hope very soon proved deceptive. The Christian Socialists had participated in the first Renner government, but they had managed astonishingly well to deflect onto their partners the criticism for the republican régime's short-comings. Their non-commital attitude to *Anschluss*, to socialization, to the capital levy, and so on, was a classic example of how to participate in a coalition without accepting full responsibility for its policy. That prominent Social Democrats should towards the end of 1919 have begun to 'think aloud' about the sense of such an arrangement from the viewpoint of their own party is hardly surprising.[6]

Certain changes in the socialist camp, in addition to the defection of its middle class and peasant supporters, weakened the Social Democrat position in the second Renner government. In summer 1919 the food situation had appreciably improved.[7] Fuels and raw materials were still very scarce, but plants could be increasingly supplied. The figure of 186,030 unemployed on 1 May had been a record high. By August the figure dropped to 133,362. In October and November it fell to 112,375 and 87,266 respectively.[8] Nutritional improvement and the decline in unemployment was accompanied by a subsiding of the unrest prevalent among working people during the first half-year. The defeat of the Hungarian republic also had a sobering effect on them and strengthened the Social Democrat reformist wing. After the formation of the new Coalition in October it was clear that the party had lost the dynamic impetus it had possessed in spring.

At the beginning of the Socialist-Catholic honeymoon the socialist leadership had exercised a preponderant influence on legislation. Some long-cherished ideas had been realized. The Christian Socialists had played the role of a 'moderating', loyal partner. Initially only purely socialist-inspired bills met with their cautious, later ever more outspoken objection.[9] As 1919 ran its course, the weight of parliamentary activity shifted from problems of social to financial and monetary reform. Here too it seemed as though, apart from a few concessions to the Christian Socialists' agrarian wing, Social Democrat policy would on the whole gain acceptance. In the early months of 1920 personal and business taxes were raised considerably. March saw the first preparations for introduction of a steeply progressive capital levy.[10] The government repeatedly intimated its intention to get hold in some, not precisely specified manner, of the 'hard' foreign exchange and foreign securities hoarded abroad during the months following the Empire's disintegration.

Agreement by the coalition parties on the need for total mobilization of all assets for the sake of putting the nation on its financial feet was evidently widespread. Yet agreement on the practical application of the principle could not be achieved. The Social Democrats adhered to the idea that the capital levy should serve as a bridgehead in the struggle for socialism. They insisted that the Goldscheid proposal to issue new shares on the state's behalf should form a part of the levy.[11] The Christian Socialists would not hear of it. Their ideological backbone was of course greatly stiffened by the downfall of Communism in Hungary. Far from acquiescing in an extension of state influence in the economy, it advocated a quick return to the *laissez-faire* principles of pre-war days. Moreover, the agrarian wing stubbornly resisted any attempt to impose even the most modest capital levy on their own following. Schumpeter's recovery programme had tried to harmonize the socialist and conservative standpoints. He met Social Democrat demands by proposing a capital levy requiring certain sacrifices from both urban and rural populations and he took the Christian Socialist outlook into account by envisaging a gradual return to a market economy. However, when in 1919 he published his plan, both parties felt strong enough to decline any compromise.

With the forces of Left and Right in equilibrium, the prospects for the success of a new financial reform plan were dim. The new Finance Minister, Dr Richard Reisch, a non-party expert like his predecessor, circumvented the dilemma by restricting himself in his introductory statement to undisputed commonplaces. Concentrating on individual measures such as higher taxes, foreign loans, a balanced budget and a sensible monetary policy to be followed by the establishment of a new central bank, he emphasised the long-planned requisition of securities, gold, and foreign exchange deposited by Austrian nationals in banks abroad. That earned him a sharp retort from the financial press.[12] The remarks on a capital levy seemed to comply with Social Democrat wishes because urban and rural property was to be burdened to the same degree. As big a slice of the receipts as possible was to be used for the procurement of foreign exchange, but in the main the levy was conceived as a means towards discharging the war debt, the provision of cover for current deficits, and ensuring influence for the state over undertakings that were particularly important to the economy.

As van Sickle rightly says, 'This pronouncement left ample room for disputes as to detail, and it was on details that the struggle in the cabinet, in committee, and in Parliament turned.'[13]

The minister's proposals were passed to the appropriate parliamentary committees and for the first half of 1920 remained there out of public sight. Meanwhile the food and fuel stocks, a little more plentiful in summer and early autumn, again became alarmingly scarce. The government, with only a small quantity of foreign exchange at its disposal, had no choice other than to pay for the necessary purchases with paper currency. In these somewhat unorthodox commercial practices it found itself in competition with the provincial administrations, which were still devoted to the principle of sovereignty in economic matters, as well as with various private importers engaged in illegal trading.[14]

The breakdown of the government's import controls, the uninterrupted flight of capital, and the manipulations of domestic as well as foreign speculators put severe pressure on the crown's exchange rate. Schumpeter's interventions in spring and summer had effected a certain stability. After their cessation the price of the currency began to drop at an alarming rate. At the end of August it stood at 42.50 to the dollar. Publication of the Peace Treaty boosted the dollar quotation to 67 in the third week of September. Henceforward the crown fell constantly and steadily until the first week of December when it reached a record low of 135 to the dollar.[15]

Although delay was now dangerous, the party representatives in the various parliamentary committees could still not agree on a common approach. The government had practically no option but again to turn to the Allies. On 6 December Renner, in his twofold capacity of Chancellor and Foreign Minister, appeared before the Allied Council at Paris and movingly described Austria's plight: 'In three weeks Vienna will be without bread and flour.'[16] His plea ended with an appeal not to let the country perish in a dreadful catastrophe. The Allies' immediate reaction was disappointing.[17] They arranged for 30,000 tons of bread grains to be dispatched from a stockpile at Trieste and so for a brief span to ease the food shortage. They gave their approval to the contacts made by the government with a Dutch banking group for the floatation of a private loan in foreign capital markets. And, to facilitate this move, they signified their readiness to release those of Austria's assets and receipts pledged to the victorious Powers by the terms of the Peace Treaty. This was, however, an all-too-often repeated promise redeemed only after two and half years of inflation.[18]

The poor success of the negotiations at Paris accelerated the crown's decline. At year-end the dollar stood in Vienna at 155. In January 1920 it soared to the dizzy height of 271. The next month seemed to bring brighter prospects. On 3 February the Reparation Commission announced its intention of establishing an Austrian committee in Vienna with the task of working out a detailed national reconstruction plan. At the beginning of April the government obtained a relief loan for 200,000 tons of American wheat.[19] This enabled it to resume interventionist operations on the Zurich and Vienna foreign exchange markets.[20] The dollar rate fell from its January peak to 138.57 crowns in mid-June, a reduction of almost fifty per cent.[21]

This sensational recovery was no more than the upshot of several outstandingly fortunate circumstances, but it granted the government its longed-for respite. Here was the opportunity to clear up the fundamental economic incongruities endemic to the situation. But this chance too was missed, mainly due to the continuing deadlock within the coalition. Towards the end of June the factors which had earlier had such an adverse influence on the crown's exchange rate became operative again.

Signs of the imminent dissolution of the coalition multiplied during spring. The ship of state had really been rudderless since the formation of the second Renner administration because the Social Democrats were no longer, and the Christian Socialists not yet, able to gain a decisive preponderance. In the light of the essentially conservative composition of the parliament where Christian Socialists and German Nationalists together had a majority, the transition to a policy of a decidedly conservative character instead of the prevailing dangerous drift was a logical, probably unavoidable development. Pressure for a clarification of the situation did not only come from the conservative elements. Among the Social Democrats too voices demanded withdrawal from a coalition which had ceased to be a tool of social democratic reform grew louder. A new opposition, to which not a single one of the important personalities formerly adhering to the Social Democrat left-wing belonged, gained increasing influence in the ranks of the Workers Councils.[22]

At first the new opposition was unable to influence the party's course, but in spring and early summer two events gave it greater political impact – the frustration of a right-wing extremist *coup d'état* in Germany through a general strike, and the initial successes of the Red Army in Poland. Left-wing Socialists and Communists in the Workers Councils began to co-ordinate their attacks on the Social Democrat leadership. The latter had at all costs to prevent its own defeat in the Executive Committee of the National Workers Council by the two rebellious factions. It decided finally to realize the intention which it had harboured since the cabinet reshuffle – abandonment of the coalition.[23] On 10 June Social Democrat members of the government used a trivial incident in the course of a Parliamentary debate as an excuse for announcing their resignation. A caretaker government was formed from representatives of the three big parties to carry on business until the new elections were held. Christian Socialists and Social Democrats now acted entirely independently. For the first time in the history of the Republic the conservative majority was able to make its real weight felt. The consequences were immediately perceptible.[24]

On 6 July Parliament adopted a new Grain Control Act.[25] The Grain Office was to remain the sole buyer of foreign bread grains and, as hitherto, imported foodstuffs were to be distributed to the communes for sale to licensed dealers who had to pass the official bread ration to the population at a price fixed by the government and in return for a corresponding number of food ration coupons. The Grain Office bought most of its foodstuffs abroad, but a certain proportion, fluctuating between fifteen and twenty per cent, was acquired from domestic farmers at an official price far below that of the foreign one. The supply quota of the peasantry was established by the state on the basis of the estimated harvest yields. Prior to the act the responsibility for the collection of the domestic food stocks, a slightly modified version of the hated wartime requisitioning system, had rested with the federal authorities. After the passage of the act it lay with the agricultural co-operatives. Co-operation was meant to replace coercion in relations between farmers and the government. That the price for changing methods was a serious decline in the domestic supply will be fairly obvious.[26]

The farmers' wing of the Christian Socialists had breached the food rationing system. Now the urban wing directed its attacks against the capital levy which, after protracted negotiations in the committees, at last emerged into Parliamentary daylight in summer 1920. The attitude of both parties had definitely changed since the days when it was widely assumed that taxing property was a panacea for the grossest social and financial grievances. Even Social Democrats no longer identified the levy with the profound social reforms envisaged –although in different form – by Otto Bauer and Rudolf Goldscheid.

In spring the Social Democrats had advanced in the *Arbeiter-Zeitung* a new argument for the 'objective' method of taxation. Collection of the capital levy in the form of new shares should no longer serve to establish the state as partner in the private sector of the economy, but was to be a means of effecting the levy on firms in which foreign capital had an interest. In the Budget Committee discussions Otto Bauer recommended that the state should use the foreign exchange proceeds from sale of the shares to buy fuels and foodstuffs abroad, thus easing the pressure on the crown's exchange rate. Securities that could not be sold abroad should be unloaded on the Vienna Stock Exchange, a step from which Bauer hoped for a distinct improvement in the position of the treasury. The proposals indicated, as *Der Österreichsiche Volkswirt* aptly remarked, that 'the idea of socialization' was no longer the 'prime motivation' of the proposals of this outstanding parliamentarian.[27] The enforced large-scale sale of Austrian share capital abroad would of course lead to acceleration of the control of domestic industry by foreign capital which as has been seen, started shortly after the cessation of hostilities. A capital levy aimed at the wholesale surrender of most of Austrian industry to foreign financial groups was patently the *reductio ad absurdum* of Goldscheid's famous 'levy in kind'. However there was one point where the Social Democrats appeared to persist in their original view. They still insisted on a speedy collection of the levy. For, as the party's speakers properly pointed out, the levy could only contribute to a reduction of the budget deficit if the proceeds were readily available.[28] But here too, the Social Democrats could not master the necessary majority.

The Christian Socialists had from the beginning taken the line that the yields from the levy ought primarily to be used for debt redemption. With the enormous increase of notes in circulation and the currency's rapid depreciation the funded public debt gradually lost its great weight. By July 1920 it no longer represented the budget's largest item but ranked fourth behind the food subsidies, civil servants' pay, and expenditure on state monopolies.[29] All who, for the most varied reasons, were against the levy leaped at the fact that two years' inflationary development had led to the self-liquidation of the public debt. The common basis for their negative attitude can be summarized as follows: 'The problem of July, 1920, was to meet current expenditure, not fixed charges, and for this a capital levy was not the appropriate means'.[30]

The alternative to the levy was a big international loan, for which prospects at this stage were unfavourable. The rejection of the levy was really inspired by a multiplicity of interests. Urban landlords were horrified at a measure threatening to reduce still further the diminished earnings on their properties. Owners of industrial undertakings feared that the government might be tempted to hold back, either wholly or in part, the shares issued on behalf of the state and by this means acquire far-reaching controlling rights over the industrial sector.[31] Even if this was not planned, the possibility of buying back their own shares involved the problem of procuring the necessary funds, a disquieting prospect at a time of exorbitantly high interest rates. And the farmers were adamant in their refusal to assume any financial burdens at all.

The bill passed by the rural-urban majority in the National Assembly against the votes of the Social Democrat party made considerable concessions to all three groups. The greatest problem was to agree on which method should be adopted to determine the value of the assests. The concessions made to the farmers were the most important. Van Sickle, who subjected the law to very close scrutiny, draws the conclusion that 'the peasant interest had succeeded in reducing their share of the capital levy to a symbolic figure'.[32]

The treatment accorded to urban landlords was hardly less accommodating than that enjoyed by the farmers. Rents had dropped to a fraction of their pre-war value, but the speculative potential of rental property remained considerably above that of its capitalized earning power. Nevertheless the conservative majority in parliament chose the capitalized earning power of the actual net receipts as the basis for the assessment of urban houses. The decision effectively freed this category of ownership from payment of the levy. A third privileged group comprised all firms not constituted as joint-stock or limited liability companies. Their capital equipment was to be rated at the original cost price. Raw materials inventories and stocks were to be valued at current market prices. Van Sickle rightly points out that that part of business property 'upon which the assessors could later check up was to be valued at purely nominal figures, while the part over which no real control could be exercised at a later date remained subject to the higher and theoretically correct method of valuation'.[33]

For joint-stock companies the act laid down a fifteen per cent levy on the capital stock, but it freed shareholders from any further imposts on their holdings if their income tax rate did not exceed fifteen per cent. The most important concession to joint-stock and limited liability companies related to the manner of collecting the levy. The companies were placed under no obligation to contribute the levy in the form of new shares unless this appeared advantageous to them. Walther Federn, having examined these and other provisions, inferred with some resignation. 'The reproach that the act unilaterally favours agricultural assets cannot be levelled, at any rate. It creates favourable conditions for all assets.'[34]

As far as the mass of the population was concerned, the act provided for an exemption of 30,000 crowns per person and imposed tax rates rising from 3% to 65% on all other assets. Most contemporary observers agreed that the exemption effectively protected the working and the lower middle classes from being affected by the levy.

The most that the Ministry of Finance could hope for was a reduction of the current budget deficit by an amount which would be sufficient for the government to refrain, intermittently at least, from using the banknote printing press (a habit quickly acquired). By the provisions relating to the manner of collection the act failed to achieve even this humble objective. These provisions foresaw a normal term of payment of three years from receipt of notice, but with the possibility of an extension for as long as twenty years in the event of financial illiquidity.[35] On 30 June 1920, the assessment date for all assets, the crown stood at 148 to the dollar. By the end of the year the exchange rate had fallen to 654, a downward trend that subsequently continued. The rapid deterioration of the currency robbed the act of any practical importance.

In this same summer parliament passed a series of fiscal laws. Here too the conservative majority, after revising the Cereals Control Act and shaping the capital levy to suit sundry pressure groups, made its newly-won influence felt. In view of the fact that the continuous depreciation of the crown made the replacement of fixed assets difficult for managements, the law of 15 July allowed anticipatory write-offs in certain branches of industry (mining, oil production, and electricity) if the expansion of capital equipment was undertaken between 1920 and 1924.[36]

Another statute (23 July) settled certain specific industrial problems. A not inconsiderable number of firms which had maintained branch organizations in various parts of the Empire held sizeable share packages, as the result of converting their affiliate companies into independent subsidiaries. The dividends on the firms' freshly acquired shares were subject to double taxation, in Austria and in the Successor States. The act provided that a domestic company coming into possession of, or continuing until the end of 1924 to maintain interests in, such establishments could deduct from its taxable profits an amount determined by the ratio between the capital of the former branch organizations and that of the firm's total capital.

Land tax was also given an urgently needed overhaul. Standard rates were slightly increased and certain surcharges dating from 1919 again introduced.[37] The ridiculously low cadastral yield figures of 1896, the basis for real estate taxation, were however retained.[38] The conservative majority also introduced a notable rise in certain indirect taxes.

Some income tax changes reflected in some degree the influence of both the Social Democrats and the conservative parliamentary parties. Whereas the exemption ceiling was fixed at 8,600 crowns – 'a sum way below the earning capacity of even a workman' – the marginal rate was set at 60% for incomes exceeding 1,200,000 crowns.[39] This increase was so steep that it caused some scepticism as to whether an effective implementation was at all feasible.

The Cereals Control Act led to a distinct easing of the war economy that had still been operative during the first half of 1920. Other measures followed that strengthened the trend towards returning to the pre-1914 free enterprise economy. An ordinance of 14 October facilitated the export of goods.[40] On the dissolution of the Foreign Exchange Agency more will be said in the next chapter.

The National Assembly could not disperse without accomplishing one task for which it had been given a binding mandate in the election of Februrary 1919 – the elaboration of a new constitution. A two-thirds parliamentary majority was necessary. The Christian Socialists and the Social Democrats had no choice other than to negotiate and to seek a compromise in a more conciliatory atmosphere. The so-called Kelsen Constitution – named after its author, the well-known constitutional jurist Hans Kelsen – accordingly made important concessions to the views of both parties.

In many months of discussion preceding 1 October 1920, the day on which parliament sanctioned the new constitution, far-reaching demands for provincial autonomy had been voiced by broad sections of the rural population and by the urban middle classes. In some of the provinces, Tirol and Vorarlberg in particular, there were serious efforts at complete severance from 'Red' Vienna. The Christian

Socialists were spokesmen for a more moderate group within the 'Away from Vienna' movement. They rejected separatist ambitions, supporting instead a loose federation of provinces.[41]

As against this the Socal Democrats were passionately committed to the principle of political centralism. It might indeed be described as an important component of their ideological tradition. Max Adler, one of the party's most distinguished thinkers, in spring 1920 told the Lower Austrian *Landtag* (the province's historic representative assembly) that provincial borders made no difference to the character and to the solidarity of the proletariat.[42]

Apart from these ideological considerations, there were distinctly practical motives behind the Social Democrats' dislike of provincial autonomy. They could hardly hope for majorities in the *Landtag* in the foreseeable future, but their successes in the 1919 *Nationalrat* elections proved that at the federal level a majority could be viewed as a reasonable political prospect.

The Kelsen Constitution called Austria a federal state. This definition, at least as a matter of terminology, amounted to a concession to the peasants and their Christian Socialist supporters. The country was to have seven provincial parliaments, seven parliamentary chairmen and vice-chairmen, seven separate administrative bodies, and a considerable number of additional, purely local institutions.[43] Rather a costly version of federalism, as the economist Julius Bunzl put it.[44] Nevertheless the constitution confirmed the country's unitary character as far as legal, fiscal, and economic policy was concerned. The Social Democrats could justly claim that they had had their way in matters of substance. Henceforward the provinces were prevented from behaving like independent economic entitites. Should they display after 10 November 1920 (the day on which the Constitution came into force) inclination to pursue a particularist course, the Federal Government could bring them before the Constitutional Court.

Supreme legislative authority was vested in a parliament consisting of two chambers, the *Nationalrat* (National Council), and the *Bundesrat* (Federal Council). The Christian Socialists wanted the *Bundesrat* to be constituted on the American pattern with each province, whether tiny Vorarlberg or populous Lower Austria, enjoying equal representation. This body, in which in accordance with these ideas the agrarian interests would have been the dominant political force, was moreover to have an absolute veto over the decisions of the *Nationalrat*. The Social Democrats were strong enough to thwart both these proposals.[45]

The Kelsen Constitution rested, like the provisional constitution of the two preceding years, on the principle of pure parliamentarianism. The composition of the *Nationalrat* derived from proportional representation. The *Bundesrat* was given the right of veto, but it was a suspensive veto and underlined still further the ultimate authority of the *Nationalrat*. The *Nationalrat* elected the government and exercised supreme control over the fighting forces. Every four years it was to meet with the *Bundesrat* in the *Bundesversammlung* (Federal Assembly) for the purpose of electing the Federal President. The latter was allotted solely representational functions. In this way the strictly parliamentary character of the constitution was preserved.[46] The city of Vienna was not yet given the status of a separate province, but the constitution contained the legal basis for the final separation of the federal capital from the province of Lower Austria, a move consummated in 1921. The Social Democrats were soon to lose their influence over matters at the federal level, but they retained the majority in the capital and made of it a model for many of their ideas on social reform.

A catalogue of human rights could not be incorporated into the constitution because the political parties' views on the relationship between church and state diverged too much. Nonetheless it proclaimed in some of its basic articles the principles of freedom and equality familiar to Western democracy. In its rigorous application of the universal franchise it surpassed even some of its Western exemplars.

The Provisional National Assembly, having fulfilled its principal task, pronounced its own dissolution. The switch by many middle-class and rural electors away from the Social Democrat camp was now clearly confirmed at the polls. The Christian Socialists were able to increase their share of the votes from 35.94% at the last election to 42.09% while the share of the Social Democrats fell from 40.76% to 36.30%. The Pangermans, unable during the time of the National Assembly to make a clear-cut impression, sustained a severe defeat. As a result the *Nationalrat* consisted of 82 Christian Socialists, 66 Social Democrats, and 22 Pangermans, as well as a number of representatives from two smaller parties. On 20 November the *Nationalrat* elected a purely middle-class government under the leadership of the Christian Socialist Dr Michael Mayr.[47] The liquidation of the war economy could now be continued at a faster pace.

Notes

1 See Hanns Haas, *Österreich-Ungarn als Friedensproblem. Aspekte der Friedensregelung auf dem Gebiet der Habsburgermonarchie in den Jahren 1918–1919* (Dissertation, Salzburg 1968), p. 231.

2 'On 17 October the National Assembly was notified that Bauer and Seipel had given up their membership of the commission. For practical purposes that was the end of socialization in Austria.' Klemens von Klemperer, *Ignaz Seipel, Staatsmann einer Krisenzeit* (Graz-Vienna-Cologne, 1976), p. 103.

3 Cf. Otto Bauer, 'Die österreichische Revolution', *Werkausgabe* (Vienna, 1976), Vol. II, p. 764.

4 Macartney has this to say about the estrangement of the peasantry from the Social Democratic Party: '. . . legislation could only meet their land hunger in one respect, by parcelling up the big districts which had been bought up in recent years and turned into deer forests. A law to this effect was actually passed, but its effects have remained small . . . It was far too little to counteract the embittered quarrel between town and country which sprang up immediately when the new government, in order to feed Vienna, fixed maximum prices at a rate which was usually grossly unfair to the producer and continued the hated requisitioning which had been in force during the war. The coalition between peasants and workmen soon became one of active hatred which was energetically fanned by the all-powerful country priests . . .' C. A. Macartney, *The Social Revolution in Austria* (Cambridge, 1926), pp. 139–40.

5 Friedrich Adler, 'Machtfragen und Formfragen', *Der Kampf*, May 1919, p. 242. 'Had it only been possible,' he added, 'to force this middle class to rule, that would for the working class have been the most desirable (outcome) . . .'

6 For example, 'There is surely hardly a single Social Democrat who finds the current position of social democracy in German-Austria satisfactory, but many enough to whom it seems unendurable. Nothing more natural therefore than to ponder whether an end could not be put to this ambiguous, disconcerting, and indeed not harmless situation, whether it would not be possible to free ourselves from a condition that entails only disadvantages for social democracy, but bestows on its opponents, all of them, even those who partake in the government and should therefore fully share responsibility, all the advantages.' Friedrich Austerlitz, *Der Kampf*, December 1919, p. 789 et seq.

7 This was not simply an outcome of the foreign aid programme, but also of normal free market revival. Given the circumstances of 1919, illegal trading held a high place there.

8 *Unemployment Insurance Statistics* (Federal Ministry for Social Administration, Vienna, 1920), p. 8. Actually, though, the number of unemployed was higher because, as has been stated, the extension of assistance was implemented more strictly than before. See Karl Přibram, 'Die Sozialpolitik im neuen Österreich', *Archiv für Sozialwissenschaften und Sozialpolitik* (Tübingen, 1921), Vol. 48, p. 636.

9 'Seipel's peculiar role in the matter of socialization is not explicable simply in terms of a tactical manoeuvre to undermine the programme's chances from within. For all that he constituted in the First Coalition's affairs a 'retardant element', as E. K. Winter put it, his approach to the subject had been marked by good will. If there is any reproach that can be levelled at him, then at the most it is

that of too little realism. But the coalition depended on participation in socialization, and the new government depended on the coalition. So Seipel's decision to give socialization his support was eminently political.' Klemperer, *Seipel*, p. 103.

10 Cf. Part IV, Chap. 3, p. 328.

11 At the Social Democratic Party meeting in November 1919 this demand was reinforced with the greatest emphasis.

12 Cf., Walther Federn, 'Das Finanzprogramm der Koalition', *Der Österreichische Volkswirt*, 25 October 1919, p. 69 et seq.

13 John V. van Sickle, *Direct Taxation in Austria* (Cambridge, 1931), p. 143.

14 'The import monopoly ... has long ceased to exist. Smuggling has assumed enormous proportions and employs the most various means ... Every province, every commune imports whatever it wants, exports crowns without the knowledge and agreement of the Foreign Exchange Agencys (and) circumvents all price regulations. The Styrian administration is even said to issue its own import licences to traders. That renders the foremost, the most important purpose of centralized import regulation utterly illusory ...' Gustav Stolper, 'Freigabe des Lebensmittelverkehrs', *Der Österreichische Volkswirt*, 6 September 1919, p. 927.

15 Cf. Appendix II, Table 6.

16 See Victor Kienböck, *Das österreichische Sanierungswerk* (Stuttgart, 1925), p. 13.

17 *Der Österreichische Volkswirt*, 20 December 1919, p. 229, refers to the Paris meeting.

18 'The powers concerned were 18 in number: Great Britain, France, Italy, Japan, Belgium, Poland, Portugal, Greece, Czechoslovakia, Yugoslavia, Rumania, and Siam had claims for reparations and other charges arising under the Peace Treaty at St. Germain; Great Britain, France, Italy, the USA, Denmark, Holland, Norway, Sweden, and Switzerland had granted relief credits to Austria. The Reparation Commission was competent to take a decision on behalf of the first group of states, but in the case of the second group it was necessary for each state to declare individually that it was willing to postpone its claims and to raise its liens. In several countries, in the USA, in particular, this could only be done by legislation, which involved a long and unfortunate delay. For reasons of internal politics the question was not dealt with by the Congress of the US until the spring of 1922, and it was not till April 6 of that year that the 'Lodge Resolution', which authorized the administration to take the necessary measures, was signed by President Harding.' Jan van Walré de Bordes, *The Austrian Crown. Its Depreciation and Stabilization* (London, 1924), p. 25.

19 Cf. *Der Österreichische Volkswirt*, 3 April 1920, p. 523.

20 Cf. Gustav Stolper, 'Stagnation', *Der Österreichische Volkswirt*, 31 July 1920, p. 819. Stolper included a relatively high inflow of foreign capital among the 'stabilizing' factors contributing to the crown's sensational recovery.

21 Renner's appearance before the Supreme Allied Council seems, as some authors think, to have had positive effects in the long run. To his initiative is attributed the foundation of the International Committee for Relief Credits at Paris (April 1920) through whose mediation loans to an amount of £26,686,690 had been raised by 1 August 1921. See Gottlieb Ladner, *Seipel als Überwinder der Staatskrise vom Sommer 1922. Geschichte der Entstehung der Genfer Protokolle vom 4. Oktober*

1922 (Vienna-Graz, 1964), p. 16. Also Kienböck, *Sanierungswerk*, p. 13 et seq.

22 The so-called 'New Left' in its fierce criticism of Otto Bauer and his party friends was especially resentful of his attachment to *Anschluss* and the negation of Austria's viability. 'Free us from our economic straits, let production be resumed and our goods be available for exchange in international markets and we shall no longer be a non-viable entity. There are plenty of smaller states which feel very well on their modest scale.' See Franz Rothe, 'Die Arbeitsgemeinschaft Revolutionärer Sozialdemokraten Deutsch-österreichs', *Der Kampf*, September 1920, p. 334. Leser, analyzing the motives and occurrences that led to the breakdown of the coalition, thinks that Bauer was 'not only influenced by fear of dissatisfaction and of criticism from the left', but also proceeded from the basic conviction that 'the natural place for proletarians vis-à-vis the bourgeois state was to be in opposition.' Norbert Leser, *Zwischen Reformismus und Bolschevismus* (Vienna, 1968), p. 342.

23 The decision to abandon the coalition was taken on 28 May at a meeting of the Social Democratic members of parliament. Bauer declared the step to be necessary 'because the Social Democratic position in the government had become pretty weak'. Renner agreed, but emphasized 'that the party was relinquishing all power'. Leser, *Zwischen Reformismus*, p. 431.

24 A more detailed description of the events leading to the dissolution of the coalition is contained in Otto Bauer, 'Die österreichische Revolution', *Werkausgabe*, Vol. II, p. 756 et seq. Kunschak confined himself to saying that 'a speech of mine broke up' the second coalition. See Leopold Kunschak, *Österreich 1918–1934* (Vienna, 1934), p. 62.

25 Official Law Gazette, No. 315 of 22 July 1920.

26 The food rationing system is summarily described in *Financial Reconstruction of Austria* (Report of the Financial Committee of the Council. League of Nations, Geneva, 1920), p. 29 and in Gustav Stolper, 'Freigabe des Lebensmittelverkehrs', *Der Österreichische Volkswirt*, 6 September 1919, p. 927.

27 Cf. Walther Federn, 'Die Vermögensabgabe', *Der Österreichische Volkswirt*, 7 February 1920, p. 362 et seq.

28 *Der Osterreichische Volkswirt*, 7 February 1920, p. 362.

29 In the fiscal year 1919–20 the funded public debt accounted for 11.9%, but in 1920–21 for no more than 6% of the total budget expenditure.

30 This is the quintessence of van Sickle's criticism of the capital levy. Cf. van Sickle, *Direct Taxation*, p. 144.

31 Some commentators claimed that this measure was the first step towards the sequestration of industry by the state. Cf. Gustav Stolper, 'Der neue Finanzplan', *Der Österreichische Volkswirt*, 24 June 1922, p. 936.

32 Cf. van Sickle, *Direct Taxation*, p. 156 et seq.

33 *Direct Taxation*, p. 157.

34 Walther Federn, 'Die Vermögensabgabe', *Der Österreichische Volkswirt*, 24 July 1920, p. 801.

35 Cf. van Sickle, *Direct Taxation*, p. 163.

36 Official Law Gazette, No. 313, 15 July 1920.

37 Cf. van Sickle, *Direct Taxation*, p. 85.

38 The 1896 cadastral yield figures stayed in force until autumn 1921 and were then raised only slightly. Cf. Federal Law Gazette, No. 663, 23 November 1921.

39 Cf. van Sickle, *Direct Taxation*, p. 98 et seq.

40 Official Law Gazette, No. 488, 27 October 1920.

41 'The Christian Socialists adhered to autonomy for the provinces and they were able to have their viewpoint recognized.' Leopold Kunschak, *Österreich 1918–1934*, Wien 1934, p. 38.

42 'We know that the common good is a concept that cannot be realized in a state ruled by class. What can at least be achieved is for as large a sphere as possible to be created where legal equality and legal security exist, particularly for the proletariat . . . where provincial borders make no difference to its character and its solidarity. That is why we socialists fundamentally take our stand on centralism in the state's constitution.' Max Adler, in a speech to the Lower Austrian *Landtag* on 3 February 1920, reprinted in *Der Kampf*, August 1920, p. 297.

43 The number of federal provinces was very soon to rise to nine in consequence of Burgenland (Western Hungary) being incorporated into Austria and independent status being given to Vienna.

44 'This dogged chatter about the need to find the saving formula for the relationship between the "independent provinces" and the "federation" could certainly be termed a "great piece of childishness" were it not that these federal fiddlings with eight provincial parliaments and their chairmen, vice-chairmen, councillors, chancelleries and other administrative requirements, their provincial governors and deputy governors are far too costly for an Austria skimping on the most urgent cultural needs.' Julius Bunzl, 'Das neue Österreich', *Schriften des Vereins für Sozialpolitik* (Munich, 1925), Vol. 169, p. 455.

45 Cf. Robert Danneberg, 'Die deutsch-österreichische Finanzverfassung', *Der Kampf*, June 1922, p. 199.

46 The 1929 Constitutional Law (Amendment) Act made several important changes in the functions of the Federal President.

47 Cf. Kunschak, *Österreich*, p. 65.

CHAPTER 2
Economic and Sociological Aspects
of Post-war Inflation

The Empire at the outset of the First World War had already been infected by the germ of inflation. During the later course of hostilities control over the movement of prices slid largely out of the government's hands. The internal depreciation of the crown was not however accompanied by a corresponding decline in its purchasing power abroad since trading with the outside world was marginal and movements of capital were subject to rigorous restrictions. Largely speaking it can be said that wartime inflation may be ascribed to two causes: first, the Empire's slender endowment with natural and industrial resources, which because of the duration and total nature of the war made itself increasingly felt; secondly, the irrational methods of war financing by a government that followed the line of least resistance.[1]

The level of prices, leaving aside the early part of the war when their movement stayed within relatively narrow limits, rose rapidly and at a fairly even rate. In July 1916, two years after the beginning of the war, the price index stood at about 400% above the average for the last month of peace, July 1914. A year later it had climbed to about 800%. Another year and the figure was more than 1,400%.[2] From July 1918 to January 1919 it doubled, the greater part of the accelerated increase occurring between November and January.

Such an upsurge in the cost of living during the winter months 1918/1919 indicates the existence of an acute emergency. The period succeeding the Armistice was indeed marked by an almost complete standstill in industry due to the embargo on deliveries of coal and foodstuffs from neighbouring countries as well as to the dangerous political disturbances. Especially in Vienna, which was also blockaded by its own hinterland, the available stocks of goods sank to the then lowest known point while the price level shot up even more swiftly than in wartime. Five years later Walré de Bordes brought the situation graphically home to his compatriots:

> In order to realize what Vienna had to endure at this time, one might imagine that, after a war lasting for several years, during which all stocks had been depleted, England – not possessing any coal mines – were suddenly shut off from the rest of the world. It is clear that the prices of food and industrial raw materials would rise enormously. Such was the case in Vienna in 1919.[3]

In February, thanks to the start of the relief credits, the first large-scale food transports arrived in Austria, and occasionally Czecho-slovakia made coal deliveries in exchange for raw materials. In this way the new republican government was to some degree able during spring to ensure, though at a shockingly low standard, the country's essential needs. The deterioration in the crown's domestic value entered into a quieter phase in spite of the expansion of the banknote circulation which was caused by a huge budget deficit.[4,5]

Although Austria resembled during these early post-war months a beleaguered fortress with few escape routes to the outer world, the crown's external value came under severe pressure. In November 1918 a US dollar cost 14.33 crowns, but five months later the ratio was 1 : 25. The exchange rate of the crown was now only a fifth of its pre-war value. Flight of capital and bearish speculation had been mainly responsible for this steep drop. They were not new features, but they could make themselves felt far more strongly than in wartime. In winter and spring 1919 the flight of capital accelerated considerably while the bearish speculation assumed wanton proportions. Together they reflected the deep pessimism with which the wealthier classes viewed the new state's chances of survival. Particularly in spring, when Hungary and Bavaria became the scene of radical social experiments, the exodus of assets is likely to have been substantial. Such operations were facilitated by relaxation in foreign exchange controls.

In April there was an attempt to stop the decline by interventionist measures initiated by Schumpeter, then Minister of Finance. The comparative stability that followed was also due to some extent to the slightly improved nutritional situation, but it lasted only until the publication of the Peace Treaty. In August 1919 the second phase of speedy deterioration in the crown's exchange rate began. By its close, in February 1920, the rate of the crown to the dollar was 271 : 1 or 1.8% of pre-war parity.

In November 1918 and in August 1919 a psychological factor, the widespread assumption that Austria was heading for a crisis, had been the immediate cause of the crown's rapid fall. In autumn 1919, though, there could no longer be any talk of Austria's utter economic isolation. The government, with its first major dollar credit nearly exhausted, was trying to obtain foodstuffs and coal from abroad, but in exchange had little better to offer than its paper crowns. Competing with it were provincial administrations, trying to procure urgent imports on the same terms, and private, generally illegal trading organizations. With the flight of capital and the bearish speculation continuing on an undiminished scale, the crown was subject to heavy pressure.

There were of course certain counteracting trends. Sometimes domestic and foreign speculators fancied that they saw signs of economic consolidation and chose temporarily to swim against the stream.[6]

More important was the demand for Austrian securities by foreign capital groups which contributed to the Stock Exchange boom in late spring 1919. These activities were the beginning of a tragic episode – the 'clearance sale' in which 'foreign dealers snatched for a song the raw materials stocks left to the Republic by the military administration, as well as the personal chattels and jewellry of the Viennese patricians impoverished by currency depreciation ...'[7]

The crown's continuous fall forced the Ministry of Finance constantly to make available growing quantities of paper money to pay for imported consumer goods. Consequently the budget deficit increased and the monetary circulation expanded further. The following table shows how the government had repeatedly to revise its 1919–20 estimates, primarily on account of growing outlays on consumer goods and fuels from abroad.[8]

Table 44   Federal budget, 1919–20 in crowns m.

		Supplement			
	Estimates	I	II	III	Total
Expenditure	6,546.9	4,350.7	2,381.4	3,594.4	16,873.4
Revenue	2,548.3	1,082.0	807.7	1,856.6	6,294.6
Deficit	3,998.6	3,268.7	1,573.7	1,737.8	10,578.8
Ratio Deficit to Expenditure	61%	75%		48%	63%

The inflationary process induced by wartime conditions had been determined by the volume of money, the rhythm of the depreciation process had been influenced by frequent changes in the velocity of money, due to a multitude of very diverse factors.[9] Post-war inflation, on the other hand, was linked in another causal chain: the balance of payments and the foreign exchange rate furnished the main impetus which, for longer or shorter intervals, influenced the volume of money and the level of prices.[10]

Apart from this round-about route between the crown's falling quotation and the domestic price level, there was a direct link between the falling exchange rate and rising prices at home. The authorities, as has been recounted, sold food to the population at a cost well below its purchase price. In late autumn they made a cautious attempt at closing the gap between consumer prices and procurement costs. The twofold object was to contain the enormous budget deficit and to adjust the domestic price level gradually to the international level.[11] No decisive move had at this stage been taken towards a free flow of trade, but a mechanism aiming at an approximation between domestic and foreign prices had been set in motion.

To complete the picture it may also be noted that speculation normally exercised a negative influence on the crown's external value, and that this in turn had an unfavourable effect on the domestic price level. The frequently reiterated view that the expectation of future paper money issues primarily encouraged bearish speculation is an arbitrary deduction from the numerous factors causing disequilibrium in the balance of payments, a disequilibrium hardly capable of correction in the short run. Most of the factors are already sufficiently familiar, in particular the acute lack of foodstuffs, raw materials and coal by which the young Republic seemed in its beginnings even worse hit than the war-worn Empire had been.[12]

While imports were hardly adequate to meet the country's needs they could not be matched by exports because domestic requirements and the low utilization of industrial capacities stood in the way of a revival of foreign trade.[13] For the time being there could be no reliance on receipts from tourism or other services, nor from capital imports not inconsiderable in peace-time. To a constantly increasing extent resort had to be made to the sale of paper crowns abroad, a dangerous instrument liable to undermine the health of the economic organism.

Some authors, including the well-known Austrian-born Fritz Machlup, have argued that a situation like the foregoing cannot last long because exorbitant demand for foreign goods and services must drive up foreign exchange rates and induce foreign buyers to avail themselves increasingly of the goods and services to be had in the markets affected by inflation. Domestic purchasers of foreign goods will, on the other hand, turn more and more to home products, and such a trend must sooner or later produce a new equilibrium between domestic and foreign markets.[14]

The theory cannot be denied a certain plausibility, but it lacks overall validity. It is definitely not applicable to a country that, like Austria, wages total war for a number of years and at the end goes through the catastrophe of being prised out of a big self-contained economic area. True, Austria was up to a point able, especially when raw materials and coal could be more easily procured, to turn the disproportionately rapid drop in the value of the crown to advantage as an 'export premium'. A fairly long time had however to elapse before industry was in a position to overcome the war's worst injuries – excessive wear and tear of machinery, complete depletion of stocks, lack of spare parts, and so forth – as well as the loss of complementary production that was located in what was now foreign territory. In Austria, for reasons deriving from the conditions of the immediate post-war period, the supply curves proved (in modern economic terminology) remarkably 'inelastic'.[15]

Voices in favour of complete abolition of the food subsidies which would mean passing on the full cost to the consumers became louder as this item claimed an ever larger slice of the national budget.[16] Initially the demand was rejected over a relatively broad front. The Social Democratic press objected that not only the working class but also large sections of the impoverished middle class, such as public employees and small pensioners, benefited from the system. The editorial staff of Der Österreichische Volkswirt, who very often showed deeper insight into economic complexities than most of their colleagues, argued that the financial position of the government would not be essentially improved by such a move because the savings would be offset by the rise in the salaries of the civil servants. They regarded the budget deficit simply as a sympton of disequilibrium in the economy as a whole.

This is not really the moment when a reconstruction of the national finances can be taken in hand. A general misunderstanding must over and over again be exposed. The German-Austrian economic problem is not a financial problem. All the financial evils which plague us are effects, not causes. The cause is the imbalance of our economy, and this is something which no amount of dynamic, inspired financial policy can remedy.[17]

The discussion on food subsidies continued with growing intensity until December 1921, when this system was at last terminated. The direct occasion of the decision and its far-reaching consequences, unforeseen by anyone concerned, will be considered in more detail at a later stage.

In spring 1920 the government succeeded again by repeated intervention purchases in the foreign exchange market in support the crown's value abroad. Indeed at the end of May the exchange rate underwent a sensational recovery, but with the rapid disappearance of foreign currency reserves these measures had to be stopped. That was the preliminary to the third phase in the crown's steep decline.[18] Once begun, forces came into play that lent it special impetus and increasing velocity.

By spring and summer 1920 rail transport in central and western Europe had almost attained normality. Austrian importers, thanks to the recession afflicting the Western economies, were able to replenish their raw materials and fuels stockpiles.[19] Only now could industry fully avail itself of the 'inflation premium' arising from the differential between the widely divergent domestic and world prices. Exports began to improve.[20] Nevertheless the pressure on the crown's external value mounted because of the country's craving for goods, not fully manifest until normal relations with the outside world had been re-established, and to a lesser degree because of an insufficiently developed 'inflation-consciousness'. Entrepreneurs had not yet learned to allow for the constantly rising costs of the required inputs while business people often offered their merchandise at prices which were not sufficient to cover the cost of their replacement.[21]

Foreign exchange control had been relaxed shortly after the war's close. The banks, or at any rate the more respectable among them, loyally adhered to official regulations. They were however soon aware that a large number of foreign exchange transactions were being conducted via other channels. They put, understandably, mounting pressure on the government to abolish the inefficient control system entirely. This the government, was quite correctly reluctant to do, because it imputed to the system, however damaged, a certain deterrent effect.[22] On the other hand, as *Der Österreichische Volkswirt* said in its financial section, the free market in foreign exchange had expanded to such an extent that the government scarcely had any alternative but to legalize the existing situation.[23]

With the decontrol of foreign exchange in November 1920 the last bastion against speculative dealings had fallen. The number of banks and bankers allowed to engage in foreign exchange dealings rose during 1921 to 360, according to Karl Ausch.

Most of them had only recently 'got going' and were unknown individuals, who in their greed for profit, had no scruples whatever as to their choice of methods or of customers. None of them bought foreign exchange because they needed it to pay for imported goods, but because they wanted either to hoard it or to dispose of it within a short time at high gain. Whoever managed to procure foreign exchange and for a shorter or longer period also to retain it was sure of achieving handsome speculative profits.[24]

Regrettably, so Ausch adds, the old-established banks lent support to speculative activity by extending loans to foreign exchange dealers.

Under these conditions it could hardly come as a surprise that the crown's downward trend turned into a veritable plunge. On 15 July 1920 a dollar cost 147.86 crowns. On 15 October the price had risen to 310 crowns. The next two months saw the figure doubled. The downward movement had acquired a dynamism evidently propelled mainly by illegitimate speculation – no longer by the legitimate forces of supply and demand. At year-end Walther Federn closed his obituary on the cessation of foreign exchange control with the passionate outburst: 'Never before has the foreign exchange game been so shamelessly played as now when speculators are sure of being safe from prosecution.'[25]

Soon wide circles of industry and of the financial world were drawn into the maelstrom engulfing the crown. They were far from wanting to inflict injury on the economy, but they had nonetheless to shield their private interests against the further deterioration of the currency by building up foreign exchange reserves.[26] Exporters selling their goods against foreign currency increasingly resorted to having their proceeds placed in banks abroad. Bankers reduced their cash holdings and in the same ratio expanded their foreign assets. In an address to the Royal Institute of International Affairs in London at the beginning of 1922 Sir William Goode, head of the Austrian Section of the Reparation Commission, said that Swiss bankers judged the amount of Austrian call money in hard currencies deposited in their country to stand at £18,000,000 sterling.[27] To this must be added the enormous hoards of money stored by Austrians elsewhere beyond their frontiers. 'It may be estimated without fear of exaggeration that during the years 1919–22 the Austrians increased their reserves of foreign exchange by several hundred million gold crowns every year,' says Walré de Bordes.[28] The speedy, rapidly accelerating decline of the crown, starting in autumn 1920, completely upset the government's budget estimates. In the preceding year it had made serious efforts to get a grip on the deficit. The crown's spectacular decline caused the deficit to

Table 45   Consolidated budget, 1920–21 in crowns m.

	Estimates	Supplement I	Supplement II	Total
Expenditure	33,194.5	37,395.7	10.6	70,600.8
Revenues	20,655.1	8,828.2	10.6	29,483.3
Deficit	12,539.4	28,567.5		41,117.4
Ratio Deficit to Expenditure	38%	76%		58%

grow to truly mammoth proportions.[29]

Only some of the thorniest problems with which the Ministry of Finance was faced during this critical phase can be cited. The chief difficulty was that public expenditure rose far more quickly than revenue. Certain items, the purchase of foodstuffs, tobacco, and coal, needed repayment in hard currency and grew in precise relation to the crown's devaluation. Others, like civil servants' salaries and unemployment benefits, rose with the price level, even though lagging considerably behind. A third category, outstandingly the public debt, fell in proportion to the drop in the value of the crown. In 1920 expenditure for the purchase of foodstuffs and coal was by far the most important.

Whereas the extent of expenditures was to a great extent determined by the fall of the crown, the majority of receipts were characterized by remarkable rigidity. No more than a very few tariffs were levied in gold.[30] In general they were adapted to the falling value of the crown with the help of co-efficients (or multiples). As however the co-efficient usually trailed after the rapidly declining exchange rate, the revenue from tariffs was *de facto* twenty five to thirty per cent lower than before the war.[31] Other public sources of income, such as revenue from the state railways and state monopolies, remained well behind the rising price level.[32]

In the case of direct and indirect taxation adjustment to the price level proved even less satisfactory. Changes of taxes pertained to the competence of the legislature which only met sporadically and whose decisions were seldom dictated by purely rational considerations. The collection machinery was so ponderous that, at a time of speedy currency depreciation, the value of the proceeds was constantly diminishing. The desperate situation was aggravated, in Spitzmüller's opinion, by the government's policy of unrestrained spending. 'In the Ministry of Finance it was thought that banknotes must go on being printed because without foreign financial aid, equilibrium could not be restored to the budget. And, until the moment that such a loan was extended, the ministry continued its policy of lavish spending with insistence on worthwhile economies in almost no sector.'[33]

In January 1921 it became known that the Austrian Section of the Reparation Commission had suggested to the Allies a long-term credit of 250 million dollars.[34] The so-called Goode Plan was based on the recommendations of the Brussels Financial Conference.[35] These recommendations firmly rejected miraculous cures relying only on monetary measures and prescribed for the ailing economies in central and eastern Europe a series of hard and fast reforms such as normalization of trading relations, a return to the rules of orthodox budget policy, and the pledge of certain public revenue sources as collateral for the procurement of foreign loans.[36]

The Brussels Conference also alluded to the need to close by suitable means the wide gap between supply and demand in the Successor States.[37] Sir William Goode's reform plan accordingly focused in the first place on the Austrian economy's investment needs. Drawing attention to the country's agricultural reserves and undeveloped hydraulic power, he recommended intensive utilization of these important resources and proposed that for this purpose the Great Powers should grant Austria a handsome loan of 250 million dollars, the amount he regarded as adequate to tide over its budget deficit by stages and to satisfy the large capital requirements of its industry. This recognition of the need for a *comprehensive* reconstruction – of industry, of agriculture, and of public finances – was at once more perspicacious and more realistic than the Geneva Recovery Plan that after another excruciating eighteen months was to be accepted by the Great Powers. On the other hand there were also certain similarities. Goode, for instance, thought that the Reparation Commission should assume control of the implementation of the reconstruction plan so as to give the creditor nations some guarantee for the appropriate use of their credits.[38]

Sir William Goode's proposals had an unfavourable reception from the members of the Supreme Allied Council. The main impediment was his demand for governmental foreign assistance which, since the United States had turned its back on Europe, no longer seemed feasible on a large scale. Public interest concentrated briefly on the so-called Loucheur Plan, by which an international financial group planned to extend a 200 to 250 million francs loan on very difficult, almost humiliating terms; but after a few weeks of debate the Austrian

Government put an end to this proposal.[39]

At the beginning of 1921 Dr Michael Mayr, the Austrian Chancellor, appeared before the Supreme Allied Council's representatives at Paris and made an urgent appeal for immediate financial aid. He was told in reply that the Great Powers had decided to waive, under certain conditions, their rights of lien arising on the terms of the Peace Treaty.[40] Such a step was of course a necessary prerequisite for any bigger credit operation on the part of private lenders. Even so it was at first not enough because most of the Treaty's signatory Powers took their time to act likewise. In spring a delegation from the League of Nations Financial Committee visited Vienna to obtain on behalf of the Supreme Council a closer view of Austria's position.

The recommendations of the delegation followed the lines of the Brussels Conference's decisions closely. However, its report dealt barely at all with Sir William Goode's explicit request for reconstruction loans.[41] It emphasized the need for severe curtailment of fiscal expenditure, 'particularly of expenses connected with subsidies and personnel, which reduction should be effected as speedily as possible'.[42] Budget receipts should be raised primarily by a drastic increase in tariffs and indirect taxes. Great importance was attached to the establishment of a new Central Bank which should be granted a high measure of autonomy from the political authorities. Even the most modest foreign loan should be made dependent on Austria's following a course of a 'gradual abandonment of price control, and of abolition of subsidies which should completely disappear by the end of 1922'.[43]

To guarantee punctual payment of the interest and amortization, such important sources of revenue as customs duties and earnings on the tobacco monopoly should be pledged. The country's domestic financial resources should be made available through 'a forced loan of two per cent on all private real estate'.[44] Finally the delegation demanded, in a passage reminiscent of Sir William Goode's list of measures necessary for recovery, that the Austrian Government accept foreign supervision of the implementation of the reconstruction plan.[45]

The delegation's recommendations, which eighteen months later served as the basis for the draft of the Geneva recovery project, were acclaimed by the three leading Austrian political parties. Even the Social Democrats, who had recently gone into opposition, quickly though non-committally agreed.[46] As has been noted, the materialization of the plan was conditional on the Allies' relinquishing their lien on Austrian state property, and this was to prove a slow, nerve-racking process.

The optimistic reactions of the Austrian press to the Goode Plan and to the recommendations of the League of Nations were not without effect on the currency speculation and led to a temporary stabilization of the crown. During the first six months of 1921 the dollar rate fluctuated on average around 700 crowns. When however it became clear that neither of the reconstruction plans would come to pass in the near future and that the government was not prepared to undertake any significant measures in the direction of budget reform, the exchange rate of the crown again came under pressure. The so-called *Chicago Tribune* incident gave a special spin to the dollar's spiralling rate.[47]

In autumn the pace became a dizzying one. Towards the end of November the dollar stood at 8,520 crowns.[48] The Finance Minister announced drastic anti-speculation measures and the crown temporarily recovered. At the end of December it fell down to 5,275 to the dollar.[49] This was not to last long.

During spring and summer 1922 the dollar shot upward at unprecedented speed. On 25 August it reached the record peak of 83,600 crowns. During the earlier phases of depreciation the level of prices had risen much less than the rate of exchange.[50] In the final, galloping stage of inflation this no longer held good. The business world had become inflation-conscious and begun to increase the price of goods simultaneously with the crown's foreign quotation. Broad strata of the population had lost their last trace of confidence in the currency. They tried as fast as they could to rid themselves of their cash holdings. The flight from the crown was no longer a flight into foreign media of exchange, which were accessible only to a small minority, but a flight into tangible assets of any and every kind.

What were the reasons for this final, most destructive stage? They arose from the circumstances following the stoppage of the food subsidies. The problem of food subsidies was of course most intimately linked to the development of wages in the inflation period.

The investigation of the development of wages is especially hampered by the unsatisfactory state of statistical data. The sources of information used here are the occasional inquiries by government offices as well as by employers' and employees' organizations and a series of figures published in the *International Labour Review* (see Appendix II, Table 7).

On closer scrutiny three longer periods of wages policy and wage conditions can be distinguished: wartime; the period from the signing of the Armistice to the stoppage of the food subsidies; and the brief phase of galloping inflation brought to an end by stabilization.

Of the first it must suffice to say that from 1914–19 wages rose slowly and were far outstripped by rapidly rising prices. In the fourth year of war wage-earners in almost all industries received considerable increases in nominal wages, but real wages continued to fall. To look at wage rates does not however give an adequate picture of the situation of the working class situation. War exposed the wage system to crucial change. Family allowances, cost of living bonuses, and similar forms of assistance supplemented basic wages more and more to the point where employees' incomes seemed eventually to have been subordinated to a principle of subsistence. Wage policy, in other words, aimed at providing the working population on a broadly egalitarian footing with the basic needs of life, rather than rewarding the individual employee according to performance.

Labour discipline, imposed with a rod of iron by the military authorities for the first three years, progressively deteriorated in the fourth year. After the great strike in January 1918 managements began to rely to an ever greater extent on the good offices of the trade unions who thus regained much of their negotiating power. Particularly during the latter half of summer and in autumn, there occurred widely disseminated labour unrest.[51] Next year the position showed no material change. Due to the constant rise in the level of prices, negotiations on wages took place in most industries throughout the year. As Emil Lederer stated the crucial social question was 'in what way, at what pace, and by what means pay can be adjusted to the higher prices'.[52]

There is no reliable wage data for 1919. Benedikt Kautsky, then economic expert at the Vienna Chamber of Labour, collated a small, but undoubtedly reliable, selection of figures.[53]

Table 46   Weekly wages, June 1919 in crowns

Printers	Skilled Metal Workers	Men's Tailors	Bakers	Coachmen
105	280	182	114	110

Remarkable is the wide margin by which metal workers were ahead of printers inasmuch as in pre-war days printers had been the highest wage-earners. Two reasons appear responsible for this change.

First there were the changes in the structure of consumer needs caused by the scarcities of the immediate post-war period. Just as consumers held articles of daily use in relatively high esteem in comparison with less urgently required goods, so the value set upon the skills needed to produce them was comparatively high. These shifts in consumer demand revolutionized not only the rank order of industrial occupations, but likewise that of manual and white-collar workers.

Secondly it was the discipline and fighting spirit of the trade union organization which so strikingly improved the metal workers' position in the labour force hierarchy. From 1919 onward their leaders, most prominently Franz Domes and Anton Hueber, became the main strategists in the trade union movement. They constituted the group which normally initiated wage drives which, with a certain time-lag were then adopted by other unions. The weekly wages of the metal workers must, in the absence of an official wage index, serve as an indicator for the general trend in money wages.[54]

The foregoing table suggests, since the metal workers' weekly wage in 1910 was about 28 crowns, that in June 1919 they were earning about ten times as much. Indeed their actual pay was somewhat higher because the table does not take into account family and other emergency allowances, but the total figure is unlikely to have been more than eleven or twelve times the pre-war one. In these same years the cost of living index had risen to thirty-one times its 1914 level. The admissible conclusion is that metal workers and other occupational groups who at some little distance followed them had succeeded in raising their real wages a fraction above the low of summer and autumn 1918. This 'success' was mainly due to the trade unions' enormous accretion of political power and to the fact that a bigger share of the national product was available for consumption.[55]

Though workers were receiving a slightly higher share of the national product than the year before, real wages still remained barely above subsistence level. As the level of prices was continually rising, the danger was that the wage gains might dissolve into nothing the next day. New wage agreements were usually preceded by protracted negotiations, a method manifestly unsuitable for adjusting wages at short intervals in this situation. The trade union strategists felt foiled by such a built-in handicap. They wanted a system designed to bring about an almost automatic link between wages and prices. Their dissatisfaction with existing conditions was particularly aroused by the price avalanche in autumn 1919 and they proposed a form of agreement amounting to a radical break with the past. In November

1919, at an industrial conference attended by employers' representatives and trade union leaders, State Chancellor Renner made detailed
proposals for the introduction of a sliding scale of wages linked to the
price index. Money wages should in future be divided into two parts –
a fixed wage portion, guaranteeing to every employee irrespective of
his qualifications a subsistence minimum, and a variable factor to be
tied to the cost of living index.[56]

The metal workers' union was the first to conclude a wage contract
framed along the lines of the ideas outlined by Renner. Every second
month a commission of employers' and employees' representatives
determined the increase in the cost of living on the basis of data
supplied by the Ministry of Social Administration. The higher costs
incurred by the average household during that period as against the
base month would be expressed in a percentage of the fixed factor. On
the occasion of the first calculation this factor was about 30% during
the next two years it rose to 300%.[57]

Though the sliding scale seemed to provide an ideal invention for
the protection of labour against constantly increasing prices, the
majority of trade union leaders followed the metal workers' example
only hesitantly.[58] Many were deeply distrustful of all official statistics
and held that those published by the ministry did not reflect the full
extent of the rise in the cost of living. Similar accusations were made
against an index compiled by the Federal Office of Statistics which the
working class press often called the 'fraud index'. No wonder that the
new wage system got under way very slowly and that a multiplicity of
cost of living indices came into use in the various industries.[59]

During 1920 and 1921, when the production of consumer goods
went up considerably, the metal workers and most other occupational
groups were able, allowing for some little delay, to continue the
improvement in their standard of living. At the close of 1920 the
weekly wages of skilled and unskilled metal workers exceeded those of
1914 by 5,000% and 6,200% respectively while the cost of living
index stood at about 9,000% of the base year 1914.[60]

The correctness of these data is confirmed by a special investigation
performed in winter 1920 by the Central Statistical Commission.[61]
Whereas in December food prices were 93 times as high as in July 1914
and those of other consumer goods 105 times as high, metal workers'
wages had risen only to 50 times the pre-1914 level. The real wages of
other groups were still lower, inasmuch as few had attained more than
30 to 45 times their pre-war nominal level. Even though the labour
force in the early post-war years made unmistakeable progress in the

improvement of its situation, at no point was it able to regain more than fifty to sixty per cent of its low pre-1914 standard of living.[62]

There were however other sections of the population who could rightly complain of a yet more drastic cut in their real income. Those in public employment were probably worst hit by the increases in the cost of living. An examination into their earnings reached the conclusion that in 1919 and 1920 their real income had fallen to about 14% of pre-war. In the succeeding years their position had improved a little as their real income now amounted to from a third to two fifths of the pre-1914 level.[63] Other groups too, such as industrial white-collar workers, bank officials, and members of the professions, experienced a similar loss of real income. The urban white-collar workers had therefore, unlike the manual labourers, to accept a truly decisive diminution of their share of the badly reduced national product. Up to a point the worsening of their position was caused by the rise of the trade unions' bargaining power in the post-war period. To this were added two further factors – the profound changes in the structure of consumer demand and the levelling trends characteristic of every acutely impoverished economy. For a fairly long time the urban white-collar workers were able to keep up a standard of living well above their current money incomes by selling their valuables, household possessions, and other personal belongings. During the final phase of inflation their reserves were for all practical purposes exhausted and they were forced to maintain themselves from their scanty earnings.[64]

The dreadful impoverishment of almost all strata of the urban population made the Government hesitate to abolish the food subsidies. In 1920 and 1921 it rescinded most wartime controls, but it continued to distribute at low prices bread, cereals, edible fats, beef, sugar, and milk powder rations. During the course of 1921 it became clear that the acute nutritional crisis of the early post-war period was past. Although the standard of living in towns was abnormally low, the population's minimum need for foodstuffs could be met without official intervention. Production in certain branches of industry seemed each month to be coming closer to the pre-war level. Coal output was already higher than in the last year of peace. The manufacture of many industrial and other products was continually rising, but it still did not reach the 1913 figures.[65]

With the revival of world trade, the services of domestic banks and commercial houses, the Federal railways' transit traffic, and tourism again raised foreign exchange earnings. After more than seven hectic, exhausting years the economy was returning, even if at a considerably lower level than in the last years of peace, to something of a precarious equilibrium. But in autumn 1921, when the crown began to drop at an unprecedented rate while prices and wages swiftly rose, the successes of the past two years seemed threatened afresh. Exports fell once more, the scarcity of capital made itself strongly felt, and unemployment expanded to an alarming degree.[66] On 1 December raging crowds marched through the centre of Vienna, offered resistance to the police, and looted shops.[67]

The early post-war years had not been lacking in financial reform programmes. On 21 October 1921 *Arbeiter-Zeitung* published a reconstruction plan by Otto Bauer which attracted general attention because it indicated the readiness of the Social Democrats seriously to discuss with the government the gradual abolition of food subsidies.

Bauer's plan had three major points: abolition of the food subsidies in several stages, adjustment of the capital levy to the new value of the crown, and a compulsory loan to be paid in foreign exchange and securities.[68] Perhaps no less important was the statement that foreign loans would be needed during the course of reconstruction: 'Even if all the measures proposed in this plan are executed speedily and vigorously, an unsecured deficit that can only be met by foreign loans will probably remain.' Once the waiver of the Allied lien had been attained, he added, it should prove easy to obtain such loans even without League of Nations mediation.[69]

It must be emphasized in connection with this programme that Bauer also proposed a major domestic investment loan because he feared that currency stabilization would be accompanied by a crisis in the export industry. Anticipating Keynes' employment therapy in the 1930s, he wanted the proceeds of the loan to be devoted to projects like rebuilding the federal railways, development of the telephone network and of hydraulic power, and housing.

The government, hastening to counter the Social Democrat reconstruction plan with its own reform proposals, also underlined that the basis for stabilizing the budget must be abolition of the food subsidies which, in December 1921, reached astronomic proportions.[70] The programme presented as a 'compromise' on 21 December by Dr Alfred Gürtler, the Minister of Finance, contained in addition to the definite cessation of food subsidies a foreign exchange registration bill that required owners of foreign currency to register their holdings with the ministry.[71] The reaction of *Der Österreichische Volkswirt* to the package was distinctly sceptical. Above all, it complained, no important component of the Social Democrat proposals had, apart from the food subsidies abolition, been included.[72]

The discontinuance of the subsidies within four months went ahead without the necessary accompanying measures such as new taxes, a compulsory loan, and foreign credits, all recognized as prerequisites to a comprehensive reconstruction. Moreover, all occupational groups, not simply the metal workers, were henceforward to be almost automatically secured against rising prices by inclusion of the index-based wage system in their collective agreements. After the conclusion of the two-party agreement the price-wage spiral began to move upwards with frightening speed. Prices and wages seemed to have joined in a kind of St Vitus's dance.[73]

What, it may be asked, were the true motives of the Social Democrat leaders for recommending to their followers, without immediate cause, the abandonment of the food subsidies, the last relic of the new state's emergency days? One plausible explanation for this sudden change of mind is a recognition that the worst scarcities of the post-war years, manifested by the wide gap between the demand and the supply of vital goods, had been gradually removed in the course of 1921 and that in future the provision of food and clothing could be secured without government intervention. This was a view shared of course by the government as well as by conservative economic and financial circles. Dr Wilhelm Rosenberg, managing director of Anglo-Österreichische Bank and *eminence grise* to the Minister of Finance, put it as follows: 'In the first two years since the (Empire's) collapse the Austrian economy has lived on its capital, by incurring debts, and on assistance until such time as the production crisis was overcome, that is, till it had again obtained coal and raw materials.'[74] The most important indicators appeared to confirm his interpretation and that of the Social Democrat leaders. Agricultural production had in 1921 risen far above the 1918 level. Most export branches were working to full capacity. Unemployment had fallen to a record low. The picture was less favourable however if seen in the light of the balance of payments.

Any study relating to the flow of payments to and from abroad during the years of inflation is bound to encounter great difficulties because of the extreme currency fluctuations and the lack of statistical data. The present description can convey only a rough picture of actual developments.

In 1920 the trade deficit amounted to 768.2 million gold crowns and rose the following year to 794.6 million gold crowns.[75] No estimate exists for the first post-war year, but it is probably a reasonable assumption that the deficit will have been only half that of a 'normal' inflation year because Austria's relations with the outside world were then still distinctly limited. Supposing this to be correct, the deficit for the first three years is likely to have achieved the handsome total of 2,000 million gold crowns.

The adverse trade balance was not however the sole cause for the constant flow of gold and paper money abroad. Exporters increasingly tended, as has been said before, in the face of progressive inflation to deposit a considerable portion of their proceeds in foreign banks. Substantial piles of foreign currency were maintained outside the country, the League of Nations delegation was told.[76] Large quantities of paper money were also secretly taken across the frontiers and exchanged in foreign markets for hard (or harder) currencies. All these transactions were of course inspired by speculative motives and the constantly fading confidence in the crown's recuperative power. Dividend and interest payments by Austria to foreign countries need not be considered because they remained unimportant for as long as a general settlement of Austria's foreign debts was pending.

How did the country meet its enormous balance of payments deficit? In the first place it obtained relief credits to a total of 552 million gold crowns which did not need to be paid back.[77] It was also the recipient of innumerable relief consignments donated by various charitable Western organizations. During the first three years their value probably amounted to 50 million dollars or 250 million gold crowns.[78] In addition there were invisible earnings arising from transit trade, from the services of banks and transport firms, from tourism, and from purchases of foreign visitors. The foreign exchange receipts from these sources were certainly very modest in 1919, but during the two following years they greatly grew in importance, not least under the influence of inflation. Charles Rist, the French economist, assessed the annual receipts in foreign exchange due to Vienna's intermediary position as around 200 million gold crowns.[79] An estimate by Dr Hans Schmidt, a civil servant, placed the receipts from tourism in 1921 at some 50 million gold crowns.[80] In the preceding two years they are likely to have been considerably lower.

Interest and dividend inflows from abroad during the inflation period were not large enough to merit attention. The major portion of Austrian capital investments were in the Successor States which blocked transfers except for the purchase of goods and services. The importance of two further sources of foreign exchange receipts allows no reasonable assessment. The first of these was the sale of Austrian securities and of foreign securities in domestic possession, the second consisted of short term loans by foreign banks and trading concerns which, after the beginning of the recession in western Europe, were generously extended to Austrian importers of foodstuffs, fuels, and raw materials.

From the foregoing data it is regrettably impossible to form an even partially sound, consistent picture of how Austria did succeed during the inflation years in meeting its adverse trade balance. All its receipts from long term loans, relief consignments, international services, and sale of securities may have covered about half to two-thirds of the deficit. The remainder was covered by short term credits and the export of paper money.[81]

At the end of 1921 government and opposition had agreed with surprising unanimity to abandon the food subsidies and to take a crucial step along the road of return to the *laissez-faire* system of the past. Christian Socialists and Social Democrats had naturally no illusions about the deficit on the balance of payments, but their courageous decision seems to have relied mainly on the potentially dynamic aspects of the situation. They counted, in other words, on the favourable trends of the last few years continuing, perhaps becoming intensified, in the era of stabilization. A further consideration appears also to have influenced their conclusion. Austrian and foreign observers were agreed that the beginning of stabilization would be the signal for substantial capital imports in the form of repatriated domestic moneys and foreign capital in search of investments.[82]

The inter-party agreement of 21 December was not however the prelude to the longed-for era of stabilization. Instead it led to the last, the most spectacular act in the tragedy of inflation. The events of 1922 will be the subject of Chapter 4.

Notes

1 Cf. Part III, Chap. 3, p. 205 et seq.
2 These figures are based on the Parity Commission's index of living costs (excluding housing costs). See Appendix II, Table 6.
3 Jan van Walré de Bordes, *The Austrian Crown, Its Depreciation and Stabilization* (London, 1924), p. 159.
4 In the first half of 1919 the monetary circulation rose from 4,500 million crowns to 7,398 million crowns. In the absence of any separate statements on monetary

circulation inside Austria – at this time the separation between the currencies in the Danubian area had not yet taken place – recourse must again be had to Walré de Bordes' estimates (p. 48).

5 For the first half of 1919 the budget deficit amounted to 601 million crowns. Only 84% of expenditure could be met from current revenue. Cf. Part IV, Chap. 3, p. 318 et seq.

6 To the degree that foreign investors hoarded crowns in the expectation that the Austrian currency would recover a part of its former value abroad they too had a share, although one difficult to assess, in the losses caused by inflation. Walré de Bordes' guess that this share must have been a very modest one is indubitably correct. 'The mark was, so to speak, sustained for several years by the fact that foreigners were willing to buy it, whereas the crown began to plunge down immediately at a headlong pace.' (p. 192) Nevertheless foreign banks and enterprises seem temporarily to have maintained not inconsiderable crown assets in certain major Austrian banks. One passage in an analysis of the Wiener Bankverein balance sheet runs, 'It can be assumed that of the 10,000 million [crowns] external funds administered by the bank a very large proportion consists of crowns held by foreign banks and big concerns . . . And these short-term foreign loans in the last resort meet the deficit in the balance of payments.' 'Wiener Bankverein', *Der Österreichische Volkswirt*, 4 June 1921, p. 141.

7 Otto Bauer, 'Die Österreichische Revolution', *Werkausgabe* (Vienna, 1976), Vol. II, p. 750.

8 Cf. Documents No. 516 and 667 of the Annex to the Shorthand Minutes of the Constituent National Assembly and John V. van Sickle, *Direct Taxation in Austria* (Cambridge, 1931), p. 66.

9 Cf. Part III, Chap. 3, p. 205 et seq.

10 Certain well-known economists, including Gustav Cassel, Ludwig von Mises, and Albert Hahn, have defined the volume of money as being the *determining* variable of the price level. Others, such as Karl Helfferich and M. J. Bonn, see the triggering factor for the inflationary process as residing in the negative balance of payments. Academic opinions on this point are utterly irreconcilable and have to this day exercised a certain influence on the theory of inflation. From what has been said in the present study it should have become clear that neither of these theories can claim a monopoly and that to both, given certain *historical* conditions, a certain explanatory value attaches although they somewhat simplify reality. A short, but remarkably concise, account of these conflicting opinions is found in Gerd Hardach, 'Zur zeitgenössischen Debatte der Nationalökonomen über die Ursachen der deutschen Nachkriegsinflation', in *Industrielles System und politische Entwicklung in der Weimarer Republik* (Düsseldorf, 1973), ed. Hans Mommsen, Dietmar Petzina, and Bernd Weisbroad, p. 368 et seq.

11 'So we are in the hybrid state of half reluctantly, half willingly approaching the world market level and of having in many respects already reached it while on the other hand nominally still upholding the price regulations which in the light of that programme must appear uneconomic and nonsensical.' See *Der Österreichische Volkswirt*, 24 April 1920, p. 578.

12 Cf. Ludwig von Mises, 'Die Geldtheoretische Seite des Stabilisierungsproblems', *Schriften des Vereins für Sozialpolitik* (Munich-Leipzig, 1925), Vol. 164, p. 5 et seq.

13 'From the outset the Austrian state was encumbered by heavy deficits, all the more

as a disproportionately large share of necessary foodstuffs had to be imported from abroad while adequate export set-offs could not be effected.' Emil Lederer, 'Die soziale Krise in Österreich', *Archiv für Sozialwissenschaften und Sozialpolitik* (Tübingen, 1921), Vol. 48, p. 685.

14 Cf. Fritz Machlup, *Die Goldkernwährung* (Halberstadt, 1925), p. 120 et seq.

15 The above-mentioned theory also disregards the disturbing effect of capital movements and speculative currency deals which played so important a part in post-1918 inflationary development.

16 One of the earliest, most staunch supporters of abolition was the agrarian economist and politician Siegfried Strakosch. See *Neue Freie Presse*, 23 February 1920, and *Die Börse*, 27 October 1921.

17 Gustav Stolper, 'Vor der Entscheidung', *Der Österreichische Volkswirt*, 13 December 1919, p. 210.

18 Walré de Bordes, *Austrian Crown*, p. 141.

19 The following table illustrates the rapid rise of imports in 1920:

	Bread Cereals & Flour	Edible Fats	Coal & Coke	Cotton
	in quintals			
2nd half-year 1919	2,359,571	122,036	12 m.	26,511
2nd half-year 1920	3,065,702	216,198	20 m.	63,232

Source: 'Statistische Übersichten über den auswärtigen Handel', *Statistische Zentralkommission* (Vienna, 1922).

20 'The attraction exercised by Vienna, thanks to the large gap between the crown's purchasing power and its exchange rate, between its value at home and abroad, between domestic and world market prices, restored its status of a major commercial centre ... Vienna recovered its old function as a commercial intermediary between the industrial areas of the Sudetenland and the agrarian areas of the Danube basin. And, with commerce moving again, trade and industry at last began to revive.' Otto Bauer, *Werkausgabe*, vol. I, p. 750.

21 A contemporary had the following to say about the need for converting business calculations into gold crowns: 'This conversion was one that, strictly speaking, the business man ought to have performed daily, i.e., he ought to have put his business on the basis of gold calculation. Most private businesses did not however do this – partly because they did not grasp the situation, partly because police regulations were in the way, and partly as a result of most people's inborn inertia.' Hans Patzauer, 'Die Staatswirtschaft', *Schriften des Vereins für Sozialpolitik* (Munich-Leipzig, 1925), Vol. 169, p. 266.

22 This excerpt from a memorandum by the Association of Austrian Banks and Bankers, dated 2 January 1920, is typical of the arguments used in a series of submissions filed at the Ministry of Finance: 'The association must observe that all measures undertaken by the authorities to restrict free trading have been shown to be completely ineffectual, inasmuch as on the one hand they were unsuited to the

achievement of their purpose and on the other, matters standing as they do today, the feasibility of eliminating or even curtailing this state of affairs which has supervened must be totally dismissed. Free trading in foreign exchange as well as in foreign notes and coins has become established to the most extensive degree not only in Vienna, but similarly at all larger-sized places in the provinces. Taking into consideration the constantly growing intercourse with other countries, frequently under the patronage of the Entente Powers, it has regained so many of its normal paths as to make it unthinkable today for an apparatus to be created and rules to be imposed capable in practice of controlling and guaranteeing the supervision of the regulations prescribed for dealings in foreign currencies . . . In view of the given situation the undersigned Association of Austrians Banks and Bankers has been forced to realize, and takes the liberty of drawing in the most urgent terms the attention of the High State Authority to the fact that the downright shameful conditions now prevailing as to commerce and deals in foreign currencies require the speediest abolition and that it is out of the question to allow conditions to endure whereby, as the High State Authority is not unaware, countless millions in Austria are daily converted into foreign exchange and foreign notes and coins with only *the leading banks and bankers, the best entitled agents in this line of business, being excluded from these same transactions while second-rate and often rotten elements dominate the market, unimpeded and unpunished, regardless of all existing prohibitions.*' Ministry of Finance Archives 66254/1920. (Present author's italics.)

23 Cf. Walther Federn, 'Die Freigabe des Devisenhandels', *Der Österreichische Volkswirt*, 16 October 1920, p. 35.

24 Karl Ausch, *Als die Banken fielen* (Vienna, 1968), p. 20. A British observer of the speculation against the crown gave the following description: 'An English accountant, who was in Vienna at the time of the stabilization, proved by an analysis of the figures that during one part of the inflation period it was possible to make a fortune of one million sterling in six months' time with an initial capital of £100. The process was simple. One deposited one's hundred pounds with the Credit-Anstalt and borrowed Austrian Kronen against them at the rate of 100 kronen to the £1. One then walked across the road to the WienerBankverein and bought a hundred pounds with the 10,000 Austrian Kronen. One then had £200 and one owed 10,000 crowns. As the exchange fell, one borrowed more crowns against the £200 and bought more pounds with the borrowed crowns. By the time the exchange had fallen from 100 crowns to 100,000 to the £1, one had amassed a sterling fortune and one's debt in crowns was almost wiped out.' R. H. Bruce Lockhart, *Retreat from Glory* (London, 1934), p. 114.

25 Walther Federn, 'Die Entwertung der Krone', *Der Österreichische Volkswirt*, 25 December 1920, p. 213.

26 'This certainty in the mind of Austrian commerce and Austrian industry that foreign valuta would continually rise, had the result that commerce, industry and finance set to work to cover themselves for periods continually increasing in length, and were forced to do so. If a man owes sterling abroad, which he has to pay at some later date, he does not want to buy sterling till the debt falls due; he buys today because he knows that he gets it cheapest today. The industrialist, financing his raw materials, and the merchant, who has payments ahead of him for his imports, do the same thing. The process must every day be intensified . . . At the present day industry and commerce are covering themselves for six to eight

months ahead; and financial capitalists are making provision to meet their liabilities for still longer periods ahead.' From an address by Sir William Goode on 24 January 1922 and quoted by Walré de Bordes, *Austrian Crown*, p. 190.

27 Walré de Bordes, *Austrian Crown*.

28 Walré de Bordes, *Austrian Crown*, p. 192.

29 Quoted from van Sickle, *Direct Taxation*, p. 72.

30 Patzauer, *Schriften*, p. 274.

31 Cf. Karl Přibram, *The Foreign Trade Policy of Austria* (Washington, 1945), p. 16.

32 'A state that wants to fight rising prices should not lead the way when it is a matter of increasing the costs of goods and services.' Patzauer, *Schriften*, p. 270. The author was a senior Ministry of Finance official.

33 Alexander Spitzmüller, . . . *und hat auch Ursach' es zu lieben* (Vienna, 1955), p. 333.

34 Cf. *Der Österreichische Volkswirt*, 8, 15, 22, and 29 January as well as 5 February 1922.

35 *International Financial Conference*. (Report of the Conference, Brussels, 1920).

36 'Above all the Brussels Financial Conference expressed its conviction that the solution to the problem of adverse payments balances . . . was not a matter of ingenuity. Decidedly and rightly it turned down the panaceas proclaimed by various sides, such as creation of a supranational money or a supranational accounting unit, fixing the ratio between paper money and gold, and so on.' Richard Schüller, the well-known economist and adviser to numerous Austrian Governments, 'Report on the Brussels Conference', quoted by Martha Stephanie Braun, 'Die Doppelnote', *Schriften des Vereins für Sozialpolitik* (Munich-Leipzig, 1924), Vol. 165, p. 127 et seq.

37 *International Financial Conference*, p. 11.

38 The Austrian press protested vehemently against the idea of giving the Reparation Commission the function of supervising the reconstruction plan's implementation. 'Assignment of the real sovereignty to the Reparation Commission will indeed help to destroy the last vestiges of self-responsibility and sense of duty towards a polity that will then with some justification seem no more than a colony belonging to hostile Powers.' Gustav Stolper, 'Aufbaupläne', *Der Österreichische Volkswirt*, 15 January 1921, p. 268.

39 'The only positive gain apparently secured in London is that the Loucheur Assistance Plan, which aimed at putting German-Austria into the hands of an international consortium of exploiters armed with unlimited plenary powers, seems to have run aground. It may be assumed that our ministers at Paris and at London rejected M. Loucheur's plans with the firmness to be desired.' 'Kreditverhandlungen', *Der Österreichische Volkswirt*, 26 March 1921. p. 467. See also Victor Kienböck, *Das österreichische Sanierungswerk* (Stuttgart, 1925), p. 16.

40 See *Financial Reconstitution of Austria* (Report of the Financial Committee of the Council. League of Nations, Geneva, 1920), p. 1.

41 As though seeking to excuse this omission, the final section of the delegation's report said, 'The emphasis which has been laid on the basic importance of currency reform for the revival of Austria's economy does not imply that the importance of purely economic causes is underrated.' *Financial Reconstitution*, p. 26.

42 *Financial Reconstitution*, p. 19.

43 *Financial Reconstitution*, p. 24.

44 *Financial Reconstitution*, p. 24.

45 'The principles of such supervision were granted even in political circles, on condition that it was given a form which would be acceptable to the Austrian government.' *Financial Reconstitution*, p. 39.

46 'The Association of Social Democratic Members (of Parliament) has examined the information received on the government's negotiations with the delegates from the League of Nations Financial Committee and on the government's financial programme drafted in connection with these negotiations and [it] has authorized us to communicate its views on the measures under consideration: our Party, now as heretofore, desires to support all efforts on behalf of procuring foreign loans for the import of foodstuffs and restoring a stable currency. We are also aware that this objective cannot be achieved without the restoration of equilibrium in the Republic's budget. It is however for the government to lay proposals to this end before the *Nationalrat* and for the *Nationalrat*'s ruling majority to determine the state's revenue and expenditure. It is not part of a parliamentary opposition's functions and duties to share responsibility for the government's financial management . . . The sole obligation that we, as opposition, can assume vis-à-vis the League of Nations Financial Committee's delegates is therefore that we shall, if our party should take over the reins of government, naturally regard ourselves as bound by all validly concluded international agreements.' *Die Tätigkeit des Verbandes der Sozialdemokratischen Abgeordneten der Republik Österreich*, No. 16, p. 18 et seq.

47 In summer 1921 a small group of individuals in London and Paris was told that the Congress at Washington would probably take several months yet to agree to the relinquishment of the Allied Powers' lien on Austrian property, the step essential to obtaining private loans. This initially secret information was made public through a leakage published in the Paris edition of *Chicago Tribune*. The paper also drew the conclusion that this put paid to the reconstruction plan. When on 23 July the report became known at Vienna, the previous day's dollar rate of 841 crowns soared to 958 crowns. Cf. Walré de Bordes, *Austrian Crown*, p. 141.

48 The rise in the Czech currency, starting in late summer 1921, also contributed to the depreciation because Austrian importers had to pay constantly mounting prices for Czech coal and foodstuffs. The German Government was moreover buying Western currency in all markets, Vienna by no means least, and so drove up the foreign exchange prices prevailing there. Cf. Ausch, *Als die Banken*, p. 38.

49 'The measures taken by Dr Gürtler were, however, found to be somewhat innocuous . . .' Walré de Bordes, *Austrian Crown*, p. 142.

50 From November 1918 until December 1921 the crown's depreciation in foreign exchange markets was ten times as high as the increase of the domestic price level (assessed in terms of the cost of living index). The discrepancy between the two orders of magnitude is however substantially less if July 1914 is taken as the point of reference.

51 'There is no longer any need to count up the occupations where the wage drive is under way because there is not a single occupation which is an exception. The metal workers took the lead and now all others have followed – the railwaymen, the miners, the printers, the transport workers . . . To the workers in industry there have been added the public service employees whose fixed appointment position has made it even more difficult for them to adjust to the quickly changing prices . . . They are in a condition similar to that of most civil servants. Recently

425

indeed a very lively wage trend has developed among the technical officials and employees in commerce, banks, insurance companies, and in industry.' 'Sozialpolitische Rundschau', *Der Kampf*, September 1918, p. 646 et seq.

52 Emil Lederer, 'Die soziale Krise in Österreich', *Archiv für Sozialwissenschaften und Sozialpolitik* (Tübingen, 1921), p. 687.

53 Benedikt Kautsky, 'Löhne und Gehälter', *Schriften des Vereins für Sozialpolitik* (Munich-Leipzig, 1925), Vol. 169, p. 113.

54 Cf. Appendix II, Table 7, showing the movement in the cost of living and the progress in metal workers' money wages from 1914 to 1922.

55 The improvement in the food situation in spring 1919 is perceptible from the following table:

Food Rations per Person per Week (in kg.)

Period	Bread Cereals	Flour	Cooking Fat	Sugar	Beef	Potatoes	Pork
30.9.1918 –6.1.1919	1.2	0.25	0.04	0.75	0.15	0.5	—
19.5–13.7.1919	1.575	0.5	0.12	0.75	0.15	0.5–1	0.125

See Ilse Arlt, 'Der Einzelhaushalt', *Schriften des Vereins für Sozialpolitik* (Munich-Leipzig, 1925), Vol. 169, p. 166.

56 Karl Přibram, 'Die Sozialpolitik im neuen Österreich', *Archiv für Sozialwissenschaften und Sozialpolitik* (Tübigen, 1921), Vol. 48 p. 676.

57 Přibram, *Archiv*, p. 676 et seq.

58 'As a matter of historical truth it has to be recorded that the resistance to the introduction of this, to us, new principle was far greater in the ranks of the manual and white-collar workers' trade unions than in those of managements.' See Viktor Stein, 'Zum Kampf um den Index', *Der Kampf*, September-October, 1922, p. 274.

59 Dr Max Lederer, a senior civil servant, described some of the special indexes in 'Indexziffern und Industrielöhne', *Der Österreichische Volkswirt*, 19 September 1922, p. 1,200 et seq.

60 See Appendix II, Table 7.

61 See *Mitteilungen der Statistischen Zentralkommission* (Vienna, 1921), No. 2.

62 That wages trail behind the cost of living during periods of inflation is a familiar feature. Bresciano-Urroni, writing on the inflation in post-1918 Germany, said that in its last year skilled workers' wages amounted to some half of their pre-war value. Cf. Constantino Bresciani-Turroni, *The Economics of Inflation* (London, 1937), p. 305. A similar observation for the time of the American Civil War is to be found in Wesley C. Mitchell, *History of Greenbacks* (Chicago, 1903), p. 347 et seq.

63 Arnold Madlé, 'Die Bezüge der öffentlichen Angestellten', *Schriften des Vereins für Sozialpolitik* (Munich-Leipzig, 1925), Vol. 169, p. 135.

64 Some champions of the urban white-collar class held the labour organizations responsible for their impoverishment. 'They include the majority of those whose work depends on using their brains ... proletarians representing the weaker groups of employees, white-collar workers in academic and scientific establishments ... small pensioners whose incomes ... are the scanty outcome of a whole life's toilsome labour. What have they done to deserve having their income cut,

in favour of the manual and white-collar workers' real wages, to where it drops below human subsistence level?' Siegfried Strakosch, *Der Selbstmord eines Volkes* (Vienna, 1922), p. 45.

65 It should be particularly emphasized here that in 1921 agricultural production had risen notably above the 1918 level. For further details on the performance of the economy's various sectors during the inflation, see next chapter.

66 Between October and December 1921 the number of unemployed rose from 8,709 to 16,713. See *Statistiken zur Arbeitslosenversicherung* (Ministry for Social Affairs, Vienna, 1930), p. 9.

67 Cf. *Neue Freie Presse* and *Arbeiter-Zeitung*, 2 December 1921.

68 The author of one of the most thorough studies of Austria's social history between 1919 and 1939 regards Bauer's reform plan as an exceedingly constructive contribution. 'It shows better than any theoretical propositions that the Austrian socialists were deeply conscious of their responsibility toward the whole of society and that they did their utmost to save the economy of the country and to restore normal economic life within the framework of the existing political and social order.' Charles A. Gulick, *Austria: From Habsburg to Hitler* (Berkeley and Los Angeles, 1948) Vol. I, p. 164.

69 Dr Victor Kienböck, for many years Minister of Finance and Chairman of the Austrian National Bank during the First Republic, welcomed the recognition that reconstruction without foreign loans would not be possible. 'Obviously, though,' he added, 'it was politically illogical on the one hand to recognize the repeal of the reparation lien as an essential prerequisite, but on the other to reject the Entente Powers' assistance in the procurement of credits.' Kienböck, *Das Österreichische Sanierung* p. 19.

70 'The amount of the subsidies in the 1922 draft budget was originally put at 84,000 million crowns, taking the average foreign exchange rates for the first three weeks in October as the basis of calculation. In December, allowing for the deterioration in the currency, the revised requirements were put at 250,000 millions, but the total estimates of receipts came only to 208,000 millions.' Ausch, *Als die Banken* p. 33, footnote. See also *Arbeiter-Zeitung*, 6 December 1921.

71 Federal Law Gazette, 21 December 1921, No. 705. The act offered moreover a tax evasion amnesty to all who would exchange their hoarded foreign currency against a domestic gold loan. Even this tempting offer bore virtually no fruit.

72 'The so-called compromise over the question of [food subsidy] reductions hides the fact that the Social Democratic party has completely capitulated only in the eyes of the blind.' Gustav Stolper, 'Eine ganze Niederlage', *Der Österreichische Volkswirt*, 24 December 1921, p. 302.

73 The sudden abolition of the food subsidies, for which the Social Democrats must carry the main responsibility, was rejected by the majority of the workers. They feared that the wage index system would not furnish adequate protection against the rise in the cost of living. Hereupon the socialist leadership tried in a widespread public campaign to convince their followers that relinquishment had been inevitable if a catastrophe was to be avoided. Cf., for example, *Arbeiter-Zeitung*, 23 December 1921.

74 Wilhelm Rosenberg, 'Staatsfinanzielle Fragen', *Der Österreichische Volkswirt*, 22 October 1921, p. 76.

75 See *Der Aussenhandel Österreichs in der Zeit zwischen den beiden Weltkriegen* (Austrian Central Statistical Office, Vienna, 1946), p. 9.

76 'As regards reserves of ready money, they hardly exist save in the form of foreign currency. Several estimates supplied to the Delegation appear to agree in calculating the total amount of foreign currency thus held in Vienna at one milliard Swiss francs.' *Financial Reconstitution of Austria* (League of Nations Geneva, 1926), p. 21.

77 Cf. Walther Federn, 'Die auswärtigen Anleihen Österreichs', *Schriften des Vereins für Sozialpolitik* (Munich-Leipzig, 1928), Vol. 174, p. 200.

78 Cf. Sir Arthur Salter, *Financial Reconstruction of Austria* (League of Nations, Geneva, 1926), p. 11.

79 Cf. *Revue politique et parlementaire*, 10 June 1923, p. 408 et seq. Walré de Bordes thought Rist's assumptions too optimistic. Cf. *The Austrian Crown*, p. 187.

80 Cf. Hans Schmidt, 'Berichte aus den neuen Staaten, *Handelsblatt*, March 1922. Certain fairly reliable estimates for the receipts from tourism exist for 1923. They were probably about 124 million schillings or 86 million gold crowns. From this it may be assumed that Schmidt's estimates for 1921 were somewhat too low. Cf. Hugo Zienert, 'Die Zahlungsbilanz Österreichs', *10 Jahre Wiederaufbau* (ed. Wilhelm Exner, Vienna, 1928), p. 295 et seq.

81 In the later 1920s too the adverse trade balance had to be met by considerable foreign loans, mainly on a short-term basis. H. T. N. Gaitskell, the outstanding British Labour party leader and a professional economist, assessed the amount of the loans borrowed by Austria between 1923 and 1930 as being between 3,000 and 4,000 million schillings. Cf. *Lloyds Bank Review*, May 1934, p. 199.

82 'When Austria is provided with a sound and stable currency, the financial importance of Vienna will increase, both through the development of the deposits as a result of international transactions effected in Vienna, and also by foreign deposits of capital in search of investment: foreign balances will increase and will serve automatically as credit.' *Financial Reconstruction*, p. 25.

CHAPTER 3
The Major Banks and Industry during the Inflation

During the war the crown's exchange rate had, as has been seen, fallen comparatively slowly. After the conclusion of the Armistice however, the value of the dollar rose steeply until by the close of 1920 it had overtaken rises in the level of prices and of money in circulation. In the final months of 1919, and for the best part of the succeeding year the dollar (or a gold unit of account) had approximately the same purchasing power on the Austrian market as in pre-war days. This is apparent from the following table:[1]

Table 47   Cost of living and dollar exchange rate index, 1919–20

July 1914 = 1	Cost of Living Index (without housing)	$ Exchange Rate Index
15 December 1919	31.02	30.98
15 January 1920	49.22	41.27
15 April 1920	58.42	40.69
15 July 1920	63.76	29.87
15 October 1920	69.60	62.63
15 January 1921	92.18	142.12

The dollar's purchasing power in the world market was, however, now distinctly less than it had been in the years immediately preceding 1914. The United States Bureau of Labor Statistics figures show the index of wholesale prices in 1920 to have been 200% above the level for 1913 and also show an average fluctuation during the following three years of around 150%.[2] With the dollar rate in 1920 increasing in terms of the crown at about the same rate as the Austrian price level, a unit of gold had in Austria about twice the purchasing power that it possessed elsewhere.[3] Austrian exporters were therefore able to sell their goods at a substantially lower price than their foreign competitors. For the next two years domestic industry benefited from a continually rising 'inflation premium' due to the fact that the dollar rose faster than the cost of living.[4]

Table 48   Cost of living and dollar exchange rate index, 1921–22

July 1914 = 1	Cost of living index (without housing)	$ Exchange rate index
15 January 1921	92.18	142.12
15 April 1921	111.34	128.48
15 July 1921	124.66	156.16
15 October 1921	237.76	532.73
15 January 1922	830.00	1,373.74
15 April 1922	1,089.00	1,540.40
15 July 1922	3,308.00	6,035.35
15 September 1922	14,153.00	15,029.78

The recovery of industry proceeded exceedingly jerkily even though during inflation foreign buyers were able to buy domestic goods very cheaply. The year 1919 had been one of acute coal, food, and raw materials shortages. Although no production estimates are available, output is likely to have dropped quite considerably below that of the last year of hostilities. In 1920, when modest amounts of vital raw materials could be imported, the index of industrial production stood at barely half that for 1913. Even after foreign trade became more normal, industry's progress remained sluggish. In 1923 the crown's exchange rate was no longer subject to fluctuations, yet the industrial production index is likely to have attained no more than two-thirds of its pre-war level.[5]

These overall indexes obviously conceal considerable differences. This is particularly true of coal mining which, on account of increased demand, had in 1920 already reached its pre-war level and in the next two years made rapid strides.[6] The sawmills and timber industries, chemicals and paper were able to expand output to no small extent, albeit from 1920 onward to a lesser degree. In the first year of currency stabilization all of these industries achieved or surpassed their pre-war levels.[7] The production of consumer goods, such as textiles, leather, clothing, foodstuffs and allied products, on the other hand, did not even roughly approach the 1913 figures. The difficulty of obtaining raw materials was partly responsible, but essentially the failure of output to expand was due to the drastic reduction in real incomes. Only a small privileged class, inflation's fortune hunters, was in a position to keep alive a luxury industry, throwing into ever starker relief the picture of general impoverishment.

A large part of the capacity of the iron foundries remained idle. In 1919 Alpine-Montan intermittently kept a single furnace going. The pig-iron output was 10% of that of 1913. As late as 1922, when coal supplies became fairly normal, the figure for iron production remained half that of the last pre-war years.[8] In the metal-working industry, whose workshops had undergone considerable expansion during the war, the situation was similar. Many firms in the machine-building, tool-making, motor vehicles construction, and electrical industries nevertheless could, as the trade statistics show, secure substantial foreign orders.[9]

The lively export trade due to the 'inflation premium' enabled the country to recover a place in the international market reasonably quickly and ensured for the mass of the population a more or less tolerable existence after the years of prolonged deprivation. It did not, to be sure, lead to the high investment level from which a restoration of the new political entity's material foundations could have developed. The number of factories with twenty and more workers rose from 6,283 in 1919 to 7,419 in 1922; the number of workers rose from 566,891 in 1919 to 781,888 in 1921.[10] Most of the new plants had however, as Hertz points out, only small capacities and belonged primarily to branches of the timber, foodstuffs and textile industries and to electric power generation. A great number of the new firms, especially those engaged in food and textiles manufacture, were not to prove viable in the raw climate of the stabilization period.[11]

Regardless of the rise in employment figures during inflation, it is almost certain that a large amount of industrial capacity remained unused.[12] The somewhat higher number of workers insured against accidents in 1921 than in 1913 seems to contradict this, but the apparent discrepancy vanishes when it is recalled that introduction of the eight-hour working day necessitated a larger number of employees to achieve the same volume of production.[13] The productivity of labour in some branches is, moreover, likely to have been lower at this time than before the war. Finally it must not be overlooked that 1913 too, was a recession year and consequently there was some unemployment.

What conclusions can be drawn from the scanty data on the formation of capital during these years? In 1913 some '13% of the national product was invested, twice as much as would have been necessary to keep up the stock of productive capital. Net investments were 7% of gross output.'[14] Even by international standards this was a remarkable performance, it was not to be attained again until after the Second World War. This same study by the Austrian Institute for

Economic Research assumes that gross investments during 1924–1937 were probably 7% of gross output, barely enough for the *upkeep* of the capital stock. This shockingly low level of investment was probably not appreciably exceeded during the years of inflation and the process of depletion of the capital stock, brought on by the war economy, continued.[15] 'Flight from the mark to the machine,' Beckmann called German entrepreneurial behaviour. It could hardly have been said of Austria.[16]

There is no great difficulty in understanding this disinclination to invest. Large unused capacities have been mentioned as one reason. Export 'achievements' remained, as will be seen, within comparatively narrow bounds. And there was a phenomenon labelled in the literature on the subject as a 'want' or a 'deficiency' of capital caused by inflation. Pre-war days had often enough heard industrialists complaining about 'lack of funds'. Circumstances prevailing during the post-war inflation turned shortage into a strangulating stringency.

During the war the volume of money had initially expanded faster than the level of prices. From 1917 onward the trend was reversed, although during the last year of hostilities the two were increasing at about the same rate. With the onset of post-war inflation prices raced ahead at an ever quickening pace until in September 1922 they reached four times the quantity of money in circulation.[17] The real value of the money in circulation as ascertained through dividing the stock of money by the cost of living index, had dropped to a quarter of its pre-war value.[18]

Businessmen naturally had difficulty in adapting their calculations to the constantly changing rhythm of inflation. 'The fall of the crown', runs a passage in the League of Nations report, 'may reduce profits to such an extent that capital will be lacking for the purchase of the raw materials indispensable to the continuation of work.'[19] The destruction of industrial working capital, so often deplored, was not simply a matter of businessmen's 'miscalculations'; it had to do with the relative shortage of money in the later stages of hyper-inflation. The demand for liquid resources accordingly grew without the banks being always able to satisfy industry's expanding appetite.[20] According to Professor Strigl smaller firms suffered particularly from this shortage of money:

> Smaller firms which had not previously had recourse to the banks often had to go begging for money from one bank to another only to be told again and again 'We can't enter into new connections now'. For an employer to have to pawn his family's jewellery was no rare occurrence. Shop stewards often

acted as their firm's intermediaries with all sorts of agencies so as to procure the money to pay the wages and to finance what was often a completely sound production. One undertaking actually borrowed the cash for its workers from their own trade union.[21]

The smaller firms also had to accept the handicap of exceptionally high interest rates, and in times of depreciation borrowers had to pay on top of normal interest an increasing risk bonus in the measure of the currency's vanishing value. In this respect many banks, led by those new banking houses not more than marginally concerned with everyday banking operations and concentrating mainly on stock exchange commission business, made too much of a good thing. Even banks of high repute charged their prime customers twenty to thirty per cent for overdraft facilities. Clients of smaller banks generally had to pay a substantially higher rate.[22] To this was added an 'advance commission' calculated on the basis of the maximum amount of the credit.[23] The desire of bank managements to recoup with this lending policy their own capital resources, which had severely diminished in the course of the war and the ensuing emergency, indubitably influenced their behaviour. They had, after all, an extremely tempting – or anyway enormously lucrative – alternative for the employment of their funds. They could finance stock exchange speculations: 'Up to 5% per week, i.e., 260% per annum,' reported *Der Österreichische Volkswirt*,

has been paid in the past seven days for transactions of this kind. Similar, and still higher, rates were paid months ago for carry-overs on securities and foreign exchange at the time of the catastrophic boom. When participation in the speculation receded, so did the interest rates, but in November they still stood at 1½% to 3% per week and then suddenly dropped to ½%, or 26% per annum, a rate below the current cost of credits for industry and commerce.'[24]

In this situation of tight, flagrantly dear money, many enterprises turned to foreign capital and/or capital increases by the repeated issue of new shares. The massive transfer abroad of domestic securities in 1919, inspired mainly by the acute lack of coal and raw materials, the fear of socialization and the precarious financial situation of Austrian capitalists in the Successor States, has been recorded. During the period of the Stock Exchange boom, lasting until spring 1924, the placements of new shares through the capital market assumed massive proportions, as is evident from Table 49.[25]

There can be no doubt that the shortage of capital and high interest rates seriously hampered reconstruction of the industry.[26] The table

Table 49   Joint-Stock Companies' capital increases and new issues,[1] *1919–24*

	Nominal Capital in cr. m.						Total Incr. 1919–24 in crowns m.
	1919	1920	1921	1922	1923	1924	
1. Mining and Metallurgy	147	241	836	11,530	16,655	23,740	23,593
2. Quarrying & Earth Excavation	59	85	204	4,103	11,420	26,800	26,741
3. Metal Process.	188	357	857	7,437	16,680	42,830	42,642
4. Machines & Vehicles Construction, etc.	187	516	1,421	8,125	22,610	39,850	39,663
5. Lighting, Power, and Cables Equipment	148	353	1,067	25,744	128,060	200,710	200,562
6. Building Indus.	60	78	213	2,410	3,900	10,370	10,310
7. Chemical Indus.	71	186	448	7,136	15,180	26,670	26,599
8. Paper, Printing, Publishing	111	257	568	9,463	18,100	39,680	39,569
9. Textiles	87	155	288	1,792	9,860	16,150	16,063
10. Leather, Rubber & Substitutes	32	62	96	3,480	5,790	8,590	8,558
11. Timber	14	57	350	2,477	12,810	24,876	24,876
12. Food and Allied Products	165	188	392	3,227	22,670	33,780	33,615
13. Clothing & Detergents	35	65	204	1,813	7,040	11,460	11,425
14. Banks & Other Credit Instit.	1,606	2,863	6,761	82,561	154,580	193,290	191,684
15. Insurance	59	63	93	1,185	2,540	3,040	2,981
16. Commerce	158	346	1,154	14,709	46,360	119,560	119,402
17. Transport (less Railways)	105	142	240	7,712	11,910	16,610	16,505
18. Cater. & Hotel Trade (incl. Nurs. Homes)	30	32	92	1,735	6,610	8,280	8,250
19. Other Enterprises	2	2	3	77	970	4,060	4,058
1.–13. Industry	1,304	2,600	6,764	88,737	289,775	505,520	504,216
14.–19. Banking & Other Services	1,960	3,448	8,343	107,979	222,670	344,840	342,880
1.–19. Total	3,264	6,048	15,107	196,716	512,445	850,360	847,096

[1] Not including companies whose places of business were situated preponderantly outside Austria

shows that in only a few sectors (electrical goods and the paper industry) did renewal, possibly a broadening of the capital base occur. This is quite clear in the case of iron and steel, where during the years of inflation practically no investment took place on account of the low utilization of capacity. The voluminous issuing activity in 1923 and in 1924 injected some new blood into industry, but, in consequence of the Vienna Stock Exchange slump starting in the spring of 1924, the influx was modest. The fact that in 1923, after the crown's stabilization, domestic shares were generally regarded as undervalued and therefore became 'fashionable securities for big financing groups' enabled banks and industrial firms at that time to place their new issues comparatively easily in the capital market.[27]

It is hardly possible to estimate the harm done to the economy by entrepreneurs with ready access to loan capital going into speculation because this looked more profitable than traditional business. That the losses caused by this perversion of the managerial mentality were not negligible can only be indirectly discerned by considering the excessive expansion of the tertiary sector during the inflation. Banks and other financial institutions as well as trading companies mushroomed. A contemporary report on the state of the banking system at the close of this development stated:

In January 1913 there were 26 banks and some 15 larger private bankers in the territory of what is now Austria. In 1924 – prior to the crisis – the corresponding figures were 61 and 260, leaving aside the large number of smaller firms in this field. In 1913 the number of depositors with the Vienna Clearing House Association was 342, in 1923 on the other hand 796. In 1913 the issue of Stock Exchange admission cards totalled 842, in 1923 the figure was 1,897. The growth of banks and banking establishments does not however illustrate adequately the excessive proportions assumed by the banking world. Quite apart from the fact that the 1913 figure applied to an economy with fifty million people, which by 1924 had shrunk to a country with six million inhabitants, there were also institutions active in the field of banking which before the war had kept inside narrow, well-defined limits. This was particularly true of the saving banks.[28]

The new establishments, Federn thought, were 'dominated by successful speculators and profiteers' whose ambition was to take advantage of the boom as best they could. Their method was simple – 'You owe crowns, you accumulate tangible assets, commodities, foreign exchange, securities to the greatest possible amount, and you pocket the difference between the unchanging – or practically unchanging – gold value of your investments and the vanishing gold value of your debts.'[29] It is astonishing that the authorities should have almost entirely failed to react in the face of these developments.[30] Perhaps it is only explicable in terms of the fact that broad sections of the middle class had also surrendered to the stock exchange fever in the belief that they could obtain in this way at least partial compensation for their diminished real income.

The prodigious extension of all commission functions, such as money lending, stock exchange business and parasitic commodity deals, into a hectic chase after material assets was the 'normal' effect, as it were, of any inflationary process in its advanced stage. Unhappily hyper-inflation affected Austria particularly badly because the liquidation of the large-scale financial and commercial machinery inherited by the Republic from the Empire was thereby still more delayed. When the inevitable shrinkage began, its point of departure was the 1922 inflation level and not the distinctly lower one prevailing in 1918.

The margin between the crown's domestic and external purchasing power had created the 'inflation premium', leading to a certain revival of exports. In some branches of industry this was a considerable factor.[31]

Table 50   Austrian export trade (in hundred kg.)

	Metal Goods	Machines	Leather & Leather Goods	Textiles	Paper & Paper Goods
1920	797,221	282,286	27,999	73,267	887,599
1921	772,750	411,642	40,443	98,313	957,056
1922	1,015,091	548,924	60,422	154,056	1,162,946

The vigorous expansion of the export volume was offset by a relatively slow rise – and in 1921 indeed a decline – in export earnings. For industry it was not easy, with its obsolescent equipment and the restrictive trade practices of the Successor States, to prevail in markets abroad. In 1921 moreover, a year of recession, world prices fell fairly heavily. Imports and exports developed as follows:[32]

Table 51   Austrian foreign trade, 1920–22 (in gold cr. m.)

	Imports	Exports
1920	1,704.1	935.9
1921	1,698.8	904.2
1922	1,757.3	1,103.7

These statistics show that during the inflationary period the ratio between the values of exports and imports was comparatively stable. The crown's falling exchange rate did not give sufficient impetus to a stimulation of exports nor to a restriction on imports, which would have brought about an equilibrium in the balance of trade.[33] These early years therefore witnessed a problem that was to haunt the First Republic for almost the entire term of its existence – the difficulty of establishing an economic equilibrium in its balance of trade.

In sum it can be said that while a few branches of industry derived advantages from the hyper-inflationary boom, the economy as a whole entered the period of stabilization in a distinctly weakened condition. After the end of hostilities it had looked as though industry, like agriculture, had discharged the major portion of its debt burden and had even acquired a certain cushion in the form of banking assets for the darker days ahead. Progressive inflation, though, necessitated ever greater recourse to credit. A policy of indebtedness in times of inflation can be justified because debts are repaid in devalued currency. Industry was nevertheless able to take only limited advantage of this policy, since in common with the politicians, the economists, and most of the population, it 'failed' to forecast correctly the course of inflation. Likewise the attempt to broaden one's capitalization through repeated issues of new shares, possible only for joint-stock companies, was doomed in days of rapid currency depreciation. Not until 1923, the first year of stabilization, did capital increases act as real tonics. The collapse of the stock exchange boom in the spring of 1924 put an abrupt end to that cheap form of funds procurement. A quotation from Bresciani-Turroni may perhaps fittingly close this review of the situation: 'The depreciation of the currency in an early stage (of inflation) does, in a way, stimulate production, but in a later phase it acts as an increasingly serious obstacle to production, which it disorganizes.'[34]

The major Viennese banks, in contrast to industry's halting and unsatisfactory process of regeneration, appeared to be enjoying a boom during the period of inflation. This had been the case already in the first post-war year; the external signs of a singular expansion could be observed in the years that followed.

The swift depreciation in the value of the currency at the root of the spurious boom was reflected with particular clarity in the balance sheet totals of the major Viennese banks. In 1922 those of the four biggest houses – Creditanstalt, Boden-Creditanstalt, Niederöster-reichische Escompte-Gesellschaft, and Wiener Bankverein – topped 9 thousand million crowns. The medium-sized Unionbank and Ver-kehrsbank took until 1923 to reach this figure. Österreichische Länderbank and Anglo-Österreichische Bank had passed into foreign hands in 1921 and will for the present be left out of consideration.

The foregoing totals are not strictly comparable, because the accounting methods of the banks were not identical.[35] What can be gathered is simply an impression of the general trend, which applies equally to the sequences of numerical data which follow. Creditanstalt was able during the inflationary period, with the exception of the crisis year 1919, to maintain its leading position. Only in 1923 was it outdistanced by Niederösterreichische Escompte-Gesellschaft, which had entered into particularly close association with the Municipality of Vienna. In 1924 the latter bank's balance sheet of more than 4 millions was by far the largest.

Table 52   Major Viennese banks' balance sheet totals (in 000 crowns)

	1913	1919	1920	1921	1922	1923
Creditanstalt	1,181,173	3,505,502[a]	11,560,649	84,502,590	1,449,591,333	2,376,375,589
Boden-Creditanstalt	920,114	4,097,117	6,649,675	34,783,041	1,135,445,869	1,749,162,984
Niederösterreichische Escompte-Gesellschaft	432,381	1,672,348	2,969,273	31,978,814	1,042,732,203	2,425,230,883
Bankverein	918,570	5,431,965[b]	10,318,350	79,540,998	1,105,545,907[b]	2,084,595,588[b]
Unionbank	374,526	1,151,117	2,950,764	20,230,841	279,037,692	1,443,420,657
Mercurbank	283,047	1,343,000	2,842,924	20,376,810	338,408,979	752,496,376
Verkehrsbank	306,780	1,637,569	4,456,954	20,342,134	357,832,480	1,150,643,346

[a] In 1919 practically all non-Austrian branches (thirteen in Czechoslovakia, two in Italy, one in Poland) were disposed of.
[b] Operating results and assets of branches in the Successor States converted into Austrian crowns.
Source: *Compass*, 1915–1925.
For further elucidation of the balance sheet totals, see Appendix II, Table A8 (Viennese Banks Creditors).

Nevertheless the operating results of those years, insofar as they are reflected in the balance sheet totals, look very meagre when converted into peace-time crowns. Table 53 shows the balance sheet figures for the last pre-war year as against the analogous one for the first year of stabilization.[36] (The 1923 balance sheet figures have been deflated with the use of the Parity Commission's price index without rent.)

There is reason to think that the published operating results for 1923 do not convey an adequate picture of the banks' real financial

Table 53   Major Viennese banks' balance sheet totals (in 000 gold crowns)

	1913	1923	1913 = 100
Creditanstalt	1,181,173	170,374	14.5
Boden-Creditanstalt	920,114	125,406	13.5
Niederösterreichische Escompte-Gesellschaft	432,381	173,877	40.0
Wiener Bankverein	918,570	149,455	16.0
Unionbank	374,520	103,486	27.5
Mercurbank	283,047	53,950	19.0
Verkehrsbank	306,780	82,495	27.0

situation. They are likely to have had certain hidden reserves, mainly as balances with banks in the Successor States and as undervalued securities. Nevertheless, even if the balance-sheet totals of the immediate post-war years are subjected to certain revisions, such as become necessary on the occasion of the drawing up of the gold balances, there still remains the impression of a dramatic weakening of the banking system consequent on the war, the disintegration of the Empire, and the years of inflation. The almost complete disappearance of the item relating to mortgage loans explains the striking diminution in the Boden-Creditanstalt total. In the case of Wiener Bankverein the transformation of the numerous branches in Czechoslovakia and Poland into independent joint-stock companies must be kept in mind. They appear in the balance sheet simply as share-holdings. The decline in Creditanstalt's balance sheet total, to approximately one-seventh of the comparable 1913 figure was also very drastic. As with Wiener Bankverein, it was only the – probably undervalued – stocks held in Czech, Polish, and Jugoslav banks which had replaced the former branches. A weightier circumstance was that in 1923 liabilities amounted to about 140 million gold crowns compared to 864 millions before the war. This was itself an indication of the dimensions assumed by the post-war capital shortage.[37]

A possibly still clearer picture of the loss of financial power of the banks emerges from a comparison of their share capital plus declared reserves on the two dates.

A comparison of the 1913 figures with those for 1925 would, it may be objected, reflect the situation more clearly because in the latter year, the gold opening balances were published and the process of reconstruction was somewhat farther advanced.[38] However, even the

Table 54   Share capital and declared reserves (in m. gold crowns)

	1913	1923	1913 = 100
Creditanstalt	243.6	18.4	7.5
Boden-Creditanstalt	174.5	18.1	10.5
Niederösterreichische			
Escompte-Gesellschaft	100.3	13.8	14.0
Wiener Bankverein	173.2	22.5	13.0
Unionbank	89.4	31.8	35.5
Mercurbank	72.0	8.8	12.0
Verkehrsbank	52.8	7.6	17.5

gold balances cannot be taken as 'reliable' statements because 'every bank on publication of the gold balances ... alluded to its cautious assessment, and some indeed referred expressly to the retained hidden reserves'.[39] In any case, such a comparison showed 'the enormous loss of substance sustained by the banks through war and inflation'.[40]

Table 55   Share capital and declared reserves, 1913 and 1925

	End 1913		1 Jan 1925	
	Gold cr. m.	AS m.	AS m.	1913 = 100
Creditanstalt	243.6	350.8	70.0	20.0
Boden-Creditanstalt	174.5	251.3	50.0	19.0
Niederösterreichische				
Escompte-Gesellschaft	100.3	144.4	50.0	34.5
Wiener Bankverein	173.2	249.4	60.0	24.0
Unionbank	89.4	128.7	36.0	28.0
Mercurbank	72.0	103.7	16.0	15.0
Verkehrsbank	52.8	76.1	14.0	18.0

The banks' loss of capital is on this calculation slightly less than in a comparison between 1913 and 1923. Surprisingly strong is the condition of Niederösterreichische Escompte-Gesellschaft – a circumstance that also caused some bewilderment among contemporary observers.[41]

The bank's loss of capital was probably more serious still, if one takes into account, as *Der Österreichische Volkswirt* did, the new issues paid-up during and after the war. It tried to ascertain by way of questionnaires what had been the proceeds of the banks in gold on issues placed since 1914.[42] Including these new issues, the figures were as follows:

Table 56 Banking capital 1913 plus post-1914 issues (in m. schillings)

Creditanstalt	452.5	15.7
Boden-Creditanstalt	308.4	16.2
Niederösterreichische Escompte-Gesellschaft	222.0	22.5
Wiener Bankverein	389.0	15.4
Unionbank	210.0	17.1
Mercurbank	139.0	11.5
Verkehrsbank	139.0	10.1

'What must not be forgotten,' added *Der Österreichische Volkswirt* laconically, 'is that the banks before the war had incomparably greater hidden reserves than today, probably relatively as well as absolutely in relation to the capital. The losses of individual banks fluctuate between 90% and 77.5%.'[43]

In wartime even the major banks had on occasion been barely able to resist the 'exhilaration' produced by large figures. Now the 'thousand million blessing' was regarded with scepticism and growing anxiety. It began to be realized that behind the glittering facade was an impoverished economy and a banking system acutely weakened. Policy soon after the war focused therefore on trying to limit losses wherever possible and on creating the prerequisites for a new phase of expansion. The strategic key points had become clearly discernible as early as 1919 – concentration on the Danubian area as the principal base for operations and partnership with Western banking capital.[44] In his memoirs Spitzmüller made the important statement that the government had from the beginning of the twenties 'ceaselessly fostered this expansive banking policy'.[45]

The effort to keep the loss of capital as low as possible is not apparent in the dividend policies of the major banks during the inflationary years. Yet the apparently high dividend distributions amounted to a fraction of those paid in 1913.[46]

Table 57 Major Viennese banks' profit distributions

	1920 in 000 crowns	1921	1922 in m. Cr.	1923	1923 in 000 gold Cr.	1913
Creditanstalt	50,000	312,500	10,000	56,250	3,906	15,938
Boden-Creditanstalt	21,000	168,000	5,040	43,200	3,000	10,800
Niederösterreichische Escompte-Gesellschaft	21,000	120,000	7,500	37,500	2,604	7,875
Wiener Bankverein	21,600	142,500	7,500	40,000	2,778	10,400

In 1923 Creditanstalt, just like most of the other big banks, increased its distributions nearly sixfold compared with 1922. In gold crowns this totalled barely 4 millions compared with 16 millions in 1913. Allowing for the fact that in the last year of peace 468,750 shares (nominal capital = 150 million crowns) had been issued, whereas in 1923 the Bank had 6.25 million shares (nominal capital = 20,000 million crowns) in circulation, the pre-war dividend was 34 crowns per share as against 0.62 gold crowns in 1923. Had the pre-war number of shares remained the same, the amount distributed in 1923 would have amounted to merely 8.25 crowns per share as compared with 34 crowns in 1913.[47] And it should not be forgotten that earnings in the latter year were no more than average.

From what has been said above one may conclude that the dividend policy in the early period of the Republic was rather restrained. This impression is strengthened by calculating the major banks' distributions as a percentage of the market value of their shares on two dates.[48]

Table 58   Major Viennese banks' dividends as % of their shares market value

	31 December 1913	30 June 1923
Creditanstalt	5.37	1.1
Boden-Creditanstalt	5.09	0.65
Niederösterreichische Escompte-Gesellschaft	5.44	0.76
Wiener Bankverein	6.19	1.35
Unionbank	5.67	0.80
Mercurbank	6.04	1.88
Verkehrsbank	6.02	1.60

In 1924 the banks' distributions as a percentage of their shares' market value were considerably higher, but they did not reach the pre-war level. The impression of a conservative dividend policy becomes rather doubtful, though, when it is realized that Creditanstalt's share capital plus declared reserves was only 7.5% of the analogous 1913 amount (Table 55), while the 1924 dividends stood at a quarter of the last pre-war year. It must not be overlooked, however, that in 1923 the predominant belief was that the securities holdings of the major banks were considerably undervalued. A commentary on Creditanstalt's 1923 statement of accounts contained the following passage: 'Thus securities and participations under syndicate agreements are together put at 20 million gold crowns as compared to 146 millions before the war. At current prices the Böhmische Escompte-bank and Amstelbank shares alone amount practically to this figure.'[49]

The numerous capital increases of the banks in wartime and in post-war years, at shorter and shorter intervals, were of course intended to protect their capital resources against the effects of monetary depreciation.[50] Creditanstalt had in 1918, before the cessation of hostilities, raised its capital by 200 million crowns. Between 1919 and 1923 seven further increases followed. In the first year of stabilization its share capital totalled 20,000 million crowns. Taking into account the allocations to reserves (capital, general, extraordinary, and real property), its own capital, i.e., 265,000 million crowns, was many times above the figure of its share capital.[51]

The practice of obtaining capital increases through repeated share issues had only modest success in spite of the considerable agio profits. The direct consequence of the failure to keep up with inflation was a continual worsening of the ratio of the banks' own resources to outside funds as reflected in 1921 by Creditanstalt's dangerous 1 : 45 ratio, one year later improved to 1 : 26. In the first year of stabilization it stood at 1 : 8, although this was notably less favourable than the proportion customary in pre-war times.

The repeated capital increases also furnished the basis for the foreign participations coming ever more to the fore. The acquisition of proprietary interests in Creditanstalt by American and Dutch financial circles has been mentioned.[52] A similar development could be observed in the case of other major banks. Without exception they sought backing from Western financial groups and sooner or later found such. During the inflationary period Niederösterreichische Escompte-Gesellschaft managed to establish a closer link with Comptoir d'Escompte de Genève and Banque de Bruxelles by the assignment of rather large blocks of shares. In summer 1923 it initiated a near association with Union Européenne Industrielle et Financière, a holding company on a close footing with Schneider-Creuzot, and a few months later it entered into relations with Lloyds Bank and Hambro's in London.[53] Boden-Creditanstalt, already before 1914 on intimate terms with foreign financial circles, was able to form connections with the American Morgan group and the British banking house Schroeder.[54] Wiener Bankverein relied on Société Génerale, Paris, Banque Belge pour l'Etranger at Brussels, and Handelsbank, Basle for support.[55] None of them was able to find such broad support from the international banking community as Credit-anstalt.

Österreichische Länderbank and Anglo-Österreichische Bank had obtained strong support from British and French financial groups before the outbreak of war. They did not content themselves now, like the above-mentioned institutions with merely fortifying their links with Western capital; they went right over into the other camp.[56] This sensational economic and political operation will be dealt with later. By 1923 the foreign share in the capital of all major Viennese banks was considerably larger than before the war.[57]

Table 59   Foreign holdings in % of Viennese banks' share capital

	1913	1923	
Creditanstalt	3.9	20.2	
Boden-Creditanstalt	17.8	c. 46[a]	
Niederösterreichische			
Escompte-Gesellschaft	0.7	36.0	
Wiener Bankverein	18.3	38.4	
Österreichische Länderbank	31.4	c. 70	(in French hands)
Anglo-Österreichische Bank	3.0	55.6	(in British hands)
Unionbank	1.5	c. 10[b]	
Mercurbank	3.4	60.0	
Verkehrsbank	—	37.6	
Allgemeine Depositenbank	—	16.3[c]	

[a] At the end of 1922 the foreign holding was for a time as high as 60%. (The calculation is based on the figures published in *Der Österreichische Volkswirt*, 16 and 22 December 1922, Supplements 'Die Bilanzen', pp. 83 and 312 respectively.

[b] At the end of 1923 about 80% of the share capital was in the hands of the prominent speculator Sigmund Bosel. Until March 1923 the majority holding had been in the possession of a German-Italian-Czechoslovak banking syndicate and of Camillo Castiglioni.

[c] Until spring 1922 the majority holding was in the hands of Castiglioni and Banca Commerciale Italiana.

That a certain resistance to this massive inflow of foreign capital became apparent among the banks' shareholders is hardly surprising. A Ministry of Finance report refers to an intervention at a Credit-anstalt general meeting by Dr Emil von Hofmannsthal.[58] His proposal was to instruct the board 'to work out a way, compatible with the statutes, to protect the right of minority holders, because the capital increases based on the inflow of foreign funds must in time lead to a control by foreign capital which could reduce the influence of the Austrian members of the board'. The ministry representative recorded that the meeting rejected the motion 'by an overwhelming majority'. His closing sentence defined the official attitude:

The strong foreign participation in domestic undertakings is indeed a deplorable fact, but in the prevailing economic circumstances almost inevitable. Many companies, especially banks, could not exist without this outside assistance. The Federal Ministry of Finance therefore holds that administrative or statutory provisions opposing too rigorously a participation by foreign capital in general should be very warily approached.[59]

In the case of Creditanstalt, the dramatic decline of liabilities during the decade 1913 to 1923, with the concomitant weakening of its earnings capacity, has already been observed. Tables 60 and 61 show this development to have been in greater or lesser degree characteristic of the whole banking world.[60]

Table 60   Accounts payable of major Viennese banks (in 000 gold cr.)

	1913	1919	1920	1921	1922	1923
Creditanstalt	783,725	63,145	123,351	121,670	116,621	143,831
Boden-Creditanstalt	282,933	70,428	66,451	48,201	91,322	101,092
Niederösterreichische Escompte-Gesellschaft	254,473	24,798	30,077	40,739	84,800	154,389
Bankverein	514,638	98,353	106,113	114,587	88,289	118,376
Unionbank	194,694	18,368	30,023	27,857	21,169	67,498
Mercurbank	143,926	22,716	27,543	28,710	25,767	39,160
Verkehrsbank	164,805	25,513	41,187	28,017	27,431	69,920
Total	2,339,194	323,321	424,745	409,781	455,399	694,266

Source: *Compass*, 1915–1925

Table 61   Major Viennese banks' deposits and cash certificates (in 000 gold cr.)

	1913	1919	1920	1921	1922	1923
Creditanstalt	80,382	3,168	1,452	328	190	1,128
Boden-Creditanstalt	—	—	—	—	—	—
Niederösterreichische Escompte-Gesellschaft	23,924	1,127	575	140	113	469
Bankverein	133,248	11,611	7,362	1,395	756	2,646
Unionbank	28,530	1,796	1,130	259	248	656
Mercurbank	42,938	2,598	1,556	385	430	3,043
Verkehrsbank	71,829	4,742	3,273	660	651	2,011
Total	380,851	25,042	15,348	3,167	2,388	9,639

Source: *Compass*, 1915–1925

Understandably, deposits declined drastically during the years of inflation because they belonged to small savers who, with growing

445

awareness of inflation, tried to invest their reserves in as stable a form of asset as possible. Not until 1923, when the depreciation of the crown was stopped, did the public at large begin to find this mode of saving more palatable. Accounts payable similarly reveal very clearly the economy's impoverishment. These changes mainly reflect the state of the banks' current transactions, which from 1919 onward were to a growing extent absorbed by the financial institutions of the Successor States, in which Austrian capital had interests of varying size.

There was another way in which the item accounts payable differed from pre-war days. During the course of inflation the proportion of funds in foreign currency grew and at times probably accounted at some banks for as much as half of their total.[61] In 1923 Creditanstalt's accounts payable in foreign currency are said to have amounted to two-thirds of all these items.[62] The explanation for this unprecedented state of affairs is to be found in the new operational structure of commercial banks. Post-war conditions forced them to conduct a considerable portion of current business in foreign currency, mainly that of the Successor States. In addition, Western banks, attracted by the high interest rate prevailing in Vienna, were increasingly ready to give short term credit to Austrian clients. For Creditanstalt, with its excellent Western links, it was particularly easy to attract this highly volatile money.

How, under these conditions, did the loans business look? In the first place it needs to be said that the debtors item too was subject to an unprecedented process of shrinkage during the inflation.[63]

Table 62   Major Viennese banks' accounts receivable (in 000 gold cr.)

	1913	1919	1920	1921	1922	1923
Creditanstalt	734,811	55,210	112,315	116,996	108,975	138,209
Boden-Creditanstalt	326,407[a]	62,982	62,463	46,764	84,815	100,728
Niederösterreichische Escompte-Gesellschaft	288,031	25,922	29,473	44,228	71,734	132,274
Bankverein	519,959	75,824	85,480	106,294	77,987	122,669
Unionbank	191,669	17,070	26,796	26,027	16,061	74,520
Mercurbank	143,565	23,949	27,309	26,910	22,809	42,462
Verkehrsbank	174,565	25,564	42,982	25,653	24,605	75,135
Total	2,379,007	286,521	386,818	392,872	406,986	685,997

Source: *Compass*, 1915–1925

In 1923 some 500,000 million crowns, more than a quarter of Creditanstalt's loan total, is known to have belonged to assets including foreign exchange holdings deposited at other banks.[64] The holdings with banks abroad by other major banks were on a similar scale, although it must be assumed that in this year of stabilization some repatriation of capital was already under way. The existence of these considerable foreign exchange holdings, which were, of course, a protection against losses arising from inflation, was repeatedly a cause of angry criticism, which will be discussed in the next chapter. Even a statesman like Dr Beneš, then Czechoslovak Foreign Minister, was quoted as saying that

he saw himself forced to point out that it must not be forgotten, if it is a matter of helping German-Austria, how certain circles in German-Austria dispose of enormous capital resources invested in various parts of Europe, including Czechoslovakia and that for the most part these circles are not inclined to invest this capital at home and to render it productive for their own country.[65]

The dimensions of the contraction process to which accounts receivable – the major part of the banking assets – were subject varied greatly. Whereas Creditanstalt and Wiener Bankverein, starting from a very high level in 1913, suffered palpable losses, the atrophy was much less in the case of Boden-Creditanstalt and Niederöster-reichische Escompte-Gesellschaft. Certain items on the debit side of the accounts experienced – as can be seen from the example of Creditanstalt – important changes during the inflationary period.[66]

Table 63   Creditanstalt earnings (in 000 gold cr.)

	1913	1919	1920	1921	1922	1923	1923 as % of 1913
Interest	25,475	1,046	1,825	1,968	2,461	5,647	21.9
Issuing & Syndicate Business	2,411	583	869	756	939	6,322	262.2
Commissions & Merchandise	7,597	442	786	2,128	3,048	8,224	108.3
Foreign Exchange Ops.	322	294	950	645	546	1,754	213.4
Gross Profit less Carry-Forward	36,622	2,368	4,432	5,497	6,993	21,946	59.9
Net Profit less Carry-Forward	20,683	999	1,325	1,415	1,849	5,397	26.1

Regardless of the high margins customary during the years of inflation, interest earnings between 1913 and 1923 dropped sharply.

This was of course connected with the shrinkage in the amount of credits. Profits on other items (especially securities and foreign exchange) were in part substantial, but they could in no way compensate for the deficit on income from loans. Yet what was really responsible for the reduction in net profits to approximately a quarter of pre-war was the rise in operating costs and in taxation. In 1923 Creditanstalt employed 2,300 individuals. Before 1914 its employees for the whole of the Monarchy had numbered 1,600.[67] The higher figure, typical of the entire banking system, was derived from the artificial expansion of business at a time of securities and foreign exchange speculation as well as from the regulations pertaining to this type of business; it placed an excessive burden on the banks. With regard to taxation it is sufficient to say that the tax burden on the Bank in 1923 was almost as great as in 1913 when the net profit had been fourfold. Table 64 vividly illustrates how inflation affected the relative importance of certain items as sources of profit.

Table 64   Creditanstalt earnings as ratio of gross profit (less carry-forward)

	1913	1919	1920	1921	1922	1923
Interest	70.3	44.2	41.2	35.8	35.2	25.7
Issuing & Syndicate Business	6.6	24.6	19.6	13.8	13.4	28.8
Commiss. & Merchand.	20.7	18.7	17.7	38.7	43.6	37.5
Foreign Exch. Ops.	2.2	12.4	21.4	11.7	7.8	8.0

These figures do not require any comment. Nothing better characterizes the abnormality of banking in those years than the drop in interest earnings (mainly on current operations) from 70% in 1913 to a quarter of total receipts in 1923. The record income from securities and syndicate business also demonstrates an unusual constellation of circumstances. So do the huge earnings on foreign exchange which in 1920 accounted for a fifth of gross earnings – at a time when precisely this type of activity had become popular among a number of licensed and unlicensed dealers.

Creditanstalt's company promotions during the Republic's first year fell to practically nil. Later there was a certain revival in what had during the last years before 1914 been an outstandingly important line of business. Although sometimes a source of quite lively issuing activity, it only rarely brought about an expansion of real capital.[69] As has been made clear before the scope of this business was conceived from the beginning on an international basis. The take-over of Anglo-Österreichische Bank and Österreichische Länderbank by British and French interests was motivated by a similar objective; it was an attempt to initiate under guidance from London and Paris company promotion activity throughout the Danubian area.[70]

At a time of adaptation to what in every respect was a radically changed political and business world, Creditanstalt's stock flotation activity naturally lacked the system and continuity typical of the last pre-war years. Soon, however, certain pivotal points of interest became clear. In the first place there was the effort either to consolidate or to broaden, partly in conjunction with foreign houses, the Bank's operational base in the Successor States. In 1921, together with Ungarische Allgemeine Kreditbank (Budapest), it founded Slowakische Allgemeine Kreditbank at Pressburg (Bratislava) so as to gain a firmer footing in the Slovak economic sphere. A portion of its former influence was retained in south-east Poland by taking over shares from Hypothekenbank at Lemberg (Lvov). The foundation in the same year of Schlesische Kreditanstalt A.G. at Bielitz, jointly with Warschauer Disconto-Bank and a group of Silesian industrialists, proved a successful venture. Other bank promotions in the Successor States were Kreditanstalt für Handel und Industrie at Ljubljana (capital of Slovenia) and Agrar- und Industriebank at Belgrade. In 1923 closer relations were established with Rumänische Creditbank at Bucharest.[71] Other associates were Bosnische Landesbank at Sarajevo, Kroatische Allgemeine Kreditbank at Zagreb, Banque Balkanique at Sofia, Bank für Auswärtigen Handel-Deutsche Orient-bank at Berlin, and the banking firm of Schneider & Münzig at Munich. The last connection was severed again in 1923. At home there was participation in certain banking houses like Steierrmärkische Escomptebank and Allgemeine Montanbank.[72]

The management's success in binding Western capital more closely to the Bank by a cession of shares has been mentioned already. Hand in hand therewith went the creation of financial bases in Holland and in the United States for the mobilization of Western capital for the purpose of a stronger participation of the Bank, above all in the Danubian area. The Amstelbank was founded, in cooperation with Nederlandsche Handel-Maatschapij and Hope & Co., both of Amsterdam, on 24 November 1920. The Austrian Rothschild house and Creditanstalt subscribed fifty per cent each of the capital stock of 3 million, later raised to 6 million, guilders.[73] On the occasion of the first capital increase, in 1921, Živnostenská banka and Böhmische

Escompte-Bank und Kreditanstalt became additional partners in the venture. Their interests were however modest.[74] In the same year the Bank and the Austrian Rothschilds put up $125,000 each towards the foundation of International Acceptance Bank, a venture with the objective of extending loans to European firms for the purchase of raw materials. In addition, the American participants insisted on a payment of $750,000 in securities or cash, which 'will have to serve as the special cover for the acceptance credits to be furnished to Austrian borrowers'.[75]

Because the Reparation Commission had first to release the necessary funds, the transaction needed in principle the Commission's agreement. A document giving the definitive permission states that for the time being the Austrian interest was to be treated confidentially 'as it must remain strictly secret in America that the shares are passing into Austrian hands'.[76] Allgemeine Waren- Treuhand AG, recently founded by the Bank, was to be responsible for the technical aspects of the business. From the prospectus annexed to the document one learns that this firm stood in close relationship to Deutsche Waren-Treuhand AG in which the banking house M. M. Warburg & Co. had a participation. In the spring of 1921 the Reparation Commission released another $1 million of securities so as to raise the ceiling for the grant of loans to domestic firms.[77] The other participants in International Acceptance Bank were Guarantee Trust Company and Kuhn, Loeb & Co., both of New York, as well as M. M. Warburg & Co., of Hamburg.[78] The American firms, with interests in Creditanstalt since 1920, were represented on the board by Max Warburg.

In the Republic's initial period, when economic developments were to a great extent distorted by hyper-inflation, the shortage of coal and raw materials, and the protectionist policies of the Successor States, it is understandably difficult to discern the focal points in the Bank's promotion business. All too often measures had to be taken to ensure the bare survival of enterprises with which Creditanstalt had been on close terms for years. The dust stirred by wartime and post-war events had not settled enough to make the outlines of future developments clear. What banking seemed to require most was the art of improvisation and the courage for experimentation.

The crippling energy shortage rendered one vital field of promotion more or less self-evident – speedy expansion of the national hydraulic power resources. Accordingly it is stated in the Annual Report: 'We have vigorously fostered – through organizational and financial assistance – organizations founded as joint-stock companies for the expansion and utilization of hydraulic power resources *which are now generally recognized as being of importance to the economy.*[79] A subsequent report reviews the Bank's participation in the issue of shares and bonds for the following corporations: Wasserkraftwerke AG (WAG), whose chief shareholder was the Municipality of Vienna, Niederösterreichische Elektrizitätswerke AG (NEWAG), Oberösterreichische Wasserkraft- und Elektrizitäts AG (OEWAG), Steirische Wasserkraft- und Elektrizitäts AG (STEWEAG), and Vorarlberger Landeskraftleitung AG. Finally, in 1923, the promotion of Tiroler Wasserkraft AG (TIWAG), together with Boden-Creditanstalt and Niederösterreichische Escompte-Gesellschaft, was recorded.[80] The further development of the Alpine hydraulic power resources met with resistance from certain Successor States. 'The delivery of necessary pit-coal for the Federal Railways was made dependent on the temporary suspension of electrification or the construction of power stations.'[81]

Creditanstalt was at pains to rebuild in a new form its business with Galician oil, the complete loss of which seemed to be threatened by the events of 1918. In this connection Erdöl Industrie-Bank AG, Vienna, was founded in 1920 in order to finance 'the export of Polish mineral oil products and the supply of all necessary materials to the Polish and Romanian excavation industry'.[82] Two years later this establishment founded subsidiaries at Lvov and Bucharest to make direct contact with the sources of supply and the principal markets.[83] The Bank was moreover a joint participant with its Hungarian business associate, Ungarische Allgemeine Kreditbank, in Mineralölraffinerie AG, Budapest and its subsidiary, Budapester Mineralölfabriks AG. The year 1920 also witnessed the formation (along the lines of Mundus-Bugholzmöbelfabriken)[84] of N.V. Nederlandsche Petroleum Maatschapij 'Photogen', with headquarters at Amsterdam, a Dutch holding company in which the Dutch banking houses closely connected with Creditanstalt were participants.[85] One of the firms in the sphere of influence of the new enterprise, Naphta AG, Lvov, very soon became 'the leading concern among the Polish crude oil producers'.[86] The shares of this company were introduced at the Vienna and Warsaw Stock Exchanges by Creditanstalt.

Another oil firm controlled by the Dutch holding company, and therefore indirectly by the Bank, was Mineralölindustrie AG, Fiume, which, after the city's annexation by Italy in 1922 and its own integration in Raffineria di Olii Minerali S.A., Rome, knew how to take material advantage of the tariff protection afforded in Italy to crude oil processing.[87] The majority of the shares was in the hands of the Italian Government. Mineralölraffinerie AG, Budapest also had subsidiaries at Oderberg in Czechoslovakia. These were converted, in conjunction with Živnostenská banka and Böhmische Escompte-Bank und Kreditanstalt, into 'Odra' Mineralölindustrie AG. At the close of 1923 the plants of this company were transferred to a Romanian joint-stock company.[88] Other important interests and business connections established in 1923 were Erdöl-Industrie AG, Berlin; Galizische Karpathen Petroleum AG, formerly Bergheim & McGarvey; and 'Schodnica' Petroleum Industrie AG.[89] Within a relatively short time Creditanstalt, closely linked to western and central European financial groups, had managed to build up an important position for itself in the Polish oil industry.

The Bank's stock flotation activity was initially more modest in timber processing, which used a raw material domestically available in large quantities. In 1920 the Bank acquired interests in two companies – the newly founded Holzindustrie Hugo Forchheimer AG at Innsbruck and the Steirische Holzverwertungs AG, Leoben, in collaboration with the Frankfurt industrialist Hugo Forchheimer.[90] The Bank also joined in the capital increase of a foreign firm, Holzexploitations- und Holzindustrie AG, Budapest.[91] It had, on the other hand, in 1918 sold its holdings in the Romanian 'Tisita' Waldexploitations AG. In 1923 it assumed a closer interest in Timber-Holdinggesellschaft für Werte der Holzindustrie, an enterprise founded in 1920 for the purpose of bringing under a common roof the Holzhandels AG subsidiaries situated in the Successor States and on whose behalf Unionbank had first acted as banker.[92]

The modest scope of activity in the iron and steel industry is hardly surprising. In 1923 the Bank joined an international group engaged in transforming Ternitzer Stahl- und Eisenwerke Schoeller & Co. into Schoellerwerke AG. Two years later, with the Bank's assistance, a merger between Schoellerstahlwerke and Bleckmann-Werke produced the new undertaking Schoeller-Bleckmann Stahlwerke AG.[93] Promotional activity in the fields of paper and textiles likewise remained within narrow bounds. Artificial silk manufacture was the object of the founding, with Böhmische Escompte-Bank und Kreditanstalt, of Böhmische Glanzstoff-Fabrik, Prague in 1921. In 1923 'Awestem' Band- und Stoffindustrie AG, Vienna became associated with the Bank.[94] In the same year the latter joined in a notable capital increase for Leykam-Josephtal AG für Papier- und Druckindustrie, and decided to take a permanent interest in this company. The funds deriving from the capital increase were used for a 'comprehensive investment programme'.[95] Papier-Industrie A G Olleschau, domiciled in Czechoslovakia, belonged to the Creditanstalt group.[96]

The export gains due to inflation in the machine-building, the motor construction, as well as the metal and electrical goods industries explain the rather more active promotional activity in these sectors. Österreichische Daimler-Motoren A G, Vienna, which in the early 1920s entered into a close pooling agreement with Puchwerke A G and Österreichische Automobil-Fabriks A G formerly 'Austria-Fiat', had progressed quite satisfactorily and until the beginning of the recession in 1923 had many orders from Britain, Belgium, and Holland.[97] Österreichische Flugzeugfabrik A G, Wiener Neustadt, had after the war switched to the production of automobile bodies, primarily meeting requirements of Österreichische Daimler-Motoren A G. In 1924 Daimler swallowed it whole.[98] The Linz shipyard enterprise, formerly allied with Stabilimento Tecnico Triestino, was after 1918 included by the Bank along with other participations in the founding of a new company, Schiffwerft Linz A G, which in 1922–23 turned to a new production programme concentrating mainly on motor construction and steel foundries.[99] The working agreement made a year later with Mars-Werke A G, Liesing led in 1926 to a merger of the two enterprises under the name Climax Motoren Werke und Schiffswerft Linz A G, Vienna.[100] The Bank displayed particular interest in N. Heid, Stockerau, a firm which at the beginning of the twenties increased its capital on several occasions and was the recipient of large-scale investment loans.[101] Maschinen- und Waggonfabriken L. Zieleniewski at Cracow, Lvov, and Sanok was one of the foreign machine-building enterprises in which the Bank took special interest.[102] Close relations continued to be maintained with Ringhoffer-Werke A G, Smichow.[103]

The development of the hydraulic power resources and the electrification of the railways gave a vigorous impetus to the domestic electrical industry and during the years of inflation good business was done in that branch. Thanks to repeated injections of capital, to which Creditanstalt contributed substantially, A E G-Union was able to uphold its leading position in this sector.[104] The expansion of its production plant was undertaken in agreement with the Berlin A E G parent company, the management of which thought that 'in consequence of the economic discrimination against Germany after the war a partial shift of operations . . . to Austria is necessary'. As it later turned out, however, the plant of the Vienna subsidiary 'had been expanded on far too large a scale by reason of assumptions that never materialized' and that 'their capacity could never be even half-way utilized'.[105] As early as 1923 'Ericsson' Österreichische Elektrizitäts AG, formerly Deckert & Homolka, another firm belonging to Creditanstalt's industrial group, began the production of radios and, with its associate company in Hungary, was able to report full order books.[106] Evidently there was at this early stage in the Republic's history no lack of important technological innovations. The trouble was that they were not numerous enough, nor did they make sufficient impact to change the generally unfavourable climate of investment.

Berndorfer Metallwarenfabrik Arthur Krupp AG was the most important of the many metal manufacturers closely associated with the Bank. During the war Krupp AG had worked almost exclusively for the state. Immediately after the cessation of hostilities it began to channel its activities into the production of consumer goods, and to this end it had to make repeated approaches to the capital market. In 1921 the conversion process could provisionally be brought to a close.[107] Nevertheless in the following years the Bank had to assist Krupp with substantial investment loans.[108] Other important consumer goods firms in association with the Creditanstalt industrial group were Vereinigte Brauereien Schwechat, Gösser Brauerei AG, Brauerei Zipf AG vormals Wm. Schaup, G. Stölzle's Söhne AG für Glasfabrikation, Vienna, Milchindustrie AG, Vienna, and the big Bohemian and Moravian sugar refineries. To be sure the Czech firms had performed most of their banking transactions with the major Czech banks since 1919. The connection of the Bank with Sascha Film-industrie AG at first showed results satisfactory to both parties.

At an early date the management saw the need for Creditanstalt to extend appropriate assistance to the wholesale trade either directly or through establishments specifically created for the purpose. The Bank repeatedly partook in the capital increases by Internationale Export-und Import AG, Vienna, which was engaged in overseas trade 'even more than formerly and with the same success'.[109] Allgemeine Waren-Treuhand AG was founded in 1920. In close connection with the German company of the same name, its main objective was to function as trustee in arranging foreign loans on behalf of Austrian industry and industry in the Successor States.[110] The promotion of International Acceptance Bank to finance imports from the United States has been described. The connection in 1922 with Bank für Auswärtigen Handel of Berlin also aimed at furthering domestic export interests.[111]

In pre-war years Creditanstalt had been on good terms with two leading retailers, A. Gerngross A G and the Viennese groceries chain Julius Meinl established in the middle of the 19th century. In September 1919 the management reported that Meinl was 'going public'; the Bank bought a block of shares totalling 6.25 million crowns.[112] The later Annual Reports repeatedly mention capital increases on behalf of the two companies. In May 1921 the Bank decided to participate with 5 million crowns in the promotion of Wiener Messe A G, the undertaking in charge of the Vienna Trade Fair which was to make an important contribution to upholding the city's status as a centre for central and eastern European trade.[113]

Long term public loans had before and during the war tied up a considerable amount of the banks' funds. Now, in the light of the crown's depreciation and because of the uncertainty of the mode of redemption of these bonds, new issues could hardly be placed on the capital market. Creditanstalt had taken a fair share of the first government loan floated in December 1918.[114] The Treasury's additional, constantly growing needs had to be met through the issue of bills which landed in the portfolio of the central bank after making the round through the major banks. In the face of protests from representatives of the Successor States', the central bank made ample use at the beginning of its discount facilities. Nothing short of a perfect mechanism for an unlimited increase in the volume of money had been set in motion.[115]

The proceeds from the 4% Lottery Loan issued in 1920 were mainly intended for the redemption of the First War Loan, due on 1 April of that year.[116] It was divided into three blocks of 400,000 numbers at 1,000 crowns each; the lots in the third block were taken over *in toto* by the Postal Savings Bank.[117] A lengthy pause in the issuing activity of the Federal Government followed. Not until the close of 1922 did the Bank have an opportunity to partake in transactions of this kind within the framework of the League of Nations reconstruction programme. The next chapter deals in greater detail with the League of Nations loan and the concomitant financial operations. While during the inflationary period the Treasury met its financial requirements principally with the aid of three-month bills, other public authorities, in particular those of the federal capital and other cities, some of the federal provinces, and the Federal Housing Fund, made repeated approaches to the capital market. A syndicate, of which Creditanstalt was a member, assumed responsibility for the placement of these securities.[118]

In spite of the substantial issuing activities of the major banks during the inflationary period in the fields of banking and wholesale trade, in particular in the Successor States, the loss of capital consequent upon the Empire's downfall could not remotely be compensated. This is illustrated by a comparison of the following figures:[119]

Table 65   Major Viennese banks' securities and syndicate accounts (in 000 sch.)

	1913	1923	Gold Opening Balance, 1 January 1925
Creditanstalt	187,766	28,604	62,026
Boden-Creditanstalt	48,010[a]	22,527	58,304
Niederösterreichische Escompte-Gesellschaft	83,298	34,017	42,914
Wiener Bankverein	123,562	20,104	29,962
Unionbank	65,390	23,593	30,210
Mercurbank	34,582	6,640	11,294
Verkehrsbank	29,527	6,031	9,946

[a] Only securities because syndicate participations were booked under debtor items

Creditanstalt's gold opening balance figures – attaining roughly one third of pre-war – certainly come closer to the 'truth' than the strikingly low amounts shown in the 1923 securities and syndicate accounts which – as has been repeatedly emphasized – included large amounts of hidden reserves. More favourable was the balance presented by Niederösterreichische Escompte-Gesellschaft, with figures for 1925 standing at around fifty per cent of their pre-war level. Wiener Bankverein adopted a decidedly cautious accounting method and puts its investments at barely more than a quarter of the 1913 total. Comparable information is lacking for Boden-Creditanstalt.[120]

Such varying estimates of their loss of assets by the major banks show that these losses differed greatly between one bank and another, and that an element of subjectivity was inherent in the methods of assessment. Even outside of banking circles there was much talk about this phenomenon. At the beginning of February 1924 a confidential report by the US Consulate to the Department of State reveals that estimates of the losses sustained by the banks fluctuated between 10% and 70%.[121] If a connection is seen between the losses of its proprietary capital and the losses on participations and other investments – the existence of such a nexus can certainly not be ignored – the more pessimistic estimates seem likely to be the more probable.

Perhaps, though, posterity's judgment is clouded by knowledge of the calamitous events climaxed by Creditanstalt's collapse in 1931.

The banks had, as has been seen, succeeded in their efforts to secure the co-operation of well-known Western establishments to maintain their former extensive radius of operation. The government authorities were, especially since the formation of a conservative administration, frankly sympathetic towards endeavours for stronger support from Western capital, although they refrained from exercising direct influence over the negotiations. The take-over of Anglo-Österreichische Bank and Österreichische Länderbank by British and French interests, respectively, bore from the outset, however, the hallmark of a political exercise; the initiatives originated with the Bank of England and the Quai d'Orsay.[122]

The Entente Powers – with France and Italy in the lead – had, during the first post-war year, been able to acquire important economic positions in Austria and in the Successor States. Nonetheless the plan for the anglicization and frenchification of the two Viennese banks was distinctly different from what had hitherto been relatively unsystematic operations. It envisaged the systematic penetration of the Danube area by the Western Powers parallel with the political supremacy created on the basis of the Peace Treaties. The reasons why these two Vienna banks seemed suitable spring-boards for British and French ambitions are not difficult to appreciate.[123]

Anglo-Österreichische Bank and Österreichische Länderbank belonged to the exclusive circle of Viennese crédit mobilier banks. Both could look back on half a century of successful activities. Both controlled an extensive industrial group, a network of branch offices, and associated banks in the Successor States.

The Anglo-Österreichische Bank Group (1922)[124]
36 Branches (20 in Vienna, 11 in the Federal Provinces, 3 in Hungary, 2 in Romania)
Bank Participations:
> Anglo-Česka Banka, Prague (c. 75%)
> Bank für Handel, Gewerbe und Industrie, Zagreb
> Kroatische Escomptebank, Zagreb
> Siebenbürgische Escomptebank, Romania
> M. L. Biedermann & Co. Bankaktiengesellschaft, Vienna
Important Industrial Participations:
> Elin AG (jointly with Wiener Bankverein)
> Enzesfelder Metallwerke AG
> Hirtenberger Patronenfabrik (jointly with Creditanstalt)

457

Universale Bau AG
Atlantica Trust AG, Budapest
Julius Meinl AG (jointly with Creditanstalt)

In all some seventy firms in the banking and industrial worlds, about half of them situated outside Austria.

The Österreichische Länderbank Group (1922)[125]

25 Branches (19 in Vienna, 6 in the Federal Provinces)
Bank Participations:

Bank für Handel und Industrie, ehemals Länderbank, Prague (80%)
Allgemeine Kreditbank, Poland
Rumänische Kreditbank
Serbische Kreditbank
Slavenska Banka DD, Jugoslavia
Ungarische Escompte- und Wechselbank

Important Industrial Participations:

Trifailer Kohlenwerke, Jugoslavia
Ungarische Allgemeine Kohlenbergbau AG
Erste Brünner Maschinenfabrik AG
Österreichische Siemens-Schuckertwerke
Austria-Email
Waagner-Biro
Zementfabrik AG Perlmoos
Solo-Zündwarenfabrik
Denes & Friedmann AG (Swiss Machine-Building Holding Company)
Wienerberger Ziegelfabriks- und Baugesellschaft (via Perlmoos, jointly with Creditanstalt)
Schönpriesener Zuckerraffinerie
Zentralmährische Zuckerfabriken

In all some seventy firms in the banking and industrial worlds, about half of them with their headquarters or main establishments situated outside Austria.

Foreign capital had played a considerable part in the foundation of the two banks.[126] Whereas before the war Anglo-Österreichische Bank was mainly in Austrian hands, in 1913 the foreign (mainly French) interest in Österreichische Länderbank is likely to have accounted for almost a third of the share capital.[127] Both establishments had considerable Western debts before 1914, a circumstance that coupled with the progressive decline in the value of the crown seemed to cast doubt on their future prospects. The provisions of the Peace Treaty rendered the Austrian state liable for the payment of debts to foreign creditors in valorized crowns, and this was partly why Austrian authorities countenanced the pending expatriation.[128] The Ministry of Finance met repeated expressions of anxiety, lest the banks' transition into foreign possession would bring about control of the economy by foreign capital with the argument that this kind of trend could not be counteracted by 'statutory regulations'. The Ministry looked on 'control of the Austrian economy by foreign capital as a long accomplished fact because it was natural under the economic conditions arising from the war' and beyond its competence to remedy.[129]

The British and French Governments had at their command mechanisms of wartime control over the capital market which were not repealed until the mid-1920s. In France the traditionally close relations between the Quai d'Orsay and the big French banks had evolved during the course of the nineteenth century. In Britain a similar rapport between the most important issuing houses and the Bank of England developed during the last decade before outbreak of the First World War. Even in 1924 when the British government again permitted the free export of capital, the Bank of England and its forceful governor, Montagu Norman, reserved for themselves certain possibilities of influence over capital transactions.[130]

A letter from the chairman of Anglo-Österreichische Bank to Dr Karl Seitz, a leading Social Democrat politician and subsequent mayor of Vienna, shows that Norman took a personal hand in the negotiations for the anglicization of the institute. The governor's attitude is described in some detail in this letter:

When in August I arrived in London in my capacity as financial expert to Dr Reisch, then Minister of Finance, Sir Herbert told me that his friends did *not* wish to participate in the conversion of the Czech branch offices. They were however not disinclined to facilitate Anglobank's transformation into a British establishment. The reason for this forthcoming attitude, which was something of a surprise to me, became clear when I introduced myself to the Governor of the Bank of England, Mr Montagu Norman, a step that I had to take as the bank is our major creditor (we owe it about £1,600,000). Mr Norman, a pronounced pacifist who said to me that his task is to build up, not to tear down, at once revealed himself to be a very warm, most zealous friend of Austria. The touching way in which he displayed his sympathy for our position and suffering, his remarks about the Successor States and how he wants to avoid anything that could widen the gap between them and Vienna, his complete understanding of the difficulties which the wretched state of our currency causes us, the satisfaction that he took in the relief operation for Austria in which the Bank of England will to all appearances be prepared to take a leading part, together with the consideration that he proposes to show in the liquidation of our debts, are manifest proof of how correct my initial impression was. The willingness of the British to be helpful stems probably from the feeling that Austria has been grossly wronged by the Peace Treaty, and their high regard for Vienna's commercial probity . . . would enable us to transform our debts into working capital, a step tantamount in substance to Britain lending Austria the amounts owed by Anglobank and Länderbank. Since these amount to £4 million, they represent quite a tidy sum towards improvement of the Austrian balance of payments, if the deal comes off. If it does not, however, the balance of payments will inevitably deteriorate as we have to withdraw our entire assets from current operations and pay the British. I can of course *not* adopt the posture that, should such an arrangement not come about, Anglobank would be lost. But it is certain that, instead of the healthy position in which it is today, it would be a body bled white and hardly in a condition to render the Austrian economy great service any longer.[131]

The letter goes on to emphasize that, in its new role as a British establishment with close relations with Austria, Anglo-Österreichische Bank would enjoy a quasi-monopolistic mediatory function between Western capital and the Successor States, all the more so because the German banks (Deutsche Bank, Berliner Disconto-Gesellschaft, and Dresdner Bank) were not being allowed to resume their operations in London. 'Nothing', the letter stresses, 'can contribute so much to securing Vienna's position than Romanian, Polish, Hungarian, Czech, and Italian firms being forced to turn to Vienna for credit connections abroad.'

Norman's intentions were not confined to ousting German influence in the Danubian area by means of a British crédit mobilier bank. He intended for Anglo-Österreichische Bank and its subsidiaries to play an important part in putting the public finances of the countries of eastern central Europe on a sound footing. Anglo-Austrian Bank did, indeed, act as the agency for reconstruction credits furnished to Austria within the framework of the Geneva recovery programme.[132]

The ambitious hopes were not, however, to be fulfilled. As early as 1925 the decision was taken to close up Anglo-Austrian Bank and to sell its assets to Creditanstalt. The failure was partly due to the lack of familiarity of British bankers with central European business methods and their notorious inability to adapt themselves to the ethics practised in the region. The merger with Creditanstalt closed 'an interesting chapter in Austrian post-war history', said *Wirtschaftsstatistiches Jahrbuch 1926*. The bank, conceived as 'intermediary between western European capital and the Austrian economy', had not been able to fulfil this function. 'Instead of bringing foreign funds to Austria, it had to export Austrian capital for the conduct of its operations . . . The attempt to conduct from Britain a bank in Vienna without paying sufficient attention to the special character of Austrian business miscarried . . . completely.'[133] Nonetheless, according to Professor Teichova, the Bank of England knew how to turn 'defeat' into 'victory':

> . . . the shift of British direct capital participation from the Anglo-Austrian Bank to the Austrian Creditanstalt in Vienna meant that the Bank of England, with Treasury approval, decided to operate through a stronger bank, which channelled fixed and working capital to a large sector of Austria's industry, in the hope of making financial facilities available for Anglo-Central European trade.[134]

The transfer abroad of joint-stock companies necessitated, according to Austrian law, their domestic liquidation. The process involved considerable outlay in fees and in other costs. But the contemplated expatriation, especially that of the Österreichische Länderbank, met with strong resistance, especially from the Pan-German Party. Although as opposition it could exercise no crucial influence on this matter, the Social Democratic Party also viewed it with a certain reserve, an attitude reinforced by the so-called Stern-Ziegler expertise.[135]

In October 1921 the Austrian parliament sanctioned the transfer of the old Austrian establishments to British and French ownership respectively.[136] As so often before, the Pan-Germans had after some initial hesitation given way to their stronger coalition partners, the Christian Socialists. An arrangement was reached which 'in substance consisted of the British and French banks' claims being transformed into shares held in Anglobank and in Länderbank. This meant that the majority of share capital passed into foreign possession and that the banks' headquarters were transferred to London and to Paris.'[137] The name of Anglo-Österreichische Bank was now Anglo-Austrian Bank Limited; 55.6% of its share capital was held by a syndicate under the leadership of the Bank of England. 70% of the shares of the Österreichische Länderbank were after the expatriation in French hands. It was re-named Banque des Pays de l'Europe-Centrale.[138]

Unlike its fellow-expatriate, Banque des Pays de l'Europe-Centrale could maintain its independence until 1938 – at the price of an exceedingly cautious business policy. This self-restraint on the part of its management was presumably the main reason for the ability of this institute to survive the severe convulsions to which central European banking was subject at the beginning of the 1930s.

The profound changes in the structure of ownership of the major Viennese banks have been described in the case of two 'textbook examples'. Most banks tried to broaden their capital base through backing by well-known Western financial groups. The managers of the Creditanstalt, Boden-Creditanstalt, Niederösterreichische Escompte-Gesellschaft, and Wiener Bankverein were however, able to retain their independence to a very large extent, since the major foreign shareholders had neither a sufficiently large number of shares nor the necessary experience of central European banking to exercise dominant influence.[139] The formal transformation of Anglo-Österreichische Bank and Österreichische Länderbank into foreign companies was another matter. Foreign syndicates had the majority of the share capital in both establishments. The managers of the Vienna branch offices were bound by directives from their respective London and Paris headquarters.[140]

A third group of banks succumbed to the influence of inflation-profiteers and large-scale speculators. This happened to Unionbank and Allgemeine Depositenbank. The two banks first fell into the hands of Camillo Castiglioni, but it proved possible to dislodge him from both. Castiglioni's meteoric career has been described earlier.[141] In spring 1922 he was replaced at Allgemeine Depositenbank by a triumvirate consisting of Paul Goldstein as general manager; Arthur Drucker the timber industrialist; and Siegmund Sachsel, a government surveyor.[142] At Unionbank he was followed in March 1923 by Sigmund Bosel, another notorious stock exchange speculator.

The management of Unionbank saw to a strict division between banking operations and their major shareholders' speculative trans-actions. Bosel's downfall could therefore be weathered without appreciable losses.[143] On the other hand Allgemeine Depositenbank was ruined by the activities of its former chairman. The ruin was not brought about by the gigantic losses which resulted from his speculations against the French franc, but by the irreparable damage dating from his time on the board.[144]

Castiglioni had known how to create a 'group' of his own within a few years. He sat on the board of many well-known enterprises like Alpine Montan-Gesellschaft, Semperit AG, Schoeller-Bleckmann, Felten & Guilleaume, Brown Boveri, Daimler Werke, Papierfabrik Leykam-Josefsthal, in addition to the innumerable smaller companies which did not 'go public' until the inflation. His method of operation was simple – he took out loans with Allgemeine Depositenbank, the house entrusted to his care. On his resignation he owed the bank 819 million crowns, i.e., about a third of its capital. Many months later he returned that sum in devalued crowns.[145] Such instances were not isolated. 'Instead of the major shareholders putting their resources at the disposal of the banks they dominate, it is the banks who have to present their resources to the major shareholders for their private deals.'[146] Vast losses accrued to Allgemeine Depositenbank from such practices. Other major banks were largely compensated for the losses arising on current business by the higher price levels of the stocks in their portfolios. Allgemeine Depositenbank was increasingly immobilized because, with the acceleration of the inflationary process, the working capital of its industrial enterprises dwindled ever further and the resort to bank credit expanded accordingly.[147]

This development by no means came to an end with Castiglioni's departure in the spring of 1922, when he was allowed to retain only a minority holding of some 300,000 shares.[148] His elimination was accompanied by an agreement with the board on a division of the bank's industrial group. Valuable packets of shares went to Castiglioni; the bank was left with the less vital interests.[149] Then the three new major shareholders insisted that the bank should furnish loans to the firms with which they were associated.[150] It became ever more difficult to obtain funds, inasmuch as on Castiglioni's departure the credit-lines to Banca Commerciale Italiana were also cut. After the bank's collapse it turned out that it had been paying its creditors twenty and more per cent interest – evidence of its desperate situation.[151]

By December 1923 Allgemeine Depositenbank's bill presentations at the Austrian National Bank had attained such proportions that the governor declined further acceptances.[152] The downfall of this bank was precipitated by the failure of the franc speculations undertaken with the bank's credit by the principal Board members. Rumours emanating from Czechoslovakia, regarding the size of the losses, caused panic withdrawals. They could not be met, especially since an attempted capital increase had fizzled out shortly before. The majority underwriting group did not have the funds to pay up the shares. The result was that, together with the remainder of the older issues, about three million shares (of a total 7.5 million) were left unplaced. The 70,000 million crowns, which would have accrued to the bank from the proceeds of the last capital increase, had merely sufficed to meet the withdrawals of the first seventy-two hours.[153]

By the end of April 1924, a few days after the withdrawals had begun, Allgemeine Depositenbank could not continue operations. The Austrian National Bank refused acceptance of its bills and demanded endorsement by the major banks. A declaration of limited liability was issued to the bank's creditors after prolonged negotiations between its directors and representatives from the National Bank and from the major banks. On 5 May Allgemeine Depositenbank was taken over by Creditanstalt, Boden-Creditanstalt, Niederösterreichische Escompte-Gesellschaft, Wiener Bankverein, and Unionbank.[154]

This step was, of course, not entirely altruistic. A statement of bankruptcy by Allgemeine Depositenbank would have invoked the danger of a general panic and have put other big banks in a difficult situation also. The National Bank, moreover, exerted pressure in the direction of a take-over by underlining the perils entailed for the currency through a large-scale drain of capital abroad. Furthermore, Allgemeine Depositenbank seemed in only temporary difficulties, but the time was too short for close investigation.

Only later did it emerge how substantial the losses had been. Mr George Stern, the vice-chairman of the Banking Commission calculated a deficit of approximately 300,000 million crowns, a figure far in excess of the bank's capital and visible reserves.[155] In the circumstances there could no longer be any thought of salvage. Withdrawals continued undiminished in spite of guarantees from the major banks. Originally they had earmarked 75,000 million crowns for the purpose. By the beginning of June another 280,000 millions had to be contributed.[156] On 5 June the new management requested an order of receivership and the fate of Allgemeine Depositenbank was sealed.

The extent to which Castiglioni (and his successors) were responsible could never be properly established. The bank's books were 'in utter disorder, the most important written agreements have disappeared, and the oral information on these operations is contradictory'.[157] A part of the files damaging to Castiglioni vanished inexplicably from a room in the bank's building used by the examining magistrate for his investigations.[158] The dimensions of the losses connected with Castiglioni were revealed in a single instance. In 1919 Allgemeine Depositenbank had had an interest in an alcohol export syndicate formed in Czechoslovakia. When the enormous profits on this business became known in March 1921, a remarkable transaction took place. The bank's interests were, without a penny of compensation, assigned to an 'Investment Trust Company' of Zurich – this company's sole shareholder was Camillo Castiglioni. The bank was thereby deprived of any profits, admittedly losing more than 40 million Czech crowns. In reality the losses are likely to have been much greater.[159]

The bank scandal was followed by a legal scandal.[160] Castiglioni was not brought before the courts, notwithstanding his manifest breaches of the law.[161] No indemnification of Allgemeine Depositenbank was imposed on him.[162] Machinations against major banks by ruthless speculators were not rare in the years of inflation. Boden-Creditanstalt too was the target for one such unprovoked operation.[163]

Notes

1 Cf. Appendix II, Table A6.
2 The situation in the major Western European markets was characterized by a higher inflation level than in the USA.
3 It has to be borne in mind that the Bureau of Labour Statistics' wholesale price index and the Parity Commission's cost of living index were not comparable. Even on the assumption that the Austrian wholesale prices stood around twenty per cent above the cost of living index – and there are indications to support this assumption – the difference between the purchasing power of a monetary unit at home and abroad must have been considerable.
4 The fall in world prices during 1921 somewhat reduced this 'premium'.
5 Putting the 1913 volume of production at 100, the index in 1920 (according to the estimate of the Austrian Institute for Economic Research) stood at a mere 45.6 and in 1924 at 69.8. The figures for the years between were 49.6, 56.0, and 57.1 respectively. What clearly emerges is that during the first year of stabilization industrial production practically stagnated, but that in 1924 it recorded a rise of more than 20%. Cf. Kausel-Nemeth-Seidel, 'Österreichs Volkseinkommen 1913–1963', *Monatsberichte des Instituts für Wirtschaftsforschung*, Special Issue No. 14 (Vienna, 1965).
6 Cf. *Wirtschaftsstatistisches Jahrbuch 1925*, p. 7 et seq., published by Kammer für Arbeiter und Angestellte, Vienna.
7 During the early post-war years there was a flourishing export trade in cut and sawn timber as well as, to a lesser degree, in iron ore and other minerals. In 1921 timber exports amounted to 436,000 tons or 41 million gold crowns and in 1922 rose to 814,000 tons or 66.5 million gold crowns. This was approximately a third of all export volume and about 6% of the total export value. The corresponding figures for minerals were 15% and 2% respectively. See *Der Aussenhandel Österreichs in der Zeit zwischen den beiden Weltkriegen*, p. 10, published by Österreichisches Statistisches Zentralamt (Vienna, 1966).
8 The following table throws light on iron and steel production during the years of inflation:

		Production in ooo tons			
	1913	1919	1920	1921	1922
Pig-Iron	607	62	100	236	323
Steel	890	162	229	351	481

Sources: *Wirtschaftsstatistisches Jahrbuch 1925* and Josef Dobretsberger, *Konkurrenz und Monopol in der gegenwärtigen Wirtschaft* (Vienna, 1922), p. 78.

9 In 1921 the value of machinery, electrical equipment, vehicles, and miscellaneous metal goods exports amounted to 177.7 million gold crowns and in 1922 increased to 213.2 million gold crowns. This represented some 20% of overall exports in those two years. See *Der Aussenhandel Österreichs*, p. 10.

10 Friedrich Hertz, *Zahlungsbilanz und Lebensfähigkeit Österreichs* (Munich, 1925), p. 20 et seq. The author mentions (p. 21) that the number of workers insured against industrial accidents was not recorded in 1922, but he adds that the hours worked in that year were higher than in the preceding one. None the less there are grounds for thinking that 1922, the year of hyper-inflation, was marked by a certain rise in unemployment.

11 Creditanstalt's activity in the line of company promotions, including certain parts of the capital goods industry, will be discussed in another connection.

12 This was a circumstance emphasized in certain studies. 'At the present time the factories are making large profits, although none of them is working at more than 50% of its capacity.' Cf. *Financial Reconstitution of Austria*, Report of the Provisional Delegation of the League of Nations (Geneva, 1921), p. 32. In summer 1923 the Vienna Chamber of Labour put industrial employment at 48% to 60% of peace-time capacity. See Hertz, *Zahlungsbilanz*, p. 32 et seq.

13 In 1913 and in 1921 the numbers of accident insured workers within the territory of the Austrian Republic were 771,729 and 781,888 respectively. Hertz, *Zahlungsbilanz*, p. 21.

14 Kausel-Nemeth-Seidel, *Monatsberichte*, p. 17.

15 The general manifestation of material assets' losses, still more underlined by many industrialists' deficient adjustment to inflationary development, was in contrast to a certain growth of capital in individual sectors. Hertz says, for example, that 'the investment of capital in hydroelectric power stations alone from 1921 to 1924 is assessed at about 200 million gold crowns, with two-thirds of that figure deriving from domestic sources. Of the stations begun since 1921, such with about 150,000 horse-power capacity had been completed by the end of 1924 while others, with a further 70,000 horse-power capacity, were under construction.' See Hertz, *Zahlungsbilanz*, p. 37, footnote 2.

16 Cf. the discussion on the formation of new capital by German farmers during the inflation, *Schmöllers Jahrbuch für Gesetzgebung, Verwaltung und Volkswirtschaft* (Leipzig, 1924), p. 123. The same conclusion was reached by Walther Federn, 'Die Kreditpolitik der Wiener Banken', *Schriften des Vereins für Sozialpolitik* (Munich-Leipzig, 1925), Vol. 169, p. 65: 'Whereas German industry after the war invested enormous sums so as to achieve technical improvement and to fill the gaps in production structure caused by territorial disruptions, in Austria such investments occurred only in a few quite isolated instances.'

17 See Appendix II, Table A6.

18 If the value of the currency is calculated on the basis of the dollar exchange rate,

the finding is considerably less. The dollar value of the notes in circulation, according to Bresciani-Turroni, amounted in August 1922 to 90 million gold crowns, approximately a *sixth* of its pre-war value. Cf. Constantino Bresciani-Turroni, *The Economics of Inflation* (London, 1937), p. 162.

19 Cf. *League of Nations, Financial Reconstitution*, p. 32.

20 The inability of banks to deal equitably with all legitimate calls for loans was also caused by factors which must be left for later treatment.

21 Richard Strigl, 'Das industrielle Kapital', *Schriften des Vereins für Sozialpolitik* (Munich-Leipzig, 1925), Vol. 169, p. 79.

22 Federn, *Schriften*, p. 64.

23 It is interesting to note that during the time of inflation there appears to have been no connection of any kind between the central bank's discount rate and the interest charged by commercial banks:

Discount Rates of the Austro-Hungarian Bank
(since 1920 under Austrian management)

1 January 1918–31 December 1920	5%
1 January 1921–13 April 1921	5%
14 April 1921–28 November 1921	6%
19 November 1921–31 December 1921	7%
1 January 1922–3 September 1922	7%
4 September 1922–31 December 1922	9%

Source: *Ein Jahrhundert Creditanstalt-Bankverein* (Vienna, 1957), p. 342.

24 'Die Geldknappheit', *Der Österreichische Volkswirt*, 10 February 1923, p. 493.

25 Max Sokal, 'Die Banken', *Schriften des Vereins für Sozialpolitik* (Munich-Leipzig, 1925), Vol. 169, p. 51.

26 'It was, and is, one of the worst troubles plaguing Austrian industry that usually it cannot work to full capacity, and primarily responsible for this is the fact that the funds for procurement of the raw material, often indeed for the payment of wages and salaries, cannot be raised.' Federn, *Schriften*, p. 65.

27 Federn, *Schriften*, p. 61.

28 Sokal, *Schriften*, p. 31.

29 Federn, *Schriften*, p. 54.

30 'The Association of Austrian Banks and Bankers had recognized the un-healthiness of this development and it pressed for remedial measures. Most of the newly founded banks too were not accepted by the association as members. They formed a separate organization, the so-called 'Banking Federation', which subsequently ... was dissolved.' *Ein Jahrhundert Creditanstalt-Bankverein*, p. 157.

31 Adele Wieser, 'Die Verwertungsmöglichkeiten der Arbeitskraft in der Industrie', *Schriften des Vereins für Sozialpolitik* (Munich-Leipzig, 1925), Vol. 169, p. 101 et seq.

32 *Der Aussenhandel Österreichs in der Zeit zwischen den beiden Weltkriegen*, published by the Austrian Central Statistical Office (Vienna, 1946), p. 9.

33 See Part V, Chapter 2, p. 418 et seq.

34 Bresciani-Turroni, *Economics of Inflation*, p. 173.

35 A commentary on the Creditanstalt 1922 balance sheet remarked that the total would be considerably higher if 'it were not for the fact that, as happened last year, debtor and creditor accounts in the same currency have been set off against

one another and included only with the value at something below the market rate on the date of the date of the balance sheet.' 'Die Bilanzen', *Der Österreichische Volkswirt*, 19 May 1923, p. 253.

36 Allgemeine Depositenbank stopped payments in 1924 and has been excluded from this and the following tables.

37 In reality the creditors item was larger than the figures published in the statement, because creditors and debtors in foreign currency were set off against one another and only the balance shown in crowns. When the Creditanstalt management altered its accountancy practice in this respect, the creditors item rose from 2,000 million crowns in 1923 to 3,600 million crowns in the following year.

38 The Gold Balance Act was to allow a preparation of schilling balances with a tax-free revaluation of assets. Its main purpose was visualized as being the elimination of tax payments on imaginary profits and consideration for banks' credit rating abroad. Cf. Franz Rust, 'Das Österreichische Goldbilanzgesetz', *Mitteilungen des Verbandes österreichischer Banken und Bankiers*, 15 July 1925, p. 97.

39 *Der Österreichische Volkswirt*, 26 June 1926, p. 1,074.

40 Table 55 has been taken from the article quoted. The details about the ratio of the 1925 figures to those for 1913 have been added by the present author. Niederösterreichische Escompte-Gesellschaft's capital, put by *Der Österreichische Volkswirt* at 93.6 million gold crowns, was adjusted in accordance with the 1913 balance-sheet figures.

41 Discussing this bank's balance sheet, the same publication remarked that it had preserved some 30% of its pre-war capital and of such as had later been paid up by shareholders 'which is more than in the case of all other Viennese banks. How far other banks' valuations may possibly have been still more cautious, so that the ratio of hidden reserves to those before the war would be somewhat less favourable than in this instance, is beyond telling.' 'Die Bilanzen', *Der Österreichische Volkswirt*, 26 June 1926, p. 302.

42 Outsiders would hardly have been in a position to make a compilation of this kind in view of the exchange rate fluctuations.

43 *Der Österreichische Volkswirt*, 26 June 1926 p. 1,075.

44 As early as 1921 a discussion of the Creditanstalt balance sheet noted that the bank had 'proceeded according to an apparently clear plan to put its entire business activities on a broad international basis'. See 'Die Bilanzen', *Der Österreichische Volkswirt*, 16 July 1921, p. 167.

45 In the light of this circumstance Spitzmüller deprecated in the sharpest terms the criminal proceedings against Creditanstalt managing board members in the wake of the 1931 catastrophe. 'There was no justification whatever for involving bank directors, and in particular the directors of Creditanstalt in criminal liability after the eventual breakdown of the banking system. I regarded this course of action, for which the Buresch government was mainly responsible, as downright disgraceful.' Alexander Spitzmüller, . . . *und hat auch Ursach' es zu lieben* (Vienna, 1955), p. 357.

46 The growth of Creditanstalt's dividend distribution was as follows:

	Crowns ·	%
1914	22	6⅞
1915	32	10
1916	36	11¼
1917	39	123³⁄₁₆
1918	20	6¼
1919	38	11⅞
1920	50	15⅝
1921	200	62½
1922	3,200	100

Source: *Ein Jahrhundert Creditanstalt-Bankverein*, p. 342.

47 Cf. 'Die Bilanzen', *Der Österreichische Volkswirt*, 31 May 1924, p. 264 et seq.
48 *Records of the Department of State Relating to Internal Affairs of Austria-Hungary and Austria*, Roll 51/C.465, Microfilm Publication No. 695, National Archives, Washington.
49 'Die Bilanzen', *Der Österreichische Volkswirt*, 31 May 1924, p. 265.
50 The frequency of capital increases in this period is revealed by, among other things, the 1922 Creditanstalt Annual Report. The Bank during that year participated in twenty underwriting syndicates including, to name but a few, the issue of shares by Stabilimento Tecnico, Melichar, Meinl, Sascha, Helios, AEG-Union, and Vereinigte Färbereien AG. In a 1924 *Nationalrat* session Wilhelm Ellenbogen, the Social Democratic member, reported that during 1923 no fewer than 227 capital increases and new issues had taken place. See *Nationalrat* Shorthand Minutes, II. Legislative Period, Meeting of 20 May, p. 1,100.
51 The 1923 Creditanstalt Annual Report mentions (p. 6) that by reason of a resolution passed at the Extraordinary General Meeting held on 14 November 1923, the face value of the share capital was raised from 1,500 million crowns to 15,000 millions. The shares' par value was simultaneously raised from 320 to 3,200 crowns. 'The enormous internal reserves which Creditanstalt had at its disposal due to its securities and such held under syndicate agreements is illustrated by the fact that for the revaluation by 13,300 million crowns only two securities holdings, Pečeker Zuckerraffinerie and Mundus Holz shares, had to be called upon.' 'Die Bilanzen', *Der Österreichische Volkswirt*, 19 May 1923, p. 253.
52 Cf. Part IV, Chapter 4, p. 354.
53 Cf. 'Die Bilanzen', *Der Österreichische Volkswirt*, 12 April 1924, p. 206.
54 Boden-Creditanstalt's foreign shareholders and friends were described as 'the world's leading financial group' in 'Die Bilanzen', *Der Österreichische Volkswirt*, 12 May 1923, p. 245. A study based on British and French sources says, 'However, during the winter of 1922/3 when the bank increased its capital by an issue of a million shares, about half were taken by Schroeders in conjunction with J. P. Morgan & Co and possibly Baring Brothers. The cost to the western syndicate was thought to be £70,000 but a trade credit may also have been involved.' Philip C. Cottrell, *Aspects of Western Equity Investment in the Banking Systems of East Central Europe*, in *International Business and Central Europe, 1918–1939*, ed. A. Teichova and P. A. Cottrell, Leicester, New York, 1983.

55 'Die Bilanzen, *Der Österreichische Volkswirt*, 17 June 1922, p. 231.

56 The two transactions recall the Goethe phrase, 'Half she drew him, half he sank'. Both the proponents of the Western capital groups and the directors of the two banks had an interest in the expatriation.

57 *State Department Records*, Roll 51/C. 344 et seq., 692, and 734. This compilation by the economic experts of the United States Consulate at Vienna served as the basis for the table. Amplifications and/or corrections were undertaken with the assistance of *Compass*, 1925, Vol. I as well as various balance-sheet analyses and discussions in *Der Österreichische Volkswirt*.

58 A cousin of the well-known author Hugo von Hofmannsthal.

59 Ministry of Finance Archives File 32954/1921.

60 For the nominal development of creditors and deposits, forming the basis for the calculation in gold crowns, see Appendix II, Tables A8 and A9.

61 Cf. Federn, *Schriften*. p. 66.

62 'Die Bilanzen', *Der Österreichische Volkswirt*, 31 May 1924, p. 265.

63 For the nominal development of debtors, see Appendix II, Table A10.

64 'Die Bilanzen', *Der Österreichische Volkswirt*, 31 May 1924, p. 265.

65 'Kreditverhandlungen', *Der Österreichische Volkswirt*, 26 March 1921, p. 468.

66 For the nominal earnings, see Appendix II, Table A11. It is once more pointed out that the figures have been deflated with the help of the Parity Commission's price index, but outlays on rent omitted.

67 Wiener Bankverein had over 4,000 employees at this date, but had indeed still a large number of branch offices. Cf. 'Die Bilanzen', *Der Österreichische Volkswirt*, 28 April 1923, p. 229.

68 'Die Bilanzen', *Der Österreichische Volkswirt*, 31 May 1924, p. 266.

69 There is no need to reiterate here the reasons for the voluminous issuing activity of the inflation years. It suffices to say that the banks' participation in the transformation of multiple frozen credits into share participations frequently led to unwanted property in these assets.

70 This was what the new majority shareholders *intended*. Actually, as *Der Österreichische Volkswirt* noted, this 'dependency status' during the first years 'crippled both banks ... in their progress'. Österreichische Länderbank had 'since its conversion into a French establishment not brought off a single large-scale deal.' Anglo-Österreichische Bank had only in 1924 'carried out its first big industrial transactions'. See 'Der Rücktritt des Generaldirektors Kraus', in 'Die Bilanzen', *Der Österreichische Volkswirt*, 29 May 1924, p. 195.

71 Cf. 1923 Creditanstalt Annual Report. Creditanstalt Archives.

72 Cf. 'Die Bilanzen', *Der Österreichische Volkswirt*, 19 May 1923, p. 253.

73 'Director Neurath reported that, having obtained official Austrian authority, we are establishing jointly with Messrs S. M. von Rothschild a bank at Amsterdam under the name of "Amstelbank" which with a capital of 3 million guilders will be devoted mainly to foreign exchange business. The Dutch licence for this bank, in which Messrs Rothschild and ourselves are engaged to fifty per cent each and on whose board besides these two firms there are represented Nederlandsche Handels-Maatschapij as well as Hope & Co., Amsterdam, has already been issued.' Board Meeting Minutes, 17 November 1920, Creditanstalt Archives.

74 'Die Bilanzen', *Der Österreichische Volkswirt*, 16 July 1921, p. 169. The board consisted of the Dutchmen Dr van Alst and Mynheer C. E. ter Meulen, head of Hope & Co., who was later to play a leading part in the League of Nations

Financial Commission, and the Austrians Louis von Rothschild, Friedrich Ehrenfest, Dr Paul Hammerschlag, Dr Hans Mauthner, and Dr Wilhelm Regendanz. The first official Creditanstalt reference occurs in the 1921 Annual Report: 'The Amstelbank, founded last year, is making satisfactory progress.' Creditanstalt Archives.

75 Ministry of Finance Archives, File 80.242/1920.

76 Ministry of Finance Archives, File 105.707/1920. At this date Austria counted in the United States still as an 'enemy state' and its nationals were therefore forbidden to acquire holdings in American companies.

77 Ministry of Finance Archives, File 35.428/1921 and 52.278/1921. A list annexed to File 80.242/1920 gives the names of the borrowers, a sizable number of textile enterprises, G. Roth AG, and Kruppwerke Berndorf, in the main therefore firms associated with Creditanstalt.

78 Cf. *Ein Jahrhunder Creditanstalt-Bankverein*, p. 164. See also Hans Buchner, *Dämonen der Wirtschaft. Gestalten und dunkle Gewalten aus dem Leben unserer Tage* (Munich, 1928), p. 20 et seq.

79 Creditanstalt 1921 Annual Report, p. 8 et seq. Creditanstalt Archives. (Present author's italics.)

80 Creditanstalt 1923 Annual Report, p. 7 et seq. Creditanstalt Archives.

81 Cf. *Ein Jahrhundert Creditanstalt-Bankverein*, p. 153.

82 Creditanstalt 1921 Annual Report, p. 16 Creditanstalt Archives.

83 Creditanstalt 1922 Annual Report, p. 11. Creditanstalt Archives.

84 Part IV, Chapter 4.

85 Amstelbank acted as 'Photogen's' banker. The other participants in the holding company were the Vienna and Paris Rothschild banking houses, Ungarische Allgemeine Kreditbank, Count Larisch, and the Parisian petroleum firm Deutsch de la Meurthe. See *Der Österreichische Volkswirt*, 16 July 1921, p. 169 and 13 October 1923, p. 11 et seq.

86 Creditanstalt 1923 Annual Report, p. 14. Creditanstalt Archives. See also 'Die Bilanzen', *Der Österreichische Volkswirt*, p. 110.

87 Creditanstalt 1923 Annual Report, p. 14. Creditanstalt Archives.

88 'Die Bilanzen', *Der Österreichische Volkswirt*, 13 October 1923, p. 11.

89 Creditanstalt 1922 Annual Report, p. 12. Creditanstalt Archives.

90 Creditanstalt 1921 Annual Report, p. 17. Creditanstalt Archives. Chairman of the Board was Prince Ernst Rüdiger Starhemberg, subsequently leader of the fascist Heimwehr organization.

91 Board Minutes, 31 July 1920. Creditanstalt Archives.

92 'Die Bilanzen', *Der Österreichische Volkswirt*, 23 January, 1924, p. 125.

93 Creditanstalt 1923 Annual Report, p. 11. Creditanstalt Archives.

94 *Ein Jahrhundert Creditanstalt-Bankverein*, p. 341. 'Awestem' was purchased from the assets of the insolvent Wiener Kommerzialbank. See *Compass*, 1925, Vol. I, p. 375.

95 Creditanstalt 1923 Annual Report, p. 16. Creditanstalt Archives.

96 From the board minutes for 4 January 1922 it emerges that the Bank had a two-thirds share in the company's capital increase from 6 million to 9 million Czech crowns. Creditanstalt Archives.

97 'Even before the breakdown of the Monarchy the idea of an amalgamation with the Fiat works, likewise belonging to the Castiglioni group, . . . and the Puch works . . . had cropped up . . . In 1920 the board was authorized to implement

the merger, or pooling agreements, . . . with these car companies . . . The board decided for reasons of taxation in favour of creating a pooling agreement. This is not only of a financial, but also of a commerical and technical nature. The buying and sales organizations were combined and joined in the Daimler-Werke while the manufacturing processes were made more effective through specialization.' *Compass*, 1925, Vol. I, p. 800.

98 *Ein Jahrhundert Creditanstalt-Bankverein*, p. 341. The Creditanstalt Board Minutes for 21 September 1921 recorded that the Bank had participated to 15% in a Daimler Motoren AG capital increase from 120 to 300 million crowns. In this way it managed to extricate the firm from 'control' by Castiglioni mentioned in an earlier chapter.

99 In the critical year 1922 the management told the board that the overall indebtedness of the shipyard had reached the alarming figure of 1,200 million crowns. See Board Minutes, 5 April 1922. Creditanstalt Archives.

100 Cf. *Ein Jahrhundert Creditanstalt-Bankverein*, p. 341.

101 'Maschinenfabriks-Aktiengesellschaft N. Heid, whose capital was increased by raising the face value of its old shares to Cr. 700,000,000 and through an issue of 500,000 shares to Cr. 1,200,000,000, had large sales due to important foreign orders and consequently satisfactory results.' Creditanstalt 1923 Annual Report. Creditanstalt Archives.

102 The consistently good state of employment in these works was noted in a number of the Bank's annual reports, e.g., those for 1921 and 1923.

103 A 1923 Bank report mentions that 'Ringhoffer-Werke AG has through an exchange of shares included Nesselsdorfer Wagenbau-Fabriks AG, Smichow in its sphere of interest'. Creditanstalt Archives.

104 The Creditanstalt 1923 Annual Report states that AEG-Union had promoted separate joint-stock companies for operations in the individual Successor States and that the parent company at Vienna had had to be reorganized and expanded. P. 10 of the report recounts that the share capital had to be increased from 100 to 225 million crowns. By October 1922 the Bank's AEG receivables were 1,700 million crowns. At this date, though, the debts of the other concerns belonging to the Bank's group were substantially bigger: Shiffswerft Linz, 6,000 million crowns; Krupp AG Bernsdorf, 4,000 million crowns; AG der Lokomotivfabrik Wiener Neustadt vorm. Sigl, 5,000 million crowns, and so on. See Board Minutes, 4 October 1922. Creditanstalt Archives.

105 'Die Bilanzen', *Der Österreichische Volkswirt*, 23 July 1923, p. 405 et seq.

106 In 1923 'Austrian Ericsson' had 'the highest level of employment since its foundation'. See Creditanstalt 1923 Annual Report, p. 10, Creditanstalt Archives.

107 'The conversion of all the plants to the manufacture of peace-time goods has been completed and an increase in production has been recorded.' Creditanstalt 1921 Annual Report, p. 10. Creditanstalt Archives.

108 The Board Meeting Minutes of 30 June 1922 stated that the Krupp AG Berndorf receivables now amounted to 1,000 million crowns. Three months later the firm's debts had quadrupled. Krupp AG was all the more dependent on the Bank as a source of funds inasmuch as its expectations of British and French firms' participation – particularly as regards an extension of foreign currency loans – were disappointed. See 'Die Bilanzen', *Der Österreichische Volkswirt*, 17 February 1923, p. 154.

109 Creditanstalt 1921 Annual Report, p. 10. Creditanstalt Archives.

110 Creditanstalt 1921 Annual Report, p. 14.

111 In 1922 the management decided on a participation in the Berlin house whose capital at this juncture was being raised from 250 million to 1,000 million marks. See Creditanstalt 1922 Annual Report, p. 8. Creditanstalt Archives. Shares in the Berlin bank were acquired in conjunction with Creditanstalt by Amstelbank and Böhmische Escompte Bank und Kreditanstalt. See *Arbeit und Wirtschaft*, 1 January 1923, Col. 30.

112 Board Minutes, 16 September 1919. Creditanstalt Archives.

113 Board Minutes, 27 May 1921. Creditanstalt Archives.

114 Board Minutes, 17 December 1918. Creditanstalt Archives. The Bank's participation amounted to 11.5 million crowns of the total 150 million crowns German-Austria State Loan.

115 At the outset the interest rate on three months' Treasury bills was 2.5%; in 1920 it was raised to 6%.

116 Act of 23 June 1920, published in Federal Law Gazette, No. 42.

117 Cf. *Compass*, 1925, Vol. I, p. 198.

118 The interest on the bonds was remarkably low. That on the tax-free City of Vienna 1921 Loan (to a nominal amount of 1,000 million crowns) was 5%. The same applied to the City of Vienna 1922 Domestic Dwellings Loan.

119 To facilitate comparison between pre- and post-war figures the securities and syndicate accounts have been added together. The conversion into schillings was made so as to be able to allow for the results of the gold opening balances.

120 A commentary on the Boden-Creditanstalt 1913 balance sheet made the criticism that 'the erratic development of the debtors item . . . has to do with its inadmissible combination of receivables and syndicate payments. Adding to this was the rise in the number of debtors during the past year. The payments on the Austrian and still more on the Hungarian bonds, the purchase of the shares majority in Cantiere Navale Triestino, and its quota in the syndicate to acquire the majority of the Oriental Railway shares, have tied up substantial resources.' 'Die Bilanzen', *Der Österreichische Volkswirt*, 7 March 1914, p. 87.

121 Estimates of the banks' losses current in Austria varied widely. One alleged that by the end of 1923 the banks had been deprived of fifty to sixty per cent of their pre-war assets. Another spoke of a ten per cent loss. The American experts thought that too low. A third, propounded by Dr Alfred Gürtler, the former Minister of Finance, put the overall loss of all Austrian joint-stock companies at seventy per cent. The companies had however through capital increases between 1918 and 1923 again doubled their assets, so that in this view the actual loss was forty per cent. The Americans regarded a loss of fifty per cent as a realistic estimate. *State Department Records*, Washington, Roll 51/C. 450 et seq.

122 'The two projects – transformation of Anglo-Österreichische Bank into a British establishment and the Länderbank into a French bank – had been mutually agreed, and Paris and London helped each other with its implementation.' Marie-Luise Recker, *England und der Donauraum 1919–1929. Probleme einer europäischen Nachkriegsordnung* (Stuttgart, 1976), p. 61, Footnote 99.

123 'In common with industrial and banking circles the British and French governments were aware at the end of the War that the most effective means of entrance to trade, finance and industry of Central and Southeast Europe would be through the great Viennese joint stock banks with their large ramified

interests.' Alice Teichova, 'Versailles and the Expansion of the Bank of England into Central Europe', in *Recht und Entwicklung der Grossunternehmen im 19. und frühen 20. Jahrhundert*, ed. by Norbert Horn and Jürgen Kocka (Göttingen, 1979), p. 371. The author cites in this connection communications between the British Legation, Vienna, and London as well as between the Foreign Office and the French Ministry for Foreign Affairs. See also Recker, *England*, p. 61.

124 Sources: *Compass*, 1925, Vol I, p. 413 et seq.; balance-sheet commentaries in *Der Österreichische Volkswirt*; Österreichische Länderbank 1923 Annual Report; *State Department Records*, Washington, Roll 51/C.751 et seq.

125 Sources: *Compass*, 1925, Vol. I, p. 338 et seq.; balance-sheet commentaries in *Der Österreichische Volkswirt*; *State Department Records*, Washington, Roll 51/C.696 et seq.; Recker, *England*, p. 65 et seq.

126 See Eduard März, *Österreichische Industrie- und Bankpolitik in der Zeit Franz Josephs I* (Vienna, 1968), p. 125 et seq. and p. 222 et seq.

127 *State Department Records*, Washington, Roll 51/C.344; *Compass*, 1918, Vol. I, p. 525.

128 The preamble to the bill which was to become known as the 'Länderbank Act' contained the following passage: 'They are encumbered with very large foreign debts which, expressed in crowns, have now multiplied greatly as against the original amount. These foreign debts would need to be settled through the process of examination and composition wherein the Federal Government is jointly liable with the debtor as against foreign countries. The Federal Government would accordingly have to pay the entire foreign debts of these enterprises and would have redress against them only. It is more than doubtful whether the Federal Government could, in view of these enterprises' financial conditions, claim this redress. It is indubitable however that the Federal Government would suffer a very severe loss through the process of examination and composition. If, on the other hand, such enterprises came to an arrangement with the foreign creditors as regards their debts, then these are omitted from the clearing (claims) and the public funds are discharged. Assistance by foreign capital on behalf of such companies is consequently highly desirable in the national financial interest.' Cf. the Ministry of Finance draft, Ministry of Finance Archives, File 2530/1921.

129 Annotations to the bill's preamble, Ministry of Finance Archives, File 2530/1921. The ministry expert drew the conclusion – it sounds somewhat strange to modern ears – that through the impending transaction 'control of the economy by foreign capital' would be 'retarded' inasmuch as the banks by converting their foreign debts 'into shares or long term warrants' avoided the necessity 'to sell for the procurement of foreign exchange the packets of industrial stocks held in their portfolio'.

130 Cf. D. E. Moggridge, *British Monetary Policy 1924–1931. The Norman Conquest of $4.86* (Cambridge, 1972), p. 201 et seq. See also Cottrell, *Aspects of Western Equity Investment*, p. 335 et seq.

131 AVA, Social Democratic Parliamentary Party Documents, Box 45, File 71. Letter of the President of the Anglo-Austrian Bank, Siegfried Rosenbaum, to Karl Seitz, dated 13 July 1921.

132 See Recker, *England*, pp. 60 and 66.

133 *Wirtschaftsstatistisches Jahrbuch 1926* (Vienna, 1927), p. 373 et seq., published by the Vienna Chamber of Labour.

134 Teichova, in *Recht und Entwicklung*, p. 385.
135 The various expert and supplementary expert opinions are available in AVA, Social Democratic Parliamentary Club Documents, Box 45. The essence of them was that the losses with which Österreichische Länderbank and Anglo-Österreichische Bank were threatened by their foreign creditors had been vastly overestimated.
136 Federal Law Gazette, 7 October 1921, Nos. 541 and 542.
137 Karl Ausch, *Als die Banken fielen* (Vienna, 1968), p. 26 et seq.
138 *State Department Records*, Washington, Roll 51/C. 692 and 734.
139 As late as 1928 a partner in the Berlin banking house Mendelssohn & Co. at an Austro-German economic conference championed the view that the influence of Western financial groups in Austria was not 'dominant in the sense that your banks do not know how, within the framework of the general dependency of a financially weak country, to uphold the independence of economic decison. Dependency does not go that far. Your banks rightly conduct their business self-confidently and autonomously.' Minutes of the Joint Conference between Deutscher Industrie- und Handelstag and Österreichischer Kammertag at Vienna on 21–22 September 1928, published at Vienna in 1929 and retained in the Vienna Chamber of Commerce Archives as Document 28833 I, p. 48 It was kindly put at the author's disposal by Dr Karl Haas, Institut für Zeitgeschichte, Vienna.
140 This circumstance led only a few years later to serious disputes between the headquarters and the Vienna branch office of Österreichische Länderbank. During the course of them the general manager, Max Kraus, and his deputy, Markus Rotter, resigned. See *Der Österreichische Volkswirt*, 29 May 1924, p. 195.
141 See Part IV, Chapter 4, p. 211 et seq. and 358.
142 See 'Der Rücktritt Castiglionis', *Der Abend*, 18 April 1922.
143 'Die Bilanzen' (Unionbank), *Der Österreichische Volkswirt*, 7 June 1924, p. 271. Later it transpired that Bosel had financed his transactions with the help of loans from the Postal Savings Bank. See Ausch, *Als die Banken fielen*, p. 247 et seq.
144 In spring 1924 Castiglioni was not so much in debt to domestic banks as heavily committed abroad. 'Der Fall Castiglioni', *Der Österreichische Volkswirt*, 4 and 18 October, pp. 20 and 64 respectively.
145 Ausch, *Als die Banken fielen*, p. 59 et seq. Between June and August 1922 alone the crown lost some seven-eights of its value.
146 'Der Fall Depositenbank', *Der Österreichische Volkswirt*, 10 May 1924, p. 967.
147 *Der Österreichische Volkswirt*, 12 June 1924, p. 1,249 commented that Castiglioni had himself never financed any bigger firm of his 'group'. 'His system was always to leave the procurement of loans to others.'
148 *Neue Freie Presse*, 21 April 1922. The group, of which Banca Commerciale Italiana had been a member, had with a holding of more than a million shares earlier been in the majority.
149 'Depositenbank', *Der Österreichische Volkswirt*, 28 June 1924, p. 1,195.
150 According to *Neues Wiener Tagblatt*, 8 October 1922, the new chairman of the board, Goldstein, on the occasion of the Extraordinary General Meeting contradicted the rumour that the bank's industrial group had shrunk after Castiglioni's elimination. On the contrary, it had grown 'because the new

475

members of the board have already affiliated a part of their enterprises to the bank'.

151 'Depositenbank', *Der Österreichische Volkswirt*, p. 1,194.

152 From the evidence provided by the governor, the former Minister of Finance Dr Richard Reisch, in the Vienna Commercial Court. *Neue Freie Presse*, 24 February 1925.

153 See Ausch, *Als die Banken fielen* p. 163; 'Depositenbank', *Der Österreichische Volkswirt*, p. 1,193 et seq.; *Der Österreichische Volkswirt*, 28 February 1925, p. 588; *Neue Freie Presse*, 24 February 1925. Ausch says that the Goldstein-Drucker-Sachsel syndicate alone owed 96 million crowns for subscribed shares.

154 *Der Österreichische Volkswirt*, 28 February 1925, *Neue Freie Presse*, 6 May 1924 and 25 February 1925.

155 *Arbeiter-Zeitung*, 25 February 1925. Nevertheless in June 1924 the major banks had still calculated an assets surplus of 20,000 to 50,000 million crowns. See 'Depositenbank', *Der Österreichische Volkswirt* p. 1,194.

156 *Der Österreichische Volkswirt*, p. 1,193.

157 'Strafanzeige gegen Castiglioni', *Der Österreichische Volkswirt*, 7 June 1924, p. 1,099.

158 'Die Geheimnisse der Depositenbank', *Der Österreichische Volkswirt*, 27 September 1924, p. 1,562 et seq.

159 *Der Österreichische Volkswirt*, 19 July 1924, p. 1,278 and 'Strafanzeige gegen Castiglioni', *Der Österreichische Volkswirt*, 2 August 1924, p. 1,340 et seq.

160 Already on 28 June 1924, when the truth about Allgemeine Depositenbank's failure had not yet properly come to light, the U.S. Embassy, Vienna, reported to the Department of State, 'It now appears certain that the demoralization has extended into larger banks and that conditions prevail there which under English or American banking laws would send many of the directors to jail.' *State Department Records*, Roll 51/C. 477/78.

161 After the proceedings against the last of the accused had been quashed, *Der Österreichische Volkswirt* wrote. 'The Castiglioni Case will live on as the worst of the many Austrian legal scandals in this time and the term 'Castiglioni justice' will be used to denote a judicature influenced by political and economic forces, like saying "Panama" when parliamentary financial corruption is meant.' 'Castiglioni', 17 October 1925, p. 65.

162 Shortly after he had paid off Allgemeine Depositenbank with $200,000, Castiglioni had published in a German newspaper that his personal fortune after the deduction of all losses still amounted to at least $20 million (about 100 million gold crowns) and that he was planning the implementation of larger-scale projects in Germany. *Der Österreichische Volkswirt*, 22 November 1924, p. 203; *Berliner Zeitung (BZ) am Mittag*, 13 November 1924; Central State Archives, (ZStA), Potsdam, 09.01 AA 40341, p. 8.

163 Boden-Creditanstalt had to undertake a capital increase quite simply to rid itself of a speculator who had purchased 200,000 of the bank's shares. Rudolf Sieghart, *Die letzten Jahrzehnte einer Grossmacht* (Berlin, 1932), p. 196. The author does not give the speculator's name; he was Sigmund Bosel. In a similar instance Creditanstalt's management reacted in a more relaxed manner. Heinrich Bronner, another well-known speculator, obtained several hundred thousand of the Bank's shares in 1923. See *Der Österreichische Volkswirt*, 1

March 1924, p. 653. At a board meeting von Neurath announced that 'the Management . . . sees no cause to put any motion'. Board Minutes, 5 July 1923. Creditanstalt Archives.

CHAPTER 4
Hyperinflation and the Geneva Recovery Programme

During January 1922 the value of the crown dropped at an un-precedented rate. Whereas at the beginning of the year the dollar had stood in Vienna at 5,765 crowns, by 23 January the price was 10,000. The government, with the abolition of the food subsidies and certain other, fairly ineffectual anti-inflationary measures seemed to have shot its bolt for the moment.[1] The Minister of Finance, Dr Alfred Gürtler, and his adviser Dr Wilhelm Rosenberg therefore pushed vigorously ahead with their efforts to set in motion an international loan operation.

Its prospects had become far rosier since Austria and Czecho-slovakia had by the Treaty of Lana undertaken to respect the political and territorial changes effected by the Treaties of Saint-Germain and Trianon. The unrelinquished lien of the Allied Powers on Austrian property still barred the way, but there was a distinct change of attitude by the Czechoslovak Government towards Austria after 16 December 1921, the day when the treaty was signed. The endeavours of Chancellor Dr Johannes Schober and his successor Seipel were supported with growing sympathy and firmness.[2]

The renewed international appeal by the Austrian Government soon showed positive results. On 7 February the British Prime Minister, David Lloyd George, announced in the House of Commons that the British Government had decided to extend a loan of £2 million sterling to Austria. Next day a loan agreement for 500 million Czech crowns was signed at Prague. Simultaneously talks began with French and Italian finance committees about an emergency loan of 55 million francs and 70 million lire respectively.[3] The total of all these credits must be called modest and the terms and the conditions attached to the British loan, were exceptionally harsh. Thus a certain Mr Young, a British diplomat, was sent to Vienna to supervise the observance of the agreement.[4] Austria had at any rate gained a breathing-space to take in hand its long postponed financial reform.

478

In spring 1922 improvement seemed to be in the offing. The prospect of early financial aid led to a brief recuperation of the currency. The dollar receded from its high-water mark on 23 January to 6,200 crowns on 15 February. For a moment too the price level steadied. The government knew of course that this was no more than a passing amelioration, yet paradoxically it seemed more concerned to acquire new and larger loans than to tackle the overdue reform of the public finances. Criticizing the odd mentality behind this policy of drift, Spitzmüller wrote:

At the Ministry of Finance everything . . . was staked on the card of outside financial aid. Until such arrived, the crown was deliberately left to slide. Departmental Head Dr Schwarzwald in particular took the line that the introduction of a financial (reform) plan based primarily on external assistance at the nadir of the crown's devaluation was a justifiable, indeed desirable thing. With exception of the food subsidies, he rejected any deflationary measures.[5]

At the beginning of April President Harding put his signature to the decision of Congress to grant Austria a twenty-five year moratorium on 126 million Swiss francs owing to the USA 'in the expectation that other states still hesitant to make such a move would follow this example'.[6] It looked like a good omen for Austria to present its case at the conference meeting at Genoa in the same month to discuss primarily the German reparations problem. The conference furnished the Austrian Government with the ardently desired opportunity to renew negotiations with the signatories of the Peace Treaty about relinquishing their lien on Austrian property. Chancellor Schober said in his reports to the Parliamentary Foreign Affairs Committee on 9 and 24 May that Genoa had produced a clarification of this problem. This would of course have greatly improved the prospects for securing international credits soon. The Chancellor seems however, as Ladner has shown, to have interpreted too favourably the statements of Yugoslavia and Romania, which at this point still hoped for reparation payments from Austria.[7] He had in any case no further chance to prove the success or failure of his Genoa excursion because his loss of support from the Pan-Germans forced him to resign shortly after his return to the capital.[8] The hopes pinned by Austrian public opinion on the journey therefore gave place to a mood of deepest pessimism when it became known that the British loan had been expended within a matter of weeks. A short review of the central bank's discount policy is necessary to understand this rapid dissipation of the sterling credit.

For the first two post-war years the 'Austrian Department' of the

Austro-Hungarian Bank had been inclined to act with reserve towards requests from the private sector of the economy, but it had unhesitatingly accommodated the far-reaching requirements of the state. In spring 1921 the bank raised the discount rate from 5% to 6%, a move of little significance when private borrowers were paying between 30% and 50%, and tightened up conditions for obtaining short-term commercial loans. This accounts for its bills portfolio fluctuating between spring and autumn 1921 around a mere 1,000 million crowns, while banknotes in circulation during the same period rose from 38,000 to 61,000 million crowns.

When Dr Gürtler assumed office in autumn 1921 the Central Bank's practice was radically altered. From the outset he and his adviser Rosenberg tried to ease as far as possible the acute scarcity of capital affecting the business world. Under their influence the Central Bank liberalized its credit policy and extended considerable loans to commercial banks and industrial enterprises. As early as the beginning of December the bank's bills portfolio had expanded to 14,000 million crowns. By the end of the month it stood at the record figure of 29,000 millions.[9] Naturally it was not always possible to distinguish between legitimate and illegitimate demands and thus a large number of speculative purchases of foreign exchange must have been defrayed with the help of cheap Central Bank loans.[10]

The situation will be better understood if it is realized that the Foreign Exchange Agency was under the control of the Ministry of Finance, not, as would have been normal, of the Central Bank. Even though Spitzmüller, then governor of the Austro-Hungarian Bank, repeatedly protested against what he called 'the monstrous condition of separate management of bills discount and foreign exchange control', no change was made.[11] In spring 1922, with a temporary stabilization of the crown, the ministry ordered an extensive liberalization in foreign exchange dealings and permitted the export of crown notes. It had doubtless been expected that this would further contribute to a stabilization of the situation in the foreign exchange market. Quite to the contrary the liberalization caused its rapid destabilization since the Foreign Exchange Agency's holdings, which had been replenished by the proceeds of the British loan, were exhausted within the shortest space of time. Walré de Bordes reports that in three weeks the entire £2 million credit had been used up.[12]

In these circumstances it hardly comes as a surprise that the negotiations with the American banking house of Pierpont Morgan, begun in February through the good services of Montagu Norman, the governor of the Bank of England, were broken off after a few months. The Austrian Minister in London claimed that the bankers 'wanted to see the larger questions in a clear light, before they committed themselves to granting any credits to Austria'.[13] It seems likely that the government's amateur handling of financial affairs must have largely helped to bring about the failure.[14]

In May the crown resumed its accelerating downward course. The dollar quotations in late spring and summer demonstrate the rapid pace of depreciation.[15]

Table 66   Dollar/crown exchange rates, 1922

15 May	14 June	14 July	14 August	15 September
10,000	19,400	29,875	58,400	74,450

The level of prices soared inversely to the fall of the crown.

Table 67   Cost of living index (less rent), 1922
1914 = 1

15 May	15 June	15 July	15 August	15 September
1,364	2,339	3,308	7,422	14,153

How the ordinary Austrian, inherently easy-going, reacted to this phase of hyperinflation is described by Walré de Bordes, a trained economic observer:

Thrifty housewives invested their money in stocks of sugar, coffee, and other perishable goods, or spent it on clothes and furniture; others squandered it recklessly – would not wine be dearer on the morrow? On days when there was a sharp rise in prices there would be a run on the shops. Prices would then increase from hour to hour, and the public were content to buy whatever they could lay their hands on. On such days one would witness those ludicrous scenes in which some old bachelor would be seen buying swaddling clothes, because the local shop had no other wares left for sale, or another would invest in four dozen tooth-brushes simply to get rid of his money by some means or other.[16]

The struggle for existence became ever more difficult too for businessmen and producers. They restricted production, they took measures to stop the speedy disappearance of their stocks, and both increased prices in proportion to the rise of the dollar. Whereas earlier there had been a considerable lag between the dollar's upward move and the rise of prices, in summer 1922 this was no longer so. Prices shot up even quicker than the dollar or the rates for other hard currencies.[17]

Table 68   *Increase of dollar rate and cost of living, 1922*

	Dollar Rate % Increase	Cost of Living Index % Increase
15 May–15 June	94	71
15 June–15 July	54	41
15 July–15 Aug	97	124
15 Aug–15 Sep	21	91

The repeal of the food subsidies had been accompanied by the universal use of wage indexing. During the first quarter of 1922 prices had risen comparatively slowly, creating no insuperable difficulties for the adjustment of wages to the cost of living index. A different situation arose when prices began to climb at break-neck speed. Now it was extremely difficult, and for some smaller firms quite impossible, to raise sufficient cash to pay the inflated weekly wages.[18] Many industrial enterprises had either to cut working hours or temporarily to close their doors.[19]

The problems facing the government were no less serious than those of the business community. Initially it had been the unbalanced budget which had released the forces responsible for the price increases and the currency's depreciation. Now the crown's swift depreciation made it virtually impossible for the Minister of Finance to put his house in order. Every effort to adapt public revenue to the rapidly growing expenditure proved futile in the light of the enormous price and exchange rate movements.[20] The size of the deficit is shown in Table 69.

On 31 May, amidst these turbulent events, a new government under

Table 69   *Federal budgets, 1921 and 1922 in 000 m. crowns*

	Revenue	Expend.	Deficit	Revenue as % of Expendit.
1 July–31 Dec 1921	78,036	218,762	140,726	36
1 Jan–31 Dec 1922	3,455,242	6,770,273	3,315,031	51

Mgr Dr Ignaz Seipel was confirmed in office by a parliamentary majority. Innumerable articles and an impressive number of books have been devoted to the personality of this Federal Chancellor and prelate, who had served as a minister in the last imperial cabinet. No attempt will here be made to deal with the character of an undeniably great and complex personality who maintained a certain distance, indeed unapproachability, even with his intimates. Otto Bauer, in an obituary which cost him the sympathy of many of his followers, did his best to draw the portrait of his great antagonist in historic perspective. To him Seipel was 'by far the most outstanding personality of the Austrian bourgeoisie, the only statesman on a European scale whom the Republic's conservative parties have produced'. Seipel, Bauer said, had placed his 'exceptional talents' at the service of the existing bourgeois society. 'That he succeeded in 1922 at the height of inflation in obtaining help from the League of Nations, which had shortly before been refused, was the outcome of a daringly intrepid, but exceedingly skilful foreign policy manoeuvre.'[21] These words can serve as introduction to the following description of Seipel's road to Geneva.

The new Minister of Finance was Dr August Ségur, former financial department head of the Lower Austrian Government. Not regarded as an expert, his appointment as the exponent of financial policy at this critical juncture roused misgivings even among conservative economists and journalists.[22] Seipel, who had little economic experience of his own, probably believed along with Ségur that he would have a number of first-class specialists at his disposal. One was Dr Alfred Grünberger, a trained economist as well as his Minister of Foreign Affairs, and another Dr Richard Schüller, a senior permanent official under Grünberger. It emerges from Seipel's diaries that he also frequently consulted the lawyer and financier Dr Gottfried Kunwald who may be called his *éminence grise*. Ségur's appointment seems however to have contributed still more to the national feeling of insecurity for now the fall of the crown, under the influence of unbridled bear speculation, turned into a breakneck plunge.[23]

Ségur did not immediately present to the public his reconstruction programme although already on 1 June he had submitted to the cabinet the main outlines of a financial plan.[24] On 7 June, with panic growing in the country, Seipel discussed the possibility of launching a diplomatic operation.[25] This he was prepared to undertake with his Minister of Finance so as to put strong moral pressure on the Great Powers to come forth with the long-promised assistance.[26] It was the first occasion on which he contemplated using drastic political pressures to obtain the international loan which he thought indispensable to Austria's recovery.

Some hopes were raised at the meeting between members of the government, representatives from the major political parties, and representatives from the big Viennese banks called by Seipel on 13 June.[27] Spitzmüller has in his memoirs left a very detailed account of these talks at which feelings appear to have run high. Here it is sufficient to recapitulate the emergency measures which were proposed on this occasion.[28]

It was feared that foreign currency for the import of Czech coal could no longer be obtained in the near future and thus Vienna's industrial enterprises would become immobilized. The Social Democrats therefore proposed that 'the big financial establishments should make available their gold and foreign exchange reserves in order to put an end to the rapid fall of the exchange rate. The banks should perhaps be persuaded to make these reserves "voluntarily" available to a new central bank to be founded by them. Over and above this, budget expenditure should be further curtailed.'[29] The major banks agreed to these proposals and it looked as though at last there was hope for a solution to the desperate state of financial affairs. On this basis, Spitzmüller adds, a comparatively modest amount of foreign assistance would have been sufficient as a first step toward the stabilization of the budget.

The decision of 13 June, although of an informal character, seemed to have prepared the way for a new, constructive programme. On 21 June Ségur expounded to parliament a plan largely based on the ideas of the two major parties.[30] The focal point was the foundation of a new bank of issue, with a share capital of 100 million Swiss francs that would furnish cover for sixty per cent of the banknotes in circulation. The Viennese banks and savings banks had promised definitely to take over 24 million francs for own account and to underwrite the acceptance of another 36 millions. The remaining 40 millions would be subscribed later. Because the new bank was to refrain from the issue of unbacked banknotes, from the first day of its operation the government had to provide for an interim fund from which to pay current expenditure until such time as budgetary receipts and outlays were again in equilibrium. The fund, it was hoped, would be financed by a 400,000 million crowns domestic loan to be secured by a tax on landed property as well as by higher indirect taxes and tariffs. The remainder of the Czech loan and the as yet unreleased French and

Italian credits were to be devoted to the same purpose.[31] Budgetary equilibrium was to be restored by severe economies comprising primarily abolition of the Federal Food Ministry, merger of the communications directorates (railways, post and telegraph systems), and far-reaching reductions of the civil service generally.[32] The long-standing Social Democratic idea of 'giving state enterprises an independent commercial status' was finally to be realized.[33] No less important were the increased receipts that were envisaged from new duties, a new tax on timber and wine, and a turnover tax. Unfortunately the parliamentary majority insisted on making a package deal of the stabilization measures and the founding of the bank of issue.[34]

The government, to ensure quick subscription of the new Central Bank's capital, decided to safeguard the value of this investment in real terms. In addition the income from the duties was to be allocated to a special fund set aside for future interest payments in case of a loss incurred by the Central Bank. The provision was however of small practical importance as long as the Allied Powers refused to repeal their lien on state property. This cardinal problem of Austria's credit rating remained still open, regardless of the promises to the Austrian delegation at the Genoa Conference.

The government now struck out along a hitherto untried path by asking the Reparation Commission to release a restricted number of Austrian assets so as to furnish funds for the Central Bank. The tactic proved successful. On 22 July the Reparation Commission announced that it had released for a period of ninety years proceeds from federal forests, salt works, customs revenues, and agricultural domains. The income on the tobacco monopoly was also put at the government's disposal to enable it to pledge this against a foreign loan.[35]

Preparations for the foundation of the new bank dragged on in spite of the partial success with respect to the matter of the liens. The Viennese banks, which the government had invited to take up the greater part of the capital of the new Central Bank, made their agreement dependent on the participation of foreign financial circles in the project. The government was thus forced to enter into negotiations with the representatives of the two former Austrian banks, Anglo-Austrian Bank Limited and Banque des Pays de l'Europe Centrale.

The Viennese managements of these institutes had been members of the Founding Committee and had agreed to the articles of association approved by the *Nationalrat* on 27 July 1922. The reaction of the London and Paris boards of the two banks came as a complete surprise to the Austrian government. The requested important changes in the articles already sanctioned by parliament, including permanent representation on the General Council, elimination of the veto of the Chairman against the Council's resolutions and a reduction in the powers of the state commissioner. Moreover, as if the interests of the foreign investors were not already adequately safeguarded, sixty million Swiss francs, an amount equivalent to the capital of the Bank, were to be deposited abroad and repatriated only by unanimous agreement. Rudolf Freund, who has dealt with this episode in detail, concludes the story by saying that on this capital of sixty million francs the two foreign banks were 'prepared to take over one million each – and that pittance on such conditions!'[36]

The contribution which the two banks were in fact prepared to make totalled nine million francs, not as Freund erroneously stated only two, but Ausch is probably right in saying that the government should never even have considered these requests. This amount could assuredly have been raised at home.[37] At this time, though, the government was hardly in a position to ignore the demands of two foreign banking houses in direct contact with British and French government circles.

The unfortunate linking of the budget reconstruction with the bank of issue had tied the government's hands. Inflation seemed now to have acquired the strength of a natural force against which everyone was totally helpless. Of Ségur's recovery programme there remained nothing except the compulsory loan which could be carried out only in a modified form and moreover was completely ineffective as a result of the rapidly accelerating inflation.[38] The system of strict foreign exchange control in force prior to Gürtler's irresponsible liberalization measures was re-introduced.[39] This abrupt return to the emergency régime in the form of the revived Foreign Exchange Agency did not however produce the desired effect, because the few happy owners of foreign currency were no longer prepared to part with their holdings. At the beginning of August the crisis seemed to approach its zenith. As a foreign observer versed in local affairs reported,[40]

the long-prophesied final collapse then appeared to be inevitable. There was no very clear idea as to what form it would take, but it was generally expected that the Austrian paper money would soon lose both its internal and external purchasing value, and it was feared that famine and anarchy must supervene, that some of the neighbouring states would invade the country and that it would ultimately be divided between them.

At the beginning of August the government was still trying to secure the participation of the foreign banks on the bank of issue project. But these went even beyond their earlier rather excessive demands and requested that the new bank must constitute an integral part of a reform plan, the most important element of which would be a foreign loan. The views of the two banks are known in detail because they are recorded in a letter by two of Anglo-Austrian Bank's directors to Lloyd George, at this time chancellor of the exchequer. The following are the crucial passages:

The financial situation in Austria is growing worse every day, and in particular the stabilisation of its currency can only be effected by the adoption of a joint plan, the essential points of which are:—
1. That the Budget shall be made to balance,
2. That steps should be taken to reduce the deficit on expenditure,
3. An internal loan,
4. Foreign credits,
5. The establishing of a Bank of Issue.

The authors of the plan which did not substantially differ from that of the Minister of Finance, added these significant words: 'These measures are intimately connected with one another and can only come into force effectively if the scheme is adopted in its entirety.' The letter ends on the following ominous note:

In view of the fact that the shareholders of these concerns cannot consent to take up unassisted the burden of measures which would be inoperative if they are undertaken piecemeal, the French and English directors of the banks regard it as their duty to approach their respective governments with a view to asking them to take the necessary steps for protecting their assets and properties in Austria against force majeure from any quarter.[41]

Presumably this last paragraph was inspired by rumours about domestic unrest and dangers of intervention from abroad. One must conclude that the two banks were determined to make foreign credits a *sine qua non* for their participation in Ségur's reconstruction programme.

Was it the foreign banks alone that made their participation conditional on outside help or, as is often alleged, were the domestic banks also behind them? A final answer is hardly possible on the basis of the sources at present available. Samuel Pressburger, historian of the Austrian National Bank, says that the banks were prepared to underwrite the new Central Bank's capital, but 'in spite of Seipel's insistent request' refused 'to subscribe to a loan to restore monetary soundness'.[42] The possibility that the approach of the two foreign banks to Lloyd George had the support of the whole Viennese financial community cannot be excluded.

The major Vienna banks maintained, as will be recalled, considerable assets in foreign currency in neighbouring countries. The policy served the twofold purpose of ensuring against losses of capital caused by inflation, and of safeguarding certain assets earmarked for repayment sooner or later to foreign creditors of valorized crown liabilities.[43] Still more was the fact that since the days of the Empire's demise an important portion of banking activities had shifted to the Successor States. The banks, initially involuntarily, then with well-considered forethought, had put their business policy on a trans-national basis. This orientation was a subject of argument from the outset. Spitzmüller especially, saddled with the difficult task of liquidating the Austro-Hungarian Bank, warned banks repeatedly against trying to uphold their Central European status.

As I saw it, in Czechoslovakia, in Poland, in Yugoslavia, and in Hungary too these positions should have been liquidated. The main advantage would have been the inflow of a large quantity of foreign exchange which would have made possible the creation of a solid, though modest, foundation for the Austrian economy. This would admittedly have entailed a substantial reduction of the excessively large banking system, but that would in turn have avoided the subsequent serious bank crashes.[44]

Whether the rapid liquidation of the banks' foreign assets would have assured a rich influx of foreign exchange is open to question, because in the immediate post-war period the absorptive capacity of the international capital market was assuredly limited. The early association of the Viennese banks with financially powerful Western banking houses must moreover have nurtured the illusion that it might be possible to conduct business successfully in central and eastern Europe as a joint venture. At the beginning of the 1920s no one could anticipate that the recovery phase in the Danube area would ultimately prove weak and short-lived, ending in the catastrophe of the Great Depression.

A certain scepticism on the part of the banks, and not only the foreign ones, towards the self-help endeavours of the Schober and Seipel governments was therefore not illogical although perhaps not wholeheartedly patriotic. Their readiness for self-sacrifice was impaired by the instinct for self-preservation. No government could have furnished them with guarantees that the provision of extensive gold and foreign exchange reserves for the establishment of a bank of issue and a domestic loan would have been sufficient to constitute a sound basis for the reconstruction of the economy. On the other hand every further loss of capital could not but seriously jeopardize their capacity to compete successfully in the hotly disputed terrain of the Successor States.[45]

During the course of July it became clear that the Seipel-Ségur recovery plan, conceived principally along lines of self-help, would have to be dropped. Once again desperate efforts were made to obtain generous financial assistance from abroad. Yet the fact that the government, after the Signatory Powers had partially relinquished their lien, could now dispose of such rich sources of revenue as tariffs and earnings on state monopolies was not enough in the eyes of potential foreign lenders. What they wanted was a formal Allied guarantee of full indemnification against loss of their Austrian assets. That left the government no choice other than to turn once more to the Supreme Council.

This important step was preceded by certain preparatory talks in Vienna. The most detailed information on the content of, and in part the actual words spoken at, one of these discussions has survived.[46] Present at the meeting, under the chairmanship of the Frederal Chancellor, were Vice-Chancellor Dr Felix Frank, the Minister of Finance, the Minister of Foreign Affairs, two of the latter's senior officials, and Dr Rosenberg, chairman of the Anglo-Austrian Board.[47]

As the Allied Council was to meet in mid-August in London for one of its periodic sessions, it was decided – on Franckenstein's advice – to address to it a memorandum. The terms were to be drafted by Rosenberg. The representation of Austria's interests was to be entrusted to Franckenstein. Schüller, the Ministry of Foreign Affairs department head, would travel to the British capital to assist him. Opinion was unanimous that the memorandum should culminate in the statement that without foreign aid 'the Austrian Government can no longer assure the functioning of the state; it will reject any further responsibility at a coming meeting of parliament and will address the Austrian people, and the world, with a declaration to this effect.'

A rather longer debate seems to have taken place on the purpose of this statement. The meeting's minutes record that the formula was by no means intended as either 'the threat of a Soviet regime' or an 'announcement of *Anschluss*', but simply to make known the impossibility of upholding the state brought into being by the Treaty of Saint-Germain. Nevertheless, they continue, neither the Federal Chancellor nor the Minister of Finance 'held that the existence of Austria as such' would cease, and the Minister of Finance even said that he really could not imagine 'what is, properly speaking, meant by the so-called collapse'. Food supplies were for the time being covered by a reserve of 70,000 tons of grain and the coming harvest. Thanks to the Czech credit it would be possible to pay the salaries of the civil service. Even without foreign loans the situation 'could be held until the middle of September'.

The meeting then dealt with what was actually to be done if the request for aid was rejected. Here too a certain amount of confusion appears to have prevailed. If a government 'must reject the responsibility' for further developments, as the memorandum puts it, that seems to leave open only the possibility of immediate resignation. It does not look, though, as if this was Seipel's intention since he declared that the reaction to a negative answer by the Allied Council would be the adoption of dilatory tactics. Moreover, 'regardless of the threat contained in the memorandum's final sentence, the government's resignation must at all events be avoided. It will simply tell Parliament that Austria in its present form can no longer be continued. Parliament will then have to speak its mind, and perhaps the government will tender its resignation.' It sounds as if Seipel regarded the resignation of his cabinet, should the Allies respond negatively, as merely one among several options.[48]

Franckenstein and Schüller (who arrived in London on 6 August) were faced with a difficult, almost insoluble task. The only item on the council's agenda was German reparations. Here matters seemed already to have reached an impasse, Franckenstein reported, because recently Anglo-French differences on this subject had hardened.

The position for Austria was rendered as bad as could be, inasmuch as Britain wanted to see the Austrian problem solved only in the context of German reparations. Primarily, says Ladner, it was owing to Schüller that the government's memorandum was placed on the agenda, more or less at the last moment. Schüller had prepared the ground in Paris by a number of statements, the principal point of which was a warning of Austria's impending collapse. Now he and Franckenstein made strenuous rounds of each of the Western delegations. The most amenable proved to be the French, the first to agree to discuss the meorandum. The Italians were somewhat aloof, distinctly sceptical about Austria's Cassandra cries, and wanting more clarification of the previously-aired possibility of a currency and customs union between Austria and Italy.[49]

The most difficult however were the British. Their attention was riveted on the menace of an international crisis over German reparations. It needed another urgent note, and Franckenstein's remarkable diplomatic touch to obtain an interview with Lloyd George in his capacity as chairman of the Inter-Allied Conference. The note delivered by the minister read almost like an ultimatum:

The finance plan of the Austrian Government, worked out on its own initiative and sanctioned by the Federal Parliament – a scheme which is almost identical with the plan set up by the Powers for the financial reconstruction of Germany – cannot be carried out and will have to be dropped, because, in spite of the release of the liens, the foreign credits cannot be obtained, although they have been repeatedly promised to Austria since the signing of the Peace Treaty of Saint-Germain. *For this reason the Austrian Government must resign.* No other government can replace it. The further destinies of Austria must be placed in the hands of the Allied Powers. The responsibility for all the consequences must rest with them.[50]

Initially even this last effort seemed to have been in vain. Lloyd George's personal assistant, Mr (later Sir) Edward Grigg, told Franckenstein that the British Government and the City believed that 'in view of current political uncertainty, the possibility of a French invasion' (of Germany), 'and of highly critical entanglements, assistance for Austria outside this context was impracticable'.[51] Nevertheless, shortly before the final session of the conference, a brief talk was arranged with Lloyd George who concentrated mainly on the wasted British credits to Austria. Franckenstein chiefly relied on the force of his political argument emphasizing the international as well as domestic turmoils that must be expected in case of the government's resignation.

Ultimately the Austrian memorandum was indeed discussed at the conference's last session, although without the slightest prospect of a positive outcome. The advice to Austria to turn to the League of Nations was therefore the sole and, as at first it appeared, unsatisfactory upshot of this diplomatic sally. Lloyd George's reply to Franckenstein's note contained the following passage:

The representatives of the Allied Governments have therefore come to the decision that they are unable to hold out any hope of further financial assistance to Austria by their Governments. They have agreed, however, to a proposal that the Austrian situation should be referred to the League of Nations for investigation and report, the League being informed at the same time that there is no prospect of further financial assistance to Austria from the Allied Powers unless the League were able to propose a programme of reconstruction containing definite guarantees that further subscriptions would produce substantial improvement and not be thrown away like those made in the past.[52]

In the light of the experience of recent years, little was to be expected from an appeal to the League of Nations. Lloyd George's frank, even if politely worded refusal to assist Austria with massive financial aid may have had its roots in some scepticism concerning the stability of the new order in Central Europe established by the Paris treaties. Britain, some observers have suggested, would not have looked on Austria's impending breakdown as a catastrophe, because that would of necessity have brought up the question of a new order for the Danubian area.[53] What soon became obvious was a strong objection to the British position by those nations – the French and the Czechs, in particular – who saw in the maintenance of an independent Austria a corner-stone of the European post-war order. Seipel realized that his strategy must proceed from this key consideration. The Austrian question had assumed an urgent political character.

On 20 August Seipel began a journey taking him to Prague, Berlin, and Verona.[54] The sequence was anything other than accidental and the selection of these sites revealed careful political planning. At Prague he could count on a reception which would largely be consonant with his own views. Dr Beneš, as he subsequently told his cabinet, assured him that 'Czechoslovakia places itself entirely at (Austria's) disposal for the intervention at the League of Nations. It will, together with France, underwrite a political guarantee and, if the other Great Powers want it, a financial guarantee too.'[55] The visit to Berlin was in the prevailing circumstances of little practical significance. Like Austria, Germany was in a critical financial condition and that robbed the *Anschluss* question of any topicality for the near future. Seipel's brief stay was interpreted as an act of diplomatic courtesy. The purpose of the trip to Verona, where he met the Italian Foreign Minister Karl Schanzer, was not at first stated.[56] From conservative circles it was very soon learned that the Chancellor had again proposed to the Italian Government the formation of an Austro-Italian customs union.[57]

The day before his departure Seipel had a talk with Spitzmüller and asked him for suggestions as to 'how to put a stop to the crown's depreciation as reflected in the rise of foreign exchange rates'.[58] Spitzmüller still clung to a programme of self-help, a position shared by the Social Democrats. That point of view was the diametric opposite of Seipel's recently evolved opinion that massive foreign aid must be the focal point of a new recovery project. What Spitzmüller had to say was accordingly received with bad grace. An offer of co-operation a few days later from the Social Democrat's side remained unanswered.[59]

Seipel's visit to Verona is unlikely to have been intended as a step toward reducing Austria to the modest status of an Italian province. He was in no way concerned with a realignment of foreign policy. The spectacular gesture was intended to draw the attention of the European community of nations to Austria's disastrous plight and thus to force through the League of Nations loan.[60] A stronger link with Italy, on the eve of the Fascist *coup d'état*, would moreover have given offence to broad sections of the Austrian public still in sympathy with the *Anschluss* plans of the Social Democrats and the Pan-Germans. The Federal Chancellor was undoubtedly prepared, as argued by Count Ottokar Czernin, the former Imperial Foreign Minister, to abandon his half-heartedly pronounced purpose of engaging in closer economic relations with Italy if his loyalty to the *status quo* in central Europe were duly rewarded. When he returned to Vienna, it looked as though his 'daringly intrepid, but exceedingly skilful foreign policy manoeuvre', to quote Otto Bauer again, would produce the hoped-for results. The dollar, on 25 August standing at the dizzy height of 83,600 crowns, rose no farther.[61]

The Geneva work of reconstruction has been the subject of many studies.[62] No fresh attempt will be made here to do justice to its complex economic, financial, and political aspects. Instead attention will focus on those parts which were of special importance for the speedy restoration of a balanced budget, and which thus paved the way for a new chapter in the history of the Republic – the period of stabilization.

On 6 September the Federal Chancellor appeared before the Council of the League of Nations and appealed for quick, effective financial aid. His arguments, advanced with dignity and eloquence, are not likely to have told the assembled statesmen anything funda-mentally new. One passage, in which he expressed his readiness to accept a system of supervision as part of an international assistance plan, was calculated to arouse still more keenly the uneasiness with which the Social Democratic leadership had viewed this diplomatic excursion.[63] After the speech the League's machinery was set in motion without delay. The council created an Austria Committee consisting of representatives of the three Great Powers, of Czechoslo-vakia, and of Austria.[64] The reconstruction plan was drafted and finally implemented under the supreme authority of this committee. The consultations preceding the programme's official publication lasted a short month during which it proved possible to compose the differences between the French, Czechoslovak, and Italian veiwpoints. On 4 October the plan was presented to the accompaniment of the usual oratorical flourishes.

The Geneva Protocols consisted of three documents formulated with exemplary clarity.[65] The first solemnly endorsed the validity of Article 88 in the Treaty of Saint-Germain. Austria undertook to maintain its national integrity, while the Signatory Powers pledged themselves to respect the sovereignty of Austria and not to seek to obtain exclusive economic or financial advantages which might prejudice, directly or indirectly, this independence. The passage showed a remarkably quick change of mind in the case of Italy.

The second document authorized the Austrian Government to float a loan of 650 million gold crowns on the international capital market. The four chief guarantor nations were to guarantee the annual debt service up to a maximum of 84%, the rest of the League's members guaranteeing the remainder.[66] The safeguards incorporated into the protocol (mainly customs dues and income from the tobacco monopoly) were however so comprehensive as to render recourse to the guarantee clause extremely improbable.[67]

How had the League experts arrived at the round figure of 650 million gold crowns? Their recommendations were based on assessments that in the next two years – the anticipated reform period – the budget deficits would run to 520 million gold crowns. This assumption proved too pessimistic, as the budget losses for 1923 and 1924 totalled only 119 millions.[68] In addition Austria was to receive 130 millions to repay the main guarantor nations the credits extended during 1922.

Article 7 of Protocol II provided for the establishment of a Control Committee of the guarantor nations which was to be represented in ratio to the loan amounts underwritten by them. This clause ensured the leading guarantors a predominant position in the committee. As they were also among the League's principal members, they made thus certain that their policy in the end determined the character and the scope of the reconstruction project. Normally the committee exercised its authority through 'recommendations' to the commissioner-general, but Article 7 prescribed that it could issue directives straight to the Austrian Government if the latter proposed to enter into loan agreements outside the plan's provisions.[69]

A commissioner-general was to be the senior authority for the plan's implementation (Article 4). He would be appointed by the League Council, which alone had the power to recall him; he would have his seat in Vienna. His expenditure and that of his staff would have to be defrayed by the Austrian Government. Austria moreover was bound not to utilize any funds from the loan or to undertake any transactions anticipating the proceeds from the loan without his express permission. This clause gave the commissioner-general an absolute right of veto over all economic and financial measures of the Austrian government. The government could afford to incur his displeasure only at the price of foregoing the further utilization of the loan.[70]

The clause would appear to ensure the Austrian Government's uncompromising readiness to co-operate. There remained however the danger that a recalcitrant parliament might refuse to put into practice a reform programme that was dictated by an outside authority. Article 3 of Protocol III therefore laid down that the Austrian Government must submit to parliament a bill that would empower every government in office during the next two years to take, without need for a further approach to parliament, all measures within the provisions of the programme which it felt to be necessary to restore budgetary equilibrium by the end of this period. In everyday language it meant that parliament should relinquish one of its oldest rights, that of sanctioning the budget. For the duration of the reconstruction plan the budget would have to be based on ordinances without the consent of parliament. To invest the government with such authority required the passing of a constitutional law, so that this part of the reform project depended on the consent of the opposition. Since temporary 'financial dictatorship' was regarded as an integral part of the recovery programme, the socialist leadership was placed in a very uncomfortable position. If they said 'No to Geneva' they would be held responsible for depriving Austria of the fruits of the international loan, with all the unforeseeable consequences resulting therefrom.[71] Perhaps it had been taken into account at Geneva that the temporary exclusion of parliament would provoke resistance among certain sectors of the population. For article 7 of the same document contains a provision unusual in a treaty of this kind: 'The Austrian Government will take all measures necessary for the preservation of public order.'

After his return to Vienna the Federal Chancellor fired the opening shot in a political offensive to win over public opinion to his reform work. His argument can be concisely summarized as 'Foreign Aid or Catastrophe'. The Pan-Germans may have had qualms about identifying themselves with a plan the realization of which was bound to a renewed, solemn affirmation of the will to national independence. Nevertheless the spectacle of the German economy infected by the bacillus of inflation and the fear that Austria without foreign aid would be unable to resist this infection induced them to support the Chancellor unconditionally.

For the Social Democrats the hour of decision had arrived. In their manifesto of 23 August they had proclaimed:

> The government still hopes for outside assistance. It uses dangerous means to attain this end. If Seipel's methods are at all suited to obtaining a foreign loan for us, then it would only be at the price of intolerable conditions signifying Austria's complete subjection to foreign control and loss of the last remnants of political independence. It will be up to us to defend ourselves against this sell-out of our independence.[72]

The socialists realized of course that 'the road to Geneva' meant more than merely surrendering every hope of an early *Anschluss*. They feared hardly less the political preponderance which their Christian Socialist opponents would gain from their close association with the guaranteeing nations. They properly surmised that a reconstruction programme under League auspices would be modelled on the conservative version of budgetary reform which they had so tenaciously resisted since the Republic's earliest days. Instead of capital taxation, requisition of hoarded gold and foreign currency, valorization of the compulsory domestic loan, and so on, a conservative budget reform envisaged in the first place, as they very well knew, a drastic increase of indirect taxes and a one third cut in civil service personnel.

Consequently a violent Social Democratic campaign against the Geneva treaty was started. The government was accused of 'high treason' and 'selling' Austria into foreign hands. Not entirely without justification the Socialists charged the government to take advantage of foreign control in order to consolidate its political power *vis-à-vis* the Social Democrats and the working class. Yet the leadership seemed to be increasingly aware that it would be hardly less onerous to assume responsibility for the Geneva plan's failure than for its consummation.

The dilemma emerged very clearly in Otto Bauer's great speech on 14 October to the party congress.[73] He began by saying that there was no *economic* compulsion for raising a large-scale loan abroad. The road to self-help still lay open if Austrians only had the will to take it. The line of argument is familiar. Once more he pleaded for borrowing gold from the banks and for imposing on the propertied classes a compulsory loan (in crowns) which, together with the government's stocks of gold, would yield 215 million gold crowns. He conceded that a self-help programme, in the form of higher fiscal dues and tariffs, excise taxes, and other indirect taxes, would impose heavy sacrifices on the masses. He thought that in the given political situation the Socialists lacked the strength to give effect to such a programme. At the same time he made it clear that the mere rejection of the Geneva Protocols without the guarantee of a practicable alternative must hurl the country into a catastrophe.[74]

While Bauer demonstrated quite clearly his party's predicament, nevertheless the consequences that he deduced from it appeared paradoxical. The party must, so ran his peroration, stick to its 'No'. 'We shall not make it easy for these gentlemen to pilot their Geneva Enslavement Treaty through parliament.' But for all the rhetoric the outlines of a compromise became visible. The real issue, Bauer concluded, was not so much whether parliament ratified the protocols or not. 'That is merely a question of empty form. The protocols are simply the framework which is now to be given its content.' With this statement it was no longer the protocols as such that were to be opposed, but the struggle was to centre on how the program was to be executed. Thus the real decision was left open.

Probably right from the start Karl Renner judged matters more soberly. In the talks he had in Prague at the end of October with the Czech Social Democrat leaders he made it clear that his party was in an extremely critical situation because Seipel 'wants to use the implementation of the Geneva programme to overthrow Social Democracy and to destroy the achievements of the revolution.' In this situation Renner thought it essential not to accept the exclusion of the Socialists from the Geneva negotiations, but to insist on taking part in the experts' preliminary talks. To this end he sought the help of Czech Social Democrats and, via their mediation, the support of Beneš. As he later told the party executive, and as his Czech friend Stivin informed Marek, the Austrian Minister to Prague, Beneš agreed to Renner's representations and assured him of the Czech delegation's support.[75]

Renner explained his strategy perfectly straightforwardly in a conversation, arranged by Sir Arthur Salter, with Owen Philpotts, a member of the British Diplomatic Service. Salter had expressed a wish to discover the real attitude of the Social Democratic Party to the Geneva Loan because the London market was in any case unenthusiastic about the project. 'One of the main features which . . . they consider will deter the foreign investor is the attitude of the Austrian Socialist Party.' Renner's remarks to Philpotts are the subject of a report on 6 November 1922 by the British Ambassador, Keeling.

According to Renner, Keeling wrote, the Social Democrats were in a 'state of flux. The Geneva protocols were capitalist in spirit, but if the leaders of the Party were given a little time and support, so that their right wing got the upper hand, the Party would be able to swallow them.' There could be no question of *carte blanche* support for the government because of the latter's political bias. A special Parliamentary Commission, entrusted with the implementation of the Geneva plan, should therefore be constituted. 'If some such arrangements were made, his Party would probably be willing to enable the Government to get the two-thirds majority which was, constitutionally, really necessary for the investment of government with the plenary powers required by the protocols, and a little later would perhaps be willing to enter into a coalition in order to co-operate in the carrying through of the scheme.'[76] On entirely the same lines, according to the Ambassador's report, a conversation was held between Karl Seitz (First President of the National Assembly and Head of State, 1919) and Seipel. The former held out the prospect of a two-thirds majority for the constitutional bill while Seipel talked of possibly including a Social Democrat in the government as Minister without Portfolio.

As regards Renner's proposed parliamentary commission, his attention was drawn to the fact that this idea contravened the provisions of the protocols. The eventual solution of a 'cabinet council' was nevertheless based on the same idea. It seems certain therefore that the concept of the compromise originated with Renner and it was prosecuted by him with the utmost vigour. A confidential British report on the crucial session of the Socialist Party Executive on 4 November also confirms this conclusion.[77] Renner, supported by Seitz, was again the main speaker. To thwart the Geneva treaties was, he declared, out of the question. All that could be done was to exercise the maximum amount of influence on their implementation. The opportunities for that were not at all bad because some of the Socialist's demands, particularly in respect of taxation, were backed by industry, while others had the support of the Pan-Germans. Both Seitz and Renner had carried away from their conversations with Seipel the impression that he was much more willing than before to co-operate and that the overall situation had improved.

No opposing viewpoint seems to have been voiced at this meeting, just as the name of Otto Bauer never occurs in these records and no special policy identified with his name emerges. So the British observer was probably right in saying that the discussion was lively, but that eventually the opposition appeared to reconcile itself to Renner's conciliatory course. For Bauer there was nothing left to do, in his speech to the party council on 23 November, except confirm the retreat. He frankly admitted that the attempt to find allies at the last moment for a policy of rejection by enormous popular protest had failed.[78] Yet he believed that 'a number of partial successes have been brought home. In one respect,' he added, 'we have gained a notable victory. We have foiled the plan for a financial dictatorship by the government.'[79] His reference was to the so-called Extraordinary Cabinet Council responsible for implementation of the recovery programme. This council consisted, apart from the non-voting ministers, of twenty-six members of parliament ('State Councillors') and decided by simple majority on the most important reform measures. The Social Democrats could of course be outvoted, but they were able to air their views on every step planned by the government and to wrest one or another concession from it.[80]

A two-thirds majority was needed to pass the bill creating the council. On 26 November the motion was unanimously accepted. The Geneva Protocols and the Reconstruction Bill, on the other hand, were approved only with the votes of the two government parties. The preparatory process for the work of reform was ended.

At the beginning of November a League of Nations delegation had arrived in Vienna to inaugurate the comprehensive reform programme which had been worked out by the government representatives and the Finance Committee. On 4 November the government submitted its Reconstruction Bill to parliament. The concept of the proposed reconstruction is already familiar in its main points. Starting from the principle of strict austerity, it imposed heavy sacrifices not only on the working class, but on practically all strata of urban society.[81] Only the farming community, spoiled child of all European conservative parties, was spared financial sacrifices and was even promised more protection by an increase in agrarian tariffs. The programme as a whole corresponded to the train of thought dominant in contemporary academic economics. An economy weakened by the disease of inflation, this theory pronounced, could be restored to health only by severe fiscal and monetary discipline. The same outlook was to prevail in subsequent reconstruction programmes – in Hungary, in Poland, in Germany, in France, and in Britain.

The most important provisions of the Reconstruction Bill can be subdivided into three sections: economies through administrative reform, reorganization of state enterprises, etc.; increase in public revenue from customs dues, state monopolies, excise taxes, direct taxation, and by the introduction of a turnover tax; and finally the cancellation of subsidies from the federal budget to the provincial and communal authorities.[82]

The repeatedly announced steps to dismiss and/or pension off one third of all civil servants (some 100,000 individuals) were to be carried out inside two years. State enterprises, like the railways and the tobacco monopoly, were to be placed on a commercial footing. That, it was hoped, would create the prerequisites for the gradual economic recovery of these enterprises plagued by recurrent deficits. Should the reorganization show no positive outcome, their lease or sale to private interests must be contemplated. Some of them, like the railways, the tobacco industry, and the federal forests, held an important position in the economy and their purchase by foreign capital – and only foreigners would have been able to raise the necessary funds – would have contributed to the acceleration of the process of foreigners gaining control over the Austrian economy.[83] The need for disposal of these public enterprises did not however arise during the succeeding years.

Consumers as well as civil servants could look forward to heavy sacrifices. The Reconstruction Bill anticipated a rise in receipts from customs dues in the first year from 40 to 80 million gold crowns, in the second year from 80 to 100 million gold crowns. It provoked Walther Federn's comment that six and a half million Austrians were expected to provide about half the customs income that in pre-war days had come from fifty million of the Empire's subjects.[84] However, the Socialists succeeded, in their negotiations with the government, in preventing for the time being the restoration of prohibitive agrarian duties. The revenue from customs dues could consequently be kept down to 80 million gold crowns.[85]

A distinctly heavier burden on the consumers was imposed by the turnover tax. It affected all commodities with the exception of exports. The bill's first draft established a rate of 1% in the first year and 2% in the next. From the beginning a rate of 12% was envisaged for luxury goods. The total burden to be born by the consumer, even when consumption was confined to vital necessities, was in fact considerably higher than the 2% rate introduced in 1924, because the tax was levied cumulatively at all intermediate stages of distribution before it reached the final consumer. In 1929 one estimate was that the consumer's total expenditure had gone up by 3.5% as a result of the turnover tax.[86] Critics also pointed out that the effect on export trade must be unfavourable even though formally it was exempted. The effect flowed naturally from the fact that the tax was levied at all stages in the process of production in so far as they involved exchanges between separate firms. It is certain that with this tax a considerable new source of income had been created for the state. In 1927, leaving aside the profits on state enterprises, the receipts accounted for approximately a quarter of the total federal revenue.[87]

Higher duties and the turnover tax were only part of the burden put on consumers and industry. The Reconstruction Bill also provided for a notable rise in various excises on sugar and alcohol for instance, as well as a sizable increase in the prices charged by all public utilities. The burden of direct taxation, on the other hand, was lessened. The business tax was appreciably reduced and the top income tax rate dropped from 60% to 40%. Later the notoriously high corporation tax also went down.[88] Finally the government proposed, in agreement with the recommendations of the League Delegation, to abolish certain grants made by the federal government to provincial authorities that found themselves in financial difficulties; they should seek the solution to their financial obligations via heavier local levies.

The government and the League Delegation were sanguine that a conscientious implementation of all the parts of the reform package would soon lead to the elimination of the budget deficit. A handsome surplus was expected for 1925, and in anticipation of a constant growth of the public revenues the government drew up the following budget estimate.[89]

Table 70   *Austrian federal budgets, 1922–25 (in gold cr. m.)*

	1922	1923	1924	1925
Fed. Outlays	672.5	552.7	458.4	370.0
Fed. Receipts	215.1	332.3	448.2	489.3
Deficit/Surplus	−457.4	−220.4	− 10.2	+119.3

These estimates did not completely agree with the League experts' original assumptions on which the big international loan had been based. But the actual development of the budget in the following years diverged drastically from these estimates. In particular the receipts grew so rapidly that critics were to speak of 'excessive taxation'.[90]

Its work on the Reconstruction Bill done, the League Delegation turned its attention to certain other aspects of the reform plan.[91] Following suggestions by the Financial Committee at Geneva, it began to draw up a draft for a new Central Bank. Already in the preceding summer preliminary planning work had been done on this subject at the time when the government had made its last, stillborn effort at stabilization. The principles elaborated in July were now as a whole confirmed. The bank was to have far-reaching independence *vis-à-vis* the Federal Government which would be guaranteed by two articles in its charter. The President of the bank would be appointed by the President of the Republic on nomination by the Federal Government, while the principal executives were to be elected by the shareholders. The bank's activities were to have a purely commercial character. Neither the Federal Government nor the provincial or municipal authorities would be allowed to issue any more paper money or to borrow directly or indirectly any funds from the bank unless they paid in gold or foreign exchange.[92]

The original proposals had foreseen a capital of one hundred million Swiss francs. The League experts now thought that thirty million gold crowns should be sufficient and that this amount should be raised entirely by private subscription. Initially the metallic cover was put at 20%, but it was to be successively increased to $33\frac{1}{3}\%$ although this did not apply to that part of the fiduciary circulation which represented loans previously made to the state by the Austro-Hungarian bank.[93] Conduct of the bank's affairs would rest in the hands of thirteen general councillors (board members) of whom no more than four could be foreign nationals. Neither the President nor any of the general councillors could veto the council's resolutions as had in the preceding summer been demanded by the representatives of the two foreign banks. Thus the independence of the new bank from interference by government or by foreign financial interests seemed assured. On 14 November the amendments to the charter were sanctioned by parliament. On 22 December the Constituent General Meeting took place. The following day there was held the first general council meeting of the Austrian National Bank.[94]

The foreign banking world, which had made its participation in the new bank dependent on unusually restrictive conditions had still retained, as was soon to be seen, several trumps. In April 1923 Dr Victor Kienböck, successor to Ségur as Minister of Finance, arrived in London to negotiate with the City on the issue of the League of Nations loan. The success of the transaction, he was given to understand, turned on the fulfilment of an important prerequisite – the appointment of a 'Foreign Adviser' to the National Bank. Kienböck had no choice but then and there to agree to an alteration of the Bank's charter. On 26 April the *Nationalrat* confirmed the appointment of such an adviser to be invested with far-reaching rights of control over the Bank's management.

A. F. Zimmermann, a Dutchman, had on 16 December 1922 assumed the office of League of Nations Commissioner-General for the Financial Reconstruction of Austria. A few months later Karl Schnyder von Wartensee, a Swiss national, was at the wish of the City installed in the Austrian National Bank as its Foreign Adviser. It is no exaggeration to say that European history knows no other instance of an international financial transaction hedged with such excessive economic and political conditions. What a contrast to the more recent Marshall Plan![95]

The circumstances under which the bills relating to the National Bank were drafted may be of some interest. Since 25 August, when the first news about the League's impending intervention broke, the crown's exchange rate had remained remarkably stable. In September, with Seipel's successful appearance before the League Council, confidence in the crown grew and the supply of foreign currencies increased visibly. In October, when political conflict seemed to jeopardize the Geneva project, a contrary trend made its appearance. During both months the Foreign Exchange Agency pursued a policy aimed at stability. It intervened in the foreign exchange market with sufficient crowns or foreign exchange to meet the respective requirements of the situation.[96]

While the crown was displaying a stability novel in its post-war history, the Ministry of Finance continued its familiar policy of borrowing money from the central bank against the security of treasury bills. In this way the quantity of banknotes in circulation rose from 914,000 million crowns in August to 3,133,000 millions in November.[97] As long as the financial authority insisted on pursuing its inflationary policy, the danger persisted that the hesitant return of public confidence, based mainly on the prospect of the large-scale international credit operation, could again change into a mood of scepticism, if not indeed of despair. To preclude such a development, the League Delegation decided on the risky step of forbidding the issue of unsecured banknotes although it was well aware that many months would pass before the international loan could be floated.

On 19 November 1922 inflation, which had lasted for over eight long, bitter years, abruptly ended.[98] Instantaneously the question cropped up of how the budget deficit could be met until the distant day when the government would be in a position to satisfy its financial requirements from the proceeds of the Geneva loan. The Ministry of

Finance extricated itself from this predicament by making a move long recommended by Gustav Stolper among others. It solicited help from domestic financial circles in the form of a short-term loan of sixty million gold crowns with six months' maturity. The return to orthodox methods of past years proved, as could be expected, a full success. In November thirty million gold crowns were subscribed by the banks, the rest by the public during the succeeding months. The ministry was moreover able to mobilize foreign resources, namely what remained from the French, Italian, and Czech advances.[99] Finally the League Council authorized the government on 1 February to float a short-term loan on the international money market which yielded £3.5 million sterling.[100] With the help of these improvizations the most pressing public obligations could be met until the time of the issue of the Geneva loan in the summer 1923.

The loan consisted of eleven slices made out in ten different currencies. The face amount was 789.4 million gold crowns while the net yield was 631 millions or some 80% of the face amount. (The net yield therefore lagged by nearly 20 million gold crowns behind the anticipated total of 650 millions.) Austria had consequently to pay interest on and to redeem almost 160 millions more than it received. This exceptionally big difference was due to the loan's low issue price. The actual interest rate fluctuated, according to the various foreign currency slices, between 9.46% and 10.20% and must, in view of the Great Powers' guarantees and the provisos, be described as strikingly high.[101]

The crown's speedy stabilization in the wake of the Geneva recovery programme looked to some contemporaries like a positively supernatural performance. For many years inflation had been the dominant factor in economic life. Its sudden stop was at first accepted hesitantly, almost incredulously. The normalization process did not however begin in autumn 1922, but, as has been seen, had already been set on foot in the course of 1921. The unbalanced budget was simply a manifestation of the struggle over the distribution of a badly shrunk national income. In the last analysis the Geneva reconstruction created the political preconditions for upsetting the balance of social forces which for so many years had obstructed a comprehensive budget reform. The middle class had now become the decisive political factor. Naturally the reform reflected the preferences of the foreign financial experts and their conservative Austrian colleagues. No wonder that it was the Socialists' right wing which made possible in parliament the passing of the bill concerning the Extraordinary Cabinet Council and so of the entire reconstruction plan.

One thing is clear. The Geneva Protocols and the Reconstruction Bills did not deal with the deeper causes of the Austrian economic malaise. This is the essential difference as against the post-World War II American aid programme (ERP). The new state's serious infirmities, its acute coal scarcity, its outdated industrial plants, its backward agriculture, its precarious foreign trade position, and all the rest, were meant to be left to a subsequent, as it were automatic process of convalescence for which the recovery programme was regarded as the indispensable prerequisite. The reformers had, as the following statement shows, a fairly lucid notion of the magnitude of the unsolved problems, but they believed their solution to lie outside their own sphere of action:

If the appropriate financial policy is adopted and maintained, the Austrian economic position will adjust itself to an equilibrium, either by the increase of production and the transfer of large classes of its population to economic work, or by economic pressure which will compel the population to emigrate or reduce it to destitution. At the worst, this would be better than the wholesale chaos and impoverishment of the great mass of the town population which must result from the continuance of the present financial disorganisation, which affords no basis for such economic adaptation as is possible.[102]

Notes

1 Apart from the repeal of the food subsidies, the measures were directed primarily at official registration of hoarded foreign notes and coins. Cf. Part V, Chap. 2.

2 'Its former distinct hostility to Austria now turned more and more into the opposite until in August and September 1922 Beneš came forward as the outspoken supporter of the Austrian recovery programme.' Cf. Gottlieb Ladner, *Seipel als Überwinder der Staatskrise vom Sommer 1922. Zur Geschichte der Entstehung der Genfer Protokolle vom 4. Oktober 1922* (Vienna-Graz, 1964), p. 24.

3 Cf. Rudolf Freund, 'Die Genfer Protokolle', *Sozialwissenschaftliche Forschungen* (Berlin-Leipzig, 1924), p. 36.

4 Cf. *Chronique des Événements Politiques et Économiques dans le Basin Danubien, 1918–1938* (Paris, 1938), p. 164.

5 Alexander Spitzmüller, . . . *und hat auch Ursach' es zu lieben* (Vienna, 1955), p. 335.

6 Ladner, *Seipel*, p. 28.

7 Ladner, *Seipel*, p. 29.

8 In 1930 *Der Österreichische Volkswirt* accused Seipel of having brought down his rival Schober after certain Great Powers at Genoa had promised the latter the extension of a large international loan. In a letter to *Volkswirt* Seipel disputed the

correctness of this account, but in its reply the paper stuck to its allegation 'as this comes from completely reliable sources'. See *Der Österreichische Volkswirt*, issues of 5, 15, and 22 February 1930. Karl Ausch, in *Als die Banken fielen* (Vienna, 1968), p. 49 et seq., dealt with the incident in detail and referred to several statements by Schober which apparently supported *Volkswirt's* version. Even if it seems plausible, Schober's confident assertions that the Great Powers were prepared to grant him 'personally' a large loan need not necessarily be unconditionally accepted. Just at this time there was in fact, especially in Britain, a shift of opinion *against* Austria. Klemperer too confirms, though indirectly, that Seipel had in May 1922 decided to take the reins of state into his own hands. 'Did Seipel want, as he was accused by Stolper's periodical *Der Österreichische Volkswirt* of doing, himself to reap the credit for Schober's long and difficult spadework so as eventually to appear as Austria's saviour? More likely is that Seipel dropped Schober when he recognized that Schober was not up to mastering foreign and domestic problems simultaneously . . . It may therefore be assumed that it was this not so mysterious reason which finally decided Seipel to discard Schober and that Schober's fall was by no means a sign of Seipel's ambition or propensity for intrigue, but more probably of his determination to obtain a strong Parliamentary basis for foreign policy.' Klemens von Klemperer, *Ignaz Seipel, Staatsmann einer Krisenzeit* (Graz-Cologne, 1976), p. 146 et seq.

9 Interesting comments on the central bank's discount policy are contained in 'Zinsfusserhöhung der Österreichisch-Ungarischen Bank' and 'Devisenpanik', *Der Österreichische Volkswirt*, 3 December 1921, p. 229 et seq. and 17 June 1922, p. 916 respectively.

10 'It was an open secret that a large part of these credits, which were granted by the Bank of Issue at a rate of interest much below that of the open market, was employed to buy and hold foreign exchange.' Jan van Walré de Bordes, *The Austrian Crown. Its Depreciation and Stabilization* (London, 1924), p. 203.

11 'When on Dr Gürtler's assumption of his ministerial duties I had succeeded in convincing him that the downright monstrous condition of separate treatment for bills discount and foreign exchange business must be done away with, Schwarzwald immediately intervened and induced the minister to go back on the promise he had given me that foreign exchange control would be included within the bank management's competence.' Spitzmüller, *Und hat auch Ursach*, p. 335 et seq.

12 Walré de Bordes, *Austrian Crown*, p. 142. This episode, as Bauer commented, was to have very serious consequences. 'Not only . . . was the most advantageous moment for cleaning up the public finances missed, but abroad it created the impression that extending loans to Austria was useless without putting Austrian finances under strict control. To a large degree the fateful mistakes made in February and March 1922 were responsible for the onerous conditions of the Geneva Treaty in October 1922.' Otto Bauer, 'Die österreichische Revolution', *Werkausgabe* (Vienna, 1976), Vol. II, p. 821.

13 See Sir George Franckenstein, *Facts and Features of My Life* (London, 1939), p. 244.

14 'Norman,' says Ladner, following up Franckenstein's remark, 'was . . . unable to conceal that confidence in Austria's possibility of recovery and efficiency had suffered a severe set-back through the recent events.' Ladner, *Seipel*, p. 31.

15 Cf. Appendix II, Table A6.

16 Walré de Bordes, *Austrian Crown*, p. 163.

17 The percentage increases shown in Table 68 were calculated on the basis of the respective preceding months.

18 During the critical period from May to August 1922 the weekly wages in certain important branches of industry rose as follows:

	May	June	July	August
Metal Workers	47,550	79,200	111,672	249,000
Building Workers	40,320	69,120	97,459	218,260
Printers	33,382	52,409	73,927	175,597
Cotton Spinners	27,900	50,000	70,500	157,920

See *Monatliche Mitteilungen*, published by the Vienna Chamber of Labour and quoted by Dr Max Lederer, 'Indexziffern und Industrielöhne', *Der Österreichische Volkswirt*, 19 September 1922, p. 1,200.

19 The unemployment figures for the months May–August 1922 were somewhat lower than for the first quarter. It has however to be borne in mind that during the whole of the inter-war period late spring and early summer were characterized by increased industrial activity as a result of the seasonal upswing in certain branches of industry. The exceptionally feeble improvement in the employment situation during the second quarter of 1922 is evidence of special factors. Cf. Federal Ministry for Social Affairs, *Statistiken zur Arbeitslosenversicherung* (Vienna, 1930).

20 A. Gratz, *Die österreichische Finanzpolitik 1848–1948*, in the Mayer ed., Hundert Jahre österreichische Wirtschaftsentwicklung, Wien 1949, p. 278.

21 *Arbeiter-Zeitung*, 3 August 1932.

22 'I did indeed all I could to help Count Ségur, which was no easy matter seeing that he had no real claim to conduct the financial department and was in particular devoid of any practical experience.' Spitzmüller, *Und hat auch Ursach*, p. 338. *Neue Freie Presse*, 31 May 1922, also commented that, as far as financial affairs went, Seipel would have to lean very heavily on 'others'.

23 Rather more than a week after Ségur's accession to office there appeared the criticism that 'to appoint as Minister of Finance at this moment of greatest emergency a man who lacks any economic training or financial experience, who has never concerned himself at all with the country's problems of state finance, can be fatal for us'. *Der Österreichische Volkswirt*, 10 June 1922, p. 885.

24 AVA Cabinet Minutes 191, 1 June 1922.

25 'Those in the know, who always know everything and are reliably initiated into the deepest secrets of high politics, are now letting it out that the Supreme Council at Paris has already taken tragic decisions with regard to Austria's future. Contact has been made with the Czechoslovak Government about the acceptance of an international mandate to take effect in case of a political and economic catastrophe (in Austria) . . .' *Die Reichspost*, 8 June 1922, quoted by Ladner, *Seipel*, p. 43.

26 AVA Cabinet Minutes 194, 7 June 1922.

27 The initiative for the meeting, Bauer reports, was taken by the Social Democratic side. 'On 13 June the Executive Committee of the Social Democratic parliamentary club went to the Federal Chancellor and told him that the Social Democratic party could no longer accept any responsibility for the behaviour of

the working masses, driven to despair by the increase in prices, unless the government ordered the banks to place their accumulated foreign exchange, no matter in what form, at the state's disposal within twenty-four hours. The threat worked.' Bauer, *Werkausgabe*, Vol. II, p. 823.

28 Spitzmüller, *Und hat auch Ursache*, p. 338 et seq.

29 Spitzmüller, *Und hat auch Ursache*, p. 339.

30 Cf. *Wiener Zeitung*, 22 July 1922.

31 Cf. Gustav Stolper, 'Der neue Finanzplan', *Der Österreichische Volkswirt*, 24 June 1922, p. 935 et seq.

32 'Civil Service retrenchment was a particularly thorny problem for the government. It involved the reduction by ten to fifteen per cent of the state's approximately 250,000 paid officials in order to economize some 30,000 million crowns on staff expenditure.' Ladner, *Seipel*, p. 49.

33 Cf. Bauer, *Werkausgabe*, Vol. II, p. 820.

34 Cf. Ladner, *Seipel*, p. 50. 'The Social Democratic opposition warned (the government) most urgently against linking the two. It demonstrated that the tax and compulsory loan laws must first be implemented, because they were the prerequisite to bringing the banknote printing to a halt, and only then, as the last step in the whole reconstruction process did the establishment of a bank of issue become topical.' Ausch, *Als die Banken fielen*, p. 59.

35 *Chronique des Événements*, p. 73.

36 Freund, in *Forschungen*, p. 41.

37 Cf. Ausch, *Als die Banken fielen*, p. 60.

38 The compulsory loan indubitably constituted an important element in the new minister's programme. As originally conceived, it was to be levied on the approximately 400,000 domestic agricultural farms. The final bill, due to objections from the agrarian wing of the Christian Socialists, saw the contribution extended also to industrial and other business assets. The swift progress of the crown's depreciation deprived the measure of any significance. See Federal Law Gazette, 27 July 1922, No. 491 and Gustav Stolper, 'Die innere Anleihe', *Der Österreichische Volkswirt*, 8 July 1922, p. 987 et seq.

39 The appropriate ordinances were published in the Federal Law Gazette issues of 19, 20, 25, and 30 July, Nos. 439, 488, 505, and 559 respectively.

40 See O. S. Philpotts, Report on the *Industrial and Commercial Situation of Austria to August 1923* (London, 1923), p. 7.

41 PRO/FO 371/HN01157, Letter from Anglo-Austrian Bank Limited, 8 August 1922. The full text is reproduced in Appendix I.

42 Siegfried Pressburger, *Österreichs Notenbank, 1816–1966* (Vienna, 1966), p. 363.

43 Two generations later there is no precise telling how far Spitzmüller's remark was justified that 'in the post-war years a spirit of speculation and greed for profit' had made headway and had 'thrust the old circumspect management of affairs into the background'. Spitzmüller, *Und hat auch Ursache*, p. 323.

44 Spitzmüller, *Und hat auch Ursache*, p. 332.

45 Ladner, an (almost) unbounded admirer of Seipel, condemns the conduct of the major banks utterly. 'At the end of June matters stood pretty well as far as the financial programme was concerned. But while the government struggled solely for the state's good repute, which it regarded as an absolute value, and while it invited all to join in an Austrian Loan front, the Viennese banks showed reserve

even if . . . in mid-June they had been keenly interested in the establishment of a bank of issue. I have various evidence which clearly goes to prove that Austria's economic crisis from 1918 onward was largely rooted in the Viennese banks' hostile attitude to the state and that likewise in 1922 the lack of faith abroad in (the strength) of Austria's economy mainly arose from the disloyal behaviour of the principal Vienna banks.' Ladner, *Seipel*, p. 54 et seq.

46 Haus-, Hof- und Staatsarchiv, NPA, K 346.

47 How great the government's lost freedom of action was, *vis-à-vis* foreign financial circles, is illustrated by the invitation to attend this meeting extended to the highest official of a bank with a majority foreign ownership who, for all that he was an Austrian national, could hardly be regarded as an impartial representative of Austrian interests.

48 Haus-, Hof- und Staatsarchiv, NPA, K 346. The Austrian Memorandum is reproduced verbatim in Appendix I. It contains in essence a description of the budget problem and the various attempts at its solution.

49 Austria transmitted 'to the Italian minister (in Vienna) at the end of June two proposals for closer economic co-operation. The first envisaged a customs and currency union . . . The second proposal aimed at speedy and vigorous implementation and development of the economic resolutions agreed at Porto Rose and Rome.' Ladner, *Seipel*, p. 64.

50 PRO/FO 371/HN 01157, 14 August 1922. (Present author's italics.) It will be observed that Franckenstein in this note describes the government's resignation as inevitable if the international loan operation does not come to pass, whereas Seipel at the aforementioned meeting merely regarded this as one of several options.

51 Ladner, *Seipel*, p. 84.

52 PRO/FO 371/HN 01157, 15 August 1922.

53 Thus Franckenstein reported, after a talk with Sir Basil Blackett, 'As for Austria, the view of the government here is that it should be awaited whether we can perhaps after all help ourselves or whether our downfall, with all its consequences, will hasten a new solution of the Central European problem.' Quoted by Ladner, *Seipel*, p. 88.

54 Seipel's diplomatic journey has been so often described, in its most thorough detail by Ladner, that the account here is confined to a few of the outstanding facts.

55 AVA Council of Ministers Minutes, 28 August 1922, and Ladner, *Seipel*, p. 93.

56 The London *Daily Telegraph* was the first paper to publish a report on the impending negotiations between Vienna and Rome on a currency and customs union. The news, *Der Österreichische Volkswirt* expressly noted in its issue of 26 August, p. 1, 165, was *not* denied by the Austrian Government.

57 Count Czernin epitomized Seipel's strategy in the following terms: 'We proposed to Italy a customs and trade alliance. Our calculation was that either this comes off – no ideal solution, but if affords us viability and prevents intervention by neighbours – or Europe does not want to concede this, in which case it has only one means of stopping it and that is by ample aid to cure us of our wish to join Italy. The calculation was correct and Geneva is the outcome of the action.' Quoted by *Der Österreichische Volkswirt*, 2 December 1922, p. 219.

58 Spitzmüller, *Und hat auch Ursache*, p. 341.

59 Admittedly the 'offer' was couched in such peremptory terms that it could

scarcely be the subject of realistic negotiations. A manifesto published after a party conference on 23 August proclaimed, 'Only when the bourgeois parties at last recognize the danger of the complete breakdown of our economy, only when they become aware of the fact that when everything breaks down the propertied classes too will not be able to save themselves from the wreckage, only when fear of this catastrophe forces the propertied classes to make the necessary sacrifices and renders them ready to fulfil our most important and urgent demands and to renounce their sabotage of all economic and social necessities, then, and then only, is there a chance of effecting in agreement with the bourgeois parties what has to be effected, then, and only then, could a temporary co-operation with the bourgeois parties be for us a means of rescuing the Republic and the national economy out of the most dire danger.' See Bauer, *Werkausgabe*, Vol. II, p. 826 et seq.

60 Cf. Viktor Reimann, *Zu gross für Österreich. Seipel und Bauer im Kampf um die Erste Republik* (Vienna, 1968), p. 115.

61 'Suddenly a whirl of worried suggestions and earnest plans for Austria swept the Continent. The most important were undoubtedly the negotiations held at Marienbad by the (Foreign) Ministers of the Little Entente . . . It was decided to request the Great Powers to grant Austria an adequate credit to be underwritten by the Little Entente too.' Ladner, *Seipel*, p. 100.

62 Important older studies include, in addition to *The Financial Reconstitution of Austria* (League of Nations, Geneva, 1922); Freund, 'Die Genfer Protokolle', *Forschungen*, Victor Kienböck, *Das österreichische Sanierungswerk* (Stuttgart, 1925); Friedrich Gärtner, 'Die Stabilisierung der österreichischen Krone', *Schriften des Vereins für Sozialpolitik* (Munich-Leipzig, 1924), Vol. 169, p. 49 et seq.; and Maurice Pillet, *Le Relèvement financier de l'Autriche* (Paris, 1928). More recently Ladner, Stadler, Reimann, and Ausch (see bibliography) have dealt in varying degrees of thoroughness with the subject.

63 Nonetheless Otto Bauer himself had, in connection with the Gürtler episode, expressed fear of the impression being created abroad that 'extending loans to Austria was useless without putting Austrian finances under strict control'. Bauer, *Werkausgabe*, Vol. II, p. 821. See Note 12.

64 The original members of the Austria Committee were Messrs Balfour, Beneš, Hanotaux, Imperiali, and Seipel.

65 The complete text of the Geneva Protocols is to be found in several of the above-mentioned works, including *The Financial Reconstitution of Austria*.

66 See Protocol II, Article 5.

67 It was assumed that the cost of the redemption service would be below 70 million gold crowns. On the other hand the receipts from the tobacco monopoly and from customs dues totalled 125.64 million and 184.47 million gold crowns in 1923 and 1924 respectively.

68 The Financial Committee did not, though, regard it as likely that the Austrian Government would have recourse to the entire sum of 520 million gold crowns in foreign exchange. One of its reports to the League Council says, 'This is a budget deficit and, in the first instance, it is Austrian currency, not foreign currency, which is required to meet it. It may be expected, therefore, that once Austria's internal credit is re-established, a considerable proportion of the deficit will be covered by internal loans.' See Report of the Financial Committee and Resolution of the Council.

69 This was one of the clauses inspiring the following irritated reaction by Rudolf Freund: 'Everywhere it can be read that the purpose of the whole project is the recovery of the Austrian economy. Only occasionally ... is there a hint of Austria's reconstruction being mainly to serve as prerequisite to the safe investment of foreign capital.' Freund, in *Forschungen*, p. 53.

70 The government was entitled to appeal to the League against supposed misuse of the commissioner-general's powers. The provision was of little practical avail, seeing that collaboration free of friction between the Austrian authorities and the commissioner-general was an absolute condition for the operation's success.

71 There has been much guesswork as to the origin of the plan to eliminate parliament temporarily, in order to be able to undertake in quick succession the measures regarded as necessary to put the budget in order. Seipel repeatedly denied responsibility. Gulick, on the other hand, says, 'Through this proposal to exclude parliament Seipel had secured the incorporation of a pet scheme which he had first published on May 26, 1919, and which had been sharply criticized by the conservative *Neue Freie Presse*. His subsequent denial that his plan constituted an exclusion of parliament ... deserves no credence.' Charles A. Gulick, *Austria from Habsburg to Hitler* (Berkeley and Los Angeles, 1948), Vol. I, p. 167. Gulick's conjecture finds confirmation on the part of Dr Otto Ender, a Christian Socialist who was for many years Governor of Vorarlberg and Federal Chancellor, 1930–31. In autumn 1922 a German diplomatic report to Berlin quoted Ender as saying, 'Geneva Protocol III envisages in concealed terms a two years' dictatorship by the government to implement the measures, but it refrains from specifying the means necessary to that end. Questioned about that, Dr Seipel did not reply, but smiled meaningfully. From this Dr Ender concludes that in this respect a secret agreement has been reached with the League Council, but he likewise does not regard it as impossible that recourse might be had to the *Heimatwehren*' (later *Heimwehr* = local militias who developed into the para- military body symbolic of Austro-Fascism) 'if resistance were to be encountered from Left radical elements. That in this respect there exists agreement between Dr Seipel and the *Heimatwehren* leaders is something I have heard from another reliable source too.' ZStA Potsdam 09.01 AA 41773, p. 271a – German Passport Office, Bregenz to Ministry of Foreign Affairs, Berlin, 19 October 1922.

72 *Arbeiter-Zeitung*, 24 August 1922.

73 Otto Bauer, 'Der Genfer Knechtungsvertrag und die Sozial-demokratie', *Werkausgabe*, Vol. II, p. 461 et seq.

74 'Short of suicide and casting ourselves into the catastrophe of famine, we can reject Geneva only by simultaneously undertaking the most vigorous financial policy. That we can do only if we constitute a strong power centre, a strong government. The constitution of such a government is however at this time virtually impossible, and that is the real predicament. Not, as the bourgeois representatives assert, that it would not be feasible to save the country by its own exertions. Economically it is feasible. A predicament exists because the energy to take the rescue in hand is lacking. This predicament derives not from the country's inability to help itself, but from the bourgeois parties' betrayal of the nation.' Bauer, *Werkausgabe*, p. 480.

75 Haus-, Hof- und Staatsarchiv, NPA, K. 345, confidential report by Ferdinand Marek, Minister at Prague, to the Federal Ministry of Foreign Affairs, 28

October 1922 and based on information passed by a Czech deputy, Stivin.

76 PRO/FO 371, HN 01206, British Minister, Vienna, to Lord Curzon, Secretary of State of Foreign Affairs.

77 PRO/FO 371, HN 01206, *Central European Summary*, No. 965.

78 'Great as our campaign has been, we have not been able to strike among the bourgeoisie the slightest spark of feeling for national independence and autonomy nor have we managed to arouse among the property-owning classes resistance to the policy of betrayal at Verona and at Geneva. On the contrary, the bourgeois parties and the property-owning classes have merged in a united front the like of which we have not before seen.' Otto Bauer, as quoted in *Arbeiter-Zeitung*, 23 November 1922.

79 Friedrich Austerlitz, editor of *Arbeiter-Zeitung*, in a lengthy contribution to the ideological organ of the Social Democrat party, summarized the party's official attitude towards the Geneva agreements. 'In its present form the Constitutional Act goes far beyond what Seipel was originally prepared to concede. No more of course than a makeshift substitute for parliament, it is nevertheless a substitute and in the hands of Social Democracy it will continue to become so more and more. So Social Democracy was fully justified in regarding the act as a mitigation of Seipel's financial dictatorship, in so far as it was at all possible, and in regarding this constitutional law which does away with parliament's exclusion as a great success for its resistance; and therefore the party had to vote for it. Since it could not prevent the passage of the protocols, voting for the act expunged the very worst of the Geneva agreement.' Austerlitz, 'Die Sozial-demokratie im Kampf gegen Genf', *Der Kampf*, November 1922, p. 354.

80 Pertinax (pseudonym of the well-known Social Democrat publicist Otto Leichter) has in a different context described his party's strategy in terms that are also applicable here. 'The arms episode of spring 1927 at any rate illustrated one of Social Democratic policy's characteristics – first to threaten the utmost resistance, yet eventually to negotiate and, in an admittedly altered situation, to concede a great part of that to which decisive resistance had previously been announced.' Pertinax, *Österreich 1934. Die Geschichte einer Konterrevolution* (Zurich, 1955), p. 44.

81 *Der Österreichische Volkswirt* laid special emphasis on the dangers to industry ensuing on rigid adherence to this programme. 'The crucial argument against this programme is however . . . the concentric attacks launched by all parts of this plan on industry's competitiveness. The turnover tax, protective tariffs, multiplication of rents, higher bread prices, higher railway fares, and increased gas and electricity prices [will] drive up industrial costs on every side in such a way as to make it impossible to think of maintaining the competitiveness of the vast mass of Austrian products.' Issue of 11 November 1922, p. 148.

82 *Report of the Provisional Delegation of the League of Nations* (Geneva, 1921).

83 In this respect too the government's proposed measure closely followed the Financial Committee's recommendation: 'State industrial enterprises should be either suppressed if merely useless, or run by the state upon a commercial, i.e., paying, basis, or, in suitable cases, transferred to private management by concessions.' *Report*, Geneva 1921.

84 Walther Federn, 'Das Finanzprogramm', *Der Österreichische Volkswirt*, 28 October 1922, p. 88.

85 'The restoration of the agrarian duties would not only have entailed the most

monstrous increase in food prices, but also an attack on the conditions vital to industry's existence. In this respect we have achieved a complete victory . . . The government is simply empowered, with the agreement of the Extraordinary Cabinet Council, to raise the duties of the revenue tariff so far as to attain a total yield for all duties of eighty million gold crowns. On the other hand the general customs tariff of 1906, and the ordinances issued in connection with it, remain in force until such time as a statutory change occurs.' Otto Bauer, *Arbeiter-Zeitung*, 23 November 1922.

86 Alexander Spitzmüller, 'Das österreichische Steuersystem des Bundes, der Länder und Gemeinden und die Kapitalbildung', *Schriften des Vereins für Sozialpolitik* (Munich-Leipzig, 1928), Vol. 174, p. 268.

87 Spitzmüller, *Schriften*, p. 267.

88 The lowering of income tax accompanied simultaneously by the considerable rise in indirect taxation was also, as a matter of social policy, a cause for fierce criticism in the liberal-minded *Der Österreichische Volkswirt*: 'The financial programme's undisguised class character must arouse moral misgivings.' Gustav Stolper, 'Der Kampf um Genf', 11 November 1922, p. 147.

89 Kienböck, *Sanierungswerk*, p. 28 et seq. The description given here, following the example of Karl Ausch, represents a certain simplification.

90 'In Austria before the war total public expenditure amounted to about 13 per cent of the taxable national income. In 1927 the share of public revenues in the national income was in Austria about 31 per cent or more.' Cf. Friedrich Hertz, *The Economic Problem of the Danubian States* (London, 1947), p. 87.

91 'The force of circumstances and some delay in the appointment of the commissioner-general compelled it [the League Delegation] to take a wider responsibility than the mere elaboration of a program.'

92 Report by the Provisional Delegation of the League of Nations at Vienna, quoted in Sir Arthur Salter, *Financial Reconstruction of Austria* (League of Nations, Geneva, 1926), p. 196.

93 Cf. *Der Österreichische Volkswirt*, 18 November 1922, p. 182.

94 Cf. Pressburger, Österreiche Notenbank, p. 371.

95 Zimmermann did not prove to be a personality who knew how to exercise a pacifying effect on the political dissensions which had been fanned to an intolerable point by the Geneva preliminaries. This should have been clear to the Foreign Office already in February 1922 when it considered sending Zimmermann on a special mission to Vienna. '(He) was appointed the crown burgomaster of Rotterdam nearly twenty years ago and is now likely to be replaced by someone else as his views are too conservative . . . He has had no practical financial experience . . . his somewhat domineering character seems to suit him for position of chairman rather than of adviser to committee.' Sir C. Marling, British Minister at The Hague, to Foreign Office, PRO/FO 371/HN 0119, 23 February 1922.

96 'During August, 1922, notwithstanding the tremendous rise of the foreign exchange rates, the D.Z.' (Foreign Exchange Centre) 'had paid out £624,000 in foreign exchange from its reserve. In September £346,000 was returned to it by the public. In October it had again to supply £283,000 to the market and a further £59,000 between November 1 and 18.' Walré de Bordes, *Austrian Crown*, p. 207.

97 See Appendix II, Table A6.

98 Cf. 'Chronik', *Der Österreichische Volkswirt*, 25 November 1922, p. 207.
99 Report of the Provisional Delegation, in Salter, *Financial Reconstruction*, p. 197.
100 Salter, *Financial Reconstruction*, p. 38.
101 Cf. Rudolf Karl, *Die österreichische Völkerbundanleihe* (Vienna, 1929), p. 3 et seq. Also Ausch, *Als die Banken*, p. 98 et seq.
102 League of Nations, *Financial Reconstruction of Austria*, p. 186. A concise but informative summary of the recovery programme's effects is also contained in Felix Kreissler, *Von der Revolution zur Annexion Österreichs 1918 bis 1938* (Vienna-Frankfurt-Zurich, 1970), p. 110 et seq.

CHAPTER 5

Initiatives for Reconstruction

Austria had shrunk to the dimensions of a small state, but it was the home of a numerically important, matchlessly productive intellectual élite inspiring initiatives which took effect far beyond its borders. In this chapter the focus will be fixed on the country's material reconstruction, and emphasis directed towards three important sectors of the economy: development of the national hydraulic resources; electrification of the railways; and promotion of technical research.

The new state's viability was disputed in many quarters. Its notorious lack of coal was seen as a congenital, therefore irreparable, defect. A small group of pioneers, including economists, engineers, politicians, and senior civil servants, had however at an early stage drawn attention to Austria's water resources and the potential significance of this natural force.

Before the First World War no integrated organization for the generation of electric power had existed. Private enterpreneurs had built small hydraulic and steam power stations designed mainly for the requirements of individual industrial undertakings. The large coal resources in the north of the Empire constituted an additional, secure, and above all cheap store of energy for the Alpine territories' industrialized areas.

Wartime difficulties with coal supplies furnished the first impetus towards examining the idea of a hydraulic power and electricity development programme. The 1917 project of the Seidler cabinet for vitalizing the economy envisaged for a start measures to increase the utilization of these resources.[1] In this context the Austrian Engineers and Architects Association held in the winter of 1917–18 a series of discussions concerning guidelines for the power supply at regional and central levels. Well-known engineers like Brock, Engelmann, Grohmann and others aired their views on the subject. As a result of these consultations a plan was adopted to link Alpine hydraulic power with the northern coalfields by means of an 'Empire Power Line'. The promotion of undertakings jointly owned by private and public capital was recommended for the implementation of these large-scale designs.

With the Empire's disintegration the Alpine provinces were deprived of what had been their main energy resources and became dependent on the development of hydraulic power. Rich as the new Austria was in potential energy reserves, it was poor in respect of actually developed capacities. In 1924, at the First World Energy Conference, the country's gross low water hydraulic power was assessed on the basis of a 1907 register at 2,710 MW. Only 1,210 MW were regarded as productive.[2] Very much later it turned out that the true potential was 15,150 MW, five and a half times as great.[3]

At the end of 1918 power plants, including caloric power stations, numbered 380. Their hydroelectric capacity was 241,240 kW.[4] This represented some 4% of the capacity installed at the beginning of the 1870s.[5] It will not do to ascribe this backwardness solely to the abundance of coal in the nearby Sudeten provinces, now no longer a part of Austria. This had undoubtedly slowed down the development of hydraulic power, but the negative influence of this factor in the Alpine territories was increased by lack of capital. The indications are that the major banks hesitated to lend support to such newfangled ideas as hydroelectric power stations. They had invested substantial funds in the Empire's black coal industry; they could hardly be enthusiastic about development of a second major source of energy, 'white coal'.[6]

Strong, easily traceable resistance to electrification was offered by the military. They had, as in Prussia, considerable influence over the development of transport and communications. For strategic reasons they repeatedly raised objections to electrification plans by the Ministry of Railways. Because of their demand, among other things, for a complete steam locomotive replacement depot for electrified lines, most projects were doomed for lack of profitability. In 1902, for example, the Railway Minister, Heinrich von Wittek, invited tenders for the electrification of certain highly important stretches south of the main Alpine chain. Thanks to an army veto, the Empire's three biggest electrical firms, Siemens-Halske AG of Vienna, Ganz & Co. of Budapest, and Allgemeine Union Elektrizitätsgesellschaft, had to discontinue the long-prepared technical and organizational preliminaries.[7]

A crucial impediment to the intensive use of hydraulic power is likely to have been the small scale structure of Austrian industry. According to the 1902 industrial census only 27.6% of industrial employment was accounted for by enterprises with more than 100 employees. Industrial production altogether accounted for only 122,890 kW installed, or 51% of existing, capacity.[8] The limited size of the average industrial unit must be regarded as an important factor favouring the use of solid fuels as against electrical power. The installation of steam engines could be suited to the scale of individual firms at the site while electrical power offered no such advantage. Very often the problem of excess capacity meant that an otherwise promising project had to be abandoned. In the absence of a grid system the use of electricity in medium- and small-sized plants, now a matter of course, was not practicable to the same extent before 1918.

So much for the sad state of affairs at the outset of the Republic's history. Only large imports of fuels could keep Austria's industry and transportation going. In 1920 coal imports represented one seventh of total imports and yet were not enough to meet industrial and domestic demand fully.[9] The development of hydraulic resources was all the more urgent because the country's energy supply was mainly thermal-based. Fuel imports necessarily placed an increasing burden on the trade balance.

Thus it was soon realized that the development of hydraulic power must be taken in hand immediately. In January 1919 WEWA (Wasser- und Elektrizitätswirtschaftsamt = Water and Electricity Supply Board) and in March the Austrian State Railways Electrification Board were established.[10] Great importance was attached to the former in particular. The board members were directly responsible to the government and permanent members were the Ministers for Agriculture, Public Works, Transportation, and Trade, Industry, and Commerce (or their nominees) as well as two representatives of the federal provinces. Wilhelm Ellenbogen, the Social Democratic parliamentarian, became chairman of WEWA.[11] On its Advisory Commission sat representatives from the electrical industry, from industry in general, and from large and medium-sized banks.[12] Technical expertise was contributed by members of the Electrical Engineers Association and the Chamber of Engineers. Hans Kelsen, the author of the Federal Constitution, was the State Chancellery's delegate.

The establishment of WEWA shared the desire to end regional

particularism in the fields of electricity and water and to create conditions for a co-ordinated policy under central government authority. The board's structure and membership, it was hoped, would facilitate co-operation between the federal government and the provinces and ensure the funds for development projects. If initially attention centred on provincial particularism, two other topics' dominated the Board's deliberations from the middle of 1919 until the mid-1920s – the problem of foreign financing and the debate on socialization of electric power.

First, though, the matter of provincial particularism. The federal provinces viewed the establishment of WEWA with the deepest misgivings, regarding it as a centralist organization aimed at divesting them of control over their water resources. WEWA, in turn, was extremely anxious to foster accord so as, by way of a cautious negotiation strategy and skilful personnel policy, to avoid any possible obstruction of its work.[13] Yet eventually every effort to gain acceptance of the general principle of centralized administration was wrecked by the provinces' resistance. Any surviving hopes were buried when on 28 January, 24 May, and 27 June the Styrian, the Upper Austrian, and the Salzburg legislatures respectively passed the draft of an amendment to the Water Usage Act declaring ownership in, and development of, all hydraulic power plants part and parcel of provincial authority.[14] Had these amendments in fact had the anticipated consequences, the result would have been complete fragmentation of all efforts at electrification.

Unmistakably the action of the provinces was directed against Vienna. Lacking adequate water resources, it was in this matter dependent on the provinces. As however Vienna alone was in a position to furnish funds on an adequate scale, and in subsequent years the assistance of Viennese banks had to be enlisted for the development of hydroelectric plants, the provinces ultimately changed their pigheaded attitude.[15] Nevertheless one of the brightest projects fell victim to separatism. The plan for Vienna to obtain current from, and to contribute most of the costs towards, the erection of a major power station on the Upper Enns foundered on its rejection by the Styrian parliament. Not until Upper Austria had shown readiness to supply the capital with electricity from the Lower Enns and an agreement satisfactory to both sides had been negotiated, did Styria indicate that it was prepared to allow the current needed by Vienna to pass its boundaries.[16] A compromise had been achieved at the cost of valuable time, but the signal for the struggle between the country's centrifugal and centripetal forces had been given. In a sense this development, intimated by a dispute about hydroelectric power, was symptomatic of the new Republic's political situation – the provinces put limits on the Vienna government's centralism, which in view of the existing balance of power it had to accept. Full exploitation of the potential capacity of the river Enns had to await the Second World War and was not completed till the end of 1973.

The second, certainly no less urgent task of WEWA was to work out plans on how to finance hydraulic power plants and to implement existing projects.

Some of the proposals relied on the principle of self-help, and revolved around the use principally of domestic capital in the form of bond issues and consumer vouchers called 'electrocoupons'. This idea had been evolved before the war by Dr Ernst Ruzicka, an engineer. Vouchers would be bought by electricity consumers (industrial firms were presumably to be the most important) and would be accepted in payment for bills accruing subsequently. The objective was to create an outstandingly cheap method of capital procurement for the construction of generator stations. But in times of inflation it could hardly prove practicable.[17]

A second group of proposals advocated the establishment of public utilities in which the participation of foreign capital was regarded as possible, or in any case desirable. However the banks adopted a waiting attitude, especially as the interest rate on long term capital was difficult to bring into line with the crown's rapid deterioration.[18] In 1920 two major electrical enterprises were promoted. OÖ (Oberösterreichische = Upper Austrian) Wasserkraft- und Elektrizitäts AG (OEWEAG) was launched with Boden-Creditanstalt assistance, but the shares of Salzburger A.G. für Elektrizitätswirtschaft (SAFE) were subscribed by Salzburg province, a large number of Salzburg communes as well as private subscribers, and Württem-

Table 71   Electricity corporation bonds

Issue Year	Interest	Name	Nom. Amount (Cr.m.)
1921	5%	STEWEAG	300
1922	5½%	NEWAG	1000
	5½%	OEWEAG	1000
	5%	STEWEAG	4400
	5%	WAG	4000

bergische Elektrizitäts A.G. at Stuttgart.[19] From 1921 onward the major banks did, to a greater or lesser degree, participate in the founding of hydraulic power enterprises and in 1921 and 1922 a series of bond issues were floated with their help on behalf of electricity corporations.[20]

Many thought, in view of the banks' reserved attitude, that to seek foreign capital was the sole alternative. Such an outlook predominated, interestingly enough, among Social Democrats. It may well have reflected their conviction that Austria was not viable and therefore not capable of developing its hydraulic resources without foreign aid. Otto Bauer tried in his capacity as Minister of Foreign Affairs to interest financial circles abroad in this field of activity and Richard Schüller, his department head, proposed to WEWA that development of the national 'white coal' resources should be left to American exploitation as compensation for foreign relief credits.[21] On the board of WEWA the Social Democrat Ellenbogen was one of the most enthusiastic supporters of foreign assistance. The notion of using the young state's idle but potentially important riches to obtain the urgently needed food supplies was natural enough. There seemed to be no other choice than to turn abroad for capital.

WEWA was so zealous in the pursuit of this concept that it conducted negotiations with a number of interested groups simultaneously. The resulting annoyance simply caused the project to fall between all stools. At the beginning of 1919 Ellenbogen had asked Creditanstalt to sound out, via a United States banking connection, American backers who might be interested in the development of domestic hydraulic resources. In December negotiations began in Amsterdam between the government and Messrs Stone & Webster. The latter, behind whom stood the powerful National City Bank and American International Corporation (AIC), made it a condition that until mid-January the Austrians should enter into no parallel negotiations.[22] Nevertheless Ellenbogen and the Minister of Finance, without thinking it necessary to tell Stone & Webster, started at the same time discussions with a British financier who had submitted a tender for a big power station construction project.[23] Other foreign interests as well as the Americans shied away from such dubious commercial practices. Different, perhaps weightier reasons for the failure of WEWA's efforts were the uncertain economic situation as well as the unallayed fear in business circles of socialization measures.

Foreign investors were of course mainly concerned to invest as profitably as possible. Frequently they insisted on conditions that would have amounted to an encroachment on the sovereignty of national economic policy. All insisted on being able to set prices which, apart from meeting their costs, would guarantee a normal return. Mostly they also demanded guarantees for an inviolable monopoly position.[24] A United States mission, having failed to obtain collateral security from domestic banks for American food credits, suggested that Austria should repay food and raw materials credits in crowns, not dollars, which would then be used by the Americans for development of the domestic hydraulic resources – prices would be left to the foreign investors to fix at will so as to ensure their profit.[25]

Another project, emanating from negotiations between the Ministry of Finance and an American tobacco corporation, tried to combine the development of power resources with the reorganization of the state tobacco monopoly. An important advantage of this project seemed to be a cut in unemployment, because only domestic firms were to be engaged for construction of the power stations and supply of the technical equipment for production of the current. The funds would come from the establishment of an Austro-American consortium in which the Guarantee Trust Company of New York would have a majority holding. The consortium would promote an Österreichische Wasserkraft AG, the capital of which was to be paid in US dollars. For the conversion into crowns the following procedure was designed: Österreichische Wasserkraft would pay out of its dollar fund for the leaf tobacco to be delivered by International Planters Corporation (IPC), an American concern, while the Austrian Tobacco Monopoly would compensate Wasserkraft AG in crowns. IPC would in return guarantee the sale of Austrian tobacco products in the United States. The project did not get beyond its preliminary stages in spite of the Austrians being prepared to make major concessions. (The Tobacco Monopoly was even ready to undertake from its American export proceeds the interest payment on Wasserkraft bonds for the period of the power stations' construction.) Apart from the catastrophic inflation a stipulation that seemed to impair the foreign firms' 'appropriate' profit was decisive in the breakdown of negotiations –the Ministry of Finance insisted on having some say in fixing the charge for power supply.[26]

Thus all attempts to mobilize foreign capital for the development of Austria's hydraulic resources proved abortive. Besides the above-mentioned amateurish behaviour of the Austrian negotiators and the lack of coordination between the agencies concerned, there were also other reasons for this failure. One of them was uncertainty as to repercussions from the terms of the Peace Treaty. An open question appeared to be whether or not the Reparation Commission could claim disposal rights over public property, such as water resources, if this had already been pledged as security for loans.[27] It is now difficult to say what part plans to socialize the power industry, as envisaged by the Socialization Commission, played in negotiations with Western capital though the Austrian Authorities repeatedly had given assurances that socialization would be foregone if foreign funds became available.

There was indeed in 1919 and 1920 a great deal of talk about socialization of electric power. Innumerable bills were drafted. The first, submitted in April 1919 by the Socialization Commission, allowed for the desire of the provinces for autonomy by proposing the formation of provincial electricity agencies to be integrated in a State Electricity Agency. The local bodies were to be organized as public utilities in accordance with the provisions of the basic law on non-profit corporations. In addition the draft proposed that no more licences should be issued at the local level to private electricity enterprises.[28] A commission official explained to the WEWA Board that socialization would be 'hardly conceivable' if the licensing system were to be retained.[29] Six months later, when a project to be financed by foreign capital was in the stage of discussion, the same official, supported by Ellenbogen, evinced readiness to abandon socialization for the benefit of the investment.[30]

No lesser man than Otto Bauer accurately defined the Social Democratic attitude in the matter.

> Expansion of the hydraulic resources was impossible without a mobilization of foreign capital. At first we thought that we would be able to make over the whole of power generation and distribution to a non-profit-making corporation, the task of which would then be to found semi-public enterprises for the development and operation of the individual plants by raising foreign funds. But all negotiations with foreign financiers showed them to be suspicious of socialization even in this form. So it was thought impossible to risk socialization of the hydraulic resources without compromising their development.[31]

Abandonment of socialization did not however attain its purpose. Except in Vorarlberg, where Swiss and later German capital played a notable part, foreign participations during the inflation years were trifling.[32] The major banks' growing interest was in no small degree due to their close links with the electrical industry.[33] The hesitant commitment of the Federal authorities had a retarding effect. In view of the slender funds available, astonishing progress was achieved in the field of power plant construction and railway electrification, but in the late twenties these activities dwindled to a complete stop.

What was actually achieved in the decade 1919–1929?

The water rights law of all federal provinces contained expropriation and reversion clauses in their own favour. Carinthia, Tirol, Upper Austria, Lower Austria, and Styria made the use of water rights by private persons dependent on provincial authorities' agreement. In Salzburg and Lower Austria they even ensured for themselves a title to all unused water rights and concomitant resources.

Very soon the task of creating a statutory groundwork for the whole federal territory was taken in hand in order to put the development of power resources on a firm legal footing. By the constitutional law of October 1920 (State Law Gazette, No. 450) water rights policies became subject to federal regulation although their implementation and enforcement was left within the competence of the provinces. The Federal Law of 13 July 1921 (Federal Law Gazette, No. 409) 'on the promotion of the hydraulic resources and power supply (Hydraulic Resources Promotion Act)' offered holders of hydro-electrical power bonds a number of advantages in order to encourage the public to buy such securities and to promote the development of these resources. The tax benefits offered a specific attraction. Subsidies were given only to firms which by deliveries of power to third parties served non-profit purposes.

On 7 June 1922 the bill 'on electrical installation (Electricity Systems Act)', Federal Law Gazette, No. 348, passed into law. It tried, in so far as possible within the narrowly confined constitutional scope, to counter any trends towards fragmentation and in part harked back to a bill submitted in February 1918 by the Seidler Cabinet. Paragraph 3 imposed public responsibilities on firms which had communications and expropriation rights. The act's second section regulated expropriation rights in the case of cable equipment being installed, and the third section dealt with the licensing of power plants.[34] It was supplemented by the so-called Power Ordinance of 12 July 1922, Federal Law Gazette, No. 436.[35]

The Federal Act of 28 October 1922, Federal Law Gazette, No. 786, laid down the terms for the provision of federal funds to the construction of large-scale power plants.[36] Against acceptance of shares or bonds on the best available terms, the Ministry of Finance was authorized to put federal funds to an overall total of 20,000 million crowns, at the disposal of firms accorded preference under the

Hydraulic Resources Promotion Act, if they had on 1 January 1922 already started on such construction work. The text was submitted to the parliament, and passed even before ratification of the Geneva Protocols.

These legal measures satisfied the formal requirements for the creation of semi-public electricity corporations able to supply energy for entire federal provinces. A corresponding volume of production could until then only be claimed by the power stations planned by the State Railways and financed by the Ministry of Transport. The semi-public undertakings now assumed responsibility for supplying rural areas, industry, and small business. The public sector was represented by the provinces, the municipalities and the state; the private sector by industry and the banks. In addition there existed certain small power stations of no more than local importance. Born of private initiative, they mostly derived from an expansion of small industrial units' own plant.

A cursory survey of developments in the individual provinces gives the following picture:

On 23 September 1921 the Vienna City Council, after protracted negotiations, agreed unanimously to the founding of a power plant corporation (WAG) in which the city and a consortium of major Viennese banks should participate to 50% each. The original share capital of 200 million crowns was very soon doubled on account of currency depreciation. The ratio of participation shifted at the same time to 75 : 25 in favour of the banks. The most important projects were the Ybbs power station with 13,230 kW average annual load, and the station, with its distribution mains and auxiliary plant, beside the Lunz-Gaming aqueduct.[37] The two existing caloric Viennese power stations, producing totals of 88,200 kW and 34,545 kW respectively, continued in operation.

After Vienna had ceased to be a part of Lower Austria and acquired the status of a federal province, NEWAG, the Lower Austrian Electricity Corporation, took over the provincial electricity works Wienerbruck and St Pölten which supplied current for the St Pölten-Mariazell railway, the St Pölten industrial area, and all consumers along the main east-west railway line as far as Pressbaum, just outside Vienna. Immediately after its founding NEWAG acquired all the Wiener Neustadt electricity works as well as the Stollnhofer and Traisental plants. A start was made on developing the Erlauf river channel in a terraced gradient; by 1923 the station was in operation. Finding the funds did not prove difficult. NEWAG shares were willingly purchased by its customers and the banks. The municipalities of Krems, Melk, and Wiener Neustadt as well as state-owned enterprises like the industrial works at Wöllersdorf or the Waldviertel electrical co-operative association were also keenly active.[38]

In Upper Austria, as related earlier, 1920 witnessed the founding of OEWEAG, the Upper Austrian Hydraulic Power and Electricity Corporation. While in pre-war days Stern & Hafferl, an important private firm in the electrical sector, had secured for itself the western part of the province and the whole of the Salzkammergut (the lake district which constitutes part of Salzburg, Styria, and Upper Austria) the newly-founded OEWEAG was now responsible for the supply of the north and the east of Upper Austria. The two main delivery points were sited at Linz and Steyr.[39]

STEWEAG, the Styrian Hydraulic Power and Electricity Corporation, was founded in 1921 by the combined forces of all the major Viennese banks, the Styrian provincial government, and communal associations. The building programme encompassed the construction of ten major power stations to ensure the supply of current along the whole of the north-south main rail line, for all Styrian broad and narrow gauge railways, and for the Styrian iron, steel, and machine industries whose nerve centre was badly affected by the coal scarcity.

SAFE, the Salzburg Electrical Corporation, as previously mentioned, had to enlist foreign assistance for development of the Fusch power station (output = 7,350 kW). An agreement was signed with Kontinental-Stickstoff AG at Munich which envisaged the immediate construction of this station and thereafter that of Austria's first nitrogen factory.

In Carinthia there were, apart from the rail power station at Mallnitz, only six small private electricity works under development. This was far from enough. The Provincial power agency created at Klagenfurt shortly after the cessation of hostilities worked out a general development plan for the whole of the Carinthian hydraulic resources, but it was not until January 1923 that the Kärntner Wasserkraft AG (Carinthian Hydraulic Resources Corporation) was founded. Soon afterwards the construction of three major power stations was undertaken.

Among the federal provinces Tirol alone did not have an electrical corporation of its own and, for lack of capital, was unable to get beyond some very old projects. Only the Federal Railways were able to undertake extension of the Reutzbach station and, in 1924–27, to complete the development of the Achensee station.[40]

As long ago as 1909 there had been moves in Vorarlberg to reorganize the hydraulic power sector on rational lines. In 1912 a committee of the Vorarlberg Technical Association tried to found a co-operative society to take over the power stations, at that time mainly in Swiss hands. The failure of this scheme to materialize was all the more to the province's disadvantage since the charges of the Swiss undertaking were high.[41] During the war the State Railways had secured water rights to Lake Spuller; yet the foundation of two provincial undertakings came to pass only after years of negotiation. The large company was the outcome of an agreement between Schwäbische Elektrizitätswerke (German), Bundener Kraftwerke-AG (Swiss), and the Vorarlberg authorities. The plan centred on the development of the Ill's upper reaches and of the Lüner Lake's stations. The small company, in which Vorarlberg had a 52% interest, was financed mainly with foreign capital.[42]

The share of the semi-public provincial corporations in the development of the country's hydraulic resources was as follows: in 1921 towns and communes held the lead in terms of major power projects under construction. If however the size of the annual average load is taken as the appropriate gauge, then the semi-public corporations were at that date already drawing level; in 1922 they drew clearly ahead. Only in the matter of company-owned installations did a further important expansion take place while the role of the towns and communes as well as of the private electrical undertakings faded completely into the background by the end of 1924. During 1924 the same trend can be observed in respect of company-owned installations. This structural transformation from very small, operational units into combines is attributable not least to the Hydraulic Resources Promotion Act. It had been virtually tailored for semi-public enterprises.[43]

In 1921 the construction of large-scale power stations had been begun with a planned annual average load of 69,825 kW.[44] In 1922 the output of projects under construction was 44,835 kW, in 1923 it was 26,460 kW, and in 1924 no more than 16,391 kW. The decline reflects the unfavourable condition of the economy in the two latter years. At the end of 1924 there were under construction sixty-eight large-scale stations with an average capacity of 157,511 kW.[45] Between 1919 and 1929 the capacity of large-scale power stations expanded from 241,240 kW to 604,790 kW or by 151%, while the production of current rose only from 1,279 million kW hours to 2,479 kW hours, an increase of 94%. This means that the capacity of the newly completed stations was much higher than before.[46] In proportion to the ambitious plans of the early post-war years the actual development was rather modest.

Statistics show that in 1928, complementing the large-scale power stations with the caloric stations and those of enterprises with a capacity under 370 kW, there existed 627 electricity companies with an average annual output of 943,660 kW. More than half this total came from nine stations. 59% of stations were operated by hydraulic and 28.4% by steam power.[47]

The Federal Railways and their transition to electrification merits a brief account. The Imperial and Royal State Railways were after 12 November 1918 called the German-Austrian State Railways, as from 21 October 1919 the Austrian State Railways, and as from 1 April 1921 the Austrian Federal Railways. After the end of hostilities their deficit grew from month to month. In 1918–19 the loss amounted to some 20% of the invested capital.[48] The reasons for the reduction were drastically reduced traffic, coal scarcity, suspension of operations, thefts, and, by no means last, the apparently intractable repair shops problem. Practically all the Empire's railway repair shops had been located in the territory of the new Austria. In post-war days, particularly when the repair jobs on the locomotive and coach fleets had been finished, there were huge overcapacities. The same applied to the Austrian locomotive factories which during the Empire met four-fifths of all requirements and after 1919 could be employed to only a tenth of their capacity.[49]

Not before 19 July 1923 did the Austrian Federal Railways come into being as an independent economic unit. Till then the state had constantly to pump high subsidies into the hopelessly indebted sytem.[50] The Ministry of Transport was responsible for its administration. On 1 March 1919 the Ministry established the Austrian State Railways Electrification Board.

The first director of the Board, Paul Dittes, in collaboration with the competent Minister, Herr Paul and the president of WEWA, Ellenbogen, worked out an electrification programme for the railways even before any legal provisions had been made for this purpose.[51] The plan provided for the electrification in two stages of the following lines within ten to fifteen years:

a. Lindau-Vienna, including Feldkirch-Buchs and Bregenz-St Margarethen;
b. Schwarzach/St Veit-Villach;
c. Amstetten-Selzthal-St Michael-Villach, including St Valentin-

Klein Reifling and St Veit a.d. Glan-Villach;

d. Selzthal-Bischofshofen;

e. Attnang/Puchheim-Stainach/Irdning;

f. Wels-Passau;

g. Linz-Selzthal;

h. Hieflau-Eisenerz-Vordernberg.

On the basis of the preparatory work done in the years 1911–1914 it was decided to start construction first on the Innsbruck-Blundenz and Attnang-Stainach stretches. On 20 December 1919 and on 20 May 1920 parliament passed the two laws enabling electrification of the two stretches to be begun and completed by the end of the initial development stage.[52] In 1925 a new programme was drawn up, providing for the electrification of the Kufstein-Innsbruck-Brenner, Wörgl-Salzburg, Tauern range, and Salzburg-Vienna stretches. The Kufstein-Brenner and Wörgl-Salzburg stretches were implemented. In 1927 continuation was abandoned on account of the sharp drop in coal prices on the world market. No fresh start was made until the thirties when creating employment was a powerful incentive. Whereas after the end of the First World War some 3.6% of the entire system had been electrified, by the time the Second World War began the figure was approximately 16.7%.[53]

The legal basis for railway electrification was the Act of 13 July 1920 'on the introduction of electrical train transport on the Austrian Republic State Railways'.[54] The measure envisaged the construction and the enlargement of four large-scale power stations:

1. the Lake Spuller station in Vorarlberg with 3,234 kW annual average capacity;
2. the Ruetz station in Tirol with 4,925 kW annual average capacity;
3. the Stubach station in Salzburg with 4,355 kW annual average capacity;
4. the Mallnitz station in Carinthia with 5,513 kW annual average capacity.

These stations supplied the current for the above-mentioned stretches. To meet the requirements of the Salzkammergut Line (Attnang/Puchheim-Stainach/Irdning) the Steeg station on Lake Hallstadt belonging to the firm Stern & Hafferl was included.

In addition to the foregoing authorities, the Austrian Engineers and Architects Association contributed greatly to the railway electrification. Always concerned for Austria's technical progress, the Association had in 1909 joined the newly-founded Water Economy

Association, in 1911 advocated electrification of the Vienna Metropolitan Railway, and in December 1917 established a standing committee for organization of the water supply.[55] It was therefore logical that after the founding of the Republic, which was plagued by the lack of fuel, the utilization of the country's ample water resources became one of the main concerns of the association. In April 1919 the association prepared an opinion on the draft electricity bill, and another was presented in February 1921 on the Electrical Communications Act.[56] The association formed groups of experts for the planning and development of hydraulic power stations. Ardent support was given to the establishment of a Federal Ministry of Public Works, regarded by the association as an indispensable prerequisite for the promotion and co-ordination of large-scale power projects. In 1920 the association protested vehemently to the government against the merger of ministries and the reduction in credits for the electrification programme.

In 1924 the association tendered WEWA a memorandum on the further development of hydraulic resources. Impelled by the foreseeable end to the initial expansion period at the beginning of 1925, its principal idea was that private domestic and foreign capital should be offered sufficient inducement to invest in this sector. The authors of the memorandum thought it unlikely, even though desirable, that federal funds or remnants of the League of Nations loan would be provided for the purpose. The most important proposal, urged by the association's chairman, Fritz Brock, was extension of the tax-free depreciation period from fifteen to forty years.[57] Another suggestion was a reduction of the social welfare levies for the workers engaged on hydraulic power stations' construction; they amounted, according to Brock's calculations, to 2% of the investment costs.[58] The memorandum further advocated exemption from taxation for twenty years and abolition of the power tax on industrial firms, or at least their uniform treatment as part of an overall federal law.[59] Finally there was a plea for reducing loan interest because this was the only way to uphold the competitiveness of hydro-electric power, endangered as it was by the fall in coal prices. The association's memorandum met with little understanding among those responsible for energy policies.

The association concerned itself with numerous other matters vital to Austria's continued technical progress. Innumerable petitions to ministries, expert opinions, memoranda, recommendations and protests testified to its untiring activity since its foundation in 1848, and this professional confraternity must be accorded high social and political ranking.[60]

A not inconsiderable number of architects belonged to the association's various groups of experts and committees. After the creation in 1906 of the Austrian Reinforced Concrete Committee, the association set up a similar panel which in 1913 became one of its standing committees. Other such bodies were the Central Heating Committee and the Methods Testing Committee for bridge construction and boiler damage. Early in 1919 a Socialization Study Committee, formed in spring, worked out a draft bill on forestry policy and placed it at the disposal of the Socialization Commission.[61] The committee considered the administration of forest property a task for the community as a whole and proposed the constitution of provincial co-operatives to whom overall planning for timber utilization should be entrusted. Management of the co-operatives was to be assigned to representatives of forestry owners, the timber industry, timber dealers, workers and employees organizations, the provincial governments, and the provincial forestry inspectorates. At the national level the co-operatives should merge into a single umbrella organization.[62]

Initiatives of a scientific-technical nature in the early years of the Republic must be seen as a continuation of similar efforts during the days of the Empire. Technical research had then been almost exclusively at the service, and devoted to the promotion, of industry. Financial support came in the first instance from private sources and principally derived from the Lower Austrian Industrial Businessmen's Association with whose name that of Wilhelm Exner is intimately connected.[63] With the assistance of the association he had, for the advancement of technical efficiency, and despite official indifference, founded the Technological Museum in 1879. In 1891 this museum was involved in an official project to promote the Empire's small-scale industries. In 1909 Exner was appointed chairman of the Technical Research Board. Next year the bill on technical examination and materials testing, which he had fathered, passed into law and remained known as the 'Exner Act'.[64]

Since the end of the last century research and testing institutes had sprouted in ever greater numbers. The oldest was the Building and Machine Materials Research Institute attached to the Technological Museum at Vienna. Many others were affiliated to technical colleges and industrial schools. Some were founded as associations. Others, like the well-known Materials Testing Office of the cast steel plant at Kapfenberg belonging to Gebrüder Böhler & Co., were private endowments. Their task was to test and to give expert opinions on industrial and commercial products. Their attestations had the character of official documents and could be substituted for expert evidence.[65]

Before 1918 more than forty authorized research institutes existed throughout the Empire, many in the territories of the future Successor States. Certain ones had therefore to be replaced urgently in the new Austria. The Textile Industry Research and Testing Institute is one example because, following the loss of the Sudeten areas, all analogous institutes were beyond the borders.[66] In 1921, on the application of Exner in his capacity as its chairman, and with the support of the Ministry for Trade, Commerce, and Industry, the research institute founded during the war to examine substitute materials for the textile industry received a non-recurring subsidy of 500,000 crowns from the Ministry of Finance, and the same amount as an interest-free loan.[67] A research department was also established by the textile factories, by the Association for Chemical and Metallurgical Production, and by Klein-Neusiedler Papierfabriks-AG to develop the processes necessary for the manufacture of staple fibres and the textiles to be home-produced from domestic timber, cellulose, and chemicals.[68] Subsequently the Silk and Wool-Drying Institute and a textile finishing plant passed into the possession of the Textile Research Institute.

With the ratification of the Geneva recovery programme a difficult time began for the research institutes, inasmuch as the Economy Commission formed by the government gave notice of their impending dissolution. As a counter-measure a Technical Commission was constituted under the aegis of the Lower Austrian Industrial Businessmen's Association. Many members and chairmen of the authorized research institutes joined this new body, the financing of which cost the association a sizeable allocation from its funds.[69] In 1923 *Neues Wiener Tagblatt* published a register, compiled by Exner, of research institutes whose establishment was assured. In the field of materials testing the most important, apart from those already mentioned, were the Technical Research Institute of the Technical University, Vienna, existing since 1901; the Mechanical-Technical Research Institute at the Technical University, Graz, founded in 1921; the paper testing institute at the Technical Museum; the Leather Industry Training and Research Institute as part of the Federal Educational and Research Institute for the Chemical Industry at Vienna; the Physical Research Institute; and the Chemical Research Institute.[70] To these was added in 1925 the Austrian Pharmaceutical

Research Institute which from the start came under heavy demand from its parent industry.[71] With the onset of the Great Depression the remarkable initiatives shown in the early days also waned in this area of activities.

Notes

1 Oskar Vas, *Grundlagen und Entwicklung der Energie-Wirtschaft Österreichs.* Official Report by the Austrian National Committee to the World Energy Conference (Vienna, 1930), p. 26.

2 Vas, *Grundlagen*, p. 24.

3 R. Partl and K. Knauer, 'Eine Neubestimmung des Wasserkraftpotentials von Österreich', *Österreichische Zeitschrift für Elektrizitätswirtschaft* (Vienna, April 1970), p. 18.

4 Vas, *Grundlagen*, p. 28.

5 Today's capacity is 5,875 MW or 5,875 mill. kW. Cf. Partl/Knauer, *Neubestimmung*, p. 18.

6 Resistance to the hydraulic power expansion in the early days of the Republic came mainly from the Czech coal interests. When as part of the Geneva recovery programme the issue of a hydraulic power loan was discussed, the Czech side raised objections. Cf. Karl Ausch, *Als die Banken fielen* (Vienna, 1968), p. 80. The same groups later tried to stop electrification of the federal railways.

7 Hanns Stockklausner, '50 Jahre Elektro-Vollbahnlokomotiven in Österreich und Deutschland', in a special issue of *Eisenbahn* (Vienna, 1952), p. 11.

8 The rest was apportioned between power supply undertakings (44%) and railway power stations (5%). Vas, *Grundlagen*, p. 28.

9 Friedrich Hertz, *Zahlungsbilanz und Lebensfähigkeit Österreichs* (Munich, 1925), p. 23, says that in 1920 imports totalled 1,704 million gold crowns. Some 50% were attributable to foodstuffs, and about 4% to fuels (coal and oil). Cf. also Hubert Overbeck, *Währung und Handelsbilanz Österreichs in den Jahren 1914–1928* (Saarbrücken, 1930), p. 36.

10 AVA/WEWA/Miscellaneous File, Box 39, Z.99/1919, WEWA articles of association.

11 As long ago as 1906 Ellenbogen had pointed out the importance of hydraulic power to the economy. At a trade union congress in 1921 he gave it as his opinion that 'with our hydraulic power resources we could, apart from being able easily to electrify all Austrian railway lines, to a considerable extent meet industry's requirements'. See Jacques Hannak, 'Die Wirtschaftliche Lage Österreichs', annex to *Österreichs Volkswirtschaft und die Sanierung* (Vienna, 1923), published by Gewerkschaftskommission Deutsch-Österreichs, p. 37.

12 Prof. Julius Landesberger-Antburg and Ludwig von Neurath, Anglo-Österreichische Bank and Creditanstalt respectively, were the representatives for the large commercial banks while Paul Goldstein, director of Allgemeine Depositenbank, sat on the commission for the medium-sized banks.

13 The appointment of Jodok Fink as representative of the provinces, not originally envisaged, had a calming effect.

14 AVA, Z. 161, 700, 467/WEWA/1919.
15 E. Kurzel-Runtscheiner, *Österreichs Energiewirtschaft und die Ausnützung seiner Wasserkräfte* (Vienna, 1923), p. 15.
16 Kurzel-Runtscheiner, *Energiewirtschaft*.
17 Ministry of Finance Archives, 9691/1918.
18 This led Ellenbogen, the WEWA chairman, to describe the Viennese banks on one occasion as 'pretty bourgeois' and 'very timid'. AVA, Z.884/WEWA/1920.
19 *Compass*, 1925, Vol. I, p. 1,125.
20 About the banks' growing interest in this category of investment an American Embassy, Vienna, analysis remarked that a number of new corporations had been founded, the capital obtained via the issue of shares and bonds, and an intensive publicity campaign conducted at home and abroad by the banks. *Microfilm Publication No. 695*, Roll 51/338, National Archives, Washington.
21 AVA, Z.68/WEWA/1919, Minutes of the 3rd Meeting, 20 January 1919.
22 AVA/WEWA/Miscellaneous File, Z. 1382/1920 and Z.1014/WEWA/1919, annexes 1–3.
23 AVA/WEWA/Miscellaneous File Z.463/1920.
24 Vickers Ltd., London, for a short while interested in developing the hydraulic resources required to supply Vienna with power, included the following conditions: 'It would be necessary for the Austrian Government to undertake that no Water Power Scheme be developed which would enter into competition with the objects of this Scheme. It would also be necessary that the Organization suggested should take over the Supply Stations (coal or water) at present owned either by the State or Civil Authorities upon terms to be approved. This would be essential to provide against future competition which would certainly arise in the event of conditions governing the supply and cost of coal becoming considerably more favourable.' Ministry of Finance Archives 107.125/1920, Letter to the Austrian Minister, London.
25 AVA/WEWA/Miscellaneous File Z. 4768/1919.
26 Ministry of Finance Archives, 107.125/1920. The investment capital was to consist to only a small part of shares, the main portion being raised by the issue of dollar bonds. (Four million shares of the anticipated $48 millions capital were to be issued at the most. Bonds totalling about $44 millions would have an 8% coupon.) The government claimed no more than the right to subscribe, together with other public bodies and private domestic interests, an amount of $1 million of the share capital. The technical execution of the development projects was to be in the hands of a consortium, the so-called Foris Group, whose members included the Dreyfuss, Thyssen, and Schneider-Creuzot enterprises as well as the Milanese bank Credito Italiano. The group was prepared to raise one third of the investment capital.
27 AVA, Z.1097/WEWA/1920.
28 Licences for the construction of own plant and equipment were to continue. AVA, Z.186/WEWA/1919.
29 AVA, Z.186/WEWA/1919.
30 AVA, Z.95/WEWA/1920.
31 Otto Bauer, 'Die Österreichische Revolution', *Werkausgabe*, Vol. II, p. 722 et seq.
32 The Trade Union Commission Report presented at the Second Trade Union Congress, 1923 said that during the course of domestic hydraulic resources

development since 1919 a series of companies had been founded 'in which, together with big domestic banks, foreign capital has participated although with moderate amounts'. Hannak in *Österreichs Volkswirtschaft*, p. 38.

33 Close relations existed between Creditanstalt and AEG-Union, between Niederösterreichische Escompte-Gesellschaft and Brown, Boveri, as well as between Wiener Bankverein and Siemens-Halske.

34 When the bill was being debated by the *Nationalrat*, the German Consulate reported to Berlin: 'It accords with the wishes long pressed with the utmost vigour by the electrical industry and the experts alike. There is no doubt whatever that to secure an overhead line system for electric cables is also in the public interest . . . The more the long distance transmission of electric current develops technically, the more palpable is the lack of a code regulating electrical communications.' German Consulate, Vienna, to German Ministry of Foreign Affairs, 13 April 1922, ZStA (DDR Central State Archives), Potsdam, 09. 01 AA, 41771 BL. 212.

35 Kurzel-Runtscheiner, *Energiewirtschaft*, p. 18.

36 Kurzel-Runtscheiner, *Energiewirtschaft*, p. 20.

37 Average annual load signifies the average load actually produced during a year. A station's real load or capacity generally exceeds by far the average load.

38 Kurzel-Runtscheiner, *Energiewirtschaft*, p. 30 .

39 Ministry of Finance Archives, 75.174/1920. OEWEAG was founded on 19 July 1920 with a share capital of 50 million crowns apportioned as follows: Province of Upper Austria, 16 millions; Municipality of Linz, 4 millions; Republic of Austria, 10 millions; and the private enterprises Österreichische Waffenfabriks-gesellschaft, Vienna and Tramway- und Elektrizitätsgesellschaft, Linz-Urfahr with 10 millions respectively. Development of the Grosse Mühl's hydraulic resources was planned as the original project. The rapid currency depreciation soon rendered a capital increase of 200 million crowns necessary, whereupon the ratio of public to private participation shifted even more in favour of the former. (Province of Upper Austria, 64 millions; Municipality of Linz, 40 millions; Republic of Austria, 40 millions; Waffenfabriksgesellschaft and Tramway- und Elektrizitätsgesellschaft, 28 million crowns each). Loans of 100 million crowns each, to be extended by Allgemeine Österreichische Boden-Creditanstalt and Oberösterreichische-Kommunal-Kreditkasse respectively, were expected as coverage for the constructional outlays.

40 See *Der Österreichische Volkswirt*, 24 September 1927, p. 1,379.

41 Kurzel-Runtscheiner, *Energiewirtschaft*, p. 40.

42 Kurzel-Runtscheiner, *Energiewirtschaft*, p. 41.

43 'Statistik des Ausbaues der Grosswasserkräfte bis Ende 1924 der Republik Österreich', issued by WEWA and published as a reprint by *Die Wasserkräfte* (Vienna, 1925).

44 Large hydraulic power stations are such as have a turbine capacity of more than 370 kW or 500 horsepower.

45 'Statistik des Ausbaues der Grosswasserkräfte'. Cf. also Federal Act of 13 July 1921, Federal Law Gazette, No. 409.

46 Vas, *Grundlagen*, p. 29

47 Vas, *Grundlagen*, p. 35.

48 Hans Freihls, *Bahn ohne Hoffnung. Die österreichischen Eisenbahnen von 1928–1938* (Vienna, 1971), p. 20.

49 Freihls, *Bahn ohne Hoffnung.*
50 The well-informed German Legation had the following to say on the Austrian railways: 'The Federal Railways have for a long time been the deadweight on the Austrian budget. Without them the budget would be almost in surplus. The subsidy which the state has to contribute to the management of the Federal Railways is almost as large as the entire budget deficit.' German Legation, Vienna, to the German Ministry of Foreign Affairs, 26 May 1923, ZStA, Potsdam, 09.01 AA, 40126 BL. 47.
51 Stockklausner, in *Eisenbahn*, p. 16. Also Wilhelm Ellenbogen in *Arbeiter-Zeitung*, 23 March 1920.
52 Paul Dittes, 'Die Einführung der elektrischen Zugförderung auf der österreichischen Bundesbahnen', *10 Jahre Wiederaufbau* (Vienna, 1928), p. 522.
53 Cf. Alexander Fibich *Die Entwicklung der österreichischen Bundesausgaben in der Ersten Republik (1918–1938)*, Dissertation, Vienna University, 1977, p. 139 et seq.
54 Kurzel-Runtscheiner, *Energiewirtschaft*, p. 23.
55 *Festschrift* of the Austrian Engineers and Architects Association on the occasion of its 75th anniversary, Vienna, 1923.
56 *Festschrift*, 1923.
57 AVA, Z.190/WEWA/1925.
58 AVA, Z.191/WEWA/1925.
59 Industrial firms' use of electric power was burdened by a so-called power tax. Many firms therefore were prepared to build their own plants rather than to use public current supplies.
60 *Festschrift*, 1923.
61 AVA/WEWA/Miscellaneous File, Box 19.
62 AVA/WEWA/Miscellaneous File, Box 19.
63 Before 1914 there were in addition four hundred credit co-operatives for promotion of small business. Cf. Kamillo Pfersmann, 'Der Wiederaufbau der österreichischen Gewerbeförderung', *10 Jahre Wiederaufbau*, p. 467.
64 Wilhelm Exner, *Erlebnisse* (Vienna, 1929), p. 174.
65 Herbert Conrad, 'Das technische Versuchs- und Materialprüfungswesen', *10 Jahre Wiederaufbau*, p. 479.
66 Exner, *Erlebisse*, p. 184.
67 Ministry of Finance Archives, 107.792/1921.
68 Ministry of Finance Archives, 107.792/1921.
69 Exner, Erlebnisse, p. 180.
70 The chemical branch of research testing was, alongside that for materials, the oldest. Exner, Erlebnisse, p. 182.
71 Conrad, in *10 Jahre Wiederaufbau*, p. 482.

CHAPTER 6
The Economy During the First Year of Stabilization

'The news that the League of Nations intended to start a recovery programme for Austria,' wrote Dr Richard Reisch, for many years Chairman of the Austrian National Bank, 'was enough to stop the crown's farther slump and to allow it to pick up by about 15% from its worst low of around 16,000 crowns to the Swiss franc on 25 August 1922 to around 13,500 crowns at the end of October.'[1] Henceforth the Foreign Exchange Agency was able to stabilize the exchange rate through market interventions. For the monetary authorities the Swiss franc remained the lead currency for another six months. When at the beginning of May 1923 it began to fluctuate rather strongly against the gold standard currencies, they abandoned it for the dollar. On 18 May the price for the latter was fixed at 71,060 crowns. From 6 August 1925 onward the rate was left free to float.[2]

During the final months of 1922 the feeling of successful stabilization effected a strong reflux of foreign exchange which lasted almost the whole of 1923.[3] The inflow came mainly from private sources.[4] With a weekly call rate of around 5% and in the face of a stabilized external value for the crown, clinging to stocks of speculative foreign currency was bound to result in losses.

The abundant influx of foreign exchange led between January and December 1923 to a 70% rise in the volume of money without endangering the stability of the crown's external value.[5] Nonetheless an increase on this scale aroused among certain well-known experts fears that inflation had not been completely averted. The currency's external value, they reasoned, had been fixed at a level unfavourable to the Austrian economy. Spitzmüller was one of the principal critics. Like Keynes, he took for his point of departure the stabilization of the domestic price level and he therefore observed the rapid rise in the volume of money with growing alarm.[6] In a series of articles and addresses he advocated a higher rate of exchange,[7] which, in his

536

opinion would also facilitate the redemption of Austria's considerable foreign indebtedness.

Defenders of the Central Bank policy, apart from the Chairman and Viktor Brauneis, the Governor, included outstanding economists like Joseph Schumpeter and Ludwig von Mises. But Reisch was mainly concerned about the restrictive effects of a higher exchange rate of the crown.[8] He defended the enormous increase of currency in circulation on the ground that the higher cash holdings by banks as well as by private individuals attested to a notable diminution in the velocity of money since the days of hyperinflation. An international comparison of per capita stocks of money, he added, also spoke against the assumption of 'currency abundance'. In terms of dollars the amount of money in circulation per capita at the end of January 1924 had been $14.60 in Austria, $8.70 in Czechoslovakia, $38.20 in Switzerland, $40.30 in Britain, and $44.40 in France.[9]

Schumpeter was vigorously opposed to any alteration in the exchange rate, arguing that the consequences of a deflationary policy were not merely very dubious, but would greatly increase social tensions and might cause a new crisis of confidence.[10] Mises too was against deflation. To those who argued that it could cancel out the regroupment of assets effected by inflation, he replied, 'Those who benefit from the rise in the value of money are not identical with those who during inflation suffered from its fall, and those who have to bear the costs of this policy are not the same as those who derived advantage from depreciation. The consequences of inflation are not rescinded by practising deflation.'[11]

Among the opponents of any deflationary measures were likewise the Social Democrats. They had of course a pre-eminent interest in maintaining the economy's competitiveness, a view also popular with the public because already towards the close of 1922 a distinct decline in the export boom, due to inflation, was making itself felt.[12] Cessation of the 'inflation premium' was not however the only circumstance which in 1923 affected the Austrian economy unfavourably.

The repercussions of the occupation by France of the Ruhr play an important role in this context. Some authors have erroneously ascribed to this event a stimulating effect for Austria's external trade. True, certain big enterprises, with Alpine-Montan of course in the van, were able to augment their exports to Germany as a result of the paralysis affecting the Rhineland's heavy industry.[13] Leaving aside the iron and steel industry, though, the economy as a whole suffered very badly. Rising coal and iron prices, due to the major breakdown in German deliveries, increased costs of industrial production.[14] The swift decline of the mark in foreign exchange markets meant a severe handicap for exports to Germany.

Similarly trade with Hungary and Poland was in 1923 very unfavourably affected by the currency crises in those countries. The following table gives the most important figures for the exchange rate and for foreign trade between Germany, Hungary, Poland, and Austria:

Table 72   Foreign exchange ratios (in cr. per respective currency units)

		January	July	December
Germany	high	9.45	0.4	0.016[a]
	low	2.35	0.056	0.014[a]
Hungary	high	26.50	7.80	3.73
	low	23.90	2.20	3.72
Poland	high	3.55	0.70	0.019
	low	1.75	0.32	0.009

a = for 1 million marks

Table 73   1923 External trade (in m. crowns)

		Exports to	Imports from
Germany	1922	166.4	392.0
	1923	132.6	360.3
Hungary	1922	141.6	188.5
	1923	85.1	209.4
Poland	1922	95.4	45.9
	1923	83.7	118.7

Source: *Compass* 125, Vol. I; Statistitsches Handbuch für die Republik Österreich (4th & 5th publ. years)

The analysis of external trade factors does not however complete the picture of negative influences during the first year of stabilization. The deflationary effects of the Geneva programme now began to make themselves felt in a decline of business activity. In addition, certain aspects of bank policy, which will be discussed later, proved detrimental to the situation.

The League of Nations plan was to eliminate within two years the budget deficit. A surplus could therefore be expected for the second half of 1924.[15] In fact, astonishingly enough, a surplus existed from November 1923 onward. Primarily this was due to the unexpectedly rapid rise in tax receipts.

Table 74   1923 Budget Development (in m. schillings)[1]

	Ségur Draft 6.11.1922	Kienböck Draft 17.2.1923	Estimates	Final Figures
A. Federal Exp.	701.9	627.5	647.8	787.1
Adminis. Rev.	326.9	466.5	493.5	763.2
B. Monopolies/Net Cash Payments	117.7	125.5	89.2	91.4
C. Fed. Enterpr./ Net Cash Subs.	230.3	201.0	201.3	225.3
Total Deficit[2]	529.4	237.5	266.4	158.2

Source: Kienböck, op. cit., p. 43.
[1] 10,000 crown notes = 1 schilling; 1 gold crown = 1.44 sch.
[2] If 1923 expenditure is amended by the transitory item Contributions to Provinces and Communes, the budget already has a surplus. That goes to show the recessionary effects of the Geneva reconstruction in an even more drastic light . . . See Fibich, op. cit., p. 9 et seq. and p. 170.

The introduction on 1 April 1923 of a turnover tax contributed substantially to the restoration of the budgetary balance. During its first year of operation it brought in receipts totalling about 105 million schillings.[16] As against this figure the outlays on investment for the whole of 1923 were only some 76 million schillings, the major part of which, i.e., about 60 million schillings, was used for electrification of the Federal Railways.[17] On the expenditure side the positive effect of the quick reduction of civil service personnel made itself felt even though the mechanical approach to reorganization of the administrative establishment detracted quite considerably from the possible economies.[18] Those who were not pensioned simply enlarged the ranks of the unemployed because the chances of obtaining any other employment were, in consequence of the stabilization crisis, extremely slim.

Inflation had left the economy with the heavy legacy of an exorbitantly high rate of interest. The Central Bank's discount rate was 9% and the major banks' overdraft rate for the most creditworthy fluctuated between 20% and 30%.[19] The stock exchange boom, beginning in spring with great vehemence and continuing almost undiminished to the end of 1923, was the most important reason for the banks maintaining their high interest rates after inflation had ceased.[20] Stock exchange speculators, at home and abroad, held that the true value of domestic securities far exceeded their market price at the time of stabilization. In September 1922 the currency's external value had sunk to a fourteen thousand four hundredth of pre-war days whereas, they emphasized, the share index (January–June 1914 = 1) then stood at merely 502.[21] The index developed, month by month, as follows:[22]

Table 75   1923 Shares index for domestic securities (January–June 1914 = 1)

	I	II	III	IV	V	VI	VII	VIII	IX	X	XI	XII
All Shares	893	751	882	1,176	1,284	1,479	2,214	2,292	2,540	2,584	2,336	2,586
Bank Shares	100	105	124	205	209	298	345	341	378	363	337	424

Source: Statistisches Handbuch für die Republik Österreich (5th publ. year, 1923)

This 'revaluation boom' on the Vienna Stock Exchange faced the banks with an exceptionally strong demand for credit which they could only meet by trying to increase their share of the deposits sum by a high interest rate.[23] Inflation had left behind an acute capital shortage which was due to the fact that the major part of business and private savings had been wiped out. Undoubtedly the interest rate charged by banks would, even in the absence of the loans demand fed by the stock exchange boom still have been above the level of 'normal' times.[24] The unusually low state of deposits with savings banks makes this plain. At year-end 1922 they stood at no more than 9.1 million gold crowns, some 0.3% of the figure for 31 December 1913.[25] Yet, as Walther Federn underlined, upholding a high interest margin was also of course to the advantage of the banks, all of which were anxious to compensate as fast as possible the loss of real assets suffered during the war and the period of inflation.[26]

The burden of high interest cost on production was the subject of an investigation held in April 1923 at the instance of the Federal Chamber of Labour. At this conference, under the chairmanship of the Ministry for Social Welfare (*sic*!), the banking representatives rejected all suggestions for a lowering of the interest level on the grounds of the high deposit interest rates and their own increased overheads.[27] Gustav Stolper held this approach to be economically unfounded because the interest rate was not determined by high costs. Conditions in the money and foreign exchange markets were, in his view, driving up the interest level and rendering it possible for banks and savings banks to maintain an unduly inflated administrative apparatus in comparison with pre-war days.[28]

For industry and commerce, faced with growing difficulties in foreign as well as domestic markets, the high cost of interest was, on top of the Ruhr crisis, unfavourable exchange rates, and a deflationary budget policy, yet another handicap, inevitably harmful to the economy's competitiveness. Clearly these factors could not but prove particularly adverse to investment activity at a time when all available energy ought to have been concentrated on reorienting and restructuring production. Consequently the first year of stabilization, which should have been devoted to reconstruction, was instead characterized by a crisis in the capital goods sector. Certain economic indicators bear eloquent witness to the fact. In the first place there is the dramatic worsening of the labour market situation as shown in table 76.

Table 76 Unemployed in receipt of assistance (end-month, in 000s)

1922[a]	33.6	42.9	42.2	44.3	38.6	33.3	30.9	31.2	38.0	58.0	82.9	117.1
1923	161.2	167.4	152.8	132.2	108.0	92.8	87.2	83.9	78.8	75.0	79.3	98.0

[a] = less Burgenland
Source: Statistisches Handbuch für die Republik Österreich (4th & 5th publ. years)

Rising unemployment figures were accompanied by an increase of short-time workers. Figures published in *Arbeit und Wirtschaft* show that in August 1923 the number of short-time workers in certain sectors like the metal industry or the timber and wood-working industry distinctly exceeded that of normal workers.[29]

External trade stagnated. Exports rose as against 1922 merely by some 7%, corresponding to the increase in wholesale prices, while imports went up almost 21%. The general import expansion was however accompanied by a standstill, or even decrease, in the import of capital goods. A decrease was thus evident in the customs tariff classifications 'Oil, Lignite, Shale Tar', 'Iron and Iron Products', 'Chemical Accessories and Chemical Products', while 'Machines, Equipment and Parts' remained at the preceding year's level.[30] The relatively strong rise in imports of consumer goods confirms repeated observations of contemporaries that a big portion of the assets gained by stock exchange speculation was squandered abroad by the importation of luxury goods.

The 1923 drop in business activity is reflected in the industrial production and the Federal Railways' performance figures. Lignite production fell by 13% to 2.7 million tons. Industry's consumption of pit coal, lignite, and coke went down 16%. The Federal Railways' payload tons/km receded by 13.5% to 3,200 million kilometres.[31]

The output of consumer goods industries demonstrated a similar retrograde trend, indubitably in consequence of restricted export opportunities, feebler domestic purchasing power resulting from high unemployment, and a decline in tourism.[32] The fall in mass consumption is vividly illustrated by the decrease in sales figures for cigars, cigarettes and sugar, and the low production of beer-worts.[33]

The extent of the stabilization crisis can be judged from data relating to industrial capacity utilization, expressed in percentages, as tabulated from Ministry of Trade surveys:[34]

Iron and Steel Works	40
Machine-Building Industry	40
Motor Vehicles and Bicycles Industry	50
Iron and Metal-Working Industry	30–60
Electrical Goods Industry	50
Leather Industry	50
Textile Industry	30–60
Paper Industry	76–80
Timber Industry	70
Chemical Industry	70–80
Glass Industry	20

The figures confirm the economy's markedly recessionary trend. Many of the circumstances responsible for this condition, such as limited export opportunities, a domestic market inhibited in its absorption capacity by a restrictive budget policy, the high costs of capital, and so on, were to remain decisive elements in the economic development of later years.

The business development in 1923 of the major banks, in particular that of Creditanstalt, has been dealt with. It should be kept in mind that the nature of their activities was crucially different from pre-war days: The increase of profits from securities and syndicate activities was insufficient to compensate for the decline of interest yield. Total earnings therefore lagged distinctly behind those in 1913. A great part of the exceptionally high receipts from stock exchange business ceased when in 1924 the market boom crumbled. The decreased profits on current business now began to have extremely adverse effects.

Issuing operations were not simply of importance for the current profit and loss account. Securities remaining in banks' portfolios after the promotion of new joint-stock companies or as a result of capital increases raised the value of their assets at a time of rising stock exchange prices. In a sense these transactions constituted a compensation for the losses sustained in the line of current business through monetary depreciation. Herein lay the significance of the reply given by the director of a major Viennese bank to an American economist: 'The chief Vice President of one of the leading banks was asked recently by an American economist whether the banks did not know when they lent money during the period of depreciation that such loans would be repaid in crowns of a lower value and that therefore the banking business in such a time was being conducted at a loss. He replied that the bankers were very well aware of the probable course of the Austrian crown but that there were two motives compelling them to make loans notwithstanding. One was their tradition of responsibility for keeping business going: a refusal to lend would have been economic sabotage of the country at large and might have precipitated the gravest social disorders. The second motive was that most of these loans brought to the bank an increased share in business and industrial enterprises. *What the bank lost as a money lender it more than made up in the enhanced value of its share of controlled enterprises.*'[35]

The close relations which in the period before the First World War had been established between banks and industry consequently became even closer in the phase of post-war inflation. Especially the years after 1920 were marked by a hectic promotion activity that in 1923 reached its zenith.[36] The extent of speculation can be judged by the increase of domestic companies quoted on the Vienna stock exchange which increased from 75 at the end of 1913 (market value equals $531.9 million) to 186 at the end of 1923 (market value equals $491.0 million).[37] No data exist for unquoted companies but it is a safe assumption that their number multiplied even faster. Contemporary estimates suggest that there were probably 2800 of such companies at the end of 1923.[38]

The reason for this new wave of 'going public' was the ever more stringent lack of working capital resulting from snowballing inflation which forced even well-known, long established firms to seek support from banks. 'Hundreds of enterprises which had prided themselves for years or even generations on being strictly private or family businesses with a large degree of individual initiative and absolute independence as to finance, policy, and control, have found themselves compelled through the dwindling of their operating capital to resort to the banks for financial help. The price they paid was practically without exception the bitter one of losing independence. The most usual procedure has been conversion into a stock company and the taking over of a large block of the stocks by the bank appealed to. Some of the stocks would be sold at the market price but some, usually enough for control, would be kept in the securities portfolio of the bank. Other firms, already incorporated before the war, also fell into the sphere of influence of the banks as a part of new issues was sold to them after the war.'[39] It was calculated that the number of firms controlled by the ten largest Viennese banks rose between 1913 and 1923 by at least ten to fifteen per cent, and it was noted that the new, smaller banks in particular were at pains to build up an 'industrial empire'. '(But) the bigger and older banks have not been so taken up with that kind of business as the newly founded smaller banks, many of which concentrated their efforts into forming "Konzerne", i.e., groups of industrial enterprises at least partially under their control.'[40]

An interesting point is that the issuing activities of the major banks were not confined to their home ground, but included enterprises in the Successor States and to some extent in Germany and western Europe.[41] In some fields, like banking or the oil industry, the foreign investments seem to have been undertaken with a long term view in mind. Not infrequently the interest in a promotion was the outcome of participation in a foreign financial concern. The ratio of Credit-anstalt's new domestic to foreign commitments developed as follows:[42]

Table 77   Important Creditanstalt promotions and participations, 1919–23

	1919	1920	1921	1922	1923	1919–1923
Domestic	4	6	13	10	12	45
Foreign	5	9	8	7	6	35

These acquisitions were, from a *qualitative* standpoint, offset by losses leading to an impairment of the structure of the industrial groups controlled by the banks. In the Successor States it was precisely the biggest and the most important undertakings affiliated to the major Viennese banks that were affected by the waves of 'nationaliz-ation' identical in many cases – as we have shown – with a transition of control to Western capital: Skodawerke, Breitfeld, Danek & Co.,

Vereinigte Maschinenfabriken at Prague, the mining and Metallurgic Company in Czechoslovakia, Stabilimento Tecnico Triestino, Austrian Lloyd and Austro-Americana in northern Italy, Krainische Industriegesellschaft in Yugoslavia, Resita-Werke (as part of the STEG Company) in Romania, and so on.[43] The loss of these substantial interests reflects primarily the banks' inability to assist these large firms with a sufficient amount of loans.[44] Through the Amstelbank, founded in 1920, and thanks to its excellent inter-national connections, Creditanstalt was no doubt better able than the rest to maintain its position abroad. But in view of unfavourable exchange rates and its drastically reduced capital resources it could hardly have been able to meet the credit requirements of, say, Skodawerke or Vereinigte Maschinenfabriken over a longer period.

Yet, all in all, the big houses did successfully manage to defend a considerable portion of their old sphere of influence in the Successor States, especially in the sugar and textile industries. During the years of inflation a cautious counter-offensive was being prepared through the acquisition of new interests. In the immediate post-1918 period the conversion of former branches into independant institutes and the subscriptions for sizeable quotas of share capital issued by the new domestic banks secured fresh, strategically important positions. However, without the injection of substantial Western capital in the form of participations and, even more important, extremely flexible short-term loans, the Viennese banks' traditional role in the Danube area could scarcely have been continued during the 1920s.[45]

The changes in the structure of industrial assets held by the banks between 1913 and 1923 can be illustrated by the example of Creditanstalt.[46] The indicators adduced for this analysis are of a very rough quantitative nature, they nevertheless admit of certain con-clusions (bearing in mind the criteria of quality noted above) regarding the altered composition of interests contained in the Bank's portfolio or booked as securities held under syndicate agreements.[47]

The number of enterprises belonging to the Creditanstalt group had by 1923 increased to 136 as against 102 in 1913. Only 57 of those who in the latter year had been in a close relationship with the Bank still belonged to its sphere of influence in 1923.[48] A number of larger share packets, including interests in 'Tisita' Waldexploitations AG, Ostrauer Bergbau AG, Mürztaler Holzstoff AG., Wilsdorfer Gerbextraktwerke AG, and Österreichische Hypothekenbank, were sold during the war.[49-53] Other firms, like Brünner Stearinkerzen-Fabriken and the textile firm Gebrüder Rosenthal AG, were during the same time liquidated.[54-55] An entirely false picture would result from a purely arithmetical comparison of the interests in the machine-building and metal goods industry where, as far as numbers went, there was practically no change. In reality only twelve of the companies who in 1913 had been part of the group still belonged to it after the war. Precisely the most important and largest had been lost. Also the regional distribution had shifted as can be seen from the following figures showing the location of the major production plants:

	Austria	Successor States (incl. Italy)
1913	6	14
1923	10	9

Table 78 Composition of the Creditanstalt Group, 1913 and 1923 (Number of Participations)

Sector	1913	1923	Retained since 1913	New Participations and/or Promotions
Banking	5	20	2	18
Insurance	4	3	2	1
Commerce, Transport, Other Services	8	13	3	10
Oil Industry	3	10	2	8
Mining/Foundries	5	6	2	4
Machine-Building & Metal Goods Industry	20	19	12	7
Electrical Industry & Power Stations	5	5	3	2
Build. Materials & Ind.	6	7	4	3
Textile Industry	8	7[a]	5	2
Misc. Consumer Goods	4	7	3	4
Foodstuffs Industry	1	3	1	2
Spirits Industry	7	7	5	2
Breweries	4	4	4	—
Chemical Industry	7	7	4	3
Paper Industry	6	5	2	3
Timber and Wood-Working Industry	4	5	2	3
	6	8[b]	2	6
Total	103	136	57	69[c]

[a] Incl. 2 holding companies
[b] Incl. 1 holding company
[c] The difference between this and the preceding table is that, in the latter, minority participations in syndicates for electrical concerns were also included.

The most striking change compared to 1913 relates to bank

interests. Only two institutes had been part of the Creditanstalt group before World War I, namely Österreichische Kontrollbank and Landesbank für Bosnien und Hercegovina. Three institutes (Kreditanstalt für Handel und Industrie at Ljubljana, Böhmische Escompte-Bank und Kreditanstalt, and Warschauer Disconto-Bank) had come into existence through the reorganization or change of status of former branches. The remaining fifteen represented Creditanstalt's post-war participations. The following compilation shows the regional distribution of Creditanstalt's banking interests:

Austria	6	Österreichische Kontrollbank für Handel und Industrie[56]
		Bankanstalt der Ersten österreichischen Sparkasse (promotion, 1922)[57]
		Steiermärkische Escomptebank (participation, 1922)[58]
		Erdöl-Industrie-Bank (promotion, 1920)[59]
		Österreichische Holzbank (participation, 1921)
		Allgemeine Montanbank (promotion, 1922)[60]
Jugoslavia	4	Landesbank für Bosnien und Hercegovina[61]
		Kreditanstalt für Handel und Industrie, Ljubljana (promotion, 1919)[62]
		Kroatische Allgemeine Kreditbank (participation, 1921)[63]
		Agrar- und Industriebank, Belgrade (promotion, 1923)
Poland	3	Warschauer Disconto-Bank (promotion, 1919)[64]
		Galizische Aktien-Hypothekenbank (promotion, 1919)[65]
		Schlesische Kredit-Anstalt (promotion, 1921)[66]
Czechoslovakia	2	Böhmische Escompte-Bank und Kreditanstalt (promotion, 1919)[67]
		Slowakische Allgemeine Kreditbank (promotion, 1921)[68]
Romania	1	Rumänische Creditbank (promotion, 1923)[69]
Bulgaria	1	Banque Balkanique (participation, 1916)[70]
Germany and Western Europe	3	Amstelbank (promotion, 1920)
		Bank für auswärtigen Handel (participation, 1922)[71]
		Société Financière Danubienne (Swiss investment trust) (participation, 1923)[72]

In 1923 the Bank's interests in the oil industry held an important place among its industrial holdings. In the case of the enterprises comprised in the sector 'Commerce, Transport, Other Services' the emphasis had shifted to commercial establishments. (Interests in the shipping companies now located in Italy were sold in 1919.) In the electrical industry the shares of Österreichische Elektrizitäts-Lieferungs AG and of Kerka-Werke (in Czechoslovakia and Yugoslavia respectively) had been unloaded and replaced by connections with the new Austrian hydroelectric power companies.[73] In 1913 the main weight of the industrial group had lain in the capital goods sector; by 1923 this trend had been accentuated.

Table 79   Creditanstalt Group breakdown (no. of enterprises)

	Capital Goods Industries	Consumer Goods Industries
1913	48	37
1923	60	40

To assess the Bank's business policy in post-war years the distribution of its spheres of influence in Austria and abroad – the Successor States, in particular – is of importance. For this purpose it is not a matter of the firm's headquarters which is crucial, but the location of the main centres of operation.

Table 80   Creditanstalt Group, 1923 geographical distribution (no. of enterprises)

	in Austria	Abroad
Industrial Enterprises	36	64
All Group Enterprises	54	82

Of all the major Viennese banks Creditanstalt seems in 1923 to have been the most active as regards the reorganization of its assets abroad.[74] This applies especially in the field of banking.[75] Other financial houses too, though, had to a remarkably high degree maintained their old ties with industrial enterprises now situated in the Successor States. A series of reports in 1924 by the American Consulate at Vienna to the State Department makes this apparent.[76] Most of the foreign undertakings with which the domestic banking world had closer relations lay in industrially more highly developed Czechoslovakia. On its heels followed Hungary, Yugoslavia, and Poland. By sectors the pivotal ones were machine-building and metal goods (52 participations, according to American reckoning), banking (51), mining and foundries (41), textiles (40), chemicals (31), electrical goods and electricity supply companies (23), building materials and the construction industry (21).[77] For individual banks, taking the number of their interests as a gauge, the emphasis was spread as follows:

Creditanstalt	Banking
	Machine-Building and Metal Goods
	Oil
	Timber and Wood-Working
Boden-Creditanstalt	Textiles
	Mining and Foundries
	Oil
	Machine-Building and Metal Goods
Niederösterreichische	Machine-Building and Metal Goods.
Escompte-Gesellschaft	Chemical
	Mining and Foundries
	Electrical Goods
Wiener Bankverein	Mining and Foundries
	Building Materials and Construction Industry
	Textiles
Österreichische	Machine-Building and Metal Goods
Länderbank	Banking
	Chemicals
Anglo-Österreichsiche	Machine-Building and Metal Goods
Bank	Mining and Foundries
	Banking

Table 81   Market values of the Viennese major Bank Groups (in $m.)

	Market Value 31.12.23	Market Value 1.10.24	1923 Balance Sheet Valuation of Portfolio Investments and Securities held under Syndicate Agreements[a]
Creditanstalt	34.7	13.7	4.0
Boden-Creditanstalt	28.7	11.5	3.4
Niederösterreichische Escompte-Gesellschaft	20.5	8.2	4.8
Wiener Bankverein	19.7	10.4	2.8

[a] Included among the portfolio investments and securities held under syndicate agreements were also other stocks, particularly League of Nations Loan holdings, hydroelectric corporation bonds, et cetera, so that this item cannot be directly compared with the value of group shares. An impression can however be gained of the order of magnitude of hidden reserves held by the banks.

The economic staff of the American Consulate tried to determine the market value of the shares kept by individual Viennese banks in their portfolios. As the basis of their calculations they took stock exchange quotations where available and for unlisted securities they used their own estimates. A 'normal' interest was assumed to be a fifteen per cent holding in industrial enterprises and a ten per cent one in banks. Were the quotas demonstrably higher, the corresponding values were allowed for.[78]

The foregoing table illustrates the dramatic drop in prices (on average some 60%) which in 1924 occurred on the Vienna Stock Exchange and which brought about an abrupt fall in the banks' hidden reserves. It was the first sign of the incipient crisis that was chronically to affect the Austrian banking system and, accompanied by a progressive immobilization of its resources, was to attain its climax with the convulsions experienced at the beginning of the 'Thirties.

The major Viennese banks had after the end of the war assumed the character of multinational concerns. On the one hand their field of operations extended to the new states, on the other hand in all of them Western capital had considerable interests. This feature was reflected in the composition in 1923 of the Creditanstalt Board on which the Hamburg banker Max Warburg sat as representative of the American banking group together with Oscar H. List, director of Guaranty Trust & Co., London.[79] Since summer 1920 there had existed alongside of the Board a 'Voting Committee', consisting of Warburg and one representative each of Creditanstalt and the American banks. It was responsible for important decisions at management level.[80] The interests of Böhmische Escompte-Bank und Kreditanstalt were entrusted to Director Otto Deutsch who in 1922 was co-opted on the Board.[81]

Louis Rothschild's election as Chairman took place on 29 July 1921. 'Baron Rothschild,' said Philipp Gomperz on that occasion, 'brings us the glamour of his family name, the international status of his dynasty, and above all the distinction of an outstanding personality. With the dreadful downfall of Austria nothing has survived in the esteem of people abroad other than the firm position of our major banks. By the acceptance of this election Baron Rothschild affirms not only his attachment to our establishment, but likewise fulfils a patriotic duty.'[82] The move was undoubtedly meant to impress the West with the fact that Creditanstalt, even under the new, so dramatically altered circumstances, enjoyed the backing of Europe's most respected private banking house. Since 1859, when Anselm

Rothschild had resigned the appointment of Creditanstalt's first vice-chairman, none of the family successors had been willing to play a leading part in the Bank's affairs although the firm S.M. v. Rothschild was always represented on its Board. It is probably a fair assumption that the Rothschilds attached importance to not being too closely identified with the policy of the leading major Austrian bank. Whether Louis Rothschild was well-advised to break with the old tradition of his house just at a time of reorientation and general uncertainty is a matter of opinion.

In 1923 Creditanstalt's management consisted of six members. Ludwig von Neurath was at the head and his most important task at this juncture was undoubtedly the reorganization of the industrial and financial empire spread all over the Successor States. Dr Paul Hammerschlag, perhaps the most notable among the leading personalities of the day, was mainly concerned with financial transactions. In addition he looked after legal and staff matters. Of the four other members, Friedrich Ehrenfest, Paul Lechner, Sigmund Löwy, and Wilhelm Regendanz, the last, who in wartime had in particular attended to business relations with the neutral and Balkan nations, retired in May 1923 for personal reasons, but shortly afterwards was co-opted on the Board.

In retrospect the year 1923 already manifested all the economic problems that were to lead to the crisis of the early 1930s. The difficulties revealed during the first year of stabilization, such as mass unemployment and a high degree of under-utilization of capacities, made themselves felt in later years too. They can be ascribed in our opinion mainly to two factors: the sluggish pace of Western and Central European economic development and the Successor States' highly protectionist commercial policy. A further element was that in a number of countries, including Austria, a strongly restrictive course was followed in economic policy, weakening still more the feeble upswing trends in the 1920s.

The deficit on Austria's balance of payments, which during the whole decade stood at a disquietingly high level, was the most important symptom of the country's chronic economic malaise. In this way it remained to a high degree dependent on the import of Western European and American capital. The inflow of foreign funds was reinforced by the fact that the banking system assumed the function of intermediary between East and West. The conversion of short term deposits from Western banks into long term loans to enterprises in the Successor States allowed the Viennese banks to maintain, at least in part, their old spheres of interest. On the other hand they became in growing measure dependent on the investment policy of Western banking capital. An international crisis, as certain contemporary observers asserted at an early date, could not but hit Austria with particular severity.

During the last three decades preceding 1918 the *crédit mobilier* character of the Austrian banking system had been the basis for the Empire's dynamic industrialization process. The generation of financial experts who had learnt their craft at this noontide of the economy naturally adhered to the 'missionary' role of banks even in the altered post-war circumstances. The close links between banking and industry had however fateful consequences for the former in the face of the adverse circumstances of the 1920s. The collapse of Creditanstalt in 1931 was the tragic climax to the admittedly necessary process of contraction and change in the pattern of banking practice that seven years before had begun with the liquidation of Allgemeine Depositenbank.

Notes

1 Richard Reisch, 'Aufgaben und Entwicklung der Österreichischen Nationalbank in den Jahren 1923 bis 1928', in *10 Jahre Wiederaufbau* (Vienna, 1928), p. 283.
2 Reisch, *Wiederaufbau*, p. 287. The Austrian National Bank's foreign exchange policy managed until 1931, the crisis year, to keep the exchange rate close to the legal parity.
3 In November and December 1922 the foreign exchange reserves rose by some £3.2 million or 45,000 million crowns, in 1923 by more than 3,100,000 million crowns. J. Walré de Bordes, *The Austrian Crown, Its Depreciation and Stabilization* (London, 1924), p. 205 et seq.
4 In 1923 only ten per cent of the foreign exchange inflow derived from tranches of bond issues accruing to the government. Walré de Bordes, *Austrian Crown*, p. 207.
5 In absolute terms the banknote circulation rose by more than 3,100,000 millions to 7,100,000 million crowns.
6 J. M. Keynes, *A Tract on Monetary Reform* (London, 1923), p. 36.
7 Alexander Spitzmüller, 'Die Geldwertpolitik der Öesterreichischen National- bank', *Mitteilungen des Verbandes österreichischer Banken und Bankiers* (1924), p. 81 et seq., and *Neue Freie Presse*, 26 January 1924.
8 Richard Reisch, 'Stabilisierung oder Steigerung des Kronenwertes' and 'Meine Replik in causa "Geldwertpolitik" ', both in *Mitteilungen*, pp. 1 et seq. and 93 et seq. respectively.
9 Reisch, *Mitteilungen*, p. 93.
10 *Neue Freie Presse*, 30 January 1924.
11 Ludwig von Mises, 'Über Deflationspolitik', *Mitteilungen*, p. 16.

12 Otto Bauer, 'Die Wirtschaftskrise in Österreich. Ihre Ursachen – ihre Heilung', Werkausgabe, Vol. III, p. 253 et seq.

13 In 1923 the export of rails to Germany went up more than 30,000 tons, due mainly to deliveries by Alpine-Montan to the Prussian State Railways. Cf. *Arbeit und Wirtschaft*, 15 February 1923, col. 159. The economic effects of the occupation of the Ruhr are described in detail in *Der Österreichische Volkswirt* from 20 January 1923 onward.

14 *Arbeit und Wirtschaft*, 15 March 1923, col. 192.

15 Victor Kienböck, *Das Österreichische Sanierungswerk* (Stuttgart, 1925), p. 27.

16 *Statistisches Handbuch für die Republik Österreich*, 1923.

17 Kienböck, *Sanierungswerk*, p. 44.

18 Karl Ausch, *Als die Banken fielen* (Vienna, 1968), p. 101 et seq.

19 Walther Federn, 'Die Kreditpolitik der Wiener Banken', *Schriften des Vereins für Sozialpolitik* (Munich-Leipzig, 1928) Vol. 169 p. 64.

20 'It became more and more difficult to procure money and tolerable conditions for legitimate production needs because people on the stock exchange, where high profits could be expected in a matter of days, were without a moment's thought ready to agree to, so to speak, any interest rate. The result was to deflect those members of the public, reduced in numbers anyway, not directly engaged in securities' dealings from the solid methods of savings capital formation and induce them to carry their money to bucket-shops and jobbing offices so as to invest in carry-over business (advances against the speculative purchase of stocks).' Cf. Viktor Brauneis, *Die Entwicklung der Österreichischen National-bank* (Vienna, 1924), memorandum prepared for the information of the League of Nations delegates.

21 Ausch, *Als die Banken fielen*, p. 120.

22 A really satisfactory explanation for the negligible revaluation of bank shares is difficult to find.

23 Walther Federn reports that small banks had to procure resources for carrying on business by acceptance on the stock exchange of call money and weekly deposits against collateral, and were paying rates of thirty to fifty per cent interest. These funds were then passed, with suitable premium of course, to their customers. Cf. Federn *Schriften*, p. 64.

24 The rates for credits in foreign currency were distinctly lower than for crown loans. In 1923 sterling credits were obtainable at about 8%. Cf. *Mitteilungen des Direktoriums der Österreichischen Nationalbank* 1923 (Nos. 1, 4, 5–7) and 1924 (No. 1).

25 Walther Schmidt, 'Die Sparkassen', *Schriften des Vereins für Sozialpolitik* (Munich-Leipzig, 1925), Vol. 169, p. 28.

26 Federn, *Schriften*, p. 64.

27 *Der Österreichische Volkswirt*, 14 April 1923, p. 726 et seq.

28 *Der österreichische Volkswirt*, p. 727. Apart from the supply and demand factors, Stolper cites the international agio business which also attracted considerable funds.

29 *Arbeit und Wirtschaft*, 15 September 1923, col. 685 et seq.

30 *Statistisches Handbuch*, 3rd and 4th years of publication.

31 *Statistisches Handbuch*.

32 In 1923 the number of visitors to Viennese hotels dropped by about 26,000 to 413,849. Cf. *Statistisches Handbuch*, Vol. III and IV.

33 *Statistisches Handbuch*, ibid.
34 Friedrich Hertz, *Zahlungsbilanz und Lebensfähigkeit Österreichs* (Munich, 1925), p. 33.
35 Microfilm Publication No. 695, *Records of Department of State Relating to Internal Affairs of Austria-Hungary and Austria 1910–1929*, Roll 51/C. 504 et seq., US Consulate, Vienna, to Department of State, 10 September 1924, National Archives, Washington. (Present author's italics.)
36 In 1921 already 'there were at times such big turnovers on the Stock Exchange that the registry could no longer work in an orderly fashion; the brokers were able to fix the price only two hours after the closure.' Franz Baltzarek, *Die Geschichte der Wiener Börse* (Vienna, 1973), p. 119.
37 *State Department Records*, 51/C. 459 US Consulate, Vienna, to Department of State, 1 February 1924. Oskar Morgenstern, 'Kapital- und Kurswertveränderungen der an der Wiener Börse notierten österreichischen Aktiengesellschaften 1913 bis 1930', *Zeitschrift für Nationalökonomie* (Vienna, 1932), p. 252, came to a different conclusion. He put the market value of shares belonging to Austrian enterprises in 1913 at over 4,100 million schillings (about $840 million). The comparable values in 1923 are missing in his compilation and he gives only the actual earnings on the capital increases, 1913–1923. According to *Compass*, 1925, Vol. I, p. 1,635, the total of domestic and foreign shares listed on the Vienna Stock Exchange was 273 in 1913 and 429 in 1923.
38 State Department Records, 51/C. 459 et seq. The development 1919–1923 can also be judged from the following compilation (Baltzarek, *Geschichte*, pp. 121 and 124):

	Requests to Vienna Stock Exchange for			
	New Listings		Admission of Capital Increases	
	Settled	Pending	Settled	Pending
1919	33	12	22	18
1920	22	12	84	47
1921	50	30	167	34
1922	84	13	236	25
1923	68	not known	151	not known

39 *State Department Records*, 51/C. 508, US Consulate, Vienna, to Department of State, 10 September 1924. The conversion of private firms into joint-stock companies often proceeded not entirely free from pressure by banks. One example is the motor-car company Perl which in 1923 became a joint-stock company with Creditanstalt assistance. See Ehrenfest Proceedings, Vienna Provincial Court, Case File 26d Vr. 6373/31–37.
40 *State Department Records*, 51/C. 459, US Consulate, Vienna, to Department of State, 1 February 1924.
41 The export of capital to Germany and the West in the form of direct investments began on a larger scale only after the crown's stabilization. 'In recent weeks', noted *Der Österreichische Volkswirt*, 11 November 1922, 'a development for which the way has been long prepared has attracted general attention – the

participation of Viennese banks and banking firms in Berlin (market affairs). It is not long ago since the movement of capital proceeded in the opposite direction . . . Now the page appears to have been turned and fresh cases of participation in Berlin firms by Viennese houses are constantly becoming known.' Special reference was made to Creditanstalt's participation in the Bank für auswärtigen Handel, Berlin.

42 Compiled from information in *Compass*, 1925, Vol. I, Creditanstalt Annual Reports 1912–1923, and company balance sheet commentaries in *Der Österreichische Volkswirt*. By 'notable' promotions and participations are meant industrial enterprises with more than 100 employees and banks of more than local importance.

43 See Part IV Ch. 3, p. 348 et seq.

44 'During the period of inflation the Viennese banks were in no position to extend loans to foreign enterprises . . . Only after stabilization of the . . . currency were creditor-debtor relations resumed on a larger scale.' Walther Federn, 'Der Zusammenbruch der Österreichischen Kreditanstalt', *Archiv für Sozialwissenschaft und Sozialpolitik* (Tübingen, 1932), Vol. 67. p. 410.

45 As early as 1926 the university lecturer Sigmund Schilder gave warning of the dangers inherent in this policy. 'What must indeed not be overlooked is that the numerous short-term loans extended in particular during 1925 must always, because of the possibility of their immediate recall or non-renewal, darken the Austrian sky like a thundercloud.' Sigmund Schilder, *Der Streit um die Lebensfähigkeit Österreichs* (Stuttgart, 1926), p. 21.

46 For 1913 see Part I, Ch. 6 p. 160 et seq. The criteria mentioned there have been applied to determine the banks' sphere of influence in industry.

47 As share capital and declared reserves at the time of inflation represent a barely comparable order of magnitude, their citation as a criterion has been deliberately omitted. A comparison of that kind would seem to make sense only after the establishment of balances in terms of gold.

48 They included several cases of company mergers and of holding companies that controlled a number of enterprises which were in the Bank's ownership in 1913.

49 Supplement 'Die Bilanzen', *Der Österreichische Volkswirt*, 21 June 1919, p. 146.

50 Österreichische Berg- und Hüttenwerke in 1916 acquired the Bank's holding (14,000 shares) through Boden-Creditanstalt. See *Compass*, 1920, Vol. I, p. 1,332.

51 The shares majority was purchased in 1917 by a syndicate including Nettingsdorfer Papierfabrik A.G. and Carl Schweizer A.G. See *Festschrift der Österreichischen Wirtschaftsunternehmungen im Interessenkreis der Creditanstalt-Bankverein. Als Ehrung für Generaldirektor Dr. Josef Joham zum 60. Geburtstag* (Vienna, 1949), p. 173.

52 In 1918 the shares passed into the the hands of Anglo-Österreichische Bank and Verkehrsbank. See *Compass*, 1920, Vol. I, p. 1,421.

53 Verkehrsbank acquired the shares majority in 1918. See *Compass*, 1921, Vol. I., p. 199.

54 *Der Österreichische Volkswirt*, 3 April 1915, p. 440.

55 See *Compass*, 1920, Vol. I., p. 713.

56 Together with other major Austrian banks.

57 Interest probably 50%.

58 Chief shareholder was Niederösterreichische Escompte-Gesellschaft. Other

major shareholders were Böhmische Unionbank and Bayerische Vereinsbank (about 9%). Creditanstalt's interest, together with Amstelbank, was about 10%.

59 Joint promotion with Bankhaus Hardy & Co. Ges.m.b.h., Berlin.

60 Together with foreign firms and banks.

61 With Wiener Bankverein and Ungarische Allgemeine Kreditbank.

62 Probably a majority holding.

63 Promoted by Boden-Creditanstalt. Participation together with Böhmische Escompte-Bank und Kreditanstalt ('Bebka').

64 A 30% interest.

65 A 30% interest.

66 Promoted with Warschauer Disconto-Bank and Silesian industrialists.

67 A 22.5% interest. Chief shareholder was Živnostenská banka; another big shareholder was Niederösterreichische Escompte-Gesellschaft. Minority holdings were also in the hands of Kuhn, Loeb & Co., M. M. Warburg & Co., International Acceptance Bank, Banque de Bruxelles, and Kleinworth, Sons & Co., London.

68 Together with 'Bebka' und Ungarische Allgemeine Kreditbank.

69 Shares acquired from Anglo-Austrian Bank.

70 Participation in 1916 with Wiener Bankverein and Ungarische Allgemeine Kreditbank. After 1918 a French banking group exercised predominant influence.

71 Joint participation with Amstelbank and 'Bebka'.

72 Other shareholders included Ungarische Allgemeine Kreditbank, Ungarische Escompte- und Wechslerbank, and the London banking house Foster.

73 Creditanstalt's underwriting shares in the big domestic electricity enterprises were not considered to establish a sphere of influence inasmuch as they did not include any control rights over the firms in question.

74 The passivity of Boden-Creditanstalt's management met with criticism. Of all the big Vienna financial houses it had after the end of the war 'shown the least initiative' and 'provided no large enterprise with funds'. See Supplement 'Die Bilanzen', p. 89, Der Österreichische Volkswirt, 23 December 1922.

75 'Creditanstalt has not taken in hand the severance of branches simply as a necessary process of liquidation. It has, simultaneously and apparently in accordance with a clear plan, gone about putting its entire business on a broad international basis.' Supplement 'Die Bilanzen', p. 167, Der Österreichische Volkswirt, 16 July 1921.

76 State Department Records, 51/C. 540 et seq. The statements about the individual banking groups are nonetheless full of gaps. In the case of Creditanstalt only 90 participations are recorded instead of 135. Similarly the size of the Österreichische Länderbank group is likely to have been underestimated. The American data speak of 40 firms as against 69 quoted by Alice Teichova, 'Versailles and the Expansion of the Bank of England', Recht und Entwicklung der Grossunternehmen im 19. und frühen 20. Jahrhundert (Göttingen, 1979), p. 374.

77 Let it be once more stressed that the mere number of enterprises is of course simply a very rough gauge for analysing group structures.

78 State Department Records, 51/C. 541, 572, 616, 654, 657. The market value of Anglo-Österreichische Bank participations amounted at year-end 1923 to $13.6 million and those of Österreichische Länderbank to $15.3 million. Comparable figures for October 1924 are not available.

79 Until November 1922 Sigmund Metz acted as representative of the American banking houses. (See Board Minutes, 22 November 1922, Creditanstalt

Archives). But neither Metz nor List, his successor, took part in board meetings. During the whole of the period 1920–1923 Warburg attended only once.

80 Board Minutes, 14 June 1920, Creditanstalt Archives. Accounts or intimations of the Voting Committee's activities have not survived in the Bank's records.

81 Board Minutes, 22 November 1922, Creditanstalt Archives.

82 Board Minutes, 29 July 1921, Creditanstalt Archives. Rothschild's election seems to have followed a deeper involvement of the famous old banking house in Creditanstalt. On 5 January 1921 Dr Samuel M. Singer, head of the firm Samuel Singers Erben and chairman of A.G. der Baumwollspinnereien zu Theresienthal und Kleinmünchendorf, was co-opted and at the motion of Dr Otto Fuchs, proxy for the Rothschild banking house, definitively elected as a member of the board at the General Meeting held on 29 July 1921 (Ministry of Finance Archives, File 81.756/1921). On 25 October 1922 the board elected him to the Directors Committee on the chairman's proposal (Board Minutes, 25 October 1922, Creditanstalt Archives).

APPENDIX I

Documentation

1. Register of Shareholders entitled to vote at the 57th Ordinary General Meeting of Creditanstalt on 4 April 1913

Augenfeld J. Leo

Bäck Dr Adolf
Bankverein Schlesischer
Baum M.
Behrendt Max
Behrens L. & Söhne
Benedikt Norbert
Beruth Hans
Bisteghi Rudolf
Bjehavy Paul
Blum Julius
Boeger Paul
Bölke Wilhelm
Bogdanowicz Wiktorya
Breisach Eduard
Brunner Lucian
Burjas Josef

Cohnheim Willi

Demuth Karl
Doderer Wilhelm Ritter von
Domaszewski Dr Waclav

Eckel Dr Hermann
Economo G. & Figlio
Eichhorn Franz
Elsinger Friedrich
Engel F. A.
Ervin Koloman

Faber Moriz
Faltis Carl
Feuerstein Ignatz
Fisch Ignaz
Fischel Arthur
Flandrak Carl
Frankl Ignatz
Freise Conrad
Friedl Carl
Fritz Carl
Fürth Ed.
Fürth Dr Hugo

Gartenberg Josef
Gerlach Ernst
Gerngross Albert
Gerngross Hugo
Gerngross Paul

Gerngross Robert
Gerstl Emil
Gerstmann Alois
Gomperz Max Ritter von
Gomperz Dr Philipp
  Ritter von
Gotthelf Benno
Gottlieb Heinrich
Gross Dr Siegfried
Gruder Dr Ludwig
Grünbaum Julius
Grünwald & Co.

Hafner Rudolf
Hardegg Franz Graf,
  Exzellenz
Hilbich Friedrich
Hinrichs Wilhelm
Hofmann Albert
Hofmannsthal Dr Emil
  Edler von
Hofmannsthal Ivan
  Edler von
Homolka Robert Oskar
Horowitz Eduard
Horváth Elemér von

Janotta Heinrich

Kanitz Otto
Karplus Dr Siegmund
Kaufmann Josef
Keinz Josef
Kern Robert
Khuen-Belasi Dr Karl Graf
Klein Ign.
Klein Julius
Königsgarten Ludwig
Kohn Julius
Kornfeld Dr Felix
Kornfeld Dr Ignaz
Kornfeld Baron Paul
Kovács Géza
Kroll Otto
Krupp Arthur
Krzisch Baltasar
Kubinzky Albrecht, Marquis
  von Hohenkubin
Kuffler Dr Karl

Langer Leopold

Lederer Dr Moriz
Lévai Ignácz
Lichtenstern Michael
Lieben Richard
Lieske Oswald
Löw Richard
Löwy Leopold
Löwy Moritz
Lukács Josef von

Margulies Dr Otto
Mastny Heinrich August
Mauthner Dr Hans
  Ritter von
Mauthner J.
May Leopold von
Medinger Eduard
Medinger Hans Edler von
Medinger Dr Wilhelm von
Mendelssohn & Co.
Mendl Max
Mérey Alexander von
  Kaposmére, Exzellenz
Mikosch Dr Ignaz
Miller Vinzenz Ritter von
  und zu Aichholz
Müller Heinrich
Münzer David

Neumann Alois
Nostitz-Rieneck Erwein Graf,
  Exzellenz

Pacher von Theinburg
  Friedrich
  Exzellenz
Pacher von Theinburg Gustav
Pallavicini Eduard, Mark-
  graf, Exzellenz
Parnas Dr Josef
Pereira-Arnstein Hans Frei-
  herr von
Philippsohn J.
Pichler & Schück
Pollack Leopold Edler von
  Parnegg
Pollak Richard
Prager Gustav

Quittner Max

Redlich Carl
Regenhart Ernst
Reich Dr Otto von
Robitschek Stefan
Rode Leon
Róna Sigmund
Rosenbaum Julius
Roth Max
Rothschild Baron Louis
Rothschild S. M. v.
Ruzička Dr Alois

Sapieha, Fürstin Mathilde,
  Durchlaucht
Sarlós Sigmund
Schelhammer & Schattera
Schey Paul Freiherr von
  Koromla
Schoeller & Co.
Schostal Wilhelm
Schostall Adolf
Schramek Ad.

Schreiber Alexander von
Schwarz Hugo
Schwarz Julius
Schweiger Alois
Sebesta Klaudius
Sietz Felix
Singer J. H. Nachfolger
Singer Dr S. M.
Skoda Karl Ritter von
Smolin Aurel
Sobotka Josef
Spanner A. C.
Spiro Dr Rudolf
Spitzer Dr Alfred
Steinhauser Dr Robert
Stern Gustav
Stukhart Leopold

Tannenberger Hermann
Taussig Dr Hugo
Taussig S.
Teubner Carl

Theimer Dr Stanislaus
Thielecke Julius

Ullmann Adolf von
Unger Josef

Wagenmann Otto
Wagner Wilhelm von,
Wahlberg Friedrich
Wečerz Wilhelm
Weiss Dr Adolf Ritter von
  Tessbach
Weisweiller Dr Moriz
Werner Sigmund
Wiesenburg Adolf von
Winternitz Max
Wollheim Ludwig
Wollisch Ignaz

Zarda Heinrich
Zidek Karl
Živnostenská banka, Filiale
  wien

Source: AVA Ministry of the Interior 254/1910

2. Attendance List of Shareholders at the Extraordinary General Meeting of Creditanstalt on 2 March 1911

The shareholders whose names are marked with a cross, accounting for 599 shares in all, were no longer represented at the 1913 Meeting

Shareholder	On Own Behalf	As Proxy	Total Votes	Proxy Holder
Weiss Julius	24+		24	
Pollack Leopold Edler von Parnegg	9		9	
Pollack Bernhard	4+		4	
Klein Ignaz	2		2	
Basch Dr M.	1+		1	
Farchy Sal. R.	2+		2	
Remhart Anton	1+		1	
Flandrak Karl	6		6	
Schostal Wilhelm	4		4	
Berlyak Franz	16+		16	
Hofmann & Co.	4		4	
Pacher von Theinburg Friedrich	16		16	
Wolf Ernst	12+		12	
Ernst Dr Adolf Ritter von	5+		5	
Goldberg Dr Adolf	2+		2	
Laden H.	2+		2	
Münzer David	30		30	
Lechner Dr Max	3+		3	
Schreiber Alexander von	2		2	
Schoeller & Co.	4		4	
Goetz Dr Rudolf	1+		1	
Bjehavy Paul	1		1	
Forster Felix F.	7+		7	
Demuth Karl	4		4	
Wiess Dr Adolf Ritter von Tessbach	22		22	
Fürth Dr Emil Ritter von	1+	229	230	
Kovács Geza	20			Dr Emil Ritter von Fürth
Róna Sigmund	20			Dr Emil Ritter von Fürth
Lévai Ignácz	20			Dr Emil Ritter von Fürth
Kornfeld Paul Baron	16			Dr Emil Ritter von Fürth
Sebesta Klaudius	16			Dr Emil Ritter von Fürth
Erwin Koloman	16+			Dr Emil Ritter von Fürth
Lücke Paul	121+			Dr Emil Ritter von Fürth
Lamel Victor	4+		4	
Kollin Karl	1+		1	
Medinger Hans Edler von	2		2	
Thomasberger Carl	3+		3	
Blau Heinrich A.	8+		8	
Thuretzky Moritz	1+		1	
Hofmannsthal Ivan Edler von	4		4	
Hofmannsthal Dr Emil Edler von	1		1	
Fischer Robert	2+		2	

Shareholder	On Own Behalf	As Proxy	Total Votes	Proxy Holder
Fürth Ed.	4		4	
Faber Carl	8+		8	
Sobotka Josef	18		18	
Medinger Eduard	8		8	
Friedl Julius	1		1	
Mauthner Dr Hans Ritter von	10		10	
Fritz Karl	4	444	448	
Rothschild Louis Freiherr von	40			Karl Fritz
Pollak Richard	4			Karl Fritz
Rothschild S. M. v.	400			Karl Fritz
Czerny Heinrich	2+		2	
Fürth Dr Hugo	84	64	148	
Lukács Joseph von	32			Dr Hugo Fürth
Klein Julius	32			Dr Hugo Fürth
Schubert Franz	4+		4	
Dostal Josef	2+		2	
Schramek Adolf	20		20	
Philippsohn J.	1+		1	
Schmid Johann	1+		1	
Schneider Adolf	1+		1	
Lenz Guido von	1+		1	
Wölfler S.	4+		4	
Feldmann Brüder	10+		10	
Helbig Carl	8+		8	
Stein Ignaz J.	4+		4	
Barber Dr Max	2+		2	
Hardegg Franz Graf	2		2	
Krupp Arthur	2		2	
Lederer Dr Moriz	2		2	
May Leopold von	2		2	
Mérey von Kaposmére Alexander, Exzellenz	2		2	
Schey Freiherr von Koromla Paul	2		2	
Gomperz Dr Philipp Ritter von	80		80	
Reich Dr Otto von	40	34	74	
Nostitz-Reineck Erwein Graf, Exzellenz	34			Dr Otto von Reich
Spiro Dr Rudolf	40	190	230	
Wiesenburg Adolf von	10			Dr Rudolf Spiro
Kohn Ernst	21+			Dr Rudolf Spiro
Janotta Heinrich	40			Dr Rudolf Spiro
Vitali Lazaro	20+			Dr Rudolf Spiro
Pacher von Theinburg Gustav	20			Dr Rudolf Spiro
Behrens L. & Söhne	17			Dr Rudolf Spiro
Gerlach Ernst	10			Dr Rudolf Spiro
Freise Conrad	8			Dr Rudolf Spiro
Lieske Oswald	3			Dr Rudolf Spiro
Bankverein Schlesischer	40			Dr Rudolf Spiro
Heimann E.	1+			Dr Rudolf Spiro
Winternitz Max	60	34	94	
Ullmann Adolf von	2			Max Winternitz
Horváth Elemér von	32			Max Winternitz

Shareholder	On Own Behalf	As Proxy	Total Votes	Proxy Holder
Doderer Wilhelm Ritter von	120	177	297	
Brecher Dr Franz	4+			Wilhelm Ritter von Doderer
Janotta Heinrich	5			Wilhelm Ritter von Doderer
Gögl Zeno	1+			Wilhelm Ritter von Doderer
Pallavicini Eduard, Markgraf, Exzellenz	2			Wilhelm Ritter von Doderer
Stern Gustav	40			Wilhelm Ritter von Doderer
Ullmann Adolf von	40			Wilhelm Ritter von Doderer
Mendelssohn & Co.	76			Wilhelm Ritter von Doderer
Feuerstein Ignatz	7			Wilhelm Ritter von Doderer
Fisch Samuel	2+			Wilhelm Ritter von Doderer
Margulies Dr Otto	48		48	
Bisteghi Rudolf	24		24	
Breisach Eduard	24		24	
Langer Leopold	24		24	
Schwarz Julius	24		24	
Feldmann Alphons	40+		40	
Elsinger Friedrich	20	258	278	
Mendelssohn & Co.	80			Friedrich Elsinger
Kohn Ernst	178+			Friedrich Elsinger
Karplus Dr Siegmund	20		20	
Kohn Julius	20		20	
Robitschek Stefan	20		20	
Kaufmann Josef	20		20	
Gross Dr Siegfried	20		20	
Kornfeld Dr Felix	20		20	
Kornfeld Dr Ignaz	20		20	
Löwy Leopold	20		20	
Taussig Dr Hugo	20		20	
Weissweiler Dr Moriz	20		20	
Blum Julius	34	84	118	
Mendelssohn & Co.	45			Julius Blum
Cohn Georg	16+			Julius Blum
Hinrichs Wilhelm	13			Julius Blum
Boeger Paul	10			Julius Blum
Faber Moriz	34		34	
Benedikt Norbert	34		34	
Gomperz Max Ritter von	42		42	
Mikosch Dr Ignaz	34		34	
Wollheim Ludwig	34		34	
			2890	

Source: *1913 Creditanstalt Annual Report*, Creditanstalt Archives.

3. Joseph Schumpeter: The Basic Lines of Financial Policy for Now and the Next Three Years (Vienna, 1919)*

I

The foremost principle of financial policy must be that *not a single bank or treasury note that directly or indirectly serves to meet the government's needs may continue to be issued*. German-Austria has unquestionably reached the stage where any further issue of unbacked paper money will lead to a state of utter anarchy. The economy's productive activity can only begin again when a stop has been put to the depreciation of money and the consequent economic demoralization.

The touchstone for any financial policy in Austria today is whether it can meet the government's needs *without the issue of paper money*. If it can, it is correct. If it cannot, it is a further step along the road to disintegration of the productive capacity and of the social order.

II

The first and immediate care of financial policy must therefore be to meet government expenditure in the coming years without the issue of paper money.

Restoration of the economy, given intensive application on the part of all, will require a period of three, possibly four years. Until then the state faces expenditure that has risen on a gigantic scale, without current income approaching anything like sufficiency.

Putting the budget in final working order is a long-term task if the economy is not to be throttled. Nonetheless this objective must now already be attempted sincerely and straightforwardly. Every measure directed towards this goal would however be so much paperwork if it were meanwhile necessary to issue, directly or indirectly, fiduciary money to meet current needs.

The war has fleeced us and the Peace Treaty imposes an annual interest burden of 250,000 million crowns. Properly to appreciate what this figure means, it has to be realized that before 1914 the Austrian Empire's total revenue (after deduction of the state enterprises' running costs) amounted to 200,000 millions. On a per capita reckoning German-Austria's share was 500 millions, with interest on the public debt accounting for only 110 millions. So German-Austria's national debt interest has increased *more than*

*Slightly abbreviated version of the original document.

566

twentyfold. It represents more than fivefold the former overall tax capacity although it is in fact mainly a matter of domestic indebtedness where interest payment and redemption render the economy no poorer.

Naturally the enfeebled economy's reaction to such an excessive burden is monetary depreciation. That causes other official expenditure to shoot sky-high. Salaries and wages have to be raised so as to allow civil servants to pay for the bare necessities of life with the deteriorated currency. Apart from this, the economy's stagnation through war and defeat means that subsidies of every kind (to uphold existence during the period of transition) must be continued until such time as the economy has adjusted itself to the upheaval. At present the annual deficit probably involves 8,000 million crowns. *Grant the state's employees salaries corresponding to no more than a fraction of current monetary value* – which *has* to be done, if the state machine is to function – and we are confronted by a deficit of approximately 11,000 millions, many times over the former public debt's interest cost, albeit in depreciated currency.

True, it can be assumed, without being excessively optimistic, that within the coming three years a considerable portion of this deficit will on the expenditure side be reduced and a part, even if a smaller one, be met from the revenue side. But the conclusion to be drawn from expert calculations is that during the next three to four years, until the economy's recovery and the restoration of an orderly budget, the state will require *20,000 millions*, which will have to be raised without paper money and will not be provided by the state's own revenues.

III

There is only one way to meet this immense need and to arrive at orderly conditions – through credit. *The problem of financial policy today is the problem of credit. All financial policy must be put at the service of credit.*

IV

It is not however the state alone that needs credit. So, above all, does the economy. Stocks have been exhausted, the agricultural capital investments impoverished and pillaged, industry stripped of all raw materials. The nation has to import foodstuffs and raw materials and it cannot pay for these imports with its own production before production is again in full swing.

For the state to help itself solely through *domestic* credit would be insufficient, even if it could be done, which is more than doubtful. Even supposing that it were possible by way of domestic credit to stop the source of domestic disruption and not to issue any more paper money, this state of affairs would necessarily lead to the economy's total decline. The economy must pay for its imports. As long as it cannot do so from current receipts and from production, the burden on our foreign exchange will be intolerable and not capable of being compensated by any other means but the foreign acquisition at an increasingly cheaper price of our national resources, our shares, estates, buildings, art treasures – in other words, the economy would have to pay for its current needs from its *capital*. That means the nation's dispossession, the inflow of foreign capital to expropriate, not to stimulate, the economy, and thus the extirpation of the roots from which in better days the state could derive the strength to prosper again. Meanwhile the rate of exchange would inevitably drop ever further, the level of prices in general be driven up ever further, the claims on the state swell ever more, and the issue of paper money become imperative over and over again.

Only the procurement of credit *abroad* can avert this danger, and that only if our national wealth is not acquired by foreign countries, but foreign credit is extended on account of our economy's national wealth.

It is a matter of obtaining foreign assets in sufficient quantity to meet the requirements of the economy till working activity has been fully resumed. Herein lies the sole means for the restoration of our economic life. No foreign assets, then no stabilization of our currency and no restoration of an orderly budget. The other way about, first to proceed towards order at home and then to obtain credit abroad, means being bled dry, which has happened often enough before with financial policy. The vicious circle of errors – no foreign credit, no domestic order; no domestic order, no foreign credit – must be broken. The nation *must* find foreign credit, however heavy the sacrifices it imposes on itself and on its people.

V

The problem having been identified, it is in the first place clear what must *not* be allowed to happen.

Any policy that seeks by way of any *force majeure* (national bankruptcy, coupon tax, diminution of banknotes' or government bonds' face value) to nullify what has irreversibly occurred will result in ruin. The burden of debt imposed on our country through the war and its unhappy outcome *must be accepted. Spontaneously and of our own accord, on whatever pretext, not to recognize our obligation would mean complete ruin of our credit standing.* Should we seriously consider such a measure, we would in coming years be unable to obtain a single loan. A country capable of completely rehabilitating its economy through bankruptcy might perhaps risk such a step. On the other hand, a country that, in order to achieve such rehabilitation, *first* NEEDS *a loan, cannot be allowed* to indulge itself in bankruptcy. Everything that impairs credit-worthiness makes recovery impossible.[1]

It is not true that monetary depreciation is inherently a declaration of bankruptcy. Not only for us is monetary depreciation a fact of life, but, even if to a lesser extent, for the victorious and neutral nations too. Only with the help of credit, which forbids us to adopt a policy of bankruptcy, can we – in so far as it is possible at all – counter this evil and all the others that it brings upon us.

[1] Among the questions needing to be approached solely from the viewpoint of the paramount credit problem is the treatment of the War Loan.

Not only would curtailment of the coupon rate be a suicidal breach of credit standing, but so would the acceptance of war bonds in tax payment at a price lower than that of their issue.

Whether or not War Loan is acceptable as payment for taxation depends on the state's financial situation, its monetary exigencies. Nobody can either force or even expect the state prematurely to repay money lent to it through such acceptance in lieu of ordinary payment. What however constitutes disguised bankruptcy is for the state to accept in payment the claim on itself only at a DIMINISHED VALUE. For a state to invite new loans from its nationals precisely at the moment when it repudiates its own bonds and wants to pay less for them than it originally obtained would be as useless as it would be unseemly. For its acceptance of the War Loan in payment there is *only one rate for the state to recognize*, and that is the RATE OF ISSUE which it received itself.

VI

Currently, whether at home or abroad, the state lacks credit completely. To hope that foreign governments could help us by backing loans politically would be a mistake. The claims of America's own allies have priority over ours. Many years would pass until it was our turn. All that can be hoped for is *private* initiative among the Entente Powers. Private assistance, though, demands interest and confidence on the part of business.

At present there is no such confidence in our country. No confidence whatever either in our country's domestic affairs or in its financial reliability.

Precisely that is why it is Utopian to hope *just now* that the state will obtain credit when it is, by way of socialization, procuring holdings in enterprises and issuing bonds on the strength of this. Credit can be hoped for only from *private* funds in the Entente countries. Their financiers have no confidence in the working of socialized enterprises or in such which are administered, or even co-administered, by our state authorities. Not until socialized enterprises have been in orderly and successful operation for a considerable length of time will credit be obtainable on that basis. Socialization can be supported without being blind to the fact that today, when the state in the first place needs credit, the socialization of enterprises destroys existing collaterals without concurrently creating new ones.

No one challenges the right of socialized capital in later years to acquire credit standing through progressively sound work and through actual achievements.

Crucial, though, is the current emergency. If we are not utterly to disrupt our economy through fiduciary issues, we need credit *immediately. Only private firms and fortunes at present constitute a possible collateral for foreign credit. Today, to save the country, there is only one collateral for credit – not that of the state, nor that of socialized capital, but* SOLELY THAT OF PRIVATE FORTUNES.

German-Austria *does* have one asset that can help it – the credit internationally reposed in its nationals and in its institutions as a result of a century-old relationship. Nobody abroad today can or wants to lend the state of German-Austria anything. Unshaken, though, remains the credit standing of its old firms, its respected nationals, its established institutes. This credit is all, in the catastrophe which has convulsed us, that we have been able to salvage from the work of centuries. *It is our last. And this last must help us.*

At this moment of direst need, when the state has to woo the world for credit, it can place reliance only on its nationals' good name. It must proffer the nation's wealth as its collateral for credit, not by confiscating nor by socializing it, but by leaving it intact in the hands of its credit-worthy owners and by engaging their active co-operation and guarantee. The possessors of large fortunes are in a position, through making use of their existing business connections and through entering into new ones, to induce other countries to view this extension of credit as a sound and promising business.

VII

The enlistment of private fortunes as collateral for credit to serve the needs of the state during the period of transition must be affected in conjunction with the capital levy.

By German law the owner of a very large fortune has to employ his capital to the benefit of the economy. If it brings him more than around 5% – which is approximately what, in the case of very large assets, the annual annuity on thirty years' payment of the capital levy amounts to – he is allowed to keep the increment. If it brings him less, he is fractionally and successively depossessed by the state.

The Austrian capital levy is likewise intended to enable the owner to retain for economically useful purposes his working capital intact by permitting payment, although on special terms, over thirty years.

The exigency of the state forces us to impose such terms. At the moment, a nation crushed and burdened beyond capacity, we need collaterals for credit. Nothing can serve us so well as the private fortunes in the hands of credit-worthy owners.

Big fortunes are to *continue undisturbed as incomparably credit-forming units*. They are not to be thrown into disarray by an immediate capital levy or by one imposing payment at short intervals. BUT this applies ONLY IF THEY PROVIDE THE STATE WITH WHAT IT NEEDS FROM THEM – COLLATERAL. If they do *not* provide this, they must for the state's purpose be *straightaway assessed to the limit of the capital levy*. They are then in the present emergency of no public benefit; they have no legitimate existence. And the capital levy must then be paid WITHIN THE THREE YEARS' EMERGENCY PERIOD.

VIII

From the foregoing the following principles for the link between credit procurement and capital levy ensue:

1. The successive payment in thirty annual instalments in the case of fortunes totalling over a million crowns is only permissible if the owner undertakes *to procure* for the state *by his personal guarantee* a foreign credit redeemable not before five years *to an amount not less than forty per cent of his own assets and to furnish the foreign lender the requisite material security*

to forty per cent of his own assets. The *simple expression of readiness* on the part of the taxpayer to procure the credit by his personal guarantee shall suffice for him to enjoy the preferential treatment of payment in thirty annual instalments.

This simple expression of readiness does not however by itself solve matters. For foreign credit really to reach us involves the active co-operation and the united effort of all well-to-do nationals. Special advantage must attach to the attainment of this purpose.

The proposal is therefore that if the credit is *actually* obtained by the taxpayer, meaning that his guarantee engages him in liability, he shall instead of the standard payment be allowed for all time a 5½% capital levy interest rate for that part of the fortune equivalent to the credit procured.

For example, let the owner of a fortune totalling five millions declare that he undertakes to furnish the state with a two millions' foreign loan and he will enjoy the preferential treatment of paying the capital levy in thirty annual instalments. If thereafter the credit of two millions is on the strength of his guarantee *actually obtained* abroad, then he will additionally be entitled to pay the amount of capital levy due on two millions in such manner that he undertakes to contribute for all time to the interest on the foreign loan the 5½% rate of interest on his capital levy assessment.

The taxpayer shall moreover be obliged to contribute a quarter to any interest burden in excess of 7% so as to engage his interest not merely in the loan's procurement, but in its procurement at the cheapest possible rate.

Steps will be taken to ensure that, as soon as the capital levy has on this basis passed into law, all financial establishments and persons of means shall co-operate for the purpose of participating in the procurement of foreign credit and that the impending currency bond issue shall in this way be placed abroad for large-scale amounts.

Any *domestic* subscription to this foreign loan will as a matter of course not be allowed. *Foreign exchange inside the country cannot be invested in this issue*. The restriction is essential so as not to achieve the opposite of what is intended. The objective is the procurement *on credit* of assets abroad *without* the surrender of crowns, *without* increase in the foreign exchange rate, *without* pressure on our foreign exchange market. Were the payment of foreign exchange inside the country permissible as a method of subscription, it would let loose an unbridled scramble for foreign exchange, the wildest forms of black market deals, and an upsurge in foreign exchange rates without creating foreign assets.

2. A connection must also be established between domestic credit and the capital levy. Currently the state enjoys no credit at home. The rumours of bankruptcy, the reports about reduction of banknotes' face value, the concern about a dividend tax, and the public disparagement of pledges have sapped the roots of state credit.

Even though fortunes of less than one million crowns, leaving aside associative mergers, hardly come into question for the purpose of foreign loans, they are nonetheless of supreme importance for domestic credit. Here too the state must link the thirty years' payment of the capital levy with the availability of credit. That is why small fortunes joining in the procurement of credit must also be conceded transformation of the capital levy into a permanent interest burden.

For a new domestic government bond issue an interest rate of 6% must be regarded as normal. A 4% loan shall be issued and the thirty years' payment tied to the condition that this loan is to be subscribed at its nominal value to at least a quarter of the fortune in question and with something over a third (precisely 36½%) of the amount subscribed counting as paid-up capital levy. This 36½% of his subscription will have been paid up by the taxpayer as capital levy inasmuch as he himself permanently contributes 5½% of this 36½%, or 2% of the loan amount, to the interest burden on the subscribed loan. Obviously the owners of large fortunes will be allowed to avail themselves of this procedure for partial discharge of the capital levy if either the procurement of foreign credit proves impossible because the would-be guarantor's security is not accepted abroad or if he wishes wholly or partially to discharge by subscription to the domestic loan that portion of his fortune over and above 40%. The owners of small fortunes can also of course elect to participate in the guarantee of foreign credit instead of subscription to the domestic loan provided that their security is accepted abroad.

IX

The amount of foreign assets that will accrue to the state from this co-operation on the part of its nationals cannot be forecast in figures. The assumption is nevertheless very well-founded that – given domestic peace and order – its success will prove satisfactory.

Not that the appeal should be expected to bring in anything like *all* that we need. The mere figures matter however little as soon as the proposed method, releasing on behalf of the state's requirements the latent forces in our economy, has led to the achievement of general co-operation for the purpose of reconstruction. Even if only the lesser half of the needed foreign assets is met in this manner, there remains a lasting basis for the further procurement of credit abroad. A state that can count on its nationals' assistance with their personal guarantee, their reputation, their business acumen and initiative furnishes the best proof of its trustworthiness.

In this way the foundations for additional state loans abroad will be laid, especially as in the course of time it will prove far easier to attain agreement on the collaterals to be provided. At present the state could not with the requisite promptitude find whatever security might be demanded because, for instance, any pledge of its sovereign rights requires international agreements, under the terms of the Peace Treaty. The realization of such agreements takes a long time, during which our economy and our public finances must not be allowed to be destroyed through the continued issue of paper money.

The procedure indicated here is therefore surely the best to obtain, successively and with the minimum of sacrifices for the economy, the necessary foreign credits.

X

In the light of the foregoing the answer to the hotly contested question of how the levy is to be employed is conclusive and self-evident.

To the degree that a taxed fortune is enlisted for the procurement of credit, the interest on this portion of the levy contributes to the payment of interest on the credit itself. For the rest, capital having been siphoned off, the levy must in accordance with the norms of sound financial policy be used only for reduction of the war debt burden.

The principle enunciated here should be strongly impressed on the nation and faithfully adhered to. Were all those who are today prepared to make a heavy sacrifice for the state's salvation to believe that they were simply helping to fill a bottomless pit or that they were having to pay taxation for purposes with which they do not all agree, then the levy would not be capable of implementation at all in the state's present condition. For that reason already the *Länder*[a], in particular, must be assured of independent control over use of the levy's yield by the establishment of a commission wherein they are all represented.

Just as cogent is the answer to the question about using War Loan for payment of the levy. *The subscribers of War Loan* must in all circumstances be assured that acceptance *in payment for the levy* will be at the rate of issue irrespective of whether the taxpayer takes advantage of the thirty years' instalment procedure or settles at earlier dates. The burden of War Loan must, consonant with popular demand, be spread justly among all those who can carry it.

[a] The German-language terms *Land* (pl. *Länder*) must be used here because 'province' fails to convey the autonomous status of these territorial units according to the Federal Constitution as revised in 1921: 'Art. 2 (1) Austria is a federal state. (2) The federal state is composed of the autonomous *Länder* (territorial units) of Burgenland, Carinthia, Lower Austria, Upper Austria, Salzburg, Styria, Tirol, Vorarlberg and Vienna.' (*The Austrian Federal Constitution*, translation published on behalf of the Federal Ministry of Foreign Affairs, Vienna, 1972.) (Translator's note)

XI

The *objective of the capital levy* determines its extent and the principles of its assessment.

The capital levy must preserve us from utter destruction of the public and the national economy. The levy and that portion of the monetary depreciation to which we must resign ourselves are a manifestation of the enormous burden left by the war. Let the taxpayers meet the onus of procuring credit for the state and the levy will be transformed into a permanent sinking fund for future interest payments. It must however in any case be high enough to help the state and the economy, whether by credit procurement or whether by debt redemption, out of the present desperate situation. Otherwise it has no justification. Too low a levy would be nothing other than a concession to political propaganda.

That is precisely why the German capital levy rates will not do for us. The unprecedented strain on our public economy will make the capital levy the *financial backbone in coming years*. In Germany it is merely a social measure complementary to financial legislation. For us it serves the absolute preservation of the public economy; in Germany, the notion of social adjustment, appeasement of the social conscience.

With us, let it be emphasized, an all-too-detailed progression is not recommendable. In Germany, with its high degree of honesty among taxpayers and its firm confidence in the bureaucratic machine, a detailed progression may be tolerable. Given our national temperament, a few, clear rates are necessary.

The proposal is for a capital levy which, starting with 10% for fortunes between 30,000 and 100,000 crowns, in sharp, swift progression attains 25% for those between 100,000 and 1,000,000 crowns, 40% between 1,000,000 and 5,000,000 crowns, and in cases of those of more than 5,000,000 crowns approaches asymptotically the rate of 65%.

This burden on private fortunes undoubtedly is *tremendously* onerous. It corresponds, though, to the state's overwhelming exigency. The state must *in all circumstances* surmount the credit emergency of the next years.

Nonetheless the capital levy must not be allowed to become an impediment to the economy's productivity. The principle must therefore be established that the assets of any business – provided, of course, that the owner collaborates in the procurement of credit and thus saves the state the peremptory necessity for earliest collection – shall against payment of the interest be without security granted respite from the levy for as long as the business employs at least as many individuals as it did *before* the war or, should the number during the war have been higher, at the time of greatest employment *during* the war.

The benefit of mere interest payment shall moreover – always on condition of collaboration in the procurement of credit – be without special security extended permanently to those amounts *freshly invested* in businesses for the increase of their productivity.

Linking the capital levy to the procurement of credit involves – along with many other reasons – the application of the purely *subjective* method of collection.

With joint-stock companies and partnerships the level will have to be directly assessed on, and collected from, the business assets since organized capital with its enhanced productivity and credit rating must be rendered directly serviceable to the state. The levy paid by a joint-stock company shall be proportionately deducted from the amount of the levy stipulated for collection from each individual shareholder.

The principle to be applied for collection of the levy will be assessment of assets at their market value. Such a method would however be erroneous where, as a result of the now prevailing circumstances, a large portion of a business' assets derives its market value from the potential of providing maintenance for the owner. Seeing that this market value is transitory, far in excess of the assets' lasting value, such an assessment would lead to an inordinate rating due to a transient sale opportunity and would consequently place an unjust burden on those pursuing a business of the utmost economic and social value, possibly leading to extremely questionable shifts in ownership. Consideration will have to be given to these special circumstances and, among other things, the principle will have to be established that medium- and smaller-sized agricultural businesses, such perhaps as do not employ more than twenty workers and such as where the owner – or, should he be incapacitated, a near relative – is himself active, shall not be assessed according to market value, but on the basis of capitalizing the continuing proceeds. That the bill will have to take account of the precepts constituting the modern social doctrine (consideration of the number of children, and so on) as well as of the plight caused by depreciation of the currency to pensioners of small means who are already suffering so greatly (lifelong respite from the levy, et cetera) is obvious.

XII

Prerequisite to the success of the credit operation is:

1. The quick passage of the capital levy. As long as the main features have not been settled, there is no prospect whatever of any consolidation in credit affairs, let alone of any large-scale co-operation by banking capital in the procurement of credit for the state.

Naturally details of the levy depend on whether the concept presented here is accepted by the whole government and by parliament. Should this not be the case and if a different plan to overcome the current financial emergency is adopted, the capital levy will have to be constructed *along other lines*. That is why a speedy decision and a speedy legislative procedure are necessary.

2. A swift *preliminary* assessment of the capital levy.

a. This objective will be served in the first instance by approval of a *provisional lump sum assessment* by the taxpayers themselves. The latter shall be given the benefit of a 5% reduction provided that within a month they hand in a provisional self-assessment and that this does not fall by more than a quarter below the final statement of assets ensuing on the declaration to be submitted later.

b. The law shall also stipulate that the tax authorities must forthwith institute an official provisional assessment of the levy based on personal income taxation. In so far as the existence of assets by way of capital resources, real estate, and ownership of buildings or business assets emerges from personal income tax and special profits tax declarations, the amount of the levy shall be *provisionally* prescribed on the strength of these assets. The calculation must be effected in accordance with a straightforward scheme founded on the declared income from ownership of assets. The files for this assessment are on hand in the tax offices and therefore this preliminary operation – which must have priority over all other business – can be concluded within a brief period.

XIII

The most important step towards the stabilization of our currency will have been taken as soon as the procurement of foreign assets has, consistently with this plan, been successfully introduced. These assets will then constitute the *last line reserve* of our national wealth, the final residue of national credit accumulated through centuries and enlisted to meet a desperate situtation. The state needs the money obtained by this means. It must not be spent on creating in the markets an artificial demand for Austrian currency and driving up its price. The ultimate effect of that would be nil. With this reserve exhausted, the state would again be on the brink of ruin. The historic mistake of Austrian, and not only of Austrian, financial policy at all times of severe crisis has been to waste its best efforts in the hopeless attempt to produce a favourable rate of exchange artificially. As soon as the reserves are used up, the artificial rise will inevitably give way to an even greater fall. The interdependence between economic factors cannot be eliminated by artificial devices.

Our sole job must be to see that the essential and *non-recurring* imports of raw materials and foodstuffs, which are likely to have to cover the requirements of about eighteen months, not only do not adversely affect the foreign exchange market, but that the interest on this present once-and-for-all need for these assets as capital for the economy's reconstruction is regularly paid to the foreign creditors and that neither our currency nor consequently our economy is unbalanced by the burden of this single capital payment.

The foreign assets in the state's possession will also serve to cushion the temporary effects of sudden upsets to our currency through adverse rumours, unloading of securities, or similar operations. Over and above that no expectations should be attached to money market activities.

The primary purpose of these assets will be their gradual realization against goods imports. Through its cash assets the government will be in a position to regulate foreign trade far more efficiently than is feasible through foreign exchange agencies and through prohibitions. Stronger than any vapid prohibition that will be transgressed at every street-corner is the fact that it is the government which has foreign assets and releases them at the same steadily maintained price for such purposes as appear advantageous to it economically. What the government will have to see to is that in the case of all foodstuffs and raw materials imports the employment of labour and of raw materials is to a large part devoted to the production of exports so that the outlays on them will be periodically turned into fresh assets abroad. For the state – not for the economy – the foreign assets will over the years automatically and progressively be converted into domestic assets in so far as its current needs necessitate this. The slow, automatic transformation will exercise a constant upward pressure on our currency which, as soon as the monetary stabilization has been statutorily fixed, will be revealed by an *automatic inflow of gold into Austria* rendering possible the establishment of our future exchange rate. Yet long before this target is in sight, perhaps as soon as the proposed measures have created reassurance and confidence, the FOREIGN EXCHANGE AGENCY, this institution which is regarded as such a hardship, must be DONE AWAY WITH. In conjunction therewith the other obstructions to an orderly system of international payments must be dropped. A foreigner, if he is again to think well of the crown, must be able to dispose of the assets that he has here freely. Likewise our exporters must be able to sell abroad against crowns, for no currency can survive a boycott by its own nationals. In recent months the financial authorities have aimed at cautiously loosening these fetters, as far as that was possible in the prevailing panicky atmosphere, and so preparing for transition to the normal conditions indicated.

The rate of exchange for our currency will show a vigorous recovery as soon as the foreign assets parry the pressure on it and the payment for imports is channelled via the government's foreign currency holdings in the banks instead of via the foreign exchange market. Stabilization will have to be effected when the currency has risen as high as will be feasible without prejudice to our export capacity at *constant* domestic prices and wages. This will be the moment, *no sooner and no later*, to proceed to the new currency statute that will lay down the crown's new gold content.

Forecasts as to the parity at which our currency will be stabilized – assuming the creation of adequate foreign assets – can at present be merely subjective estimates. Nevertheless even today all public policymakers must aim at an exchange rate which should not be fixed at the highest possible level but at a *sound* one that *reflects existing* domestic wage and price ratios.

The war *must* be paid for somehow, and undoubtedly it will to a large extent have to be paid for in our currency. That means, as in the case of all major breaks in economic development, that it is above all *the rentier class*, i.e. people with unearned incomes, who have to carry the burden.

XIV

Initially German-Austria's currency will continue to consist exclusively of the banknotes already in circulation. After conclusion of the Peace Treaty these will have to be converted into official promissory notes.

The formation of a German-Austrian bank of issue is one of financial policy's earliest, most urgent tasks. Without an institution authorized to issue money and discount bills the revival of the economy is impossible.

At first, however, this establishment will have to operate on a modest scale. The prime principle that must be enunciated upon the bank of issue's foundation is that it shall be denied any link whatsoever with the central government finances. The bank must be absolutely forbidden – and for this purpose perhaps put under special control by the *Länder* – to allow advances to the central government in any form whatever or even to accept government securities as collateral. Every other kind of collateral will be a matter for the bank itself to decide. Its natural and most important function will consist of bills discount business.

As soon as the statutory ratio has been fixed, the bank will be allotted the task of buying the gold and silver (which, given a cautious enough establishment of this ratio, is bound automatically to flow in) and so of obtaining subsequently a bullion as well as a banking cover for the notes that it will issue.

The withdrawal of the official promissory notes in circulation can on no account be taken into consideration at an earlier point. To act now would only represent some kind of *compulsory* measure, like devaluation of the notes' face value or something similar, that would neither serve any useful purpose nor be regarded as other than frivolous.

XV

The urgent tasks of the moment, credit procurement and defence of the currency, must not allow the final shape of the national budget, after the three to four years' transition period, to be relegated into the background just now.

The annual deficit can be assessed currently at more than 8,000 millions. As a contribution to the *lasting* consolidation of the budget the capital levy can be taken into account solely with respect to its interest accrual; this is offset however by the continuous interest burden to meet the requirements of the emergency years.

To the foregoing deficit there has to be added, though, a most important item.

No financial programme would even merit discussion if it did not provide for the *salaries of all state employees to be adjusted as soon as possible to the shrunken value of money*. The monetary depreciation, so far as it is actually manifested *in domestic transactions*, in living costs, and not for instance in current foreign exchange rates, is a final, irreversible consequence of the war. The inability of its civil servants to uphold the standard of living commensurate with their status, the compulsion for them to run into debt or to earn on the side, and the consequent distraction from their conscientious zeal, saps the strength of the state organism more than anything else. Unquestionably the sense of duty which, in spite of all deprivations, still permeates this class is admirable. But civil servants and state employees must be left in no doubt that their salaries will, as quickly as possible and without being confined to the lower divisions, be *continually adjusted to monetary depreciation*; thus these salaries have to be increased to approximately three times the present income.

The state machine cannot function properly and good order in the budget is impossible, unless civil servants are paid in full. The restoration to civil servants of their full pay imposes on the present budget an additional expenditure of 2,500 millions for which *full* allowance must be made. At the moment this increase in civil servants' pay is, as a result of the state's emergency, not feasible. For the present civil servants' readiness for self-sacrifice must continue to be called upon. But the slightest delay beyond the stage at which the increase becomes at all practicable without the issue of paper money would be an act of iniquity against the foundations of the state's existence.

The full rise cannot, for example, be postponed for three years. It must without deferment be fully implemented to the degree that the results of the proposed credit operations permit.

The state's uncovered annual requirement, mentioned at the outset, would accordingly amount to 11,000 millions.

The national income, even allowing for monetary depreciation, cannot stand a burden of such magnitude. The state organism has a load capacity whose elasticity cannot be stretched beyond a certain point. For German-Austria this point can *in the case of money's present value* not be assumed as being higher, even should the economy have fully recovered, than – assuming the *utmost* strain – 8,000 millions annually. Of these a little more than one thousand million already comes in from current taxation. This figure is admittedly only an estimate, but an estimate which certainly – in so far as a very distant future is left out of consideration – represents the *extreme* limit of what is attainable.

An absolute postulate of orderly fiscal policy must therefore be that the surplus of more than 7,000 millions of the 11,000 million deficit must undergo reduction from the *expenditure* side.

Official outlays originating purely from the state of temporary stagnation in production and from the general adjustment to the monetary depreciation are prime targets for reduction. 2,300 millions of the budgeted outlays and such as are still to be considered therein derive from transitory items, such as unemployment assistance and losses on foodstuff distribution.

Not that this will entail any sacrifice on the part of the working classes, for it will be the state's business through its management of social policy to bring influence to bear on the adjustment of wages to rising living costs. The financial authorities will inexorably urge, however, that all those outlays regarded as expedients to render the transitional economy possible shall be energetically and swiftly slashed.

Even then there remains an uncovered expenditure item of about 1,750,000 millions. There is only one way to cut this down – *economy*. German-Austria is encumbered with an outsize number of civil service departments and officials dating from its former Great Power status. Experience shows that an excessive number of civil servants does not add to the productivity of their labours. Quite to the contrary, it diminishes this because it reduces the responsibility of the individual and accustoms departments to sluggish procedures. The pruning of posts, the simplification of administration, the early retirement of all supernumerary civil servants, and the eradication of all budget items going back to former days is absolutely necessary to clean up the budget.

Allowing for the fact that in the case of civil servants' payment in full (in correspondence with the monetary depreciation) will constitute an item of

3,750 millions, expenditures can during the period of transition be successfully reduced through economy measures by more than a full thousand million.

Even then the budget's complete equilibrium is not possible of achievement. The most earnest exertion of taxation effort and the most rigorous exercise of economy will still leave five hundred thousand uncovered annually. We must hope that the restored national economy will after three to four years, in spite of the capital levy's heavy burden, leave so much to spare each year as to render possible the coverage of this national need by way of domestic credit and eventually, in the more distant future and given further consolidation of the economy, to bring about the bridging of the gap from the budget's own receipts.

XVI

The annual deficit, according to the foregoing, amounts to 7,000 millions which are to be met from taxation and from receipts by the state for its own account. It is absolutely essential to determine *now and axiomatically* how this enormous requirement is to be raised.

The state can surmount the present desperate situation by calling upon ownership to render services of the most extreme and difficult kind, extending far beyond the German example, and by full mobilization of its entire capabilities, immaterial as well as material.

A mistake, though, would be to think that the credit which we seek, and which we must find, could be obtained unless people abroad are at the same time convinced that good order will after this critical period be restored in the national finances and that not only the property-owning classes, who must now bring sacrifices and who must now help, but all classes will be called upon and will answer the call. The capital levy is the backbone of the temporary efforts at relief. *All* classes of the population will have to contribute to the *subsequent lasting* good order.

The main burden of the war and the war's outcome is being carried by the rentier class. The monetary depreciation, manifestation of the war burden, has at this stage reduced all fixed interest incomes to *at least* a tenth of their real assets value.

Throughout the world the war has led to a diminution in the value of money to less than half of its pre-war level. Were it even possible to raise the crown's value to a parity of 20 Swiss centimes, this would still only signify a fifth of the global money value, i.e., *a tenth of the domestic peace-time money value*. Let the most optimistic expectations be fulfilled and prices at home will still stay ten times as high as they were before the war. In other words, all those who draw a fixed income have *lost in terms of purchasing power nine tenths of their real income*.

To try and somehow fight against the force of this monstrous fact would be self-deception. The burdens of the war have in our own country to be borne by the rentier class which has in the course of developments been hit by an automatic, silent tax of ninety per cent. On top of this raise the taxation on personal incomes to the highest rates economically endurable here and then there still will have to be tapped *earned income* so as to meet the state's routine outlays, which through monetary depreciation have risen to thousands of millions.

It is compatible with our country's social structure, the reasonably fortunate distribution of income scales, and the highly graduated integration based on intelligence, education, and organization of working people in this social structure that about *half of the current public outlays* must be borne, if they are to be borne at all, by the working population in the widest sense of the term. State expenditure has risen to such a degree that, given our social structure, it cannot possibly be imposed on a single element in the body politic. The state must lay its hands on *every* income so as to skim off *its* income. Were it to pluck only the higher incomes, were it even to confiscate all income above a certain limit, then the higher the lower classes' standard of living and the mightier the rise in their social position the less could it satisfy its needs.

For technical reasons the calling upon of the lower income brackets must be effected by way of consumption taxes. Indirect taxation is intrinsically nothing else than the downward spread of income tax. Taxation of the individual would however at a certain level of income entail cost and machinery rendering the result a financial mirage.

In the light of ownership's huge prior encumbrance through the capital levy and of the uttermost strain being put on the income tax potential, the annual deficit of 7,000 millions will have to be met, if it is to be met at all, by some 3,000 millions arising on consumer taxation in the lower categories, 1,500 millions on the utmost yield attainable from direct taxation, 500 millions by special consumer levies in the higher categories, and 2,000 millions by a burden on commerce and communications.

XVII

Among the various forms of direct taxation, land tax and transfer tax do not constitute an item for exploitation by the central authorities because they will be ceded to the *Länder* and communes. The *Länder* authorities can be expected to increase vigorously these levies whose closer local context makes the link between expenditure and income more palpable than in the case of the state.

The *building tax* can hardly be raised, but it will be complemented by a special direct consumption tax for certain categories of dwellings. The Rent Restriction Act's strong and timely intervention has entirely eliminated the effect of monetary depreciation on rentals in existing buildings. The poor are not to be deprived of this advantage. Those who are better off, though, are at least to share it with the state while the owner of such existing buildings cannot be allowed more than some compensation for their increased maintenance cost.

Personal income tax is undoubtedly capable of expansion in the medium brackets. A far faster and sharper progression will need to be introduced.

This year's legislation has in the top brackets provided for the economically admissible limit. This ceiling of 33.5% shall however be altered so as to take effect not only when an annual income of 6 millions, but already one of 400,000 crowns has been reached.

On the other hand, corresponding to monetary depreciation, the tax-free subsistence minimum will be raised to 10,000 crowns. This income figure shall in principle be regarded as having been brought in via direct taxes and it shall consequently enjoy exemption in the higher brackets too.

Thereafter the assessment rate will start straightaway at 10% and rise to 33.5% in five clearly graduated and readily comprehensible brackets. The 15% surcharge for households in easier circumstances will remain.

The capital levy imposes stringent rates on *unearned* income. In cases where it comprises only interest on assets, it appropriates the yield to the uttermost endurable limit of close on two thirds. For the *current* annual budget the capital levy, irrespective of whether it is paid immediately or successively or is converted into permanent interest payment, comes into effect of course merely by way of the interest amount.

Death duties (estate and legacy duties) require a very far-reaching increase. The devolution on marriage partners and on children, constituting three quarters of all reversions, are at present especially taxed too lightly. The German example will serve as guidance.

XVIII

Commerce and communications shall undergo taxation by an increase in rail tariffs and postal charges as well as by a reform of stamp duties.

The increase in rail tariffs will have to be such as to ensure that the *full* cost price is covered. The high deficit on the state railways' operations is a familiar fact. Tariffs will need to rise until this deficit has been completely wiped out.

The postal services too are working at a loss. The increase in charges will have to be adjusted in stages to the monetary depreciation. Here (contrary to the railways' operation) the state will obtain a source of real and considerable income.

Stamp duties are to experience thorough reform. There are two possible approaches. One is imitation of the German model whose incidence falls on the turnover of goods as such. This would require not only a fresh and comprehensive collection machinery, but it would probably prove to be not altogether compatible with our national outlook. The other is to extend our system so as to make all agreements involving future disbursals subject to stamp duty if they are to be legally binding. Taxation on turnovers will have to be developed along one or the other of these lines.

XIX

Taxation of the lower income brackets by indirect taxation will in the main have to be confined to a few consumers' goods. It would be wrong to complicate the collection machinery by distributing the tax over as large a category of articles as possible.

The *operative* principle in the case of a heavy impost on certain few articles must be that the increase of indirect taxation shall not occur all at once, but in *successive*, three or four, *stages during the three years' transition period*. This is necessary so that there does not ensue an impairment in the standard of living and a complete radical change in the way of life in consequence of a very sudden, surgical, operation. What should and must however here and now *be clearly and honestly stated is the aim of taxation in the long run* so as to prove to people abroad and to our own population the seriousness of our fiscal policy and our readiness for sacrifice, our financial viability and our genuine credit-worthiness.

Indirect taxation shall provide for semi-luxuries as to render possible *an automatic progression also of indirect taxation* so that its incidence shall likewise fall lightest on those who are in greatest difficulty and poorest, heaviest on those whose living is more comfortable and less restricted. Obnoxious are those indirect taxes on absolutely essential consumption goods which hit the most impoverished as badly as the better off, the thrifty as much as the spendthrift. The same economic principle that in the case of the capital levy requires preferential treatment wherever assets are actually devoted to fresh production, must in the case of indirect taxation lead to encouraging those who save and hurting those who waste. Imposts on absolutely essential necessities would contravene this principle.

Admittedly, in view of the utmost exertion of our economic potential, the burden on penurious households cannot *altogether* be avoided. A consumption tax of 2 crowns per kilogram of meat and an adjustment to current money value of the sugar tax in the form of a 2 crowns' levy per kilogram will have to be brought forward. These commodities at least guarantee, even if within narrow bounds, a certain automatic progression at the expense of the better off. *In all events* there must be avoided taxation on absolutely essential articles of consumption like flour, eggs, and fat. Let it be pointed out that, inasmuch as this most extreme possibility is refrained from, there cannot in good conscience be talked of intolerable burden.

The main burden of indirect taxation must fall with full impact on the taxation of semi-luxuries, meaning tobacco and in particular *spirituous liquors*.

Statistics show that consumption of alcohol increases absolutely and percentagewise among the working classes with the growth of prosperity. The taxation of spirituous liquors automatically creates an onus on small people in easier circumstances as against the worse off.

The consumption of spirituous liquors constitutes the little man's luxury outlay. Its taxation represents a progressive levy on small households. It leaves thrift beneficial to the economy untouched and affects only that part of income which is not conducive to additional production and the creation of credit resources in the form of savings. It is the *perfect consumption tax*.

Taxation on spirituous liquors must be exceptionally far-reaching. The principle should be established that *on average a full third of what the population spends on spirituous liquors shall accrue to the state*.

If the principle is established that *on average a third* of the amount spent on spirituous liquors is to come into the state's coffers, there emerges a different treatment for beer and for wine.

Tobacco prices will during the three transitional years similarly have to be successively increased. The state tobacco monopoly is currently operating at a loss as it obtains its raw materials exclusively from abroad and, apart from the depreciation of the currency, the higher foreign prices are of crucial influence. The successive increase in tobacco prices will have to be successively implemented till such time as a complete adjustment to the changed monetary value has been achieved.

XIX

Taxation of the small man's luxuries will have to go hand in hand with an *exceptionally high* tax on luxury outlays by the wealthy. The intention is in this instance to go well beyond the German example. Social conscience requires that if the luxury of the have-nots is taxed to a third of what is spent, then the expenditure on luxuries by the haves, particularly the enjoyment of foreign wines, maintenance of costly means of transport, and consuming sumptuous meals, as well as running de luxe business premises, and so on, shall be subject to 100 to 150% taxation.

XX

The foregoing has described the principles of taxation to be applied in coming years. Requisite for the immediate future is indeed no more than the decision on the capital levy because tax receipts to facilitate our needs in any substantial way can currently not be counted on. Nevertheless it is absolutely essential that even now a decision on the principles to be applied to taxation shall be solemnly and finally taken, putting an end to vague intimations and the accumulation of lifeless piles of paper. It is necessary not only for the capital levy and its link to the procurement of credit to be decided on, but that at least the most important and heaviest indirect taxation measures, particularly the taxes on spirituous liquors, should be determined *here and now in toto*.

It would have been easy to restrict this financial plan to the steps at present necessary and to the basic concept of linking the capital levy to the procurement of credit. Such a procedure would however have been too perfunctory. We must evince complete and sober determination not only to survive for the present without the issue of paper money, without national bankruptcy, and without breach of faith, but also to take upon ourselves in the more distant future the requisite sacrifices to attain and to preserve the provisionally achieved good order. This financial programme rests on the conviction that we can help ourselves. The haves must put at the state's disposal what they possess, not merely the largest part of their personal wealth, but also their credit rating and their good name so as to enable the economic order to be upheld. The have-nots must by their assumption of all the sacrifices entailed by indirect taxation render possible the continued existence of the economy without the creation of paper money. Foreign countries must be shown that we are ready to help ourselves. Only then will and can they be prepared to help us.

4. Letter from the Anglo-Austrian Bank to Rt. Hon. David Lloyd George

ANGLO-AUSTRIAN BANK LIMITED

24–28 Lombard Street,
London, E.C.3.
August 8th 1922.

The Rt. Hon. D. Lloyd George, M.P.
First Lord of the Treasury,
10, Downing Street, S.W.1.

Sir,

We have the honour to inform you that the foreign banks established in Austria on the same footing as the great Austrian banks and Messrs. Rothschild, have been called upon to participate in the formation of a new Bank of Issue.

The English and French directors of these banks have met in order to come to a decision upon the matter. They examined the situation at length from every point of view, and they unanimously came to the following conclusion:

"The financial situation in Austria is growing worse every day, and in particular the stabilisation of its currency can only be effected by the adoption of a joint plan, the essential points of which are:

1. That the Budget should be made to balance,
2. That steps be taken to reduce the deficit on expenditure,
3. An internal loan,
4. Foreign credits,
5. The establishing of a Bank of Issue."

These measures are intimately connected with one another and can only come into force effectively if the scheme is adopted in its entirety.

The conditioning element of success however, beyond all others is that Austria should be definitely promised foreign credits. Under whatever form these credits may be given they pre-suppose the assistance of foreign governments, whether directly or as guarantors. The recent decision of the Reparation Commission has now made the way clear for such assistance. It would be sheer illusion to imagine that the mere creation of a new Bank of Issue could improve the situation, or even stabilise the currency, unless the other measures of the joint plan under consideration are put into execution at the same time.

Moreover, if and when the Austrian and other foreign banks established in

Austria definitely take up or guarantee the first instalment of the capital required for the new Bank of Issue up to a total of 60 million Swiss francs, no lasting results will be achieved, and the final effect will merely be to weaken those private institutions whose strength is one of the essential factors in the restoration of Austria.

The English and French directors of the Anglo-Austrian Bank and the Banque des Pays de l'Europe-Centrale therefore consider that the private interests which they represent cannot see their way to take up their proportion of the requisite contribution to the Bank unless the adoption of the other items of the scheme is guaranteed. In view of the fact that the Shareholders of these concerns cannot consent to take up unassisted the burden of measures which would be inoperative if they are undertaken piecemeal, the French and English directors of the banks regard it as their duty to approach their respective governments with a view to asking them to take the necessary steps for protecting their assets and properties in Austria against force majeure from any quarter.

They have the honour to draw the attention of their governments to the urgent importance of granting the Austrian government external assistance which is the only means of forestalling a grave crisis with which private resources will be unable to cope.

We are, Sir,

Your obedient servants,
for ANGLO-AUSTRIAN BANK LIMITED.
(SD) H. A. LAWRENCE
Chairman.

(SD) P. BARK[a]
Director.

Source: Public Record Office, London, FO 371/7339/HN 01157.

[a] Peter Bark, a former Czarist Minister of Finance who fled to Britain during the October 1917 revoluton and who held this appointment as a protégé of Montagu Norman.

5. Memorandum by the Austrian Government on the Financial Situation of Austria, August 1922

Minutes of the Meeting

At the meeting held under the chairmanship of the Federal Chancellor on 3 August from 9.30–11.00 a.m. it was resolved, at the motion of the Federal Minister of Foreign Affairs, to instruct Head of Department Dr Schüller to travel to London immediately after the announcement of the lifting of the liens on Austrian assets by the Reparation Commission (expected for Friday) to assist Minister Franckenstein. The Federal Minister of Finance stated on the subject of the draft budget calculated on a gold basis that the result was not very encouraging, since exceptionally high deficits must become apparent in the state enterprises and even more in the central administration. The contents of the Memorandum were briefly outlined. Board Chairman Rosenberg undertook to submit the finished version by five o'clock. It was to culminate with the statement that in the absence of help the Austrian Government can no longer keep the state going, will reject the responsibility for it at the meeting of parliament to be convened, and will turn to the Austrian people and the world with a corresponding declaration.

During the afternoon session from 5.00–7.30 p.m. the more exact circumstances and the consequences of such a declaration were discussed. There was agreement that this is not to mean either a proclamation of *Anschluss* nor the threat of a Soviet régime, but that it shall express the impossibility of maintaining Austria as created by the Treaty of Saint-Germain. Germany will not perish if no one worries about it. We however shall perish if we are NOT worried about. Neither the Federal Chancellor nor the Minister of Finance held that the existence of Austria will cease as such. The state will have to be kept going. The Minister of Finance in particular could not really imagine what is, properly speaking, meant by the so-called collapse. Board Chairman Rosenberg interposed that the crown will simply be no longer accepted as currency and we shall consequently be unable to obtain foodstuffs. To this was countered that for the present there was still on hand the 70,000 tons stockpile, the domestic harvest was on the point of being gathered, and that the Czechoslovak loan instalments – 41 millions in August, 60 in September, the rest in October – indirectly took care of civil servants' pay.

The Federal Chancellor mentioned sanctions against foreigners and requisition of foreign property so as to induce the Entente to intervene, but he added right away that such an idea could hardly be taken seriously. To be considered, on the other hand, was whether or not we should publicly announce that we shall no longer bother with the Peace Treaty.

The Federal Chancellor raised the question as to how we would act if the crown were to rise. The Minister of Finance said that without foreign credits the financial plan could not be implemented. Even the tiniest of upward movements by the crown will in the eyes of the world deprive us of the moral right to launch a disaster operation. Board Chairman Rosenberg remarked that the crown could only rise if we were to be granted foreign credits, or rumours about a grant of credits would be circulated, or, finally, if the Entente's attitude towards Germany underwent substantial change and the world at large then regained confidence with respect to developments in Germany and in Austria. The Minister of Finance observed that even without foreign credits the situation could be held till mid-September. This led the Federal Chancellor to ask what were to happen if the London Conference turned down our request. Then we should have at first to play for time. In any event, regardless of the threat intimated in the memorandum's last paragraph, the government resignation must be avoided. It will only tell parliament that Austria in its present form can no longer be continued. Parliament will then have to speak its mind and perhaps the government will tender its resignation. The state must however be kept afloat as long as feasible. The nation must be roused by the resolute series of moves and talks will have to take place with all possible partners as to how matters shall proceed.

After the dissolution of the meeting Board Chairman Rosenberg asserted that the index law is the ultimate nail in our coffin. 'I am now very pessimistic. Even if we get the credit. We shall achieve recovery only via catastrophe.'
Those present:
The Federal Chancellor
the Vice-Chancellor
the Federal Minister of Foreign Affairs
the Federal Minister of Finance
Board Chairman Rosenberg
Minister Pogatscher
Minister Wildner

Text of the Memorandum
The Austrian state finances are in danger of immediate breakdown unless external help arrives in the *very near future*.

The breakdown is caused by the budget's huge deficit. It constantly necessitates fresh recourse to the printing of banknotes. This inexorably results in deterioration. In consequence of this constantly increasing deterioration of the currency the growth of receipts cannot keep level with the expenditure, the deficit becomes ever larger, and the printing of banknotes has continually to be expanded, leading to the continuous deterioration of the currency.

Everyone admits that there is only one way of escape from this cycle —

foreign loans to meet the deficit remaining after the increase of taxes and other national sources of receipt. That must at the same time have a favourable effect on the rate of exchange. The deficit must be met and the currency be stabilized by bringing into play three factors – thrift in the budget, high taxation, and credits.

The disintegration of the Austrian budget, in so far as it is not due to the war's events, is a direct consequence of the former state's breakdown. The Monarchy, due to the refusal of the Powers to conclude peace with the then Austria-Hungary, suddenly split into its constituent components. All at once today's Austria was cut off from its coal resources. Its entire industrial population together with those engaged in commerce and trade were virtually thrown out of work.

The Austrian Government, in charge of a state half of whose population was unemployed, naturally had to provide food subsidies on a large scale and to introduce unemployment benefit. That is one of the two main reasons for the state finances' collapse. The other derives from the hypertrophic condition of the civil servants and public employees, in large part also a consequence of the Monarchy's breakdown inasmuch as the German-language civil servants and public employees streamed back from the distant parts of the Empire to today's small Austria and had to be accommodated here. The post-war legislation on social policy required moreover a great number of employees. The higher costs of public enterprises could not however be met by higher charges and higher prices to match the state's services because domestic industry, not for lack of good will, but for lack of raw materials, was unable to operate.

To the Great Powers it was from the outset clear that in these conditions, fully familiar at the time of negotiations in Saint-Germain, foreign aid would have to be extended to render the state's existence feasible. This explains the promise of assistance in the Cover Note to the Peace Treaty of Saint-Germain.

The chairman of the Vienna contingent of the Reparation Commission, Sir William Goode, did indeed work out a plan for assistance, but this did not obtain the approval of the Powers. On the contrary, the Allied Powers decided to entrust the Austrian problem to the Financial Committee of the League of Nations. The delegates of the League's Financial Committee in agreement with the Austrian Government elaborated a financial plan the implementation of which appeared to promise complete success. The assurance was given that resources had been earmarked for a considerable loan to the Austrian Government provided that the liens on Austrian assets existing in accordance with the terms of the Peace Treaty and the Relief Convention for a period of at least twenty years were waived. The ordeal which the Austrian Government went through in order to gain acceptance of this waiver is common knowledge.

After more than eighteen months of endeavour the waiver of these liens appears to have been at last attained. The League of Nations' aid operation has however evaporated meanwhile and no one doubts but that the plan is now no longer capable of implementation.

In the interim the Austrian Government has tried to negotiate with a powerful Anglo-American financial group about the extension of a loan against the security of various state receipts (above all the customs duties). As is well-known, these negotiations came to nothing, the main reason being that private lenders shrink from taking the political risk which they see in the grant of a loan to the Austrian state. The problem of this state's viability and the problem of its political fate are in their eyes far too unclear for them to want to venture the conclusion of a loan with this political entity even if the security offered seems adequate as such.

The Austrian Government has certainly not failed during the intervening time to employ measures of self help. Before the middle of 1921 measures in that direction were impossible. When, however the world coal position improved and eventually Austria also became the recipient of such deliveries, the factories were able to work, trade was given a vigorous impetus, and about October, when it turned out that the League of Nations assistance could not be extended in time, the Austrian Government took the *Draconian decision* to abolish *all food subsidies*, causing the price of bread to rise straightaway around tenfold. A series of new taxes and levies were at this point, the end of 1921, introduced to meet the deficit.

Throughout this time, though, the unfavourable development with regard to the rate of exchange continued its alarming course. The generous assistance by the British Government in the form of a £2,000,000 advance was sufficient for several months to underpin the price of the crown, but it proved to be insufficient in the long run *when the Conference at Genoa again failed to effect the suspension of the liens.*

With a constantly falling crown rate of exchange and the threat to European economic conditions created by the situation in Germany, the present Austrian Government, undaunted, has continued to concentrate the entire national energies on paving the way for order in the budget. On the one hand public confidence in the domestic currency is to be raised by the establishment of a new bank of issue which will be expressly forbidden to grant any credit to the central authorities. On the other, budget receipts are to be augmented by at least meeting the running costs of the state's services in the telegraphic, telephonic, postal, and rail communications sector and by the realization of substantial profits through sharp increases in the field of the state's financial monopolies, especially tobacco products. Levies on mass consumption goods are to be stepped up enormously; heavy alcohol taxes are to be introduced and *customs dues are to be paid in gold.* In addition a forced levy, from which proceeds of about 400,000 million crowns are to be expected, is to be imposed on both agriculture and mobile capital. Banking circles have moreover been induced to guarantee to the amount of approximately £3 million the capital for the new bank of issue which has to be paid up in cash. The central bank is to be established by mid-September.

Everyone familiar with prevailing circumstances will confirm that this financial plan, set down already in legal form, represents *the uttermost effort of which today's Austria is capable.*

The full result for the budget of these laws can be seen in the appendix to this Memorandum. Separating the budget's outgoings and receipts into permanent and transitory categories, it becomes apparent that the permanent outgoings of 573.7 million gold crowns are offset by receipts of 557.5 million gold crowns, signifying a deficit of 16.2 million gold crowns that could be met by domestic financial operations on the part of the government.

As against this the transitory outgoings show an amount of 256.6 million gold crowns offset by receipts of no more than 11.1 million gold crowns.

This means a deficit of 245.5 million gold crowns, which can only be met by foreign loans. If a stabilization of the Austrian currency renders further budgetary measures possible, the deficit could be made to disappear within the course of eighteen months, indeed successively during this period, so that *on average* only the transitory deficit for one year would need to be met by loans. The government believes that a recovery of the state finances in the interim is possible if foreign credits meet the transitory deficit for one year. On the other hand it is convinced that, failing this, the present plan must likewise prove impracticable and that it would be impossible to stop the complete disintegration of the Austrian state finances.

This state of affairs can of course not be kept from business people and the public at large. With no visible foreign aid in sight and the apparent danger of the state's destruction commerce, industry, and private individuals tend to act on the principles of *sauve qui peut.* Consequently everyone's sole object is to buy foreign exchange without anyone, in particular neither industry nor commerce who receive such, being prepared to make it available. To this is to be added the distrust felt in widest circles of the population about the domestic currency which, to secure their savings and their property, they invest in foreign currencies.

A continuation of these circumstances must soon result in *the impossibility of raising* foreign exchange for the import of vital commodities. The imposition of sanctions hold out no promise because it would simply shatter what confidence there remains among the nationals of this political entity.

The Austrian Government is convinced that today's Austria, its economy having for nearly four years accommodated itself to the prevailing state of affairs, is viable if foreign assistance is forthcoming. Its condition without such foreign assistance is hopeless. Whether they wanted to extend this assistance is now a matter for the Great Powers to decide.

Austria is today still what it has been for centuries, a bulwark of Western civilization, an element of peace and order in central Europe, inhabited by a peace-loving, industrious, and skilful population. The Austrian Government, responsible as it is for the preservation of the ancient cultural assets represented by Austria, and especially Vienna, cultural assets irreplaceable for the whole of Europe, and indeed the whole world, must reject this responsibility if disintegration follows because of failure to afford timely assistance in spite of all the efforts made by this country, ready moreover as it is to subject itself to any and every financial control. The loss hereby inflicted on all humanity and the peace of Europe as well as of civilization bears no relation at all to the small amounts needed by the Great Powers to rescue the country and whose repayment within the foreseeable future is more than likely. The Austrian Government owes complete truth and candour to itself, to the population of this severely tried country, and to the whole of Europe. Should therefore assistance not follow as early as possible, it would have to convene the *Nationalrat* and publicly decline the responsibility for further events.

Source: Haus-, Hof-und Staatsarchiv, NPA, K 346.

APPENDIX II

Tables

Table A1: *Summary of Subscription totals to War Loan Issues I–VIII, Participation by Banks, and distribution of subscribed amounts*

Subscriptions to		Loan Issue I		Loan Issue II	
		No.	Face Val.	No.	Face Val.
Total		418,912	2,200,746,900	384,991	2,688,321,800
Banks & Exchange Off. (for own account)			229,293,100		345,114,300
Pte. Persons & Bus. a) via Pens. Sav. Bank		33,027	3,370,500	11,690	1,954,600
b) Other Subscriptions					
up to	100 crowns	54,949	5,494,900	35,682	3,568,200
up to	200 crowns	51,756	10,351,200	41,506	8,301,200
300 to	500 crowns	66,514	28,732,500	68,255	27,146,200
600 to	900 crowns	24,622	17,700,300	31,614	25,861,000
1,000 to	1,900 crowns	79,830	95,313,000	80,082	107,017,700
2,000 to	9,900 crowns	81,330	289,214,500	86,834	306,209,600
10,000 to	49,900 crowns	22,972	339,236,800	24,452	382,727,600
50,000 to	99,900 crowns	2,235	123,893,300	2,699	142,281,000
100,000 to	499,900 crowns	1,480	220,549,300	1,931	286,642,800
500,000 crowns and over		197	174,483,300	246	225,091,200

Loan Issue III		Loan Issue IV		Loan Issue V	
No.	Face Val.	No.	Face Val.	No.	Face Val.
582,326	4,202,600,200	673,671	4,520,292,000	438,205	4,467,940,000
	673,848,400		728,030,100		678,984,000
35,288	5,438,400	19,689	1,135,000		
145,540	14,554,000	258,249	25,824,900	106,112	8,917,200
60,305	12,061,000	68,022	13,604,400	38,171	7,634,200
72,531	27,745,600	56,865	20,306,900	39,996	15,465,400
30,518	22,782,700	27,237	20,066,600	33,066	22,417,500
93,879	111,618,900	99,723	107,837,900	103,970	105,239,000
93,423	344,549,300	99,898	317,166,200	81,484	251,386,000
41,746	615,716,100	35,696	527,592,200	27,410	444,042,000
5,135	279,987,600	4,740	276,918,300	4,256	247,414,200
3,591	494,688,800	3,201	447,526,800	3,268	498,348,400
370	402,332,400	441	578,214,900	472	541,354,000

Subscriptions to	Loan Issue VI		Loan Issue VII		Loan Issue VIII		Total	
	No.	Face Val.	No.	Face Val.	No.	Face Val.	No.	Face Value
Total	396,134	5,189,066,000	394,390	6,045,896,000	288,780	5,814,000,000		35,128,862,900
Banks & Exchange Off. (for own account)		779,909,750		1,004,430,200		973,388,850		5,412,998,700
Pte. Persons & Bus.								
a) via Pens. Sav. Bank								11,898,500
b) Other Subscriptions								
up to 100 crowns	116,314	10,613,550	86,085	7,440,850	60,766	5,994,600	863,697	82,408,200
up to 200 crowns	50,216	9,997,250	53,479	10,227,000	32,354	6,462,200	395,809	78,638,450
300 to 500 crowns	34,300	12,426,350	40,196	15,816,100	21,822	8,083,500	400,479	155,722,550
600 to 900 crowns	17,094	12,394,250	17,103	11,805,900	15,537	11,330,450	196,791	144,358,700
1,000 to 1,900 crowns	75,691	83,362,150	85,131	89,356,650	62,280	65,911,500	680,586	765,656,800
2,000 to 9,900 crowns	65,998	239,899,000	66,854	227,285,900	55,340	207,958,400	631,161	2,183,668,900
10,000 to 49,900 crowns	27,112	507,928,950	33,863	536,745,650	31,321	491,762,800	244,572	3,845,752,100
50,000 to 99,900 crowns	4,952	306,499,700	6,682	372,397,600	5,087	301,633,950	35,786	2,051,025,650
100,000 to 499,900 crowns	3,664	580,429,950	4,286	668,558,300	3,690	589,222,150	25,111	3,785,966,500
500,000 crowns and over	748	759,600,850	711	813,904,800	583	726,938,950	3,768	4,221,920,400

Source: Max Sokal, *Die Tätigkeit der Banken*, p. 8 et. seq.

Table A2: Recourse to the Austro-Hungarian Bank by the Austrian and Hungarian Financial Authorities, 1914–18

Categories		Date	Austria		Hungary	
			Amount	Used up	Amount	Used up
Coll. Loans		14. 8.1914	1,272,000,000	15.10.1914	728,000,000	28.10.1914
Prom. Notes		⌠ 7.10.1914	1,272,000,000	24. 4.1915	728,000,000	1. 5.1915
		⌡12. 4.1915	508,800,000	4. 5.1915	291,200,000	5. 8.1915
Open Market						
Loans	1.	15. 7.1915	954,000,000	12.10.1915	546,000,000	6.11.1915
	2.	16. 9.1915	954,000,000	6. 5.1916	546,000,000	3. 4.1916
	3.	24. 2.1916	954,000,000	7. 9.1916	546,000,000	1. 8.1916
	4.	31. 5.1916	954,000,000	7.11.1916	546,000,000	16. 9.1916
	5.	21. 9.1916	954,000,000	22.12.1916	546,000,000	30. 8.1917
	6.	23.11.1916	954,000,000	2. 7.1917	546,000,000	1.10.1917
	7.	19. 5.1917	954,000,000	7. 9.1917	546,000,000	2.11.1917
	8.	30. 8.1917	954,000,000	6.10.1917	546,000,000	29. 4.1918
	9.	28. 9.1917	954,000,000	14.11.1917	546,000,000	1. 7.1918
	10.	24.11.1917	954,000,000	27.12.1917	546,000,000	17. 8.1918
	11.	20. 3.1918	954,000,000	12. 4.1918	546,000,000	19. 9.1918
	12.	15. 4.1918	954,000,000	30. 4.1918	546,000,000	7.10.1918
	13.	29. 4.1918	954,000,000	29. 5.1918	546,000,000	4.11.1918
	14.	1. 6.1918	954,000,000	22. 6.1918	546,000,000	23.11.1918
	15.	27. 6.1918	954,000,000	12. 7.1918	546,000,000	28.11.1918
	16.	15. 7.1918	954,000,000	29. 7.1918	546,000,000	20.12.1918
	17.	1. 8.1918	954,000,000	27. 8.1918	546,000,000	24.12.1918
	18.	29. 8.1918	954,000,000	11. 9.1918	546,000,000	31. 1.1919
	19.	11. 9.1918	954,000,000	27. 9.1918	546,000,000	17. 2.1919
	20.	26. 9.1918	954,000,000	12.10.1918	546,000,000	19. 3.1919
	21.	14.10.1918	954,000,000	30.10.1918	546,000,000	—
Cash Certs. in Circ.		31.10.1918	1,966,513,908	—	1,125,489,092	—

Central Bank Claims on 26 October 1918 against

	Austrian	Hungarian
	Financial Authorities	
Syndic. Loans	510,000,000	297,500,000
Coll. Loans	1,272,000,000	728,000,000
Prom. Notes	1,780,800,000	1,019,200,000
Open Mar. L.	19,634,000,000	6,798,000,000
Cash Certs.	1,862,997,276	1,066,243,724
Total	25,059,797,276	9,908,943,724

Source: Alexander Popovics, *Das Geldwesen im Kriege*, p. 79

Table A3: Banknotes in circulation and actual gold and foreign currency holdings by the Austro-Hungarian Bank, 1914–18

Date	Banknote Circulation	Cred. Balances	Total	Gold Bars & Coins	Gold Bills Abroad & For. Notes	Assets with For. Banks	For Ex. & For. Notes	Total
1914								
31 July	3,061,925	367,302	3,429,227	1,094,938	54,872	119,289	845	1,269,944
31 August	3,850,327	1,002,309	4,852,636	1,119,511	44,857	87,771	287	1,252,426
30 September	4,469,435	1,001,939	5,471,374	1,119,210	21,704	80,464	2	1,221,290
31 October	4,827,402	1,029,625	5,857,027	1,099,098	16,769	74,978	2	1,190,847
30 November	4,930,201	1,614,620	6,544,821	1,079,032	14,085	73,129	2	1,166,248
31 December	5,136,694	1,427,076	6,563,770	1,055,069	14,087	67,028	3	1,136,187
1915								
31 January	5,158,947	1,344,897	6,503,844	1,023,951	10,680	74,455	2	1,109,088
28 February	5,246,319	989,154	6,235,473	977,572	9,914	97,214	8	1,084,708
31 March	5,537,862	940,518	6,478,380	940,885	6,297	95,306	6	1,042,494
30 April	5,907,937	1,247,753	7,155,690	915,754	5,698	82,018	31	1,003,501
31 May	6,026,838	1,268,428	7,295,266	859,128	5,305	104,475	40	968,948
30 June	6,385,419	753,389	7,138,808	778,023	5,232	98,932	81	882,268
31 July	6,400,530	658,622	7,059,152	755,302	5,128	145,498	1,023	906,951
31 August	6,571,621	833,785	7,405,406	750,623	24,543	171,379	1,047	947,592
30 September	6,859,875	814,895	7,674,770	715,655	60,000	141,823	1,695	919,173
31 October	7,109,008	1,228,702	8,337,710	705,985	58,153	124,142	2,640	890,920
30 November	6,961,134	1,455,311	8,416,445	694,453	27,261	103,934	3,569	829,217
31 December	7,162,355	272,809	7,435,164	684,885	60,000	128,459	5,710	879,054
1916								
31 January	7,254,598	1,077,175	8,331,773	649,231	40,281	105,200	3,774	798,486
29 February	7,378,921	1,658,134	9,037,055	617,033	21,138	239,685	4,485	882,341
31 March	7,599,425	1,696,026	9,295,451	583,468	29,401	174,945	4,680	792,494
30 April	7,942,731	1,463,750	9,406,481	544,170	24,626	232,873	4,200	805,869
31 May	7,884,870	1,746,475	9,631,345	503,065	60,000	273,437	13,685	850,187
30 June	8,265,216	1,398,693	9,663,909	469,183	60,000	249,952	25,154	804,289
31 July	8,618,370	1,342,288	9,960,658	401,027	60,000	183,575	6,411	651,013
31 August	9,091,889	1,032,610	10,124,499	391,958	36,453	195,044	2,350	625,805
30 September	9,800,990	1,380,640	11,181,630	352,624	35,669	135,577	1,746	525,616
31 October	10,426,903	1,152,234	11,579,137	318,441	13,361	129,768	1,834	463,404
30 November	10,805,530	1,418,517	12,224,047	298,997	8,448	127,422	1,673	436,540
31 December	10,888,619	424,498	11,313,603	290,024	5,644	160,318	2,188	458,174

1917

31 January	10,886,850	2,318,794	13,205,644	290,737	17,364	259,260	9,097	576,458
28 February	11,150,474	1,995,488	13,145,962	281,862	41,893	261,207	8,289	593,251
31 March	11,609,169	1,791,614	13,400,783	272,278	50,032	307,789	6,120	636,219
30 April	11,921,655	1,567,681	13,489,336	262,709	46,723	310,178	4,781	674,391
31 May	12,107,800	1,894,957	14,002,757	253,233	60,000	353,800	6,686	673,719
30 June	12,688,955	436,082	13,125,037	252,436	60,000	373,615	11,284	697,335
31 July	13,255,920	1,302,252	14,558,172	252,632	60,000	334,991	26,771	674,394
31 August	14,392,465	976,336	15,368,801	253,192	60,000	494,969	36,653	844,814
30 September	15,463,222	1,282,539	16,745,761	253,586	60,000	552,099	15,508	881,193
31 October	16,825,711	1,556,523	18,382,234	253,733	60,000	575,072	53,436	942,241
30 November	17,722,001	1,547,671	19,269,672	257,012	60,000	533,847	89,896	940,755
31 December	18,439,695	1,958,349	20,398,044	265,136	60,000	631,233	85,190	1,041,559

1918

31 January	18,541,116	2,088,567	20,629,683	264,816	60,000	716,445	115,097	1,156,358
28 February	19,013,262	1,725,492	20,738,754	264,970	60,000	717,234	147,211	1,189,415
31 March	20,095,552	1,272,900	21,368,452	265,201	60,000	684,750	220,155	1,210,106
30 April	21,445,625	1,431,328	22,876,953	265,312	60,000	661,611	197,232	1,184,155
31 May	22,559,518	1,209,231	23,768,749	265,429	60,000	599,768	205,456	1,130,653
30 June	23,873,037	1,563,754	25,436,791	265,505	60,000	480,293	208,040	1,013,838
31 July	25,365,591	1,709,436	27,075,027	265,461	60,000	378,046	111,405	814,912
31 August	26,990,451	1,609,230	28,599,681	265,763	60,000	360,133	31,573	717,469
30 September	28,646,034	2,458,547	31,104,581	267,659	12,948	354,634	12,699	647,940
31 October	31,483,231	3,362,314	34,845,545	267,711	17,764	340,555	13,991	640,021

Source : Alexander Popovics, *Das Geldwesen im Kriege*, Appendix, Tables II and III

(The figures in brackets signify the number of companies included)
BG = Gross Profit RG = Net Profit

Business Groups		1913	1914	1915	1916	1917	1918
				Austrian Crowns			
Coal (6)	B.G.	26,819	23,715	26,934	33,704	35,570	35,926
	R.G.	14,128	10,486	14,154	16,231	14,587	13,590
Oil, Petroleum (3)	B.G.	15,045	16,537	12,472	41,770	49,835	55,221
	R.G.	3,779	4,080	−2,041	22,050	21,570	21,657
Mining, Metallurgy (5)	B.G.	76,767	58,810	80,688	112,772	122,008	130,859
	R.G.	38,823	19,465	39,003	51,848	40,072	30,080
Mills (3)	B.G.	1,157	3,555	2,822	3,308	3,474	2,916
	R.G.	293	1,712	1,707	1,269	1,502	928
Beer (7)	B.G.	33,507	33,045	33,126	35,366	18,257	32,604
	R.G.	3,950	3,622	4,695	3,937	3,258	6,547
Sugar (5)	B.G.	39,014	37,779	45,017	45,804	55,766	50,987
	R.G.	4,229	3,563	6,918	8,437	8,393	7,459
Alcohol (1)	B.G.	1,101	1,025	1,151	1,412	1,630	1,703
	R.G.	353	271	382	466	450	464
Textiles (8)	B.G.	22,355	22,465	27,868	43,029	41,822	49,303
	R.G.	2,672	3,858	8,767	12,638	13,558	7,472
Leather (2)	B.G.	2,164	3,451	6,892	8,647	6,317	5,520
	R.G.	408	678	3,168	4,285	2,179	1,878
Arms & Munitions (5)	B.G.	15,724	24,301	54,302	76,545	106,291	108,170
	R.G.	8,534	14,624	25,968	38,816	36,855	21,157
Machines, Rolling Stock (9)	B.G.	9,621	14,718	25,242	41,290	56,033	65,921
	R.G.	1,946	5,992	12,128	18,525	17,029	11,909
Metal Goods (8)	B.G.	19,504	17,978	25,841	46,766	58,407	69,130
	R.G.	8,741	7,487	13,109	20,828	19,707	17,323
Automobiles (2)	B.G.	2,070	2,601	4,263	7,184	13,234	22,371
	R.G.	576	610	1,178	1,787	2,395	2,579
Electrical Goods (7)	B.G.	28,489	26,499	29,489	37,044	47,333	61,516
	R.G.	7,017	4,403	6,935	10,201	9,854	6,718
Bricks	B.G.	18,929	13,482	6,695	8,365	14,653	19,266
	R.G.	5,275	2,222	−404	974	3,860	4,494
Glass (3)	B.G.	3,072	2,157	2,995	5,475	7,070	9,236
	R.G.	423	−241	489	1,866	2,076	2,815
Paper (5)	B.G.	7,242	7,427	5,872	10,815	14,523	15,745
	R.G.	3,543	−343	−3,082	4,725	5,636	5,795
Chemicals (7)	B.G.	21,724	21,095	31,608	53,719	57,291	61,878
	R.G.	7,861	7,842	15,102	28,566	24,603	24,390
Banks (8)	B.G.	187,403	177,473	197,316	249,923	325,400	351,808
	R.G.	96,807	70,223	100,360	119,753	141,941	89,386
Wholesalers (5)	B.G.	14,579	13,264	17,154	23,458	28,530	34,791
	R.G.	3,188	2,442	5,552	8,269	9,134	8,173
Communications Enterpr. (4)	B.G.	54,552	54,443	60,819	68,984	66,829	63,975
	R.G.	34,096	31,774	37,873	43,716	36,227	29,153

Business Groups		1913	1914	1915	1916	1917	1918
				Per Cent of Net Profit			
Coal (6)	M.Z.	100	69	54	28	13	7
	R.G.%	53	44	53	48	41	38
Oil, Petroleum (3)	M.Z.	100	108	−36	262	111	69
	R.G.%	25	25	−16	53	43	39
Mining, Metallurgy (5)	M.Z.	100	48	60	37	15	7
	R.G.%	51	33	48	46	33	23
Mills (3)	M.Z.	100	567	368	116	71	23
	R.G.%	25	48	60	38	43	32
Beer (7)	M.Z.	100	91	80	31	12	15
	R.G.%	12	11	14	11	18	20
Sugar (5)	M.Z.	100	83	111	64	30	17
	R.G.%	11	9	15	18	15	15
Alcohol (1)	M.Z.	100	76	74	42	19	12
	R.G.%	32	26	33	33	28	27
Textiles (8)	M.Z.	100	138	193	133	72	56
	R.G.%	12	17	31	29	32	15
Leather (2)	M.Z.	100	161	457	352	84	48
	R.G.%	19	20	46	50	34	34
Arms & Munitions (5)	M.Z.	100	192	214	160	74	27
	R.G.%	64	67	54	55	38	22
Machines, Rolling Stock (9)	M.Z.	100	293	361	263	120	49
	R.G.%	20	41	48	45	30	18
Metal Goods (8)	M.Z.	100	82	86	65	31	16
	R.G.%	45	42	51	45	34	25
Automobiles (2)	M.Z.	100	99	111	74	54	33
	R.G.%	28	23	28	25	18	12
Electrical Goods (7)	M.Z.	100	60	60	43	20	9
	R.G.%	25	17	24	28	21	11
Bricks, Cement (6)	M.Z.	100	39	−4	4	9	6
	R.G.%	28	16	−6	12	26	23
Glass (3)	M.Z.	100	−53	63	106	64	49
	R.G.%	14	−11	16	34	29	30
Paper (5)	M.Z.	100	−8	46	34	22	13
	R.G.%	49	−5	−52	44	39	37
Chemicals (7)	M.Z.	100	96	127	119	47	28
	R.G.%	29	37	40	46	39	36
Banks (8)	M.Z.	100	68	56	30	19	7
	R.G.%	52	40	51	48	44	25
Wholesalers (5)	M.Z.	100	72	95	62	37	19
	R.G.%	22	18	32	35	32	23
Communications Enterpr. (4)	M.Z.	63	87	60	31	14	6
	R.G.%	100	58	62	63	54	46

Source: Wilhelm Winkler, *Die Einkommensverschiebungen in Österreich während des Krieges*, pp. 166–70.

Table A5: Development of the ten biggest Viennese banks' own resources, 1913–18

	1913	1914	1915	1916	1917	1918
Anglobank						
a) Own Capital	100,000,080.—	100,000,080.—	100,000,080.—	130,000,080.—	130,000,080.—	150,000,000.—
b) Reserves	26,708,929,02	29,708,929,02	30,208,929,02	51,414,438,18	54,414,438,18	77,886,322,08
c) War Losses Res.	—	5,000,000.—	5,000,000.—	5,000,000.—	5,000,000.—	5,000,000.—
Bankverein						
a) Own Capital	130,000,000.—	150,000,000.—	150,000,000.—	150,000,000.—	150,000,000.—	180,000,000.—
b) Reserves	43,164,287,24	48,212,661,02	41,331,760,61	41,900,990,40	42,861,421,68	58,825,144,12
c) War Losses Res.	—	8,740,526,08	8,740,526,08	8,740,526,08	8,740,526,08	8,740,526,08
Boden-Creditanstalt						
a) Own Capital	54,000,000.—	54,000,000.—	54,000,000.—	63,000,000.—	63,000,000.—	75,000,000.—
b) Reserves	111,121,231,12	113,798,831,12	115,548,831,12	145,094,831,12	148,444,831,12	192,810,831,12
c) War Losses Res.						
d) Premium Funds	9,600,000.—	9,600,000.—	9,600,000.—	9,600,000.—	9,600,000.—	9,600,000.—
Creditanstalt						
a) Own Capital	150,000,000.—	150,000,000.—	150,000,000.—	170,000,000.—	170,000,000.—	200,000,000.—
b) Reserves	93,616,044.—	96,116,044.—	96,116,044.—	112,695,690.—	115,195,690.—	148,724,176.—
c) War Losses Res.	—	5,000,000.—	5,000,000.—	5,000,000.—	5,000,000.—	5,000,000.—
Depositenbank						
a) Own Capital	33,000,000.—	33,000,000.—	33,000,000.—	40,000,000.—	60,000,000.—	80,000,000.—
b) Reserves	11,656,955,47	12,644,144,66	11,316,356,09	13,861,008,98	23,323,682,33	36,690,936,73
c) War Losses Res.	—	3,051,870,14	3,051,870,14	3,051,870,14	3,051,870,14	3,051,870,14
Escompte-Gesellschaft						
a) Own Capital	75,000,000.—	100,000,000.—	100,000,000.—	100,000,000.—	100,000,000.—	100,000,000.—
b) Reserves	25,386,668,84	45,483,346,87	46,375,336,79	47,998,842,59	49,670,129,93	52,411,850,64
c) War Losses Res.	—	—	—	—	—	—
Länderbank						
a) Own Capital	130,000,000.—	130,000,000.—	130,000,000.—	130,000,000.—	130,000,000.—	160,000,000.—
b) Reserves	18,866,282,05	20,873,668,30	16,608,819,17	21,592,096,34	24,935,955,77	28,858,881,27
c) Premium Funds	5,222,771,97	5,222,771,97	5,222,771,97	5,222,771,97	5,222,771,97	16,181,760,93
d) War Losses Res.	—	—	8,500,000.—	8,500,000.—	8,500,000.—	8,500,000.—
Mercurbank						
a) Own Capital	50,000,000.—	50,000,000.—	50,000,000.—	50,000,000.—	66,000,000.—	80,000,000.—
b) Reserves	22,000,000.—	22,750,000.—	23,000,000.—	24,000,000.—	31,600,000.—	39,600,000.—
c) War Losses Res.	—	2,000,000.—	2,000,000.—	2,000,000.—	2,000,000.—	2,000,000.—
Unionbank						
a) Own Capital	70,000,000.—	70,000,000.—	70,000,000.—	70,000,000.—	100,000,000.—	100,000,000.—
b) Reserves	19,386,028,72	20,130,631,01	20,130,631,01	20,713,961,67	35,667,267,96	36,863,267,78
Verkehrsbank						
a) Own Capital	42,000,000.—	50,400,000.—	50,400,000.—	60,200,000.—	65,000,040.—	75,040,000.—
b) Reserves	10,852,364,41	13,636,528,03	13,816,528,03	16,712,500.—	19,358,228.—	26,265,473.—

Source: Max Sokal, *Die Tätigkeit der Banken*, p. 26 et seq.

Table A6: Post-war inflation, November 1918–December 1922

		Banknote Circul. (Cr. m.)	Banknotes Increase (2,500 Cr. m. = 1)	Cost of Living[a] Month. Av. (Jul. = 1)	Vienna Dollar Rate
1918	November	(32,915.8)	13.17	16.40	14.330
	December	(34,889.0)	13.96		16.160
1919	15 January	(35,944.2)	14.38	28.37	16.027
	15 February	(37,572.2)	15.03		19.128
	15 March	(37,408.2)	14.96		20.522
	15 April	5,122.3	10.25[b]		26.79
	15 May	5,663.5	11.33		24.50
	15 June	6,532.4	13.07		30.19
	15 July	7,578.4	15.16	31.02	32.25
	15 August	8,571.5	17.14		39.—
	15 September	9,382.7	18.77		60.75
	15 October	10,075.6	20.02		85.—
	15 November	11,034.3	22.07		101.10
	15 December	11,508.3	23.02		153.33
1920	15 January	12,307.7	24.62	49.22	204.43
	15 February	13,389.7	26.74		279.17
	15 March	14,793.0	29.59		227.14
	15 April	15,379.7	30.76	58.42	201.42
	15 May	15,137.4	30.27		205.—
	15 June	16,329.2	32.27		138.57
	15 July	17,451.1	34.90	63.76	147.86
	15 August	18,665.8	37.33		206.25
	15 September	20,566.3	41.13		238.33
	15 October	23,539.6	47.08	69.60	310.—
	15 November	25,978.0	51.96		430.—
	15 December	28,935.5	57.87		620.58
1921	15 January	32,501.0	65.00	92.18	704.—
	15 February	36,590.4	73.18	99.56	665.—
	15 March	38,774.3	77.55	111.74	682.—
	15 April	42,394.5	84.79	111.34	636.—
	15 May	44,274.4	88.55	118.80	584.—
	15 June	47,208.6	94.42	118.95	675.—
	15 July	50,435.3	100.87	124.66	775.—
	15 August	55,247.6	110.50	123.52	1,020.—
	15 September	61,322.7	122.65	150.61	1,600.—
	15 October	79,292.2	154.58	237.76	2,637.—
	15 November	103,129.0	206.—	374.37	5,950.—
	15 December	142,871.8	286.—	661.—	6,450.—
1922	15 January	193,749.4	387.—	830.—	6,800.—
	15 February	238,665.7	477.—	980.—	6,300.—
	15 March	271,757.9	544.—	989.—	8,050.—
	15 April	321,325.7	644.—	1,089.—	7,625.—
	15 May	351,460.8	703.—	1,364.—	10,000.—
	15 June	439,463.6	879.—	2,339.—	19,400.—
	15 July	616,861.1	1,234.—	3,308.—	29,875.—
	15 August	913,932.4	1,828.—	7,422.—	58,400.—
	15 September	1,700,865.4	3,402.—	14,153.—	74,450.—
	15 October	2,590,414.3	5,181.—	12,965.—	73,510.—
	15 November	3,132,670.8	6,265.—	12,158.—	73,400.—
	15 December	3,711,593.4	7,423.—	11,737.—	70,450.—

[a] Without rent.
[b] Compared with pre-war circulation of 500,000,000 crowns within the territory of the later Austrian Republic.

Sources: Banknote Circulation = Walré de Bordes, *The Austrian Crown*, pp. 47–50
    Cost of Living = *Statistische Nachrichten*, December 1923, p. 195.
    Dollar Rate Quotations = Walré de Bordes, *The Austrian Crown*, pp. 115–35.

Table A7: Development of real wages in the machine-building and metal goods industry

	Metal Workers Min. Wk. Wage[a]		Wk. Wages Ind.		Living Costs Index[b]
	Skilled Worker	Unskil. Worker	Skilled Worker	Unskil. Worker	
July 1914	28	21	1	1	1
June 1919	280	—	10	—	28.37
December 1920	1,411	1,301	50	62	89.00
March 1921	1,603	1,469	57	70	111.74
June 1921	1,841	1,677	66	80	118.95
March 1922	16,368	14,784	584	704	989.00
June 1922	43,296	40,128	1,546	1,911	2,339.00
September 1922	241,824	227,712	8,636	10,843	14,153.00
December 1922	218,016	206,208	7,786	9,820	11,737.00

Source: International Labour Review, Vol. VIII, July–December 1923, p. 92.
Benedikt Kautsky, 'Löhne und Gehälter', Schriften des Vereins für Sozialpolitik, Vol. CLXIX, p. 113
[a] in crowns.
[b] without rent.

Table A8: Liabilities of the Viennese Banks, nominal development (in 000 crowns)

	1913	1919	1920	1921	1922	1923
Creditanstalt	783,725	2,916,659	10,442,881	80,432,792[c]	1,368,786,427[c]	2,006,152,282[c]
Boden-Creditanstalt	282,933	3,253,062	5,625,753	31,860,558	1,071,845,319[c]	1,410,025,114[c]
Niederösterreichische Escompte-Gesellschaft	254,473	1,145,417[a]	2,546,300[a]	26,928,183[a]	995,299,371[a]	2,153,411,591[a]
Bankverein	514,638	4,542,934	8,983,531	75,742,303	1,036,250,292[c]	1,651,109,305[c]
Unionbank	194,694	848,424	2,541,728	18,413,707	248,456,165[c]	941,464,322[c]
Mercurbank	143,926	1,049,257	2,331,776[b]	18,977,068	302,430,082	546,202,233
Verkehrsbank	164,805	1,178,450	3,482,861	18,519,498[d]	321,954,109	975,250,484[c]

Source: Compass, Vol. I for the years 1915, 1922, 1923, and 1925
[a] Liabilities as well as Loans and Advances in foreign currencies were till 1920 converted at peace-time exchange rates. From 1920 onwards accounts in identical currencies, in so far as they offset one another, were entered in peace-time crowns and only the balances adjusted to the rate on the balance sheet date.
[b] Successor States balance sheet items adjusted at par.
[c] Loans and Advances in foreign currencies largely set off against Liabilities in foreign currencies; only the balances converted into crowns.
[d] Old accounts adjusted to peace-time parity; new ones approximately to daily rate. Czechoslovak assets were converted at Cz. Crown 1 = Aust. Cr. 1.
[e] No set-offs effected.

Table A9: Deposits and cash certificates at Viennese Banks, nominal development (in 000 crowns)

	1913	1919	1920	1921	1922	1923
Creditanstalt	80,387	146,327	122,938	216,910	2,228,550	15,733,626
Boden-Creditanstalt	—	—	—	—	—	—
Niederösterreichische Escompte-Gesellschaft	23,924	52,040	48,676	92,228	1,330,970	6,545,108
Bankverein	133,248	536,310	623,255	922,381	8,872,367	36,900,081
Unionbank	28,530	82,967	95,679	171,504	2,909,116	9,148,459
Mercurbank	42,938	119,988	131,729	254,789	5,049,164	42,439,091
Verkehrsbank	71,829	219,025	277,051	435,958	7,638,742	28,042,950

Source: *Compass*, Vol. I for the years 1915, 1922, 1923, and 1925.

Table A10: Loans and advances by Viennese Banks, nominal development (in 000 crowns)

	1913	1919	1920	1921	1922	1923
Creditanstalt	734,811	2,550,135	9,508,570	77,334,561	1,279,045,305	1,927,737,512
Boden-Creditanstalt	326,407[a]	2,909,153	5,288,131	30,910,875	995,470,564	1,404,955,742
Niederösterreichische Escompte-Gesellschaft	288,031	1,197,336	2,495,180	29,234,578	841,941,737	1,844,961,313
Bankverein	519,959	3,502,288	7,236,706	70,260,602	915,332,318	1,710,990,422
Unionbank	191,669	788,467	2,268,581	17,203,835	188,502,532	1,039,398,738
Mercurbank	143,565	1,106,190	2,311,956	17,787,621	267,712,152	592,262,865
Verkehrsbank	174,565	1,180,798	3,638,826	16,956,596	288,790,573	1,047,985,383

Source: *Compass*, Vol. I for the years 1915, 1922, 1923, and 1925.
[a] Inc. Syndicate Business. See also Notes to Table A8.

Table A11: Creditanstalt earnings, nominal development (in 000 crowns)

	1913	1919	1920	1921	1922	1923
Interest	25,475	48,318	154,542	1,300,787	28,884,300	78,765,677
Securities & Syndicate Bus.	2,411	26,917	73,586	499,493	11,015,300	88,172,544
Commissions & Merchandise	7,597	20,395	66,508	1,406,891	35,771,960	114,703,202
Foreign Exchange	822	13,567	80,435	426,319	6,411,024	24,466,312
Gross Profit[a]	36,622	109,375	375,171	3,633,490	82,082,484	306,107,735
Net Profit[a]	20,683	46,138	112,179	935,176	21,698,943	75,278,979

Source: *Compass*, Vol. I for the years 1915, 1922, 1923, and 1925.
[a] Without Carry Forward

Sources and Bibliography

Index to German-Language Abbreviations, Place-Names, and Terms used in the Bibliography

ABBREVIATIONS
Bd., Bde. = volume/s
Ders. = idem
Dies. = idem
Hrsg. = edited by,
       published by
Jg. = year (of public.)
Nr. = no.
s.d. = see under

PLACE-NAMES
Brüssel = Brussels
Brünn = (post-1918) Brno
Bukarest = Bucharest
Genf = Geneva
Köln = Cologne

TERMS
Aufsätze = Articles
ebenda = ibid.
Gesammelte Werke = Collected Works
Heft = number, issue
Sonderheft = special issue
Werkausgabe = Collected Works
von, vom = by
zitiert nach = quoted from

München = Munich
Prag = Prague
Rom = Rome
Warschau = Warsaw
Wien = Vienna
Zürich = Zurich

Sources and Bibliography

1. Archivalische Quellen (Archives)

AVA (Allgemeines Verwaltungsarchiv), Wien (General Administrative Archives, Vienna) .

Ministerium des Inneren 2544/1910–17476/1916.
Handelsministerium HL 1390/zu 17476/1914–PZ37175/1914–5698 KP/1914–34714/1914–37175/1914–38155/14 G/1914–39799/1914.
Korrespondenz Renner K 65a.
Sozialdemokratischer Parlamentsclub, Karton 45, Mappe 71.
Ministerratsprotokolle 191–194.
Sammelakt WEWA 1919, Karton 19 und 39 – Z. 68/99/161/186/467/700/1014/4768.
Sammelakt WEWA 1920, Z. 95/463/884/1097/1382/92190.
Sammelakt WEWA 1925, Z. 190/191.
Finanzministerium 14167/1916 Beilage B – 1629/1917 – 31 617/1917.

Archiv des Finanzministeriums, Wien (Ministry of Finance Archives, Vienna)

1914: 2091/1726–915/82894/92190.
1915: 789/54907.
1916: 13438/40968/79129/84508/90822.
1917: 20199/36848/45929/47965/55726/65507/98166.
1918: 9691/24941/25621/33434.
1919: 603 Präs/619 Präs/2291 AP/35472/53645/57606/83623/87111/87794.
1920: 21623/46707/55021/66254/75174/80242/101096/105707/107125.
1921: 2530/30976/32954/35428/52279/81756/107792.

Haus-, Hof- und Staatsarchiv, Wien (Dynastic, Court, and State Archives, Vienna)

PA, Karton 312, 314, 511.
NPA, Karton 261, Nachlaß Otto Bauer, 345, 346, 349.
Ad. Reg. Karton 69.
Neue Ad. Reg. Karton 263.

Archiv der Creditanstalt, Wien (Creditanstalt Archives, Vienna)
Verwaltungsprotokolle und Geschaftsberichte 1914–1923.

National Archives, Washington

Microfilm Publication No. 695 'Records of Department of State Relating to Internal Affairs of Austria-Hungary and Austria 1910–1929', Roll 51.

Public Record Office, Foreign Office, London
FO 371/HN 00981/HN 01008/HN 01119/HN 01157/HN 01206/HN 02382/HN 10960.

SOURCES AND BIBLIOGRAPHY

Zentrales Staatsarchiv der DDR, Potsdam (Central State Archives, Potsdam)

09.01 A.A. (Außenamt) 40126/40341/41773.
31.01 RWM (Reichswirtschaftsministerium) 663/15691/15729.

Archiv der Wiener Handelskammer, Wien (Vienna Chamber of Commerce Archives, Vienna)

Nr. 28833 I — Verhandlungsschrift der gemeinsamen Tagung des deutschen Industrie-und Handelstages und des österreichischen Kammertages in Wien, 21. und 22. Sept. 1928.

Landesgericht, Wien (Provincial Court Records, Vienna)

Prozeßakte Ehrenfest, 26d Vr. 6373/31–37.

2. **Protokolle** (Parliamentary Proceedings)

Stenographische Protokolle des Hauses der Abgeordneten, 1917.
Stenographische Protokolle der Konstituierenden Sitzung der Nationalversammlung, 21. 10. 1918.
Stenographische Protokolle des Nationalrates, Erläuterungen, Beilagen, 1922.

3. **Gesetzblätter** (Law Gazettes)

RGBı *(Reichsgesetzblatt)*
1912: 236.

BGBı *(Bundesgesetzblatt)*
1920: 42.
1921: 409/705.
1922: 439/488 491/505/559/872.

LGBı *(Landesgesetzblatt)*
1921: 127/128.

StGBı *(Staatsgesetzblatt)*
1918: 20/74/122/138.
1919: 112/114/150/152/162/191/268/281/283/381/395/581.
1920: 153/313/315/488.

4. **Statistiken und Dokumentationen** (Statistical and Documentary Sources)

Anbaufläche und Ernteergebnisse in der Republik Österreich im Jahre 1918. Hrsg. vom Staatsamt für Land- und Forstwirtschaft, Wien 1919.
Bericht der Metallzentrale-Aktiengesellschaft über ihre Tätigkeit in den ersten drei Geschäftsjahren, Wien 1917.
Bericht der Niederösterreichischen Handels- und Gewerbekammer über die Wirtschaftsverhältnisse 1914–1918, Wien 1920.
Bericht der Österreichisch-ungarischen Bank, Wien 1917.

Bericht über die Industrie, den Handel und die Verkehrsverhältnisse in Niederösterreich während des Jahres 1910. Hrsg. von der Niederösterr. Handelskammer, Wien 1911.

Bericht über die Tätigkeit der Oezeg, Wien 1917.

Chronique des Événements Politiques et Économiques dans le Bassin Danubien 1918–1938, Paris 1938.

Compass. Finanzielles Jahrbuch, Jg. 1905–1925.

Der Außenhandel Österreichs in der Zeit zwischen den beiden Weltkriegen. Hrsg. vom Österreichischen Statistischen Zentralamt, Wien 1946.

Die Tätigkeit des Verbandes der sozialdemokratischen Abgeordneten der Republik Österreich, Heft 16, Wien 1922.

Die Wohnungspolitik der Gemeinde Wien. Hrsg. vom Gesellschafts- und Wirtschaftsmuseum Wien, Wien 1929.

Ein Jahrhundert Creditanstalt-Bankverein, Wien 1957.

Festschrift der österreichischen Wirtschaftsunternehmungen im Interessenkreis der Creditanstalt-Bankverein. Als Ehrung für Generaldirektor Dr. Josef Joham zum 60. Geburtstag, Wien 1949.

Festschrift des Österreichischen Ingenieur- und Architekten-Vereins aus Anlaß seines 75jährigen Bestehens, Wien 1923.

Financial Reconstruction of Austria. Report of the Financial Committee of the Council. League of Nations, Genf 1922.

International Financial Conference. Report of the Conference, Brüssel 1920.

Materialien zur österreichischen Produktions- und Betriebsstatistik. Zusammengestellt im Auftrag des k.k. Handelsministeriums vom k.k. Österreichischen Handelsmuseum, Wien 1916.

Mitteilungen der Handelspolitischen Zentralstelle der Vereinigten Handels- und Gewerbekammern und des Zentralverbandes der Industriellen Österreichs, Wien 1914.

Mitteilungen der Statistischen Zentralkommission, Wien 1921.

Mitteilungen des Direktoriums der Österreichischen Nationalbank, Jg. 1923 und 1924.

Mitteilungen des k.k. Finanzministeriums, Wien 1917.

Nachrichten des Staatsamtes für Soziale Verwaltung, Wien 1920.

Österreichisches Biographisches Lexikon.

Österreichisches Jahrbuch, Jg. 1920 und 1923.

Österreichische Parteiprogramme 1868–1966. Hrsg. von Klaus Berchtold, Wien 1967.

Österreichisches Statistisches Handbuch für die im Reichsrat vertretenen Königreiche und Länder. Hrsg. von der k.k. Statistischen Zentralkommission, Jg. 1905, 1914, und 1915.

Report of the Provisional Delegation of the League of Nations, Genf 1921.

Statistik des Ausbaus der Großwasserkräfte bis 1924 in der Republik Österreich. Hrsg. vom Wewa. Sonderdruck der Zeitschrift, 'Die Wasserkräfte', Wien 1925.

Statistisches Handbuch für die Republik Österreich, Jg. I–V, 1921–1924.

Statistische Monatsschrift, Jg. 1906, 1913 und 1914.

Statistische Nachrichten. Hrsg. von der Statistischen Zentralkommission, Jg. 1915, 1923 und 1925.

Statistische Rückblicke aus Österreich. Hrsg. von der k.k. Statistischen Zentralkommission, Wien 1913.

Statistische Übersichten betreffend den auswärtigen Handel der wichtigsten Staaten in den Jahren 1903–1907, 1907–1911. Hrsg. vom Handelsstatisstischen Dienste des K.k. Handelsministeriums, Wien 1910 und 1914.

Statistische Übersichten über den auswärtigen Handel. Hrsg. von der Statistischen Zentralkommission, Wien 1922.

Statistiken zur Arbeitslosenversicherung. Hrsg. vom Bundesministerium für soziale Verwaltung, Jg. 1920, 1925 und 1930.

Tabellen zur Währungsstatistik. Hrsg. vom k.k. Finanzministerium, Wien 1904.

Verhandlungen der vom k.k. Handelsministerium veranstalteten Kartellenquéte, Wien 1912.

Wirtschaftsstatistisches Jahrbuch 1925. Hrsg. von der Kammer für Arbeiter und Angestellte Wien.

Wirtschaftsstatistische Materialien über Deutsch-Österreich. Hrsg. von der Niederösterr. Handels- und Gewerbekammer, Wien 1919.

5. Zeitungen und Zeitschriften (Newpapers and Periodicals)

Archiv für Sozialwissenschaften und Sozialpolitik, Jg. 1921–1932.

Arbeit und Wirtschaft, Jg. 1923.

Arbeiter-Zeitung, Jg. 1913–1923 und 1932.

Bankarchiv, Jg. 1971.

Berliner-Zeitung am Mittag, 13 November 1924.

Christlichsoziale Arbeiterzeitung, 10 November 1921.

Der Abend, Jg. 1917 und 1922.

Der Kampf. Sozialdemokratische Monatsschrift, Jg. 1914–1923.

Der Österreichische Volkswirt, Jg. 1913–1930.

Der Tresor, Jg. 1912.

Die Börse, Jg. 1921.

Die Fackel, Nr. 514–518, 1919.

Die Furche, 27 November 1971.

Die Gewerkschaft, Jg. 1920 und 1921.

Die Reichspost, Jg. 1918, 1919 und 1922.

Lloyds Bank Review, May 1934.

Mitteilungen des Verbandes österreichischer Banken und Bankiers, Jg. 1923–1925.

Neue Freie Presse, Jg. 1912–1924.

Neues Wiener Tagblatt, Jg. 1922 und 1925.

Pester Lloyd, 15 February 1920.

Revue politique et parlamentaire, 10 June 1923.

Schmollers Jahrbuch für Gesetzgebung, Verwaltung und Volkswirtschaft, Jg. 1906 und 1924.

Schriften des Vereins für Sozialpolitik, Bd. 158 (1919), 162 (1921), 164 (1923), 165 (1924), 169 (1925) und 174 (1928).

Wiener Zeitung, 22 July 1922

Zeitschrift für Nationalökonomie, Jg. 1932.

Zeitschrift für Volkswirtschaft und Sozialpolitik, Jg. 1922.

6. Literatur (Bibliography)

Adler, Freidrich, Machtfragen und Formfragen, in: Der Kampf, V/1919.

Adler, Viktor, Um den 4 August, Diskussionen der Wiener Vertrauensmänner nach Kriegsbeginn, in: Viktor Adler der Parteimann, Reden und Aufsätze, Heft IX, Wien 1929.

Aldcroft, Derek H., Die Zwanziger Jahre. Von Versailles zur Wallstreet 1919–1929, München 1978.

Allmayer-Beck, Max von, Materialien zum österreichischen Kartellwesen, Wien 1909.

Almond, Nina, und Ralph Haswell Lutz (Hrsg.), The Treaty of St. Germain. A Documentary History of its Territorial and Political Clauses, Stanford 1935.

Arlt. Ilse, Der Einzelhaushalt, in: Schriften des Vereins für Sozialpolitik, Bd. 169, München-Leipzig 1925.

Ausch, Karl, Als die Banken fielen, Wien 1968.

Austerlitz, Freidrich, Die Sozialdemokratie im Kampf gegen Genf, in: Der Kampf, XII/1922.

Ders., Können wir nicht anders? in: Der Kampf, XII/1919.

Bachinger, Karl, Das Verkehrswesen, in: Die Habsburgermonarchie 1848–1918, Bd. 1, Wien 1973.

Bairoch, Paul, Europe's Gross National Product 1800–1975, in: The Journal of European History, V/1976.

Baltzarek, Franz, Die Geschichte der Wiener Börse, Wien 1973.

Bartsch, Franz, Statistiche Daten über die Zahlungsbilanz Österreich-Ungarns vor Ausbruch des Krieges, in: Mitteilungen des k.k. Finanzministeriums, Wien 1917.

Basch, Antonin, The Danube Basin and the German Economic Sphere, New York 1943.

Bauer, Otto, Bolschewismus oder Sozialdemokratie, in: Werkausgabe, Bd. 2, Wien 1976.

Ders, Das Selstbestimmungsrecht der österreichischen Nationen, in: Der Kampf, IV/1918.

Ders., Die österreichische Revolution, in: Werkausgabe, Bd. 2.

Ders., Die Sozialisierungsaktion im ersten Jahr der Republik, in: Werkausgabe, Bd. 2.

Ders., Die Teuerung, in: Werkausgabe, Bd. 1, 1975.

Ders., Der Weg zum Sozialismus, in: Werkausgabe, Bd. 2.

Ders., Der Genfer Knechtungsvertrag und die Sozialdemokratie, in: Werkausgabe, Bd. 2.

Ders., Einführung in die Volkswirtschaftslehre, in: Werkausgabe, Bd. 4, Wien 1976.

Ders., Die Wirtschaftskrise in Österreich. Ihre Ursachen – ihre Heilung, in: Werkausgabe, Bd. 3.

Ders., Imperialismus und soziale Revolution, in: Werkausgabe, Bd. 6, Wien 1979.

Berchtold, Klaus (Hrsg.), Österreichische Parteiprogramme 1868–1966, Wien 1967.

Berend, Iván T., und György Ranki, Ungarns wirtschaftliche Entwicklung 1849–1918, in: Die Habsburgermonarchie 1848–1918, Bd. 1, Wien 1973.

Bienenfeld, Rudolf, Die neuen Bestimmungen über Preistreiberei, in: Der Österreichische Volkswirt, 28. 4. 1917.

Böhm-Bawerk, Eugen von, Unsere passive Handelsbilanz, in: Neue Freie Presse, 6., 8. und 9. 1. 1918.

Bosl, Karl (Hrsg.), Versailles-St. Germain-Trianon, München-Wien 1971.

Brady, Robert A., The Rationalization Movement in German Industry. A Study in the Evolution of Economic Planning, Berkeley 1933.

Braun, Martha Stephanie, Die Doppelnote, in: Schriften des Vereins für Sozialpolitik, Bd., 165, München-Leipzig 1924.

Brauneis, Viktor, Die Entstehung der Öesterreichischen Nationalbank – Memorandum verfaßt zur Information der Delegierten des Völkerbundes, Wien 1924.

Bresciani-Turroni, Costantino, The Economics of Inflation, London 1937.

Brügel, Ludwig, Geschichte der österreichischen Sozialdemokratie, Wien 1925.

Brusatti, Alois (Hrsg.), Die wirtschaftliche Entwicklung (= A. Wandruszka, P. Urbanek, Die Habsburgermonarchie 1848–1918, Bd. 1), Wien 1973.

Bunzel, Julius, Das neue Österreich, in: Schriften des Vereins für Sozialpolitik, Bd. 169, München-Leipzig 1925.

Cagan, Philipp, The Monetary Dynamics of Hyperinflation, in: Studies in the Quantity Theory of Money, ed. by Milton Friedman, Chicago 1956.

Charmatz, Richard, Österreichs innere Geschichte von 1848 bis 1907, Leipzig 1909.

Conrad Herbert, Das technische Versuchs-und Materialprüfungswesen, in: 10 Jahre Wiederaufbau, Wien 1928.

Cottrell, Philip C., Aspects of Western Equity Investment in the Banking Systems of East Central Europe, in International Business and Central Europe, 1918–39, ed. A. Teichova and P. Cottrell, Leicester, New York, 1983.

Czedik, Aloys von, Der Weg von und zu den österreichischen Staatsbahnen, Teschen-Wien-Leipzig 1913.

Danneberg, Robert, Die deutsch-österreichische Finanzverfassung, in: der Kampf, VI/1922.

Deutsch, Julius, Der Geist der Koalition, in: Der Kampf, X/1919.

Dittes, Paul, Die Einführung der elektrischen Zugförderung auf den österreichischen Bundesbahnen, in: 10 Jahre Wiederaufbau, Wien 1928.

Dobretsberger, Josef, Konkurrenz und Monopol in der gegenwärtigen Wirtschaft, Vienna 1929.

Drage, Geoffrey, Austria-Hungary, London 1909.

Einzig, Paul, World Finance 1914–1935, New York 1935.

Ellenbogen, Wilhelm, Die österreichische Staatsschuld, in: Der Kampf, IV/1914.

Ders., Sozialisierung in Österreich, Wien 1921.

Ellis, Howard S., German Monetary Theory 1905–1933, Harvard-Cambridge 1937.

Exner, Wilhelm (Hrsg.), 10 Jahre Wiederaufbau, Wien 1928.

Ders., Erlebnisse, in: ebenda.

Federn, Walther, Die auswärtigen Anleihen Österreichs, in: Schriften des Vereins für Sozialpolitik, Bd. 174, München-Leipzig 1928.

Ders., Die Kreditpolitik der Wiener Banken, in: ebenda, Bd. 169, München-Leipzig 1925.

Ders., Der Zusammenbruch der österreichischen Kreditanstalt, in: Archiv für Sozialwissenschaften und Sozialpolitik, Bd. 67, Tübingen 1932.

Ders., Aufsätze, in: Der Österreichische Volkswirt
  Wirtschaftliche Rückschau, 2. 1. 1915.
  Die Zinsfußermaßigung der österr. -ungarischen Bank, 17. 4. 1915.
  Die Teilnahme der deutschen Banken am Effektengeschäft, 12. 6. 1915.
  Die Kurssteigerung auf dem Effektenmarkt, 14. 8. 1915.
  Die Devisenzentrale, 28. 10 1916.
  Österreich-Ungarn zum Jahreswechsel, 30. 12. 1916.
  Der Prozeß Kranz, 7. 4. 1917.
  Die Berichte der Staatsschulden-Kontrollkommission, 29. 9. 1917.
  Österreichische und ungarische Finanzfragen und die 7. Kriegsanleihe, 3. 11. 1917.
  Die siebente Kriegsanleihe, 10. 11. 1917.
  Der Finanzausschuß über Kriegsschulden und die österr. -ungarische Bank, 8. 12. 1917.
  Die österr.-ungarische Bank im Kriege, 22. 12. 1917.
  Österreich-Ungarn zum Jahreswechsel, 5. 1. 1918.
  Die Umschichtung auf den Devisenmärkten, 12. 1. 1918.
  Kriegsanleihen und Inflation, 23. 3. 1918.
  Daz finanzielle Chaos, 25. 1. 1919.
  Der Staatsvoranschlag Österreichs, 8. 2. 1919.
  Die Währungstrennung und der Wert der Krone, 15. 2. 1919.
  Die Sicherung der Vermögensabgabe, 22. 3. 1919.
  Die finanzielle Liquidation der Monarchie und Deutschösterreichs Finanzen, 31. 5. 1919.
  Defizit aus staatlicher Ernährungswirtschaft, 31. 5. 1919.
  Das Finanzprogramm der Koalition, 25. 10. 1919.
  Ungestempelte und falsch gestempelte Banknoten, 1. 5. 1920.
  Die Vermögensabgabe, 7. 2. 1920.
  Die Wiener Banken, 17. 7. 1920.
  Die Freigabe des Devisenhandels, 16. 10. 1920.
  Die Entwertung der Krone, 25. 12. 1920.
  Wohlleben und drohende Katastrophe, 13. 8. 1921.
  Das Finanzprogramm, 28. 10. 1922.

Fellner, Fritz, Die Pariser Vororteverträge von 1919/20, in: Versailles-St. Germain-Trianon, München–Wien 1971.

Fibich, Alexander, Die Entwicklung der österreichischen Bundesausgaben in der Ersten Republik 1919–1938, Diss. Wirtschaftsuniv., Wien 1977.

Fink, Krisztina Maria, Die österreichische Monarchie als Wirtschaftsgemeinschaft, München 1968.

Fischer, H., Die Maschinenindustrie in Österreich, in: Die Großindustrie in Österreich, Wien 1908.

Fränkel, Elise, Zwei Wiener Arbeiterhaushaltungen während des Krieges, Diss. Wien

1921; quoted by Wilhelm Winkler (see Winkler, Wilhelm).

Franckenstein, George, Facts and Features of my Life, London 1939.

Freihls, Hans, Bahn ohne Hoffnung. Die österreichischen Eisenbahnen 1918–1938, Wien 1971.

Freund, Rudolf, Die Genfer Protokolle, in: Sozialwissenschaftliche Forschungen, Berlin-Leipzig 1924.

Fritz, Hedwig et al., 150 Jahre Sparkassen in Österreich, 5 Bde., Wien 1969–1971

Gaitskell, H. T. N., Austrian Economic Development, in: Lloyds Bank Review, May 1934.

Gärtner, Friedrich, Die Stabilisierung der österreichischen Krone, in: Schriften des Vereins für Sozialpolitik, Bd. 165, München-Leipzig 1924.

Gerlich, Rudolf, Die gescheiterte Alternative. Sozialisierung in Österreich nach dem 1. Weltkrieg, Wien 1980.

Gerschenkron, Alexander, An Economic Spurt that Failed, Princeton 1977.

Goldscheid, Rudolf, Sozialisierung der Wirtschaft oder Staatsbankrott, Wien 1917.

Ders., Staatssozialismus oder Staatskapitalismus, Wien 1919.

Gomperz, Heinrich, Theodor Gomperz. Ein Gelehrtenleben im Bürgertum der Franz-Josefs-Zeit, on the basis of narration by Heinrich Gomperz, selected and edited by Robert A. Kann, Vienna 1974.

Good, David F., Stagnation and Take-Off in Austria 1873–1913, in: The Economic History Review, Vol. XXVII., No. 1, 1974.

Ders., The Cost of Living in Austria 1874–1913, in: the Journal of European Economic History, Jg. 1976.

Goode, William, Economic Conditions in Central Europe, London 1920.

Gratz, Alois, Die Österreichische Finanzpolitik 1848 bis 1948, in: Mayer, Hans (Hrsg.), Hundert Jahre österreichische Wirtschaftsentwicklung, Wien 1949.

Gratz, Gustav, und Richard Schüller, Der wirtschaftliche Zusammenbruch Österreich-Ungarns, Wien 1930.

Dies., Die äußere Wirtschaftspolitik Österreich-Ungarns, Wien 1925.

Gross, Nachum Th., Die Stellung der Habsburgermonarchie in der Weltwirtschaft, in: Die Habsburgermonarchie 1848–1918, Bd. 1, Wien 1973.

Gruber-Menninger, Ignaz, und Gustav Thaa, Daten zur Zahlungsbilanz, in: Tabellen zur Währungsstatistik, Wien 1904.

Grünwald, Paul, Das Finanzsystem Deutsch-Österreichs, in: Schriften des Vereins für Sozialpolitik, Bd. 158, München-Leipzig 1919.

Gulick, Charles A., Austria: From Habsburg to Hitler, Berkeley and Los Angeles 1948.

Haas, Hanns, Österreich-Ungarn als Friedensproblem. Aspekte der Friedensregelung auf dem Gebiet der Habsburgermonarchie in den Jahren 1918–1919, Phil. Diss., Salzburg 1968.

Hannak, Jacques, Die wirtschaftliche Lage Österreichs – Anhang in: Österreichs Volkswirtschaft und die Sanierung, hrsg. von der Gewerkschaftskommission Deutsch-Österreichs, Wien 1923.

Hantos, Elemér, Das Geldproblem in Mitteleuropa, Jena 1925.

Hantsch, Hugo, Die Geschichte Österreichs, Wien-Graz-Köln 1962.

Hanusch, Ferdinand, und Emanuel Adler (Hrsg.), Die Regelung der Arbeitsverhältnisse im Kriege, Wien-New Haven 1927.

Hardach, Gerd, Zur zeitgenössischen Debatte der Nationalökonomie über die Ursachen der deutschen Nachkriegsinflation, in: Industrielles System und politische Entwicklung in der Weimarer Republik, Düsseldorf 1973.

Ders., Der Erste Weltkrieg, München 1973.

Heiss, Der nationale Besitzstand in Böhmen, in: Schmollers Jahrbuch, Bd. 30, Leipzig 1906.

Hertz, Friedrich, Die Produktionsgrundlagen der österreichischen Industrie vor und nach dem Kriege, Wien-Berlin 1917.

Ders., Ist Österreich wirtschaftlich lebensfähig?, Wien 1921.

Ders., Zahlungsbilanz und Lebensfähigkeit Österreichs, München 1925.

Ders., The Economic Problem of the Danubian States, London 1947.

Hickel, Rudolf (Hrsg.), Rudolf Goldscheid, Joseph Schumpeter, Die Finanzkrise des Steuerstaates. Beiträge zur politischen Ökonomie der Staatsfinanzen, Frankfurt 1976.

Hirsch, Julius, Grundriß der Sozialökonomie, zitiert bei Heinrich Wittek, Die kriegswirtschaftlichen Organisationen und Zentralen in Österreich, in: Zeitschrift für Volkswirtschaft und Sozialpolitik, Wien 1922.

Hoffmann, Alfred, Grundlagen der Agrarstruktur der Donaumonarchie, in: Alfred Hoffmann (Hrsg.), Österreich-Ungarn als Agrarstaat, Wien 1978.

Hoffmann, Robert, Die wirtschaftlichen Grundlagen der britischen Österreichpolitik 1919, in: Mitteilungen des österreichischen Staatsarchivs, Sonderdruck 30, Wien 1977.

Ders., Die Mission Sir Thomas Cunninghames in Wien 1919. Britische Österreichpolitik zur Zeit der Pariser Friedenskonferenz, Phil. Diss., Salzburg 1971.

Hoffmannsthal, Hugo von – Leopold von Andrian, Letters, Frankfurt 1968.

Horn, Norbert, und Jurgen Kocka (Hrsg.), Recht und Entwicklung der Großunternehmen im 19. und frühen 20. Jahrhundert, Göttingen 1979.

Jaszi, Oscar, The Dissolution of the Habsburg Monarchy, Chicago 1929.

Jefferson, Michael, Inflation, London 1977.

Kann, Robert A., The Habsburg Empire, New York 1957.

Karl, Rudolf, Die österreichische Völkerbundanleihe, Wien 1929.

Kausel, Anton, Österreichs Volkseinkommen von 1830–1913, in: Geschichte und Ergebnisse der zentralen amtlichen Statistik in Österreich 1829–1979, Wien 1979.

Kausel, Anton, Nandor Nemeth und Hans Seidel, Österreichs Volkseinkommen 1913–1963, in: Monatsberichte des Instituts für Wirtschaftsforschung, Sonderheft Nr. 14, Wien 1965.

Kautsky, Benedikt, Löhne und Gehälter, in: Schriften des Vereins für Sozialpolitik, Bd. 169, München-Leipzig 1925.

Kerschagl, Richard, Die Währungstrennung in den Nationalstaaten, Wien 1920.

Keynes, J. M., The Economic Consequences of the Peace, London 1919.

Ders., A Tract on Monetary Reform, London 1923.

Kienböck, Victor, Das österreichische Sanierungswerk, Stuttgart 1925.

Kleinwächter, F. F. G., Der fröhliche Präsidialist, Wien 1925.

Klemperer, Klemens von, Ignaz Seipel. Staatsmann einer Krisenzeit, Graz-Wien-Köln 1976.

Klenner, Fritz, Die österreichischen Gewerkschaften, Bd. 1, Wien 1951.

Klezl, Felix, Die Lebenskosten, in: Schriften des Vereins für Sozialpolitik, Bd. 169, München-Leipzig 1925.

Kola, Richard, Rückblick ins Gestrige, Wien 1922.

Koren, Stephan, Struktur und Nutzung der Energiequellen Österreichs, in: Österreichs Wirtschaftsstruktur gestern – heute – morgen, Bd. 1, Berlin 1961.

Korsch, Karl, Das sozialistische und syndikalistische Sozialisierungsprogramm, in: Schriften zur Sozialisierung, Frankfurt 1969.

Kreissler, Felix, Von der Revolution zur Annexion Österreichs 1918 bis 1938, Wien-Frankfurt-Zürich, 1970.

Krizek, Jurij, Die wirtschaftlichen Grundzüge des österreichisch-ungarischen Imperialismus in der Vorkriegszeit, 1908–1914, Prag 1963.

Kunschak, Leopold, Österreich 1918–1934, Wien 1934.

Kurzel-Runtscheiner, E., Österreichs Energiewirtschaft und die Ausnützung seiner Wasserkräfte, Wien 1923.

Ladner, Gottlieb, Seipel als Überwinder der Staatskrise vom Sommer 1922. Zur Geschichte der Entstehung der Genfer Protokolle vom 4. Oktober 1922, Wien-Graz 1964.

Lammasch, Marga, und Hans Sperl (Hrsg.), Heinrich Lammasch. Seine Aufzeichnungen, sein Wirken und seine Politik, Wien 1922.

Landes, David S., The Unbound Prometheus. Technological Change and Industrial Development in Western Europe from 1750 to the Present, Cambridge 1969.

Landmann, Salcïa, Erzählter Bilderbogen aus Ostgalizien, München 1975.

Layton, W. T., und Charles Rist, Die wirtschaftliche Lage Österreichs, Wien 1925.

Lederer, Emil, Die soziale Krise in Österreich, in: Archiv für Sozialwissenschaften und Sozialpolitik, Tübingen 1921.

Ders., Friedensdiktat und Sozialismus, in: Der Kampf, V/1919.

Lederer, Max, Indexziffern und Industrielöhne, in: Der Österreichische Volkswirt, 19. 9. 1922.

Leichter, Käthe, Erfahrungen des österreichischen Sozialisierungsversuches, in: Käthe Leichter. Leben und Werk, hrsg. v. Herbert Steiner, Wien 1973.

Leichter, Otto (Pertinax), Österreich 1934. Die Geschichte einer Konterrevolution, Zürich 1955.

Ders., Otto Bauer, Tragödie oder Triumph, Wien 1970.

Leser, Norbert, Zwischen Reformismus und Bolschewismus, Wien 1968.

Lewinson, Richard (Morus), Die Umschichtung der europaischen Vermögen, Berlin 1925.

Licht, Stefan Edler von, Die Kriegszuschläge zu den direkten Steuern, in: Neue Freie Presse, 15. 3. 1918.

Lloyd, George D., Memoirs of the Peace Conference, New Haven 1939.

Lockhart, R. H. Bruce, Retreat from Glory, London 1934.

Löffler, Alexander, Der Einfluß der Gesetzgebung auf die Kapitalaufzehrung, in: Schriften des Vereins für Sozialpolitik, Bd. 169, München-Leipzig 1925.

Lohner, L., Der Waggon- und Automobilbau in Österreich, in: Die Großindustrie Österreichs, Wien 1908.

Lopuszanski, Eugen, Die neueste Entwicklung des österreichischen Bankwesens, Vortrag, gehalten 1907 in der Gesellschaft österreichischer Volkswirte.

Loewenfeld-Russ, Hans, Die Regelung der Volksernährung im Kriege, Wien 1926.

Löwe, A. K., Österreichs Banken im Jahre 1905, in: Statistische Monatsschrift, Brünn 1906.

Macartney, C. A., The Social Revolution in Austria, Cambridge 1926.

Machlup, Fritz, Die Goldkernwährung, Halberstadt 1925.

Maddison, Angus, Phases of Capitalist Development, Rom 1977.

Madlé, Arnold, Die Bezüge der öffentlichen Angestellten, in: Schriften des Vereins für Sozialpolitik, Bd. 169, München-Leipzig 1925.

Mann, Thomas, Gesammelte Werke, Bd. XIII, Frankfurt 1974.

Marx, Karl, Herr Vogt, in: Marx-Engels-Werke, Bd. 14, Berlin 1961.

März, Eduard, Österreichische Industrie- und Bankpolitik in der Zeit Franz Josephs I., Wien 1968.

Ders., Zur Genesis der Schumpeterschen Theorie der wirtschaftlichen Entwicklung, in: Festschrift für Oskar Lange, Warschau 1973.

März, Eduard, und Karl Socher, Währung und Banken in Cisleithanien, in: Die Habsburgermonarchie 1848–1918, Bd. 1, Wien 1973.

März, Eduard, und Fritz Weber, Verstaatlichung und Sozialisierung nach dem Ersten und Zweiten Weltkrieg. Eine vergleichende Studie, in: Wirtschaft und Gesellschaft, Jg. 4, Nr. 2, Wien 1978.

Matis, Herbert, und Karl Bachinger, Österreichs industrielle Entwicklung, in: Die Habsburgermonarchie 1848–1918, Bd. 1, Wien 1973.

Matis, Herbert, Österreichs Wirtschaft 1848–1913, Berlin 1972.

Mayer, Hans (Hrsg.), Hundert Jahre österreichischer Wirtschaftsentwicklung 1848–1948, Wien 1949.

Mejzlik, Heinrich, Die Eisenbewirtschaftung im Ersten Weltkrieg, Wien 1977.

Mendershausen, L. H., The Economics of War, New York 1941.

Milward, Alan S., Der Zweite Weltkrieg, München 1977.

Mises, Ludwig von, Die geldtheoretische Seite des Stabilisierungsproblems, in: Schriften des Vereins für Sozialpolitik, Bd. 164, München-Leipzig 1923.

Ders., Über Deflationspolitik, in: Mitteilungen des Verbandes österreichischer Banken und Bankiers, Jg. 1924.

Ders., Die Störungen des Wirtschaftslebens der österreichisch-ungarischen Monarchie während der Jahre 1912/13, in: Archiv für Sozialwissenschaften und Sozialpolitik, Bd. 29, Tübingen 1915.

Ders., Der Wiedereintritt Deutsch-Österreichs in das Deutsche Reich und die Währungsfrage, in: Schriften des Vereins für Sozialpolitik, Bd. 158, München-Leipzig 1919.

Mitchel, Wesley C., History of Greenbacks, Chicago 1903.

Moggridge, Donald E., British Monetary Policy 1924–1931. The Norman Conquest of $4,861, Cambridge 1972.

Mommsen, Hans, Dietmar Petzina, Bernt Weisbrod (Hrsg.), Industrielles System und politische Entwicklung in der Weimarer Republik, Düsseldorf 1973.

Morgenstern, Oskar, Kapital- und Kurswertänderungen der an der Wiener Börse notierten österreichischen Aktiengesellschaften 1913–1930, in: Zeitschrift für Nationalökonomie, Jg. 1932.

Müller, Stefan von, Die finanzielle Mobilmachung Österreichs und ihr Ausbau bis 1918, Berlin 1918.

Novak, Karl F., The Collapse of Central Europe, London 1924.

Neurath, Otto, Vollsozialisierung und gemeinwirtschaftliche Anstalten, in: Der Kampf, II/1922.

Oppenheimer, Francis, Stranger Within. Autobiographical Pages, London 1965.

Otruba, Gustav, Bauer und Arbeiter in der Ersten Republik, in: Geschichte und Gesellschaft. Festschrift für R. Stadler, Wien 1974.

Overbeck, Hubert, Währung und Handelsbilanz Österreichs in den Jahren 1914–1928, Saarbrücken 1930.

Palla, Edmund, Ein Jahr Arbeitslosenfürsorge in Österreich, in: Nachrichten des Staatsamtes für Soziale Verwaltung, Wien 1920.

Pard, R., und K. Knauer, Eine Neubestimmung des Wasserkraftpotentials von Österreich, in: Österreichische Zeitschrift für Elektrizitätswirtschaft, Wien, April 1970.

Pascu, Stefan, Constantin C. Giurescu, Josif Kovács und Ludovic Vajda, Einige Fragen der landwirtschaftlichen Entwicklung in der österreichisch-ungarischen Monarchie, in: Die Agrarfrage in der österreichisch-ungarischen Monarchie, Bukarest 1965.

Pasvolsky, Leo, Economic Nationalism of the Danubian States, New York 1928.

Patzauer, Hans, Die Staatswirtschaft, in: Schriften des Vereins für Sozialpolitik, Bd. 169, München-Leipzig 1925.

Pfersmann, Kamillo, Der Wiederaufbau der österreichischen Gewerbeförderung, in: 10 Jahre Wideraufbau, Wien 1928.

Phillpotts. O. S., Report on the Industrial and Commercial Situation of Austria to August 1923., London 1923.

Pillet, Maurice, Le Relèvement financier de l'Autriche, Paris 1928.

Popper-Lynkeus, Nach dem Kriege – die allgemeine Nährpflicht, Dresden 1915.

Popovics, Alexander, Das Geldwesen im Kriege, Wien 1925.

Ders., Die Neuregelung des Verkehrs in ausländischen Zahlungsmitteln, in: Neue Freie Presse, 23. 2. 1916.

Pressburger, Siegfried, Österreichische Notenbank 1816–1966, Wien 1966

Pribram, Karl, Die gesetzliche Regelung der Arbeitslosenfürsorge, in: Der Österreichische Volkswirt, 3. 4. 1920.

Ders, Die Sozialpolitik im neuen Österreich, in: Archiv für Sozialwissenschaften und Sozialpolitik, Tübingen 1921.

Ders., The Foreign Trade Policy of Austria, Washington 1945.

Rašin, Alois, Die Finanz-und Wirtschaftspolitik der Tschechoslowakei, München-Leipzig 1923.

Recker, Marie-Luise, England und der Donauraum 1919–1929. Probleme einer europäischen Nachkriegsordnung, Stuttgart 1976.

Redlich, Josef, Schicksalsjahre Österreichs 1908–1919. Bearbeitet von Fritz Fellner, Graz-Köln 1945.

Ders., The Austrian War Government, New Haven 1929.

Reik, Walter, Die Beziehungen der österreichischen Großbanken zur Industrie, Wien 1932.

Reimann, Viktor, Zu groß für Österreich. Seipel und Bauer im Kampf um die Erste Republik, Wien 1968.

Reisch, Richard, Aufgaben und Entwicklung der Österreichischen Nationalbank in den Jahren 1923 bis 1928, in: 10 Jahre Wideraufbau, Wien 1928.

Ders., Meine Duplik in causa 'Geldwertpolitik', in: Mitteilungen des Verbandes österreichischer Banken und Bankiers, 6 Jg., 1924.

Ders., Stabilisierung oder Steigerung des Kronenwertes, ebenda.

Renner, Karl (Synoptikus), Staat und Nation. Zur österreichischen Nationalitätenfrage. Staatsrechtliche Untersuchung über die möglichen Principien einer Lösung und die juristischen Voraussetzungen eines Nationalitätengesetzes, Wien 1899.

Ders., Die Wirtschaft als Gesamtproseß und die Sozialisierung, Berlin 1924.

Ders., Marx oder Mazzini?, in: Der Kampf, V/1918.

Ders., Österreichs Finanzen und der Krieg, in: Arbeiter-Zeitung, 14. 12. 1915.

Reidl, Richard, Bemerkungen zu den deutsch-österreichischen Friedensbedingungen, Wien 1919.

Ders., Die Industrie Österreichs während des Krieges, Wien 1932.

Rosenberg, Wilhelm, Staatsfinanzielle Fragen, in: Der Österreichische Volkswirt, 23. 10. 1921.

Rothe, Franz, Die Arbeitsgemeinschaft revolutionärer Sozialdemokraten Deutsch-Österreichs, in: Der Kampf, IX/1920.

Rothschild, Kurt W., Wurzeln und Triebkräfte der österreichischen Wirtschaftsstruktur, in: Österreichs Wirtschaftsstruktur gestern – heute – morgen, Bd. 1, Berlin 1961.

Rudolph, Richard L., Banking and Industrialization in Austria-Hungary, Cambridge 1976.

Rumpler, Helmut, Das Völkermanifest Kaiser Karls vom 16. Oktober 1918, Wien 1966.

Rust, Franz, Das österreichische Goldbilanzgesetz, in: Mitteilungen des Verbandes österreichischer Banken und Bankiers, 7. Jg., 1925.

Sack, A. N., Le Mode de Repartition des Dettes Autrichiennes, Paris 1927.

Salter, Arthur, Financial Reconstruction of Austria, League of Nations, Genf 1926.

Schausberger, Norbert, Der Griff nach Österreich, Wien 1978.

Schiff, Walter, Die sozialpolitischen Aufgaben der Gengenwart und der nächsten Zukunft, in: Der Österreichische Volkswirt, 23. 11. 1918.

Schilder, Sigmund, Der Streit um die Lebensfähigkeit Österreichs, Stuttgart 1926.

Scheffer, Egon, Das Bankwesen in Österreich, Wien 1924.

Schmidt, Hans, Berichte aus den neuen Staaten, in: Handelsblatt, März 1922.

Schmidt, Walter, Das Sparkassenwesen in Österreich, Wien 1930.

Ders., Die Sparkassen, in: Schriften des Vereins für Sozialpolitik, Bd. 169, München-Leipzig 1925.

Schmölders, Günther, Psychologie des Geldes, Hamburg 1966.

Schüller, Richard, Die Handelsbilanz Österreich-Ungarns, in: Zeitschrift für Volkswirtschaft, Sozialpolitik und Verwaltung, Wien 1912.

Ders., Wirtschaftliche Bestimmungen des Friedensvertrages von St. Germain, in: ebenda, Wien 1921.

Ders., Bericht über die Brüsseler Konferenz, zitiert nach Martha Stephanie Braun, s. d.

Schumpeter, Joseph, Die Krise des Steuerstaates, in: Hickel (Hrsg.), Die Finanzkrise des Steuerstaates, Frankfurt 1976.

Ders., Sozialistische Möglichkeiten von heute, in: Archiv für Sozialwissenschaften und Sozialpolitik, Tübingen 1924.

Ders., Theorie der wirtschaftlichen Entwicklung. Eine Untersuchung über Unternehmergewinn, Kapital, Kredit, Zins und den Konjunkturzyklus, 2. Auflage, München-Leipzig 1926.

Ders., Zur Soziologie der Imperialismen, in: Aufsätze zur Soziologie, Tübingen 1953.

Schwoner, Alfred, Die Kriegskosten und die Geldentwertung, in: Der Österreichische Volkswirt, 25. 8. 1917.

Segré, Roberto, La Missione Militare Italiana per l'Armistizio Dicembre 1918 – Gennaio – 1920, Bologna 1929.

Seipel, Ignaz, Das Recht des Volkes, in: Die Reichspost, 19. 11. 1918.

Ders., Das Wesen des demokratischen Staates, in: ebenda, 20. 11. 1918.

Ders., Die demokratische Verfassung, in: ebenda, 21. 11. 1918.

Ders., Das Volk und die künftige Staatsform, in: ebenda, 23. 11. 1918.

Sickle, John V. van, Direct Taxation in Austria, Cambridge 1931.

Sieghart, Rudolf, Die letzten Jahrzehnte einer Großmacht, Berlin 1932.

Sokal, Max, Die Tätigkeit der Banken. Separatdruck aus dem Bericht der n.ö. Handels- und Gewerbekammer über die Wirtschaftsverhältnisse 1914–1918, Wien 1920.

Ders. Vom österreichischen Bankwesen, in: Schriften des Vereins für Sozialpolitik, Bd. 162, München-Leipzig 1921.

Spitzmüller, Alexander, Das österreichische Steuersystem des Bundes, der Länder und Gemeinden und die Kapitalbildung, in: Schriften des Vereins für Sozialpolitik, Bd. 174, München-Leipzig 1928.

Ders., Die Geldwertpolitik der österreichischen Nationalbank, in: Mitteilungen des Verbandes österreichischer Banken und Bankiers, 6. Jg., 1924.

Ders., Der letzte österreichisch-ungarische Ausgleich und der Zusammenbruch der Monarchie, Berlin 1929.

Ders., Die Kriegsanleihe, in: Neue Freie Presse, 26. 11. 1914.

Ders., ... und hat auch Ursach' es zu lieben, Wien 1955.

Sommeregger Franz, Die Wege und Ziele der österreichischen Agrarpolitik seit der Grundentlastung, Wien 1912.

Stadler, Karl R., Hypothek auf die Zukunft, Wien 1968.

Stein, Viktor, Zum Kampf um den Index, in: Der Kampf IX/X/1922.

Steiner, Friedrich, Notenbank und die staatliche Anleihepolitik in den Nachfolgestaaten Österreich-Ungarns, in: Schriften des Vereins für Sozialpolitik, Bd. 166, München-Leipzig 1924.

Stockklausner, Hanns, 50 Jahre Elektro-Vollbahnlokomotiven in Österreich und Deutschland, in: Sonderheft der Zeitschrift 'Eisenbahn', Wien 1952.

Stolper, Gustav (Hrsg.), Schriften des Vereins für Sozialpolitik, Bd. 162, München-Leipzig 1921.

Ders., Der Friedensvertrag von St. Germain in seinen wirtschaftlichen Wirkungen, in: ebenda.

Ders., Deutsch-Österreich als Sozial- und Wirtschaftsproblem, München 1921.

Ders., Aufsätze in: Der Österreichische Volkswirt
Wehrreform und Finanznot, 11. 10. 1913.
Politisches Resumé, 15. 11. 1913.
Handelsbilanz und Wirtschaftspolitik, 4. 4. 1914.
Handelsbilanz und Kreditpolitik, 11. 4. 1914.
Die Industrie im Kriege, 10. 4. 1915.
Zur Beurteilung der Wirtschaftslage, 24. 4. 1915.
Die zweite Kriegsanleihe, 8. 5. 1915.
Eine amtliche Teuerungsstatistik, 18. 9. 1915.
Die Neuregelung des Getreideverkehrs, 7. 6. 1919.
Freigabe des Lebensmittelverkehrs, 6. 9. 1919.
Vor der Entscheidung, 13. 12. 1919.
Das ungarische Bündnisangebot, 21. 2. 1920.
Donauföderation, 29. 5. 1920.
Der neue Finanzplan, 24. 6. 1920.
Stagnation, 31. 7. 1920.
Aufbaupläne, 15. 1. 1921.
Eine ganze Niederlage, 24. 12. 1921.
Der neue Finanzplan, 24. 6. 1922.
Die innere Anleihe, 8. 7. 1922.
Der Kampf um Genf. 11. 11. 1922.

Strakosch, Siegfried, Der Selbstmord eines Volkes, Wien 1922.

Strigl, Richard, Das industrielle Kapital, in: Schriften des Vereins für Sozialpolitik, Bd. 169, München-Leipzig 1925.

Strong, David F., Austria, October 1918–March 1919. Transition from Empire to Republic, New York 1939.

Svennilson, J., Growth and Stagnation in the European Economy, UN, Genf 1954.

Szinai, Miklos, Zur Geschichte der Beziehungen zwischen der ungarischen Räterepublik und Österreich. Otto Bauers Brief an Béla Kun, Budapest 1972.

Teichova, Alice, An Economic Background to Munich. International Business and Czechoslovakia 1918–1938, Cambridge 1974.

Dies., Versailles and the Expansion of the Bank of England into Central Europe, in: Recht und Entwicklung der Großunternehmen im 19. und frühen 20. Jahrhundert, Göttingen 1979.

Temperley, Harold W. V., A History of the Peace Conference at Paris, 5 vols., London 1920–1924.

Tremel, Ferdinand, Der Binnenhandel und seine Organisation, in: Die Habsburgermonarchie 1848–1918, Bd. 1, Wien 1973.

Vas, Oskar, Grundlagen und Entwicklung der Energie-Wirtschaft Österreichs. Offizieller Bericht des österreichischen Nationalkomitees der Weltkraftkonferenz, Wien 1930.

Verosta, Stefan, Joseph Schumpeter gegen das Zollbündnis der Donaumonarchie mit Deutschland und gegen die Anschlußpolitik, in: Festschrift für Christian Broda, Wien 1976.

Wagner-Herr, Ernest, Die Wohnungsverhältnisse, in: Schriften des Vereins für Sozialpolitik, Bd. 169, München-Leipzig 1925.

Waizner, Ernest, Das Volkseinkommen Alt-Österreichs und seine Verteilung auf die Nachfolgestaaten, in: Metron, Internationale Statistische Zeitschrift, Bd. VII, Rom 1929.

Walré de Bordes, Jan van, The Austrian Crown. Its Depreciation and Stabilization, London 1924.

Weber, Wilhelm (Hrsg.), Österreichs Wirtschaftsstruktur gestern – heute – morgen, 2 Bde., Berlin 1961.

Wegs, James, R., Austrian Economic Mobilization During World War I, with Particular Emphasis on Heavy Industry, Diss. Illinois 1970.

Weissel, Erwin, Die Ohnmacht des Sieges. Arbeiterschaft und Sozialisierung nach dem Ersten Weltkrieg in Österreich, Wien 1976.

Werfel, Franz, Barbara oder die Frömmigkeit, Berlin 1929.

Wieser, Adele, Die Verwertungsmöglichkeit der Arbeitskraft in der Industrie, in: Schriften des Vereins für Sozialpolitik, Bd. 169, München-Leipzig 1925.

Winkler, Wilhelm, Die Einkommensverschiebungen in Österreich während des Krieges, Wien 1930.

Wittek, Heinrich, Die kriegswirtschaftlichen Organisationen und Zentralen in Österreich, in: Zeitschrift für Volkswirtschaft und Sozialpolitik, Bd. 2, 1922.

Ders., Die österreichischen Eisenbahnen vor und nach dem Kriege, in: Schriften des Vereins für Sozialpolitik, Bd. 162, München-Leipzig 1921.

Wysocki, Josef, Die österreichische Finanzpolitik, in: Die Habsburgermonarchie 1848–1918, Bd. 1, Wien 1973.

Zeuceanu, Alexander, La liquidation de la Banque d'Autriche-Hongrie, Wien 1924.

Zienert, Hugo, Die Zahlungsbilanz Österreichs, in: 10 Jahre Wiederaufbau, Wien 1928.

Zöllner, Erich, Geschichte Österreichs, 6. Aufl., Wien 1979.